DATE DUE			

THE CHRISTIAN FAITH AND
NON-CHRISTIAN RELIGIONS

THE CHRISTIAN FAITH
AND NON-CHRISTIAN
RELIGIONS

By

A. C. BOUQUET, D.D.

LECTURER ON THE HISTORY AND COMPARATIVE STUDY OF RELIGIONS
IN THE UNIVERSITY OF CAMBRIDGE, 1945-56
HULSEAN LECTURER, 1923-24
STANTON LECTURER ON THE PHILOSOPHY OF RELIGION, 1931-34

GREENWOOD PRESS, PUBLISHERS
WESTPORT, CONNECTICUT

Library of Congress Cataloging in Publication Data

Bouquet, Alan Coates, 1884-
   The Christian faith and non-Christian religions.

   Reprint of the ed. published by J. Nisbet,
Welwyn, Eng., in series: the Library of construc-
tive theology.
   1. Christianity and other religions.
2. Religions. I. Title. II. Series: The
Library of constructive theology.
[BR127.B64 1976]   261.2   76-13920
ISBN 0-8371-7974-2

Copyright © 1958 by Alan Coates Bouquet

First published in 1958 by James Nisbet & Co., Ltd., Welwyn,
Herts

Reprinted with the permission of James Nisbet & Company Ltd.

Reprinted in 1976 by Greenwood Press,
a division of Williamhouse-Regency Inc.

Library of Congress Catalog Card Number 76-13920

ISBN 0-8371-7974-2

Printed in the United States of America

IN PIAM MEMORIAM

ELIZABETHAE BOUQUET

MATRIS OPTIMAE

GENERAL INTRODUCTION

BY THE EDITORS

Times change, and our words change with them. The passage of thirty years, crowded with events which have shaken the foundations of our society, makes necessary some addition to the original Preface to this series. From a new vantage point further down the stream of time, earlier landmarks take on a new perspective. There are phrases in the original Preface which their authors, writing afresh today, would not now employ, not because they would repudiate their meaning, or feel constrained to some major retraction, but because the continually changing vocabulary of theological conversation has rendered blunt and inapt words which were formerly clear-cut and apposite.

About the main stresses of their original intentions the Editors remain convinced and very sure that the 'Library of Constructive Theology' has still an important work to fulfil. That silent crisis of our time, which they saw to involve not only a questioning of authority but a revolt against it, has not only persisted but intensified in such manner as to sharpen the questions facing Christian men as they seek to bring home their message to a largely estranged contemporary mind. It is true that the last decades have seen an important return to authority, a return in many churches to positive elements in the holy tradition of the past, in the revival of dogmatic theology in Continental Protestantism, in the increasingly fruitful Ecumenical conversation, and in the emphasis on the dogmatic content of Biblical theology.

In part this has been a result of the context of the time: the new perils and heresies, and notably the challenge of the totalitarian ideologies, have driven Christian men to consider the great unchanging affirmation of their faith. They have also been the logical consequences of the explorations of historical, dogmatic, and Biblical studies themselves, pursued by a generation of scholars. But if theological studies have advanced, new knowledge has accumulated in the field of science, new problems of philosophical discussion, such that in itself a return to authority can only sharpen the acuteness of the crisis provoked by the relation of Christian belief to the modern mind. 'The effort to think out anew, in the light of modern knowledge, the foundation affirmations of our common

Christianity' is not less but rather more urgent than in the years before the rise of National Socialism and the Second World War, and the recent discussions about 'De-Mythologizing', and the problems raised by 'Logical Positivism' have shown that the Christian enquiry may turn out to be even more drastic and thoroughgoing than a previous generation had envisaged.

The Editors stressed the value and validity of religious experience, widely defined to include the moral and spiritual experience of the whole human race. Now 'existential' seems to be replacing 'experience' in the jargon of the schools. Modern philosophic discussion has pursued the lines of a century-old debate, but it too has been drastically affected by the shattering experiences of contemporary life, in a disrupted, shattered world where the old familiar stable patterns of existence have been dissolved, and where the age-long problems of the human soul have to be reconsidered against a life setting of pain and anxiety and frustration thrust in upon the human consciousness by events which the individual cannot alter and control, driving him to ask old questions with a new depth and poignancy. But here again the change of emphasis and vocabulary, and the new problems provoked for Christian exposition, have not altered but rather brought into deeper analysis the fundamental concern of religion, amid all the preoccupations with human solidarities, with the lonely and the contrite heart, and with a God who addresses men and women at the deepest level of their personal existence. It remains true that 'theology cannot exist without the religious consciousness and reflection upon it.'

Finally, the need for studies of these things which shall be intelligible to the general reader is as urgent as ever. Twenty years ago it was right to speak of a gulf between the pulpit and the pew: now perhaps we might add the perils of a gulf between the study and the pulpit, beside the great divide which separates the pew from the street. The problem of Christian communication meets us within and without the Church, hampering the endemic responsibility of the whole Christian community from carrying out at every level an ever-renewed and renewing theological conversation, and, above all, imperilling the evangelical commission to the Churches to bring their gospel home to the heart and mind of a bewildered, distraught, and hungry age.

*　　　*　　　*

The Editors of this series are convinced that the Christian Church as a whole is confronted with a great though largely silent crisis, and also with an unparalleled opportunity. They have a

common mind concerning the way in which this crisis and opportunity should be met. The time has gone by when 'apologetics'
could be of any great value. Something more is needed than a
defence of propositions already accepted on authority, for the present
spiritual crisis is essentially a questioning of authority if not a revolt
against it. It may be predicted that the number of people who are
content simply to rest their religion on the authority of the Bible or
the Church is steadily diminishing, and with the growing effective-
ness of popular education will continue to diminish. We shall not
therefore meet the need, if we have rightly diagnosed it, by disserta-
tions, however learned, on the interpretation of the Bible or the
history of Christian doctrine. Nothing less is required than a
candid, courageous, and well-informed effort to think out anew, in
the light of modern knowledge, the foundation affirmations of our
common Christianity. This is the aim of every writer in this series.

A further agreement is, we hope, characteristic of the books which
will be published in the series. The authors have a common mind
not only with regard to the problem but also with regard to the
starting-point of reconstruction. They desire to lay stress upon the
value and validity of religious experience and to develop their theology on the basis of the religious consciousness. In so doing they
claim to be in harmony with modern thought. The massive achievements of the nineteenth and twentieth centuries have been built up
on the method of observation and experiment, on experience, not on
abstract *a priori* reasoning. Our contention is that the moral and
spiritual experience of mankind has the right to be considered, and
demands to be understood.

Many distinguished thinkers might be quoted in support of the
assertion that philosophers are now prepared in a greater measure
than formerly to consider religious experience as among the most
significant of their data. One of the greatest has said, 'There is
nothing more real than what comes in religion. To compare facts
such as these with what is given to us in outward existence would
be to trifle with the subject. The man who demands a reality more
solid than that of the religious consciousness seeks he does not
know what.'[1]

Nor does this estimate of religious experience come only from
idealist thinkers. A philosopher who writes from the standpoint of
mathematics and natural science has expressed the same thought in
even more forcible language. 'The fact of religious vision, and its
history of persistent expansion, is our one ground for optimism.
Apart from it, human life is a flash of occasional enjoyments lighting

[1] F. H. Bradley, *Appearance and Reality*, p. 449.

up a mass of pain and misery, a bagatelle of transient experience.'[2]

The conviction that religious experience is to be taken as the starting-point of theological reconstruction does not, of course, imply that we are absolved from the labour of thought. On the contrary, it should serve as the stimulus to thought. No experience can be taken at its face value; it must be criticized and interpreted. Just as natural science could not exist without experience and the thought concerning experience, so theology cannot exist without the religious consciousness and reflection upon it. Nor do we mean by 'experience' anything less than the whole experience of the human race, so far as it has shared in the Christian consciousness. As Mazzini finely said, 'Tradition and conscience are the two wings given to the human soul to reach the truth.'

It has been the aim of the writers and the Editors of the series to produce studies of the main aspects of Christianity which will be intelligible and interesting to the general reader and at the same time may be worthy of the attention of the specialist. After all, in religion we are dealing with a subject-matter which is open to all, and the plan of the works does not require that they shall delve very deeply into questions of minute scholarship. We have had the ambition to produce volumes which might find a useful place on the shelves of the clergyman and minister, and no less on those of the intelligent layman. Perhaps we may have done something to bridge the gulf which too often separates the pulpit from the pew.

Naturally, the plan of our series has led us to give the utmost freedom to the authors of the books to work out their own lines of thought, and our part has been strictly confined to the invitation to contribute, and to suggestions concerning the mode of presentation. We hope that the series will contribute something useful to the great debate on religion which is proceeding in secret in the mind of our age, and we humbly pray that their endeavours and ours may be blessed by the Spirit of Truth for the building up of Christ's Universal Church.

[2] A. N. Whitehead, *Science and the Modern World*, p. 275.

PREFATORY NOTE BY THE AUTHOR

My first acknowledgement at this point must be to the Vice-Chancellor and Council of Andhra University for the great courtesy and hospitality shown to me, in allowing me to reside for several months at this progressive Indian University, and to be able to ponder and check and correct the proofs of this book in a genuinely Asian atmosphere, facing out across the Bay of Bengal towards the Buddhist world, and in a region of perpetual sunshine. For all this I am deeply grateful.

I would like to pay tribute to those who have so kindly taken the trouble to read this work in manuscript and to make so many helpful suggestions: to wit, the three General Editors of the series, Dean Matthews, Professor Rupp, and Dr. Daniel Williams; Professor S. G. F. Brandon of Manchester University; and last but not least the Rev. R. A. K. Runcie, Dean of Trinity Hall, Cambridge, who discussed with me the chapter on the Doctrine of the Logos in detail. I have endeavoured to profit by all their criticisms, and have accepted their suggestions wherever possible. A work of this kind is usually undertaken by a team, but since in this case it was decided that one man should carry it through, I have not scrupled to seek advice and information far and wide. The suggestions of the Rev. George Appleton about modern Buddhism in particular have been most helpful.

I must also express my sincere gratitude to the Rev. H. A. Williams of Trinity College, Cambridge, and the Rev. R. A. K. Runcie of Trinity Hall for looking again through the proof sheets during my absence from England; and to Professor K. Satchidananda Murty for many kindnesses, and for some wise and charitable criticism.

I hope I have not committed any serious errors in the spelling of Asian or African words. In the case of the latter I have followed Dr. E. W. Smith, to whose editorial work on African matters I must again express my deep indebtedness. In the case of the former, I have tried to keep reasonably up-to-date, but changes are so rapidly occurring, that it is impossible to avoid falling behind. Thus 'Banaras' is a spelling which I was told to adopt three years ago, but I am now informed that Indians wish to write it Varanasi! Meanwhile Ceylon wishes to be called Lanka, Siam, Thai, and so on. We are even faced with the possibility that Egypt may re-entitle herself Misr, which is already the name by which for centuries she has been known in India, and which in its dual form of Mizraim is familiar to readers of the Hebrew Old Testament.

I must repeat here what I have said at various points throughout the book, that any criticisms, whether of Christians or non-Christians, are not made in any spirit of antagonism or from any wish to hurt or to score, but solely in the attempt to appraise what is true. I owe too much in particular to the courtesy and hospitality of Indian friends to wish to wound their feelings in any way. But I think they would wish me to be frank, and I am confident that frankness is the best way in which to help them in dealing with a situation the delicacy of which I am sure they feel as much as I do. Somewhat the same I should wish to say with regard to my many valued American friends.

Finally I must express my thanks to Mr. J. Mackenzie Wood of Messrs. Nisbet for his ready and sympathetic counsel, and for the patience with which he has waited for the completion of the MS.

A. C. BOUQUET

Andhra University,
Waltair,
Andhra Pradesh,
India.

CONTENTS

INTRODUCTION

This is a work in a series which is concerned with Christian theology. It may therefore be assumed by some who pick it up (and put it down again without having read it) that it is merely concerned with the confirmation of a prejudice. Non-Christian faiths, indeed! Any answer about their relation to Christianity made by an Anglican clergyman is bound to be loaded beforehand! The universalistic Christian claim was put forth in the limited world of the Mediterranean, before much was known about the great Asian systems. Forged thus in comparative ignorance, how can it be substantiated in these latter days, when we know so much more about Asia, not to mention Africa, than anybody in Europe did during the first four centuries of our era?

My preliminary answer to this must be to urge caution. In the first place the early Christians were far more acquainted with non-Christian systems than some might hastily conclude. Such systems lay at their doorstep in the Mediterranean, and even India was not to all of them entirely a *terra ignota*. It was from a Hellenistic philosophy and paganism strangely resembling that of India in many respects[1] that those who were not Jews were converted, and as we shall see later, they had their own theory about the relationship of their new faith to the traditions and speculations which they had discarded, and this theory has actually been transmitted to us by the Christian Church, so that its examination must necessarily occupy a whole preliminary section of the present book.

But in the second place, however, we have to face certain empirical facts.

1. Hinduism until recently never put forward any universalistic claim. It was as much a religio-social nationalistic system as Judaism, and it only enlarged its borders by (a) the actual expansion of its population, e.g. towards what we now call Indonesia; (b) the incorporation of subject peoples and primitive tribes within its

---

[1] 'To the Greek mind God is impersonal, rather like all-pervasive aether; an Absolute transcending all differences; almost a complete Blank. The Ultimate Reality is the One who is one and all alone, and evermore shall be so.' (J. S. Whale, in *Christian Doctrine*, ch. iii, p. 54.) In one of the plays of Aeschylus occur the words: 'Zeus is air, Zeus is earth. Zeus is heaven, Zeus is all things, and whatsoever is higher than all things.' These statements might easily come straight out of one of the Hindu Upanishads. Moreover, like many Indians, Greeks held a cyclic view of events, and did not regard the historical as significant (see A. E. Taylor, *Gifford Lectures*, vol. II, pp. 326–8). The passage in the Epistle to the Colossians 2:20–3, whether or not it is of Pauline authorship, pre-supposes an acquaintance with religious observances akin to those in some forms of Hinduism.

borders as additional castes.   Whatever we may think of it, neo-Hinduism of the type which invites disciples from other lands is a modern construction inspired by patriotism and stimulated by rival faiths—Christianity and Islam—and it involves the abandonment of much which the old orthodox Hinduism would have regarded as *de rigueur*.

2. Buddhism, though universalistic so far as Eastern Asia is concerned, has not until the last forty years seriously considered the conversion of Europe or America, and in its Theravada form is a mysticism so rarefied as to seem to many observers simply an Asian type of humanism, while even so ardent an advocate as Mr. Christmas Humphreys quite frankly and honestly confesses that he does not expect a landslide towards it on the part of the West.[1]   All he claims is that it should be recognised and respected as an alternative to Christianity by those who like it, or find it interesting and attractive.

3. Islam, it is clear, was led to make its universalistic claim by the influence of the Christian movement which had gone before it. Whether Mohammed would have acted as he did if he had not known of the existence of that movement we cannot tell: but knowing it, even though from the outside and only imperfectly, he clearly conceived his Asian Protestantism as a Catholic religion.   His claim is therefore hardly an original one, but must be taken in conjunction with that of the Christians themselves.   Moreover, Islam, despite its specially Arab features, its fervent over-emphasis upon the transcendence of Deity (derived and extended from Hebrew prophetic monotheism), its reduced Christology and its deviationist morality, still bears a remarkably close resemblance to a Christian heresy, and Mohammed himself has been described not inaptly as a Semitic Luther.[2]

4. Whatever may be my readers' opinion about it, the Christian movement, as observed fact, is the *one* religious system which has right from the outset to the present day consistently made a universalist claim, and by its adherents has been believed, in effect, destined to be in some form or other the common world religion for

---

[1] *Buddhism* (Pelican Books, A.228), p. 230.

[2] My own personal experience, for what it is worth, certainly tends to put modern Islam, as far as I have seen it, within the category of a book-centred Protestantism. The Senussi *zawya* which I visited at Zliten in North Africa had the mixed atmosphere of a Bible college and an early medieval Benedictine monastery.   The neat and clean little green and white mosques of Libya remind one of nothing so much as rural dissenting chapels, while the Sheyk in charge of the Temple area at Jerusalem was a dear venerable old man who talked and behaved and even looked rather like a nice elderly evangelical clergyman whom I once met in Birmingham.   Of course part of this may be due to a kind of friendly rivalry with the Christian church; but that it is possible seems evidence that between Christianity and Islam there is a strong relationship.   I hope to develop this theme in my chapter VII.

all time.[1] As observed fact also it is the one and only system which has succeeded in making disciples and establishing centres of influence all over the globe. The quality of these various centres may vary, and in many cases, in so far as they are indigenous, they only form minority movements in the countries where they exist, as for example in Iran. It is, however, indisputable that the Christian movement, though still relatively young in comparison with the age of the earth, the age of the human species and the age of some other religions, has within the past 150 years really for the first time entered upon its truly ecumenical phase, and has for the first time reached a position when the evangelisation of the planet, as distinct from portions of it, can seriously be taken in hand, without the accusation being levelled at it of ulterior political motives. It has made good its claim at least to be believable and practicable alike by Arabs and Eskimos, Irish and Panjabis, Chinese and Italians, Nigerians and Australian aborigines—and so on: and this not because of European dominance, since a good deal of missionary expansion is being carried on by the peoples of the countries concerned. South Indians are ardently evangelistic. So are many West Africans. In Jordan, some of the most effective gathering-in of converts from Islam was being achieved in 1952 by an old Arab priest.

The above facts being as they are, why should any wish to put blinkers on themselves? It is surely worth while enquiring *why* the Christian movement has expanded in this way. May there not be some inherent reason for its success?—May not at least *some* of its affirmations be justified?—Why has it so confidently and consistently put forward its universalist claims?—and what in point of fact do those claims amount to? It cannot be improper to raise such questions, and to consider them in the widest possible context.

[1] We are today getting to know much more about the early spread of the Christian movement in Asia and North Africa, over a thousand years ago. It is a chastening story, because we are able to see how through fundamental defects in both cases it failed to maintain itself. But the striking fact remains that this early Christianity was quite as much convinced as that of the nineteenth century that it held a mission to the world of its own day, taken as a whole, and that it was its bounden duty to expand; and it is only neglect to study the distance travelled on a map of the world, which can prevent us from recognising the scale on which it laboured, and the immense areas which it covered. Attention also may reasonably be drawn to the actual names by which the various religions are known.
  Hinduism means 'the religion of Hind', i.e. of the Indian sub-continent.
  Buddhism means 'the system of enlightenment' (i.e. of being *buddhi* or awakened to the truth).
  Islam means 'submission'.
  Christianity means the faith centred upon the Person of Christ, but for centuries it has called itself 'the Catholic Faith' the inference of which is obvious.
It is thus only Christianity which has *called itself* 'the common world-religion'. This, however, while making it unique, does not establish its claim, which is bound to rest on other grounds. Islam, copying Christianity, makes, but does not substantiate, a similar claim, being still most itself among purely Arab, African, and Asian peoples round the terrestrial heat-belt. One notes the inauguration of a Moslem Missionary Society, financed largely by one of the deportees from Ghana.

What I propose for re-examination in fact is a situation which already exists, rather than one which Christians would undoubtedly wish to exist.

Nevertheless it would be wise to avoid exaggeration. Some of the diffusion may have been favoured by subsidiary causes. The survey made in recent years by Dr. Latourette is a magnificent *tour de force* in so far as it is an actual survey of the various expansions of our faith which have occurred. But it does not deal as much as one would wish with either the quality or the character of the various forms of such expansions, or consider the diverse motives which may have at times prompted their promoters.

In any case the evangelisation of the earth's populations can only be described as a long way from completion. It is quite right to speak of 'the unfinished task'. In 1920 the world population was estimated at a total of 1646 millions. After nearly forty years it may rise to anything between 1700 and 2000 millions. The population of China alone, estimated in 1920 at about 400 millions, is said to be increasing at a rate of 15 millions a year, and will soon reach the total of 700 millions. Indeed the Chinese Minister of Health has said that family planning must be speedily introduced in China on a wide scale if that country is to be able to feed and maintain her immense population at a reasonable standard of living.[1] The accession of new members to the Christian movement is certainly not keeping pace with this kind of birth-rate—even if that accession be still in progress, as it certainly is; so that there are actually more non-Christians in the world than there were on the day of Pentecost, in spite of all the centuries of evangelism which have intervened: while in the lands where Christianity has been longest established there have been serious losses, and in the past whole areas have ceased to be Christian, or where a Christian community has endured within them it has become little more than a museum piece, a grotesque and pathetic survival, devoid of evangelising power, and yet entitled to some respect because it has often maintained a witness to Christ under depressing conditions, and has refused to let itself be liquidated or syncretistically absorbed.

It is possible that some parts of such 'problem' areas were never more than superficially converted. In any case, entire groups and classes, whether in Russia, France,[2] or England, stand at the present time completely outside Christian membership, and exhibit the most serious challenge which any branch of the contemporary Church has to face. Leaving out of count for our present purpose Africa and

[1] See note on Hoyle's discussion of the population problem.
[2] In France it is said that only 7 million out of 42 million citizens ever perform their obligation to hear Mass.

Western Asia, we may look at the situation for an example in Eastern Asia. Here the population is estimated at 1230 millions, a fairly large slice of the whole population of the planet. Of these the Christian element is estimated to be about 40 million, that is to say an average of about three per cent.

Eastern Asia must be declared without prejudice to have been a great area of landlordist and capitalist exploitation, with the money-lender unpleasantly prominent. Though it is fairly rich in resources, abject poverty is widespread, and Marxist agitators are finding it a fertile soil for their propaganda.[1] It cannot therefore be guaranteed that Christian expansion in that area will continue even at its present moderate pace, and it may even diminish. The distribution of Christians in Eastern Asia varies very much. In India it averages two per cent, though the membership is much larger in the south than in the north. In the Philippines it is much higher, 18 out of 20 millions. In Thailand, a country where the profession of Buddhism tends to be equated with patriotism, it is very small, 70,000 out of 18 millions. A good deal of Asian nationalism, both in Burma and Ceylon is, as we shall see, leading to a furbishing up of Buddhist institutions, an observance of Buddhist anniversaries, and a collation of Buddhist sacred texts. Hinduism, says Nicolas Zernov the Russian Christian, 'is not a dying religion. Its mystery and pageantry appeal to the lower classes, and its philosophical systems to the intellectual'. There is some truth in this, though it may be queried whether this popularity will be able to survive the growth of Indian literacy, and the development of education in the physical sciences. Islam has been written into the constitution of new states, Pakistan, Indonesia, Jordan, and Libya; while federations of Moslem states, especially those linked with Egypt, at least pay lip-service to their religion as a politically unifying cement.

Beside these facts the Christian claim somewhat shrinks.

And further. Overshadowing all, Christian and non-Christian alike, broods the great new force of Marxism. Though avowing enmity for all religion, the Dialectic Materialism of Marx proposes itself as an alternative force of human integration, in the same way that Christianity did in the first and second centuries. The Christians themselves, as is well known, were called 'atheists', and they un-doubtedly sought the disintegration of the popular religion which they encountered. Marx's own attitude breathes the tradition of rabbinical, if not of prophetic Judaism, towards the religion of the *goyim*. As developed in Russia at any rate, Dialectic Materialism is an immanentist mystical philosophy which rejects theism

[1] See further, Chapters X and XI.

(Khruschev: 'We don't believe in God') but replaces it by a devotion to the ultimate Life Force, which is irresistible, and to which surrender must therefore be made. Zähner's recent estimate of it is most just. He sees in it a system very close indeed to the non-theistic systems of Asia, which are centred upon an Absolute, but not upon a Personal God. No survey of the world-situation can therefore be reasonably undertaken if we ignore the challenge of Marxism. Many questions, however, are bound to arise. For instance, is Marxism merely a materialistic humanism, and not really to be classified as a religion? We might ask the same question about Theravada Buddhism. Again, is there any evidence of a syncretism beginning between Marxism and other existing systems? What is happening in China for instance?—And are there in Russia or for the matter of that in Europe or America an appreciable number of Christians who are trying to be Communists, and even to accept a certain amount of dialectic without ceasing to be Christian?—It is a grave question whether at least some kind of economic Communism has not come to stay in Asia. Let no one underrate the confidence of the Chinese leaders, whose people may in time come to be a greater influence in the world than the Russians. Liu Shao-Chi, who in prestige is perhaps second only to Mao-Tse-Tung, said recently to a British member of Parliament: 'Your children will grow up in a Communist world.'[1] The implications of this I shall try to discuss in Chapters X and XI.

One thing has become clear. Orthodox Marxism does not tolerate deviations. It is not satisfied that one should be a humanist, or even some form of socialist. 'Reformist' is a term of reproach. There is to be only one true socialistic humanism, and that is held to derive from the Dialectic Materialism of Marx as interpreted by Lenin. All other sorts are in varying degrees dismissed as heretical, but chiefly because they are gradualist; for the orthodox Marxist holds that no true change can be effected without conflict. 'Reform' means compromise, in which the reactionaries manage to hold on to something. It is only discontinuous revolution which can really make a clean break with the old order.

How strange it would be if in the face of a rationalistic scientific humanism Marxists found themselves driven into the same camp as Christians. It must be quite clear from the story of the Lysenko controversy that pure science is not by any means always on the side of the Marxist, that the attempt to force everything into a dialectical

---

[1] Mr. Dulles, of course, would not agree with this: he thinks Marxism in China to be a phase which will pass, more especially because of the strong individualism of the Chinese character. But this is a very debatable proposition. See Chapter XII, sect. iv.

framework will not succeed, and that the promise of a Marxist millennium is based upon faith and hope, upon prophetic prediction of what one would like to happen, rather than upon rational demonstration. If the Marxist hope were to fail, and its faith to prove a false guide (and this looks like happening), then the Christian socialist might be the residuary legatee of the desire for a true faith and a sure hope, since basically the Christian religion is itself revolutionary.

Rudolf Otto once said that even in the event of the triumph of Christianity none of the great non-Christian religions ought to be allowed to vanish without its own special features having first been studied with reverent care and generous appreciation, in order to see whether they might not have something to contribute to the fullness of the Christian faith. It will be my purpose therefore in these pages to give due consideration in turn to each non-Christian complex of faith, and to enquire what might fitly be preserved and incorporated into a true Christian Catholicism. But here it is necessary to be cautious. Changes are taking place within the Asian religions themselves away from what may be called their classic expression. The latter may continue to survive in all sorts of places which are less accessible to the influences of modernity, but the sort of Hinduism, Islam, and Buddhism now to be encountered among educated Asians is likely, judged by classical standards, to be heretical or modernistic,[1] and often of an unprecedented character, full of new attempts at syncretism.

Bishop Neill has this year challenged Christians to make stronger efforts to penetrate the minds of believers in the non-Christian religions, and to seek to understand why they have seemed to many to provide a rich and satisfying inner life. The answer suggested here will be that in these great religions there is a *relatedness*, that they do not stand in complete isolation from one another, but that through them runs a kind of golden thread, however much it may be tarnished

---

[1] Dr. Max Warren has written to me: '... However much the Ahmadiyyah sect may officially be denominated a heresy in Islam, its influence (or the influence of a similar mental outlook) is increasingly widespread. The local mullah on the North West frontier of Pakistan or in Meshed in Iran, or in one of the villages of the Delta in Egypt may be fanatically orthodox, but the Foreign Minister of Pakistan is likely to be one of the Ahmadiyyah, and the Effendi class over most of the Middle East has long since passed from anything approaching orthodox Muslim belief. Its link with Islam is the link of culture, custom, and tradition, not of deep inner conviction. Allow for the fact that that statement is a little exaggerated, there is, I think, substantial truth in it.
'Again, take Hinduism. No doubt there are Hindus who can only properly be approached through the medium of a sympathetic understanding of the great classics of Hindu thought, but the vast majority of Indians who are likely to be met with by any missionary are quite unmoved by the classics, and certainly are not the adherents of strict Brahmin doctrines. For example, your devotional type of young Indian today, in so far as he is a Hindu, tends towards the tenets of the Ramakrishna Mission rather than towards strict Hinduism. The politically minded young Indian follows Gandhi, and today Vinoba Bhave, and is in effect following a way of Hinduism which has been profoundly modified by the Christian Gospel.'

and obscured here and there through expression in an unfamiliar idiom, or through a covering cloud of superstition. The one Reality is sought. The seekers are themselves all the creaturely off-spring of the one Reality. Human creatures can only be addressed by that one Reality within the limitations of human faculties, and can in turn only practise and maintain communion with the one Reality through such a technique as is possible to the human species. It would be surprising if there were not a good many similarities in religious practice, but it is not so much the practice as the content of belief on which attention should be fixed, since it may well be that only one such content of belief fully satisfies the conditions for the full expression of the character of the one Reality. The effect of what we may call Dionysian mystical theology and technique has undoubtedly been widespread, and accounts for a good many of the similarities which we observe; but a rich and satisfying *inner* life need not be the highest and best form of religion. It could and still can be an intensely selfish spirituality, no doubt extremely agreeable to persons of a certain kind of temperament, who like living on mounts of Transfiguration, but who feel no urge to battle for social righteous-ness, and tend to leave Lazarus just where he is, even though they may provide him with a dole.

In general it may be said that whereas fifty years ago the non-Christian religions were on the defensive, it is no exaggeration to say that in many instances they are now on the attack. Dr. Dewick has described the spectacle which he witnessed not long ago in Ceylon during a celebration in Kandy, when a vast statue of the Buddha was flood-lit, and an illuminated inscription placed over it: 'The True Light of the World.' The Imam of the Ahmadiyya Mosque at Woking has said that Christians should not monopolise Jesus Christ, 'since he also belongs to Islam'—a statement which of course is in one sense true. The gentle polemics of Sir Sarvepalli Radhakrishnan are fairly well known.[1]

Anyone can see, however, that the facts have not altered. One may become an enthusiast for a belief because one is inspired by a sense of emancipation, of renewed national dignity, and of pride in one's own cultural inheritance, and with that enthusiasm it is im-possible not to sympathise. One should even feel a respect for it. But such enthusiasm does not affect the basic relation of one's belief to other beliefs, since they must needs all be judged on their merits

---

[1] Dr. Dewick has quoted an amusing remark of Radhakrishnan that different religions are like different public schools. One expects the Eton boy to say, and to believe sincerely, that Eton is the best school in the world: and the Harrovian to say the same of Harrow: and that is sound loyalty. But one does not expect the Harrovian to praise Eton, or vice versa!

alone, and ought not to be modified in any way for purposes of argument so as to assimilate them to Christianity, but should be taken exactly as they have independently developed. Moreover, fundamental principles may be betrayed by more than one set of people. It is the principles that need long-term examination rather than their unworthy exponents. If it was an ostensibly Christian nation which first engaged in nuclear warfare, it was a predominantly Buddhist nation which committed the treachery of Pearl Harbour and the atrocities of Malaya. 'All have sinned and fallen short of the glory of God.'

One must, however, in honesty, say that part of the attack on Christianity consists in two things. First, in judging by Christian standards. The very illogicality of this is impressive. Why should a Buddhist or a Moslem judge the adherents of another religion by standards which are not necessarily his own? The fact that such a judgment can be made is something which should provoke deep shame and humility on our part, since it suggests that our faith is better than we are, and that our critics are aware of this, even if they do not say so. And in the second place, part of the defence of non-Christian faiths clearly consists in a re-writing of their credentials so as to make them more like Christianity. But if those who hold to them believe them to be good enough in themselves to deserve loyalty, why should they wish to alter or adapt them in this way? It can only be because of a covert suspicion that the Christian faith possesses some treasure which they themselves have not.

I do not write the above in any spirit of animosity; but it seems clear to me that here is one of those cases in which it is a bounden duty to 'speak the truth in love', and where a truth needs to be thought over honestly, and its implications faced with courage.

But we must now go back to where we started, i.e. that this is a work of *Christian* theology. Christian theology, however, is, or at least claims to be, a part of truth. If it distorts or ignores what is true, it is condemned at the outset. There may be different aspects of truth. Many will remember Dr. Westcott's remark about its being not less than a perfect cube. But there cannot be different brands of truth. Truth is fact, and even if of infinite extent, must possess unity and consistency. Its various branches must cohere, must fit together, and must make sense. We may grant that if a Being of the nature of a self-existent super-Personal Deity is to be assumed, the whole truth could be only knowable and known to such a Being. But no department of the whole truth could be of such a character that it could be at variance with or in contradiction to other departments of the whole truth. If then Christian theology is a part of truth it must be congruous with and related to all other departments of truth.   Sometimes it may be possible or necessary to iron out (so to speak) seeming inconsistencies, but it must be the duty of any responsible Christian theologian to aim, before everything else, at writing the truth, and to avoid the inclusion of what seems to be doubtful or erroneous, whether in the exegesis of Biblical texts, in doctrinal expositions, or in the writing of Church history.   No doubt humanly speaking it is not easy to divest one's self of the prejudices which one inherits from one's upbringing, one's family, national and ecclesiastical traditions, or from the preferences of temperament. But the effort has to be made, and since what is true only exists by the will of God and proceeds from the mind of God, it is the theologian's duty to love truth and to pursue truth at all costs, knowing that since truth is of God, the pursuit of truth, though it may sometimes seem to lead him away from God, can never do so in the long run, and that a generous acceptance of fact, and a scrupulous rejection of theories which seem inconsistent with known and observed fact, as well as an equally scrupulous acceptance of those which appear to be consistent with it, are plainly his solemn duty.   It must be admitted that these are very exacting conditions, and that human frailty forbids anyone to claim that he has perfectly observed them.   But in a world dominated by the sciences, no other course is open to any theologian than to aim steadfastly at fulfilling them.

It would be difficult in this book to avoid some reference to geography as conceived at the present day, and even to astronomy, since the general view of the universe can hardly be left out of a survey which is already committed to the consideration of mankind from China to Peru.   I admit that this may seem rather like the behaviour of a man who in writing the History of England started with the creation of the world.   But in view of various remarks which in our day and age have been made by astronomers, it seems hardly possible to avoid this course.[1]   It will also be impossible to avoid a reference to analytical philosophy, since some of its exponents have seen fit to challenge the validity of any religious experiences, non-Christian and Christian alike, and to query whether statements made anywhere by anyone about any sort of religion can in any sense at all be meaningful.

---

[1] The way in which almost all theologians except Dr. Inge have in the past thirty years ignored the work of the astronomers is perhaps only matched by the curious way in which it gets left out of much popular thinking.   This is not a rational exclusion, but is due to emotional prejudice against thinking uncomfortable thoughts, and is also partly due to human inability to concentrate on matters which don't lie close to us. Perhaps I myself should not have been so much impressed with its importance had I not happened to live as I do opposite the University Observatory and Solar Physics Research Station, with Sir Arthur Eddington as my neighbour for a good many years.   I cannot go out of my front gate without being reminded of the existence of the astronomers.

Before we embark on these various undertakings it is only right that one should define one's standpoint clearly.

The Christian starts from a very simple but profound decision for Christ. The phrase has unfortunately become rather hackneyed, and has been bandied about by the enthusiasts of a certain group. It might even seem to suggest a certain patronising adoption of the Master, since it is He who chooses us, rather than we who choose Him. Yet in accepting the choice it is believed that a certain personal surrender must be made.

> 'A Man of sorrows, of toil and tears,
>   An outcast Man and lonely—
> But He looked on me, and to endless years
>   Him I must love, Him only.
>
> And I would abide where He abode
>   And follow His steps for ever,
> His people my people, His God my God,
>   To the land beyond the river.
>
> And where He died would I also die,
>   For dearer a grave beside Him
> Than a kingly throne among living men,
>   The place which they denied Him.'

There can be no mistaking the sense of that, and it is the point from which the Christian sets out. It is fair to say that although there have been many faithful disciples and followers of the other great sages and prophets of mankind, it is impossible to find anything as searching as the above written by any one of them about his own leader. Whatever one's opinion about it may be, it is quite certain that the disciple who follows Jesus of Nazareth finds himself more deeply and more emotionally involved with Him as a personal leader than the most ardent Buddhist or ardent Moslem finds himself in relation to his own sage or prophet. The demands made are greater; the identification to be achieved is unparalleled.

Now the reasons for starting out from this decision are clear. The Christian, like the Marxist, believes profoundly in the union of theory and practice. He is sure that one can only know the full truth of Christianity by living inside it experimentally. ('If any man willeth to do the will of Him that sent me, he shall know of the teaching, whether it be of God.') An act of will to *follow* without reserve and without prejudice must therefore precede every other activity. The self must be surrendered, as in the famous First

Spiritual Exercise of St. Ignatius Loyola.[1]   Once this surrender of the will has been made, then, and then only, can there be complete intellectual freedom, since He to whom surrender has been made *is* the Truth.   This, it will be seen, is something quite different from and much profounder than the surrenders which are often substituted for it, i.e. decisions to submit to an infallible Church or an infallible Bible.   It is said that though these two surrenders look like intellectual suicide, they work.   So they do, up to a point, just as any other religious act of submission works by delivering the individual from self-centredness, and reorganising the ego round a spiritual centre outside the self.

But decision today, if it is to be any good at all, must be made within the world as we see it, and not within the obscurantism of the Middle West, or the naïve romanticism of the Midi.   It must be made within the bounds of a society which, during the lifetime of children of ten who are now at school, may become something like that pictured by Sir George Thomson in a recent book.   The words of Cowper have today a prophetic meaning which he can hardly have intended when he wrote:

> 'He who wore the thorn-crowned head and bleeding brow
> Rules universal nature.'

Surrender to the claims of Christ has to be made intelligently within that world of universal nature which modern researches have revealed to us, and since all knowledge is in some sense revelation, we are bound to take what is progressively being discovered about the external universe, in all its departments and on all its levels of being, as in itself a progressive revelation.   Moreover, since He who calls, calls His disciples to love God with their minds, part of their surrender, and indeed a very large part, must be the dedication of their minds to follow truth wherever it may lead.

Sir George Thomson, in a public utterance, has reminded us that truth in science is in two parts, truth of fact, and truth of interpretation.   In the former case, there can in the last resort be only one thing that is true, i.e. the fact itself.   In the latter, there may be a number of theories interpreting fact, and most of them will perhaps be sincerely framed and in themselves respectable.   But some will be better interpretations than others, and in the last resort there may be only one which possesses the maximum truth of interpretation.

---

[1] One notices the testimony of Dr. Schweitzer at this point, when he writes: 'Anyone who ventures to look the historical Jesus straight in the face and to listen to what He may have to teach him in His powerful sayings soon ceases to ask what this strange-seeming Jesus can still be to him.   He learns to know Him as one who claims to have authority over him.'

In his address he went on to draw an analogy between truth in science and truth in religion, and implied that the existence of a number of religions did not necessarily mean that one was good and true and that all the others were false and evil, nor even, at the opposite extreme, that all were equal, or that each necessarily shared one or more sides of the truth, though not the whole truth. It might still be possible for one of them to supersede all the others as the *most* true. I feel that at this point it needs to be added that since religion deals with God as Fact, no finite being could ever expect in this life to attain to complete knowledge of the whole Fact, to the same extent to which a scientist might expect to attain complete knowledge of a physical fact. Even here he might only attain to the 'what' and the 'how', but not to the 'why' and 'wherefore'. Thus before one ever got to the stage of interpretation in religion one would find the way blocked by the impossibility of reaching complete factual knowledge. But is not this just what we find in dealing with one another as persons? I may live many years with a man without really knowing the facts about him, unless he chooses to *confide* in me, and I may therefore hopelessly misinterpret his motives and purposes in what he does. How much more difficult must it be for any finite being to know and interpret Deity unless the Latter is pleased to take the initiative. Something like this has of course often been said before, and yet how little account is taken of it in considering the general problem of religion! We can only expect to proceed safely along lines of interpretation so long as we start from the right facts, however partial and limited. If we include among our data any wrong facts, to that extent our interpretations will also be defective, and therefore useless.

Why is it still alleged (probably with justice) that we have not yet found the correct technique for communicating the Christian message to the scientifically trained and educated members of the public in general?

One reason is that the latter are still far from convinced that we are taking the scientific study of our own religion seriously, let alone that of others. They observe the antique formularies, with their pre-Copernican and pre-Darwinian assumptions, to be still in use (this does not apply to all Protestant denominations) although those who recite them in worship sometimes tell the public to put a free interpretation upon the words, which involves (as an intelligent student once put it): 'that we say what we don't mean'. They occasionally listen to sermons, and for the most part find them naïve. They reflect that the largest single body of Christians is still timid as to the free study of the natural sciences, and also in regard to biblical criticism, and that it totally rejects the idea of family planning, scientific birth control, and eugenics. They hear very little about any liberal or modernist Christianity, and often seem hardly aware that it exists. They therefore assume that by and large the Christian movement is still opposed to all the best that they stand for. While they may sometimes deplore the world-negating systems of Asia, especially if they themselves are socialists, they nevertheless think some of them to be less opposed to science than Christianity.

The above considerations need to be taken seriously. Asia and Africa today are accepting from the West a great deal of scientific technique and outlook. The relation of the Christian faith to science is therefore quite as important as its relation to the old faiths of Asia and Africa. Popular Hinduism and Buddhism, as well as popular African religion, are in process of being liquidated by modern education and the deliberate spreading of literacy, as well as by the use of radio programmes, especially in villages.

Religious broadcasting can be a danger as well as a blessing. If it is undertaken by authorities whose policy is to prevent spiritual battles in search of the truth from being fought in public, then quite obviously persons of an honest and enquiring mind will turn sadly away from it. It is quite reasonable that one might desire people to make a decision at some point to live as Christians, and to hazard all for Jesus at a clap, and not simply to drift along vaguely and hopefully. But in a world of young people, a large mass of whom are either practising or being trained as technicians, it is idle to suppose that such persons, whether in India, China, Africa, or Europe, will be able to arrive at a good and intelligent as well as a firm decision, if the terms of the invitation presented to them seem irrelevant to the new order of society in which they live, and are couched in language which does not appear to them to be meaningful.

I earnestly desire, as did the writers of *Lux Mundi* nearly seventy years ago, to speak in the way that the Church to which I belong would have me speak. Anglicans, as Charles Gore then said,[1] are so free from the obscurantist fear of historical enquiry, that they are more likely than those in any other part of the Church Universal to arrive at determinations on the subject of religion such as will be of material service to the whole of Christendom. I return humble thanks that I have been enabled during some forty years to join frequently during University terms in collective study of the text of the New Testament, and for fifty years to engage in pastoral duty as an ordained minister of the Church of England, twenty-three of them in one single parish of plain folk. These twin occupations have

[1] In *Lux Mundi*.

guarded me from the dangers of mere superficial attachment to the Christian faith. No one can claim to be more fully aware of what that faith is *from the inside* than I can, or more conscious of the sense of personal inadequacy which such knowledge brings with it. Both my parents were heirs of a very long and honourable Christian tradition, and, on my father's side, I inherit a tradition of those who once left their homeland and became 'displaced persons' for con-science' sake. But on the other hand, from the time when at the age of fifteen I heard Romesh Dutt lecture in London on the Ramayana and the Mahabharata (which latter of course includes the Gita) I felt that here was great literature about the implications of which the Christian Church must inevitably come to a fair and just decision, and my interest in the religious experience of India, and indeed of Asia in general, has never waned since that time.

Nevertheless, the majesty and complexity of the subject here to be treated fill one with misgivings. Had I not twice been asked to undertake the task of composing this book, I am sure I should never have dared to attempt it. My only excuse is that having once tried (in 1941) to write a straight and detached account of the history of the development of global religion considered objectively, one owes it to the public to say why and in what sense and for what reasons one wishes to be considered a Christian, and to try to do justice to one's own share in the Christian religious experience.

Let no one suppose that I wish to promote Christianity simply because it *is* my own religion. I only do so because at the end of a long and full lifetime I still believe more than ever that it is the true and best of all faiths, rich in marvellous recuperative powers and in the capacity for objective self-criticism. I see it still developing, and I want it to succeed, because I believe it to be what it claims to be, and to be good and positive, offering a better general explanation of the problems of life, especially the tragic ones, than does any other religion. I do not pretend that it is the whole of the truth. That would be foolish as well as arrogant. But it is, I believe, the *essential* truth for life as God wishes and permits us to know it, and in the knowledge of that it is abundantly possible to live and die. If a common world-faith is to be possible, this is it, even though it may not yet have reached its fullness of form, and may still be in a some-what adolescent stage. We need have no hesitation in granting that the Living God has spoken to mankind 'by divers portions and in divers manners'; but we are still abundantly entitled to claim that the Decisive Word has come to us in a Single Person, in a precise spatio-temporal historical setting. At the same time, while I am sure that a common world-faith is necessary, and that the evidence is in favour of that world-faith being some form of Christianity, I do not think that, taken as a whole, Christianity as it stands, is yet quite fit to fulfil that function.

The plan of this book should now be set forth. I propose to begin by stating some presuppositions which will put the subject, so to speak, within its cosmic and geographical context, and in due proportion. I shall then proceed to a brief historical survey, aimed at giving as clear and concise an account as may be of the development of religion in the world both prior to and apart from the Christian movement. But since that movement has now diffused itself into many parts of the planet, I shall make no apology for interrupting the argument at this point in order to consider the meaning and principles of diffusion as they appear to the anthropologist. I shall then go back to the historical survey, and consider in some detail the manner in which the Christian movement from its inception related itself to the religious systems already existing in the world into which it emerged. This section will be of decisive importance for my main argument, because it is precisely at this point that some very learned and earnest Christians today have disagreed about the principles which should guide the movement in the face of non-Christian religions as they at present exist. It will of course be necessary to say something about the origin and past history of what have been called the great *founded* religions, other than Christianity. Volumes have been written upon these, and it will be necessary to avoid becoming entangled in detail: but a clear picture must if possible be given. It must be recognised, however, that these systems are now changing with such rapidity that it is idle for anyone to study them as they were, and to suppose that when he meets them in the field they will still be like that. One item must therefore be to give some account of these changes, and to consider as fairly and reasonably as one can how these modified systems come to look beside Christianity. But at this point it will be only too easy to get tripped up. With which type of Christianity are they to be compared?— The Christian movement has been and still is going through many changes, and even though still hardly beyond its adolescence, as I have said, has grown already from an insignificant seed into a mighty organism, just as the Founder predicted that it would. The problem thus presented cannot simply be looked at and passed by. Something constructive has got to be said about it, even at the risk of error. Perhaps the best plan will be to consider how different types of Christian thinkers have in the past hundred years or so undertaken a theological revaluation of their religion, viewed against the background of other beliefs. This I shall undertake in my final chapter;

and it will I fear show that there is a serious divergence between two main groups in their approach to the problem.

But before doing so, it will be necessary to consider the pressing problem of Marxism. Finally one may venture, greatly daring, to estimate the possibilities of the future. Here there will be still greater risk of going off on the wrong track. Yet again the attempt must be made; and since a large part of my purpose is to stimulate both non-Christians and would-be Christians, as well as those who already claim to be Christian believers, to think and to go on thinking, perhaps it will not much matter if some of the things written in this final section provoke discussion and even disagreement. It is certainly a part of Christian belief that truth is a goal as well as an inheritance, and that the Spirit of the Living Master will according to His promise guide us into all truth, and even show us things to come. But it is also the confident hope of Christian believers that these things to come will not detract from the glory of Christ, since, if as the Word of God He is already reigning over universal nature, future discoveries can only make explicit what has already been there implicitly.

Let us therefore approach our task with the words on our lips of the *gayatri*, that famous Indian prayer, which is so easily capable of a Christian interpretation:

'LET US MEDITATE UPON THE MOST EXCELLENT LIGHT.
MAY HE GUIDE OUR MINDS.'

N.B.—It ought to be said that this book had been planned, and a large part of it written before I had had any opportunity of reading Dr. Hendrik Kraemer's latest work. Many resemblances to it are therefore to be attributed to the fact that we have been working (although independently) upon the same subject. But I gratefully acknowledge the stimulus and advantage which I have derived at a later stage from being able to study the text of his book; and even where I dissent from his conclusions, I am bound to pay a respectful tribute to their eminent author, who has led me to modify and amplify some of my own.

Finally I would wish to say that I profoundly deprecate the practice that has sometimes prevailed of abusing non-Christian religions in respect of their weaker features. By all means let there be a dispassionate survey of weaknesses, Christian as well as non-Christian. But let what is true and best quietly take the place of what is less good and true, as happens in the case of scientific theories and human techniques. Wasting time in abuse is both uncharitable and unseemly. All that the missionary really need say is: 'And behold I show unto you a more excellent way.'

CHAPTER I

PRESUPPOSITIONS

THE UNIVERSE AROUND US

Let us begin by trying to look at ourselves objectively. That we can do so is in itself a matter for wonder, since we have no experience of any other living organisms that seem able to do it, or that show any interest in trying to make what it is fashionable to call 'meaningful statements' about themselves and their surroundings.

Our present dwelling-place is on a spherical body, slightly flattened at its poles, and commonly known to its inhabitants as the earth. This body mainly consists of mineral substances in a state of solidity, interspersed with water, but it seems clear that at some remote period in the past these substances were in a gaseous condition.[1]

We must needs consider the general lay-out of the universe of which our earth forms a minute part. What we call the solar system is considered to form a section (though a rather small and suburban section) of a vast concourse of stellar objects in various stages of condensation, grouped together in the shape of a dinner plate. This *galaxy*, as it is called, may possibly contain within its limits, besides substances which are either in a gaseous condition or which have not the right temperature, something like 100,000 or a million bodies (the real number may lie somewhere between the two extremes) upon which organic life could develop, is developing, or has developed. But there are, on a rough estimate beside our own particular system, 100 million others of various shapes and sizes existing in the universe which are within the range of observation, the nearest of these, 700,000 light-years away, being the galaxy connected with what astronomers know as the constellation of Andromeda. Possibly there may be a further indefinite number of other such galaxies which lie beyond the range of observation, and to each several galaxy there might be a million planetary systems, and thus a possible total of 100 million million systems for the observable part of the universe alone, without counting the rest of it which is beyond.

There have been two main attempts at explaining how the earth first came to have a separate existence. Some thirty years ago it was

[1] It is nearly 8000 miles in diameter, almost 25,000 miles in circumference, and weighs 6×10^{21} tons.

18

thought that the sun, in very remote antiquity, had been approached by another star, which by the force of attraction had drawn away a large piece from it, and that this piece, continuing to rotate, had split up into the various planets which now revolve round the sun as a centre. This theory was found to have certain flaws in it, with the technical details of which we need not concern ourselves; and more recently it has been replaced by another. According to the latter, the sun and another star, called a supernova, formed what is called a binary system, and revolved round one another until the second star reached a point of disequilibrium which caused it to explode, and so to divide up, the larger fragments forming the planets, and the smaller the moon, the planetary satellites, and a quantity of lesser meteoric bodies.

There is no necessity to believe that this second theory will prove to be the final one which satisfies all conditions, but for the present it holds the field, and is less open to objection than its predecessor. According to the earlier theory it seemed likely that there must be remarkably few places in the whole universe where atmospheric and other conditions would be favourable to the development of living beings at all like ourselves ('Very few babies in other cradles' was the picturesque way of putting it). But the later theory favours the possibility that in every galaxy (and we have seen that of these there are a vast number) it would be possible for planetary systems to develop through the explosions of supernovae, in which organic life could emerge at some points, and continue to evolve until creatures of the same type as the human species appeared on them as well, and not improbably would pass through similar experiences.

Again we have no right to say that this later theory is destined to be the final one. It might be modified again in twenty years time, though the likelihood of this, on the evidence available, does not seem to be very great. Meanwhile it holds the field, and its most popular spokesman has had his own picturesque way of describing it:

'On this basis, every event, no matter how impossible, must be repeated at different places in the universe, so that even now in some distant spot another fellow like me may be broadcasting to an audience exactly like you, about an identical subject.'[1]

There is, however, one interesting point which both these theories have in common. They both predict the ultimate extinction of life on the earth. The earlier one held that because the sun was gradually cooling, a crisis would eventually be reached at which the

---

[1] Professor Karl Jaspers even hazards the conjecture that in some cases the explosion of a supernova might be due to its quasi-human inhabitants reaching the same stage as ourselves, and proceeding to the further fatal step of destroying themselves by nuclear fission!

temperature of the planet would fall below that necessary for any organisms to remain alive, much less to breed. The one at present prevailing predicts that before the real cooling of the sun begins there will be a contrary process, in which the hydrogen-supply in the sun will be converted into helium, thus greatly increasing its luminosity and its emanation of heat. The effect of this will be to raise the temperature on the earth's surface beyond the point at which the continuance of organic life can remain possible.[1]

Either way, the answer is death. Man as an individual is already only too conscious of his destiny. He may be finding ways of increasing his expectation of life, but he knows that he must sooner or later reach the frontier. Modern astronomy will not allow him even the positivist's hope of racial immortality, or endorse the Asian idea of reincarnation in human or non-human organisms. All life is to go; over all organisms, whether rudimentary or complex, hangs the doom of extinction whether by freezing or burning, and the expectation that some day the earth will be a dark and wholly lifeless planet. An existentialist like Heidegger will have it that this absolute fact of extinction is something which it is before all things necessary to face. Life is a brief space of existence between original nothingness and the return to nothingness. In this, of course, he is no innovator. The speech of the ealdorman before King Edwin of Northumbria, spoken some thirteen hundred years ago, has a very modern ring about it:

'I will tell you, O king, what methinks man's life is like. Sometimes when your hall is lit up for supper on a wild winter's evening, and warmed by a fire in the midst, a sparrow flies in by one door, takes shelter for a moment in the warmth, and then flies out again by another door, and is lost in the stormy darkness. No one in the hall sees the bird before it enters, nor after it has gone forth; it is only seen while it hovers near the fire. So it is, I ween, with this brief span of our life in this world; what has gone before it, what will come after it—of this we know nothing. If the strange teacher can tell us, by all means let him be heard.'

The sparrow is now not merely mankind in particular, but, as we shall see the whole of stellar matter in general. The old story of Philip of Macedon and his slaves, and of Saladin and the inscription which was hung over the table at his feast, not to mention the curious dialogue between a man and his slave which has been discovered on a most ancient tablet in Mesopotamia, are evidence in themselves that long ago leaders of men sufficiently recognised the shrinkage of

[1] Another suggested possibility is that as the rotation of the earth on its axis is known to be slowing down, it will eventually cease to rotate, so that one-half of it will become too hot, and the other too cold, for living creatures to survive on its surface.

values which comes with death; though, of course, since they were not modern astronomers, they did not know how sweeping its effects were going to be for the whole race. It is, however, equally important to note that mankind in general has ever refused to sit down submissively under the Fact. It has always felt that if the latter really were what it appears to be, then there would be something radically wrong with the universe. Let us leave the matter at this point, and continue our objective survey.

The idea of the dialectic materialist that one starts ultimately from the conception of primordial matter in motion cannot be accepted without demur, since matter itself cannot be taken as beyond the need of definition. The astronomers, Hoyle and Lyttleton, while they reject Jeans's earlier theory of a purely one-way system of running down or entropy in the material universe, cautiously put forward, as being more in harmony with the evidence, a kind of eternal cyclic system, involving the continual expansion of galaxies to the point at which they fade out, and an indefinite condensation of new galaxies to replace those that are disappearing. They thus posit a continuous and eternal creation of material substance, but they will not allow that this material substance is primordial, since observations, they say, contradict this possibility. Material substance capable of observation seems, they say, to crystallise into being from nowhere. 'At one time the various atoms composing the material do not exist, and at a later time they do.'[1] 'May it not be that it is a property of space that wherever space occurs, then matter may appear in it from nowhere, and to just such an extent in total throughout the observable universe as to balance the loss over the frontier horizon of the universe? That is, new material created from nothing, throughout space.'[2]

This remarkable conclusion is of course put out without any consequent theological deduction of a Creative Mind which, from eternity to eternity, is engaged in bringing material substance into existence *ex nihilo*. Nevertheless, the obvious inference must be that Something brings it into existence without being dependent on anything else, and this is only another way of saying that that Something, whatever it is, is Self-Existent. But since before material substance is in a condition in which it can be observed, it does not appear to be there at all, the implication is that that which is Self-Existent is invisible, as well as being unobservable by human apparatus. Hoyle refuses to accept any idea that the material of the universe is infinitely old. He says it could not be, since if it were,

---

[1] Hoyle.   [2] Lyttleton.

there could by this time be no hydrogen left in the universe, and as is well known, there is a great deal of the latter.[1]

The final conclusion then would seem to be unavoidable, that there is an inexhaustible source of Invisible and Self-Existent Energy which brings the observable spatio-temporal order of the universe into being, and that since the less cannot create the greater, this Self-Existent Source cannot be impersonal or sub-personal, since in that case it could not be responsible for the evolution of beings possessing even finite personality.   It is therefore not improper to say that it must be in essence super-personal.   To say that the impersonal is superior to the personal is an irrational error of thought; which could never have come to pass if the Self-Existent had not become degraded by association with anthropomorphic myths; and the sooner it is discarded the better.   Yet even along anthropomorphic lines, by the contemplation of that which is best in man, it is still possible that something may reasonably be learned about the nature of the Self-Existent.

Coming now nearer home, we turn our gaze upon the earth itself.   It is not, of course, today exactly as it was in the earliest stages of its separate existence.   Indeed it has altered a very great deal even within our own lifetime, and certainly very much since it cooled down sufficiently for its surface, marine or otherwise, to be able to accommodate living organisms.   Its contours have changed: the position and elevation of its various land-masses have shifted (although we know very little as yet about the possibilities or ultimate effects of what is called continental drift): and the depth and area of its seas, rivers, and lakes have also been subject to variation, consequent upon the occurrence of what are known as ice-ages, which may have been due to a tilting of the axis of the planet which has transferred arctic regions away from the poles, and tropical areas away from the equator.   The nature and distribution of its human inhabitants have also been subject to changes, although certain features about them have remained surprisingly constant.

One of these, which is the main subject of our concern in this volume, is their persistent and frequently expressed desire to establish a satisfactory working relationship with the 'Self-Existent', i.e. with

[1] One gathers that this theory of ubiquitous continual creation (either *ex nihilo*, or out of the non-observable), although still in its infancy, has the most promise for successful development at present, of any theories put forward.   It is interesting to compare at this point the reflections of Mr. Aldous Huxley upon the matter.   After describing the laboratory experiments which demonstrate what is known as the PK effect (psychokinetic) upon matter, he continues: 'if a human mind can directly influence matter not merely within but outside its body, then a Divine Mind, immanent in the Universe or transcendent to it, may be presumed to be capable of imposing forms upon a pre-existing chaos of formless matter, *or even perhaps of thinking substance as well as forms into existence*' (the italics are my own).   The above was written some time before the statements of Hoyle and Lyttleton were issued.

that Ultimate which is its own *raison d'être*, and which, because it does not depend on anything else, must be more than just the mass of visible and fluctuating phenomena of nature. Of course, such a desire and such a working relationship began by being expressed and manifested in the crudest and simplest forms, and were concerned at first with an attempt at the conservation of the simplest and crudest values. But they are not to be evaluated simply by being referred back to their lowest terms, but rather by the consideration of what they have grown into, and any objective survey of these attempts at adjustment to the Self-Existent must take account of some very elaborate thinking and of some very magnificent types of cultus.

Perhaps the question of the Ultimate requires closer attention. If I am talking to someone with a modern scientific education who is a serious-minded enquirer, but who says that the word GOD does not signify anything within his own personal experience, what should I say?

There are, of course, certain preliminary points to be made, and the first of these is that one is really starting with the wrong word. GOD to many persons means a sort of invisible 'super-daddy', and the scientifically trained person may well say that he has no acquaintance with such a being. He looks through his life, and is not conscious that at any point he encountered such a personality. Better start with some other word which has not the same associations. We might try the Self-Existent. Now the latter has been quite real to many who have not conceived of It anthropically, e.g. some of the Hebrew prophets, and certain Hindu mystics and Chinese sages. Even the orthodox Christian definition of It is 'one, living, and eternal, without body, parts or passions'; in fact a unique super-personal Mind, creating and controlling the entire universe. It seems inevitable that people should have experience of this category of the Self-Existent in a number of different ways, and a fuller account of these will be provided in Chapter II; but it will be enough to give a few here as examples. Some clearly experience the Self-Existent as a continuously creative system or stream of life; others as a directing Super-Mind; others again as beyond definition, since we, being part of It, cannot see it objectively or in a detached manner so as to be able to define it, but are only conscious of our identity with it. But in no case do they feel disposed to conceive of the Self-Existent anthropically. Even Christian philosophers have considered themselves forbidden to do that. There is, however, a specific Christian experience, which I am confident is shared to some extent by the adherents of other religions, and that is that along with the *ultimacy* there may also be some kind of *intimacy*, so that one cannot but be conscious at times of living under the controlling and purposive guidance of the Self-Existent, and of exercising one's freedom within the sphere of an over-ruling Providence. I would venture to suggest to the scientist that he may be in contact with this Self-Existent Providence without being aware of it, and that he is often nearest when he is engaged in one of his most characteristic occupations, e.g. the surgeon when, scalpel in hand, he is at the moment of beginning a delicate operation in the theatre, or the physicist when he is at the climax of some decisive experiment in nuclear research.

There is, however, a very definite difficulty about certain of these conceptions of the Self-Existent, and it is on the whole a moral difficulty, and was brought out with great clarity by Dr. Schweitzer in his now largely forgotten Selly Oak lectures of 1923, in which he pointed out that if one accepts the pantheism of India, the polytheism of ancient Japan, the nature worship of ancient China, the various polytheisms of the Mediterranean or the Middle East, the deism of Islam—and he might now have added the evolutionism of the humanist, or the pragmatism of the Marxists—we are left in the end without any standard of right and wrong, good and evil. If the Self-Existent be a group of deities, some of them will be favourable, some persuadably neutral, some hostile; and right and wrong as such will not be guaranteed by any of them, for they are little more than men and women of a larger growth, with all the amiable qualities, the lusts, the passions, and the weaknesses of human beings magnified. If the Self-Existent be an immanent Life-Force, whatever contributes to its progress will be right, whatever hinders, wrong, and its ultimate purpose may not emerge until the end of the process—whoever will be there to observe it is not simple. If the Life-Force be as the Marxist dialectician describes it, then the reason for the relativism of his morals will in fact be abundantly simple. A thing is right if it ministers to the working out of the process. Hence to be shocked at a lie is absurd, if that lie helps the process, for that process is a long war, and in war all is fair. And again, if the Self-Existent is the Allah of the Moslems who is not to be enquired as to what he does, then everything 'shall be as Allah pleases', and the truth, mercy, and righteousness cease to have any fixed meaning. Allah, according to the holy Qur'ān, can and does deceive and plot, and mislead whom he will, so why should not we?

These positions seem only to have to be stated in order to establish their unsatisfactory nature. If the Self-Existent really be non-moral in the sense of being wholly indifferent to the highest spiritual values known to us, then there can be no alternative but to defy It.

The Christian view of Reality, on the contrary—perhaps not unrelated to those of Zarathustra, Socrates, and the Hebrew prophets—is that the creaturely is endowed by the Self-Existent with varying degrees of self-determination, that the purpose of the Self-Existent is always that of righteousness conceived at the very least in the highest terms known to mankind, so that the gift to the creaturely of the capacity to win and use freedom may lead either to co-operation or conflict with the righteous purpose of the Self-Existent. This co-operation will nevertheless involve the possibility in an open universe such as the one we inhabit, that suffering may have to be endured and constructively accepted. Deity does not coddle us, but expects us to share in His own adventure, which may include a species of 'cosmic Calvary'.

But to continue our objective survey in terms of physical geography. Let us suppose a sort of universal observer who is also an airman, and possibly one who is able to make a girdle round the earth in forty-five hours. Looking down from his vantage point in the sky as he travels, he will observe that the greater part of the surface of the earth is submerged beneath sea-water. The actual relative proportions in volume are said to be 99·976% solid, 0·024% fluid, but the water, of course, is spread out over a wide surface. We must assume, I think, that our observer has got somebody with him who can tell him what it is he is looking at down below. He will observe the existence of what used to be called the Eastern and Western hemispheres, that is to say, two main masses of land as distinct from water, one a good deal larger than the other, but in both cases divided in the middle. The greater hemisphere has its two portions divided on a broad front, and except at one point (the Suez Canal) the division is effected by small natural belts of sea; the lesser hemisphere has its two parts joined by a narrow neck of land artificially pierced by the Panama Canal. This description of land-surface is not, however, entirely satisfactory or exhaustive, as there are considerable tracts of the earth at the southern pole which are entirely detached from either hemisphere, and which are completely icebound; but since they have no resident population, they do not matter much for our purpose. More serious is the fact that the large detached island-mass of Australia, and the smaller islandmasses of New Zealand and the various islands of the Pacific, do not now really belong to either hemisphere, although they cannot be neglected, since they have a substantial and at some points increasing population. Returning to the study of the larger hemisphere it is necessary that the relative size and position of some of its parts should be realised. Those who travel little and who seldom study maps do not always realise what our universal observer is bound to see, namely that what is known as Europe is virtually a Western projection of Asia, and that taken as a whole India and China is each on the scale of Europe, so that generalisations about them must be made on that basis. It is manifestly improper to discuss India, with its enormous varieties of race, language, and physical configuration, as though it were the size of England; and much the same is true of China, where the differences in climate between North and South and of elevation in East and West profoundly affect the temperament of its population. In size, again, Europe and Asia taken together are pretty well matched by the African continent, which, when it is able adequately to solve its two problems of feeding and keeping healthy its vast population, must surely have a great future ahead of it.

In actual size, Great Britain is seen to rank very low. Though rather heavily populated, its total land area seems to be not much bigger than that of the newly constituted State of the Gold Coast (Ghana) in West Africa. Our observer as he looks down upon the U.S.S.R. may be reminded that it has been styled for some time the

Socialist sixth of the world, but it will be clear to him that if its satellite states[1] and China be added in, its influence as a State controlled by Marxist influence extends today over more like one-quarter of the world, not to mention small pockets of influence in other countries; but he will do well to remember that within it are still considerable bodies of persons who are trying to maintain the Christian way of life. He will perhaps have it pointed out to him that what is called the Moslem block runs mainly round the heat belt, and while it includes two new states with a considerable density of population (Pakistan and Indonesia), it is largely made up of desert areas, of which there are enormous ones in Northern and equatorial Africa as well as in Arabia and Iraq.

Crossing to look at the western hemisphere, our observer will no doubt be reminded that by far the greater part of its population has come from Europe, northern Europeans being largely in the majority in the United States and Canada, and southern Europeans vastly predominant in South America, although Brazil is now receiving numbers of Dutch and German colonists. There will be certain qualifications, such as the increasing number of people of Latin race in the population of the United States, and the presence there also of a considerable negro element. In South America rather more of the original Indian population has survived and even interbred with Latins, while in certain areas such as Guiana, Indians from Asia have come in, as well as a number of negroes. Chinese colonists have spread into Malaya, and Japanese are to be found on the Pacific coast of North America.

The size and proportions of some of the better-known states of the world need to be borne in mind. Size is no doubt a dangerous criterion to employ in judging importance; but it is worth recognising that a number of areas whose influence today is not what it used to be are nevertheless very extensive, and once carried much more considerable populations.

Take, for example, Iran. Today one thinks of it mainly as an oil-producing area with a number of interesting antiquities such as the city of Persepolis, and a great tradition of craftsmanship in the form of wonderful blue tiles and exquisite rugs and carpets; but in its distant past it saw great religious creative periods, the age of Zarathustra, the age of Mani, and the age of the Persian Moslem poets and painters. Were we to try to travel round Iran we should find that it covered some 620,000 square miles, and was perhaps

---

[1] Even if some of them show signs of strong deviationist tendencies, and, like Jugo-Slavia, develop Communisms of their own, it must not be supposed that their governments necessarily eschew all Marxist doctrines.

three or four times the size of Great Britain, yet with only a population of 18 millions as against England's 41 millions.

The United States of America has an area of nearly 3 million
square miles, with a population in 1952 of about 166½ millions, but
Brazil is larger, covering about 3½ million square miles, and, although
its population is steadily on the increase, has as yet only 52 million
inhabitants, and an enormous forest area.

The Union of Socialist Soviet Republics has a total area of over
8 million square miles, and an estimated total population of 193
millions.

Beside these the Scandinavian States and Holland, which give
ballast to the world, look exceedingly tiny. The modern state of
Egypt, which, like Iran, includes some desert areas, is only about half
the size of the latter, but has a slightly larger population of 19
millions, confined to a relatively small space, the Nile valley.
Canada is slightly larger than the United States of America in area,
over 3 million square miles, and therefore to be compared with
Brazil, though less than half the size of the U.S.S.R.; but it includes
regions within the Arctic circle, and is still under-populated, with
only 13 million inhabitants. Saudi Arabia, though larger than Iran,
with 800 thousand square miles, only supports a population of just
over 6 million, largely because of the desiccation of areas which
centuries ago were fertile and productive. India is as large as
Europe: so is China: and both have dense populations of over 400
million, still increasing.[1]

The influence of some small areas on the earth's surface is
altogether out of proportion to their size. On the map, the famous
Fertile Crescent from which so many of the permanent features of
ancient and modern civilisation have sprung, looks a most minute
portion of the total surface of the earth. Again, large areas on the
planet seem as though they will always with difficulty support any
substantial population, or make any very striking contributions of
their own to its culture. If they ever do, it will be the result of future
conquests of the desert by irrigation, or of the polar regions by
adjustment to conditions of extreme cold, and in other tracts by the
eradication of endemic disease.

Again, who would expect countries like Britain, Greece, and
ancient Israel to have made such noteworthy contributions, when
one views their limited territories? It is, I think, wholesome that
we should realise that the inhabitants of eastern Asia do not always
view these contributions with the same appreciation as do the inhabitants of Europe and America. Asia would probably say, and

[1] See Chapter XI at the end.

not unjustly, that for her, Indian religion and philosophy, and perhaps Indian art, had been as vital in forming her culture as anything contributed by ancient Hellas to that of Europe.

We have then the spectacle of a particular group of living organisms distributed rather unevenly on the surface of the earth, and consisting of a considerable number of different physical types, embracing many species, but possessing enough common characteristics—perhaps like the genus 'dog'—to justify our classifying them together. These creatures, who have developed a brain-system of remarkable complexity and efficiency, have come to speak of themselves as possessing also an element which operates through this brain system.[1] They give it many names, and have many different ideas as to its nature (one soul or a number of souls) and they disagree as to its relation to the bodily structure[2]; but in this they agree, that it exists, and they have been engaged throughout many millennia in a series of experimental adjustments of it to the Self-Existent, and for the most part have resolutely refused to live the lives of mere featherless though rather ingenious mammalian bipeds, content with a limited and wholly material objective; but on the contrary have been for ever struggling to find a true and adequate meaning and interpretation of their leasehold existence, to discover some compensation for the grim fact of the Frontier, and to establish a relationship with the Self-Existent that will lift them beyond the condition of 'Brutes, which nourish a blind life within the brain'.

Can they be said so far to have in any measure succeeded? What shape does the story of their efforts assume when briefly told? This will be the subject for the next chapter. In the meantime it may suffice to remind ourselves that some candid critics are sceptical about the value of any of these efforts; while on the other hand the standard Christian claim has been that the Self-Existent is not only responsive to them, but actually inspires them, and that there is a certain *relatedness* about all man's attempts at discovery; but that at a precise and definite period there occurred a special discontinuous Initiative on the part of the Self-Existent, centred upon a specific

---

[1] Cf. for example Professor Gilbert Ryle's re-statement in *The Concept of Mind*.
[2] I am bound for reasons of space to omit discussion of the very interesting problem dealt with by Mr. Leslie Paul in his *Nature into History*, as to the way in which simian and anthropoid creatures developed into characteristically human beings. But he is quite justified in stressing the remarkable and mysterious discontinuity between the human and the sub-human species. Whether it be that anthropoids began to walk on their hind-legs in order to protect their abdomens against getting wet and cold by dragging through herbage on all-fours, so that the ones who continued the latter form of locomotion died off as the result of chronic gastric troubles, while the erect ones survived, we can never be sure; nor can we do more than speculate whether keeping in such an erect posture may have contributed to a special development of the cerebral region. What seems certain is that the transition from anthropoid to true man was a discontinuous one, though what was involved in that discontinuity may remain for ever hidden from us.

character in history, which has not only given a significance to the sequence of all historical events, but has in itself permanently modified the relation between the human race and the Self-Existent, and cut the history of the planet into two distinct portions.

The two astronomers previously quoted make it quite plain that, proceeding by the methods of abstraction proper to their own department, they themselves have been able so far only to arrive at a blank. 'Here we are,' declares one of them, 'in this wholly fantastic Universe, with scarcely a clue as to whether our existence has any real significance.'[1] His colleague, writing perhaps with rather more restraint, says: 'There is one final question that occurs to us all in response to some deep cosmic emotion when we are confronted at whatever level by the wonder of the Universe, and one that has so often been asked before, namely: "What is the meaning and object of it all?" This is the question that down the ages has puzzled all the thinkers and all the philosophers, without any real satisfactory answer being found. And now it seems only science is left to appeal to, and what science says is that there is no indication whatsoever in the whole cosmos that there is any discernible purpose at all.'[2]

Statements such as these would probably receive at least a measure of endorsement from workers in other departments of physical science.

It is not enough to complain that these various departments are only concerned with the investigation of *how* things happen, and that they ought to press on to the further investigation into *why* and *to what purpose*, if any, they happen. The investigators would say that their technique and apparatus can only discover and record the 'how', and that so far as they can see, the same technique and apparatus are incapable of discovering and recording the 'why'.

It is necessary to ask therefore at this point whether any other means or technique is within man's scope, by which he may be enabled to determine the meaningfulness of life as it is known to him.

Here it would seem that whether they like it or not, all the great religions of the world stand broadly on the same side of a dividing line. All submit and claim that meaningfulness is capable of being sought and reached by a quality of the personality of men which is not merely that of pure and isolated deductive reasoning, or which is dependent upon the use of instruments external to and operated by man.

Hinduism calls this quality *vidya* or intuitive knowledge, and says that the first to acquire it were the ancient *rishis* or seers, who

[1] Mr. Hoyle.   [2] Mr. Lyttleton.

perceived certain cosmic vibrations, the meaning of which they transformed into language.

Buddhism speaks of vision, enlightenment, or of being *buddhi*, as a state of consciousness in which meaning appears clearly to the individual during meditation or *jhana*.

Christianity claims that while mankind has always been questing, and Deity has always been responsive, the peak of all the self-disclosure of the Latter was reached in the activity of one unique human life, which, like many of the greatest achievements in art or in literature, has come once, not necessarily late in time, but at the precise moment when the situation was ripe; and has not come again.

Islam declares that its one great Prophet received his message by an inward call, by *wahj* or revelation. This is only another instance of the Semitic claim which appears again in the lives of the Hebrew prophets, that the Self-Existent, Yahweh, 'spoke' to them. 'Whatsoever I give thee, that shalt thou speak', is a claim which recurs among Christian Jews, such as Paul and the author of the Apocalypse; and it is clear that the Founder of Christianity was from the first believed to stand in a similar position, although 'more than a prophet'. But others, outside the area of the Semitic peoples, have experienced this sense of givenness. In Iran Zarathustra implies that Ahmuramazda has revealed truth to him. In ancient China, Kung-fu-tze declares that Heaven has entrusted him with a mission, and that what he speaks, he speaks in accordance with a 'heavenly mandate'.

The situation has renewed itself in discussion during the past forty years by the French Jew Bergson's insistence upon 'deux sources' for religion and morality, one of these being 'intuition'.

The question therefore demands an answer: 'Is it legitimate to assume that besides the abstract methods of Science there exists another equally abstract method by which *meaningfulness* for life can be reached?' The discussion of this might in itself occupy a whole volume. But it must suffice to say here that at least *one* of these intuitive attempts has up to the present afforded satisfaction to a greater variety of human beings than any other, and that its claims, though not yet conceded by a majority of the earth's inhabitants, for that reason only merit further dispassionate investigation. Yet that investigation requires that the phenomenon studied should be placed beside others of a like character, and that when this is done, certain facts of 'relatedness' should be recognised between various objects in the group.

Meanwhile, some more shrewd words of that versatile self-constituted lay theologian, Aldous Huxley, are worth pondering.

In the introduction to his anthology, *The Perennial Philosophy*, he writes:

'It is a fact, confirmed and re-confirmed by 2 or 3 thousand years of religious history, that the Ultimate Reality is not clearly and immediately apprehended, except by those who have made themselves loving, pure in heart, and poor in spirit.   This being so, it is hardly surprising that a theology based upon the experiences of nice ordinary unregenerate people should carry so little conviction.   This kind of empirical theology is on precisely the same footing as an empirical astronomy based upon the experience of naked-eye observers.   With the unaided eye a small faint smudge can be detected in the constellation of Orion, and doubtless an imposing cosmological theory could be based upon the observation of this smudge, but no amount of theorising, however ingenious, could ever tell us as much about the galactic and extra-galactic nebulae as can direct acquaintance by means of a good telescope, camera, and spectroscope.'

This, of course, although written earlier than the utterances of Hoyle and Lyttleton, is a possible answer to their difficulty.   But it can only satisfy such scientists as the latter, provided that they are prepared to concede the existence of another abstract method than that of what Eddington used to call 'pointer-readings', whereby the meaningfulness of the total universe may be ascertained, a method which is only open to saints and sages who have by detachment and purification intensified certain intuitive faculties with which they happen to be naturally endowed, and which provide them with the self-validating certainty of direct awareness.

We can never in so many words, *prove* these people to have been right—and, of course, they differ from one another in their findings partly (though not entirely) because they speak different languages, use different media, and live in different cultural contexts, partly because they see only a portion of the whole field, or see it from a special angle.   The most we can do is to examine the pragmatic effects of experimentally accepting their deliverances to test them by the light of reason, and to consider whether the latter are in any way confirmed by the sciences as not improbably true.

We shall then find ourselves back again at the conclusion of the great Bishop Butler, that for most folk *probability* is and must be the guide of a life lived under normal conditions.   Most of us only 'see through a glass darkly'.   The great religious geniuses see a little more of the outline.

What if One saw more than the others, was more surrendered than all the others, and by the same token was able to release more of the action *of the Divine Word upon the world than any of the others?— It might be true.*

In such an event, when two dimensions of being, the Self-Existent

*and the finite, achieved a unique contact, something might well occur
which would deserve to diffuse throughout the planet as a normative
condition of the well-being of its populations.*

Of course there have been in the past many claimants who have
asserted that the nature of the Self-Existent can be known infer-
entially, as well as through intuitive experience, namely through
logical deduction from the structure of the human mind, and through
observation of the external world.   The whole sequence of the well-
known 'five proofs' of God's existence depends upon the validity of
such assertions.   But these proofs have been severely criticised from
the time of Immanuel Kant to that of C. D. Broad, and it would
seem that the only one which has survived the test with any credit is
the teleological.   For myself, I feel that the 'proofs' are capable of
re-statement in such a way as to recover a good deal of their validity:
but at the most they can only be inferential.   They tell us probabili-
ties about God, but they do not provide any adequate substitutes for
real *encounter*, for the conviction of being guided and used, for the
effect of contact with the eternal Jesus, or even for the sense of simple
awareness.

One has always to remember that in religious belief there is a
combination of a number of elements, the traditional, the natural, the
rational, the moral, and the affective, and that the last is best described in the burning words of Pascal: 'Dieu d'Abraham, Dieu
d'Isaac, Dieu de Jacob, non des philosophes et des savants.   Certitude.   Certitude.   Etc., etc.'

Additional note 1

A word may perhaps fitly be added by way of comment upon the distinction which Mr. Hoyle draws between formal religion and the
religion of direct experience.   One can see what he means.   It is the
age-long contrast between the 'deposit of faith' of 'dead dogma',
which is unchangeable; and direct living experience.   Dr. Hoyle
contrasts fixed religious dogma unfavourably with the constantly
changing and provisional hypotheses of science, which are gradually
leading on towards some not yet attained truth in the future.

Now no one would wish to reject his description of the way in
which scientific progress is made.   But the antithesis is not quite just.
In the first place the so-called fixed dogmas are attempts to express
and codify direct religious experience, and they are intended not to
give final truth, but often to conserve actual past experience from being
jettisoned or ignored.   One admits that this is not true of all of them,
and that sometimes dogmas have been rather perversely promulgated.
But generally speaking, they are not the opponents of direct experience so much as statements of the area within which that direct experience may still take place, since if the area (the discovery of which is
itself the result of past direct experience) were not defined, further
direct experience would not be possible.

The physicist himself has to set out from some dogmatic presuppositions, to wit (among others) that there is an external universe to be observed, that his senses are competent to undertake those observations, and that the universe is all of a piece, so that if examined and observed by human reason it will yield rational results, even though these may alter from time to time as rational apprehension increases.

On the other side, the Christian—to speak only for him—while also starting from certain presuppositions which are the direct result of past religious experience of a direct character, namely the historicity of Jesus, and His unique impact upon humanity, is also progressing in rational and in experimental apprehension of what Jesus means to the world. It can hardly be maintained that the spear-point of progressive Christianity conveys on its tip the same kind of teaching as it did even a hundred years ago. This does not mean that it has reduced its claim, but that it has come to state its claim in a different way. Even the 'semper eadem' of Rome has changed so much recently that it has actually been heard said: 'You never know what is going to happen next.' But the great Roman Church is nothing if not realist, and despite her aberrations into obscurantism, is fully sensitive to the needs of the age and the developments which are taking place outside her. May she, in the interests of Christian unity, and the progress of honest religion, go on to discard falsehood and take the lead in promoting a common world faith worthy of the acceptance of thinking men!

Mr. Hoyle in his most recent work has deserted his astronomical last for an attempt (quite justifiable, since it was asked of him) to emulate the illustrious author of the *Novum Organon*, and to take all knowledge for his province. In the course of his survey he appears of necessity to do a good deal of provisional thinking and labelling. Thus his Self-Existent would seem to be 'electricity', whatever that is, and human minds he regards not as independent intrusions into matter, but as 'electricity organising itself in a special way'. The inference does not seem to be drawn that if this is so, it must inevitably tell us something decisive and perhaps unexpected about the nature of electricity. Again, in his final chapter, Mr. Hoyle favours the identification of God with 'the Universe'; but it does not appear that at the same time he defines 'the Universe'.

One feels great sympathy with very many of the reflections which he offers about the purpose of life, the absolute necessity for an intelligently conducted one-power world, the urgent call for a sane selective control of world-population, and the pressing need for extending the operation of the Christian ethic to communities as well as individuals. It is also abundantly and unhappily true that elements in traditional Christianity are survivals from what later on I shall call 'pre-axial religion'—they are like weeds clinging round a beautiful statue which has been dredged up from mid-ocean—and that it is the curious conservatism of human beings, agrarian quite as much as and even perhaps more than non-agrarian, which makes their retention part of the 'dangerous fossilisation' of mankind of which Mr. Hoyle speaks. But one also feels that were he to explore more fully into the realm of the philosophical theology (let us say) of the last half-century, he might find that some thoughtful Christians had been in the field before him, and that their outlook was not so greatly at variance with his own.

Additional note 2

Professor John MacMurray, in broadcasting on 'What religion is about', leads us back to it as indissolubly bound up with personality; and since personality cannot properly develop without *relationship*, religion, he says, involves relationship, its maintenance, its interruption, and its restoration. So far, one can agree with him, but he seems to hesitate at this point, as though he meant by relationship only that which exists between the finite members of a group. In this he seems to be unduly influenced by what Durkheim and others have called 'group-theories of religion'. One feels he ought to go on to state that the Ultimate Relationship is that between finite individuals or groups *and the Self-Existent*, however the latter be conceived.

LOGICAL ANALYSIS

The most immediate challenge to philosophical theology during the past quarter of a century has come from those who in some degree are associated with what is known as analytical philosophy, or in its earlier stages as logical positivism. This is not to say that the latter have not rendered a real service in clearing away a jungle growth of jargon, and compelling people to speak and to write in plain language. But by insisting upon certain restrictions they have exposed themselves to the very reasonable criticism of having excluded from their purview some legitimate experiences.

The analytical philosopher goes behind the actual statements themselves, and queries the vocabulary employed in describing the various types of religious phenomena. He asks whether what he and his colleagues call the Verification Principle, which they insist on applying to statements made by metaphysicians, should not equally be applied to those made by theologians, whether Christian, Hindu, Buddhist, or Moslem. This principle asserts that propositions have meaning if, and only if, they are verifiable by sense-experience. The analytical philosopher declares that many theological terms have neither direct empirical relevance such as may be attributed to the simple names given to sense-data like book, car, bag, or pill, nor indirect empirical relevance such as may be predicated of scientific terms like positron, potential, nucleus, or isotope. He concludes therefore that theological words such as deity, grace, sin, logos, agapē, and their near equivalents in Sanskrit, Pali, Chinese, or Arabic cannot be meaningful, and in consequence that the alleged experiences they profess to describe, or with which they are connected, are unworthy of a philosopher's attention.

It is fair to ask why the Verification Principle should be limited thus to physical sense-experiences. No doubt the meaningfulness of such a sentence as: 'I have burnt my finger by touching the electric fire' is simple enough. But the sentence 'Charles is in love with Jane' need not necessarily be limited to physical sex-experience, while it is equally certain that Otto's Numinous can be and is the object of mental and of very strong internal emotional experience, whatever it really may be.   There are indeed more sensations in heaven and earth than those connected with burnt fingers or physical procreation.   Surely the Queen's dedication of herself to public service meant something more than: 'I propose presently to go to London and sit upon a piece of very cold granite which some people say ought to be returned to North Britain.'[1]

It is also fair to point out what is certainly true, but is often ignored, i.e. that all language is not the same language, but that there is one vocabulary for physical sense-data, another for scientific terms, and another for religious and moral concepts, and that if we confuse or mix these different grades or classes of vocabulary, although we may sometimes do so when we speak, as we say, in terms of metaphor, we are liable in doing so to commit what Professor Gilbert Ryle has called 'a category mistake', such as happens in the stock case where a musical composition for violin and piano is described in terms of mechanics, and the nonsense of the result is patent.

If then we admit that there is a kind of hierarchy[2] of terms, we may justly assert, as Professor Ian Ramsey has said (in effect) that it is legitimate to classify the word 'Deity' and the phrase 'Self-Existent Being' as in each case constituting an apex term and an apex formula, presiding over a total language-map.   Any proposition that contains either the word 'Deity' or the phrase 'Self-Existent Being' will thus have a unique but also a legitimate logical status.   It will not be meaningless, nor will it be incapable of verification in some kind of conscious experience, provided that the latter be taken to include *mental experience* of categories of being.

In an earlier work I have ventured to assert that religious problems are not created by religious dogmas or practices, but that certain categories of experience have provided the raw material out

[1] A critic has commented: Not all philosophical analysts would now accept the Verification Principle, and there is considerable discussion as to its meaning going on. Many would now reject its restriction to physical sense-experiences.

[2] These paragraphs were part of a lecture delivered at Birkbeck College, London, and in the discussion which followed, an analytical philosopher in the audience objected to the use of the term 'hierarchy'.   I saw his point, i.e. that even if one admitted the existence of different vocabularies, it was not a necessary consequence that one vocabulary should be graded as more important or higher than another. Each vocabulary, in its own sphere and for its own specific purpose, might well be deemed as important as any other.   I felt quite ready to concede this point, so far as the *internal* value of each vocabulary was concerned.   But the relation of these various vocabularies to one another seems to me to be calculable in terms of the various activities or occupations which they describe, and common sense seems to demand that the occupation of shaving can hardly be graded on the same level as that of sacrificing one's life to save another's.

of which have sprung the practices, the dogmatic formulas, and the problems. I will now go further, and assert that the existence of these categories being in each case verifiable from mental experience, any proposition which contains a word describing or reflecting upon one or more of these categories will be a meaningful proposition.

I would submit, for example, (1) if a Chinese were to make up a sentence which included the word Tao, and which was in effect a statement about the Tao, that statement could be described as logically meaningful, since it is clear that a Chinese sage had mental experience of a category to which he gave the name Tao. (2) If a Western philosophical theologian were to make up a sentence containing the phrase 'Self-Existent Being' or the word 'Deity', in each case, for the same reason, such a sentence could be logically meaningful. In both examples the object of direct mental experience might be at first inarticulate, and then mystically, and only much later rationally described.

Analytical philosophers, while they can hardly deny the existence of such categories when they are actually faced with them, certainly seem in practice to ignore them; and therefore, to give in consequence an inaccurate account of religion. For example, Professor Morris, of the University of Chicago, says (pp. 126–7 in *Signs, Language and Behaviour*) that we can discern sixteen different ways of discourse. That may well be so, and with his definition of *scientific* discourse which follows, no one need quarrel. He says:

'Scientific discourse is made up of statements which constitute the best knowledge of a given time, that is, statements for which the evidence is highest that the statements are true.... Any statement which cannot be confirmed or disconfirmed has no place in scientific discourse, for science seeks knowledge, and knowledge requires evidence. If it is impossible to obtain evidence (direct or indirect) that a statement is true or false, the statement in question falls outside science.'

Again I say that in one way, no one need quarrel with this. But of course everything depends upon what is meant by evidence. Is it evidence of pointer-readings, or of observation with instruments or the naked eye, or is it the evidence of the consensus of mental experiences of reputable people? It must be evident that the Professor does not mean the latter; since, when he comes to speak of *religious* discourse, he does not define it in terms of evidence, but says that religious discourse is that which lays down a pattern of behaviour—which is to be made dominant in the total orientation of the personality, and in terms of which all other behaviour is to be assessed; so that a statement in a religious discourse is merely a statement about behaviour. The inadequacy of such a definition may not be entirely his own fault. It suggests that he has been fed to repletion with a diet of sermons upon the text 'Be good', or that he has taken the phrases 'moral uplift' or 'moral rearmament' in their literal sense, not recognising that the word 'moral' in each case is sometimes only a reverent (dare one say timid) substitute for the phrase 'that which is involved in encounter with the Living God', even if it is not, as it often is, merely a stupid cliché. But Professor R. B. Braithwaite of Cambridge University has recently said much the same thing. In an address to the University Theological Society he has declared that a religious statement is a statement about the desirability of behaving in a certain specific way, e.g. a Christian religious statement would be one concerned with the desirability of behaving in what he called an 'agapeistic' way. Yet he has seen a little further than this, for he considers that a religious statement is normally commended by having a story attached to it. He asserts, however, that such a story need not be true. It may be fiction. Its value for the production of a behaviour policy consists in its being believed.

Now one fancies that when Professor Braithwaite said 'story' he was thinking either of the Christian Gospel story, or the story of the righteous king in the Hindu Ramayana. 'Story' is not quite adequate by itself. 'Dogma interpreting a story' would be better, or even 'dogmatic assertion'. Thus 'agapeistic conduct' is normally commended by the simple assertion 'Deity is Love', and that is a dogmatic statement based on the story in the Christian Gospel.

In India, conduct imitating that of Rama may be commended by the proposition 'Rama was the incarnation or avatar of the god Vishnu. Vishnu is the Self-Existent Being in its beneficent aspect, therefore conduct such as that of Rama is cosmically correct.' This again is a dogmatic statement, though it is based on a story which it claims correctly to interpret. But the story itself may be mythical, and not historical in the sense in which the story of Jesus is historical, and Indians do not seem to think that if it were demonstrably unhistorical it would be any the less valuable for purposes of edification; while as a matter of fact in the form in which it has most religious significance, it is heavily loaded with myth.

It seems that there is a tendency here to begin at the wrong end in the analysis of religious language. The speech of religion is primarily concerned with certain categories of experience which are encountered by the conscious human mind and which the latter then proceeds to interpret. No doubt these encounters may lead on to the commendation of certain sorts of behaviour, but a religious statement, primarily and *sui generis*, is a statement about one or more categories of mental experience. In different religions and in different national groups such statements may be expressed in different languages, and by the use of different words, but they are none the less descriptions derived from encounters with elements in the raw material of human consciousness.   Thus when a Marxist rejects the Christian Doctrine of God, but affirms the doctrine of the Dialectic Process, he is not rejecting a category of experience, but merely changing the name given to the fundamental category of Self-Existent Being which is common to both Marxists and Christians, and to many millions of human beings who are neither Christians nor Marxists.   We are bound to add, however, that he is not experiencing the category of Self-Existence in the same way as the Christian but is rather shifting his attention from one category of experience to another.

Various lists of these categories of religious experience are possible.   In an earlier work I have adopted a tentative list of six, i.e. the external world, other selves, the Self-Existent, conflict, escape or rescue from conflict, and values, which it is felt important to preserve or promote even at the sacrifice of one's life.   Perhaps one might now add a seventh, i.e. vacuum, produced by flight from the Self-Existent Being. Mlle Simone Pétrement has lately given another enumeration: 'Primordial pattern, Self-Existence, struggle, escape, choice.' These two lists are quite independent of one another, yet it will be seen that they have certain features in common. It may be said that as they stand they are rather (in the words of Bradley) 'a bloodless ballet of categories', but it is obvious from the history of religion that mankind soon gives them (so to speak) flesh and blood, not necessarily in the form of myths,[1] as for example a material hell as representing the vacuum, and a material heaven as representing Eternal Life, but also in the form of attributes and actions.   Thus, one very important attribute given to the Self-Existent Being is that of responsiveness, activity, or initiative.   This is no arbitrary or artificial bestowal, but is derived from actual experience.   Mr. Blanco Posnet may be a figment of Shaw's imagination, but when Shaw makes him say that 'God has got him' the worthy dramatist is only reproducing in dramatic fiction what plenty of human beings have found and recorded as fact.   Whether it be a Hebrew prophet saying: 'The hand of Yahweh was heavy upon me' or Mohammed declaring that Allah spoke to him saying 'Recite Thou', or Saul of Tarsus struck to the earth, crying 'Who art Thou,

[1] Some of us will feel that the myth is not an entirely satisfactory embodiment of a category, but may still have its uses as a symbol of 'what eye hath not seen'.   Buddhists apparently call it 'hormon' (see pages 298–9) and say that it is valuable for teaching the unsophisticated.   But Christianity is deeply rooted in the spatio-temporal order, and cannot allow its experience to be wholly dissolved into edifying fiction.

Lord?' or an Indian Saivite bhakta singing: 'with mother-love He came and made me His', or John Wesley feeling his heart 'strangely warmed', or the blind Presbyterian, Matheson, composing his hymn: 'O Love that wilt not let me go', or the Catholic beggar on the streets of London, Francis Thompson, writing 'The Hound of Heaven', in this at least all are one, that for them the Self-Existent Being does not repose in its own majesty, but goes out to seek and call. It is no light matter to ignore the significance of a sentence like that of St. Augustine the Great: 'Thou hast touched me, and I am on fire for Thy Peace.' I must confess that the latter seems to me a perfectly meaningful proposition.

There would seem to be two clearly distinct kinds of religious discourse:

(a) that based on alleged facts unsupported by evidence and interpretation,
(b) that based on facts supported by evidence and interpretation.

Professor Braithwaite has said that behaviour inculcated by any religious system may be based equally well on either (a) or (b), so long as either is believed to be true. It all turns on what is meant by 'equally well', for one supposes that a line of behaviour, unless wholly automatic, is always ultimately reproduced by some sort of belief. I move my belongings out of the house because I believe that at a certain time tomorrow there will be a high tide which will flood it. My belief may be due to a hoax, or to imperfect, even though honest observation, though as long as I believe, for whatever reason, I go on moving my furniture with equal celerity; but once my reliance upon the information on which my belief was based is shaken, I cease to act fervently in accordance with that belief, so that the belief in a fiction, though it may work to some degree in any case, only works *as well as belief in a fact*, up to a point at which the fiction becomes unveiled and recognised for what it really is.

So with religious belief. I may be reluctant, for conservative reasons, to give up a shaken belief or a time-honoured observance; but once I get a suspicion that either is based upon a fiction, my reliance upon it will grow inevitably weaker. If one kills the goose that lays the golden eggs of belief, no more eggs come to be laid, and the behaviour based on faith gradually peters out.

But here a critic may object that certain dogmatic statements, though belief in them may have efficacy in commanding and producing behaviour, may still prove to be based on fiction. On what grounds, says the critic, do you commend the behaviour based on the dogmatic statement God is Love, other than that it probably

4

makes everybody a bit easier to get on with? (I submit that the
latter result is in itself a curious bit of evidence about the nature of
the Universe. Why should we wish everyone to be a bit easier to
get on with? A society based upon tribal feuds, and living in an
habitual state of internecine warfare, might not bother about this.)

A reply to this criticism might be along the following lines:

(i) All scientific statements rest ultimately upon acts of faith, upon
assumptions such as that scientific observation is possible. But such
assumptions are often of the nature of unproved hypotheses, or at any
rate of hypotheses for which the evidence is low.

(ii) The verification of such assumptions is not the cause of the
observation, but is the result of the discovery that the assumptions
connected with the observation lead to constructive and positive consequences, and are therefore probably correct, whether they be the
assumptions which preceded the observation, or the further assumptions which followed it, and which were derived from it as deductions,
and then assumed in making further experiments.

(iii) A preliminary assumption which precedes a piece of scientific
observation may be a very simple one, such as 'there is an external
object E for me to observe', but it is similar in nature to an act of
religious faith, since apart from some coherence test, complete proof
of the existence of the external object is not to be had any more than
complete proof of the experience of a religious category.

(iv) A good statement about religion will thus be good in the same
way that a species of scientific statement is good. It will, of course,
not be a statement concerning physics or chemistry, but concerning
one or more categories of mental experience, but if it is to be a good
statement it must be confirmed by evidence. Now the evidence for
the credibility of a statement in physics will be based on observation
and experiment, made over a sufficiently protracted period, and under
conditions which guard as much as may be against error, so that the
probability of the correctness of the statement will be strong. Similarly, I would submit, the evidence for a good religious statement will
have to be the fruit of a sufficiently long-term period of observation
and experiment, furnishing results which, if not wholly conclusive, can
provide an extremely strong probability for the truth or correctness of
the statement, so that they can be the basis for a reasonable faith.

(v) Any general theory of religion must therefore be based upon an
empirical study of the experiences connected with the different religions, an analysis of the language in which they are recorded, and an
investigation into the circumstances under which they arose: e.g. it is
useless in studying the Sikh religion to ignore the certainty that it is a
hybrid product of Hinduism and Islam, and therefore a hybrid product
of Hinduism and the religions out of which Islam itself emerged, to
wit, Judaism and Christianity.

(vi) But lastly, any experiment must be a real one. One ought not to
give up experimenting before one has passed through and checked the
vital experiences of a given religious complex. Thus, to give full
weight to Moslem belief, I am sure that one must face and experience
the seeming ruthlessness of life, leading to the possible conclusion:
'Allah is not to be enquired as to what He does.' It is equally certain
that the Christian claim, 'Deity is Agapē', which depends upon the

interpretation of a specific piece of history, has to be tried out experimentally over a long period. Many persons abandon the experimental practice of Christianity either well on this side of Calvary, or in the middle of Calvary, and they thus never reach its maximum experience of Victory through Calvary, while others reject the statement 'Deity is Agapē' without trying it out over a long stretch of a lifetime, and studying it in all its bearings, and especially in the context of a belief in freedom delegated to and generously bestowed upon the creature by the Creator. That seems a pity, if only because it is imperfectly scientific.

DISHARMONIES

It has usually been said that central to the Christian position is a conviction that there is a sense of uneasiness, distortion or perversion, bound up with human life as we know it, that even in the sub-human forms of organic life there are evidences of this, and that among human beings it takes the form of something which produces a separation and disharmony between them and the Self-Existent Being. It is also said that while on the one hand this consciousness of a disharmony may become an obsession, on the other hand among pantheists it hardly exists. This is not wholly true. Quite clearly the Buddha was only too well aware of the existence of unhappiness and suffering all around him, but he put it down, as most Indians have, not to the *misuse* of selfhood, as Christians have done, but rather to ignorance of the way in which to resolve the disharmony, namely by the technique of what modern philosophers call a particular kind of behaviour-policy. Judaism and Islam, the other two religions of transcendence, are quite as conscious in their way as Christianity that there is something about human lives which sunders them from fellowship with their Creator.

The question naturally arises whether there is any sense in which this consciousness of disharmony can really be meaningful, or whether it is a misperception or misreading of the data of existence. In a work referred to elsewhere[1] occurs an essay by the famous physical anthropologist, the late Dr. Duckworth, on 'Man's Origin and his Place in Nature', treated from the standpoint of a student of biological science. In this he presents two conclusions. First that we can no longer base man's pre-eminence in nature upon grounds of physical conformation. In structure man resembles the beasts that perish, and his claims to a supreme position must rest upon his mental rather than on his physical character. He has in fact so far surpassed the beasts in intellectual development that superficially at least comparisons hardly seem to hold, although the human mind, whatever it is, has been evolved from lowly beginnings, and we can

[1] Page 359.

see this evolution to some extent repeated before our eyes as we watch its growth in infants and small children. Secondly (says Duckworth) the past history of man fails to reveal evidence of a sudden degradation like that implied in the expression 'Fall'. On the contrary, the general tendency has been upwards, though the path has been by no means straight; deviations have been numerous, and mistakes frequent. Instances occur of degeneration, with loss of adaptive power, sometimes leading to the final result of a stable condition of degradation, and in a number of cases to the final result of extinction.

This no doubt represented the position held fifty years ago, and it was natural that this view of man's status and prospects should lead to the conclusion that most, if not all, of the disharmony in human life was due to the survival of sub-human instincts and habits, which might have been less harmful and even appropriate in the beasts, but which it was man's business to get rid of. No doubt this is one aspect of the truth, but the last half-century has convinced many that it is not the only aspect, and that it is a mistake to continue to assume that it is. The disharmony results quite as much from the evil acts which man invents, and the evil habits into which he grows. Nor is virtue indiscerptibly connected with knowledge, or evil conduct with ignorance. The famous words of St. Paul (Romans 7:14–21) are as true today for most people as when they were written.

In view of this, some observers, Mr. Aldous Huxley for instance, have reverted to an idea which has appeared more than once in the past, and which is certainly to be found in the pages of the seventeenth-century German mystic, Jakob Boehme, namely that the emergence of the creaturely from nothingness into a state of finitude is in itself a Fall. But this does not seem to be quite properly put, and it certainly conflicts with such a statement as 'God saw all that He had made, and behold it was very good'. Yet there is something to be said for it. The statement would surely be better put if it were said that emergence into finitude involved the *possibility* of a Fall, or at least of a *falling short* of the glory of God's purpose for His creation; and we note that it is this 'falling short' of which St. Paul accuses the human race. Yet even 'falling short' does not seem adequately to describe some of the things which we see happening day by day in the world. We see human beings wilfully deviating from the obviously correct path, and perversely setting out on a line which involves the development of new and often horrible sorts of conduct. And yet without the freedom to do this there could be no freedom to invent new forms of virtue, which is certainly what we see happening in the case of many of the saints. The latter actually initiate new forms of holiness and spiritual beauty which, however much they may have been implicit in the behaviour-policy of their Master, were never before their time explicitly to be seen in the world.

Certain conclusions seem to follow from this.

(1) It is misleading, and even incorrect, to speak of the Fall as a spatio-temporal event in history. I think naturally of a terse sentence thundered at me in a garden at Bonn by Karl Barth: 'Adam ist uns!' This may be compared with a sentence in lectures on Christian Doctrine by the Rev. John Whale: 'Eden is on no map, and Moses is no nearer to the Fall than we are.' Every man is his own Adam. The possibility which passes, all too soon, into actuality, of being in a state of fallenness or disharmony, due to self-centredness or the misuse of one's selfhood, is a universal human experience, and belongs in a measure to organic life as such, and in the form which Christians call 'sin', to the human race taken as a whole, even though they may not always be aware of it.

(2) It does not follow that because some human beings misperceive the circumstances, or even fail to see them at all, that this fact of sin is not the basic truth. No doubt it is capable of exaggerated statement, as when poor little Steve Fairbairn was shut up in the billiard-room by his aunt to meditate upon the fact that he was a 'child of wrath'. Probably economic and social conditions of a favourable character can sometimes breed in human beings a sense of complacency and false optimism. It is said that in China the natural goodness of human beings was one of the main cardinal doctrines of Confucianism; but even in China there were sages who did not agree that man was naturally virtuous, and it is said that Kung-fu-tze himself experienced much sadness at the end of his life, because he found that so many of his countrymen perversely refused to respond to his teaching of virtue and gentleness.

(3) Although some scientists who chiefly regard the situation from the point of view of biology may be inclined to say that the concept of sin introduces an unnatural element into the picture of evolution, it is not unfair to ask them to think again. Many years ago a Cambridge biologist[1] spoke of the two tendencies in organic life which he labelled 'anabolic' and 'katabolic', and he held that these were present throughout its whole sphere sub-human as well as human, so that they were responsible on the one hand for the development of new and beautiful forms, and for the success of the co-operative as against the merely predatory types, and equally on the other for the development of supineness, parasitism, and degeneracy. If this be borne in mind, we can hardly be surprised at the existence of disharmonies and shadows in the lives of human beings; and if

[1] S. A. Macdowall.

amid many diversities there is an essential unity in the structural nature and evolution of stellar matter throughout the Universe, it would not be a matter for further surprise if there existed similar disharmonies on any planetary bodies on which beings similar to ourselves came to develop; although this, as far as we can see, is bound to be a matter of speculative deduction, in spite of the assertions of optimists about the future possibilities of space-travel. The hazard of disharmony may thus have to be regarded as the price that has to be paid in the Cosmos for the gift of winning and developing freedom. It may even be (as a possibility) a necessary condition for the development of such freedom, for without it freedom could not be real. Something like this has been said many times in the last forty years, but that does not mean that it need not continue to be said, since the implications of it do not seem to have sunk into our day-to-day thought as much as they should. If it is the price, we may reasonably contend that it is a fair one.

How much does the deadly sin of pride blind the cocksure scientists (of whom there certainly are some), as much as the cocksure theologian, to the glory and infinitude of the Divine Mystery?

The Jew ends by seeing God as of unutterable ethical holiness and mercy, and believes that righteousness is to be sought in the fulfilment of the Torah, the observance of which frees from guilt (only it may be said that one-hundred-per-cent fulfilment is impossible).

The Moslem sees the human race as disobedient and often ungrateful, and therefore called to make total submission to the divine Fiat of Allah.

The Indian, whether Hindu or Buddhist, sees the uneasiness to proceed from ignorance, *avidya*, which may be resolved by following the doctrine of the *rishi*, *yogi*, or *guru*; and the latter, being a kind of spiritual director, may also take upon himself the wrongdoing of the disciple, known as his bad *karma*, and so relieving him of the consequences of it, the *geru* himself nullifying it by his own righteousness.

Jesus would probably not have denied altogether any of the foregoing explanations; but He has given an explanation of the uneasiness which is additional and more fundamental. This is the self-centred lovelessness of man, who does not love enough either his God or his neighbour, and needs to be redeemed from this self-centredness by a jolt not wholly unlike that proposed by a Zen Buddhist, a jolt which, by a look at the Crucified One, who reveals the Divine Love, jerks him out of darkness into light, and from the power of Satan into the service of the Living God, a service which is essentially world-transforming, and which is maimed and distorted when it is represented as limited to mere individual salvation— 'Glory

for me'.   Dynamic Christianity is not introvert, and its *love* is not the
mild benevolence of the Stoic or Buddhist, beautiful as these are in
their way; but an ardent passion to convert society as well as the
individual, to change the world, and not to despair of it, or to assent
to its remaining as it is.

Our final presupposition is that the present situation is one of
great urgency.   If, as many have urged from standpoints as different
and as widely separated as those of Professor Julian Huxley and
Professor Gregor Smith, mankind has in recent generations reached
an unprecedented stage in his career, in which the population of the
whole planet, and not merely a bit of it, has arrived at a condition of
Sturm und Drang such as is commonly associated with the early
adulthood of the individual, then as never before has man to face the
challenge of meaningfulness, and supremely the twin challenge of his
own grandeur and misery.   Just at the very time when his many
inventions render him in one way full of a sense of being *capable de
tout*, he is also beset by an equal sense of disbelief both in himself and
in the entire universe.   The latter seems to offer him nothing but
ultimate emptiness, and to evacuate him of even the most meagre
degree of self-respect.   Under such conditions, with one deadlock
after another arising between nations and functional classes, it is
difficult to see how anyone without the Christian hope can carry on
at all.   Probably a great many do not, and simply break down, or
deaden their senses by absorbing some sort of tranquilliser, or by
setting up a protective mechanism of escape.   But in this age of
violence and disorder, the Christian does manage to carry on without
escapism, and in the belief that world-transformation is still his duty;
and he has therefore some right to claim a hearing, since he still
finds that what he believes has efficacy, whereas the humanist has
nothing to offer in its place except the old remedy of time-honoured
notoriety—endeavouring to pull one's self out of the slough into which
one is slowly sinking, by resolutely tugging at one's own bootlaces.

One cannot but feel much sympathy for Dr. Julian Huxley in
his efforts, rather different from those of his brother, though no less
earnest, to find a religious integration for life, regarded from the
standpoint of the professional biologist.   Where one fails to agree
with him is in his use of terms.   'Religion' is a concept which
necessarily involves a relationship between the finite and the
Absolute, and it will not do to say that some forms of religion are or
can be 'godless', implying thereby that they have liquidated one term
in the relationship.   What Dr. Huxley means, I think, is what some
Buddhists have said to me, that they have in effect liquidated the
idea of a quasi-human God, anthropically conceived.   They have

still kept two terms in the relationship, but the Absolute is on principle not defined, except perhaps as Cosmic Law. But an Absolute self-expressed in terms of Cosmic Law is rationally inconceivable except as possessing a purposive intelligence resembling human intelligence raised to the nth. The use of the word 'religion' to describe something in which the relationship between the two such terms does not exist seems to me one without meaning. I do not consider therefore that Dr. Huxley's tentative forecast of what a new religion would be like and what conditions it would be necessary for it to fulfil in order to succeed and prevail, preserves the fundamental concept which would make it a religion at all. He declares that it must be centred upon the fulfilment, both for the individual and the race, of the ideal possibilities of life, regarded as sacred. It must be a universal faith. In place of eternity (presumably thought of as static), it must have the enduring background of evolution, with the possibility of thousands of millions of years for its possible future flowering. The core of its need will be belief in human possibilities of physical, mental, and spiritual enrichment. It will be based on scientific reverence for fact, and inspired by an expanding vision of destiny.

But none of these high-sounding phrases contains the actual germ of a new religion. It would not be difficult to show that the conditions could be fulfilled by a modernist Christianity. It is indeed arguable that the epoch for the emergence of any really new religion has gone by for ever (much as the emergence of a new scientific epoch which coincides with the work of Charles Darwin has gone by for ever), and that as Hermann von Keyserling once declared, mankind stands now in the shoes of all possible ideals. All it can do is to choose which way it will walk. But Huxley is right in so far as he sees that whichever way mankind chooses to walk, it will have to do so under the conditions he has outlined. Not a few of us are convinced that it would be possible to do this and still to remain essentially Christian, and we are trying to do so. That a good many of our fellow Christians are not as yet accompanying us makes no difference. Someone has got to start moving on the new way.

A recent reviewer has said that Dr. Huxley seems to regard belief in God as a purely intellectual hypothesis; but that to the believer God is not a metaphysical entity but the central object of his worship, a belief which arises from his interior personality. This I would strongly endorse. I do not think that anyone who has had personal experience of being used and guided by the Self-Existent can have any doubt that the latter is in some very real sense possessed of the characteristics of Personality, and this has nothing whatever to do with what is stigmatised as superstition, or mere anthropism.

CHAPTER II

A BRIEF HISTORICAL SURVEY OF RELIGION UP TO THE EMERGENCE OF THE CHRISTIAN MOVEMENT

(i) GENERAL OUTLINE

In giving a historical account of the development of religion upon the earth, it is now usual to recognise certain broad divisions in the subject. These cannot rigidly be adhered to, since the existence of the factor known as the time-lag, and the problems created by expansions due to trade or to migrations of population somewhat blur its edges. In the main, however, the story of human religion may be conveniently divided into pre-axial, axial, and post-axial. This division depends upon the title given by Professor Karl Jaspers to the period roughly extending from 800 to 200 B.C., which he has called 'the axial age'.[1] I should myself prefer the extension of this age to about 300 A.D. as I think did also Christopher Dawson and Dr. Inge, whose work preceded that of Jaspers; while if we knew more than we do about the *sebayit* literature of Egypt, we might have to push it back considerably behind 800 B.C. When the content of this age comes to be examined, it is found that it arrives earlier in some spots on the earth's surface than in others, and that its main occurrence, even within the limits proposed by Jaspers, is only to be observed in certain countries which, within those dates, managed to achieve some measure of relatively stable civilisation. If we are able to speak about the arrival of the axial age in other countries outside this area we can only say that it was brought to the Western hemisphere by colonisation and conquest, and to the African continent by the spread of colonialism. People in the pre-axial stage were still to be found until quite recently not only in Africa but in certain out-of-the-way parts of India and South-East Asia, and in a number of islands. War and colonisation have abruptly transferred some of these peoples from the pre-axial to the post-axial condition, though it is perhaps fair to say that missionary expansion, whether Christian, Buddhist, or Moslem, has generally brought people to the axial stage. Dr. Margaret Mead, in her recent account of how she revisited the people of Manus in the Pacific, after the war between the United States and Japan had passed over them, vividly describes

[1] For further definition of this see pages 56 and 405; readers may like to know that Jaspers' most interesting work, *The Origin and Goal of History*, is now available in an English translation, published in America.

47

how the inhabitants, who a few years ago were in a very early pre-axial stage of development, have now suddenly and discontinuously passed into a condition in which they are familiar with all the so-called advantages of modern civilisation, and modern ideas of community life, and even of democracy.

The story of the pre-axial age of mankind is of course a very long one, and cannot possibly be given here in detail.[1] As fully developed it generally seems to be pluralistic, and to consider the universe as controlled not by a single Power but by a number of different Powers, some of them beneficent, some capable of being persuaded to be favourable, and others again hostile and uniformly maleficent. There is still considerable controversy as to how mankind emerged into this pluralistic conception of the Self-Existent Supernatural. The evidence is conflicting, and some have regarded it as certain that the earliest creatures we could call human 'by a pure jet of their spiritual nature'[2] contrived to conceive of Deity as one, personal, supreme, and good. According to them, pluralism represents a falling away from a primitive ideal. That there is evidence here and there of an extremely naïve and primitive type of monotheism cannot be gainsaid, but we are bound to write off some of it as faint memories of contacts with monotheists of a more highly developed culture. Nevertheless in certain instances it is undoubtedly a primitive and independent development, though it is a remarkable fact that those who profess it seem to find it hard to maintain any effective contact with it as a belief, and tend to regard what is known as the High God (or Goddess) as a recognised assumption, rather remote and shadowy, Who is not very active in government, and Who is therefore not so important as the considerable number of minor supernatural beings who are also believed to exist. Other anthropologists have positively affirmed that the pluralistic stage is the normal one which must have existed in the remotest antiquity. They regard the development of the primitive High God (or Goddess) here and there as an early piece of theological speculation, or perhaps as the promotion of one particularly important supernatural being to the position of 'President of the Immortals'; but they consider that pluralism, until the arrival of the axial age, is the normal condition of mankind, although it varies immensely according to the standard of culture. In its naïve earlier stages it is described as animism, and polydaemonism, and is an affair of nomads, hunters, cave-dwellers, and primitive villagers. Others again see a great deal of this early religion as pre-animistic on the one hand, or as simply

[1] Reference may usefully be had to such a work as that of Dr. E. O. James, *Prehistoric Religion*, or to the various books by the late Dr. R. R. Marett.
[2] Father Martindale, in a small pamphlet published by Benn.

a cult of the dead on the other.[1] With the arrival of urban civilisations and the development of elaborate architecture, painting, and
sculpture, with the growth of temples, liturgies, ritual accessories, and
music, pluralism assumes very elaborate forms; but its naïve background is still there, especially in its mythology, and basically there
is little to differentiate it from the pluralisms to be found in existence
among such tribes as those in the interior of New Guinea, with their
arrested development. Certain features develop and persist during
this long period, of which the chief are: (1) the conception of the
necessity of sacrifice, either feeding, showing gratitude to, or pro-
pitiating the God (which will take on a different aspect according to
the nature of the supernatural being or beings to whom it is offered,
whether beneficient, persuadable, or maleficent); (2) the development
of a class of sacred persons whose *métier* it is to offer the sacrifices or
to practise divination, and to interpret the intentions and wishes of
the supernatural beings to the remainder of the population; (3) the
accumulation of a certain number of prohibitory injunctions (often
labelled *taboo*, the word being a Polynesian one, and meaning
'strongly marked').

This state of human religion, though in a multiplicity of varied
forms, appears to have satisfied mankind over a very long period,
and for those who lived under its sway it must have seemed both
normal and permanent. In certain areas it began to break up in or
about the seventh century B.C. and the axial age came in in those
countries as an internal development. In other parts of the world it
maintained itself right up to the twentieth century, and it is only
during the past one hundred and fifty years that it has given way to
either Christian or Moslem invasion. But it is true that these
invasions would not have carried the new order into pluralistic areas
if there had not first been an internal breakaway from pluralism in
some of those countries where it prevailed. In any case, the breach
with pluralism has seldom been wholly complete, since the new forms
of religion have often actually tolerated the existence of pluralists, as
in India, where the sophisticated monist will declare that the worship
of a number of different gods by means of idols is a perfectly permissible and innocent affair for illiterate peasants or jungle tribes, who
are not on a sufficiently advanced cultural level to be able to understand anything higher; or as in Buddhist, Christian, and even perhaps Moslem countries, where the craving for pluralism is satisfied
by permitting the cultus of a substantial number of saints, some of
them historical, but others survivals of older minor deities, who have
been made respectable by reduction of status and change of name.

[1] See the chapter on the Problem of Africa.

In any case, the sages, prophets, and reformers have usually been in a minority, and it is not often that they have succeeded in capturing the entire population for their advanced ideas. Sometimes there have been compromises, voluntary or involuntary, involving what is known as syncretism. Sometimes the reformers have been killed or driven away into exile. Sometimes they have tolerated pre-axial beliefs and practices without regarding them as essential. This of course has specially been the case in India.

Having thus divided our subject into its three sections, we must now devote ourselves to a closer study of each of them.

(ii) THE PRE-AXIAL PERIOD

Pre-animism, animism, and polytheistic pluralism

Religion in its naïve earlier stages, is frequently described as animism, and sometimes as polydaemonism, the attribution of personality to a multiplicity of external objects, such as trees, streams, and mountains; and of course the recognition of the existence of a number of disembodied spirits, such as ancestors. It is an affair of nomads, cave-dwellers, food-collectors, or hunters, and of primitive villagers. A good many of these primitives have a dim belief in a High God, but they do not appear to credit Him with any present concern for their welfare, and it is not certain whether this belief originated on the spot, or whether it has come in as the result of contact with monotheists.

Whereas, however, experts like Karsten consider that the earliest kind of reaction towards the supernatural was the veneration of ancestral spirits, or at any rate a primitive pluralism, others like Marett consider the evidence to favour what they call a *pre-animistic* stage of belief, in which the Sacred Self-Existent is thought of as a rather vague potent and terrifying Impersonal Force. The technical name given to this Force is another Polynesian word, *mana*, but there are a good many other names by which it is known in different countries.[1] There are certain difficulties about accepting this as final. In the first place it would seem to presuppose a certain capacity to make generalisations, such as we do not expect to find among savage peoples. With them the concrete usually comes first, and the abstract much later, but even supposing that this vague *mana* is believed in as immanent in a number of different objects, it does not always seem to be equally or universally distributed.[2] Thus a

---

[1] In Morocco, *baraka*; among the Japanese, *kami*; among the Iroquois Indians, *orenda*; in Madagascar, *andriamanitra*; among the Yaos of Nyasaland, *mulungu*; to the Romans of old, *numen*; to the Akikuyu of East Africa, *n'gai*; to some West Africans, *dzo*, to others, *juju*.

[2] It is So-and-so's *mana*, not *mana* generalised, and so really a kind of rudimentary pluralism rather than a rudimentary monism.

spear thrower may have *mana*, and a chieftain may have a great deal of Mana, but a spear itself, or an ordinary member of the tribe, may have little or none.   It seems then that *mana* may be the equivalent of Power or rather excessive Power, but that it is only when Power is in excess that it attracts attention.   On the other hand it is not impossible that some primitive peoples may favour the conception of the Self-Existent as a distributed Impersonal Power which they are not articulate enough to define under separate names.   The whole problem is still obscure and can perhaps only be brought nearer to a solution by a number of separate careful studies of individual social groups of arrested development (we are perhaps hardly entitled to call them primitives), and these are now in process of being made, although the results of the studies are mostly locked away from the public in the technical writings of anthropologists.   In the meantime it is probably legitimate to accept provisionally the view of Dr. Paul Radin that given appropriate conditions and chance-mating, the different types of early belief and religious practice may develop *concurrently*, even within the same social group; so that for example, in a single village community may be found an individual with a tendency towards monotheism, an ancestor-worshipper, and animist, a believer in the equivalent of *mana*, and even perhaps someone who shows no interest in the supernatural at all, like the sceptical man quoted by Mr. C. R. Hopgood in the volume on *African Ideas of God* referred to in Chapter XII, p. 257.   Dr. J. H. Hutton once said that he had encountered similar scepticism among individual Nagas in Assam.

Magic, and primitive religion

Sir James Frazer's idea that magic has always preceded religion is not now so widely held as heretofore.   We probably regard more sympathetically than we used to the curious rites of the simple and unlettered (are they perhaps inarticulate, rather than simple?), and it is nearly always rather difficult to dissever religion from magic, especially if we remember the now customary definition that magic seeks to gain power over Deity, and to control and use It for its own ends, whereas religion is God-centred rather than man-centred, at maximum seeks to dedicate the self to the service of Deity, and at minimum seeks to propitiate Deity, always recognising that Deity is the verbal symbol for that which, being Self-Existent, never could or can be brought under finite control, or merely 'used'.   Who is able to say how much of even some Christian worship is entirely devoid of a small subconscious streak of magic?   And who dare say that even what seems primitive magic among savages may not have in it perhaps an unexpressed element of religion? Some of the elementary prayers which have been collected indicate a sense of thankful dependence, and some acts recorded indicate a sense of adoration, and approach very close to 'the prayer of simplicity', or 'the prayer of simple regard'.

The Christian faith, in the person of its missionaries, has done almost as much as the anthropologists to preserve for us and make us acquainted with the survivals of the pre-axial stage in man's religion. One has only to refer to the work on the Ba-Ila of Northern Rhodesia shared with Mr. Dale by his missionary colleague Dr. E. W. Smith, or the work of Dr. Capell in recording the ceremonies of aboriginal people in North-West Australia.[1] Nevertheless as a synoptic picture of these Australian beliefs I would venture to quote the summary given by Professor Radcliffe-Brown not very long before his death. He did not consider that either before or at the time when they formulated this mythology, the people he had lived with had had any contact with Christians.

Australian cosmology begins, he says, with a condition of chaos, formlessness, and unconsciousness. Then comes the Dawn Period, when consciousness begins to wake up. This period is known as the Alcheringa, or dream-time, and in it appear certain Dawn Beings. These were not created, they arose, and though plural, were quasi-Self-Existent. They did wonderful things (such as might be seen to happen in dreams), and they established the main terrestrial features, species, customs, and forms of conduct. Radcliffe-Brown saw a corroboree in Western Australia which dramatically represented the Dawn Period. Of the various Dawn Beings one (the High God) went up into the sky, but other Beings went down into the earth, and where each of them did so a totemic centre was formed. These local Dawn Beings were regarded as friendly to those living in the neighbourhood of the totemic centre, but not to strangers. For example, the Rainbow Serpent was said to have gone into a water-hole in Durham-land, and this water-hole has since become a totemic centre for the tribe living in its neighbourhood, so that if a Rainbow Serpent man has wandered away from his own neighbourhood into another area, and is dying, it is proper to send him back to his own neighbourhood, while at the same time chanting the totemic song.

It is not possible to ignore the interest which these pre-axial religious ceremonies have for investigators in general and for Christians in particular. To begin with, they demonstrate the immensely important part which dramatic action, ritual, and ceremony play among non-literate peoples; and it is abundantly clear that the

[1] Recorded in *The International Review of Missions*.

widespread attraction which such features have within Christianity for all kinds of folk is evidence that deep down within most of us lies the subconscious survival of the outlook of primitive non-literate mankind.

A good instance of this occurs in Dr. Capell's essay on aboriginal ceremonies referred to above. He describes vividly how he was allowed to be present at a rite in which each member of the congregation, after some preliminary chanting, reverently produced a piece of pearl shell of great beauty, laid it on a cloth which had been spread out, and then gazed at it, chanting quietly and ending with a soft long-drawn-out Ah!—followed by silence. The pearl-shell is a sacred object which symbolises the water from which it comes, and water is life-giving, so that the shell symbolises the mysterious source of life. Capell adds that the rapturous hush and intense devotion of his Australian friends at the Exposition of the pearl-shell could only be compared with that at a Catholic service of Benediction, when the monstrance is elevated.

A more detailed account of another ceremony is given by the late Mr. F. E. Williams, in connection with the people of the Orokolo Bay area in New Guinea. These people, before their conversion to Christianity, were pluralists, and their sacred club-house or *eravo* contained the symbols of a multiplicity of supernatural beings (individual, independent spirits known as *harihu*) and not of a single Supreme Being. The Orokolo elders admitted in fact that until the missionaries came they did not know of such a Being. These *harihu* were never departed spirits of human beings; indeed, they never had been human, but were always supernatural. There seemed to be two main classes of *harihu*, the *kovave* and the *hevehe*. The former appeared to have been a sort of mountain spirit, and individuals wearing elaborately constructed masks or costumes could impersonate it. The *hevehe*, which began by being a bush spirit in the form of a water-snake, came in time to be regarded as a monster-spirit of any kind. The ceremony connected with the *hevehe* was a cycle which took as much as twenty years to complete, and was evidently the result of a long process of ritual development, and it culminated in a magnificent pageant in which there was a procession of as many as over 120 elaborately fashioned masked figures. The people had been working on the construction of these huge images for months, and after a long period of pent-up excitement what Williams calls the day of the *revelation* arrived, and the images were carried out into the presence of an ecstatic congregation, each one accompanied by its separate guild of votaries. (One is tempted to think inevitably of processions in church of British Legion standards, or of great triennial musical festivals when each detachment of singers marches behind its own banner round a cathedral.)

Quite plainly these occasions minister satisfaction to some deep psychological need in humanity. It is necessary, however, to emphasise at this point the fundamental principle that the familiar 'fallacy of nothing but' is at all costs to be avoided. The higher must not be explained away in terms of the lower, but the lower seen to reach its gradual fulfilment in terms of the higher, of which it is but the primitive form or embryo. This is true not only of such ceremonies as have been mentioned above, but also, and perhaps especially, of the quasi-baptismal initiation rites so widely distributed, of the multitude of sacrificial ordinances with which the world abounds, the communion meals and the efforts at the consecration of time, space, material objects, individual persons, and even sound. It is equally true of the many primitive moral and ceremonial prohibitions or taboos, by which savage man has disciplined and ordered his life.

In 1895 Sir Baldwin Spencer visited Alice Springs in Australia in order to see the *Engwura*, the greatest of all the then surviving initition ceremonies belonging to the aborigines of that country. They were not a single piece of ritual, but a whole series of rites, the last of all the initiations. The word 'Engwura' is compounded of a root *ura*, which Spencer says means 'fire', and certain fire ceremonies formed part of the series. These ordeals came at the end, and when a man had passed through them he was called *Urliara*, that is, he was fully initiated, and considered able to exercise authority over the younger men. The natives said to Spencer that the *Engwura* had the power of imparting strength to all who passed through them, that by strength they meant strength of character—courage and wisdom— and that men so initiated did actually become more kindly disposed and less quarrelsome, *ahia mara okniwa*, 'men very good or great'. Here even at the stage of dynamism we have surely a *moral* worship. The Unseen Power is attentively recognised, and it is believed that to be *en rapport* with It will cause the Power to flow into one's self, and so improve one's character. The ceremonies themselves were, of course, as Spencer witnessed them, the product of long centuries of experiment and tradition as well as of arrested development, if not also of degeneration, but it is clear that their object was to get some of the 'grace' inherent in the Power into the systems of the persons taking part in them, and that this actually did happen was alleged to be proved by experience. The results were felt and observed, and the ceremonies were valued for their influence upon the characters and lives of the initiates.

It is rather sad to find Spencer writing in 1928: 'the older men are dead. The young men do not care for the ceremonies. There will never be another *Engwura*.' This would not matter so much if one could feel sure that the Christian movement in Australia was offering to all these poor people a greater and nobler form of initiation. But it is to be feared that only a portion of the blackfellows have come fully under Christian influence, and these have not always been helped to turn their religious self-expression through ceremony in a Christian direction; while the remainder, once they have lost their pride in their ancestral customs through contact with the white man's culture and his vices, have nothing left to inspire them, and so tend to die out, since they have not acquired any new way of integrating their lives.

It is certainly true all the world over that these primitive ceremonies and systems of belief do in their way perform a real service for primitive man in the integration of his life. Unless, therefore, his surviving communities are to be kept segregated somewhere as museum pieces, it seems of vital importance that whatever can be preserved of his ritual life, and without sacrifice of principle given a Christian significance, should not be abolished. It is well known that both in New Guinea and in the Naga districts of Assam some Protestant missionaries have adopted the policy of insisting that the people give up their ceremonies totally on conversion, with the result that there has been a great impoverishment of their social and artistic life, which might not have been necessary.[1]

The pre-axial condition of religion has not only a very long past history, but has persisted in a variety of forms in many outlying parts of the planet right up to the present day. In spite of many local variations it presents a remarkable uniformity, and whether we consider the relics of dead forms of it or the phenomena of living specimens, we can discern resemblances which show that whether in past or present we are dealing with the same kind of attempts at adjustment to the Self-Existent.

Thus, if we make a list of the various supernatural beings whose existence is believed in by the different groups, we shall find a certain number which are personifications of natural phenomena universally observable, like the sun and moon, or of recurring types, such as rivers, mountains, earthquakes, or volcanos. We also find the tendency to elevate outstanding personalities to the status of at any rate minor divinities, and to make up stories about the different personalities which explain or symbolise their relations with one another. Almost everywhere we find the tendency to classify the supernatural beings into beneficent, persuadable, and maleficent. We also find a number of common practices. Ruler-worship possesses certain similarities as well as differences, whether we regard it in ancient Egypt, Imperial Rome, Byzantium, or twentieth-century Japan. Almost everywhere in past and present we find that washing under certain circumstances is given a sacred value, and the consumption of consecrated food is represented as a means of sacramental union with the Divine Sacred. The use of symbolic images as visual aids in concentrating upon this Divine Sacred may very well go back at least to neolithic times. It seems that it must always have been the practice to perform some ceremony over these artefacts in order to make them effective symbols, for until this had been done it was thought that they were not effective vehicles of the supernatural. Thus in India an image which is destined for use either in a temple or in a domestic chapel or shrine, after it has been made in the work-

---

[1] This matter will be found discussed further in Chapter IX on Indigenisation.

5

shop, still has to be taken to the priest, who performs certain ceremonies over it which are called *pran pratishta*, and it is only after
these have been completed that it can be treated properly as a cult-
object.   There is, however, ample evidence that in non-Christian
areas of West Africa the same kind of practice prevails.   Stalls have
been found where images are on sale, and the vendor, apparently
holding some kind of priestly office, performs the necessary ceremonies for the benefit of any customer who chooses to buy an
image.   But this consecration of material objects to make them
effective means of contact with the supernatural has been proved by
Dr. Edwyn Bevan to have been widespread in the ancient pagan
world of the Mediterranean.   He quotes from its literature evidence
showing that a statue or a figurine had to be consecrated before it
could become a cult-object.[1]

The elaboration of all this institutional pluralism goes on for
many centuries, and involves the growth of vast masses of ritual
regulations, which are only completely known to the sacred persons
concerned with carrying them out, and which are not invariably
written down, since sometimes no script exists for the purpose.   It
looks as though in a good many cases the worshippers began after a
time not to have a very vivid idea of the supernatural beings who were
the objects of cultus, but they maintained the ritual, because they
thought it had a certain precautionary cosmic value, and that if it was
omitted the natural order of planetary life might be disturbed.

The great change

There is no exact date that can be given for the coming in of the
axial age.   Perhaps we may put it at somewhere between 800 and 500
B.C., but some think that signs of its approach are to be discerned a
good deal earlier in Egypt, perhaps even as far back as 1200 B.C.[2]   It

---

[1] See *Holy Images*, pp. 31–3.

[2] I gladly concede that Professor Brandon is right in saying that while I have paid
due regard to the *sebayit* literature of Egypt, I have not sufficiently stressed the contribution which its ancient religion made to the moral progress of mankind, by its
steadfast emphasis on the idea of divine judgment upon human shortcomings.   Although the judgment is that of a panel of gods, and is to that extent polytheistic, even
though the panel may be presided over by a supreme president, the god Osiris,
nevertheless the offences for which the individual is tried are ethical rather than ritual,
and the weighing of the soul has passed on into medieval Christianity to such a degree
that it figures in many wall-paintings.   That in this form it did not find favour with
the leaders of the Reformation is clear, and the reason is not far to seek.   The weighing
of the soul is in these paintings represented as usually carried out by the archangel
Michael, while the Virgin Mary in some cases intervenes to weigh down the scales in
favour of the defendant, and in others a demon of a distinctly Egyptian physiognomy
loads the scales against the victim with the burden of his sins.   A believer in *sola fide*
could not have had any truck with such symbolism.   Nevertheless the idea of ethical
answerability is certainly present in the papyrus of Ani, and the judgment scene is
perhaps a way of symbolising that answerability in terms of the familiar surroundings
of the law-court, which in itself is something that has passed on into the interpretation
of the Atonement by Christian theologians.   The story of the *door* that cried out
against Ani 'I know you and your wickedness' is pregnant with possibilities.

is certainly clear that in China, India, and round about the Fertile
Crescent mankind simultaneously and independently tended to throw
up a series of individuals who, as Professor Ian Henderson has said,
stood outside the pattern of life, and questioned whether it really was
the best pattern; and this questioning involved not only political
structures, but existing schemes of religion.   Of course, the movement did not begin everywhere quite at the same time, nor did it
penetrate into all levels of the population; and owing to the time-lag
it has only come to some outlying regions of the world within the
lifetime of the present generation.   In any event, pre-axial ways of
thinking and behaving have often persisted alongside the new, and
this is especially true of India.   In Africa and the Pacific islands, on
the other hand, the transition has not come for many centuries.   We
are concerned, therefore, at the moment to give only a summary
description of the main areas in which it began.   It does not seem to
have been a general popular movement, but to have been connected
with one or more outstanding personalities, and many would say that
it often transferred the interest from religion to philosophy, though
this is only partly true, since philosophy can be an aspect of religion.
Thus in Iran it would seem to have been promoted by the isolated
figure of Zarathustra, and although plainly he must have had disciples, we do not seem to have records of the names of any of them.
In Hellas there are, of course, rather a limited number of outstanding
names, Socrates, Plato, Aristotle, and Zeno, and of course the earlier
Ionian philosophers Thales and Xenophanes.   Among the Hebrews
we have preserved for us the names and utterances of a fairly long
string of *nabis*.   India, perhaps, has the largest number of spiritual
revolutionaries, and these were prolific in training and inspiring
disciples who carried on their work.   The celebrated Upanishads seem
to be mainly groups of literature or single compositions each connected with the school gathered round some outstanding teacher, and in
them we often read the names of these individual teachers, such
as Dirghatamas, Naçiketas, and Yajñavalkya.   In China there was
also a long succession of sages (one or two perhaps rather vague and
legendary) and some disciples who added comparatively little to
the teaching of their masters; but the outstanding names are those
of Kung-fu-Tzu, Meng-Ko, and Mo-Ti. (Lao-tzu is doubtfully
historical.)

Post-axial religion

The effects of this age of intellectual and spiritual revolution are
felt for many generations after the deaths of the original teachers,
prophets, and sages.   Great institutional developments occur, and

commentators and theologians extend the work of the original leaders, and seek to draw out the implications of the original revelations, while popular religion unhappily tends to corrupt, and even to distort or blanket the teaching of the Founders. In the case of Islam a whole new movement occurs which, although it bears the features of a reform movement, goes on to declare its independence, and even claims completely to supersede, though perhaps not entirely to contradict, the beliefs of Jews and Christians. In medieval India great commentators and teachers arise who have left their mark upon subsequent Hinduism. In China a revival of Confucianism also occurs, in which teachers roughly corresponding to the scholastic philosophers of medieval Europe re-issue in a philosophical form what they believe to have been the essential doctrines of an earlier generation. In Christendom and in the Buddhist world the work of two outstanding personalities is followed by long generations of theologians and philosophers who have drawn out what they think to be the implications of the original *kerugma*, and of missionaries who have sought to carry the expansion of the original movements into other parts of the planet. The personalities of Jesus of Nazareth and of Gautama the Buddha differ considerably from one another, but we are not at this point concerned to assess the significance of these differences, but only to indicate that these two persons, the one emerging early, and the other rather late in the axial age, have gathered around them a striking amount of loyalty and devotion, and have fertilised great areas of spiritual devotion. It is perhaps permissible to assert, however, that the larger expansion of Buddhism took place when the person of its founder came to have attached to it a theological doctrine to some extent resembling the logos-doctrine of the Fourth Gospel, so that although the idea of incarnation in Buddhism tends to be multiple rather than once and for all, nevertheless it exists there, and is accompanied by a doctrine of sainthood, of salvation through trust in the merits of holy persons, and in a future life which may be either bliss or torment; so that it is not unreasonable to say that the largest expansion of Buddhism has occurred in those areas where it was most like Catholic Christianity, while even in Lanka (Ceylon), Burma, and Thailand institutional Buddhism tends to assume a mixed form which combines monasticism with a public worship for the laity which is centred round reverence for sacred scriptures and their exposition.[1]

Various reasons have been given for this fundamental change in religion. It is, of course, quite possible to say that it was due to some providential activity on the part of the Self-Existent, ordering

[1] In Thailand it clearly partakes of the character of a choir-office.

the course of human affairs, and to leave the matter at that. Conversely it may be attributed to purely naturalistic causes, the growth in certain favoured areas of a non-agrarian population supported in relative leisure by an agrarian one, and for that reason able to achieve a condition of mind in which the questioning of life could go on without distractions. But this is perhaps in both directions a too great simplification of the story. To begin with, even an agrarian population, once it has begun to store food and to domesticate animals, achieves a partial condition of stability and freedom from strain, so that it is not necessary for the development of axial tendencies to be deferred or confined to an urban or non-agrarian condition of life. To refer the change without reservation to a wholly supernatural agency is tantamount to a refusal to consider any secondary causes, and there is nothing irreverent or unseemly in assuming that the Self-Existent Providence can, if desired, make use of such secondary causes as the means of achieving the end in view. But further, the explanation given in the second instance does not seem to account for the paucity or limited character of intellectual and spiritual adventure in the ancient world. The non-agrarian institutionalists are remarkably conservative. They elaborate their cultus, but they do not liberalise their theology at the same pace or in the same proportion. The modernist and revolutionary thinkers and prophets are few and far between, and are usually in hostile opposition to them, regarding them often as sterile ritualists. Specially gifted and talented people in Hellas, India, and China—and more particularly in the first of these three—are the only ones who arrive at a high degree of development; and it is by no means certain whether the price paid for such development is not a sinister amount of exploitation of masses of oppressed workers—in fact the institution which in its divers forms is known to us as chattel-slavery.

Mr. Hoyle, although he does not say so in so many words, would seem to favour the explanation of the fundamental change which we are considering in terms of what is known to physicists as 'a co-operative phenomenon'. The latter, he says, is one in which to begin with a number of individuals change themselves in some particular feature, though at first without having much effect upon the group of which they are members. Nothing happens until the ratio of changed individuals to the whole group has attained a certain proportion (he does not say how much this is). Then, and then only, a crisis is reached. As long as the ratio remains below the critical point, the properties exhibited by the whole group remain but little altered. But once the crisis is reached, there follows a discontinuous switch-over to the display of one or more new properties. The essence of a co-operative phenomenon, he says, is that the change of group-behaviour is not gradual but sudden and continuous. We might call it a 'land-slide'.

Of course in politics this is a familar phenomenon. There we call it 'the leavening of public opinion by a few earnest reformers'. These reformers may carry on what seems a thankless campaign often for many years. But by their dogged persistence they may eventually succeed in educating an indifferent public to the point of being interested in their X, whatever it is. They bring the public to a point at which it suddenly becomes X-minded. It is then no longer difficult to bring a bill before Parliament embodying the reform X which the earnest minority has so long desired, and since the constituencies are now X-minded their Parliamentary representatives feel no hesitation about voting for X. There has been a sudden shift of public opinion, and no fear need be felt about legislating ahead of it.

In the matter of religion an analogous case may be quoted. When missionary work began in Fuh-kien, China, in the early middle nineteenth century, eleven years elapsed without a single convert having been gained. During this same period two evangelists died, a third died just as a few converts began to trickle in, and a fourth died just as a persecution began on the top of this same initial success. By 1863 there were in Fuh-kien thirteen Christians and five cate-chumens, in charge of a young priest who had only been there eighteen months. Five years later, a bishop paying his first visit to the province found ninety candidates awaiting confirmation, one man ready to be ordained deacon, and some ten out-stations, already occupied by catechists. Later developments have resulted in the Fuh-kien area recording the largest percentage of Christians to the population for any province in China, with a mainly Chinese ministry, a theological college, a number of schools, and a church-membership running into hundreds.

It is therefore reasonable to see in the discontinuous changes in the religious sphere an example of a 'co-operative phenomenon' of a spiritual nature. That this was what happened is the best general way of describing and accounting for the revolutionary events in religion which occurred between 800 B.C. and 300 A.D. To put it in simpler language, when God chose to reveal Himself to expectant and enquiring minds, He used the same methods and technique as we know to have prevailed in other spheres, and even in the sub-human creation, in the same units which are the object of the physicists' attention.

But it must be borne in mind that whereas the changes occurred then in a sort of central block, they have been passing on to late-developed areas and outlying parts of the globe during succeeding centuries, while it is by no means to be assumed that the post-axial period is or need be everywhere one of fossilisation. The age of science itself, in which our lot is cast, is a projection out of the axial age, though this is by no means generally realised, and is a consequence of rational religion. So severe are its effects proving upon our modes of thought, that some have even been tempted to see in it the beginnings of a new axial age. But this would probably be a misreading of the data. The use of the methods of empirical science, as Sir William Dampier has shown, goes back to the original axial period, and is not so much a new discovery as an extension of what, but for the intervention of the so-called Dark Ages, might have been in full operation much earlier. The revolutionary religious and philosophical changes of the axial age belong to the same epoch of intellectual and spiritual ferment, and it is only the vast inertia of religious institutions preserving pre-axial modes of thought which has hindered the religious ideas of the great axial leaders from making greater headway.

Another suggestion as to the origins of early theism has come from Professor E. O. James. He sees an intimate relationship existing between such theism and the notion of a divine king; since the latter is gradually brought closer and closer into unity with the

Beneficent Creator, who otherwise tends to become remote, but by this process is re-vitalised and drawn back into the sphere of cultus. As he points out:

'to the indifferently and intermittently religious, ethical mono-theism seldom makes an appeal, and therefore it is the lesser divine beings (spirits, totems, or ancestors), that men of this type usually approach';

'. . . The Greeks found that polytheism solved their theological pro-blems more easily than monotheism . . .';

'in Babylonia henotheism, which centred in Marduk, passed into polytheism again because the people failed to regard each and every god as the highest deity';

'in Egypt a reaction in favour of the traditional gods took effect after the death of Amenhotep IV, and swept away the short-lived cult of Aton.'

These quotations from Dr. James are enough to show that the transition to monotheism under the influence of what James Adam called 'the instinct for unification' was by no means a one-way process, and that it is not always a matter of 'thinking things out', but some-times due to the purposive functioning of an emotional urge.

It is to be regretted that Professor James, in his otherwise excellent essay, leaves out of account so entirely the religious phenomena of India, which should surely have been brought into the picture if it is in any way to be complete. The major fact is that in India unification did not result, as at one time (Varuna) it seemed as though it was going to do, in a moral monotheism, but stabilised in an impersonal monism, with a more or less atheistic pluralism as the reaction against it.

Additional Note 1 *on Sir James Frazer*

It seems unnecessary to go into detail over the vast work of Sir James Frazer. In his day he certainly performed a great service in helping us to distinguish between good and bad religion, and broke fresh ground by sorting and classifying the various data supplied to him by archaeologists and anthropologists regarding the religious practices of the more primitive peoples, and compelled us to take into account similarities of myth and ritual in diverse regions of the world. Few have written with such distinction of style and such precision of scholarship as he; and yet we cannot regard ourselves as inevitably tied to some of his theories; nor can we overlook the serious gap in his studies.

He seems to have made no detailed attempt to come to grips with the problem of what we have called axial religion, or with the work of the great prophets and sages. As an expert in the classification of pre-axial religious beliefs and practices he is still of monumental im-portance; but even here, much has become available since his day which renders some of his generalisations no longer valid. In any event, he is too much disposed to minister to the fallacy of 'nothing but' for him to be really a safe guide. His chapter on the cult of Ganesa in India (who is called by him Gun-putty[1]) is both discourteous and unfair. The elephant-symbolism here denotes Divine wisdom, and is no more to be taken literally or ridiculed that that of the Lamb, enthroned and adored, in the Johannine Apocalypse.

[1] A distortion of Ganapati.

Additional Note 2 on some forms of Primitive Prayer

It is a grave error to say that savages in general know no such thing as thankfulness and thanksgiving, though it may well be that some tribes are deficient in this respect. Yet it is true, as Professor E. O. James says, that the absence of any special word for thanks in many native languages argues that the idea of thankfulness is not prominent. Nevertheless when anthropologists concern themselves with taking down and recording short and ejaculatory primitive prayers, it is frequently to be found that they express the recognition of a gift from the Divine Being. This is certainly true of some of the jungle tribes of India. Dr. Heiler, quoting from primitive African recordings, draws attention to numerous acts of worship which clearly recognise the dependence of man upon Divine gifts.

In the early stages of prayer a considerable degree of improvisation is to be found. The knack of making up songs and chants impromptu is widespread, and is extended into the sphere of religious worship. Thus Skeat, writing about the pygmy tribes of Malaya, says: 'With few exceptions they have not attained to the level of fixed formulas in prayer, but the petitioner usually contents himself with expressing his needs in quasi-conventional terms even to the greater divinities of his tribe. Many primitive prayers are of a mixed type, half spontaneous, half liturgical. Mostly beginning by being short and ejaculatory, they increase in length, partly through repetition. Emotion is often stimulated by repetitive chanting, which produces ecstasy, and leads to "God-possession", or at least puts the worshipper *en rapport* with his deity.'

Heiler calls the rudest form of worship 'chaotic mass-prayer'; and it is certainly the case that for the most part such prayer is not that of individuals but of the group, as among the Australian aborigines. It is only gradually that the leadership comes to be vested in a sacred individual. It has been noticed that among many primitive peoples such a sacred person is selected in the first instance on account of his or her psychic qualifications, or supposed susceptibility to supernatural influences, though in certain cases the leadership is hereditary. The Asiatic *shaman* is often naturally neurotic or psychic, though at times the supernormal states required of a sacred individual are induced by drinking some form of sacred alcohol, or by taking a drug. The sex of the leader is usually male, but in some cases, especially where the organisation of society is matriarchal, it may be female. Females may also be selected for psychic reasons, since the medium of the ancestral spirit is often a woman. In Melanesia, and among the Ainu of Japan, women are on the contrary excluded from participation in religious rites. Among the Galla of North East Africa the women have their own special formularies of worship. The recital of prayer by a leader is usually accompanied by silence on the part of other worshippers—sometimes very intense silence. This is only in part a question of decency and order, but is mainly due to precaution against spoiling the efficacy of the prayer or rite by the utterance of unlucky words. Thus a Kafir chief, before the offering of sacrifice, would cry: 'Let all be still'. We naturally recall the cry of the priests in ancient Rome: 'Favete linguis'. Sometimes the congregation will add a kind of refrain or response. Thus among the Ruanda in Africa the head of the family recites a prayer and it is then taken up and repeated by all who are present. Among the Magandscha, a priestess calls: 'Hear us, O Mpambi, and grant us rain', and the people reply: 'O Mpambi, hear us', which reminds us almost exactly of the story of Elijah and the priests of Baal. At the sacrifice among the Galla of Ethiopia there are similar versicles and responses. It has been noticed that while the short communal responses soon become stereotyped, the prayer in between may remain impromptu (this obviously reminds us of the habit of improvising litanies of intercession in some Christian Churches). In a limited number of cases we find an entire communal prayer chanted by the whole assembly, usually in musical rhythm. Individual prayer, though less prominent, is by no means absent, and sometimes there is a middle variety, in which, during a gathering, one speaker prays after another. The prayer of a North American Indian chief before setting out on a canoe journey was estimated to have lasted for five to ten minutes. Some such early prayer is of a relatively fine quality, and it is hard to believe that it has arisen without Christian missionary influence. Thus, at the annual thanksgiving ceremony of the Lenape-Delaware Indians in North America occurred the following, recited by a chief and recorded in the publications of the Pennsylvania Historical Commission (Harrisbury 1931):

'I am thankful, O Thou Great Spirit, that we have been spared to live until now to purify with cedar smoke this our House, because that has always been the rule in the ancient world since the beginning of creation. When anyone thinks of his children, how fortunate it is to see them enjoy good health. And this is the cause of a feeling of happiness, when we consider how greatly we are blessed by the benevolence of Our Father, the Great Spirit. And we can also feel the great strength of him, our Grandfather first, to whom we give pleasure when we purify him and take care of him, and when we feed him with this cedar. All of this together we offer in esteem to him, our Grandfather, because he has compassion, when he sees how pitifully we behave while we are pleading with all the manitto as they were created, and with all those here on earth. Give us everything, Our Father, that we ask of You, Great Spirit, even the Creator.'

It is true, of course, that this prayer is a translation which bears signs of having been made most probably by an American Protestant Christian, yet it can hardly be doubted that it represents fairly well the sentiments of the original. (It is not clear whether the *manitto* are lesser divinities or ancestral spirits; but as created beings they would seem most likely to be the latter.)

It will appear from the foregoing that most of the popular types of prayer with which Christians are familiar are already in existence among uncultured people, albeit in an embryonic state. We naturally ask whether communal or individual prayer came first. Heiler inclines to the view that in spite of man's tendency in early times to engage in *group* activities, individual spontaneous prayer came first. If this was so, then chaotic mass prayer would not have been the first kind of worship. Perhaps it is rather unprofitable to debate such a subject. Is it not more than likely that both kinds of attentive recognition of the Sacred were in operation simultaneously? It is not unreasonable to think that the first solitary prayer may have been uttered when the first sub-man found himself standing by the dead body of his mate, and the first corporate or mass prayer may have consisted of more or less crude emotional sounds uttered when a little group of sub-men found themselves face to face with some fierce wild animal or some natural disaster such as a flood, a plague, or the eruption of a volcano, which produced a sense of powerlessness. The content of such prayers is likely to be determined by emotion rather than by reflection. 'From the abundance of the heart the mouth speaketh.' Petition, being central, has rather unfortunately come to give its name to the whole of worship. The commonest petitions are of course concrete ones: first for life, health, cure from disease, safety and protection, and then for food and drink, good herds and crops, children, daily necessaries, protection against robbers and invaders, the granting of justice, the success of a spell or charm, and the gaining of victory. Propitiatory and penitential prayers are a relatively late development, though they can exist among quite primitive folk. As time goes on there is a transition from the concrete and particular to the abstract and the general, but this does not involve the abandonment of the eudaemonistic petition.

The transition to the great religions of antiquity, pre-axial, axial, and post-axial, does not however, strange to say, involve the disappearance of naïve petition, but if anything its continuance with undiminished strength and originality both in the popular cultus of the village or household, and in the official worship of the state, whether civic or sacerdotal. This is equally true, whether we consider Christian or non-Christian worship. The prayer enshrined in such worship is often the same as unadulterated primitive prayer; and it is astonishing how very little the revolutionary teaching of the great religious leaders has been able to alter it. Heiler, in his monumental work on prayer, has shown how these great teachers, from Xenophanes to the Stoics, and on through Christianity to the philosophers of the Aufklärung, have endeavoured to wean mankind away from petitions for temporal blessings, and even on occasion from petition of any kind; and yet both in individual prayers and in liturgies the naïve petition persists.

(iii) THE AXIAL AGE ITSELF

We must now devote ourselves to a closer study of the middle period, and we will take it according to its development, in each several country of its origin.

Iran

Events in this area at the beginning of the period under consideration are not easy to define clearly, and indeed the early history of Iranian religion has been the subject of much dispute. It is possible that there are three reliable dates: first, about 520 B.C., the temporary success of the prophetic reforming movement initiated by Zarathustra, and its recognition by Darius at the beginning of his reign: second, about 485 B.C., a rebellion of the religious conservatives, following on an attempt by Xerxes to make the cultus of Ahuramazda the established faith of Iran: third, about 404 B.C., the restoration by Artaxerxes of the old religion in a modified form, which paid lip service to Zarathustra, but made concessions to the very institution which he had tried to reform. Difficulties arise when we try to fill in the details of all this.   The five Gathas or early psalms which are generally accepted as the genuine work of Zarathustra tell us little.   The prophet appears to have been of priestly family, and to have been married, and he seems to have been at the outset a champion of his people, who were being plagued by cattle-lifting marauders.   He bids his fellow countrymen to be more faithful to the one righteous god, and give up polytheism.   We may perhaps compare him to leaders like Moses and Mohammed, but he does not seem to have been as successful as either of these.   In these Gathas there are seventeen separate hymns.   It is not certain at what time they were committed to writing, but it is probable that for some centuries the transmission was oral.   Scholars are in consequence very doubtful over the nature of the original text, and even when they have made up their minds about a reading, they are equally doubtful as to how it ought to be translated.   Quite often there are at least two possible readings, and sometimes a number of translations which are all equally possible and equally impossible.   These may seem to be rather depressing conclusions, but it is important that they should be recognised, since otherwise it is possible to attribute more decisive importance to Zarathustra than he really deserves.   For instance, there is some ambiguity about the extent to which he was purely a monotheist.   It may well be that there was development in his thought as he went along.   Even if he ended by being as much a monotheist as deutero-Isaiah, it is sometimes difficult to be sure whether the satellites of the Supreme God, or Amesha Spentas as they are called, to whom he refers, are subordinate divinities, or whether they are angelic creaturely beings.   Yet it is probably fair to say that although at some time in his life Zarathustra occupied a border-line position, like Plato, who sometimes speaks of 'God' and sometimes of 'the gods', he ended by centring his devotion upon one Supreme Deity, to Whom he gave a name which was already of great antiquity (Ahuramazda),[1] and Whom he conceived as ethically holy, and the Cosmic Champion of righteousness—'Good Thought'.   It was generally accepted throughout succeeding centuries that the prophet discouraged his people from offering material sacrifices. The text in the final stanza of Yasna is doubtful, and possibly corrupt, but if the translation of Duchesne-Guillemin is the right one, the stanza begins with the condemnation of false gods (i.e. of polytheism) and then goes on to deprecate the sacrifice of oxen.   Plutarch certainly repeats the tradition that Zarathustra taught the Persians only to offer 'prayers and thanksgivings'; curiously like what we read in the Hebrew Psalm 50.

[1] Found at a much earlier date on an Assyrian tablet.

The later history of this movement is of less interest.   After the compromise effected by Artaxerxes a good deal of the old ritual seems to have returned.   It is doubtful whether we ought to make too much of its alleged dualism.   It certainly appears that the Good and Bad Sacred are regarded as balanced against one another until a date in the future when the Good will be victorious and the Bad finally defeated, but this is not unlike Christian belief.   Where there is a difference it is in the treatment of the Bad Sacred as being sometimes the *object* of a propitiatory cultus.

The story of how the later Zoroastrians fled as refugees to India in order to avoid persecution by the Moslems and how they became known there by the title of Parsis (Persians) is familiar history, and most people know that the Parsi community centres its worship round temples (*atesh behram*) in which the focus of devotion is a sacred fire, and that they have the curious practice of neither burying nor cremating their dead, but of disposing of them in what are known as Towers of Silence (*dakshma*) where the corpses are devoured by birds of prey.   They have also a ceremony of initiation, during which children are invested with a sacred garment, a cross between the sacred thread of the Brahmins and the small tallith of the Jews. The sacred literature of this community, known as Zendavesta, which means 'text and commentary', has become very much swollen out with time, and the Gathas are the only original parts of it.   It is not as it stands in chronological order, and opens with a priestly document composed some centuries after the death of Zarathustra, not unlike the Hebrew books of Leviticus or Deuteronomy, in which Ahuramazda is represented as addressing the prophet, and giving him detailed ritual instructions.

Towards the beginning of the third century A.D. the Sassanian dynasty founded a new Persian empire, and for political reasons gave their patronage to the priests of the Zoroastrians, who by this time are called Magi, and this led to the translation of the sacred texts from old Persian into Pahlavi, the dialect then in use in Persia. There were also added to them a number of works of dogmatic theology, one an account of creation, and another eschatological, and containing one of the earlier efforts at a description of Heaven and Hell.   There is also a sort of Apocalypse.   Three later theological works, written after the Moslem conquest in the middle of the seventh century, exhibit the influence of Moslem theology.

What matters for us today is that the Parsi community is no longer a really missionary body.   It transmits its faith from generation to generation, and is respectful to its clergy and its religious institutions; but it is hesitant about making proselytes, and although some Parsi modernists from time to time publish works in which they emphasise the beauty and dignity of the moral monotheism of Zarathustra, they do not seem seriously to contemplate the extension of their religion throughout the world.   The conception of Deity as just and righteous, and of man's duty to co-operate loyally with Deity in the eternal battle against evil, is in itself a noble one, but since the day of Zarathustra it has been caught up into wider movements, and there seems now little justification for preserving it in a separate institution.   The actual historical value of the original teaching of Zarathustra is certainly a landmark in the emergence of monotheism, but it is now very ancient, and the words spoken by some Parsis in the ancient city of Banaras to a Christian visitor are of pathetic significance: 'What we need is a living voice.'

A good deal has been written about the influence which Zarathustra's faith may have exerted upon the Jews during their period of exile in Mesopotamia.   Thus it is thought that the idea of a Messiah, a Heavenly Man coming to deliver humanity victoriously from evil, may have its origin in Iran, and we also find the belief in angelic beings rather like Amesha Spentas developing among the Jews after 586 B.C.   It seems likely also that ideas of Heaven and Hell, and especially of the Bridge of Chinvat, a narrow causeway over which human beings had to travel to reach Paradise, and from which they were liable to fall into Hell, were transmitted from later Zoroastrianism westward into Christianity and Islam, and eastward into Buddhism.   But these are subordinate matters, and it can hardly be said that they are of great importance today.   Beside the Parsi community it is doubtful whether many Zoroastrians exist today.   There are a few thousand still surviving in modern Iran, in the cities of Yezd and Kirman, and their official clergy appear to be sent to Bombay for their education.   Some of these survivors no doubt for traditional reasons cling to their old customs, but it is not unreasonable to speculate whether they might not gain a good deal by allowing themselves to be absorbed into the main Christian movement as a kind of guild, still venerating their great prophet as Christian Jews might still venerate Moses, and preserving any of their customs which did not seem inconsistent with those of the Christian church, but adding to them others of a specifically Christian character.   Few would refuse to see in Zarathustra one in whom the Divine Logos was at work, and it is therefore no more incongruous for Christians to respect his memory than that of Amos or Isaiah. Parsis are highly cultured and industrious people, but they have for some time tended in many instances to drift into a liberal humanism, rather than to remain specifically Zoroastrian.   And yet it is hard to see why if one accepts the Christian Platonists of the seventeenth century in England as genuine members of the church of Christ, one cannot visualise the possibility of there being also 'Christian Zoroastrians'.

It is not unnatural to ask why the faith of Zarathustra has not left a greater mark on the world. Granted that Iranian influence is to be seen in Judaism, why is it that the monotheism of the Iranian prophet did not exert even as much power in his own country or in other parts of the Middle East as that of his Hebrew contemporaries? As Moulton says, he is tremendously in earnest, yet the spirit generated by him cools down immediately we get outside his own period.

Certain features stand out clearly, which seem to indicate that Zarathustra's vision of Reality and of our relation to the same was somewhat seriously lopsided.

First, as against Hinduism and Christianity as well as Buddhism, his religion, on the confession of its own teachers, stands for self-assertion, and utterly repudiates asceticism. It makes no strong call to sacrifice, definitely encourages the getting of riches, and has no place for voluntary celibacy. Zarathustra himself certainly endured hardship, and chose the way of renunciation, but there is no sign that he demanded it of his followers, and it is this absence of a strong call to self-sacrifice which explains the comparative failure of Parsi religion since his day. To quote Moulton once again: 'That it has failed it is impossible for the most kindly observer to question. For every follower that Zarathustra claims today Gautama claims thousands.'

Second, the element of love seems lacking from the relationship between the prophet and God.

Third, in the matter of sin and repentance there is an explicit statement of self-sufficiency. At the initiation ceremony a child is made to believe in the efficacy of one's own good thoughts, good words, and good acts. A Parsi has to believe that for the salvation of his soul he has to look to nobody else but himself, only to the purity of his own thoughts, words, and actions. Think of nothing but the truth, speak nothing but the truth, do nothing but what is proper, and you are saved. This must be cold comfort for the struggler who knows that the more we realise the lofty requirements of the Divine Ideal the less we can attain to it. There is no message for the man who feels the despairing experience of St. Paul.

And yet in the piety of the Parsi there is nothing on which one could place one's finger and stigmatise it as unworthy, or even, so far as it goes, untrue. It is indeed reasonable to say that the Christian faith is a logical outcome of the partial revelation made to Zarathustra, and that the Gospel in this case arrives not to destroy but to fulfil and enrich. One wonders how many Parsis refrain from borrowing from other religions and especially from Christianity. They are usually persons of a relatively high standard of education, and they often seem quite ready to form a sort of eclectic religion.

Egypt and Babylonia

Jaspers as we have seen would make the axial age begin about 800 B.C. This is roughly only a little earlier than the earliest of the great Hebrew prophets, and about the same period, it is thought, as the teaching associated with the name of the Egyptian, Amen-em-Ope. The latter is preserved for us in a papyrus bearing his name, which bears considerable resemblance to the Hebrew book of Proverbs, and in it Étienne Drioton has drawn attention to twenty-eight passages which, he considers, use the word for Deity in a monotheistic sense. It may be thought that we have here a document which shows a movement similar to that arising in Israel, and it may be questioned whether it is a separate movement, or whether it represents the influence of Israel upon at least one Egyptian moralist, or yet again whether the influence of Egypt itself was in any way exerted upon Israel. What is remarkable is that the moral treatise of Amen-em-Ope stands at the *end* of a rather long line of papyrus fragments which may go back many centuries, and in which as far back at least as about 2500 B.C. there are signs of a tendency to exalt moral conduct above ritual sacrifice, and to speak of Deity by using a neutral word with the consonants P-N-T, which does not mean any individual god like Ptah, Amon, or Osiris, but rather what we might mean by 'Providence'.[1] (It is certainly significant that in Coptic versions of the Bible, both in the Old and New Testaments, the word for God may be transliterated, with the same consonants, as *pnoutē*.) It is difficult to build up any secure conclusions from fragmentary papyri, especially when the meaning of words is in dispute, but it is tempting to speculate whether we have not here a tendency to push back the beginnings of the axial age into further antiquity.

Scholars like Kramer in America have claimed to find evidence for similar moral treatises in ancient Mesopotamia, and one such, a Sumerian tablet written in eight columns, has been found preserved in the Museum at Istanbul; but although it is said to be at least a millennium earlier than the biblical Book of Proverbs, it is only an isolated survival, and its background seems to be polytheistic. Another tablet of Babylonian origin which may be dated some time

---

[1] With the vowels added, it seems to have been something like *pâ neter*.

earlier than 700 B.C. is also a moral treatise, but again it does not seem to be monotheistic. It is unsafe to build any theories upon such fragments, and all that can be done is to refrain from saying that the kind of document found in Egypt may not yet come to be discovered in Mesopotamia.

Israel

Much of pre-prophetic Hebrew religion was admittedly of a pre-axial character, and does not fall into this section. Moreover, the story of the development of Hebrew prophecy has been worked over so often, that it seems hardly necessary to repeat it here. Nevertheless it is bound to receive mention in this survey. The earliest of the great prophetic books (that of Amos) is datable about 763 B.C., and it is one of the mysteries of antiquity that its forceful and spontaneous utterances should have come down to the present day in what appears to be in the main an authentic text.[1] After that there is a whole succession of prophets, and it is difficult to say when the line really comes to an end, since although the establishment of the Old Testament Canon puts a stop at the writing called Malachi, the Hebrew genius seems to have continued to interpret history long after that, so that we get glimpses of such interpretation in the various apocryphal apocalyptic works, and few would deny that John the Baptist stands in the true prophetic succession; while to call Jesus of Nazareth the Crown of the Prophets would seem to many to be fully justified. Even the strange figure of Karl Marx seems like the re-appearance of some old Hebrew prophet. He claims to have found the clue to history, and his interpretation of the latter, as has often been pointed out, fits in very well with the scheme of (i) a human descent into corruption, (ii) a deliverance wrought by a messianic community, and (iii) the promise of a good time coming.

India

The axial age in this great country takes a normal course, and is of considerable importance, perhaps second only to that of Israel; but we have to confess to a large number of serious gaps in our knowledge. We know that both in proto-Dravidian and in proto-Nordic India there was polytheism, and the hymns of the Rig-Veda give us some idea of what the latter of the two was like; but we cannot precisely tell when the revolutionary change began. These hymns, 1028 in number, seem to belong approximately to a period between 1500 and 1000 B.C., and it is some time after that that we get evidence of a movement connected with a number of sages and mystics who denounce ritual sacrifice, and lay stress upon blessedness

1 With, however, a substantial addition.

to be obtained through *vidya* or mystical knowledge.   The records of this movement consist mainly of a curious collection of Sanskrit documents, of which there are about fifteen principal ones; but although in these we seem to discern a certain development of thought, and some common ideas, we have only the most fragmentary information as to the historical background against which these teachers did their work, and they themselves speak of earlier sages or *rishis* about whom nothing is known.   We may perhaps give outside dates to the whole episode, and say that it began somewhere about 900 B.C., and died down a little before the commencement of the Christian era, but as in the case of the Hebrew prophets, the succession may have maintained itself for a much longer period.   The typical holy man of India is always the ascetic recluse.   Nevertheless, where we should like to know more, there are many gaps.   Thus the movement which we know as Jainism seems to have begun about 569 B.C., in the middle of the period with which we are concerned, but although its founder, Vardhamana, was a historical character, his birth, childhood, and initiation have become surrounded with legends.   We know almost nothing about the early history of Jainism, and can only deduce from various bits of evidence that it must at one period have exercised a very great influence over perhaps two-thirds of India.   The mere fact that although its members only now number about one and a quarter million it still persists and holds the allegiance of some very highly educated and cultured persons is in itself evidence that it must once have been a very strong movement. Again, the Buddhist movement emerged in the middle of the same important period, but although we know rather more about the personal history of its founder, we can only guess at his actual relationship to the Jain movement, which perhaps he overlapped by about thirty-five years.   And again, the date and composition of one of the most important Indian theological treatises, the Bhagavadgita, is greatly disputed.   In form it is very much like some of the other documents of the period, though it is obviously a late one, but whereas Radhakrishnan would place it as early as the fifth century B.C., others disagree with him and say that in the form in which we have it it may not be older than 200 B.C. or even later than that, and that it obviously contains various strata, while even its main theme seems to be an answer to Buddhist pacifism, and must therefore be post-Gautama.   Most of all, though this falls just outside even the widest dating for the axial age in India, we know next to nothing about the influence which the early Christian movement must have had on that country.   We find a Christian church in South India as long ago as the reign of King Alfred in Anglo-Saxon England, but

6

we have no information as to how it got there. It seems to have been due to missionary activity spreading from the Middle East, but no chronicle of the events of this mission have been preserved. If it came by sea, it must have arrived without touching the northern part of the sub-continent; but if it travelled overland from the north-west, it may well have left behind there a certain amount of influence, and this may possibly account for the numerous resemblances to gospel events in the traditional life of the Buddha, and also for some of the features of medieval Indian theism.

But of course this is highly speculative. We are on surer ground when we confine ourselves to a study of the fifteen principal Sanskrit documents mentioned above. These, which are known as the Upanishads, introduce us to one of the profoundest and most important revolutionary movements in the history of religion, next to that of the prophets of Israel. It is a lay movement, and most of its teachers seem to have belonged not to the priestly class, but to that of the *kshattriyas* or warriors, and their doctrines if logically followed out would seem to render the functions of the priests largely unnecessary, since ritual sacrifice is in them replaced by a technique of meditation which any layman can learn. The theology of the Upanishads reduces Deity to a single indefinable Being, who is beyond change, beyond good and evil, and yet all-pervading. The beginning of this fusion of the various divinities is thought by some to have begun as far back as the composition of at least one of the Vedic hymns, since in one of them occurs the oft-quoted verse or *brahmodya*:

> They call It Indra, Mitra, Varuna, and Agni;
> And also heavenly-beauteous-winged Garutman.
> The Real is One, though sages name It variously;
> They call It Agni, Yama, Matarisvan.

and in another the doubt is expressed as to whether any individual god ought to be offered cultus, while in a third the Self-Existent creator is declared to be prior not only to the creation of the world but also to the gods of the Indian pantheon; but with the development of the Upanishads monism clearly takes the lead. Where the situation again is obscure is as to when and why there came the pluralistic reaction which produced the familiar doctrines of Jainism; and why the Buddhist movement, which, from a study of its earlier logia, clearly began by being a branch of Upanishadic monism, went on to such a refinement of thought as to make it appear on the one hand a virtual atheism, and on the other, the purest form of identity-mysticism, identification here being effected with That which is beyond definition.

Almost everything in Indian religion from this point onwards is a matter of commentary upon the Upanishadic or Vedic documents, either reaffirming their monism, or interpreting them in a theistic sense as a modified monism, or in a third case twisting their meaning so as to make it patient of a theistic dualism, God and the soul being in this case wholly separate entities. Beyond this we get the obvious and logical reaction in the direction of an emotional relationship between God and the soul, well known as *bhakti*. But this leads us into the post-axial period.

Buddhism

Properly to understand the significance of Buddhism one has always to bear in mind that it deviated from the mainstream of Upanishadic Hinduism right in the middle of the axial period, so that whatever it subsequently became, it is not possible to understand the earliest parts of the teaching of Gautama unless one is fairly familiar with the idiom of the Upanishads. Some of the early logia of Gautama lay stress upon the existence of the Great Self. In the Maitri Upanishad one reads: 'This Self assuredly is Lord, is Becoming, . . . this assuredly one should desire to know.' Here the Self is the one Atman, the Unconditioned Absolute, into which the little self is to be absorbed by *vidya* or knowledge. But in the *Dhammapada* we find: 'The Great Self is the end or goal of the self' which gives the same idea. Other similar passages are:

(i) 'He who has the Self as Master, let him walk with heed.'
(ii) 'The Self is the protector of the self; who else could the protector be?'
(iii) 'Here is a man who has made-to-grow his actions, morals, mind, wisdom, who is not a less, who is a Great Self, who dwells in the ideal.'

In addition to these, Mrs. Rhys Davids insists on translating the dying command of Gautama: 'Live ye as those who have the Self as a lamp.' Professor Murti[1] has recently challenged this translation on the ground that the exegesis of the passage by later commentators does not appear to support it, and points out that observers and critics of both Jainism and Buddhism in early times assume that in a certain sense they are atheistic, and do not manifest belief in a Great Self. But Mrs. Rhys Davids, if she were now alive, would certainly retort to this that at the time when Gautama lived, the Pali '*attadipa*' could not have meant 'those who are lamps unto themselves', but must have meant 'those who have the Self for a lamp'. Commentators who interpreted it in a different sense must therefore have

[1] Of Banaras University.

done so after the meaning of the term had changed, and its original significance had been forgotten.

With these considerations therefore in mind we approach the specific contribution of Gautama. It seems fairly clear that the *anatta* or 'non-soul' doctrine in Buddhism is closely related in spirit to the *advaita* or 'non-duality' doctrine of Hinduism. Gautama certainly makes very little sense of the individual ego. For him it is hardly more than a string of sense-impressions, succeeding one another like the separate shots on a strip of cinema film. To live under the illusion that they are more than that, is to misperceive Reality, and so, by dwelling upon that which is fleeting and evanescent, to condemn one's self to pain, suffering, sorrow, and disillusionment, since (in the words of a Christian and not a Buddhist) 'the world passeth away and the lust thereof'. All this Gautama himself said that he saw in a sudden flash while he was seated under the Bo-tree, and he became *buddhi*, wide awake; 'Vision arose in me, light arose', he says, and this kind of experience is considered to be the essential feature of the true convert to Buddhism. No doubt it might be difficult to keep on the level of this experience for very long, but the aim of the Buddha was to help his disciples to work out a technique by which it could become habitual, or at least frequent, and the eightfold path which he prescribed was intended to provide a framework within which a certain type of character could be developed. The goal was clearly a condition in which one was perpetually *buddhi*, and this meant the 'waning out' of natural desires, or, as we should say, of the libido (in Pali, *tanha*, or craving). This state is the one which bears the technical name of *nibbana*, and was once described by a Sinhalese monk as 'bliss unspeakable'. But bliss is a meaningless term unless one assumes that there is some conscious being who experiences it. To speak of a person who is under the influence of a total anaesthetic as blissfully unconscious is a misuse of words, unless what is meant is that his escape from the sensation of being cut or pulled about by a surgeon was something which gave him a blissful sensation before he went under, or a blissful satisfaction in knowing what he had evaded, after he came round; or that he was temporarily in a condition which appeared blissful not to him but to his conscious well-wishers who were looking on at him. But at the time of the operation itself he could not properly be said to be *experiencing* bliss, unless the particular anaesthetic employed gave him a pleasant dream. It seems clear that the sensation called *nibbana* is the sensation which the professional psychologist calls that of identity-mysticism, in which the individual mystic perceives himself as identified with the Absolute, the little self identified with the

Great Self, and this identification might be symbolical rather than numerically factual.[1] The Buddha himself always refused to be drawn into arguments about the existence or non-existence of the soul and about the nature of the Absolute. Questions on these matters he always regarded as not being properly put. But it is quite clear that in this he stands in the true succession of Indian mystics for whom the nature of the Absolute can only be described by saying 'neti, neti'—'it is not this, it is not that'. To say that anything is beyond definition is not the same as saying that it has no being, and one has been struck in conversation with Buddhist monks by their steadfast refusal to define the Absolute or Self-Existent, although all the time they would say that their aim was to have complete unity with It.

Gautama does not seem to have wished to concern himself with hair-splitting questions of theology. His aim was practical, and at the same time humanistic. He did not start from the contemplation of Deity, but from the spectacle of the needs of humanity, such as one may see in walking through old Banaras today—sick beggars crying out by the wayside, corpses being carried on stretchers to the burning ghat, and multitudes of aged and infirm poor. Gautama's remedy for all these was not a change in their physical condition, but a change in their mental and spiritual outlook. It is true that in his eight-fold path one of the highest virtues is compassion or goodwill, a kind of universal benevolence clearly akin to the Hindu *ahiṃsa*. But it does not appear that this benevolence was in any way connected with a constructive reformation of the social order. Indeed, although the Buddha is represented on one occasion as saying 'He who would wait upon me let him wait upon the sick', there is no evidence, apart from the activities of the Emperor Asoka, of the establishment of hospitals, and this seems to have been limited to the lifetime of Asoka. Buddhism in modern Japan has engaged in hospital work and other kinds of social service, but it has clearly been stimulated to this by the competition of Christians, whose activities it has sought to emulate. For the Buddha the best service one could render to one's fellow man was to teach him to see the world order from the right point of view, so that he too, by a change of mentality, could attain to bliss unspeakable. There can be no doubt that a good deal of the difference between essential Buddhist and essential Christian doctrine can be set down to a misunderstanding of one another's language. My own experience has been that Buddhist monks do not understand very often the meaning of Christian theological terms, and suppose that when we speak about

[1] Quotations from St. Catherine of Genoa and Charles Wesley could easily illustrate this.

God our meaning is much more anthropomorphic than it really is. In the same way I am sure that *nibbana* is a much more positive concept than is popularly believed, and does not mean annihilation. But in general one's impression is that abstract Buddhism is much more like a form of Stoicism than it is like Christianity. If we had met Epictetus I think we might have found him in his way quite an admirable person, and yet we should have felt that we wanted to carry him a long way beyond the point he had reached, and this is how one is impressed when one concentrates upon the person of the Buddha. Undoubtedly he had a most penetrating intelligence; yet when one comes to study the *sutras* one derives the impression that he is more interested in psychology than in religion, and that if this is really the original Buddha, he cannot have had much message for simpler folk or for untouchables.

The actual nature of the Buddhist ethic on its positive side is in danger of arousing unhappy controversy. Christians who believe in the Johannine and early patristic presentations of the Logos doctrine should be glad when they find Gautama saying to his monks:

'Fare ye forth, brethren, on the mission that is for the good of the many, for the happiness of the many, to take compassion on the world, to work profit and good and happiness to daevas and men. Go not singly; go in pairs. Teach Dhamma, lovely in its origin, lovely in its progress, lovely in its consummation. Both in the spirit and in the letter proclaim ye the higher life in all its fullness, in all its purity. Beings there are whose eyes are hardly dimmed with dust, perishing because they have not the Dhamma', or: 'Whosoever waits upon the sick waits upon me.'[1]

But it is vitally necessary to face facts. If we compare the two plain stories of the lives of Jesus and Gautama, we find in the latter a very great stress upon the duty of self-development, on the perfection of one's own inner life, and on self-discipline for the perfecting of one's own character, but little or nothing about the corporal works of mercy. In fact the Buddhist theory of man perfected almost certainly over-stresses the individualistic side of morality, and says too little of the social side. Indeed Gautama seems to have felt that the core of his mission consisted in the foundation of an order of persons who should devote their time exclusively to the spiritual culture of themselves and their neighbours. Outside this order the advice given to the laity is very much like that to be found in conventional morality all over the world, and it might be paralleled from the aphorisms of Kung-fu-tze or the wisdom literature of Israel

---

[1] One cannot forbear the speculation that this particular logion may have undergone modification by someone who at a very early date had come to know the corresponding saying in the Synoptic Gospels.

or Egypt. But the ideal disciple, the Arahat, is advised in the following terms:

'Without covetousness, without deceit, without craving, without detraction, having got rid of passion and folly, being free from desire in all the world, let one wander alone like a rhinoceros.

Having left son and wife, father and mother, wealth and corn and relatives, the different objects of desire, let one wander alone like a rhinoceros.

Wishing for the destruction of desire, being careful, no fool, learned, strenuous, considerate, restrained, energetic, let one wander alone like a rhinoceros.

Like a lion not trembling at noises, like the wind not caught in a net, like the lotus not stained by water, let one wander alone like a rhinoceros.'

But of course in one of the books of the fifth Nikaya we also get the following:

'To serve wise men and to serve fools, to give honour to whom honour is due, this is the greatest blessing.

To dwell in a pleasant land, to have done good deeds in a former existence, to have a soul filled with right desires, this is the greatest blessing.

Much knowledge and much science, the discipline of a well-trained mind, and a word well spoken, this is the greatest blessing.

To succour father and mother, to cherish wife and child, to follow a peaceful calling, this is the greatest blessing.

To give alms, to live religiously, to give help to relatives, to do blameless deeds, this is the greatest blessing.

To cease and abstain from sin, to eschew strong drink, to be diligent in good deeds, this is the greatest blessing.

Reverence and lowliness, contentment and gratitude, to receive religious teaching at due seasons, this is the greatest blessing.

To be long-suffering and meek, to associate with the monks of the Buddha, to hold religious discourse at due seasons, this is the greatest blessing.

Temperance and chastity, discernment of the four great truths, the prospect of Nirvana, this is the greatest blessing.

The soul of one unshaken by the changes of this life, a soul inaccessible to sorrow, passionless, secure, this is the greatest blessing.

They that do these things are invincible on every side, on every side they walk in safety, yea, theirs is the greatest blessing.'

This in itself is good and noble: but it could almost be paralleled from the precepts of the Stoics. Obviously there is a positive side to the Dhamma, but it just stops short where the Christian way of life goes on. Thus in Digha we read that the disciple of the Tathagata should spend many hours cultivating goodwill (*mettā*) for all beings, both human and subhuman, and should let his mind pervade in this way first one quarter of the world and then another. But, as Pratt remarks, the practical-minded Westerner would prefer not quite so much meditation, and a good deal more constructive action. He continues that the Buddhist, and perhaps any Oriental, would reply that it is the inner life that matters, and that without it mere physical activity will bring but slight blessing.   This is true, most certainly true, for the Christian, in so far as his religion lays great stress upon motive and inwardness.   One can be tempted, like Becket in Eliot's play, 'To do the right thing for the wrong reason'.   The Christian is certainly taught that in prayer and meditation one should aim at cultivating, and ask for Divine Grace to continue cultivating, an 'agapeistic' habit of mind towards the world and its inhabitants. But we are not to stop there.   The Stoic was urged to cultivate a spirit of benevolence towards others, but benevolence in Stoicism and *mettā* in Buddhism seem to have a passive rather than an active connotation.   It is possible to feel sorry for people who are in the same unhappy condition as yourself, yet not to think about doing anything to change that condition—for it is perhaps unchangeable— so that one's only aim can be to teach and train one's neighbours to do what one tries to do oneself, namely, to pass through this world with a certain calm, restrained, and detached frame of mind (very much the same as the Stoic $\dot{\alpha}\pi\dot{\alpha}\theta\epsilon\iota\alpha$), knowing full well that what happens to one is indiscerptibly bound up with the constitution and course of nature, but that the wise man or Arahat is superior to this, and by his vision and enlightenment can dwell in peace, unharmed by the 'slings and arrows of outrageous fortune'.

If, on the other hand, we look at the example of Jesus, we see that his long hours of prayer and meditation were matched by almost ceaseless activity in going about doing good and healing.   He did not consider it enough, when He felt compassion for the multitude, to confine himself merely to teaching them to acquire a new habit of mind 'inaccessible to sorrow, passionless, and secure', but to changing their physical circumstances as well.   Behind Jesus stands the Hebrew prophetic tradition which desires 'a new heaven and a new earth wherein dwelleth righteousness', and from Jesus onwards the spirit of the Christian disciple, when not infected by the spirit of Oriental pessimism and life-negation, which are alien to and not inherent in it, is concerned with the making of individuals into new creatures, and the transforming of the whole world into the commonwealth of God.

A veteran missionary in India has reminded me that when Jesus is spoken of in the Gospels as 'having compassion', it is only once followed by the words: 'He began to *teach* them many things'.   On other occasions 'He had compassion and healed.'   'He had compassion—and fed.'   'He had compassion—and touched.'   There is always action of a concrete character after the compassion is felt; and the spectacle of suffering is always with Jesus an incentive to do something to relieve the sufferer.   Indeed the severest condemnations

falling from His lips are reserved for those who do nothing constructive, either shutting up food for themselves in barns, or concealing
wealth in the earth, or engaging in trivial ceremonies, instead of in
works of justice and mercy.   The vision of the Great Assize in
Matthew 25, with its judgement against those who neglect to be enterprising in constructive service, has no real parallel in the *Sutras*.
Yet supposing that Jesus and the Buddha had ever met, one can feel
sure that the latter would not have been hostile, but would have
freely recognised in the teaching and example of the Man of Nazareth
the logical fulfilment of his own *karuna*, *mudita*, and *anukampa*.   He
would not have resented the advent of one who carried further the
fruits of his own enlightenment.   Yet an honest appreciation of the
facts must lead to the admission that this 'constructive compassionate
activity' has no real parallel either in Stoicism or in Buddhism, and
of course it is the mainspring of all Christian humanitarian service.

The picture of Gautama is indeed beautiful in its love and unselfishness, up to a point.   He not only teaches that the true Bhikku
must 'cultivate a heart of love that knows no anger, that knows no
ill-will . . . let him cultivate goodwill towards all the world, a bound-
less mind of *mettā*, above and below and across, unobstructed,
without hatred, without enmity.   This way of living is the best in
the world'; but he also exhibits this unselfish love in many forms.
Yet somehow it seems to stop short, apparently because the Buddha
did not see society as worth redeeming.   It was more important to
cultivate an inner temper, than to change outward circumstances.
Contemporary secular thought did not encourage the belief on his
part that the temporal order could, or need be improved, and this in
the main seems to have been the Buddhist tradition ever since.   Hence,
for example, it is not surprising that in such a country as Burma,
Buddhists are some of the best subscribers to Christian institutions
for the indigent blind, but there is no visible sign that in past centuries
they have ever taken the initiative in founding such institutions.

The change from the ideal human being as Arahat to the ideal
human being as Bodhisattva is so remarkable that it has occasioned
much comment.   It would be ungenerous and incorrect to deny what
we have already seen to be the case, that even in the earliest logia
of Gautama is to be found the command to cultivate the spirit of
mettā towards the whole world.   But in the development of
Mahayana as distinct from Theravada Buddhism the Bodhisattva
appears as concerned not with 'wandering alone, like a rhinoceros'
in search of the perfect state of consciousness, so much as in holding
back from the attainment of the latter in order to help one's fellow
human beings out of ignorance into a better state of mind.   Yet the

Bodhisattva does not set about transforming society into the Kingdom of God.

It is alleged that under Asoka hospitals were built, but although 'remedies' for men and animals are mentioned, little or nothing is known of these institutions, nor do any seem to have survived in India to later generations. There is near Angkor an extraordinary inscription belonging to the reign of King Jayavarman VII who lived about 1185 A.D., contemporary with Henry II of England, in which the establishment connected with the great temple of Ta Prohm is described, and it is added that the kingdom included as many as 102 hospitals. It is also mentioned in the Mahavamsa that kings founded hospitals and distributed medicines, and Marco Polo apparently mentioned this as well, and said that the care of the sick was recommended by the example of the Buddha himself. That, at any rate, appears to have been what he was told.

The difficulty about this evidence is that the Jayavarman inscription is early medieval, and that Marco Polo is mid-thirteenth century; while the Mahavamsa, although begun in Ceylon as a kind of chronicle in the fifth century A.D., was continued by later writers down to the year 1750 A.D., so that in the present state of the critical study of its text we cannot be sure how much of it is late tradition, added for the purpose of magnifying the beneficence of the kings of Ceylon. Errors in it have already been pointed out by European scholars from time to time. In any case, it is quite possible for the larger developments of institutions for the sick to have been the result of Christian influence. It is well known that in the fourth century A.D. there was a great Christian hospital at Caesarea in Cappadocia, and as the Nestorian missions moved further east they would have carried with them the tradition of engaging in such work. One can only wish, in the interests of fairness to our Buddhist friends, that the evidence could have been more conclusive; certainly the swing of the pendulum from the Arahat to the Bodhisattva is mysterious, and can most naturally be accounted for by the infiltration of Christian ideas eastward from Asia Minor. If this happened, the ideas certainly fell upon ground which was ready to receive them, for there seems no doubt that improvements and developments in Indian medicine and surgery actually did coincide with the stimulating spread of the Buddhist movement in India.

The four actual terms used in Buddhist ethics are:

mettā=amity (*mitto*=friend), i.e. friendliness
kāruna=pity
mudīta=sympathy
anukampā=compassion

yet all of them seem, where unmodified by Christian influence, to be rather of a passive and negative sort. Mrs. Rhys Davids, who knew the Pali scriptures intimately, perhaps better than many Buddhists, had no hesitation in saying that there was nothing in them to match the 'loving warding of man by man, whereby after death his fate before the tribunal of the Son of Man is determined'. No definition of *mettā* anywhere, she says, approaches the rich beauty of the thirteenth chapter of the first epistle to the Corinthians in praise of agapē or charity. 'As compared with the latter, *mettā* is a very temperate relation.' This judgment, coming from one who greatly appreciated Buddhism, needs to be treated seriously.

It is only too often said that Buddhism is atheistic (I believe Bertrand Russell has even actually described Gautama as the greatest atheist in history, and recently Professor Julian Huxley has said very much the same thing). But let us get this clearly thought out. There seem to be three different kinds of Buddhism, that of Gautama, that of the Theravada, merging in these days into a humanism 'sans dieu', and thirdly the Buddhism of the Mahayana. Gautama himself is recorded as having preached to his disciples on at least one occasion a clear doctrine of a Self-Existent Being. To quote from the *sutra* in question: 'There is, O Bhikkus, that which is unborn (*ajabam*), which has not become (*abhutam*), which is uncreate (*akatam*), which is unevolved (*asamkhatam*). Unless, O Bhikkus, there were that which is unborn, which has not become, is uncreate, and unevolved, there could not be cognised here the springing out of what is born, has become, is created, and evolved. And surely because, O Bhikkus, there is that which is unborn, has not become, is uncreate and unevolved, therefore is cognised the outspringing of what is born, has become, is created and evolved.' (Udana.) Lest anyone should suspect me of giving a Christian turn to this statement, I would safeguard myself by saying that the translation is that of a Buddhist. The translator goes on to say that this Creative Force has had many names, of which he gives as examples God, Father, Tao, Allah, Brahman, Zeus, Jupiter, Yahweh, First Cause, Élan Vital, Universal Mind, Cosmic Intelligence, and Absolute, according to the group which has applied the name. He strongly deprecates what he feels to be anthropomorphism, and says that the universe is not the work of a personal Creator, but is governed by an *Impersonal Principle*, the permeating essence of all that exists. But this is not at all what is commonly meant by atheism. It is merely the strongly expressed desire not to limit the definition of the nature of the Self-Existent so as to bring it down to the level of man's emotional needs. He adds: 'We humans are weak-kneed beings; most of us still demand a God cast in our own mould, one who can give succour when approached in prayer.' One can well understand this reluctance to conceive of Deity in human terms, but it is after all no more than has been said by Jewish theologians. At the same time the insistence upon the so-called impersonality of absolute law, which is not by any means a logical one, leads easily into a humanism which entirely negates the Self-Existent. The humanism of certain modern Buddhists is not by any means certainly to be deduced from the identity-mysticism of the original Gautama. The latter is a reaction against an all-too-human theology. But the practical mind of the Buddha concerned itself not with theology, but with the need to relieve human tension and suffering, though it did so against a Background which even if not expressed is at least always implied.

In the Mahayana, although anthropomorphism is still excluded, there is certainly assumed the self-existence of an Absolute or cosmic Buddha-spirit, beyond definition of course, and yet partially knowable as expressing itself in a series of concrete Buddhas. This Spirit, among some Japanese Buddhists, bears the name of Nyorai, and the American anthropologist, Dr. Embree, in making a study of the life of a Japanese village, listened to a sermon preached by a Japanese Buddhist monk, the central theme of which was the importance of sinking one's personality in that of Nyorai. He said that most of us spend our lives beset by anxiety; but that if we surrender to Nyorai, Nyorai will take care of us, and we need have no worries about the future. The spirit of Nyorai will encourage us to live for others and forget ourselves, and being thus delivered from self-centredness we shall enter into a state of bliss here and now. It is difficult to describe such Buddhism as 'atheistic', and although we may well wonder to what extent the preacher in question had allowed himself to be influenced by some Christian sermon which he had heard or read, it is important to recognise that he felt no inconsistency as an orthodox Buddhist of the Mahayana in preaching such a doctrine, and it seems clear from a somewhat similar sermon heard a good many years earlier by Lord Redesdale when he was attaché to the British Embassy in Tokyo, that it was by no means exceptional. One does not know, of course, how far the quasi-personal objectification of Nyorai ought to be regarded as an instance of *hormon*, or accommodation to popular needs. But at least it is not unfair to say that even if Nyorai be a verbal symbol for an ineffable Reality, it could not be effective if the Reality were inferior to the symbol. The Absolute may be beyond definition, but it is contrary to reason to say that the Absolute is inferior to the symbol.

Modern Buddhists make much of Panch Sheers or the Five Principles of Buddhist life :

- (a) Refraining from injury to living things.
- (b) Refraining from taking that which is not given.
- (c) Refraining from sexual immorality.
- (d) Refraining from falsehood.
- (e) Refraining from intoxicants.

There are five other negation prohibitions, specially for monks and nuns. Devout lay-folk vow to keep five or eight of these ten commandments, and many renew their vows every Moon-day or Poya-day, four times a month. All excellent as far as it goes.

Additional note on Jainism

I hope that my Jain friends will forgive me for relegating them to an appendix; but it is difficult, even within the limits of a large book, to do justice to all.

Jainism is, as stated, professed by perhaps some million and a half of the inhabitants of India; but its status there must no more be judged by figures than that of the Quakers in England. Ostensibly Jains are not theists, but believe in and practise devotion to a number of great saints or Tirthankaras who have achieved Jiva or victory and peace through living an ethically pure and ascetic life. Some of them however say that they believe in a Paramatman or Supreme Being, within Whom all finite beings subsist: but whether this is pure deviationism on the part of a minority, or whether it represents genuine doctrinal development under the cover of Christian influence, one finds it hard to say. Jains are divided into monastic orders and laity, and at one period they may have exercised enormous influence throughout India. But the theistic reaction referred to elsewhere caused a serious shrinkage, as it did also in the case of the Indian Buddhists, and today it is rather difficult to know where the Jains stand. They are genuinely interested in the life of the various Christian monastic orders, and bear a dignified witness to a spirituality which is entirely divorced from ritual sacrifice and polytheism. Clearly they supported in the beginning an extreme reaction against both these—more extreme than the principal teachers whose work is commemorated in the Upanishads. But the stigma of atheism seems to have fastened upon them at an early date, and they have remained an isolated phenomenon in the midst of a population the leaders of which mostly prefer a monism to a pluralism. One of their greatest contributions has been the principle of *ahiṃsa* (non-violence, reverence for life, or doing no harm to any living organisms) which has become cardinal now for many orthodox Hindus, is central also in Buddhism, at least for monks and nuns, and has extended its range far outside the bounds of the Jain community, even perhaps exercising some influence upon Dr. Schweitzer!

Post-axial Indian religion

The long and rather complicated history of Indian religion from the end of the Upanishadic period onwards can only be summarised here, in so far as it bears upon the main thesis of this work, and I have dealt with it more fully elsewhere.[1]

[1] *Hinduism*, in Hutchinson's University Library.

For some still obscure reason there was a swing of the pendulum from monism towards a species of theism after about 200 B.C. The beginning of this can hardly be due to any Hebraeo-Christian influence, since it emerges before the birth of Christ. It may be part of a kind of general reaction against pantheism which is common at that period to an area of the world extending roughly from the Aegean to the Ganges valley, or it may be due to invasions coming in over the north-west frontier, bringing into India a number of tribes with a foreign tradition and a lower culture.

At any rate this theism, accompanied by the belief in *avatars* or docetic incarnations of the Supreme Being (who is usually worshipped under the form of the beneficent god Vishnu, though sometimes under that of the more dangerous god Siva) certainly appears in India towards the close of the pre-Christian era,[1] and although the influence of the Upanishadic teachers does not disappear, theism of a sort persists right up to the present century and has manifested itself in a rich variety of devotional forms. The period in India corresponding to that of medieval Europe produces in fact two main types of religion, associated with the names of two great teachers, Sankara *c.* 788 A.D., and Ramanuja *c.* 1100 A.D., who symbolise respectively the majority and minority approaches to the subject. Sankara is the apostle of non-duality or *advaita*, Ramanuja of modified duality or *vishistadvaita*, and there is even a third teacher, Madhva, who is rather less often referred to, and who sees the relationship between Deity and the soul as complete duality. Sankara has sometimes been stigmatised as a Buddhist, and he certainly upholds the pure doctrine of identity-mysticism[2] in which All is One and the One is beyond definition, while Ramanuja and Madhva in varying degrees see the relationship which exists as one between the Emanator and that which emanates from him.

The logical consequence of this dualistic relationship is the growth of an expression of dependence. In identity-mysticism there can be no *flow* of life from the Self-Existent to the finite, since the Ocean of Being is unruffled except by misperception on the part of its components, but in theism there prevails what Dr. Tennant has denominated in his philosophical theology, 'delegated activity', or 'devolved autonomy' and these bespeak the priority of the Self-Existent, the giving of life by the latter to the creaturely, and its maintenance, renewal, and re-direction when abused. Christians have various ways of expressing the sense of this priority, when they employ the

---

[1] This Bhagavata theism, as it is called, is thought by some to have been initiated by one specific teacher, but we have to confess that we know nothing about him.
[2] Professor Murty of Andhra University would dissent from this. For him Sankara also is fundamentally a theist.

term 'grace'. There is the grace of creation and inspiration, the grace of preservation, the grace of redemption, and the grace of sanctification. There is prevenient grace, and the grace which follows and makes perfect. It has for many years been noticed that the sense of dependence in Asian theism outside the range of Christianity also expresses itself in a doctrine of grace. Rudolf Otto has written a whole book on this subject, and has introduced European readers to the existence in India, to all appearances independently of Christianity, of a very real devotional theism known as *bhakti*, in which the soul is conscious of the unmerited love of God and responds to it in lyrical outbursts.

Kraemer[1] is anxious that we should not see too much resemblance in this. He holds that the relationship between the soul and God is far from identical with what is to be found in Christianity, and this criticism in a measure is just. The God worshipped is often in the popular mind merely a selected one out of a pantheon, and not the *sole* Deity—although philosophic Indians will tell one that this is only an ignorant misperception of the latter, who is seen and worshipped for the moment under a specific aspect. Again, the nature of the god worshipped is often ethnic rather than ethical, and retains many of the attributes of ruthless tropical Nature personified.[2] This is especially to be seen in the grim theophany which occurs at the end of the Bhagavadgita. The God of the Gita is the Destroyer as well as the Preserver, a fact which is often slurred over. And thirdly, the relation between the soul and God in *bhakti* is sometimes hardly dignified, but sportive and even erotic. Kraemer declares that there is no easy and direct transition from Hindu *bhakti* to Christian *bhakti*, and that the convert to the latter quickly repudiates his past. This may be true if the teaching given him follows along certain lines, but it seems more just and generous to see in Indian theism and *bhakti* a desire of the sensitive Indian soul for something which can only receive full satisfaction in the more dignified form of Christian personal religion, though in its Indian form it may sometimes approximate to the latter and display real beauty. Moreover it needs to be remembered that both among Catholic and Protestant Christians there have sometimes occurred extravagant forms of scarcely sublimated erotic devotion to Christ or the Madonna which approach rather closely to certain features of South Indian *bhakti*, while some of the Saivite hymns are sufficiently lofty in their devotion to induce speculation as to whether they owe anything to Christian influence.

[1] In *The Christian Faith in a non-Christian World*.
[2] It is not even *pure* theism, since the god in question has generally a female consort, symbolising the procreative and maternal aspects of deity.

Side by side with this emotional religion occur also new forms of theistic philosophy, and it would be unjust not to mention at least the actual teaching of Ramanuja, Madhva, and others like them, (though it is not quite clear whether Ramanuja himself was not a selective henotheist rather than a true monotheist). Mention should also be made of the school of philosophical theology in South India connected with the Saiva Siddhanta, which may conceivably have derived some influence from association with the Christianity of the Malabar coast.

A new stage in Indian religion is reached when a fresh wave of Christian evangelism enters from the eighteenth century onwards. Thenceforward it becomes still harder to dissever Hindu philosophical theology from Christian. Rabindranath Tagore was a member in early life of the Brahmo-Samaj sect whose founder owed much to Christian teaching; while both Tagore and Gandhi were friends of Charles Andrews, who infused into them much of his own refined and scholarly Christian spirit. Radakrishnan and Aurobindo Ghose were in their youth both pupils at Christian colleges, and had many friends among Christian teachers and theologians, to whatever extent in later life they may have come to pursue lines of their own. It is therefore impossible to see much of nineteenth- and twentieth-century Hinduism in isolation from western religion.

But indeed post-axial religion in India owes much to the juxtaposition of Hindus with Moslem as well as with Christian invaders. There are a number of hybrid sects which clearly owe their form to the influence of Islam, and among these is that of the Sikhs, whose early teachers undoubtedly tried to combine the best elements in both Islam and Hinduism.

Europe

The story north of the central mountain-belt is different from that to the south of it. In Hellas the transition from pre-axial to axial took place *before* the entry of Hebraeo-Christian religion into the Mediterranean. The story is already well-known. Sir James Frazer and Miss Jane Harrison led the way fifty years ago in the interpretation of pre-axial Greek religion by reference to the work of anthropologists, and created a small revolution by persuading scholars of the Greek and Roman classics to see their subject in a wider context. Frazer's edition of the *Fasti* of Ovid, as well as a large part of his famous *The Golden Bough*, dealt with it along those lines; but while we are thus now able to view the pre-axial religion of the Mediterranean world in comparison with that of ancient India as well as of Borneo and other islands in the Pacific, we are also able to see the work of the Hellenic philosophers in comparison with that of the Chinese sages and the Upanishadic teachers of India, and the resemblances are sometime striking, as well as the differences. Seldom if ever do we find in Asia long literary treatises such as occur among the Greeks. Most of the literature is of quite a different kind, and consists of strings of aphorisms rather than of reasoned arguments.

North and west of the Alps and Balkans, however, pre-axial paganism remained untouched by the work of the philosophers of Greece, and polytheism was there in possession until the impact of Christianity upon it. Thus Central and Eastern Europe, as well as Britain, remained characteristically pre-axial until they were evangelised by Christians in the way described in Chapter V of this book. This meant that there was a kind of reversal of the process of development. The Christianity which passed into Germany and the British Isles as well as into Gaul and Spain was very largely that which had developed in the fourth century A.D., and which, as those who study the work of Lucius mentioned in Chapter IX will be aware, was the result of a good deal of syncretism. Hence, although on its prophetic side it was an advance on the paganism which it supplanted, this prophetic element does not appear pure, but is much tempered in popular circles by the survival of a somewhat thinly transformed pagan pluralism. There may be some difference of opinion as to whether real prophetic Christianity does not emerge in this area until some time after the end of the Dark Ages. Some will see its emergence as the fruit of Scholasticism and the work of the Friars; other perhaps will defer it to the time of the sixteenth-century Reformers, which certainly brought it once again into prominence; and there is perhaps a good deal of oscillation in the story of Central European religion, since the age of the *Aufklärung* in the eighteenth century, at any rate in France and Germany, brings a new outburst of axial re-thinking of the whole position, and the Christian religion in Europe has never really recovered from that outburst, which for weal or woe has imprinted its influence indelibly upon all theological thought since that time. Nevertheless the classic axial age for Europe still remains the age of Socrates, Plato, Aristotle, and the Stoics. The pioneer work of these has indeed shaped the thought of educated Europe ever since, and has even inspired, by its freedom and independence, and by insistence upon observed fact, the later work of empirical scientists.

China

The story of religious thought in China is probably the longest on record, longer even than that of India. Its pre-axial polytheism goes back at least as far as that of Egypt, and possibly further, and, as in Egypt, probably contented the inhabitants of that country for a period considerably longer than that of the whole of Christian history up to date.   But the axial age seems to have come in somewhere about the time of the birth of Kung-fu-tze, i.e. about 550 B.C., and it continues down to perhaps 221 B.C., though again its fringe this end is rather ragged.   The Buddhist movement did not enter the country until the sixth century A.D., and within a hundred years after that we get the arrival of the Manichaeans, and of the Nestorian Christians.   The crucial period therefore is from Kung-fu-tze, through what is often called 'the Age of the Hundred Philosophers', down to minority movements which arose a little before the beginning of the Christian era.[1]

It is difficult to get very much theology out of the obiter dicta of Kung-fu-tze, but it does not do to say that he was not religious. While he shows little interest in the multiplicity of Chinese divinities which have come down perhaps from the Bronze Age, he certainly recognises what we may perhaps call Providence, and declares that this Supreme Power has entrusted him with a mandate to teach, and that It also bestows its mandate upon rulers and governors.   If, however, they abuse the authority so entrusted to them it may be right to deprive them of it, and in this case the mandate of Heaven ceases so far as they are concerned.   The fact that Kung-fu-tze believed in his mission carries with it the implication that Heaven sets the seal of its approval upon his moral teaching, so that when he tells people to behave courteously and to manifest the quality or virtue which he calls *jên* in all their dealings one with another, he is speaking with the approval of Heaven.   The misfortune is that so much of the teaching of King-fu-tze appears to be bound up with the preservation of the relations between individuals which clearly belong to a patriarchal, feudal, and monarchist order of society, that it has seemed very difficult to find a place for it within the bounds of a republican democracy.   And yet in spite of this it seems as though within the limits of his own day Kung-fu-tze did recognise the worth of the ordinary individual, and the rights of the common man, since, *jên* is not wholly a class virtue, but is intended to be universal in practice, and one of the most famous aphorisms of Kung-fu-tze, often quoted, runs: 'Treat everyone you meet in the street as though he were an honoured guest, and that which you would not wish to be done to yourself, do not do to others.'   Again there is another aphorism which, although it seems patient of several different

---

[1] Reference may be made by the reader to Marcel Granett's *La Pensée Chinoise*, or to the writings of E. R. Hughes and Arthur Waley.

translations, generally has the same significance: 'There being instruction there will be no distinction of classes.' Kung-fu-tze is very fond of defining his ideal man. He calls him the princely man (*chün-tzu*), which somewhat reminds us of the high-minded man of Aristotle. Thus he says: The *chün-tzu*, contemplating the world, is free from unreasonable likes and dislikes. He stands for what is right. The man of honour makes demands upon himself: the man without a sense of honour makes demands on others. And once more: 'Men of true breeding are in harmony with people although they do not agree with them; but men of no breeding agree with people, and yet are not in harmony with them.' 'A man of true breeding sets his heart on spiritual power within himself: the man of no breeding sets his heart on land.' 'The man bent on public service, if he be the human-hearted kind of man (lit. full of *jên*) under no circumstances will he seek to live at the expense of his *jên*. There are occasions when he will lay down his life to preserve his *jên*.'

But what is *jên*?

The significance of all the *logia* lies in this one key word, the story of which is as important for the study of Chinese ethics as the story of ἀγάπη is for Christian ethics. *Jên* before the time of Kung-fu-tze is not really common even in literary Chinese, but where it occurs it is almost the equivalent of *largesse*, the bountiful kindness of a superior to his inferiors. It also means 'man', but the two ideograms, although pronounced in the same way, are written quite differently. The result of this similarity had been to lead some translators to interpret the ethical term as 'humaneness', or 'human-heartedness'; but it is said that this cannot be the correct translation, since it does not account for the later development in the meaning of the word. There can be no doubt that Kung-fu-tze used the word in a new sense which was all his own. Thus, when he was asked the meaning of *jên*, he replied in the terms of the negative golden rule given above. This rule, however, is negative only in form, Chinese style preferring a kind of understatement. That this is so may be seen from another passage in the Analects: 'To be able from one's own self to draw a parallel for the treatment of others—this may be called the method of *jên*' (benevolent love). He also defined it by the word 'reciprocity' (*shu* in Chinese). Sometimes Kung-fu-tze used the word as the synonym for perfect morality, very much as St. Paul says 'He that loveth another hath fulfilled the Torah.' Yet as we shall see, *jên*, as used by Kung-fu-tze, is not the same as equal love to all men. It is benevolence operating within the scheme of the feudal China of Kung-fu-tze's day. The result of this has been that *jên* has come to be exercised in a graded manner, and indeed is often defined as 'graded love'. This has made the Confucian ethic unpopular in Republican China, partly because it gives a certain aristocratic flavour to benevolence, and at the same time commends the tendency to love and benefit one's relatives and parents more than other people, so that in the classical work known as The Doctrine of the Mean we read of 'the decreasing measures of love to more distant relatives'.

At this point it is necessary to speak about Mo-Ti (*c.* 475–393). Mo was born about the time when Kung-fu-tze died, and as he grew up he was trained in the Confucian school. But he developed considerable independence of thought, and disagreed with the principle of *graded* love.

> 'A thief loves (*ai*) his own family and does not love other families; hence he steals from other families in order to benefit his own family. Each grandee loves his own clan and does not love other clans, hence he causes disturbances to other clans in order to benefit his own clan. Each feudal lord loves his own state and does not love other states, so he attacks other states in order to benefit his own state. The causes of all disturbances ... lie herein. ... It is always from want of equal love to all'.

So spoke Mo, and throughout his writings, which were carefully preserved and even chanted over by his disciples, he develops his distinctive idea of universal benevolence. Heaven, he says, loves all equally, and desires the wellbeing of all, and therefore we ought to behave like Heaven. (Anyone can see that this comes remarkably close to the teaching of Jesus, when He says that the Heavenly Father is kind to the unthankful and evil and sends His rain upon the just and unjust alike.) Mo invented a word for his new kind of benevolence, which was to be equal and universal, by adding to *jên* the suffix *ai*, which is the Chinese word for ordinary sexual love, the compound being capable of transliteration as *jienai*. This uncompromising teaching led to a controversy between the Confucians and the Mohists which went on for almost 200 years. Meng-Ko who sided with Kung-fu-tze and who flourished from 372 to 298, said that equal love for all was unnatural. Everyone has certain special duties towards his own family, and if one does not recognise these one is actually less than human, and no more than a beast. The teaching of Mo is therefore bestial. As the result of the strong influence of Meng-Ko, filial piety became elevated to the position of a key virtue, and since it involved a form of graded love, Mo became relegated to the position of a heretic. It was conceded that in the golden age of the past there might have been such a thing as universal benevolence, but it was clear that graded love was the only suitable attitude for persons living in the contemporary world. The effect of this in politics was disastrous, for it led straight to corruption. The adoption of the Confucian ethic meant that rulers, magistrates, and government officials generally always tended to put their relatives into high positions. The whole bureaucracy became corrupt, and for a time Taoism and Buddhism increased in influence. But after about six centuries there came a revival of Confucianism at the hands of the scholastic teachers, and these neo-Confucians, while reviving the use of the unmodified term *jên*, gave it more or less the meaning which *jienai* had for Mo. One of these scholastics, who lived in the eleventh century A.D. said that to practise *jên* one must be completely impartial (*gung*). This seemed to open up a good prospect for revived Confucianism, and a few years later another scholastic writer declared that there was no justification for any selfishness. 'He who enlarges his mind is able to treat equally all living beings in the universe.' He also revived Mo's term *jienai*, and popularised the ancient saying 'All within the four seas are brothers.' This is paraphrased in what is known as the *Western Inscription*: 'All people are my brothers, all things are my relations.'

Unfortunately the Chinese found it hard to maintain such a high ideal, and the greatest of the scholastics Chu Hsi (1130–1200) compromised by saying that the two virtues of 'graded love' and 'universal love' were to be held side by side.

Anyone can see that 'graded love' as practised by the Confucians is incompatible with the practice of the Christian ἀγάπη, but it is by no means impossible to argue successfully that the *jienai* of Mo comes very close to it. It is also obvious that 'graded love' especially in regard to its practical results is bound to be obnoxious to the Communist.

In contrast to all this ethical teaching about relationships with a more or less vaguely religious background, comes the doctrine of the Taoist. Its reputed founder, Lao-Tzû, although still spoken of by some educated Chinese as though he were an historical character nearly contemporary with Kung-fu-tze, remains in fact a somewhat legendary person, and it is even doubted whether he really existed at all. There was, however, quite clearly during the part of the age of the Hundred Philosophers, a school of mystics which centred its teaching upon the belief in the great Tao, and this school, according to Dr. Waley, produced somewhere about 240 B.C. a collection of paradoxical aphorisms known as the Tao-te-King. This collection, however, is anonymous.

The importance of the Tao-te-King is to be found in its theology, which looks suspiciously as though it had been influenced from the direction of the India of the Upanishadic period. It is Quietist in essence, and expounds the view that the entire universe is pervaded by a single Cosmic Principle which is eternal, and prior even to the *shen* or super-human beings. The statement that in its unchanging and absolute character it is 'nameless', and 'like an empty vessel', reminds us of passages in the Upanishadic philosophy, and also in the Sunyata philosophy of Buddhism. 'Namelessness' would seem to be an idiomatic way of expressing unknowableness and indefinability.

The original Tao *in esse* is like the Void of the Sunyata or like the το ὄν of the Greeks; but when it gets a name it seems very much to resemble the Logos[1] of Hellenistic Greek philosophical theology.

We read: 'All pervading is the great Tao. It may be found on the left hand and on the right. All things depend on It for their production . . . we look at It and we do not see It. We listen to It and we do not hear It. We try to grasp It, and do not get hold of It. Even with these three qualities It cannot be made the subject of description: hence we blend them together and obtain the ONE.'

What should be one's relationship to this great Tao in human affairs? The Taoists themselves are quite clear. It should be that of passivity. Live according to the principles which you see around you in nature, and do not resist them. That is all that is necessary. The greatest of the Taoist thinkers of a later generation wrote:

> 'Inaction is the real part of fame, the storehouse of all plans, the responsible head of all business, the master of all knowledge. Identify yourself completely with Infinity-Eternity, and wander in the non-self. Carry to the highest what you have received from Heaven, but do not reveal your success in this. Be empty, that is all. The perfect man's use of his mind is like a mirror. He does not anticipate events, nor does he go counter to them. Thus it is that he is able to master things and not be injured by them.'

In the Tao-te-King itself occurs the maxim for statesmen and politicians: 'Let me do nothing, and the people will transform themselves. Let me love quiescence and the people will put themselves right.'

The early Taoists do not seem to have expected that they would make all the Chinese into Quietist mystics; but they clearly hoped that enough educated persons would appreciate their teaching to provide the state with a supply of persons duly qualified to serve it after the manner of Plato's philosopher king, and that the latter would rule without making their power felt, as it was said had happened in bygone days in China, in the golden age of Yao and Shun.

The basic assumption in Taoism of course is in the original goodness of man, an assumption which seems generally shared by most Chinese thinkers. It is, however, ethnic rather than ethical, and visualises no such thing as the destruction in mankind of the *imago dei*. 'Leave the people alone, and they will put themselves right.' But this doctrine, of course, in the hands of an unscrupulous tyrant, would mean that he could justify to himself whatever he chose to do as being in harmony with nature. Unless 'Infinity-

---

[1] In the English Protestant version of the Fourth Gospel into Chinese 'Tao' is actually used to translate 'Logos', but there is never in Chinese non-Christian thought, so far as I am aware, any idea of the Great Tao becoming fully embodied in a completely historical character. For instance, it is not said of Kung-fu-tze, I believe, on any occasion, that 'in him dwelt all the fullness of the Tao bodily.'

Eternity' and 'non-self' are seen to be invested with the highest moral attributes, the logical outcome of Taoism is bound to be non-moral and sub-human. That some Chinese thinkers were not incapable of seeing this seems to appear from the fragments of them which remain. Thus one of them, in the fourth century B.C. and about a century after Kung-fu-tze, taught that men are by nature not good but evil. Nature must therefore be overcome by nurture, and men must be trained to overcome their nature. Instead of praising nature as the Taoists do, he said that we ought to domesticate and regulate her. Both Confucian and Taoist teachers agreed to the extent of opposing him, but his protests remain as a witness against their one-sided views.

Later still, in the post-axial age of Chinese thought, a quasi-scholastic philosopher of the twelfth century A.D., Chu Hsi, sought to combine features from the various schools of Chinese classical thought and in the course of his work uttered the following aphorisms:

> We need not talk about empty and far-away things; if we would know the reality of Tao we must seek it within our own nature.
> Each one has within him the principle of right, what we call Tao, the road along which we ought to walk.
> The means by which we all may day by day banish human desire and return to Divine Law lie within our reach, and to use them is our duty.
> The one thing we must realise is that we must use our earnest effort and master it, get rid of its excesses, and restore the Mean.
> Virtue is the practice of moral law.
> Virtue is what is received into the heart. Before serving one's parents and following one's elder brother, already to possess a perfectly filial and fraternal mind; this is what is termed virtue.
> Love itself is the original substance of virtue; reverence is love in graceful expression; righteousness is love in judgment; and wisdom is love in discriminating.
> Sincerity is the principle of reality. It is, to be the same whether before men's faces or behind their backs.
> To be devoid of anything else is spontaneous Sincerity; to allow no deception is Sincerity acquired by effort.

Hebraeo-Christian religion

Although, considered in a detached manner, the emergence of Hebraeo-Christian religion clearly belongs to the period of the axial age, in a very important sense it stands by itself, and differs profoundly from all the other movements within that period. The unprejudiced observer cannot but be sensible that to a degree which is not present in the other movements, except perhaps in some of the works of the Upanishadic age and of the sage Mo'ti in China, it is theocentric rather than anthropocentric. It starts from the end of

God rather than from the end of man.   Like other axial teachers, the Hebrew prophets challenged the established order.   But theirs is a different kind of challenge: it is less concerned with the internal welfare of man than with the sovereign purpose of the Self-Existent. Fundamentally, unless one assumes the pantheistic outlook of identity-mysticism, the Way of the Buddha is humanistic.   Even the morality of Kung-fu-tze and Meng-Ko relegates Heaven into the far background.   The Greek philosopher, though he may sometimes speak of God and sometimes 'the gods', is avowedly concerned in the main with man as the artist of his own life.   Here and there we get little outbursts from men like Xenophanes and Socrates which sound like echoes of something from Isaiah; but in the main the spirit is man-centred.   This difference cannot fail to be recognised by anyone who looks fairly at the evidence.   The conclusions which may be drawn from it may vary, but the nature of the challenge and the claim which it involves are beyond dispute.   There is, of course, a further element in Hebraeo-Christian religion which marks it off from other developments preceding it in the axial age, and that is its emphasis upon the significance of the course of events.   We here encounter a feature which is held in common by Judaism, Christianity, and Islam.   These three are quite obviously in a state of relationship to one another, and Mr. Aldous Huxley charges them with what he calls 'an idolatrous preoccupation with the time-sequence'.[1] It does not seem to follow as the inevitable consequence of this insistence upon the importance of history that any such religion should be more violent and persecuting and less humane than those which are only concerned with eternity.   It may, in fact, not really be true at all.   Buddhism seems to have had almost no effect in checking the militarist violence of Japan, while Hinduism, being so very largely a social system, cannot be pleaded in this case, since its most ardent ultra-conservative supporters show that they are prepared to use extreme violence against any who contract out of it.   The staunchest advocate of non-violence was Gandhi, who acknowledged great indebtedness to the Sermon on the Mount; and it was the ultra-orthodox Mahasabha which murdered him.   On the other side, it is not accurate to say that the orthodox Quakers were not concerned with the profession of belief in the events of the Gospels.   They certainly were, and they used the New Testament when the spirit moved them to read or preach at Meeting, and they do so still.   It is only a modernist minority which has gone outside historical Christianity and followed a kind of Liberal Unitarian or vaguely

[1] *The Perennial Philosophy*.   There is, on the other hand, evidence that the Bhagavata movement in Hinduism, which is a little pre-Christian in emergence, concerned itself in some measure with the idea that Deity intervenes in history.

theistic line.   This does not mean any kind of defence of intolerance. But it is only too true that if pantheism is once logically followed out to its conclusion, it can and often does end by dissolving all moral distinctions and all standards of right and wrong, good and evil.   It may begin by having a charming appearance, but it can end by being very cruel, and certainly wicked.   Logically it can have no reason for seeking to abolish prostitution, exploitation, dishonesty, or fraud, since even those who indulge in such practices are equally manifestations of the Absolute with the sage or saint.   It is only when the Creator and the creaturely stand in a relationship to one another which is not that of pure identity, that evil or its possibility can have any meaning at all; and it is to be presumed that in the world in which we live it is impossible to remain satisfied without some reasonable explanation of our curious surd-like consciousness that there really are items which are indisputably evil.   Conversely, it cannot be other than most unsatisfying to regard the course of events as merely cyclic repetition without any more significance than the repeated hammering of a word or note when a gramophone record is jammed.   But if we are to choose between a linear and a cyclic view of events, and to prefer the former, we cannot in reason forgo the possibility that some events will have more significance and more far-reaching consequences than others; and that whether any one or more of these be described as either intrusions of the Self-Existent into the temporal order which is His creation, or intensifications at one or more points within that order of the creative activity of the same Self-Existent, there is no more logical connection between such a belief and coercive persecution than there is between such persecution and the belief that one is in possession of any other sort of absolute truth.   Anybody who feels strongly enough about what he knows, or thinks he knows, to be true, will always be tempted to force that belief on other people because he thinks that that will be for their good.   He will be wrong, because that is not the way in which truth is properly to be commended, but his mistaken enthusiasm, whether it be Marxist, Moslem, or Christian, is understandable.   It is only the liberal agnostic who doubts whether any truth is ascertainable, who thinks all morality is relative, and takes for granted that we are all of us doomed in this life to grope helplessly in the twilight (and perhaps also believes that the temporal order is only the surplus energy of the Absolute thrown off for his amusement), who has no temptations to persecute anybody—except perhaps those morally earnest persons who protest against the hedonism into which he sometimes sinks.   Tolerance in that form is a real throwing-up of the sponge; for it abandons any attempt at finding any real meaningfulness in life. Bertrand Russell's free man defying the universe because it fails to conform to the highest he knows, is better and nobler than such a person.

The sense of the uniqueness of Christianity is continually re-asserting itself. Its most recent form, put forward by Professor Gregor Smith, represents it as not religion at all, but as a rejection of all religion; so that when the Marxist totally condemns the latter, the Christian can almost say: 'Amen: but you have not condemned *me*.' Yet it is always possible, in asserting this uniqueness of Christianity, to go too far, farther than the evidence warrants, and to take up a stance which prohibits almost all conversation with the earnest seekers in non-Christian faiths. If Kraemer and perhaps Barth and those who follow them concede that in approaching the latter there should be a great Yea as well as a great Nay, it does seem to many of us as though the great Nay completely drowns the great Yea.

Summary

The foregoing survey will have shown the extent to which the religious leaders of the various countries during the axial age were in agreement as to certain general ideas, though this agreement does not necessarily mean actual intercommunication, even if some diffusion cannot be entirely ruled out. The inference is that in the main there was concurrent development, which was due to mankind in many areas having reached a certain stage of mental development.

The principal changes are in the direction of less anthropism, and in the development of a unitary conception of Godhead, but especially in the spiritualisation of worship, and in the development of its inwardness.

For example, the following passages show remarkable unanimity in deprecating ritual material sacrifice:

1. *From Yasna 44 in the Gathas of Zarathustra*

'The false gods, have they then been good masters?—
I ask it of those who, in their worship,
Behold the sacrificer and his attendant deliver the ox to fury,
And the chief magician cause him to yield up his life with groans,
And who do not put liquid dung (or rather perhaps "pour libations")
    upon the field to make it prosper, according to Justice.'

2. *From the Mundaka Upanishad*

'Unsafe boats, however, are these sacrificial forms,
The eighteen, in which is expressed the lower work.
The fools who approve that as the better,
Go again to old age and death.'

3. *In the Chandogya Upanishad* (Khandah 16) we get the assertion that a person's entire life is a sacrifice, and in Khandah 24 that if the Agnihotra sacrifice is made with the correct understanding, it is 'made in all worlds, in all beings, and in all souls'.

4. *In the Bhagavadgita* (IV.25) we find a whole philosophy of sacrifice stated:

'The act of offering is Brahma, the oblation is Brahma, it is Brahma that is offered by Brahma in the fire; by that to Brahma must he come through concentration on action which is Brahma.

Some Yogis worship with a sacrifice to the gods. Others celebrate a sacrifice only by sacrifice to Brahma as the fire.

Others sacrifice their hearing and other senses in the fires of restraint. Others sacrifice sound and other objects of sense in the fires of the senses.

And others sacrifice all the actions of the senses and the actions of breath in the fire of Yoga and the restraining of the self, lit by knowledge.

Others are sacrificers of wealth, sacrificers of austerity, and sacrificers of Yoga; men of restraint and of strict vows are sacrificers of their scripture-study and knowledge.

Others sacrifice their outbreathing in their inbreathing and their inbreathing in their outbreathing. They check the breath that goes in and out, intent on control of breathing.

Others restrained in food offer breaths in breaths. All these too are knowers of sacrifice, whose sins are done away by sacrifice.

Eaters of the immortal food of the remains of the sacrifice, they go to Brahma the eternal. This world is not for him who sacrifices not, much less another world, O best of Kurus.

Even thus, many and various are the sacrifices that are set up before Brahma. Know that they are all born of action, and thus knowing thou shalt be liberated.

Better than material sacrifice is the sacrifice of knowledge, O hero. Each and every action, O son of Pritha, is comprehended in knowledge.'

5. *From a Buddhist Psalm*, Samyutta i (metrical translation by Mrs. Rhys Davids)

'The sacrifices called the Horse, the Man,
The Peg-thrown Site, the Drink of Victory,
The Bolts Withdrawn, and all the mighty fuss;
These are not rites that bring a rich result.
Where divers goats and sheep and kine are slain,
Never to such a rite as that repair
The noble seers who walk the perfect way.
But rites wherein's no slaughter and no fuss,
Are offerings meet, bequests perpetual,
Where never goats and sheep and kine are slain,
To such a sacrifice as this repair
The noble seers who walk the perfect way.
These are the rites entailing great results.
These to the celebrant are blest nor curst.
The oblation runneth o'er: the gods are pleased.'

6. Also, in the *Itivuttakam*, the Buddha proclaims to his monks:

'There are two sacrifices, the material and the spiritual, and the higher, O monks, is the spiritual.'

7. And again in Samyutta viii the Buddha addressed himself to a Brahmin who is engaged in offering a sacrifice with ghee over a fire, and declares that this is not at all the kind of sacrifice that ought to be offered, and that he himself would offer. He condemns the pride and superiority of the Brahmin, and then goes on:

> 'It is the heart that is the altar,
>   and the fire thereon is my being,
>   quite submissive.'

In view of the above it is not surprising to read as one of the pillar edicts of the Buddhist Emperor Asoka:

> 'No animal may be slaughtered for sacrifice.'

8. Passages can be found in the sayings of Chinese sages, in which the inwardness of worship is commended in opposition to public and ostentatious religious ceremonies. Thus Kung-fu-tze says: 'If I am inattentive at the sacrifice it is as though there were no sacrifice'—a clear denunciation of the *opus operatum* theory.

9. With the foregoing may specially be compared the passage in the Hebrew Psalm 50:

'Thinkest thou that I will eat bulls' flesh and drink the blood of goats. Offer unto Yahweh thanksgiving, and pay thy vows unto the Most Highest.'

The same sentiment, of course, is to be found in Amos 5.22 ff., Isaiah 1.10–17, and in Micah 6.

10. Stoic writings contain much of the same nature, cutting at the roots of ritual sacrifice and replacing it by 'rational sacrifice' (λογικὴ λατρέια), which is interior and bereft of ceremony. Cicero transcribes the feelings of the Greek reformers of a former generation when he makes his interlocutor Balbus say: 'That worship of the gods is the best, that piety is the most holy and undefiled, in which we reverence them always with mind and voice, pure, blameless and uncorrupt.'

11. The Alexandrian Jew Philo in his treatise *De specialibus legibus*, when commenting upon the directions in Leviticus for the sacrifice of the red heifer, says: 'Even though the members of the congregation bring nothing more, in presenting *themselves* they are offering the best sacrifice, the perfect oblation of a virtuous life.'

And also: 'The true sacrifice (θρησκεία) is the oblation of the soul. The true altar of God is the grateful soul of the wise man, made up of perfect virtues . . . on this altar always burns the sacred light, the light of the spirit, which is wisdom.'

12. With these we may compare a classic passage from the New Testament, James 1.27: 'Pure and undefiled religion (θρησκεία) in the judgment of God the Father means: to care for the orphans and widows in their trouble, and to keep oneself from the stain of the world.' (θρησκεία is a standard word for cult-sacrifice.)[1]

It must be frankly admitted that these passages are often extracted from very dissimilar contexts, some being pantheistic, others monotheistic, one in phraseology almost polytheistic. What will probably strike the unprejudiced reader, however, will be that no single one of them refers to the inadequacy of man to attain unaided to this ethical and spiritual ideal of worship. Micah, Philo, and the author of the Epistle of James seem to assume that all that is necessary is 'simply doing right', like Mr. Belloc's young hero. So for the matter of that does Cicero. The Buddha speaks of being submissive, but omits to say to Whom one is to be submissive, and is usually held to have said: 'Be ye as lamps unto yourselves.' Even if what he may actually have said was: 'Be ye as those who have the Self for a Lamp', subsequent monastic commentators have put the other interpretation upon the Pali words.

Later Buddhism certainly develops the idea of Grace (as also does *bhakti* Hinduism), and both thus seem in this respect to have moved in the direction of Christian doctrine. But it is only Christianity which throughout its whole course has proclaimed a sufficiently lofty ideal of spiritual perfection to lead to the correlative doctrine of the inadequacy of man to reach it unaided. No one who is sincere, or who sees himself objectively can say, touching the Commandments, 'All these have I kept from my youth up.' The doctrine of the spiritual sacrifice is not to be discarded, but correlated with the doctrine that it is not we who lead the Christian life but Christ who lives it in us, once we have surrendered to Him; and that, apart from Him, all have sinned and fallen short of the Glory of God; so that, in the words attributed to Him in the Fourth Gospel: 'Apart from me, ye can do nothing.' To quote Luther's blunt and incisive translation of St. Paul: 'Wohin bleibt der Ruhm? Er ist aus!'

---

[1] Similar passages can be found in the sayings of Chinese sages, in which the inwardness of prayer and meditation is commended in opposition to public and ostentatious religious ceremonies.

The dependence of the axial changes upon outstanding individual personalities is obvious. Wherever we go, we find names called in our ears. No one thinks of remembering the name of the priest, the magician, or the medicine man: but with the prophet, the reformer, and the sage it is different. This, however, is a phenomenon which is not confined to religion, but betokens a general heightening of the stress laid on the individual, as the human race moves on its course. Nevertheless it is perhaps more marked within the sphere of religion and philosophy than elsewhere, and this feature has certainly passed on into the realm of the sciences, where we find that the authors of various discoveries have given their names to them; so that we hear of Avogadro's law, Boyle's law, Darwin's Theory of Evolution, Jeans' Theory of the Solar System, and Planck's Quantum Theory; and of the principle of relativity as specially associated with the name of Einstein.

What we cannot help noticing is that the contribution of the great Hebrew prophets to the thought of the axial age is different from that of most of the others in its attitude towards the course of events, in which it is to some extent followed by Kung-fu-tze. Chinese thought in this matter is, however, nothing like as positive and searching as that of the Hebrews.

Finally we notice that the development of the Christian movement out of the Hebrew Church is something which has no real parallel elsewhere. The nearest approach to it is the development of Buddhism out of Hinduism, and here the differences are much greater than the resemblances. The Buddha himself occupies much more the status of Socrates or Plato than of Jesus, and it is nowadays difficult not to conclude that whatever assimilation of Buddhism to Christianity may have taken place it must have been due in part to the infiltration of Christian ideas into Buddhist theories.

With the exception of the section on medieval Hinduism which the foregoing chapter contains, the major part of the discussion of post-axial religion will be found in Chapters VI, IX, X, and XI and in the sections of Chapters IV and V which deal with the expansion of Christianity.

CHAPTER III

THE PRINCIPLE OF DIFFUSION

We will start with something quite simple. There is no feature of material culture which has spread more universally than the pedal bicycle. Invented in England, it has become a normal means of individual transport all over the world. Especially noticeable is the way in which the peoples of Asia and Africa have adopted it. Wherever one goes in Arab states, in India, or in Africa, one finds crowds of folk rushing about on these useful machines. No one seems to have any hesitation about taking advantage of the convenience which they afford, in spite of the fact that their invention emerged first in a single Western European country.

I have a vivid recollection of something which I saw some years ago in the Indian capital of Delhi. By a splendid gesture of the government, the old Vice-regal Lodge with its surrounding open space had been handed over to the newly-established independent India, as the headquarters of the University of Delhi. The spacious park made an ideal University campus, and round it were rapidly growing up new colleges and lecture rooms, while the former residence of the British Commander in Chief (the Jang-i-lat-Sahib of Kipling's *Kim*) had been turned into a women's college of the status of Newnham or Girton, at which I was privileged to deliver a lecture. But right opposite the gates of the University precincts, on a piece of waste land, had been erected an enormous hoarding covered by a poster advertising the mass-produced bicycles of some Indian firm, while up and down the road passed a continuous stream of pedal cyclists of all ranks and descriptions. India, it seems, feels neither shame nor hesitation in adopting an invention of such proved utility, in spite of the fact that in origin it is essentially foreign. This seems to me to be of the nature of a parable. It is quite clear that on principle any item which is universally agreed to be both useful and beneficial ceases to be foreign in any derogatory sense, but belongs to the world. No one declines to use electrical power simply because the principles on which it is based were first discovered in Europe, nor to take advantage of radio because its invention was due to an Italian, Marconi. No one ignores Italian painting, or Chinese porcelain making, merely because they were local developments. All are examples of the general phenomenon which anthropologists have labelled 'Diffusion'. I propose in this chapter to discuss some of its features.

New items in human culture have certainly appeared from time to time in particular spots on the earth's surface. Some of these can be regarded as beneficial, and their appearance as a form of progress; some are neutral and indifferent as to their value; some are clearly signs of retrogression, or of decadence and degeneracy, and have therefore been described as evil. Such new items may sometimes be concurrent developments, appearing as it would seem independently in different areas, when similar favourable conditions render their appearance likely, if not inevitable. On the other hand one of them may arise singly in some special area, and then spread by diffusion to other localities.

If, for the moment, we confine ourselves to the consideration of material culture, it is not difficult to pick out items which are clear examples of concurrent development, and others which operate on the principle of diffusion. Thus the general practice of clothing the body to protect it against cold on the one hand or excessive solar radiation on the other clearly develops independently and concurrently in various regions, although some particularly successful form of clothing may be invented in one place, and then diffuse to or become adopted by others. Hunting implements such as the spear and the bow and arrow do not seem in their simplest form to have diffused from one area, but to be natural and inevitable concurrent developments. The chopper is almost universal, beginning with the flint hand axe and going on to metal ones mounted on hafts, but the development of molten metal tools may be something which has diffused from a central area or areas, and spread round the globe, although smelting may have been discovered and practised in a number of separate places. The first wheeled carriage is believed to have been invented in the Nile valley and to have diffused thence to other countries, but special developments of wheeled vehicles have also diffused from different places.[1] Thus the steam-driven railway train, as probably the first mechanically-propelled wheeled vehicle in the world, began in the north of England, and thence diffused itself over a large part of the planet. The motor-car began perhaps by a short priority in France, but we are all familiar with its diffusion, and although certain countries import their cars from either America or Britain, nevertheless many are now establishing factories of their own, and striving to make the manufacture of cars into an indigenous industry. Local patterns have since developed in various countries, though the difficulty of obtaining replacements and spare parts naturally tends to encourage standardisation.

It is usual to enumerate a number of different types of diffusion. Purely natural diffusion may simply be due to the natural excellence or convenience of some specific tool or machine, so that it has been easy for people in areas bordering upon the place of its invention to

---

[1] Mr. Donald Busk in his book on Ethiopia, comments on the fact that in some parts of the world the wheel itself is still an unfamiliar device, and that natives of those areas when presented with one do not see how to use it until they are taught.

copy and adopt it. A development of this natural diffusion may be diffusion by trade, as when some useful article is bartered for another one of which the inventors stand in need. Once this has taken place the object may be copied, unless patent or copyright laws stand in the way, and so the invention becomes spread through wider and wider areas.

Sometimes, however, diffusion will be artificial, as when a country invents a new material convenience and then tries to sell it to other countries, which not having been previously acquainted with it, may at first hesitate to adopt it. In this case the inventing area will send its commercial travellers to try to talk the inhabitants of other countries into accepting the new article, and sometimes they will actually train and employ persons belonging to the countries where they wish to obtain sales, and use them as propagandists. A typical example of this some years ago was the spread of the Hoover vacuum-cleaner, which was invented in America, but which its inventors wished to sell to England. For this purpose they not only sent over American propagandists, but trained and employed a certain number of Englishmen on the same task. There have always been cases of resistance to artificial diffusion. Human beings are naturally conservative, and it sometimes takes a little time to persuade them to adopt a new gadget. This will happen not only with the exporters, but also with the wholesalers who have to persuade the owners of retail businesses to take on something new, and again to the assistants in the shops who are only too familiar with what is called 'sales resistance' on the part of customers, when faced with something new and unfamiliar, even though it may be an improvement on what they have been in the habit of using. Another kind of artificial diffusion results from the conquest or colonisation of one country by another. This type of diffusion is perhaps a hybrid, and is neither purely natural nor purely artificial. Thus we can think of the diffusion of some useful devices such as central heating by the use of hypocausts, or the making of paved roads, both of which were due to the conquest and centralisation of government in Europe by the Romans; or of others the spread of which has resulted from the colonisation of various parts of the world by the British, French, Spaniards, or Germans. It is quite clear that various items were carried into central and southern America by the Spanish Conquistadors and have now so long been established there that they can almost be mistaken for native products. Again, another kind of diffusion will be due to travellers who, finding something in a strange country which they think to be either useful or pleasant, return with it to their own land and either propagate it there or persuade their fellow countrymen to encourage its import. Various fruits became diffused from the Middle East as far as Britain; African fruits are today imported into England; while that most useful vegetable, the potato, was introduced into Europe from the American continent, which has also sent the maize plant, or at least the processed seeds, to many parts of the world.

Greek sculpture is said to have been diffused eastward through the campaigns of Alexander, and to have influenced the development of Buddhist statuary. Loyal Indians tend to dispute this, and to say that India was quite capable of developing her own art-forms, and that Southern Indian sculpture in particular owes nothing to Hellas. Nevertheless some Buddhist art seems to show definite Greek influence, and it cannot be denied that specifically Greek patterns have been found carved on tombs as far east as Korea.

Let us now go on to apply these principles in the sphere of religion. As to how much ethnic religion may be a series of concurrent developments we can perhaps only conjecture. It is certainly clear that over large areas of the planet the same kind of reactions to the category of the Self-Existent, the Numinous, and the Supernatural take place; and these may be simply the result of the general construction of the human mind, which, faced in different places with similar experiences and similar problems, tends to behave in the same way, to make similar deductions, and to exhibit similar emotional reactions. Under such circumstances the stages of growth will seem to be concurrent, though with modifications due to the time-lag, which operates here quite as much in this case as in the case of diffusions. There seems no reason why animatism, polydaemonism, and the more highly developed polytheisms should not arise independently in all countries, given normal conditions of mental and social development. Some areas may be ahead of others, but it would not be a necessary conclusion that some areas had borrowed from others. Modifications such as do arise may be due to alliances, federations, or conquest, leading to the amalgamation of deities in groups. In these ways there may be modified forms of diffusion. Sir Thomas Kendrick thinks that what is commonly called druidism may have diffused from the Continent into Britian along with the expansion of the continental Celts, but it may not have been sufficiently different from the religion of the Iberian inhabitants of Britian's neolithic period to have been more than a modification of an existing pluralism; and the same thing may be said in regard to the effects of the Roman invasion and conquest, which before the advent of Christianity only led to the introduction of Greek or Roman dieties to be added to the pantheon already worshipped by the British; and it seems clear that the local British divinities, some-times under Latin names, went on being worshipped side by side with Jupiter, Juno, and Mars. The diffusion of the cult of Mithras is perhaps something rather different, since it seems to have been due very largely to the moving about of troops. The cult of Mithras was mainly a male affair, and it would seem to have been the Roman legions that carried it up to the Roman wall, while it was probably the Roman garrison in Londinium which was responsible for its existence in that city. Most of this, therefore, may be con-sidered as natural diffusion, i.e. the conveyance of religion by travel-lers, traders, soldiers, or even slaves and displaced persons, none of whom intend deliberately to engage in religious propaganda, but spread their cultures and their beliefs simply by being there. Their social habits may be copied or imitated by people in the surrounding population, for whom these, as well as their religion, may come to have a kind of 'snob value'; or they may intermarry with their neighbours, and their partners and children may come to adopt their faith. It has been said that the diffusion in Hellas of the cult of Dionysus was due to the Greeks bringing in large numbers of slaves from further East to work in the silver mines of Attica. These poor victims, who laboured in terrible conditions, not only solaced them-selves by adhering to their own religion, but also somehow com-pensated for their miserable condition by spreading the cult of Dionysus among their oppressors. One wonders how this happened. Was it that Greeks took Thracian wives or concubines from among their slaves, or did the male slaves themselves marry Greek women? Or were there other psychological reasons which favoured the spread of an orgiastic worship, which, as we know, specially appealed to women? The whole problem is a most interesting one, since Dionysus himself seems, like the Indian god Siva, to have been a specially dangerous individual, and to have excited a considerable amount of numinous awe.

What we are bound to notice, however, especially in the case of the more highly developed faiths from about the year 500 B.C. on-wards, is the counterpart to the *artificial* diffusion of material culture; namely the expansion of a religion by means of enthusiasts, votaries, or prophetic individuals, who have been so much captured by the sense of the value of their faith, that they set to work to proclaim it to others. This type of diffusion is most familiar to us in connection with Christianity and Islam, but it certainly operated in the case of Buddhism, and many of the sages of China (e.g. Mo-ti) were certainly earnest propagandists, while within a more restricted sphere still, we find individual propagandists who wish to commend a drastic modification of existing religion such as Zarathustra in Iran, and numerous teachers in India of the type exemplified by Sankara, who himself travelled widely up and down India founding religious communities and teaching his monistic religious philosophy. Yet even here in the case of the greater religions, diffusion may take on a number of other forms. Besides being due to the work of missionaries of a vocational character, whether paid or unpaid, the spread of a larger and more highly developed religion may operate along some of the great trade routes, such as the ancient caravan road running east and west across the North of India, or by casual travellers or returned pilgrims, or it may be fostered by alliances and federations, whether voluntary or forced, due either to treaties or conquests. In India many animistic tribes have become Hindus by a process of amalgamation which has turned them into additional castes within the Hindu social system. In Mesopotamia, city-states federated and combined their several civic divinities into the form of a pantheon. There have been cases where military coercion has actually been used to intimidate conquered peoples into accepting a new faith. Charlemagne is said to have employed this method in dealing with some of the pagan German tribes, and it seems clear that at one period Islam was imposed upon subject peoples by the sword. Imperialism and colonialism have undoubtedly provided the occasion and opportunity for much prophetic diffusion, though the latter, in the case of Christianity, has just as often taken place, in countries like Uganda, China, and parts of India, as well as in Japan, as the result of voluntary prophetic adventure on the part of missionaries. These have gone, sometimes at considerable personal risk, and for the love of souls as well as in obedience to their Master's command to evangelise, into sovereign states which are not their own, and where they must appear at first as alien intruders. We think naturally of the work of the Franciscan friars and Jesuits in China, of Henry Martyn in Persia, of St. Francis Xavier in Japan, of Chalmers in the Pacific, and of Hannington in Uganda. The christianisation of Ethiopia may well have been begun by the shipwreck of Aedesius and Frumentius, which must have seemed to them providential, and which they used as the occasion to commend their faith to the ruler of Ethiopia and his subjects. Colonial expansion by Indians would seem to have carried Hinduism eastward and southward, to Cambodia and Indonesia, where it is followed also by an expansion of Buddhism.

The consequence of all the above considerations is bound to be that if anything comes into existence, whether material or spiritual, which is seen to be either good or true, there can be nothing derogatory or shameful about its diffusion. The truth or value of any new item in human culture is in no way diminished by its original emergence in one spot. If truths and values of such a kind are to be of benefit to humanity they must be allowed to spread. Many circumstances, accidental, political, and even as it might seem unspiritual, may be the actual occasions which lead to, prompt, or aid the diffusion; but the only question that in the last resort demands a decisive answer is: 'Can it truly be said that the human race benefits by such a diffusion?'

If, therefore, there is anything in one or more of the great founded religions which seems to be of world-wide value and importance, that item, no matter where it comes from, is entitled to be regarded as belonging to the world. On the principle of the Logos-doctrine which will be dealt with elsewhere, it will be permissible for us to accept whatever seems to be good, or of permanent value and significance in the teaching or example of the great non-Christian prophetic sages, as that which belongs to the world. We are, however, equally entitled to consider that the unique personality and claims commonly associated with the historical Jesus of Nazareth cannot be diminished or depreciated by the fact that both He and the Christian movement originated in one small country on the borders of Europe and Asia. In the case of something supremely good, true, and beneficent, it is no longer a case of mine, yours, or his, or of something that is foreign, but of that which belongs to the whole of humanity.

At the same time the phenomenon of 'resistance' to diffusion deserves to be treated with respect. It is not surprising that the dislike of imperialism and colonialism should lead many people to hesitation or even to rejection, when they are confronted with the offer of something which in their minds has always been associated with foreign rule, and sometimes with exploitation. Self-government has seemed to them preferable even to good government, and they are therefore inclined to deduce that indigenous religion may even be preferable to good religion, if the latter is offered to them from outside. Actually one of the problems at the moment is quite plainly the intense earnestness of American Christian propaganda. The material power of the United States leads to its religious earnestness being misunderstood or suspected by the Asian world, so much of it rejoicing in its new-found freedom and independence. Having got free, that world does not want to be bought up by any other state, either materially or spiritually. It may well be unjust in doubting the good will and sincerity of some great and good Americans, but it can hardly be blamed for desiring to be cautious.

In any case the question may fairly be asked: 'Why should any single religion claim the exclusive privilege of diffusing and propagating itself?' Of course it should not. All must stand on their merits; and in the present age neither Rome nor Mecca nor Banaras nor Moscow can be justified in using coercive methods to prevent the truth from being known.

As an Indian friend once put it to me: 'We adopted the bicycle because we saw you British using it, and we liked it and saw that it was useful and efficient. You did not force it on us, or canvass us to accept it, and indeed there was no need, for its virtues as a means of transport were evident to all observers. Can't we be allowed to do the same in regard to religion?' This is, of course, an argument in favour of natural as against organised diffusion. I am not sure, however, whether if something is felt to be supremely good, its possessors are to be forbidden to cry it aloud to others. One remembers that Peter and John once said, 'We cannot but speak the things which we have seen and heard.' Yet how cry? There was once an African who said to a European missionary: 'Baas, your life shouts so loud, that I cannot hear the Gospel you preach.' The inference is obvious. It is the life that has to cry aloud, not the tongue only. Chaucer knew it as well as the Principal of any training college for the ministry, when he said of the poor parson:

> 'But Criste's lore and his apostles twelve
> He taught, but firste he followed it hymself.'

But I quite understood my Indian friend when he said that he did not object to diffusion in religion, but only to imperialism in religion. He did not mind anything that was universally true expanding; but he did not like an institution which prided itself on the number of converts it collected and ruled, nor did he think it charitable to assume that God could not have revealed himself to other people than Christians. The Logos doctrine which we are to consider is some answer to the second point. But the curious fact is that in certain special ways God *does* seem to work by diffusion from a centre. Some of the greatest gifts of inspiration He has bestowed on mankind, whether in sculpture, painting, plastic, philosophy, or law, have manifested themselves first as *local* developments, and have then been accepted by the rest of the world for what they certainly are; but have not developed everywhere to an equal extent.[1]

---

[1] I cannot forbear to quote a remarkable statement from the pen of an Indian, which appeared in an Indian newspaper on 'Republic Day' 1958:
'Closely allied to this notion of the identity of religion and culture is the view (or perhaps it should be referred to as a vague emotional attitude) that to be properly "Indian" a religion, or cultural pattern, or idea, should have been born in India. According to this view Christianity and Islam are "foreign" religions. If this notion is pressed to its logical conclusion, and if it is insisted that every country should invent or manufacture every material and spiritual thing needed for its life, we shall be in a strange situation indeed. The three or four major religions of the world are of Asian origin, and the rest of the world would have to go without a religion. We in India would have no claim on many of the scientific ideas of the modern world, nor on some of the institutions of democracy. The Russians would have no right to practise Marxist socialism, because Karl Marx was not a Russian, and *Das Kapital* was not written in Russia. Doubt might be cast on the validity of claiming anything "Aryan" as Indian, and some of the absurdities of the Dravida Kazhagam might seem to be justified.'

It needs to be remembered that the British themselves received Christianity from outside, partly by natural diffusion—Roman Christians who came to live in Britain as members of the army or civil service, or as traders—partly by artificial diffusion through earnest missionaries who came from a number of different centres: while the original gospel was not even European but West Asian—arising in a small country whose people possessed a specific religious genius.

It would not be impossible, or obnoxious, supposing that western Christianity were seriously to deteriorate, for the flame to be re-kindled, and re-diffusion thus to take place from the Church of Asia or Africa; and it would be the humble duty of the West to welcome that.

CHAPTER IV

THE RISE OF CHRISTIANITY

At the time of the establishment of the Roman Empire under Augustus, after the breakdown of the Roman republic, the general religious situation in the Mediterranean world was somewhat as follows. Greek religion had reached a stage in which it had reacted against the earlier axial free thought and scepticism of some of the philosophers, although popular attendance at religious rites showed but little revival. In certain quarters scepticism persisted, but in others it was being replaced by a rather more constructive and strongly ethical philosophy, that of the Stoics.[1] Stoicism covers a fairly long period, and indeed began much earlier than the Augustan age, but at the time we speak of it had shown development and change in expression, and had come to provide many educated folk in the non-Jewish world with a kind of working faith which could form an effective substitute for a pluralistic system obviously grown bankrupt, and hard to believe in seriously. Beginning as a kind of cosmic pantheism, Stoicism gradually developed a more theistic outlook, as may be seen in the noble address to Deity which is to be found in the famous hymn of Cleanthes. Its exponents proclaimed an ethical system which could be summed up in the phrase: 'Live according to nature', a principle strangely resembling that proclaimed by some of the Chinese sages. In its depreciation of ceremonial sacrifices it sometimes seems to proceed along the same path as that of the Hebrew prophets. The Stoic disciple may very well have considered it irrelevant and unnecessary to attend worship in a temple, or to provide a sacrificial victim of a material character to be immolated upon an altar.

Side by side with this there was also developing a mysticism which encouraged people to find satisfaction in something not unlike the *yoga* of India. This proceeds perhaps from the influence of the genuine Platonic writings, to which it adds other spurious ones, and perhaps does not fully develop until the second century of the Christian movement, but in a measure it is certainly pre-Christian. We find also the existence of a certain number of religious cults, some of then dating back a few centuries, others, like that of Mithras,

---

[1] Perhaps the best work to which to refer the reader is the German one by Pohlenz, *Stoizismus*, pub. Leipzig.

being fairly new developments more or less contemporary with the infant Christian movement.   In these the existence of a number of divine beings is assumed, and sometimes these are declared to be different aspects of one Supreme Deity; but the interest usually centres round a single one, who though usually mythical and legendary, and perhaps not quite the highest god, is believed to have an interest in the welfare of the human race, so that by becoming enrolled in the cult-community associated with this particular Being, one can as it were enter into and share the experiences of that Being, and by a kind of new birth, assure oneself of a blissful immortality. How many people joined these communities, and how much satisfaction they derived from them, it is perhaps difficult to estimate. But their very existence betokens a spiritual hunger and anxiety on the part of many people who perhaps felt the philosophical religion of the Stoics somewhat arid, and too severe and abstract as a way of escape from the troubles and uncertainties with which they found themselves surrounded.   It might suit some of them to be told that nothing could happen to them but what was in the constitution and course of nature, so that even their dissolution at death was not to be feared, but accepted and even welcomed as what was natural; but a good many undoubtedly craved for a warmer and more positive creed than this, and although the various initiations into the mysteries of the Graeco-Roman world perhaps only provided them with an illusory hope—'opium for the people'—wishful thinking tempted them to cling to it as at any rate providing an emotional satisfaction, which they felt might well have some genuine basis, if only because it was so stimulating.

Such were the quasi-religious activities of the *goyim*.   Meanwhile the Jewish people had many of them become scattered throughout the Mediterranean world.   Wherever there were enough of them to form a real community, they built themselves a synagogue, and kept themselves distinct by their loyalty to the Torah, and by the purity and regularity of their liturgical worship, in which there were no longer any blood sacrifices, but a spiritual cultus centred round the words of a sacred book.   Nevertheless, there was still in the middle of the first century a substantial community of Jews dwelling in and around Jerusalem, and for these Herod the Great had provided a magnificent new temple, designed and constructed on a gigantic scale, with a fine and dignified cycle of worship.   Short as was its duration, this temple achieved considerable renown, and the diligence with which the dispersed Jews obeyed their injunctions to pay a tax for its maintenance, and (if humanly possible) to visit it once a year, must have made it respected by even the non-Jewish citizens of the Mediterranean world. It seems certain that the comparatively high moral standard and the strict exclusiveness of the Jewish people earned for them the esteem of many gentiles, who, not without encouragement from the Jews themselves, became proselytes, accepting circumcision and adherence to the regulations of the Torah, even though they were not of Jewish race. Some, though not accepting these obligations, visited synagogues and listened to the worship taking place in them. The general situation extending roughly from Spain to the Persian Gulf was one of religious instability and expectancy, and of vague dissatisfaction with the older institutional religions, though with no very clear idea as to what could with confidence be put in their place.

Into this world there suddenly emerges the movement which we call Christian. Evidence recently discovered seems to show that it did not stand quite alone, but that there were other movements in Syria at this period which preceded it, and which, although they only had ephemeral careers, bore some slight superficial resemblances to it, in that they sought to purify the Hebrew religion of their day, and to form a closely knit spiritual community waiting in expectation for the coming of the Anointed of God, whose appearance would bring the deliverance of society.[1]

On to the stage thus set there appears the historical figure of Jesus of Nazareth. There is no need in this work to recapitulate the events of the gospels, since that has been done again and again elsewhere. What we are here concerned with is the precise general position which the great Figure of Galilee was clearly held to occupy by his immediate contemporaries. Of course it is plain that at first the greater part of the Mediterranean world knew little or nothing about him. The news of his meteoric career was for some time confined to a small band of devoted followers, a few of whom began

---

[1] Summaries of the contents of the documents discovered at Qumran and elsewhere on the borders of the Dead Sea may be found in the works by Professor T. H. Gaster, Professor Dupont-Sommer, Professor F. F. Bruce, and Mr. Allegro: but the literature dealing with them is now immense, and the issues are extremely controversial. One thing seems however quite certain. The documents are not themselves Christian, although they are probably those of a Jewish reforming sect a little earlier in date than Christianity. They illustrate the religious hopes and aspirations of the period, but they do not substantially alter our estimate of Jesus and the community which sprang from Him. Phrases like 'children of light' occur in the documents, and show that some Jewish reformers tended to talk the same sort of language as Christians; and it is quite conceivable that both John the Baptist and Jesus Himself may have known of this Qumran community. But the doctrines of the sect bear no actual resemblance to those of Christianity, and the title 'Teacher of Righteousness' ought never to have been used as a translation of the designation of the leader, and is most misleading. It should rather be 'Expounder of the Torah or Law'. The ideas of the crucifixion and resurrection of this Teacher have been read into the text, or deduced from incorrect scrutiny of the original manuscripts. Altogether a good deal of nonsense has been talked and written about these 'Dead Sea Scrolls'; though many scholars regard them as of importance as helping us still further to an understanding of the atmosphere in which Christianity arose.

to go about in the lands of the Eastern Mediterranean testifying and witnessing to what had been going on. The remarkable thing is that they testified to a Person rather than to a teaching. Teaching no doubt there was, but the main announcement was a God-story, a gospel of something that Someone had done. This announcement was declared to be on the one hand good news of deliverance to all who would accept it, but on the other a warning of judgment to any who rejected or disbelieved it. It was thus not at all like the *dhamma* of the Buddha, since in the latter case the teaching, though first proclaimed by Gautama after his enlightenment, was compact in itself, and in its earlier form not dependent upon or influenced by the person who had first delivered it. But the Christian evangelists from the first sought to bring people into an *encounter* with a Unique Person, who though fully human, spoke as never man spake, who spoke and acted with authority, who embodied the strange paradox of conquest through humiliation, whose living and victorious presence, though invisible, they believed to be still really with them, and whose mission was to all mankind. Strange though it may seem, it was evidence of this encounter which they managed to bring with them to their audiences.[1] Nothing like it had ever happened before. Here was no vague and ancient myth, but the story of a real historical person who had been crucified under Pontius Pilate, and yet was alive for ever more and had the keys of the world beyond the grave safe in his hands.

It is no part of the purpose of this book to re-write what is known of the earthly career of Jesus of Nazareth. That as we have said has been done countless times, and I have even tried myself to do it briefly elsewhere. But it is important to recognise that whatever adornments or developments may have come to be woven around His Person, whether in the way of myth (as in the apocryphal gospels) or of theology (as in the multitude of works written during the past 1900 years), and whatever conversions may have resulted all the world over from an encounter with His Living Presence, the true historical estimate of Jesus must be great enough to account for all these. To denigrate Him as some have done is to desert scholarship for prejudice, and to leave a residual figure too insignificant to convert even the smallest organism. Christianity reduced in this way cannot account for the facts of its diffusion.

It is unjust not to concede the greatness of Buddha, Kung-fu-tze, and Mohammed. They won disciples, and held their loyalty with notable magnetism, and it is foolish and idle to deny that they

---

[1] Dr. Tennant has ventured to remind us, however, that even a strong impression of a Personality depends for its communication to others upon the minds of the persons who *interpret* that impression.

achieved good, when judged against the background of their times.
But make no mistake about it. Jesus, when truly encountered and
known, did and does win and hold converts in a way that no one else
has ever done, and with greater and more constructive effects than
any other. Even in a company of great men, He sits upon a solitary
throne, higher than all. This is no partiality or prejudice. It is
plain matter of fact. A story in latter years has come from Tibet.
There a Moravian mission was joined by a monk from a Buddhist
lamassery. When asked why he had become a Christian he replied:
'The abbot of my monastery was declared to be a bodhisattva (and
therefore an incarnation of the Buddha-spirit). But I knew the
abbot too well to be satisfied, and I sought and found the full incarnation of the Divine Purusha elsewhere.'

Again, the parents of some needy Arab refugee children said to
the Christian social workers who were tending them, 'Yours must be
a wonderful Faith if it leads you to care for our boys in this way.'
But why have not the wealthy Moslems of other states shown more
zeal in helping these wretched folk? Admittedly some of them have,
but there has been no philanthropy in respect of them to compare
with that of non-Moslems, and even if this criticism were to spur some
Moslems on to greater efforts, it would still be true that the urge had
come from the Christian side. No. Take out of the world the constructive works of kindness and mercy which have been and are still
being directly inspired by the Living Spirit of Jesus, and how much
would be left?

It is not simply the supreme enlargement of Hebrew religious
belief and teaching which Jesus certainly proclaimed, but His whole
career, taken as a Revealing Act, that has to be reckoned with; and
this Revealing Act is not a mere republication of natural religion, as
some described it in the eighteenth century—not even the enlargement of Hebrew religion acknowledged above, but a great new Unveiling of Reality, and one in which the Latter is seen as taking the
Supreme Initiative; an Unveiling not completely deducible from
anything previously happening in world-history, and one which,
although it took place in the Middle East, belongs by right to the
whole world.

The original obscurity of Jesus has sometimes been urged as an
argument against any cosmic claims made on His behalf, such as a
finished act of deliverance and reconciliation for the human race in its
relation to Deity. How could something done in the heart of Palestine affect the whole world? This needs sober and unprejudiced consideration.

In the first place it must be admitted that there is no inherent objection to something new and decisive originating in a small country, but diffusing everywhere because it is subsequently seen to be of universal significance.

But in the second place, the original occurrence (one will not say whether providentially so ordered) took place in Western Asia, at a point where contact with and diffusion throughout both west and east was possible, to a degree which would have been difficult of attainment if the occurrence had been anywhere further west or anywhere further east. If it had taken place in the American continent, the isolation would have been too great for it to have had any influence elsewhere for many centuries, nor does the field of the Americas seem to show any signs that it would have been a good nursery for the early growth of Hebraeo-Christian religion. And in the third place, was Jesus, even within the world of the Levant, so obscure? He was clearly recognised by the populace as the legitimate claimant to the throne of the ancient Jewish monarchy. Beggars addressed Him with cries of: 'Jesus, thou Son of David.' He obviously had great powers of attraction and leadership—a genuinely Royal Presence; and crowds on more than one occasion wanted to acclaim Him as *melek*. No doubt He rejected such offers from the time of the Temptation; but that is just the point. One is bound to consider what might have happened supposing he had accepted the rôle of a political leader. Although as much dispossessed as young Richard Plantagenet living in a Kent village at the beginning of the Tudor period, and although brought up to a trade in the Galilean town of Nazareth, Jesus, like Gautama the Buddha, was of princely origin. Had he chosen to assert his right, and done so successfully, the history of Western Asia might have been changed as unfavourably as Eastern Europe perhaps was at a later date by the so-called conversion of the Emperor Constantine. A good deal turns upon the supposed invincibility of the Roman 'Raj'. The Jew has always been a doughty soldier, and in the days of the Maccabees he did valiantly. The curious document discovered at Qumran, known as 'the war of the sons of Light', does not appear to make very good sense if merely read mystically. It would seem much better to suppose that some unknown author in this case was thinking seriously of building up an army of liberation on the lines of a Roman legion. Jewish patriots might well have thought it possible in secrecy to assemble such a force, perhaps somewhere outside the frontier of the Empire, and to use the organisation and discipline which they already saw existing in the regiments of the *goyim* (whose personnel in Syria had already been recruited from among the inhabitants, and who were thus serving under Italian officers, and might be considered to have been drawn away from their allegiance). But such an army would have needed a symbol and leader to fight for, and if this had been forthcoming and, in addition, there had been an alliance or federation among the states of the Middle East in opposition to the Romans, a campaign might have been successfully conducted which would have ended in the establishment of a rival power to that of Rome. Legions were not always invincible. There were stories that they sometimes disappeared, as in Britain. There was also the disaster under Varus, when a whole army was beaten by German tribes. Jesus might well have ended as the ruler of a small Asian Empire.

Well, we know that it did not happen. This is the fourth point. Earthly sovereignty was, as seems clear, neither his interest nor his purpose nor his choice. If we may borrow a phrase from Dr. Tennant, which seems to imply a more reduced Christology than is really justified in the last resort, he was 'the religious genius of theism'. All the evidence of his teaching and action supports the belief that he rejected the political for what he felt to be a much higher rôle. He did not wish to be *Melek Yisrael*, but the inaugurator of the *Malkuth hashamayim*,[1] and so he set himself with determined visage to challenge the Roman 'Raj' with what Gandhi would have called 'non-violent non-co-operation'. No doubt few people at first outside Jerusalem took much notice of his execution; and yet in a few years' time a movement issuing from it began to spread which ended by capturing the peoples of the Roman Empire for a new kind of idea. Apparent defeat was seen to have had a wholly unforeseen spiritual reversal, the effects of which did not wane but went on increasing, and are still felt strongly today. The implications of this may sometimes have been rather unhappily interpreted in terms of a Roman law-court; but it is not unreasonable to see in the whole incident a decisive moment in the fortunes of the human race which was quite as much Act of God as act of man. Such at least is the belief about it which, if not universally accepted, has already obtained an almost universal *diffusion*. People out of nearly all nations and languages have without difficulty been able to receive it as the inauguration by Jesus of a new order of human beings, a potential deliverance wrought by God through him from the wrong sort of order—the mere 'kingdom of man', which would always be in sinful opposition to the Divine Will. Thus the acceptance by Jesus of the Cross was in the nature of a true deliverance for

1 Even now the centrality in the teaching of Jesus about the Kingdom of God, or the Rule of God, teaching which has no parallel or peer anywhere else in the world, does not seem to be fully appreciated. (Cf. the writings of the late Arthur Clutton Brock.)

the whole human race, a more fundamental and far-reaching one than could ever have happened if he had simply inaugurated a neo-Davidic dynasty in succession to that of the twelve Caesars.

This potential deliverance, which concerns nations as well as individuals, is still being proclaimed by the Christian movement, but can never be properly realised by force of arms. Offered in completeness by God through Jesus, it can only be appropriated through the steadfast witness of Christian disciples who are prepared to 'out-think, out-live, and out-die' the devotees of the secularist 'kingdom of man'. That is the sum of the Christian message.

> And there's another country, I've heard of long ago
> Most dear to them that love her, most great to them that know;
> We may not count her armies, we may not see her King;
> Her fortress is a faithful heart, her pride is suffering;
> And soul by soul and silently her shining bounds increase,
> And her ways are ways of gentleness and all her paths are peace.

Of course the way has not been smooth, and the journey so far has been as full of adventure and even disaster as any 'Pilgrim's Progress'. The gift of Jesus to the world has often been mis-appropriated by worldly men, and made the instrument and accessory of temporal power. It has been enshrined by others in an over-organised institution, a totalitarian state persecuting non-collaborators, so that Hobbes could see in it 'the ghost of the Roman Empire, crowned and sitting upon its throne'—and let us remember that he, in the seventeenth century, was looking at the reformed Counter-Reformation Papacy, not at that of the Medicean worldling, Leo X. But those who have eyes to see can, in the twentieth century, discern a new age opening for this same gift of Jesus to the world, the emergence, albeit through great tribulation, of a free and liberated Christianity, liberated not only from political chains but from intellectual fetters as well, and perhaps still more from the fear of sharing in Calvary, the possibility of which must be inevitably included in all true Christian discipleship. The prophetic words of the Pope in Browning's famous poem seem indeed specially to apply to the present day:

> 'What if it be the mission of that age
> My death will usher into life, to shake
> This torpor of assurance from our creed,
> Re-introduce the doubt discarded, bring
> The formidable danger back, we drove
> Long ago to the distance and the dark?
> No wild beast now prowls round the infant camp;
> We have built wall and sleep in city safe;
> But if some earthquake try the towers that laugh
> To think they once saw lions rule outside,

> And man stand out again pale, resolute,
> Prepared to die, which means alive at last?—
> As we broke up that old faith of the world
> Have we, next age, to break up this the new—
> Faith in the *thing*, grown faith in the *report*—
> When must we bravely disbelieve report
> Through increased faith in the thing reports belie?—
> Must we deny— . . .
> Recognised truths, obedient to some truth
> Unrecognised yet, but perceptible?
> Correct the portrait by the living face,
> Man's God by God's God in the mind of man.'

The thesis of this book and the outlook forecast for the world may perhaps be summed up in a single phrase therefore: 'Not a new religion but a newly expressed and renewed Christianity.'

The clearest of facts about Jesus is that he does not simply enrich our knowledge of God's essence by teaching, though of course he does that. He enriches our awareness of God's mind and purpose by what He is and what He does. He is not the purveyor of interior *vidya*, but the demonstrator of God in Action; and further, as He acts, so He expects all His disciples to act too. 'Follow me', 'Hear my call', 'Come after me', 'Take up your own cross', 'Feed my sheep', 'He that doeth', etc. These are the sort of phrases constantly on His lips. And He goes further—to the very roots and springs of action. Μετανοεῖτε 'change your minds, redirect your wills'. 'Freely ye have received, freely give.' Thus the Christian religion always consists in being and doing, in being used and being called to do—not simply in knowing. And the doing has to be 'in Christ', otherwise the deed, however well-intentioned in its beginning, is bound to fall short of what it ought to be. A revolutionary like Khruschev, however much he may desire the welfare of the greatest number of his fellow citizens, through his rejection of religion in general and of Christ in particular is bound inevitably to fail in achieving the best that he might, and so may actually do harm; while on the other hand a politician like Gandhi, because of his close association with the saintly Charles Andrews, from whom he obviously learned so much, approximated in his character and methods more and more closely to the Christian ideal, and consequently achieved a lasting influence of such a benign nature that a Hindu journalist could describe him in an obituary article as 'that Christ-like man'.[1]

The doctrine of the Two Natures of Christ needs consideration in a wider context. Radio programmes ('What think ye of Christ?') have brought into prominence once again the passages in the Gospels

[1] Of course some atheists and non-Christians have been more constructive than some reactionary Christians. See Père Daniélou's comment, quoted on p. 269.

which present the mysterious dual consciousness of Jesus, and which are not by any means confined to the Fourth Gospel. Is there, we may ask, real reminiscence here, or a misunderstanding of idiom? Or do the passages reveal development of expression and understanding on the part of the narrators? It is painful to recall the opinions of those who have seen in the Figure of Nazareth one who along with his Messianic consciousness developed a tinge of megalomania. G. B. Shaw says with his usual brutal frankness that Jesus today would have been brought before two doctors and a magistrate, and certified. But in the New Testament we are not dealing with a twentieth- or even nineteenth-century world, but with a world much more resembling that of unmodernised Asia. The comment of the Maltese upon Paul's immunity from the bite of the viper (they said he was a θεός) and that of the Lycaonians upon Paul and Barnabas (the θεοί are come down to us in the likeness of men) is almost exactly that of popular Hinduism in the nineteenth century as described by Mr. O'Malley. In such a world it was quite natural for divine beings to appear in human form and to speak in character. Even if strict Jewish rabbinical authorities forbade the idea of a man making himself God—as strictly as Mohammed in the Qur'ān—the *am haaretz* went on thinking in more popular terms, so that in the Decapolis area a possessed person could hail Jesus as υἱὲ τοῦ θεοῦ τοῦ ὑψίστου.

But there is more to it than this. Always assuming that Jesus did claim some close filial relationship with Deity even in Aramaic textual traditions, oral or otherwise, which do not survive, are there not signs that Asian holy men have never felt any difficulty or reluctance over making similar, even if lesser claims? The *yogi* who by means of his technique 'yokes himself' with the Absolute believes that it is possible to reach a condition of perpetual *samadhi* in which this unitive condition persists, instead of being intermittent and fitful. Again there is the remarkable case of the Japanese farmer, Kawate Bunjiro, who, quite independently of any biblical or Christian influences, ended by achieving a break with Japanese pluralism in the direction of a prophetic monotheism, and then went on to develop such a close relation with his One God that he often claimed to speak his logia as the mouthpiece of the Latter, yet all the time remaining an ordinary human farmer. Such instances, both in Europe and Asia, could be multiplied from among the mystics. The complete identification, which as it were turns inspiration into incarnation—if such a phrase be allowed—could no doubt be pathological if it were an affirmation in prose, which it seldom is. But in a world in which one scientist can equate 'Man' with the 'Universe', and another one can talk about our 'carrying the Universe around inside our own heads',[1] it can hardly be extravagant to suppose a condition in which the Self-Existent might find a unique Self-Expression through some choice and exceptionally pure and gifted individual. In a country in which stark monotheism was the major religious experience, such a situation might well appear blasphemous and even pathological. But even here we have to note a strange circumstance. In Moslem countries the mentally afflicted or dissociated person is often treated with a reverence which perhaps derives from a pre-Islamic world of thought, evidently because such have often been found to be clairvoyant or possessed of an unusual degree of extra-sensory perception. Yet divination is not the only function of the prophet, although the remark

---

[1] Messrs. Hoyle and Lyttleton.

of the woman of Samaria to Jesus 'Sir, I perceive that thou art a prophet' because he told her all the things she ever did, is completely in keeping with this. Nineteenth-century sophisticated English Christians were wont to say that it was the function of the prophet to declare the will of God, not to predict the future or to solve problems by E.S.P.; but I think it is now seen that this was too narrow a definition of his function, and that the completer the union between the prophet's mind and that of Deity, the greater would be his ecstatic sweep of vision, and the greater the probability of his being able to form a correct estimate of the future, and to read other people's minds.

To sum up. In the rise of Christianity we see not the development of a new abstract system, but the emergence of a Person Who dominates and goes beyond all systems, showing in Himself the clue to life on this planet, and the fundamental Nature of its Begetter.

'We are still far from grasping the whole significance of what Jesus has to say. God for Jesus, God in Jesus, is an unexplored treasure still; and for us, apart from Jesus, God is little better than an abstract noun; and to people who are serious, abstract nouns are of less and less use. Let us put it this way. If we spoke straight out, we should say that God could not do better than follow the example of Jesus. That means that Jesus fulfils our conception of God; but that is not all, nor is it enough. He is constantly enlarging our idea of God, revealing great tracts of God unexpected by us. God as interpretable in and through Jesus is unexhausted.'[1]

Those words, though written some thirty years ago, are, in the light of the experiences of the years between, no unfair statement. Yet, as Dr. Macnicol has reminded us, we have no choice as to the message which Jesus would have us deliver, or to select one theme of our own as the grain of mustard-seed from which we deem the whole structure of church doctrine to have developed. The core of His own teaching is the good news that the Rule of God is in Him breaking into history, so that wherever He is now proclaimed it is still breaking in, until the kingdoms of this world are indeed become obedient provinces in God's great Commonwealth. 'History is always being recreated from an inner centre, that is out of the experience of those who have received the Kingdom of God, and are thereby committed to the labour and conflict through which the Kingdom is revealed.'

It may be said in criticism that a fairly advanced stage in this book has now been reached without any definition having been put forward of 'Christianity' itself.

The answer is that one has deliberately chosen so far to speak of Christ, and to use the proper rather than the abstract noun. But since a definition ought now to be given, let me say that any system which places the historical Jesus in a central position has the right to be called a part of the total organism which constitutes the Christian

[1] T. R. Glover, *Jesus in the Experience of Men*, pp. 15–16.

movement. *Movement* is I am sure the right word. 'Christianity' is a way of life which derives from and is centred upon the historical Jesus, and the Gospel is one which is about Him as well as something proclaimed by Him. As has been often said in the past, it is 'good news rather than good advice'; for it declares in effect that the Nature of the Self-Existent Being has never been so clearly, richly, and decisively expressed as by the character of Jesus.

But what is 'orthodox Christianity'?

The test of orthodoxy may involve several points:

(1) belief in the continuity of the Christian society.[1]

(2) loyalty to the broad highway of teaching which is borne witness to by the canonical Scriptures, which stem from the experience of that society.

(3) fair deduction from the actions and teaching of the Historical Jesus.

(4) general consensus of belief on such matters.

With all these items it is obviously impossible to deal fully in the present book, since their re-statement belongs to that internal theological revaluation which is referred to in Chapter XIII, and which is being attempted in other volumes of this series. I will only say here that in considering the expansion of Christianity I am considering in the main the expansion of churches which hold to the four points stated above, with the recognition, however, that part of such a movement is of communities which take an independent, and perhaps schismatic or unorthodox line, yet even so without departing from the centrality given to Jesus Christ.

> It is often the case that as one goes about the world, and not least in a country like India, one finds examples of the Kingdom of God 'breaking into society' in a milieu which has hitherto not been subjected to the Lordship of Jesus. Thus I found in one place a state hospital with a Hindu matron, where the under-matron and as many as 133 nurses were practising Christians, with the resultant effect of an increasingly Christian atmosphere in the wards of an otherwise neutral institution. Again, since Christians are not naturally born but reborn or converted, one sometimes finds areas of life which have sunk into the unhappy state of being sub-Christian, and have had again to be redeemed. Thus the horribly cruel and un-Christian practices of child-labour, in mines and factories, which deformed the early industrial revolution in England, had to be removed by the devoted efforts of such Christians as Elizabeth Barrett Browning and Lord Shaftesbury.

[1] Such continuity implies first, that it is an extension of the Incarnation so that, as the Germans say: *Haupt und Leib, ein Christus* (Head and Body—one Christ); second, that it is not a voluntary association of like-minded people, but in itself part of God's Initiative, a choosing out of individuals without reference to their worthiness or suitability for transformation into a worshipping and witnessing fellowship through which the Living Christ may go on breaking into the world.

But this 'breaking in' often occurs as the result of the impact of the New Testament portrait of Jesus upon someone who encounters it freshly for the first time, and we need not expect that this impact will lead immediately to what might be called 'full denominational orthodoxy'. Why should we? After all, this was the way in which the Christian movement first began. It is a good distance from the parable of the generous Householder and the good Samaritan, and the events of Calvary and Easter, to the Chalcedonian Definition or the Augustana. Yet 'to hear Jesus gladly', as the first converts did, still carries one the first steps of the way; and Indians who do so, find the Kingdom beginning to break in on their lives just as truly and really as did those to whom Paul preached.

CHAPTER V

THE EXPANSION OF CHRISTIANITY

It is important to clear our minds upon the principles which from the first underlay the expansion of the Christian movement. A pre-critical age had no difficulty in saying what they were. Appeal was made straight away to what an eminent layman in the early nineteenth century described as 'the marching orders of the church', and the enquirer was pointed to the concluding verses of the gospels of Matthew and Mark. When, however, reputable scholars arrived at the conclusion that Matthew 28:19, 20 with its Trinitarian formula seemed to belong to a later generation than that of the Apostles, and that Mark 16:9–20 were not the original ending of the gospel, which either concluded at verse 8 or had been preserved in a damaged manuscript to which a later generation added what it thought was an appropriate sequel, a feeling of uncertainty entered into the minds of some intelligent Christians, who remembered that the Lord, at an earlier date in his ministry, had said that he was 'not sent but unto the lost sheep of the house of Israel'.

Further examination of the total corpus of Bible documents, however, has entirely removed this uncertainty. Our Lord's conversation with the Syro-Phoenician woman is clearly in the nature of oriental repartee. He sees that she is a *goy* and He sets out to test her faith. His primary ministry is, as He says, to His own people, but not to the exclusion of non-Jews, otherwise He would have rejected her appeal without hesitation. It is perfectly clear, however, that in the last stage of His ministry His immediate disciples had no doubt that they were interpreting His mind correctly when they represented Him as speaking in terms of complete universalism. The cumulative evidence of the various texts, whatever their date (and they are none of them likely to have taken shape later than the end of the first century), points to the intention of Jesus to create a common world-religion. Such an idea would not be entirely alien to the mind of observant Jews, many of whom were already engaged in making proselytes from among the nations surrounding them in their dispersion.

It will be well to look at these traditions:

In Mark 14:9 we have the logion regarding the woman with the alabaster box of ointment: 'Wheresoever this gospel shall be

123

preached throughout the whole world, this also that she hath done shall be spoken of for a memorial of her.' The phrase 'in the whole world' is here εἰς ὅλον τὸν κόσμον, and the same word κόσμον is repeated in the appendix to the gospel in chapter 16, verse 15, where, in addition, the command is to proclaim the gospel 'to the whole creation'. Then there is the logion about many coming from the east and the west, and reclining with Abraham, Isaac, and Jacob, in the Kingdom of heaven. This occurs in Matthew 8 and Luke 13, in different contexts, possibly drawn from Q; but it reads like an original and primitive saying of Jesus—the community is the Kingdom, and not the church.

The so-called little apocalypse in Mark 13 has, in verse 10, the statement: 'And the gospel must first be published εἰς πάντα τὰ ἔθνη.' In the corresponding version of this in Matthew 24:14 this is slightly modified to run: 'And this gospel of the kingdom shall be preached in all the world for a witness unto all nations; and then shall the end come.' The absence of the same verse from Luke 21 seems to suggest that the Lucan version of this apocalyptic passage may have been drawn from a slightly different oral tradition, but there is no diminution in the emphasis upon universality, since the author, right at the beginning of what he admits to be the second volume of his work (Acts 1:8), represents the Lord as saying after His resurrection, in His appearance before His ascension: 'ye shall recieve power after that the Holy Ghost is come upon you, and ye shall be witnesses of me both in Jerusalem, and in all Judaea, and in Samaria, and unto the uttermost part of the earth', and this is preceded by the statement at the end of the Lucan gospel (24:47): 'and that repentance and remission of sins should be preached in his name among all nations, beginning at Jerusalem'.

Statements similar to these do not actually occur in the Fourth Gospel, but the whole tenour of this document is universalistic. Thus Jesus quite clearly does not confine his ministry to the Jews, who are often in opposition to it, but speaks throughout of his mission to the κόσμος, as for example John 12:46, 47: 'I am come a light into the κόσμον, that whosoever believeth on me should not abide in darkness. And if any man hear my words and believe not, I judge him not: for I came not to judge the κόσμον but to save the κόσμον.'

It is probably correct to assume, since the Incarnation was real, and not a docetic Epiphany, that Our Lord's spiritual development continued throughout his Manhood, and didn't spring into being miraculously complete at His birth, (like Hera from the head of Zeus) or even end with His adolescence. His realisation of His universalist mission may therefore have continued to develop throughout His ministry. This may explain the fact, recorded in matter common to Matthew and Luke, that 'He marvelled' at the faith of the centurion, and in other similar matter, recorded by Luke in a form slightly different from that of Matthew (who in addition appends it to the episode of the centurion) that 'many shall come from the East and the West, and shall recline with Abraham, Isaac and Jacob in the Kingdom of Heaven'. An intensification of this universalism may well have resulted towards the close of His earthly career from a growing sense of His rejection by a number of conservative Jews, and have led to the logion about the children of the Kingdom being cast out, and to the bitter cry: 'O Jerusalem, Jerusalem, that killest the prophets. . . .' Nothing could be more perverse than to see in these passages Christian anti-Jewish fabrications. There is the ring of truth about them. Moreover, if this estrangement had not developed, He need never have been crucified, but, like the Buddha before Him, have died a natural death. Yet the tragedy of Calvary is attested by non-Christian authors of the period, and has never been called in question by any reputable historian.

The early chapters of Acts contain the story of Peter's hesitation in visiting Cornelius at Caesarea, with the admission of the apostle: 'God is no respecter of persons, but in every nation he that feareth Him and worketh righteousness is acceptable to Him', but it is perhaps not surprising that an untrained mind like Peter's should waver and betray inconsistency in so momentous a matter as the extension of the fellowship of the little Jerusalem community so as to include Roman officers. In any case, Peter in his first sermon is represented in Acts 2:39 as saying, presumably to a Jewish audience in the streets of Jerusalem: 'the promise is unto you and to your children, and to all that are afar off, even as many as the Lord our God shall call'. Unless we are to write off this speech as Thucydidean, we must assume that at least something like this was what Peter said. On the other hand, if the author is writing under the influence of St. Paul, whose medical attendant he was, we cannot regard it as such good evidence. Nevertheless, the long Lucan gospel passages seem to show clearly that it was believed that this kind of teaching was not confined to the Pauline circle.

The Pauline emphasis on the universality of the Gospel hardly needs exposition,[1] but it is significant that the Jerusalem community, even though with some reluctance, ended by accepting the apostle; and in the Jerusalem council at which Paul and Barnabas are present,

---

[1] It is significant that Paul does not regard his mission to the *goyim* as a personal choice, but as a *command* issued to him by Jesus (see p. 128).

James is represented as quoting the (almost certainly post-exilic) addition to the ninth chapter of Amos,[1] in which Yahweh declares His intention to include the *goyim* within His scheme of salvation. Similarly universalistic passages occur elsewhere in the Old Testament writings, e.g. in parts of the Isaianic corpus, where they may even be earlier in date. With such traditions behind them, it is unnecessary to suppose that there were not a considerable number of Jews, and these not even Christian ones, who were possessed of a universalistic outlook. It can hardly then be doubted that some at any rate of the disciples of Christ accepted from the first their Master's *intention* to establish a common world-faith, even if all of them did not grasp it fully, and their actions show clearly that from the first they proceeded to carry it into effect (e.g. the story of the Ethiopian eunuch evangelised admittedly by a man with a Greek name—Philippos). That there were conservative Jewish Christians who did not agree with this may well be admitted, and we must also confess that our documents all belong to that part of the Church which wrote and spoke Greek, while the tension which came to a head at the time of the controversy about Stephen shows that there must have been considerable reluctance on the part of even believing Christian Jews to accept the possibility that the new religious community need not be centred upon Jerusalem, or even perhaps admit Gentiles on an equality with Jews. The struggle cost Stephen his life, and shows that St. Paul, before his conversion, clearly belonged to a conservative Jewish group. That such a group could fade away and disappear as completely as it did, is further strong evidence for the intention that the Christian movement should be a universal one, and the logia previously quoted could not have established themselves in the Gospel tradition, if they had not been felt to be fundamentally consistent with the general sense of the teaching of Jesus. On the part of some commentators there has been much undue and perverse scepticism over them. Thus 'the field is the world' in the Matthaean parable of the tares (although this parable has by some been felt to be a late composition) does not look like a late phrase. Might we not rather have expected it, if really late, to have taken the form of 'the field is the ecclesia' or 'qahal'?— But it does not.

It is worth considering how some other commentators have dealt with this question of the primitive character of Christian universalism. The late Dr. Claude Montefiore, as a liberal Jew, says that

[1] This text in Acts is not as it appears in the Massoretic Hebrew, but closely approximates to the form which appears in the LXX, though it is not identical with the latter. Even the earlier strata in Amos (in Chapter I) shows the belief that Yahweh is the God of the *goyim* as well as of the Hebrew people.

Jesus did not teach universalism, and that his teaching does not go beyond that of Jonah and the Prophets. But this in itself is a considerable admission, which rather tends to nullify the force of his earlier statement. Montefiore goes on to say that Dr. Rashdall, who insists that the teaching of Jesus was consciously and deliberately universalistic, is stretching the meaning of the Gospel logia beyond that which they can bear. Yet Montefiore admits that in Hillel and other Rabbis there are implicitly universalistic passages. This makes it difficult to see why Our Lord himself could not have made universalistic statements. Why, in any case, are such universalistic sayings as have survived not more explicitly controverted even by the conservative Christians of the first century? Must it not have been because it was felt that such sayings showed the avowed intention of Jesus?

Montefiore says that conscious deliberate universalism which means saying definitely 'not merely the Jew, but all men' is not taught till we get to Paul. But this seems to involve a contradiction, since Hillel taught 'Love thy fellow-creatures, and draw them near to the Torah'. He does not say 'fellow-Jews'. Such a saying must surely have been familiar to Gamaliel, one of Paul's teachers.[1]

Bishop Rawlinson in his commentary on St. Mark says cautiously that the form of the saying in Mark 14:9 is Christian, and presupposes the process of evangelism as having already begun. The phrase 'to preach the gospel' is, he says, one which belongs to the missionary vocabulary of the Gentile church. Dr. Vincent Taylor agrees in the main with this, but adds reasons for supposing that the logion had a primitive origin. The name of the woman is omitted, and late traditions tend to provide names for the persons concerned. Moreover, the saying is prefixed by the formula 'Amen I say unto you', which seems to denote an early logion. Dr. Taylor says that Jesus can hardly have had a narrower outlook than the prophets who preceded Him, so that even if Mark has not given his *ipsissima verba* (and verse 10 certainly does interrupt what seems to be a poetically rhythmic string of sentences with a prose comment), yet the evangelist has nevertheless rightly presented the mind of his Master in this matter.

Professor McNeile, commenting on the words of the Great Commission in Matthew 24:14, says that if these words were actually those of Jesus, it is hard to account for Peter and the other Apostles acting as they are represented as doing in Galatians 2:7 and following,

---

[1] The obvious truth is that there were two contradictory elements in Jewish belief, a universalistic and a non-universalistic, just as in England there are those who hold to the logical Christian belief in the missionary duty of the Church, and those who, even while they would wish to be called Christians, 'don't hold with missions'.

and Acts 10–11:18. This difficulty has been dealt with elsewhere. It is however noticeable that even Paul did not at first accept the principle 'not merely the Jew, but all men', but said that it was Jesus risen and glorified who changed his outlook ('God revealed his son in me', and 'I am Jesus whom thou persecutest . . . I will send thee unto the *goyim*'). It must be obvious that this idea, so unwelcome to Paul before his conversion, must have presented itself to him as coming from somewhere, and where, if not from the early tradition of the teaching of Jesus, which would at that time have been orally transmitted?

But in any case the God of the Bible, as finally conceived in the Jewish Canon of Scripture, is concerned with the spiritual destiny of the *whole* human race, whatever some individual Jews may have thought about Him. The belief is expressed in the Hymn of Creation in Genesis 1 that God is Maker of the *whole* earth, while in Genesis 12:3 we read 'in thee shall *all the families of the earth* bless themselves'. Whatever their date, these passages are pre-Christian, and show the point to which the Jews were progressively led.

If we attend once again to the earlier speeches in Acts, we note that Lake and Jackson, in commenting on Acts 2:39, point out that it echoes the passage in Isaiah 57:19 . . . 'Peace to those afar off and to those that are nigh', and also the LXX, of Joel 2:32. It is, however, possible to argue that 'those afar off and those that are nigh' does not refer to *goyim* and Jews, but to Jews of the dispersion and Jews of Palestine. Lake and Jackson, commenting on Acts 15:16 and following, refer to the difficulty of supposing that a Jewish Christian could have used the LXX in defiance of the Hebrew, or that any Aramaic source should have done so either. The conclusion they say must be that the whole source of chapter 15[1] is Greek, or that the speeches at least owe their form to a Greek editor. It is strange that the reference to Simeon in the speech of James in this chapter should so generally be referred to Simon Peter in commentaries, whereas it is much more natural to see in it a reference to the utterance by the aged Simeon of the Nunc Dimittis, with its phrase: 'to be a light to lighten the *goyim*', as it is recorded in the first volume of Luke's narrative. This makes far better sense. The story of Simeon must have come to Luke in some early oral tradition, and if this was known in Jerusalem, it is not artificial to suppose that James could have made mention of it on this occasion.

There remains, then, the question of Pentecost. It is of course possible to say that the whole of the book of Acts, and especially its

---

[1] This tells strongly against Torrey's idea that there was an Aramaic source for this chapter. But of course a translator from the Aramaic into Greek could have inserted speeches. The chief alteration in the LXX is the reading of אָדָם instead of אֱדוֹם as the word to be translated.

early chapters, is composed as an apologetic by Luke on behalf of Pauline universalism, and directed towards a specific Gentile Christian, the 'most excellent Theophilus'. But it is not said that Theophilus is outside the Christian community, and that this apologetic is directed to a non-Christian for the purpose of convincing him that the Christians constitute a legitimate development of Judaism, and that they have a right to exist. On the contrary, the author claims that he is only putting into literary form a longstanding tradition, as the result of careful enquiry and research, and that the person to whom he is writing has already been instructed in that tradition, and only needs to be assured of its ἀσφάλειαν. It would not therefore have been proper for the author to introduce into his syllabus anything which was violently incongruous with that tradition, although he might at times include in his compilation some varying traditions regarding the same event.

Now it does not appear that any substantial body of Christians repudiated the Pentecost story. Doubtless it may have received a Pauline interpretation. Yet 'Glossolalia', even to Paul himself, does not seem to have been 'the gift of divers languages', but of 'an unknown tongue' (so that he himself would hardly have related the Pentecost story in the form of Acts 2:1–13, but rather in the form in which it—perhaps—reappears in Acts 4:31), and psychologists like J. B. Pratt are able to adduce abundant examples of the latter from the records of revival meetings taking place in the United States of America. There is still a good deal to be said in favour of Bishop F. H. Chase's conjecture that what happened on this occasion was the emotional recital of the Eighteen Benedictions by a large gathering of Jews, many of whom came from the Diaspora, and were permitted to use their local *patois* in making such a recitation.[1] But the whole picture we are given is of a newly-gathered religious confraternity which has suddenly become conscious of a tremendous urge ('the Power of the Spirit') to witness to a new thing which has come into their lives, and it is not so much that Saul of Tarsus converts it to a wider universalism, but that it is the confraternity itself which, by sheer spiritual coercion and readiness to endure persecution for its new belief, drives Saul to the point at which he himself is converted.

Thus the universalistic motif is indeed present right from the first. Doubtless it owes much more to the responsiveness of

---

[1] My own recollection of the audible recitation of the liturgy for Rosh Hashannah by a synagogue of orthodox Jews in Jerusalem at which I was privileged to be present in the year 1952, and which was very noisy and emotional, leads me to think that it was the atmosphere of an assembly of this kind which occasioned the adverse comments of the bystanders.

Diaspora Jews like Stephen and Philip, than to Palestinians. Yet it is hard to conceive of the substance of the speech of James the Lord's brother (in which he confesses his conviction) as constituting a sheer, deliberate falsification of the facts surrounding the Jerusalem council. Such a falsification would surely have been hotly attacked by some Ebionite Christian. But evidence of any such attack is entirely wanting.

It has been left to Dr. Latourette to remind us that even if we conclude that the words of the Great Commission were not spoken by Jesus in precisely the form in which we have them, it is abundantly clear that whoever wrote them in their present terms believed that something very much like them had been spoken by the Lord; and that in any case we have the clause in the Lord's Prayer 'Thy Kingdom come, Thy Will be done on earth as it is in Heaven', a logion which even the most sceptical would acknowledge to have been uttered by Jesus; and again that the traditions of the Fourth Gospel (much of which we are now beginning to see may be just as likely to be primitive as those of the Synoptic Gospel, even though coming from a different group of believers) contain the sayings: 'God sent not his Son into the *world* to condemn the *world*, but that the *world* through Him might be saved', and '. . . I in them and Thou in Me, that they may also be one in us; that the *world* may believe that Thou didst send Me'. Whatever κόσμος may mean in these passages, it cannot mean only Israel, and the whole tenour of the Gospel, *pace* some critics, is one of 'and Gentiles'.

It is fair to conclude then that from the outset the infant Christian community, if sometimes faltering in its witness, did believe that it had a mission to the κόσμος, even though its members could not possibly have had explicit knowledge of all of which the κόσμος consisted. As a reviewer of the book on Pentecost by H. R. Bauer has put it: '. . . Mission in its deepest and most real sense is a dimension (it might well be said *the* dimension) of the very *esse* of the church'. Admittedly the Great Commission of Matthew 28 is never referred to either by Paul or by James, who seem to take their initiative from Pentecost, and it is not clear from the evidence whether the passages Acts 1:8, Acts 2, and Acts 4:31 refer to three separate events, or whether they are all of them different versions derived from separate oral traditions pointing to one single event, which is perhaps the same as that mentioned in the fourth Gospel in 20:23. What we seem able to be sure about is that the majority in the newly formed Christian κοινωνία firmly believed that any universalist mission which had previously existed as part of the spiritual function of the Jewish people had passed on to it by inheritance as the true spiritual Israel, and that this was the intention of its Founder, as being the true M'shicha, He who should come.

In conclusion, one would wish to draw attention to the universalistic passages which occur in the worship of the Jewish Church, as manifested in some of the psalms, and pre-eminently in Psalm 96, where the lordship of Yahweh over the whole earth is strongly emphasised. Whatever the date of these psalms, it is most unlikely that they are Christian interpolations in the Hebrew psalter, and it makes but little difference that they are probably post-exilic. With such devotional songs familiar to them, it seems inconceivable that early Jewish Christians should have found any serious difficulty, apart from emotional prejudice, in believing that their Master's ultimate mission was to the *goyim*, nor is it an acceptable idea that His own outlook was more restricted than that of Psalm 96.

The full story of Christian expansion has been told by Dr. Latourette, and in a work of theology there can be no question of repeating it here in detail, as though one were engaged in the composition of church history. Nevertheless, no proper picture of the present world-situation would be complete without some outline description of that expansion. It is perhaps not unfair to say that some of the episodes in it were of an experimental nature, and that mistakes occurred. Although the programme was entered upon in all sincerity, it is quite evident that some of its results have been far from permanent, and even that missionary preaching here and there contained appeals to motives of a doubtful character, and to doctrinal statements which would not be in order today. Nevertheless, for whatever reasons, and with whatever defects in presentation, Christ was preached, and His personality brought before nations which hitherto had not known Him.

We may perhaps see ten main phases in this expansion. First, the transition from Palestine to the Hellenistic Gentile world. This in itself was not an extensive one, and was in the main confined to the shores of the Mediterranean; but on account of the principle involved in it, it was of supreme importance, for it meant an extension of the Christian movement from Palestine to other provinces within the Roman empire, and to those who were not of Jewish birth. It was, however, followed by a further extension to a few regions outside the Empire. These in the main, though not wholly, lay to the east of it, and their evangelisation involved the adoption of linguistic, devotional, and institutional forms peculiar to those regions. The languages used were neither Greek nor Latin, but such tongues as Syriac, Coptic, Armenian and Amharic (Ethiopian). The strange character of East Syrian Christianity centred around Edessa has been mentioned elsewhere.

In the third stage came the evangelisation of the Nordic invaders of the Western Empire which carried the Christian movement into Germany, Scandinavia, and the British Isles, as well as to the invaders of Gaul and Spain. Against this later expansion must be set the serious and total loss of North Africa, which will again be referred to in the chapter dealing with Africa as a whole.

After the downfall of the African church came, as some sort of compensation, the ninth-century evangelisation of the peoples of the Balkans and Crimea, of Moravia, Bohemia, and Russia. The Russian Prince Vladimir is said to have become a Christian at the end of the tenth century, partly because he was impressed by tales of the gorgeousness of the worship which his envoys saw at St. Sophia in Constantinople, partly because he gained the victory in a war he was waging and had previously vowed to be baptised if he won it; partly because he married the daughter of the Byzantine Emperor. He himself received baptism at Cherson in the Crimea, while many of his subjects underwent it in mass formation at Kiev. Having desecrated the idol of their principle deity, Peroun, they went on to lay the foundations of their enormous national Church. This episode, in itself, whatever its results, can hardly be described as wholly edifying.

The next extension, we note, began somewhat earlier, but was carried further afield than any previous one. This was the mission of those Christians who adhered at least nominally to the doctrine of the Patriarch Nestorius; and it is quite clear that their work of evangelisation led to considerable success among Zoroastrians, penetrated through Persia to India, and ultimately passed along the North Indian caravan route into China, where remains of it have been found in several places, especially in the form of a monument with Chinese inscription at Hsi-an Fu. As we shall see, there is some evidence that Christianity was known in the Indus valley even earlier than this, and it would seem also that a sea-borne transference of Nestorian Christianity also passed to the Malabar coast of South India, the latest view being that it did not arrive there overland.

After this comes a pause, and the next phase is that of the Franciscan missions in the latter part of the thirteenth century. These do not seem to have achieved much fruit among the Moslems, although their leaders no doubt made some impression upon the Soldan. The mission to China however was more successful, and maintained itself in Peking for a considerable time, until it was swamped by a fresh invasion of pagan Mongols from the north. There was very nearly some success in the realms of Kublai Khan, to whom also friars were sent; but the unhappy condition of the medieval church in the fourteenth and fifteenth centuries militated against any very vigorous missionary effort. In any case the great Khan had demanded that the missionaries, if they were sent, were to work all kinds of nature miracles for the confounding of his own native sorcerers, and this was hardly a condition for self-respecting Christians to accept.

Again there is a pause; and the spearpoint of the next expansion is that of the Society of Jesus. Initiated in the middle of the sixteenth century as part of the Counter-Reformation revival, its story is too well known to need recapitulation. Taking advantage mainly of the discovery of the New World, it sought to plant mission stations of Iberian Christianity in Mexico and Peru, in the southern regions of North America and up the Californian sea-board, as well as in various other areas of South America. The very names on the map are sufficient evidence of this. It must be admitted that the cruelties of the Spaniards in dealing with native populations greatly mar the spectacle of this mission work, yet it is abundantly clear that the Catholic missionaries were often critical of the Conquistadors and their troops, and sought to mitigate the effect of their barbarism; but of course Jesuits also went on other missionary journeys where politics did not enter in, notably St. Francis Xavier to India and Japan, and in the seventeenth century Ricci and his companions to China, where they laid the foundations of the present Roman Catholic Church in that country, translated many of the Chinese classics into Latin, and achieved considerable success.

Finally the Protestant Churches began to feel that they ought to take their share in this kind of work, and the heroism of Xavier and his colleagues and successors stimulated Christians from other groups to emulate their labours. The Jesuit missions to Asia were thus followed by others from England, Germany, and Scandinavia, during the latter part of the eighteenth century. But it is the nineteenth century which witnesses the greatest activity of all. This century opens with the despatch of the Russian church mission to Japan, and the foundation in England of the Church Missionary Society and other similar bodies, and is followed by the pioneer work of British and other evangelists, whose devoted labours led on to the greatest expansion of the Christian movement since it first began.

Looking back over this panorama, certain facts are clear, some of them only too clear.

First, the extension of the Christian faith to the transatlantic world obviously could not have happened before its existence was known to the Christian West. It is thus a matter only arising from the sixteenth century onwards, and in parts of South America is still incomplete.

Second, the extension to Central and Eastern Asia, and to Central and Southern Africa, apart from the counter-Reformation Catholic Missions mentioned above, belongs to the period from the end of the eighteenth century onwards, and part of this extension has only been achieved during the first half of the twentieth century.

Third, the circumstances leading to the extension were often not very good ones. The mixed motives of Vladimir of Russia in adopting Christianity have already been referred to. But mixed motives are to be found not only in the Dark Ages. Early in the nineteenth century the report of one missionary society in England spoke of work in India as desirable because it would make the inhabitants more subservient to discipline, and so preserve the country *under British rule*.

Fourth, the actual work of diffusion has been most generally undertaken by devoted enthusiasts. We think naturally of people like Boniface of Crediton, Francis Xavier, Peter Claver, Henry Martyn, James Hannington, and John Coleridge Patteson. The work of such may have been encouraged and supported by politicians whose motives were less worthy, but the various apostolic characters themselves were beyond doubt inspired by a genuine love of our Lord and of their fellow human beings.

A bad individual cannot really convey genuine Christianity to others, though a good one may sometimes make an occasion for his work out of the mundane and less reputable activities of his countrymen. It can hardly be supposed that St. Francis of Assisi approved of everything that the armies of the Crusaders were doing, but their presence in Palestine certainly gave him the chance of preaching to Moslems. Again, Peter Claver cannot have regarded the Portuguese slave trade with anything but horror, yet he laboured to evangelise the slaves as well as to doctor them, for some thirty-eight years. 'Why did he not attack slavery at the root?' we may well say. The charge that Christians have often contented themselves with ambulance work cannot be wholly dismissed. Both St. Francis and Claver had been trained to believe that in a fallen world things might have to go on happening which were un-Christian. Individuals could be saved out of this world, but the question of redeeming it as a whole did not enter into the programme, for it was in itself madly heading for judgment and destruction. It would seem therefore that the theological and ethical basis of much missionary work may have been defective, and that while here and there we can discern Christians who believe that society as well as the individual is included within God's plan of redemption, nevertheless the general attitude is often not very different from that represented by Charles Kingsley in one of his novels as that of a Saxon abbot shortly before the Norman conquest, who exclaimed: 'O earth full of violence and blood. O last days drawing nearer and nearer', or if we turn to the genuinely historical, that of Luther himself: 'The world is a queer fellow. Let us hope God will soon end him.'

The fifth conclusion must be that certain parts of the nominally Christian world were never more than superficially converted, that the populations of some areas were swept into the church *en masse* without possessing any deep conviction; that counting heads for the purpose of writing a report for a missionary society is a perilous task; and that while in the last hundred years the motives for evangelisation have improved beyond measure, and the numbers of workers holding the conception of a redeemed social order have increased, yet many parts of the Christian or ex-Christian world are crying out for reconversion to a better Christianity. This, once again, does not mean that one ought to regret the Christianisation of any parts of the globe (for whatever reason, Christ has been proclaimed). What one cannot help wishing is that the task had been better performed. In any case it must be clear that Christianity is still a very young and often most imperfectly understood religion, and that much of its empirical past partakes of the nature of infancy and adolescence. There can be no doubt that although pure Christianity in itself belongs to the order of what Lippmann has called 'High religion', a good deal of pre-axial material has intertwined itself with it. Nevertheless, it will never do to confuse the issue. Christian faith is ineradicably grounded upon history, and we cannot be content to treat the insistence upon the retention of this historical surd as part of the survival of pre-axial religion.

Meanwhile, just as the methods of expansion used by Moslems have mellowed and softened somewhat, so the methods of expansion of Christianity have changed for the better. Fairly successful attempts have been made to get the missionary duty to be recognised as a natural part of the life of every normal Christian community and individual. Alms-giving for evangelistic work has been inculcated as part of the natural routine of every congregation, to whom annual bulletins are issued both by sermon and by printed report, and the favourable motive proclaimed for such activities can be discerned in the hymns prescribed for singing on such occasions. Bishop Heber, great man though he was, is now heard rather less than A. C. Ainger,

Percy Dearmer, and Sylvester Horne. All this has of course a bearing upon theology. It is clear that the reasons for evangelistic work which were so clearly and uncompromisingly set forth by William Carey, are not for the most part the reasons which would be given today. Faced as he was with a corrupt and degenerate Hinduism, Carey saw the antithesis between masses perishing in darkness, and Christians rejoicing in a light of salvation. If we had been in India at that time we might largely have agreed with him. In any case St. Paul saw the situation in the first century A.D. in a somewhat similar light, at least if we are not to take as pure rhetoric some of the statements which he makes in his epistles. That there are to be found nobler elements in some of the Asian and African religions is not to be doubted; but one is sometimes tempted to wonder whether their rediscovery has not been largely due to the provocation arising from their juxtaposition with Christianity. Without that juxtaposition spurring their adherents to look again at their best treasures, might not the latter have remained buried for ever? It is said that the great value set by twentieth-century Indians upon the Gita is largely the result of a reaction provoked by Christian missionaries, and that in the day of Carey, Marshman, and Henry Martyn, this wonderful poem was very little esteemed by the great majority of Hindus. But where the finer elements in Asian religion have been rightly stressed and fairly appreciated it has been natural for Christians to regard them with respect, and to stress on their own side the place of the Logos-doctrine.

Yet in this matter the end is not yet in sight. If it is possible without prejudice to regard the social effect of the non-Christian faiths in comparison with those of Christianity, it may be confidently said that the theological basis of the latter certainly produced the nobler results in action, and that where such results are now being aimed at outside the Christian movement, as for example in the Ramakrishna mission of Hinduism, they proceed not as the logical outcome of the latter, but as an artificial grafting from Christianity on to Hinduism of something which does not properly belong to the latter.

CHAPTER VI

THE DOCTRINE OF THE LOGOS

In the year 100 A.D. there was born in Syria at Sychem (then known by its Roman title of Flavia Neapolis because founded by the Flavian emperor Vespasian) a Greek called Justin. His parents were pagans, and we know nothing about his early life; but when he appears before us in history, he is engaged in searching for truth in the old philosophical schools, and he tells us that he first went to a Stoic teacher, who informed him that it was unnecessary to know God. Justin, in no wise discouraged, passed on, and sought a Peripatetic philosopher, who scandalised him by the grasping way in which he insisted upon his fees. He then turned to a Pythagorean, but he says that before attending the lectures delivered by the latter it was clearly necessary to learn Music, Astronomy, and Geometry. So he betook himself to a Platonist, and in retrospect he declared that he considered himself to be at this stage in a better way to a knowledge of God. Who his teacher was from this point onward we do not know, except that he was 'a venerable man who led me from Plato to the Hebrew prophets', and so eventually to faith in Christ. Justin, in a dialogue which he claims to have held at Ephesus with a Jew called Trypho, declares that in the last resort he found Christianity to be 'the only philosophy that is sure, and suited to the needs of man'. He retained his philosopher's cloak (a recognisable uniform, as recognisable as the Roman toga or the yellow robe of a Buddhist monk), but travelled about as a Christian philosopher, seeking to disseminate his newly found convictions. It is, however, to be noted from the onset that his teaching groups itself round a specific term, that of the LOGOS. Justin, in dealing with Trypho, declares that whenever, in the Hebrew Bible, Deity is said to have appeared to the patriarchs, it was the Logos that did so. But in his two apologies to his gentile pagan contemporaries he goes further, and maintains that the Logos also taught Greek philosophers, and that even though some of these might be accounted 'godless' ($\dot{\alpha}\theta\acute{\epsilon}o\iota$), they were, in so far as they lived 'according to Logos', *Christians before Christ*, the latter being the supreme manifestation of the Logos. As St. Paul had said: 'In Him [Jesus] dwelleth all the fullness of the Godhead bodily', and in the anonymous epistle, 'to Hebrews' we get a similar assertion, that Jesus is the reflection or ἀπαύγασμα of God's glory.[1]

The logical implications of this teaching are so important that they deserve careful examination, since it has been affirmed that the statement about *Christians before Christ* is capable of being extended so as to embrace most of the sages of Asia, and to include, for instance, Sankara, Lao-tzu and Mo-ti and even perhaps, paradoxical as it may seem, the Jew, Karl Marx, as among those who have lived and talked 'according to Logos'.

It is certainly clear that a doctrine of the Logos was developed as the semi-official way of relating the work and person of Jesus Christ to the larger world of Mediterranean thought, and of defining His position in relation to other religious teachers. The rise of the doctrine in fact marks the first serious contact between the Christian Gospel and the non-Christian populations of the planet, and is a momentous experiment, upon which the Christian Church, for weal or woe, eventually set the seal of its approval by declaring the Fourth Gospel (where the doctrine appears in the Prologue) to be a canonical book. Further, in the worship of the Church, this Prologue came to occupy an honoured place, being selected as the proper Gospel for the day at the Christmas Eucharist, and as part of the Celebrant's private devotions at the end of Mass in the Roman Liturgy. It seems right therefore that the origins of the doctrine should be carefully traced, and that the significance and history of the use of the term Logos should be clearly understood. Why did Justin dwell upon it, and whether he acted independently, or under the influence of the Fourth Gospel, what led the author of the latter to write his Prologue in the terms in which he did? There is no convincing evidence that Justin is actually dependent upon the Fourth Gospel, and indeed the authority wielded by the latter, until we reach Irenaeus (*c.* 180 A.D.) is dubious.

The History of a Word

The Greek term Logos is in a certain sense untranslatable, and, as Dr. Inge once pointed out, Goethe, in his *Faust*, tried one word after another, and finally fell back on the neuter demonstrative pronoun. The Latins hovered between Verbum, Sermo, and Ratio, finally fixing upon Verbum, with not entirely happy results, especially for Protestantism. They had, however, some precedent for this, as we shall see in due course.

The word occurs in classical Greek from Homer onwards; but it seems gradually to have been employed in two different senses,

---

[1] See Colossians 1:15. Hebrews 1:3.

sometimes in relation to speech, sometimes to mind and personality; so that confusion is always possible. As it is quite clear that in the Prologue to the Fourth Gospel[1] and in Justin the second use is indicated rather than the first, we must trace the history of this first of all; although the idea of its equivalent, i.e. an immanent Reason in the world, is to be found in Indian, Egyptian, Iranian, and Chinese thought.

Logos as a distinctly technical term makes its appearance in Greek on the ground of philosophical theory about 500 B.C., in the works of Heracleitus of Ephesus, at a period when Greek and Indian philosophy were by no means so far apart from one another as used to be thought: and it must always be remembered that Ephesus is on the Asiatic shore of the Aegean, and is actually the place where it is believed that the Fourth Gospel was composed, though of course at a much later date. Like other Ionian physicists Heracleitus set out to consider of what the Universe consists, and what may be said to be the permanent substance lying behind its manifold and changing appearances. All these physicists agreed that there was such a common substance. Thales said it was water. Anaximenes said that it was air or mist. Heracleitus however decided that it must be fire. By 'fire' he did not mean 'flame' in the ordinary sense, but much more what we should describe as a molten gas such as hydrogen, and he said that this primordial fire transformed itself by process into fluids and solids, and then by an upward road back again by a cyclic movement into fire. Although he appears to remain a materialist, since his primordial substance is not yet conceived as anything like mind or spirit, at this point he greatly resembles some of the Indians who have spoken of the Absolute (or Brahma) as emitting, sustaining, and reabsorbing the universe.[2]

This rhythmic downward and upward process, a River of Time and a River of Space, is the condition for Heracleitus under which all things live. Yet the primordial substance is hardly what we mean by 'gross matter', since it is said to be the source of the world's intelligence. It is not really the anthropomorphic Zeus of popular Greek theology ('It will not be called Zeus, and yet it will be called Zeus'), but it is the intelligent Cause of the world, and the world-changes which it produces are neither fortuitous nor spasmodic, but occur systematically according to natural law; and this natural law is given the name of Logos, which might be paraphrased either as Cosmic Principle, or as the Absolute in the process of

---

[1] Though not invariably in the rest of the Gospel.
[2] The idea is indeed fundamental to Indian thought, and reappears in the works of the late Aurobindo Ghose.

self-expression. Here Heracleitus wavers in his description, and expresses doubt as to whether he ought to ascribe personality to the Logos.

This organic philosophy of Heracleitus has affinities with other organic philosophies which arose further East, especially in China, and also with certain others in the Western world, such as the process-philosophies of Alexander and of Whitehead, the Holism of Smuts, and even perhaps the Dialectic Materialism of the Marxists.

All things, Heracleitus tells us, happen according to Logos, and the Logos is universal, an all-pervading cosmic principle of reason. The resemblance between this and the Chinese doctrine of the Great Tao—which will be discussed in another chapter—is so striking, that some have been tempted to deduce an actual connection between the thought of Hellas and that of China, especially when it is found that Chinese moralists like Meng-ko urge people to live according to nature, which is just what the later Stoics like Epictetus did.[1]

One can assume in such a case either diffusion of an idea from a centre, or concurrent but independent development of the same idea in different areas, owing to the presentation to all human beings of the same data of consciousness, leading in turn to an emergence of similar concepts at a period in the history of the species, when the same grade of development had been reached.

The immediate successors of Heracleitus did not for the most part use this word Logos. Plato in his genuine works, as well as Aristotle, substituted for it the word Nous, which they took over from an earlier Greek thinker, Anaxagoras. There is possibly one instance in Plato where the word Logos is used in a genuine work. It is only in the spurious Platonic literature that the Logos really crops up again, and this spurious literature was doubtless known to Justin, and probably to his venerable teacher, who, like most of his contemporaries, probably accepted it uncritically as genuine.[2] Nevertheless Nous, meaning Mind or Intelligence, signifies much the same as Logos, certainly in the way in which it is used.

[1] A delightful story is told about a certain Chinese emperor, that when he was travelling with his courtiers on the royal barge, it was attacked by two river-dragons. The courtiers in a panic asked the emperor what they should do, and his reply was 'Keep calm and behave naturally, since if it is in the constitution and course of nature that you should be killed by the dragons, nothing is to be gained by behaving in an undignified way. But if it is not in the constitution of nature that you should die from the attack of the dragons, then there is nothing of which to be afraid, and so again you should keep your composure'. When the dragons heard this they went away depressed, and it is thought that they died of humiliation! This story breathes the purest Stoicism, and might just as well have been related of the Emperor Marcus Aurelius.

[2] From Justin to Proclus no philosopher doubted that the Epinomis (which is to-day reckoned as spurious) was Plato's own handiwork, and the theory of the Logos certainly appears in it.

The Stoics, Zeno, Chrysippus, Cleanthes, and later on Epictetus and Marcus Aurelius Antoninus and others, such perhaps as Cicero, although subsequent to Plato and Aristotle, genuinely derive their cosmic theory from Heracleitus, even though they may not have entirely understood his meaning. They not only return to the use of the word Logos, but equate it once again with Fire, Energy, and, in the last resort, with Deity. Plato had developed a dualistic picture of Reality which divided it into the Changeless Idea and the Changeful World of Sense.

But the Stoics reverted to a pure monism, or as Indians might say to A-dvaita or non-duality, in which the ideal and the actual were held to be one within the unity of the Cosmic Whole, so that the Cosmos and Deity were simply two aspects of It. Their 'One' was 'primal fire', which they also designated Pneuma, i.e. fire-vapour, and they seem to have gone no further at first than conceiving it as a kind of compressible gas or expansible solid—perhaps not unlike molten hydrogen, and dependent for its transformations into individual substances upon a law of Tonos or tension.

Each grade of existence was said to have its own appropriate kind of Tonos:

in inorganic subjects this is *hexis* = cohesion
in vegetable life   *phusis* = the power of growth
in the animal world   *psuche* = material soul
in man   *nous* = reason.

Each species of organism, the Stoics declare, has a kind of specific formula or local principle applicable to its nature; and just as the entire universe is said to be controlled by a central Cosmic Principle or Logos, so each species has a specific principle, to which is given the title Spermatikos Logos, the idea being that each sperma or seed contains within itself the principle of its own development, and this is its own Logos, a specific and individual formula of pneuma-tonos. Finally, as the Stoics put it, 'The intelligent Deity which is the Fire-Artifex proceeds to the generation of the whole cosmos by an orderly method, and contains within Itself all the individual Spermatikoi Logoi, in accordance with which things come into being as predestined.'

It must of course be realised that this picture of 'how things happen' was not constructed by any experimental methods of research such as those of Thomson and Rutherford, but was the combined result of observations more or less without instruments, of intelligent deduction, and of keen intuition.

So far the emphasis was on the whole on the side of a

materialistic pantheism. Nevertheless, the presence in the Supreme Logos of both intelligence and purpose compelled the Stoics gradually to concede that the Logos could hardly be represented as sub-personal.[1]

On the Stoic side again we find Cleanthes (331–232 B.C.) turning from scientific philosophy to poetry, and identifying the Sovereign Principle of the Universe with 'God most glorious, called by many a name, nature's great King, through endless years the same; omnipotence, Who by Thy just decree controllest all, hail Zeus'—and so on, in almost the manner of a Hebrew psalmist. Zeus is obviously to Cleanthes no more 'the man in the sky' than Shang-ti, the heavenly deity, was to Confucius and his successors. He represents perhaps what Varuna, the Sanskrit equivalent of the Greek Ouranos in the Vedic hymns, might have become, if religious thought in India had developed differently—the Supreme, Super-personal, Spiritual, Benevolent, and Holy Director of the universe.

But next, a logical and perhaps obvious distinction began to be drawn between this Supreme Deity in his own Being and in his Self-Expression. To know Deity internally and exhaustively one would obviously one's self have to be Deity, and thus mankind could only have a partial, external, and even contradictory knowledge of the Self-Existent. Total Deity to mankind must be unknowable and indefinable, as the Indians still say: 'neti, neti'—'It is not this, it is not that.' Only in so far as Deity chooses to be manifest in self-expression is any knowledge of Deity possible. The natural inference therefore is that only through the operations of the Logos in the spatio-temporal order can mankind have even an approximate knowledge of the character of Deity.

As we draw nearer to the Christian era, we find the tendency to associate the Logos with Hermes rather than with Zeus, and also to conceive of Logos as appearing on earth in quasi-human mani-festations, somewhat resembling the multiple avatars of Vishnu in India. Among these we note Cronos, the Titans, Eros, Atlas, Pan, Agathodemon, and Herakles.[2] The Logos-doctrine in fact, as a piece of secular thought, like that of evolution or of relativity in our own day, is present in the minds of many writers at the beginning

---

[1] In China, at a much later date, roughly contemporary with that of Aquinas in Europe, the philosopher Chu Hsi was faced with a similar dilemma. In his organic philosophy he reduces everything in the universe to Li and Chi, roughly 'Cosmic Principle' and 'Matter'. Li he sometimes represents as eternal, unconscious, change-less law, but at another time as constituting a property of mind, and at yet another as containing love, righteousness, reverence, and wisdom as its component principles, and since these can only be said to be mental attributes, it would appear that at this point Li and Mind are identified, since Li apart from Mind would have nothing in which to inhere. Li also conceived in this manner could hardly be sub-personal.

[2] See Lebreton, *History of the Dogma of the Trinity*, Engl. trans., vol. I, p. 49.

of the first century, A.D. One has only to mention Balbus, Cicero, Plutarch, Cornutus, and the pseudo-Heracleitus of the Treatise on the Homeric Allegories. Plutarch says that the goddess Isis is the Female Principle in Nature, and is styled 'the One of numberless names' because she is converted by the Logos into, and receives, all appearances and forms. Later he says that Osiris is the common Logos of all things in heaven and hell'.

The place of Cornutus in this group is somewhat significant. An African from Leptis Magna, he flourished as a Stoic teacher in the reign of Nero, and is thus a contemporary of St. Paul, though less well known than Seneca. One of his pupils, the poet Persius, pays a warm tribute to his instructor in the course of one of his Satires. Cornutus' chief work, composed in Greek, is an essay περὶ τῆς τῶν θεῶν φυσέως. Since the title is the same as that of Cicero's De natura deorum, the inference would seem to be that the educated public of the Mediterranean world was seriously concerned at this time about the need for a philosophical theology. Like many in India, they had got beyond the point of a naïve polytheism, and works were appearing which aimed at providing 'a religion for thinking men'. The 'Theology' of Cornutus is not considered by Lebreton to be popular interpretation so much as learned exegesis. It is the cult of the Logos as seen in Hermes which appeals to the multitude. Small shrines of Hermes were often to be found in the public streets of Mediterranean cities, very much as one may see at this very day small shrines to the god Şiva about every ten yards in some of the streets of Banaras, and people were able to make votive offerings to them as they went by. Hermes, however, though a subordinate deity, the messenger of the gods, is the deity of speech and eloquence, of divine communication and self-expression. Strictly speaking, according to the Stoics, the universal Logos is reason rather than speech. Hence there is a tendency to analyse the Logos into two aspects, and Cornutus tries to represent the universal Logos as Divine Reason, while the human Logos, further analysed into the interior (ἐνδιαθέτος) and manifested (προφορικός) is identified with Hermes as Divine Speech or Divine Self-Communication. But pseudo-Heracleitus says that Hermes is the one and only manifestation of the Logos, and represents both reason and language.[1]

[1] One notices that Radhakrishnan, in his new edition of the *Principal Upanishads*, p. 61, says that Hiranyagarbha in the Vedas answers to the Logos, the word of Western thought, but that the corresponding Vedic term for Logos is Vac or Vak, which means word or wisdom, and that 'the first-born of Rta is Vac', 'yavad brahma tirthati tavati vac'. He also says that Prajna, wisdom, and Logos, intellectual principle, certainly have a family likeness. The attempt at an early development of a kind of Logos-doctrine in Egypt has been referred to elsewhere; but such possible resemblances need to be regarded with caution. (See my *Sacred Books of the World*, p. 60.)

The Septuagint

Such was the situation in the Gentile world at the moment when the Christian movement emerged into view in Palestine. Obviously it did not do so in isolation from the world around, for already a certain degree of hybridisation had begun to take place between Hellenic and Hebraic ideas, and in order to understand the situation aright we must now pass on to consider it.

When, after the conquests of Alexander, a great library was set up at Alexandria, and had to be supplied with MSS., it was not unnatural that its promoters should want to have translations available of all the main works then in existence. Just as our Victorian ancestors like to have in their libraries *The Sacred Books of the East*, edited by Professor Max Müller, and considered them to constitute a proper item in the erudition of a nineteenth-century English gentleman, so the Alexandrians approved the idea of having, among other works, the sacred canonical literature of the Hebrews. It is irrelevant for our purpose whether the so-called Septuagint version first produced was or was not translated from an official or critically-selected Hebrew text. The discovery of the so-called Dead Sea Scrolls has shown that even in the first century A.D. there were in existence a number of different Hebrew texts, and the later standard or Massoretic text gives manifest signs at certain points that the Hebrew text from which the Septuagint translation was made was sometimes the same as the Massoretic, sometimes a text which appears neither in the Massoretic nor in any of the newly discovered texts. But none of these points matters. What is important is that certain Hebrew words such as (דבר: Dābār) were rendered into Greek as Logos and Pneuma. It is possible to say that this opened the way either to misunderstanding or to interpretation on the part of Gentile readers; but there can be no disagreement over the fact that interpretation, even if it were *mis*-interpretation, was bound on this basis to take place. For example, if in Psalm 33:6 it was said 'by the Dābār of Yah were the heavens made', in the LXX this ran τῷ λόγῳ του κυρίου οἱ ουρανοὶ ἐστερέωθησαν, or in Psalm 119:89: 'Thy Dābār O Yah, endureth for ever in heaven', this ran εἰς τὸν αἰῶνα, κύριε, ὁ λόγος σου διαμένει ἐν τῷ οὐρανῷ, or again in Psalm 119:115 we find in the LXX: 'Thy Logos is a lamp unto my feet and a light unto my path', where the word used meant in the Hebrew 'Thy Torah', but in the LXX Greek might also signify something different, more like the Cosmic Logos.[1]

---

[1] It would be both unwise and misleading to leave the issue of the Septuagint, without making certain qualifications.

(1) The story of its composition needs to be evaluated critically and with care. The main source, the alleged letter of Aristeas, an Egyptian courtier, to his brother

It is perfectly fair to say that דבר in the original Hebrew may not always carry the same meaning, so that LXX translators render it by as many as six different words beside that of Logos; and also to say that Logos in Greek may sometimes be the equivalent of דבר when it means Mandate or Proclamation or Command, but may easily be interpreted (or misinterpreted) in a Stoic sense, along the lines which have just been indicated.

What is quite certain is that when it comes to making a *commentary* on this LXX version of the Hebrew Bible, the interpretation of the word Logos tends to be heavily tipped in the Gentile direction. The reason for this is clear. Platonic and Stoic ideas were steadily coming to form the background for the culture of most properly-educated citizens in the post-Alexandrian world of the Levant; and when the point came for explaining to this world the LXX version of the Hebrew scriptures, it was almost inevitable that such ideas should leave their mark on the explanation.

Philo

The one outstanding commentator is the great Alexandrian Jew, Philo, and it will be seen that the attention that scholars have given to him is fully justified.

Philostates, cannot be regarded as anything but an elaborately told romance, but it has clearly an historical basis. Behind its legend about the 72 scholars and their Hebrew scroll written in letters of gold, which they translated at the command of Ptolemy Philadelphus with miraculous unanimity in 72 days, lie certain facts which are reasonably probable. Philadelphus was undoubtedly a collector of books. He founded in fact a second royal library at the Serapeion to take the surplus of the MSS. which Ptolemy Soter had accumulated at a building near the Museum and the Palace. He was also interested in syncretistic activities, and there is evidence that a Buddhist mission from the Ganges valley was permitted to visit his court. The tradition that he fostered and encouraged a translation of Hebrew sacred literature, even though it may have been undertaken in part as a popular effort by the Alexandrian Jews themselves, is therefore generally accepted by most modern scholars as a respectable one. It seems unlikely that Philadelphus 'ordered it officially to be made', since the style and vocabulary of that part of the LXX which tradition ascribes to his reign is too full of barbarisms for it to be entitled to the adjective 'scholarly'.

(2) Tradition limits this first translation to the Pentateuch (the Torah proper); and the nature of the text and vocabulary confirms this. It is indeed clear that, as a version, the LXX is by no means a unity. Thus the translation of the Psalms is later than that of Genesis, while even up to the time of Christ some of the books of the Old Testament were still only on the edge of becoming canonical, and would therefore hardly yet be candidates for translation. Again, in the different books different styles are to be detected, and in different books different Greek words are employed to translate the same Hebrew word.

(3) With the above qualifications it can safely be affirmed that approximately by the time of St. Paul the LXX had in the main taken authoritative shape, and that it now became for Christians throughout many years the standard Old Testament for their use, equally as a store-house of proof-texts, as the source of their knowledge of the circumstances of the Old Dispensation, and as food for their devotional life. This does not mean that other translations such as those of Aquila, Theodotion, and Symmachus were not sometimes appealed to, or that Christian writers did not quote inaccurately from memory, or even that they did not paraphrase LXX passages—for they certainly did, just as did also the Qumran sect, whose writings are preserved among the Dead Sea Scrolls. But when deductions have been duly made on this score, it still remains the fact that the LXX is the main source for quotations from the Greek Old Testament.

Philo came of a wealthy and influential family, and seems to have been born about 20 B.C. He took part in an embassy from Alexandria to Rome somewhere about 39–40 A.D., in order to complain to the Emperor Caligula about certain disabilities from which Jews in Egypt were suffering, so that although he does not appear from his writings to show any personal acquaintance with the Christian movement, his life-time covers that of Christ, of the Baptist, and (in part) that of St. Paul.

Philo whole-heartedly accepts the value of the ordinary Gentile scheme of education which prevailed in his day, and which was known as the Encyclia—'a good all-round training'—embracing literature, rhetoric, mathematics, music, and logic. He even compares the Encyclia to Hagar, saying that just as Abraham, when Sarah was childless, had to satisfy himself with the bondwoman, so the soul, until it is mature enough for the Divine Wisdom, must subsist upon secular education. He had plainly absorbed plenty of it himself, and when he sets to work to compose some twenty-odd treatises upon the inner meaning of the Hebrew sacred books, he does not scruple to use freely his secular cultural background. Thus he becomes the first great writer to relate the ideas of Hebrew theology to the Gentile philosophies of late antiquity.

The effect of this was profound. Once we divest ourselves of prejudice, we can have no sort of doubt in our minds that the Philonic approach is to be seen in the Johannine literature of the New Testament, if not in other places; while post-New Testament Christian writers such as Justin, Clement of Alexandria, and Origen are plainly indebted to him, and St. Ambrose used him freely. In fact the Christian church came to regard Philo as an 'anima naturaliter Christiana', a champion of the Faith, albeit unconsciously.

Dr. Kraemer is hardly just in dismissing the influence of Philo as he does. Many commentators on Johannine literature have obviously been scared at the idea of admitting that the writings of Philo could have had any influence upon it, although a classical scholar like R. G. Bury has clearly demonstrated that again and again the Fourth Gospel shows close affinities with the thought and language of Philo. Bury's work is today out of print, but it is idle to suppress (in the interests of reverence for the scriptures) the facts which he gives.

For the convenience of readers I give here a summary of his main points, the significance of which would seem to be beyond dispute.

1. Either at first or second hand the Johannine author seems clearly to have been acquainted with the works of Philo, or at least to have had some access to the same material as the latter.

2. Philo's Logos is eternal, i.e. from the beginning.

3. Philo's Logos is an essential part of Absolute Deity, it is Divine Reason.

4. Philo's Logos is nevertheless distinct from and subordinate to the Absolute, in just the way in which the Christ of the Fourth Gospel says: 'My Father is greater than I.'

5. Philo's Logos is the agent of creation.

6. Philo's Logos is 'The Holy Logos according to seven.' (The perfect number.) *Leg. Alleg.* i, 6.

Similarly, the Fourth Gospel, which is artificially constructed with great skill, has seven outstanding miraculous events, seven 'I am' pronouncements, and seven decisive quotations from Scripture.

7. In Philo the Divine Logos is full of the water of wisdom—an everflowing fount. *Somn.* ii, 37; *Migr. Abrah.* 13.

8. The Logos is sinless. *Prof.* 20 f.

9. The Manna from Heaven is a symbol of the Logos, and in the Fourth Gospel the Logos in Jesus is the Bread from Heaven.

10. Philo's Logos is designated by him, on various occasions: πρωτόγονος or First Begotten Son: θέος and not ὁ θέος (just as in John 1:1); παράκλητος; ἀρχιερεύς; ἐικὼν θεοῦ; ἄνθρωπος θεοῦ; ἑρμηνευτής; πρεσβευτής.

11. Moses is a symbol of the Logos. So is Abraham, and so is Melchizedek. It is thus only a step further to the full manifestation of the Logos in the historical Jesus. (Even the ideal sage of Stoicism is not far from being a kind of incarnate Logos.)

12. The Logos is the Shepherd King who leads his flock. *Mut. Nom.* 19 ff.

13. But whereas the Logos of Philo is mostly referred to in terms of cosmology, the essentially Christian feature is that the Logos is philanthropic, and concerned with soteriology, being, as at a later date the Creed of Nicaea put it, One 'who for us men and for our salvation came down from Heaven'.

14. Further points of resemblance are the parallel between John 9:41 and the passage in *Philo Q. Rer. Div.* xv, 'The blind class of men thinks it sees, but is sightless'; and the phrase in Numbers 20:17, 'the royal road' which is explained by Philo as signifying 'the Logos of God' or Way. We are naturally reminded of the declaration of Jesus in John 14, 'I am the Way'.

Philo and the Christians

If there is one term more than any other with which Philo makes play, it is that of the Logos, and insofar as Justin appeals to the Logos as the Inspirer of non-Christian sages, it is probably to Philo that he owes the idea, or at least it may be the case that Justin and Philo, and perhaps also the writer of the Fourth Gospel, and certainly at a later date the anonymous writers of the two separate but now conjoined works which are included within the so-called epistle 'ad Diognetum', are all using more or less independently a conception of the status and work of the Logos which was current intellectual coin at the period. Philo groups the Platonic ἰδέαι with the one term 'Logos'.

> I am quite ready to concede that ὁ λόγος σὰρξ ἐγένετο was not the kind of expression which would have been used by Philo. But then I do not for one moment suggest that the author of the Fourth Gospel is merely duplicating Philo. He was first and foremost a Christian believer, and even if he used some Philonic phraseology, his own personal belief led him naturally beyond Philo's theology.

Whatever, therefore, pagan writers and Philo may have attributed to the Logos as a unifying factor in the minds of men is clearly appropriated by early Christian teachers to what they held to be His unique manifestation in the historical Jesus. If the Stoics said, as they certainly did, that since the one Logos is present in many human souls, men may have communion with each other through the one Logos, the Christians could add, 'Yes, and this is just what we have come to feel about Jesus. He is a bond of union for all mankind; and to Jew, Gentile, Scythian, Greek, slave and free, He speaks with the same ecumenical appeal. He is undoubtedly the Light that lightens every man.' The use made by Christian writers of the word Logos would seem to be regardless of the varied shades of meaning which the pagan writers and Philo apply to it. Their intention, as Inge says, would seem to have been (to use a present-day phrase) to show that their beliefs about the historical Jesus were 'in agreement with the best modern thought'. There can in fact be no doubt that any educated Gentile, on reading the Prologue of the Fourth Gospel, whoever its author may have been, would immediately understand its allusions, while a Jew familiar with the LXX would at once feel sympathetic towards a statement which would not only remind him of the opening words of Genesis 1, and of passages in the Wisdom Literature of the Hebrew people, but would also associate the Word Incarnate in Jesus with the Hebrew Memra and the Dābār of Yahweh as rendered into LXX Greek. It is incredible how rarely commentators on the Fourth Gospel allow themselves to ask: 'What did its author hope and expect that his readers would understand from it?' His whole attitude is plainly that of one who is appealing to the Hellenistic Greek world of his day. In his twelfth chapter he introduces a story which involves an address by Jesus to Greeks. It is inconceivable that he should have begun his work with a prologue which, dependent as it is upon the introduction of the technical term, Logos, uses that term in a private sense completely misleading to his readers. However much he may wish to lead them on to an acceptance of Jesus as the Supreme Incarnation of the Logos, and to demonstrate to them that, as St. Paul would have said, 'In him dwelt all the fullness of the Godhead bodily', he cannot have meant them to understand by the word Logos anything other than what the Hellenistic world of his day had come to mean by it.

The Early Church

It is this position which after some interval received its endorsement by the early and undivided Church, and there is no good reason for doubting that Christians today ought to regard themselves as its inheritors, so that they are both entitled and indeed bound to make use of its implications in dealing with the other great systems of faith which the world has produced. Yet it must be admitted that reference to the term Logos diminishes from the fourth century onwards. The word did not find a place in the original Creed of Nicaea, nor in any of the subsequent confessional documents which received full endorsement. Probably the existence in pagan theology of expressions about the Logos which the Church could not endorse, in which he was referred to as 'a second god', or distinct from and subordinate to the supreme Deity, alarmed orthodox theologians, who feared that an indiscriminate use of Logos-theology might support the Arian heresy, and lead to a recrudescence of polytheism in a new form.[1] But no council went so far as to condemn the use of a word which had its place in the forefront of one of the most sacred and revered documents of the Church, and as we have already seen, the liturgical use of the latter has come to impress the Logos doctrine upon multitudes of Christians who would otherwise have hardly heard of it, and that during the great central festival of the Incarnation; while every priest as he concludes celebrating the Holy Mysteries has his attention called to it immediately before he leaves the altar. In our survey of the great faiths of mankind which we shall now undertake, we must therefore keep this doctrine steadfastly before us.

---

[1] It may well be that one reason for the decline in the attention paid to the doctrine of the Logos was the use of the word by docetic heretics to imply a false view of the Incarnation. In the apocryphal Acts of John, which Montagu James dates as not later than the middle of the second century, the Greek original (as distinct from the Latin version which has been purged of unorthodoxy) contains the extraordinary story of the hymn and dance of Christ and the disciples on the night of the betrayal. The hymn itself as well as the discourse in the cave which follows it is centred round the idea of the Logos, but the gist of the discourse is that 'the Lord contrived all things' (connected with the actual passion) *symbolically* and by a dispensation toward men for their conversion and salvation. Below there was the *appearance* of execution, but above the cross was the Lord Himself 'not having any shape, but only a voice'. The language is very obscure and involved, but the meaning of it seems to be that the Logos Himself did not suffer crucifixion, but that that was only endured by a human body, 'I suffered, yet I did not suffer: I suffered not, yet did I suffer: ... and so speak I, separating off the manhood. ... When He had spoken unto me these things ... He was taken up, no one of the multitudes having beheld Him.'

The Fourth Gospel, and the early Fathers of the Church

Certain general points about the Fourth Gospel should be considered here, as they have been stressed in recent British scholarship.

> Mr. C. K. Barrett points out very properly that the history of the Fourth Gospel before 180 A.D. is very obscure. References to it in writings before that date are ambiguous and doubtful, and although it seems from various pieces of evidence that it existed, its authority does not seem to have been universally accepted, and those who appear to quote from it may or may not have known it in the form in which we have it today.

We find Professor Dodd at the end of his Introductory Chapter coming firmly to the conclusion nevertheless that the primary intention of this Gospel is to expound a doctrine of the Person of Christ to a wide public consisting in the main of devout and thoughtful persons in the varied and cosmopolitan society of a great Hellenistic city such as Ephesus under the Roman Empire. Whereas Mark's Gospel seems to assume that both John the Baptist and Jesus are already known to its readers, so that they are introduced abruptly without any explanation, the Fourth Gospel begins with nineteen verses of theology, then goes on to introduce John, and only at the end of the chapter identifies the incarnate Logos with Jesus of Nazareth. It could in fact 'be read intelligently by a person who started with no knowledge of Christianity beyond the minimum that a reasonably well-informed member of the public interested in religion might be supposed to have by the close of the first century'. It is of course perfectly possible to say that the Gospel was written with Jewish as well as Gentile non-Christians in view, and there is no reason for denying that there is evidence in it of the influence of some Wisdom-literature, and that the word Logos is sometimes used, not as the equivalent of the cosmic Logos, but in the sense of the spoken word. Nevertheless the way in which throughout it the Jews are spoken of in the third person would be unnatural if the writer were confining his address to Jewish readers. It is also noticeable that the term Logos is introduced without any preamble, and the implication is that the readers will understand the allusion at once; but since in the prologue the word is used of 'being' rather than 'speech', it is difficult to avoid the conclusion that whoever wrote the prologue meant its readers to identify Jesus with the Logos in the sense in which the word was used in Hellenistic Gentile philosophical theology. It is true that at this time Jewish and Gentile meanings for the word Logos were drawing together, as is evident not only from the LXX, but also from the writings of Philo, and there is therefore nothing incongruous in the word Logos being used during the course of the Fourth Gospel with more than one meaning. Thus we read in the high priestly prayer in the seventeenth chapter 'thy word is truth'[1] where 'word' is the translation of 'Logos', and Jesus says elsewhere 'if ye abide in my word', and again 'the word which I have spoken unto you', but it is evident that in some of these cases Logos does not simply mean speech, but the *content* of the speech, i.e. revelation, command, or even principle. It is not the same as λαλία. When Jesus says 'thy Logos is truth', it is important to understand the meaning here of the word truth, ἀλήθεία. It is not simply veracity, or true evidence such as a witness swears to tell in a court of law, but the complete or real state of affairs, in fact very much what a philosopher like Bradley means when he uses the word Reality. This is clearly the meaning of the phrase 'thy word is truth', and it is also the meaning which ἀλήθεία has in the famous speech of Jesus before Pilate: '. . . that I should bear witness to the truth; everyone that is of the truth heareth my voice'[2]; and again in 8:32: 'Ye shall know the truth and the truth shall liberate you', i.e. 'you shall have liberty through knowledge of Divine Reality'. The Logos of God then is Divine Reality, and the evangelist has previously stated that it is this Logos which has become σάρξ.

Now if this was the fundamental purpose with which the Fourth Gospel was composed, i.e. to demonstrate the cosmic position of the Personality of Jesus of Nazareth, it seems clear from recent evidence that it was put into effect at a relatively early date, for from papyrus texts lately discovered in Egypt it seems that the Gospel may have been in existence soon after, if not just before A.D. 100. True it did not win its way to full acceptance very quickly, and was possibly not approved of by some more conservative Christians for a considerable time. Nevertheless in shaping the formularies of the church it fulfilled a most important rôle, and even if there seem to be difficulties about believing that in the form in which it has come down to us it is the actual composition of an eye-witness of Christ's ministry who was not only one of the twelve apostles but one of the three most intimate companions of Jesus, there seems no reason for not supposing that the compiler was closely dependent upon the testimony of such an eye-witness.

In reading the Johannine prologue and the passage in Justin which has previously been quoted, however, let us beware of identifying the *relatedness* of the various great religious systems

---

[1] The whole passage runs: ἁγίασον αὐτοὺς ἐν τῇ ἀληθείᾳ· ὁ λόγος ὁ σὸς ἀλήθειά ἐστι.
[2] It seems quite reasonable to render this passage: '. . . that I should bear witness to Reality. Everyone who is in harmony with Reality listens to me', and Pilate's rejoinder, as: 'What *is* Reality?'

11

with the *equality* of all religions. The Christian use of the concept of the Logos certainly involved the former, but it is an improper use of it to try along the lines of it to establish the latter. The Christian use of the Logos doctrine does not lead to what may be called a form of neo-Hinduism. Those who first used it had no doubt at all that what had captured them was destined to supersede all the other forms of religious belief and practice with which they were surrounded. They saw these indeed as *related to* their own faith, but they never expected them to survive and to co-exist. For them, however gradual the process, it was certain in the end to be one of the radical and complete displacement, rather than of syncretism. Take, for example, Tertullian the African. He knew and accepted the Fourth Gospel, and in one of his writings he speaks of the Logos as 'the Immanent Reason of the world, which fills it from end to end, as the honey fills the honey-comb'. Yet no one is more conscious than he is of the unique centrality of Jesus Christ, and some forms of non-Christian religion he avowedly regards as diabolical. In his Apology, chapter XLIV, and in his 'de praescriptione haereticorum' he says: 'Where is there any likeness between the disciple of Hellas and the disciple of Heaven?' Or take again the argument in the earlier half of the anonymous and composite *Ad Diognetum*. No one makes use of the Logos-doctrine more clearly than this author does in his chapter VII. Yet he goes on to say that the step taken by God when he sent Jesus is *in addition to* Creation. The Logos, as he says, is

'the very Artificer and Creator of the universe Himself, by whom He made the heavens, by whom He enclosed the sea within bounds of its own, whose mysteries all the elements faithfully observe, from whom the sun has received the measure of his daily courses to keep, whom the moon obeys as He bids her shine at night, whom the stars obey as they follow the course of the moon, by whom all things have been ordered and defined and placed in subjection . . .'

Yet he leaves no doubt that in his belief the central Christian proclamation is that this continuous creative process has been succeeded in the fullness of time by a single discontinuous action in which the same Logos is involved; and the writer explicitly declares that although this special initiative involved imparting to man a knowledge of God which he had never had before, that initiative also had its redemptive aspect. Chapter IX is almost exclusively Pauline in both language and emphasis:

'Having therefore planned the whole dispensation already in His own mind in union with the Son, He permitted us during the former time to be carried along by disorderly inclinations just as we wished, and led astray by pleasures and desires, not in any way taking delight in our sins, but bearing with them, nor again assenting to that age of unrighteousness, so that we, having then been by our own works convicted of our unworthiness of life, might now be rendered worthy by the goodness of God, and having plainly proved that we were unable of ourselves to enter into the kingdom of God, might be enabled so to enter by the power of God. But when our unrighteousness had now been fulfilled, when it had been made completely manifest, that its retribution was awaited in chastisement and death when the time came which God had ordained to manifest His own, goodness and power (O the surpassing kindness and love of God for man!), He did not hate us or reject us or take vengeance upon us, but showed His longsuffering and forbearance; in His mercy He Himself took up the burden of our sins, He Himself gave His own Son as a ransom on our behalf, the holy for the lawless, the innocent for the guilty, the just for the unjust, the incorruptible for the corruptible, the immortal for the mortal.

What else could cover our sins but His righteousness? In whom could lawless and ungodly men be justified but in the Son of God alone? O sweet exchange! O inscrutable operation! O unexpected blessings, that the lawlessness of many should be hidden in one righteous person, and the righteousness of one should justify the lawless many!'

The word *Memra* merits some special attention. It is an Aramaic noun formed from the same root as the Hebrew verb Amār, to speak, and means speech, utterance, or proclamation. But as used in the extra-Biblical literature of the Targums it is inserted between the person of Yahweh and those to whom He addresses Himself, almost as though it were an Intermediary Being. Since, however, orthodox Jews were strict monotheists, the meaning is rather that of an attribute, the Self-Expression of Yahweh. A similar expression is that of the Shekinah, the radiance or effulgence of the glory of Yahweh, which in Greek becomes $\delta\delta\xi\alpha$. In the Epistle of James 2:1 we read: 'My brethren, hold not the faith of our Lord Jesus Christ, the $\delta\delta\xi\alpha$ (or Shekinah) with respect of persons'—a bold phrase, showing that this writer, whoever he was, clearly identified Jesus with the Shekinah of Yahweh. The Prologue to the Fourth Gospel, which also refers to 'seeing the $\delta\delta\xi\alpha$' of the Logos, thus holds out a hand at this point, if not at others, in two directions at once, since it has been pointed out that, especially in its reference to the Light and in some other respects, its language has affinities with that to be found in some of the literature of the Qumran Sect. But since its clear aim was to commend the new religion to the Mediterranean Gentile world, it is the Logos as the latter understood it upon which the major emphasis is laid.

Saint Paul does not generally use the actual word Logos, but in his genuine Epistles he has all the ideas connected with it, and they are related to the historical Jesus; while some of the very terms used by Philo are to be found in his writings. Similarly, in the anonymous Epistle to Hebrews, Philonic conceptions are linked to Jesus, and the whole document is expressed in typical terms of Alexandrian theology.

We are confronted with a somewhat interesting situation when we examine the alleged Pauline letter to the Church at Colossae.

Here the author, whoever he was, comes to much the same conclusion as the Johannine writer in the course of stating his Christological belief. He uses the word σοφία as with λόγος but λόγος and σοφία elsewhere are known to have had close literary connections, and his statements about the historical Jesus are both well known and unequivocal, the relevant passages being in chapters 1 and 2.

The position may be summed up in this way. The authority and experience of the early and undivided Christian community led ultimately to the establishment of the Fourth Gospel and Colossians as canonical documents, and subsequently to the canonising of Justin as a Christian saint. It is not impossible for Protestant Christians to question the wisdom of the former,[1] perhaps after the same fashion as that in which Luther denounced James as 'a right strawy Epistle'. They may also feel entitled to ignore Justin as a saint. It is, however, most difficult for any Christian who believes that in the main highway of the experience of the Christian Church there was an actual growing into truth, to resist the implications of these two decisions. After all it is the Christ of the Fourth Gospel who is represented as telling His followers that the Holy Spirit will guide them into all truth; and even though the doctrine of the Logos may have undergone interpretation since the second century, and may still undergo further interpretation, the main outline of it stands as a permanent datum with which we have to work. Justin's literary authorities for commending heathen sages as Christians before Christ may not be critically sound, but his main thesis remains untouched. The natural reaction for Christians was to say, as did Justin and other apologists: 'What you are striving after we are able to give you, only with this difference, that whereas the manifestations of the Logos of which you speak are in ordinary persons only the result of His creative activity, or, where you claim them as special and discontinuous, they seem to us both mythical and docetic, we have but one full manifestation, and that completely and truly historical and reasoned and for the express purpose of human redemption. We are able to accept much of what you say about the Logos as the Self-Expression of the Ineffable Deity, but we feel justified in claiming that in Jesus Christ that Self-Expression, in the fullness of time, attained to its Peak and did so for a specific and unrepeatable Purpose.' This affirmation of particularity seemed for early Christians to be in no way scandalous, partly because it was historical ('sub Pontio Pilato'), but also because, like Cullmann in our own day, they

---

[1] It is noticeable that Emil Brunner asserts the right of Christians to deal freely with the Canon of Scripture, pp. 393–6.

accepted this sudden appearance of the historical Jesus as the true
and decisive dividing point in terrestrial history.

Wolfson, in the first volume of his great work on early Greek
Theology, asserts that for Justin the Logos was a subordinate mediator
and not God, at any rate not God the Father (see review of Wolfson by
Brooke Otis of Hobart College in the *American Journal of Psychology*).
I think it is going too far to say that Justin's Logos was not God in any
sense of the term, if one considers his *opera* taken as a whole; but it
is probable that he did teach the subordination of the Logos, which,
although it is capable of being distorted into an Arian form of doctrine,
can hardly be described as in itself heretical or unscriptural (see
Westcott's famous note in his commentary on the Fourth Gospel, on
the Subordination of the Son).

The idea of God's Self-Expression being in some way *inferior* to
the Essence of His Own Being, probably does not make appeal to us
today, for unlike thinkers of the second and third centuries (e.g.
Origen) we should not say that water drawn from a river was 'inferior'
to that of the river itself, or that radiation from the Sun was
necessarily 'inferior' to the actual substance of the Sun.

But whether or not the doctrine does appeal, it does not affect the
main structure of my argument, since Justin's point is that the Logos,
while certainly being $\dot{a}\pi\grave{o}$ $\tau o\hat{v}$ $\theta\epsilon o\hat{v}$, does not confine His operation to
the historical Jesus, but functions also, though in a lesser degree,
in *all* religious leaders, whose work is thus related to that of Jesus:
'Whatever men have said or done well, belongs to us Christians',
a startlingly liberal statement, yet one which the Christian Church has
never expressly repudiated in her Councils. I notice that Dr. Radhakrishnan, in the course of his Hibbert Lectures on 'The Idealist view
of Life' quotes Justin, but without going on to draw the logical inference from the passage.

Dr. Kraemer's exegesis, compared with that of others

One hesitates to cross swords with so widely read and competent
a scholar as Dr. Kraemer, but I feel bound to point out what may
be said in criticism of his exegesis of the Johannine Prologue.

His general support of Kittel, in maintaining that the Johannine
Logos is an entirely different conception from that of the Hellenistic
philosophers, I have in effect dealt with above by implication.
But even if one agrees with him to the extent of saying that of course
the human religious consciousness is marred by self-centredness,
and to that extent is incapable of a *full* recognition of God, and
often engages wilfully in a flight from His presence, it does no good
to exaggerate this by taking words in their wrong senses, and to
intensify one's argument by misconstruing Scripture passages. A
glaring instance of this would seem to be Dr. Kraemer's inter-
pretation of John 1:6. In this passage $\kappa\alpha\tau\acute{\epsilon}\lambda\alpha\beta\epsilon\nu$ has almost always
been taken by British scholars in the sense of 'overcame', and this
not for any doctrinal reason, but because it seems to be required by

an impartial exegesis. Wordsworth rendered it: 'did not surprise and overwhelm'; Westcott, 'did not overcome or eclipse it'; A. E. Brooke, 'did not conquer it'; Moffatt, 'did not master it'; R. H. Strachan, 'did not overcome it'. Bernard renders the passage for preference 'did not overcome it', but quotes in fairness the alternative, 'did not understand or appreciate it', though he suggests that the former interpretation is to be preferred because it is more in harmony with other passages, the existence of which Kraemer ignores, i.e. Wisdom 7:2, and Philo, commentary on Genesis 1:3. R. H. Lightfoot also gives both possible translations. Mgr. Knox puts in his text 'was not able to master it', and relegates the other possible word 'understand' to a footnote. Hoskyns, while saying that the double significance of the Greek verb must be given full weight, goes on to quote the R. V. margin, 'overcome', evidently preferring this, since he adds: 'the reference is primarily not to the age-long opposition of men (I Baruch 3:12, and also Psalm 36) but to the opposition of the Jews which issued in the crucifixion' and concludes: 'The Light is unconquerable' (like the Sol Invictus). Mr. C. K. Barrett feels that the author is characteristically playing here upon the double meaning of the word κατέλαβεν.

There is therefore a heavy consensus of British scholarly opinion (not, be it noted of one religious denomination) against Kraemer's rendering. Bultmann it is true supports him by taking κατέλαβεν in the sense of 'begreifen' rather than of 'ergreifen' or 'überwaltigen'. But continental scholarship seems perverse in neglecting to give full weight to the passage in John 12, which ought clearly to be taken into account here. In the second part of this twelfth chapter we find the famous passage about the 'Greeks who would see Jesus'. A natural reading of the text makes it clear that the intention of the author is to represent the discourse which it contains as an address by Our Lord to the Greek enquirers. At this point one feels bound to agree with Westcott against Brooke, since the latter considers that the enquirers were not admitted to Christ's presence. But the discourse is not spoken to Philip alone, but αὐτοῖς, and twice in the course of it 'the multitude' is mentioned. It is clearly a public and not an esoteric discourse. Whether in form it is Thucydidean or not, we cannot be certain; but common sense demands that we should see in the account the author's clear intention that his Gentile readers shall understand it as meant for them, as it was when first spoken. Indeed the passage shows signs of having been composed by the same person as the Prologue, for it is noteworthy that in 12:35 we read: περιπατεῖτε ὡς τὸ φῶς ἔχετε, ἵνα μὴ σκοτία ὑμᾶς καταλάβῃ, which includes the same three words as 1:6, φῶς, σκοτία, and the verb καταλάμβανω. The only possible way of making sense of this is to take κατελάβῃ in the sense of 'overtake', 'overcome' or 'overwhelm'. But this leads on to the inference that it is sheer perversity not to translate the verb κατέλαβεν in 1:6 by the same word, since here also it is in juxtaposition with φῶς and σκοτία.

Continental Protestantism starts no doubt with a prejudice against linking the Johannine Logos with Hellenistic ideas. But when we consider the plain intention of the Johannine author to write for Greek-speaking Gentiles, we are bound in honesty, I repeat, to ask ourselves: What did he expect his readers to understand by his use of the term Logos? Would there have been any point in employing it, but at the same time putting upon it a private meaning of his own which would not have been clear to them? It would have been tantamount to some British writer introducing a scientific term like 'relativity' into a theological work, but intending it to mean something quite different from what it would have signified when used by Einstein. To make such a supposition in the case of the Johannine author seems fantastic. Whoever he may have been, when he wrote 'Logos' he meant 'Logos', and he meant it to be taken in the sense in which a contemporary Stoic writer would have taken it. His clear purpose is to say to his Gentile readers: 'I am asking you to link up the concept of the cosmic Logos, which you know so well, with the historical character, Jesus of Nazareth, to whom I am introducing you (these things are written that ye might believe, etc.) and I do so with the more confidence because He *is historical*'. This brings us at once to the decisive assertion ὁ λογος σαρξ ἐγένετο. It is often said that this was a phrase which would have seemed scandalous to the Hellenistic readers. But is that really right?—Lebreton[1] has shown that shortly before the Christian era there had been a growing tendency not only to personalise the Logos, but further to associate him with specific epiphanies of supernatural beings. Granted these *parousiai* were docetic, and concerned with individuals around whom there clustered a good deal of mythology, the plain purpose of the Johannine author must have been to carry this idea further, following up his assertion with a series of incidents drawn from recent history, and implying, by giving the logion of John 12:24, followed by an extensive historical account of the Lord's Passion, that *here* is no mythical dying god, no Adonis or Osiris, but a *real* character from contemporary history. It is the same implication as in the Cana story. Whatever the events which lie behind it, the author means

[1] *Op. cit.*, chap. ii.

his readers to understand him as saying, 'Here is no mythical wine-creating Dionysus, but a real historical figure', as the Johannine first epistle puts it: 'That which we have seen and handled of the Logos of life' (the living Logos). σάρξ, in Jewish and non-Jewish writers of the period, other than Paul, seems to be used to mean flesh or body, and not with any adverse ethical significance. To say ὁ λόγος σάρξ ἐγένετο meant then exactly what the English translation says. In Acts 14 the Lycaonians are represented as saying that the gods have come down to them ὁμοιωθέντες ἀνθρώποις. But it must not be overlooked that in Philippians 2:7 the writer, in describing the Incarnation of Jesus, says exactly the same thing. He was from eternity ἐν μορφῇ Θεοῦ . . ., but He became ἐν ὁμοιώματι ἀνθρώπων. In Apocalypse 19:13 the triumphant hero riding on his white horse, described as the Logos of God, 'hath on his vesture and on his thigh his name written: King of kings and Lord of lords (an obvious reference to the labelling of the statues of gods and emperors in this way). This is clearly the apotheosis of the Logos of John 1:6. To say that this Logos is from the Old Testament is not enough. Which Old Testament? we ask. The answer must be: 'The LXX Old Testament'; for the latter, if read by Gentiles who did not know Hebrew or Aramaic, would have led many to the conclusion that the Jews after all had their own belief in the same cosmic Logos which was a familiar concept in their own Gentile circles, and which they were beginning to personalise. They need not have read Philo in order to draw this conclusion, and it matters little whether it was erroneous or not. The effect on them would be the same.

It is true that we have to consider Kraemer's strong emphasis on the Pauline passage in Romans 1:18–32. Here the plain meaning is that God reveals Himself in the natural order, and can not only be known by men through it, *but is known—and rejected*. Men are not incapable of apprehending God, but they actually reject That which they have apprehended. They 'hold down the truth in unrighteousness' and 'knowing God, they glorified Him not as God . . . but became vain in their reasonings'. But this is only one side of the picture. In comparison with it we read in the Johannine Prologue: 'He came unto His own, and His own received Him not, but as many as *did receive* Him to them gave He power', etc. The inference is that the author does not suggest, like Paul, that *all* have turned to their own way and rejected the Logos and the Light, but that *some* did receive Him. It is true that, further on, the Evangelist represents Jesus as saying: 'This is the condemnation that light is come into the world, and men loved darkness rather than light, because their deeds were evil.' But this passage is evidently overshadowed by the thought of the rejection of Jesus by the Jews—as indeed is perhaps the earlier passage (1:11) too. Yet it cannot be that the Evangelist meant to exclude the fact that some *did* accept, for he certainly says that they did; and Kraemer seems to ignore this, as well as the passage in Acts 28:28. '. . . αὐτοὶ καὶ ἀκούσονται'. Why should the *goyim* do this?

The interpretation of the Prologue depends largely here upon the point at which the Evangelist intends to speak of the Incarnation. Does it only come at verse 14? Or is there a covert reference to it in verses 5–11? It is often said that the Evangelist's mind is so subtle that he can write something with the deliberate purpose of putting it in terms which admit of a dual interpretation; and it may well be that this is the case here. But it is surely evident that the verses of the Prologue are primarily not all on a level, but that there is a sequence and a culmination about them, whatever secondary interpretation may be possible.

In this case the meaning will be: 'The Logos appears in the world as the Agent of creation and the Giver of inspiration, and He is not simply an intermediary between Yahweh and His creatures, but Yahweh Himself in self-expression' (as at a later date one of the writers in the *Ad Diognetum* expressly says: chapter vii). Yet although He comes thus to His creatures, they do not all choose to recognise or receive Him, though some do; and these, of whatever race or clime, are those whom Justin afterwards describes as 'Living according to Logos' and 'Christians before Christ', to whom is actually given the power to become, if they will, true sons and daughters of the Living God.

It is necessary to draw out the reasonable implications of I Corinthians 1:11. Here Pneuma seems to be employed in the same sense as the Johannine Logos, as the Power that lightens every man, and although the immediate application of Pneuma is as the Constructor of the Ecclesia which is the Soma Christou, yet the inference which can be justly drawn without any forcing of the text beyond the limits of what the author would have allowed is that Pneuma can work in a diversity of ways, some of them outside the Soma Christou; and in this case we are not far from the same idea as that in the famous passage of Justin Martyr, who seems in his own way to express the same sentiments as Paul when the latter writes (I Corinthians 12:5–6): 'there are diversities of ministrations but the same Lord; and there are diversities of workings, but the same God Who worketh all things in all'. It is this kind of passage which those on Kraemer's side seem to ignore.

Modern Implications

If, as I hold, the foregoing is the correct exegesis of the various New Testament passages, the implications for the Christian preacher to the non-Christian world, whether in his own country or in a foreign land, will be the same, and will be far-reaching and decisive. He will begin by recognising that if its inhabitants have enough serious purpose in them to want to talk to him about religion, or to listen to what he has to say about Christ, they have already within themselves encountered the Divine Logos, though perhaps unconsciously, have been found by Him and have been moved by Him to take some step towards further knowledge and towards a deeper and more explicit relationship. This is perhaps what C. F. Andrews meant when he was asked how he approached earnest Hindus, and answered: 'I always take it for granted that they *are* Christians, and as I talk to them, I often see the light of Christ come into their eyes.'

I believe this to be fundamental.

Imagine a European or American scientist who, although finding difficulty about giving any significance to the word G-O-D, is trying to live a virtuous life according to the best he knows, and has a passionate and disinterested love of truth for its own sake, and who also keeps a mind open upwards, and is receptive to anything that a Christian may be able to *show* him of the Reality which he, the Christian, has found. Such a person is clearly not far from the Kingdom, and may truly be said to be 'living according to Logos', with all that that implies.

The Pauline Writings

It will be seen that this conception, though it abates not one whit the unique glory of the once-for-all discontinuous Incarnation in Jesus, has the power of bringing Jesus and the non-Christian world together in a way which is decisive and comprehensible. I do not think that it is really incompatible with the Pauline point of view. Paul, in his speeches in Acts (and, I believe, here and there in the Epistles) shows that even his inherited Hebraic exclusiveness could make room for the same conception. At Antioch in Pisidia he uses the phrase 'a Light to lighten the Gentiles' in a way which suggests not only the Nunc Dimittis in Luke but also the 'Light' of the Fourth Gospel. At Lystra he says that although God left all nations to walk in their own ways, yet He left Himself not without witness among them. When Paul and Barnabas go through Phenice and Samaria they declare the conversion of the *goyim*, a startling thing to many Jews, as also to the many non-Jews in

Phoenicia and Samaria; and one which carried with it the necessary implication that even the *goyim* must have some preliminary motion which is impelling them towards the Living God.   Paul admits this at Athens, where he says that he is making explicit declaration of a Being Whom the Athenians worship already, though not according to full knowledge.   His hearers, we are informed on this occasion, were Epicureans and Stoics, and the latter would of course have known of the doctrine of the Logos.   The 'Man of Macedonia', whom Paul sees in a dream, is obviously not a Christian already, nor even a Jew, but a Gentile who is desirous of knowing about Christ.   Of course, like the devout Greeks of Thessalonica, he may have already been on the edge of becoming a Jewish proselyte, and could have been a σεβομένος τὸν θεὸν, interested in the message to be heard at the synagogue, though not actually one of its members. Paul in his speech to Agrippa lays some stress on the *goyim* being in darkness, and being brought to repentance and light, but in his speech at Rome he declares that the *goyim will hear*, and must therefore have that within them which renders response possible. This seems to tie up with his previous statement that in the Living God we ourselves live and move and have our being, and that He is not far from each one of us (a statement very much like the later one of Mohammed, that Allah is closer to every man than his jugular vein).   In I Corinthians Paul disclaims the tendency of the *goyim* to approach Deity through σοφία, in favour of emphasis upon the Cross, which he says is to them foolishness, but the point here is that the Cross implies the apparent defeat and passibility of the Logos, who is thus not the dangerous type of God, like Dionysus or the victorious Apollo, but 'reigns from the tree', and is *Christus Victor through* His humiliation.[1]   In Romans 2 Paul says that the *goyim*, not having Torah, are a Torah unto themselves,[2] which would surely have been impossible, if it had not been for the Logos, but the revelation of the Logos in the flesh transfers the *goyim* from their own imperfect Torah into the realm of grace, which is after all what the Johannine Prologue also says, when it concludes, after proclaiming the Incarnation, that χάρις καὶ ἀλήθεια (grace and reality) came by Jesus.   Any exclusiveness which Paul shows might well be due to his Pharisaic ancestry and upbringing, and unless we are prepared to regard him as verbally inspired (in which case we

[1] It is significant that at a later date another *goy*, King Ethelbert of Kent, raised the same objection to Augustine at Ebb's Fleet.   'You ask us to worship a god who died in fashion of a thrall.   Our gods are warriors.'   Yet even he capitulated on reflection. The light that was in him united itself with the Light presented to him from without.
[2] This seems to contradict Romans 1:18, which is rather emotionally written, and looks like a rhetorical denunciation in which, as von Hügel hints, Paul is being too sweeping.

must revert to the acceptance of his statements about the status and dress of women in the Christian congregation) we are bound not to regard this exclusiveness too seriously. He would certainly start off with an initial prejudice against the religious impulses of the *goyim*, whose popular religion he would view no doubt very much as Carey and Henry Martyn viewed the popular religion of the Hindus of their day, some of which was admittedly of a debased sort. He shows this not only in Romans, but (if Ephesians is also his work) in that Epistle also (4:17). Even if he be not the author of Ephesians, it is certainly at this point not an unfair picture of a great many non-Christians of the baser sort all the world over. And yet equally there are always not a few non-Christians who could qualify for Tertullian's famous epithet: 'Anima naturaliter Christiana'.

It should be pointed out once again that in Acts 10, Peter is represented at Joppa as publicly declaring: 'God is no respecter of persons, but in every nation, he that feareth Him and worketh righteousness is acceptable to him', a terrific admission for anyone who had been an orthodox Jew, but one which Luke, if indeed he was the author of this part of Acts, must have enjoyed writing down.

The Apocalypse

It must be pointed out in fairness that the Apocalypse is so completely overshadowed by the hostility of the Imperial Government to the infant Christian Church in the days of Domitian, that the author can only see the non-Christian Gentile world as hostile and wicked. The same contrast appears indeed as in some of the Pauline writings quoted above, and the vast mass of pagans are thus swept into one general condemnation.

But the Apocalypse cannot thus be dismissed briefly, and it seems best to reserve a special section for dealing with this strange and remarkable book and its influence upon early Christology. I do not propose to discuss problems of text, or to consider whether there has been at some early date an editing of the book or a displacement of paragraphs in it. Such matters may well be left to expert scholars of the calibre of Bernard and Charles. Let us assume that in a form fairly close to that which we now possess, the Apocalypse began to be circulated in the early Church: it is clear that a good many Christians found it both puzzling and even repellent, and that it was a long time, even some centuries, before it attained full canonicity. Yet in spite of this, hardly any New Testament book has been more quoted. The part played by

Shakespeare's *Hamlet* in enriching the English language with proverbial phrases is rivalled among Christians in the part played by the Apocalypse. 'Thou hast lost thy first love'; 'I would thou wert either hot or cold'; 'A new heavens and a new earth'; 'There was no more sea'; 'Worthy is the Lamb that was slain'; 'There shall be no more death, neither sorrow nor crying, neither shall there be any more pain'; 'He before Whom heaven and earth shall flee away'; 'New Jerusalem'. These are only a few of the many familiar and time-honoured phrases. It is the Apocalypse which has incorporated the Old Testament Trisagion into Christian worship. The language and imagery of the Apocalypse have shaped the diction and imagery of John Bunyan, and have been interpreted by the immortal music of George Frederic Handel.

The almost uncanny attraction which the book possesses has, however, led to one unfortunate result. It has tended to obscure the position which the work must have occupied when it was *new*. Here was a composition of a fairly familiar *genre* among first-century Jews, so Jewish in fact that some scholars have even held that it is a Christian adaptation of an originally Jewish work. The author is a prisoner in a small concentration camp of miners on an island in the Aegean who is nevertheless in communication with other Christians dwelling in well-known cities on the mainland of Asia Minor where there were long-established pagan centres of cultus greatly resembling those of India and especially South India. The Christian sect, although spreading already with some rapidity, is still obscure; yet the prophet of Patmos is prepared to make the most astounding, if not to say extravagant, claims for it. He assumes familiarity on the part of his readers with many kinds of contemporary pagan customs and worship of which we know little or nothing, but of the nature of which we can infer a good deal from customs in India or Japan surviving into the nineteenth and twentieth centuries. The multiple-breasted Artemis of Ephesus looks strangely like some representation of Mahadevi, the creatures full of eyes and with multiple wings are completely in the Hindu tradition of intensification by repetition, and the reference to the mark of the Beast on foreheads reminds us of sectarian marks and badges borne by Saivites and Vaishnavites. The frequency of wayside shrines in a Mediterranean city is similar to that to be observed in the narrow lanes of old Kushi (Banaras). In form the cultus of the Mikado prior to 1945 closely resembles that of Caesar.

Yet, formidable as the Christian prophet sees entrenched paganism to be, in a great sweep of inspired vision he gazes beyond it to a world subdued to Christ. So familiar has this vision been made to us by Christian oratorios and hymns, that we almost fail to see how astonishing it is, and how audacious it must have appeared to non-Christian contemporaries. If Porcius Festus could exclaim, after listening to a Christian sermon, Μαίνῃ, Παῦλε, we can well imagine the camp commandant on Patmos saying with equal justification, Μαίνῃ, Ἰωάννε.

Now what is the belief which the prophet says is going to conquer the οἰκουμένην? It is intimately linked up with the historical account which is the climax in all the four canonical gospels. 'I am He that liveth—*and was dead.*' The earthly Jerusalem, 'spiritually called Sodom and Egypt', is pre-eminently the place where the historical Jesus was crucified. No attempt whatever is made to soften down the grim circumstance. The antithesis of utter defeat and humiliation on the one hand, and of complete victory on the other, is preserved without hesitation or apology. The glorious and triumphant dweller in τὰ οὐράνια now above all authority and power, conceived as more terribly dazzling than Apollo and as a mightier wonder-worker than Dionysus, is— a Man who was hanged by order of the Imperial Government! Still more astounding, as coming from the mind of a monotheistic Jew, this historical figure is identified with the A and Ω, 'who is and was and is to come'; while the conquering Messiah of Davidic stock is nakedly and openly denominated the *Logos* of the Supreme Deity.

The inference is obvious. If there is exaggeration or extravagance, it is in the text itself, not in any reading of it by later generations. The still largely Judaic Christian movement, puny, persecuted, and obscure, is towards the close of the first century staking the claim of Jesus to be the *Logos incarnate* as understood by the *goyim*. Historians must judge whether this really was extravagance, or inspired insight.

Summary

The purpose of this chapter has been to show that the Logos of the Johannine writings is not separate from the Logos of the second-century apologists (who according to Bultmann and his supporters use the term in a different sense from John), but is a direct appropriation by him, coming very possibly through Philo, of the current Hellenistic usage, to denote the identity of Jesus with the now personalised cosmic Logos.

What Bultmann says in Volume 2 of his *Theology of the New Testament*:

'No theoretical interest in God's general relation to the world, aside from the history-of-salvation relation, exists as yet, and the Stoic conception of the Logos, which was later taken up by the apologists, is not yet put to service to explain the relation of the transcendent God to the world—not by John, either, for the Logos of his Prologue comes not from the philosophical but from the mythological tradition, and is not used to serve the cosmological interest'

simply does not seem to me to be borne out by the facts.   It seems to me that to postulate the idea of a gnostic myth is just to introduce a complication which is entirely unnecessary.   To say that any philosophical thought of the Logos as controlling the rational orderliness of the divine cosmos is quite foreign to the Johannine author, wilfully ignores the assertion: 'All things were made by Him [the Logos], and without Him was not anything made.'

Bultmann indeed seems to be arguing against himself when he admits that the title 'Logos' is not here derived from the Old Testament, because there we never find 'the Word' but always 'the Word of the Lord' or 'of God': for in that case the only real alternative source must be the secular literature of the Encyclia on which also Philo depends.   From where else could it have come, which would make it a term easily intelligible to *goyim*?   How many of the literates among the latter would know about a 'gnostic myth' compared with those who would know Logos as a familiar term in Stoicism?

But if my contention is accepted, then there is no gap or discordance between the Gospel and the apologists of the second century, and their doctrine can be said truly to represent the mind of the developing church, a mind which subsequent generations of theologians have not until recent years brought seriously into doubt.

CHAPTER VII

THE PHENOMENON OF ISLAM

Islam stands in a totally different position from the other Asian religions. Unlike them it does not claim to be of immemorial antiquity, but if we leave out Marxism for the present as a rather controversial subject, it is the one great Faith which has arisen since the beginning of the Christian era, and the one which most definitely claims to supersede Christianity. On a rough estimate the world contains something like 300 million Moslems, and these are mainly distributed round what has been known as the heat-belt—roughly one-seventh of the population of the world.

The story of the life of Mohammed, and of the rise of the movement connected with him has been told so often in recent years that it may seem somewhat superfluous to repeat it again. In a popular form it appeared in Mr. H. G. Wells's *Outline of History*, and as the latter made no pretence of being a Christian, it might be thought that his account would have been an impartial one. As it happens, however, he is inclined to be hostile to the Prophet, and (rather surprisingly) to adopt something fairly close to the traditional Christian view. Elements in this view are unfortunately (because true) inevitable, even in a balanced description of the man, but they need to be combined with other features. It is, for instance, unfair to judge Mohammed by a standard which he did not know. It is also necessary to remember that even orthodox Moslems admit that he was a fallible human being, albeit the mouthpiece of *wahj* or divine revelation. Moreover it cannot be denied that Mohammed did also display certain rather attractive features in his personality. These have been summed up in a sentence of Professor Gibb as: 'Unmistakeably a largeness of humanity, sympathy for the weak, a gentleness that seldom turned to anger save when dishonour seemed to be done to God, something even of shyness in personal intercourse, and a glint of humour.' It may be recalled that he lived faithfully and happily with his wife Khadijah until her death, that he had a number of friends who showed him to the end considerable affection and loyalty, and that some of his sayings have a clarity and power which verges upon real greatness. A man asked him how he was to commemorate his mother. The Prophet answered: 'Dig a well, and give water to the thirsty.' Even in the later parts of the

Qur'ān there are passages of a spiritual and practical nature which
are in themselves quite admirable:

'There is no piety in turning your faces toward the east or the west,
but he is pious who believes in God, and the last day, and the angels,
and the Scriptures, and the prophets; who for the love of God dis-
burses his wealth to his kindred, and to the orphans, and the needy,
and the wayfarer, and those who ask, and for ransoming, who
observes prayer, and pays the legal alms, and who is of those who are
faithful to their engagements when they have engaged in them, and
patient under ills and hardships, and in time of trouble; these are they
who are just, and these are they who fear the Lord.'

'Avoid what is forbidden, then you will be the most zealous in the
service of God; be content with what God has given you, you will be
the richest; do good to your neighbour, you will be a believer; wish
for men what you wish for yourself, you will be a Muslim; laugh not
overmuch, for much laughter kills the mind.'

According to tradition Mohammed was born in 570 A.D. as a
member of a family which is said to have been entrusted with the
guardianship of the local sanctuary.   Mecca is on a very old trade
route, and its surroundings are barren; but it was a market centre,
and the Quraish, Mohammed's tribe, are said to have been bedouin
who came and settled there, adopted a static life shortly before 500
A.D., and by the time of his birth had become urban traders.   Gibb
rejects the long-lived idea that Islam is the religion of the desert, but
I cannot help feeling that he goes too far in this respect.   In that
region of the world 'the desert' and 'the sown' are never very far
apart.   Nomads come in to urban life and drift out again from it
easily, while the memory of it is fresh in their minds.   Whether it be
Arabia, North Africa, or Pakistan, the arid desert-spaces are never
very far away, and one can travel quickly and easily into them.   The
picture given by Asad shows clearly that the Arab takes readily to
the ideal of simplicity: even when urbanised, he retains something of
it in his houses and his domestic customs, and he views critically the
complications in the city life of the Western world.   Nevertheless it
is true that young Mohammed, after being left an orphan at an early
age and brought up by his uncle, became a caravan trader, and a
business man.   By the time he was grown up, Mecca had become a
place of wealth and business, a kind of trade-link between India and
the Mediterranean.   Thus, while one is permitted to believe that the
Meccans retained a certain degree of simplicity, they were not
isolated either from the Byzantine or the Indian worlds.   There
were many Jews in the south, and especially at Yathrib, better known
by its later name of Medina (lit. *the* town—Medinat-al-nabi in full,
i.e. Prophet's-town).

How much contact Mohammed had with Christians we shall
12

never know.   It is quite certain that at this time there were Christians in Arabia, though of what sort it is difficult to be certain.   At any rate there were organised churches in the north, south, and east, and Hira on the Euphrates, the seat of a Nestorian bishopric, was an Arab town.   In the Yemen there was a Christian community which about half a century before the birth of Mohammed had called in Abyssinian Christians to aid it in overthrowing a Judaising movement.   The Qur'ān very obviously contains many quotations from the Talmud and other extra-canonical Jewish literature, and from apocryphal Christian books, such as the Protevangelium of James. Sweetman, however, is disposed to think that there are echoes of passages even from the canonical New Testament.   The misfortune is that in so far as Mohammed depended upon this literature he seems either to have misunderstood it, or to have had only a very scrappy and imperfect acquaintance with it, and it is most certain that at times he totally misconceived the nature of orthodox Christianity.   This is not to deny that there was a strong element of originality about his own mind, nor can we feel at all certain that if we had been confronted ourselves with the Christianity which he saw around him we should not have felt grave dissatisfaction with it.   But if one is seeking successfully to embark upon a great movement of religious reform, it is a disadvantage of a most serious and decisive character to start from a whole chain of misunderstandings.   It is, of course, extremely difficult to get Moslem scholars and theologians even to begin to accept the possibility of such misunderstandings, but it is certain that the attempt must be made, and that one must appeal to educated Moslems to face the facts, even if they seem unwelcome. For facts they are, and can be attested by reference to the various texts.   Hitherto it has been difficult to accustom Moslems to a critical study of the text of the Qur'ān of the kind which is an everyday and familiar matter to Christian scholars dealing with the text of the New Testament.   Once, however, this difficulty has been surmounted, it will be possible for both sides to agree in an appreciation of the evident virtues of Mohammed's character, while accepting its limitations.   Perhaps no religion starts from zero, and it is quite clear that a number of familiar words in Syriac Christianity were adapted to the use of Islam.

In the matter of the Old Testament, it should be remembered that Mohammed claimed to be spiritually (as well as physically) in descent from Abraham, and he selected a number of Old Testament characters, called by him 'prophets', linking him up with Abraham and also with Jesus.   But it is curious that among these he does not include the great Hebrew prophets like Isaiah, Jeremiah, and

Ezekiel, or even Amos, with whose utterances Christians are familiar. One would think he could hardly have known about them, and yet for the establishment of a chain of prophecy they would seem essential both to Jews and Christians.

In many ways Mohammed in his earlier phase reminds one of the prophet Amos, or of the prophet who uttered the first chapter of Isaiah. He saw clearly the darker side of Meccan society, and he was horrified and indignant at its social iniquities. He did not preach a social revolution, but he declared dishonesty in trade and business, and the oppression of hirelings, to be offences against Almighty God, and he warned those who committed them of the danger of impending Judgment. Indeed, one of the chief impressions which is produced on one by a first reading of the Qur'ān is the tremendous insistence with which the doctrine of Judgment and Hell is hammered in. No revivalist hot-gospeller could be more emphatic, and in one sense there is nothing really inconsistent with the utterances of a Christian mission preacher. When Paul before Felix reasoned of 'righteousness, temperance, and Judgment to come' we learn that Felix trembled, as well he might. But in this matter Paul was only doing in his day what Mohammed did later on, and it cannot but be noticed that the most recent Continental influence in the preaching of Christianity is in the direction of reminding us that we all stand under the Judgment of God. Where of course Mohammed was limited was in his corresponding lack of emphasis upon the redeeming love of God.

It would appear that this very simple preaching about the Four Last Things on the part of Mohammed went on for about ten years with meagre results, and the story of the beginnings of the expansion of his little movement is a curious one. Indeed it is not quite easy to see why his removal from Mecca to Medina should have made so much difference, except that the Medinans, having invited Mohammed to come to them, accepted him as their leader, and so allowed him to organise them on a pattern which up to the present had only been implicit in his mind, but now received an explicit shape. Medina in fact became the model of what Mohammed thought a Moslem community ought to be. The next step of course was to win Mecca, and for this purpose Mohammed seems clearly to have accepted it as inevitable that he should use military coercion. It is true that he never employed armed force until diplomacy had failed, but he showed no scruple about fighting and killing when these were necessary. He ruthlessly liquidated the Jews at Yathrib when he believed them to be plotting against him, and although he ended by making a compromise with the Meccans which was favourable to his own plans, he did so after blockading the city into surrender.

How far at this time Mohammed saw himself as a world leader may be doubted. He clearly imagined that there would be some kind of expansion of his movement outside Arabia, and he spent considerable pains in training his immediate followers in loyalty and zeal over the propagation of his religious and social beliefs. But the story that in 628 he wrote challenges to the Byzantine Emperor, to the Persian King, and to other potentates, is perhaps a tendentious legend. Gibb thinks that shortly before his death in 632 he was certainly contemplating some kind of action against the Byzantine empire. What seems clear is that his religious beliefs, based as they were upon a misunderstanding of both Judaism and Christianity, led him to disappointment. Neither Jews nor Christians would accept him as their leader, and this may very well have embittered him against them. It is also clear that there was in him a strong and growing element of Arab patriotism. He united the Arabian tribes in a campaign in which religious enthusiasm was combined with an enthusiasm for *Lebensraum*. If on the one side he looks when at his best something like an Arabian Luther, and indeed holds the allegiance and affection of Arabs in much the same way that Luther holds the allegiance and affection of many Central European Christians, on the other side there is an equally strong flavour about him of Hitler in his earlier stages. One people, one faith, one leader—that seems to be the slogan. But one must hasten to guard against any tendency to carry this analogy too far. No fair-minded historian can evade the conclusion that there was *some* decline in idealism during the lifetime of Mohammed, but there was never the downfall to degradation which blackens the memory of the *Führer*. To the end Mohammed remained a centre of true loyalty, and whatever weaknesses he may have shown, the final speech delivered by him shortly before his death is one which commands our respect and even admiration. It is in the old vein:

Ye people, hearken to my words; for I know not whether, after this year, I shall ever be amongst you here again.

Your lives and property are sacred and inviolable amongst one another until the end of time.

The Lord hath ordained to every man the share of his inheritance; a testament is not lawful to the prejudice of heirs.

The child belongeth unto the parent; and the violator of wedlock shall be stoned.

Whoever claimeth falsely another for his father or another for his master, the curse of God and the angels and of all mankind shall rest upon him.

Ye people. Ye have rights demandable of your wives, and they have rights demandable of you. Upon them it is incumbent not to violate their conjugal faith nor commit any act of impropriety; which things if they do, ye have authority to shut them up in separate apartments and to beat them with stripes, yet not severely. But if they refrain therefrom, clothe them and feed them suitably. And treat your women well, for they are with you as captives and prisoners; they have not power over any thing as regards themselves. And ye have verily taken them on the security of God, and have made their persons lawful unto you by the words of God.

And your slaves, see that ye feed them with such food as ye eat yourselves, and clothe them with the stuff ye wear. And if they commit a fault which ye are not inclined to forgive, then sell them, for they are servants of the Lord, and are not to be tormented.

Ye people. Hearken to my speech and comprehend the same. Know that every Moslem is the brother of every other Moslem. All of you are on the same equality.

This is what the Hadith or tradition ascribes to Mohammed as his farewell utterance, and in it we see the best of the man, as well as features which are not so good. It is clearly an address of a man to men, and no equality of the sexes is assumed; but the treatment of slaves is humanised, and made no doubt a good deal less unpleasant than it was before. Yet there is no suggestion that all individual souls are of equal worth, so that all slaves should be freed. It is only all male Moslems who are brothers.

The special features and perhaps we *must* say weaknesses of the Qur'ān have been worked over again and again. It was clearly intended by the Prophet as a counterpart and rival to the Tawrat and the Injil, and it is equally clear that it is a collection of deliverances (or Suras) not entirely made during his life-time, and that some Suras are late, others early, while some of the long ones are conflations of shorter logia. It is in fact a compilation of the same sort as (e.g.) the book of Isaiah. There is considerable repetition of a limited number of themes, which are hammered home to ensure that they are not forgotten. Some critics have described it as a dreary welter. Others have compared it to Mrs. Eddy's *Science and Health* in its verbosity and reiterations. But critics may easily be unfair. In the Arabic it rolls out impressively and with majestic rhythm, and it certainly contains fine poetic passages. If some of its doctrines fall short of enunciating Christian ideals, and if others seem perversely ignorant or mistaken; yet it also enshrines, preserves, transmits, and by recitation ensures the renewal of much fervent and sincere religious experience; and it is with the generous recognition of the latter that we must start, even if we have to go on afterwards to criticise. But with the doctrine of verbal inspiration we can have no truck. Whether in the case of the Bible or the Qur'ān, this is, of course, a superstition which has sternly to be banished.

It must ever remain a matter of deep regret that the Christian and Moslem movements drifted into opposition from the very first. The fault cannot be said to have been entirely that of Mohammed and his followers. No serious attempt within his lifetime ever seems to have been made to remove his misapprehension. To the end he was quite ignorant of the true nature of the doctrine of the Trinity. To the end he thought of it as a tritheism of God the Father, Jesus, and Mary—such an elementary error that one wonders how it could possibly have survived. Nor does he seem to have been in the least aware of the insistence upon the Unity of God in the New Testament, or the condemnation of idolatry which appears in its pages. He speaks with reverence of the *Injîl*, but he cannot have been fully aware of its contents. He repeats the non-canonical legend which is to be found in the apocryphal Acts of John that Jesus was never crucified in person, but escaped that indignity. But apart from the New Testament the Christianity which he encountered was very much open to misunderstanding; it was not only divided by controversy, but large sections of it taught doctrines about the person of Jesus which we should today repudiate—some of them verging very nearly upon Apollinarianism, others even disparaging the value of the Passion. It seems quite certain that Mohammed had no proper idea of the true Catholic doctrine of the Incarnation, although it is noticeable that he accepted the belief in the Virgin Birth. In the end he comes to think of himself not only as a successor to Jesus but as the *only* successor. It is difficult to be sure how much of this was sincere fanaticism and how much was vanity.

The assertion may sometimes be seen, that the doctrine of Mohammed actually represents an advance in the expansion of theistic belief. This is not borne out by the facts, and it is a pity that responsible scholars should lend their support to the statement. It may well be conceded that Islam was in a sense an attempt at the reformation and simplification of theism, and that some of its emphases were actually needed at the time, just as Mrs. Eddy's emphasis upon the healing ministry of the Christian Church was needed in its own day as a corrective to the under-emphasis on that ministry by orthodox Christians. But both movements were based upon misunderstandings and upon unsound intellectual foundations, and cannot therefore be said to lead to real progress. In effect, Islam represents a slight step backward, a retreat to pre-Christian Judaism, instead of an advance from it. Instead of 'the Word became Flesh' we have rather 'the Word became Book'. Although the physical limitations of Judaism are rejected, and a Moslem Church becomes substituted for a Christian Church, a new legalism is imposed, that of the Sharia, in its way quite as cramping as that of the old Jewish Torah; while there is also the promulgation of what is in many respects a lower and more easily attainable moral standard. The majesty of God is certainly emphasised, but not to any greater degree than it has in the past been emphasised by great Christians; and the sterility of the relations which prevail in Islam between God and the soul is rather curious and surprising. No Moslem has ever written, or perhaps could write, a book like St. Augustine's *Confessions*, and even where the utterances of Sufis approach most nearly to it, they seem least Moslem.

The reason why there were estrangement and misunderstanding between Islam and Christianity from the very lifetime of Mohammed onwards deserves a little closer scrutiny; and this was undertaken by the late Dr. Richard Bell. His elucidation of it may be summarised as follows.

In the first place it is very clear that however imperfect may have been Mohammed's knowledge of the Bible and of Christian doctrine, he did start from a number of ideas which belonged to the Hebraeo-Christian religious complex, and are found in Palestine in the first century A.D. For example, Mohammed lays stress upon fleeing from the *Rugz*, which is not properly translated Abomination, but rather Wrath (i.e. Divine Wrath). He speaks of this in Sura lxxiv, which is one of the shortest and earliest, and the word used comes straight out of the Syriac New Testament, being there used in Matthew 3:7 in the form *rugza*, where John the Baptist said: 'Who hath warned you to flee from the *rugza*?' Following on this we get Mohammed's tremendous insistence upon the Divine Judgment which is a cardinal feature of Jewish Apocalyptic as well as early Christian literature. The word *furqan*, says Bell, is of great significance. It means deliverance, and in the Old Testament is associated with Moses and the deliverance of Israel from the hosts of Pharaoh, and then applied to Mohammed and his deliverance from his enemies through the (divinely ordained) victory of Badr. But it is also used of the action of Allah in regard to the believer who receives a *furqan* or deliverance from judgment by the mercy of Allah, who forgives his sins. Nothing here is said about the Atonement through the Passion of Jesus. Jesus is brought into the Proclamation, but his office and function are clearly misunderstood. He is a successor of the prophets, and the believing Jews are those that accept Him, while the unbelieving and evil Jews are those who reject Him. At first sight this almost looks like an agreement with the Christian position. But then, as Mohammed goes on, he becomes more and more aware of the alleged position of Abraham as the divinely accredited begetter of a new race or seed of believers; and he then goes on further to become aware of the existence of Ishmael and the story of Abraham, as the alleged ancestor of the Arab people. At this point he begins to deviate seriously. Accepting the tradition of the Arabs as the descendants of Abraham through Ishmael, he treats them as the physical rivals of the Jews, and sees in them the guardians of the pure monotheism of Abraham, before it had become perverted by the Jews and Christians. Both these latter groups in Arabia have declined to accept him and to co-operate with him as their religious leader, and therefore he becomes increasingly hostile to them, and justifies this hostility by the foregoing legend. But of course his exegesis of the Old Testament with regard to Ishmael will not bear scrutiny, and it is in any case just as much bound up with a physical conception of vocation as in the case of the Jews. It is clear, however, that this exegesis determined Mohammed's obstinate refusal to accept the message of the Christians, and he followed this up by declaring that the message of Jesus had been as purely monotheistic as his own, but that the Christians had perverted it by deliberately corrupting the text of the New Testament: and this again, of course, will not stand critical scrutiny.

SUFISM

Various suggestions have been made as to the origin of the word Sufi, such as *safa*—purity, *sufa*—bench (i.e. poor Moslems sitting on a bench outside the mosque), and σόφος—the wise person. But none of these is as satisfactory or as likely to be correct as the simplest one, i.e. *suf* or wool, to wit the coarse woollen garment commonly worn by ascetics.

It seems clear now that although the actual origin of the Sufis is still obscure, they were Moslems who were much influenced by the austere spirituality of Christian monks and hermits, and who felt that Islam as it had been left organised by Mohammed and his immediate disciples did not meet the call to a life of spiritual perfection. The title Sufi is said to have been first borne by a Moslem who died in 778 A.D., but Sufism as a widespread movement seems to develop after the time of the great Moslem mystic, Al Ghazzali, who lived in the early twelfth century. It clearly owes much both to ascetic Christianity, to Neo-Platonism, and to Buddhism. But perhaps its real origin may be judged from the way in which some of its leaders paid a special tribute to the historical Jesus as the supreme ascetic, although the actual picture they present of him is a much exaggerated one, and shows little acquaintance with the canonical gospels, only stressing, and indeed over-stressing, some of the ascetic passages which they contain, and representing Our Lord as much more like an Indian *sannyasi*.

There can be little doubt that Sufism developed in response to a real need, and as a reaction against the legalism of orthodox Islam, and its presentation of an attainable standard for everyone. But its interest for the modern world is bound to be limited. In the first place it seems for the past hundred years to have declined very much in importance, and enquiry has elicited the fact that very few observers have come across Sufis.[1] Side by side with this, the rather loose organisation of these mystics into 'orders' of dervishes (the word 'darwish' meaning poor) has more or less ceased, existing orders in Turkey having been suppressed by order of the government.

Sufism has no practical side. It produced some superb mystical poetry, and expressed itself in terms of a mystical syncretism; while its actual doctrines are of considerable interest to those who study mystical states of consciousness. But the orders of Sufis do not seem to have occupied themselves in any corporal works of mercy, but to have indulged what must seem to many to be a spiritual selfishness. If one looks at what Miss Underhill says about non-Christian and Christian mystics in general, one can see the point at which the Sufis fall short, although one is bound to admit that even corporal works of mercy may sometimes be done from the wrong motive, and that there is a strong case for the practice of spiritual exercises in order to divest oneself of an egoism which can make even the most practical charity lose its savour.

One account of Sufism describes it as involving a three years' probation, the first being 'service of the people', though on examination this is not found to be what it appears, but only means menial attendance upon the other Sufis; the second, 'Service to Allah'; the third, 'Watching over one's own heart'. Each novice vowed obedience to his shaikh, whose office corresponded to that of the abbot in a Christian monastic house. The path or *tariqa* of the disciple varied in details, but consisted first in fasting, solitude, and silence, to bring the flesh into subjection. This was followed by a series of 'stations', or *maqāmat*, corresponding roughly to the various stages in Hindu *yoga* or in Christian spiritual exercises. The goal was deification, corresponding to the perpetual *samadhi* of the Hindu mystic, and comprised four elements; *fana*, or passing away from individuality, *baqa*, or abiding in God, *faqd*, or loss of self, and *sukr*, or God-intoxication.

[1] I much regret that information about Indian Sufis, courteously provided for me by Professor Valiuddin of the Osmania University, Hyderabad, has arrived too late for me to insert it here: but it seems fairly clear that Sufism is still active in the Moslem areas of the sub-continent.

The *dhikr* of the dervishes was a technique of singing, chanting, or moving the body rhythmically, which aimed at producing some of these states of consciousness.

Sufis, like some modern Hindus, lay stress upon the unity of all religions, without, however, showing any very intimate acquaintance with the tenets of the non-Moslem ones.

In the Divan of Jelaladdin we read:

'True Parsi and true Brahman, a Christian yet a Mussulman,
Thee I trust Supremely right: Be not far, Oh be not far.
In all Mosques, Pagodas, Churches, I do find one shrine alone;
Thy face is there my sole delight; Be not far, Oh be not far.'

Such sentiments cannot fail to excite sympathy, though it is to be noted that they are not those of official Moslem doctrine. What they imply of course is that behind all the different forms of worship there is only One Reality. But it does not follow logically that this Reality is equally well approached by all different forms of worship.

The Reverend Godfrey Phillips, Professor of Missions at Selly Oak, once wrote that it would lift a burden from many consciences if we were to recognise that it is *our* God who is approached by the most primitive savage, *our* God who is addressed in bhakti hymns, and *our* God who is the object of the yogi's adoration and of the Moslem's obedience. (I have ventured to paraphrase him.) Yet one is certain that Professor Phillips, as a Christian, would feel that in genuine Christian worship and life there was the highest approach to the One Reality. This situation expressed itself on one occasion in my own experience when I was attending an international conference, members of which belonged to most of the great religions. We felt that each day we ought to begin with prayer, and we did so by going into the chapel provided in the building, and staying there for a short space in Quaker silence. We found this a very helpful and satisfying time of worship; but we all agreed that we could not have done it together if we had tried to put, each of us, his or her act of worship into words, since in that case some of the expressions we should have used would have been not so much complementary to one another, as contradictory of one another. There would have been few, if any, words of prayer which we could have said in unison. Some of us might have used the same prayer by putting different interpretations upon it, but others would have found no such prayer capable of being used. There could therefore have been no complete unity of worship in vocal prayer. And yet in silence we could all feel that we were seeking to harmonise ourselves with the One Reality.

We may remark in conclusion that when Henry Martyn at the beginning of the nineteenth century visited Persia, he found Sufism active, and compared its devotees to the Methodists with whom he was familiar in Christian England—a remarkably interesting judgment, providing much food for thought. One's own personal experience is that the Senussi of North Africa are still more like Methodists. They are earnest and punctilious, live certainly 'according to method', and not without cause regard their non-Senussi neighbours as slack and degenerate.

THE SIKHS

The Sikh community may be taken as an example of an attempt at producing a hybrid religion out of Hinduism and Islam. Founded between 1469 and 1538 by Nanak, a Hindu from Lahore who had come under strong Moslem influence in Banaras, it has survived as a sort of social and political as well as religious unit, with a distinct costume and social customs. Anyone who hires a taxi-cab in Calcutta will probably find himself being driven by a romantic figure somewhat resembling Michel Angelo's Moses, with a huge turban and a long beard. The industry is in fact largely in the hands of Sikhs. Sikhs wherever they go wear their heads covered, and like some orthodox Jews allow their beards and hair to grow. A Sikh who applied for work in Birmingham failed in his application because he refused to shave off his beard. Such ritual intransigence may seem trivial, but it is the outward sign that Sikhs feel that they belong to an exclusive community, set apart like the Jews. They reject idolatry, and their worship consists in the recitation of their sacred scriptures, the Granth-sahib, which comprises a number of religious lyrics composed by the founder, but also a number of similar poems by various medieval Hindu saints who were theistic in their beliefs.

Somewhat earlier than Nanak there flourished a teacher from Banaras called Kabir, who also tried to form a hybrid system between Hinduism and Islam. His experiment did not lead to the gathering of a large body of adherents, but his influence is still acknowledged by a number of small sects, the largest, the Kabir-panthis, being of about the strength of a million. Hymns by Kabir are included in the Granth-sahib. His theology is eclectic, and oscillates between pantheism and theism, but he rejects the idea of avatars, the practices of circumcision and idol-worship, and the institution of caste. Some of his poems display great beauty of thought and language: but there is no finality about his position, and it is easy to see why both the Sikhs and the disciples of Kabir have remained minority movements. In 1941 the number of Sikhs was given in census returns as about $5\frac{1}{2}$ millions, mostly resident in the Panjab.

C. F. Andrews in an article on 'The Genuine Islam', 1936, sums up by saying: 'One of the greatest blessings which Islam has brought to

East and West alike has been the emphasis which at a critical period in history it placed upon the Divine Unity; for during 600–1000 A.D., Dark Ages both in East and West, this doctrine was in danger of being overlaid and obscured in Hinduism and Christianity itself, owing to the immense accretions of subsidiary worships of countless demi-gods and heroes. . . . Indeed, with the final emphasis on this truth, which Islam gains from its central position, facing India and facing Europe —it is doubtful whether this idea of God as One could have obtained that established place in human thought which is uncontested in the intellectual world today.'

I should like to cap this by a magnificent story from Moslem tradition, which shows how early Moslems were possessed by the sense of the majesty and nearness of God. It is, however, I think slightly tinged, as so many Hadith stories are, by moral influences from Christianity.

The Caliph Omar is said to have been travelling from Medina to Mecca, when he met a negro slave tending sheep. Omar asked him to sell one of his lambs. The boy said: 'No, they're not mine, but my master's.' 'But he'll never know,' replied Omar. 'You can tell him that one was snatched away by a wolf.' The negro boy answered with dignity: 'I might be able to cheat my master, but how can I cheat Allah, that Great Master who sees us, and listens to us?' Omar was so overcome that he burst into tears, went to the owner of the slave, asked how much he had paid for him, put down the money, and said: 'Set the boy free.'

Such a tale must be an inspiration to anyone, of any faith or no faith at all.

CHAPTER VIII

RESEMBLANCES AND FUNDAMENTAL DIFFERENCES

The Tariano Indians of the Upper Amazon have a grim and curious custom. When one of their great chieftains dies they cremate him. They then take his ashes and calcined bones and grinding them into a powder, mix them with their native alcohol. This potent draught is then drunk with some ceremony, and is believed to impart to them the strength and virtue of the departed hero. Sacramental acts and practices of this kind can be collected from many parts of the world, and it is always possible for the anthropologist to say that the Christian Sacrament of Communion is only another instance of the same kind of practice.

The comparative study of religions ever since the days of Sir James Frazer seems to have been associated in the minds of most people, and perhaps not altogether unjustly, with conclusions of this sort. The game is only too easy to play at. A very large number of monographs are assembled, each one dealing with the spiritual and material culture of some primitive people, the contents of the various chapters are put side by side, and the conclusion is readily arrived at that religious practices after all resemble one another in most parts of the world. Although this is really not quite the case, it is near enough to the truth to enable the observer to indulge in a little chirp of self-satisfaction, and to suppose that he has explained away Christianity by reducing the whole of it to a survival of various features from primitive religion. But the matter is not so easily to be disposed of as that, and we ought ever to be on our guard against the fallacy of 'nothing but', or of the *reductio ad minimum*.

Apparent resemblances in custom and in ceremony do not necessarily mean resemblances in thought. Not infrequently a ceremony persists with very little change or modification right through the history of the religion of a people, yet with its inner meaning changed perhaps once, perhaps more than once, during the same period. It would obviously never do to say that the very widespread custom of ceremonially washing infants always meant the same thing everywhere. Of course it does not, and it would be absurd to say that the doctrine lying behind Christian baptism was no more than that lying behind the quasi-baptismal ceremony performed by the same Tariano Indians over their young children. It

179

would even be unsafe to say that the doctrine of Christian baptism itself had remained unchanged throughout the course of the history of the Christian Church. It certainly has not, and it would be easy to show from the attempts at altering words, phrases, and prayers in the office for the administration of baptism, that variations in the interpretation of scripture and in the doctrine of man were involved in them.

Nevertheless, there is certainly some good to be got out of a study not only of the ceremonies and institutions but also of the beliefs current among the votaries of religion in various ages, partly because the resemblances tend to show a relatedness rather than an identity between the various religious systems, a universality in the prevalence of various hopes and fears, and a measure of similarity between the means adopted for the realisation of those hopes and the dispelling of those fears. Thus these quasi-baptismal rites seem to indicate a dim sense that the state of the human race is such that merely being physically born as a member of it is not in itself enough. But enough for what? There is the rub. In some very simple cases the assumption may be that there is only a kind of physical defilement to be washed off. Further experience may lead to the conclusion that the infant may be in need of some higher status being granted to it than simply that of being the child of its parents. Or there may be some idea that as soon as it is born influences from the bad sacred may be ready to pounce upon it, and that these may need to be dispelled, driven away, or nullified. It is perhaps not only in the Christian gospel that we find the idea of being born again not of corruptible seed but of incorruptible.

The study of the various types of communion meal may yield the same kind of conclusion. Right through may run the fundamental assumption that, as an Indian once said, 'no man can succeed in life alone, and he cannot get all the help he needs simply from his neighbour'. From the outset it is felt that some enhancement of our normal powers is not only to be sought but is actually obtainable from a kind of supernatural reservoir of power. How this reservoir is to be tapped and made available for our use is a question that is answered in a variety of ways. Obviously one way is to do some corporate act such as hauling, rowing, chopping, or fighting, in unison, and at the same time to chant rhythmically. This is plainly the theory behind sea-shanties, mowing and harvesting songs, and battle chants. The latter are not only intended to terrify the enemy, but to build up the strength of the singers; and it is an actual experience that rhythmical action in unison, as well as singing or shouting in unison, does in some way increase the dynamic force wielded by the actors. Again, the power of suggestion works mightily when it is a case of eating or drinking something which is believed to be a means of eating or drinking the strength of an animal-totem, a departed chieftain, or a god. It is not only the Christian theologian who is able to affirm: 'Crede, et manducasti.' But here again caution is needed. Although the technique may be one of suggestion, the result need not necessarily be due to belief in an illusion, though that will work, up to the point at which the illusion is dispelled. As long as it is believed in, it may well have some effect, but once its true nature is exposed, it will cease to be efficacious. Thus the Christian sacrament of communion does not depend entirely upon a primitive belief. The ancient sacramental technique has been grafted on to a confident hope dependent upon and justified by obedience. Obedience to Christ's injunction 'This do' carries with it the fulfilment of the promise 'He that eateth me, even he shall live by me'. The sacrament, in the words of the Anglican catechism, is the outward visible sign of an inward spiritual grace, and that grace is granted in return for obedience to the divine command coupled with the correct disposition. The ceremony is thus a moral and not a magical one, although its ancestry may have contained magical elements. It is not what the ceremony of the sacrament has evolved from, but what it has grown into that matters.

The study of resemblances in forms of worship and sacrifice, if reverently conducted, is therefore far from being unfruitful. It may teach us to deal gently with 'the sacraments of simple folk',[1] and sometimes to use them for the illustration of Christian ideas, to which it may not be difficult to adapt them. In Ceylon for example, it has been found possible and edifying to convert an animistic harvest ceremony into a Christian one, while still retaining some of its ritual. We may also gain a sense of the unity and relatedness of the acts of religious worship, though not, of course, of their identity in all respects. Thus a jungle tribe in Central India offers a sacrifice to a female tutelary deity in the following manner: A place is chosen with a flat stone, the people are assembled round it, and the pujari or sacrificing minister receives the offering of a fowl. He then kills it, sprinkles the blood, and lays the corpse of the victim for a short time upon the flat stone. All this is accompanied by certain set words which are not in the vernacular, but apparently in some archaic tongue. After the victim's body has remained on the stone for a short space, the virtue in it is believed to have been absorbed by the deity to whom it is offered, and it is then removed, cut in pieces, and eaten by the congregation, who believe that in this way

[1] The phrase comes from Dr. R. R. Marett.

they are receiving into themselves the strength of the goddess. Finally, the residue of the sacrifice is burned in a fire, the altar slab is washed clean, and the congregation disperses. In China, up to the year after the establishment of the first republic, there had been offered from time immemorial a great annual sacrifice to the Supreme God in the Chinese pantheon, together with his less eminent colleagues, and the details of this have been carefully preserved. The ceremony took place in the centre of the white marble temple of heaven at Peking, and was performed with great magnificence, the celebrant being the emperor himself, although most of the ritual was actually performed for him by proxy. The structure of this Chinese liturgy was almost exactly that of a high mass. Within a great circle approached by flights of steps were a number of altars, one for the burnt sacrifice, another for incense, and another for the burning of various votive objects. On one side stood a choir with an orchestra, and in another place a group of ceremonial dancers. The service included a number of hymns, and began with one which took the form of an introit. There was no reading or chanting from sacred books, but after the introit came a series of oblations, first that of a slain bullock, then offerings of jade, silk, wine, incense, and finally a specially composed prayer for the blessing of heaven upon the nation during the coming year. During the singing of a kind of communion hymn the emperor received some of the food and drink which had previously been offered, the drink being from the cup of wine. Following on this there was a post-communion ceremony, and the various consecrated objects which remained on the altars were put in a furnace and consumed, and the vessels cleansed. Finally, a herald, who had previously announced the beginning of the sacrifice, proclaimed that it was over, and dismissed the congregation very much in the way in which a Christian congregation has been dismissed at the conclusion of the Latin rite with the words 'Ite missa est.'

There is something strangely moving about the general similarity in structure and outline between these two sacrificial rites, the one so humble and homely, the other so stately and magnificent, and moreover between their general outline and that of the Christian eucharist as it has come to take shape throughout the greater part of the Christian world. Again, there is a relatedness; but while the general structure has remained constant, it has been filled out with an entirely new meaning.

These are only examples of the kind of resemblances which may be found throughout the religious world. It would be possible to multiply them almost indefinitely. We could stress, for instance, if we desired so to do, the similarities between a Buddhist and a Christian choir-office, with its chanting of sacred books and its sermon. Or we could draw out the fundamental similarities between the various types of wedding ceremony, in which there is almost always the rite performed by the bride and bridegroom of pledging themselves to share a common life of comradeship, together with some kind of propitiatory offering to the supernatural in order to obtain its blessing upon the newly wedded couple; but in addition to this there will be a wealth of different customs belonging to different localities, and these, although hallowed by long-continued usage, will not be of fundamental importance.

All this can be very entertaining, and indeed sometimes instructive, but a great deal of it can only be of antiquarian interest, and may merely lead the student to the acquisition of a kind of mental museum of curiosities. The more serious business begins when we go on to study the contributions of the various great prophets and sages who have founded religious systems of their own, which may have adopted into themselves many of the institutional ceremonies of previously existing religions, but which have on the whole preserved the fundamental tenets of the founders, and have sometimes modified the previously existing institutions so as to express the new ideas contributed by their founders.

When we reach this point, the divergences between Christianity and the non-Christian faiths become for us of vital importance. The tendency which one comes chiefly to associate with philosophical Hinduism, but which may be found asserted by a good many in the west today who would not call themselves Hindus (however much they may have been influenced by the teachings of some of the latter), namely that all religions have a fundamental identity, and are only different aspects of one central reality, and each as good as its fellow, is one which finds expression with easy confidence on the lips of a great many people who have not thought very deeply upon the matter, or who have not seriously considered the fundamental differences which also exist.

Thus it is all very well to compare Buddhist and Christian choir-offices; but one must not stop there, but must go on to consider the doctrines which lie behind each, and which often vary, as we shall see, so profoundly. If, for instance, a Theravada monk could say to a Christian bishop when he was asked what he was doing: 'I am praying to nobody for nothing', it is difficult to see how such a monk could logically be invited to offer vocal prayer in a Christian building side by side with theists. Or again, though there are certain Hindu and Moslem prayers which with very little

13

interpretation could be used by Christians, it is necessary to ask in what sense, and to what kind of Being, such prayers are offered by the Hindus and Moslems who habitually use them. Unless the latter are coming to modify their doctrinal beliefs under Christian influence, and are in this way developing a less distinctively Hindu or Moslem doctrine of deity, it is clear that fundamentally they mean something different from what Christians mean, and this difference is so great that both cannot be right. It is not a matter of three people seeing three different facets of one Supreme Jewel. The several ideas are actually incompatible with one another. The doctrine of deity in the Vedanta, in bhakti Hinduism, in Islam, and in orthodox Christianity is really different, and although sometimes the edges of the difference may become blurred through association (since the different religious systems live in the same world, sometimes borrow one another's language, and share in rivalry and competition), nevertheless the basic conceptions of the Self-Existent are not the same.

It is perhaps this fundamental difference which more than anything else expresses itself in the pastoral system of the Christian Church, taken in its widest sense. This does not mean that there is not spiritual leadership, instruction, and supervision supplied by Hindu gurus, Buddhist monks, and Moslem mullahs. But there is nothing in any of these systems (unless where they have begun to borrow from Christianity), which really resembles the pastoral care of Christian ministers for their flock. It is difficult to imagine a treatise or manual on pastoral theology written for Hindus, Buddhists, Moslems, Parsis, or Sikhs. Christian ministers in any denomination may fall short in the performance of their duty, but nothing can take away from them the fact that it is their duty, explicitly stated, and implied in the words of the gospels and in the example of Christ, to care for the people committed to their charge, as *God* cares for them. To put it in other words, the pastoral duty is firmly rooted in the belief that the Self-Existent Deity is a definite and particular kind of Being. The pastoral duty rests upon theology. Take away or alter the theology, and the motive for the pastoral care is deprived of its basis. Pastoral care rests upon the conviction that the Self-Existent Deity has brought creatures like ourselves into existence in order that they may be His intelligent friends and fellow-workers in the achievement of His great cosmic purposes. He loves each one of them with a discerning and loving wisdom as though each one was the only being in the world. This love is supremely shown not merely in our creation, preservation, and all the blessings of this life, but in the great self-giving action when the very God himself took a human life, and in it expressed the depth and extent of what that love could mean, i.e. a ministry of healing and compassion culminating in Calvary.   Wherever Christian ministers are at work they have before their eyes the words 'As my Father hath sent me, even so send I you', and they know with fear and trembling that God's honour is in their hands, and that his pastoral love for his creatures must be expressed through their own unworthy ministrations.   I defy anyone to read the charge which is delivered by a bishop in my communion to those whom he is about to ordain as priests without feeling his heart 'strangely warmed', and without being conscious that however noble some of the great religions of the world may seem, they have nothing in them to compare with this in its expression of a supreme belief about Deity, which lies behind it.

The practice of making sacrificial offerings is common to most early religions, and as we have seen the pattern of these ceremonial acts is very much the same everywhere, partly, one supposes, because an action in which something is given to a Divine Being can only be performed in certain ways.   If the offering is of something alive then it will have to be killed.   If it is something raw it may have to be cooked.   If it is liquid it will have to be poured out.   If it is some passive object such as flowers or cereals it is natural to put it on some kind of table.   If the offering is to be followed by a communal meal, this will take place after the actual sacrifice and certainly after the object offered has been dedicated.   We have noticed already that at the approach of the axial age one of its features is the introduction of the idea of inward and spiritual sacrifice, and in this Stoics, Buddhists, and Hebrew prophets within their own separate contexts seem to say much the same thing.   Yet the doctrine of spiritual sacrifice as taught in orthodox Christianity is unique.   It not only abolishes all the old sacrificial practices, but declares that even at their highest and best they are bound to be inadequate, since Man by reason of his position is in himself incapable of making any perfect offering.   The Christian declares that although the kind of statements made in the 40th and 50th psalms are good so far as they go, even the offering of the penitent's broken heart in Psalm 51 is not enough.   Even the self-offering of the Stoic wise man is not good enough, since the very best and wisest fall short of the ideal, and share also in the corporate sins of the society of which they are members. All man can do then is to unite himself in his obvious unworthiness and incompleteness with the full, perfect, and sufficient sacrifice of Christ; and that really means accepting and appropriating God's own gift.   At the present day the theory of the Christian sacrifice is undergoing development, and Protestant and Catholic views of it are drawing nearer together in sympathetic understanding of each other. Their approaches have been different, but they have always more in common with one another than they have with any expressions about spiritual sacrifice made by non-Christians, however noble, since the latter are either Pelagian in spirit, or, if they do stress human inadequacy and plead for faith and trust, have no historical figures on whom such faith and trust can be pinned. Amitabha is certainly mythical, and even the Indian Rama is so overlaid with myth that in the form in which his incarnation is represented as possessing the highest soteriological value, in the post-Christian writings of Tulsi Das, Rama is least historical. Exalted as are the sentiments attributed to some of the Asian saviour-figures, one cannot help being conscious that to redeem from waywardness of will costs more than to redeem from ignorance, and that some decisive action within the spatio-temporal order is imperatively needed to deliver human beings from a false egoism. No docetic or mythical deliverer can suffice for that. He can only show what mankind would like to happen, and what he shows is but a fantasy woven of wishful thinking.

Most developed religions possess some literature which they regard as sacred. The nature of this literature varies according to the status of the individual religious system. Thus a community which has no script will memorise its sacred compositions. The Navaho Indians in New Mexico possess hundreds of hymns which have never been written down, and which are passed on orally from one person to another, and chanted at their religious ceremonies. It would seem that a collection of hymns constitutes the oldest form of such sacred compositions, and where a script develops, the hymns in course of time are committed to writing. Hymn books of one sort or another are therefore to be found practically all over the world. Heiler, however, makes a distinction between various grades of hymns. There are, he says, very ancient hymns which seem to have been more or less spontaneous compositions, and which are naturally in archaic language, and therefore regarded as of the greatest importance and also potency, since their recital, even though its meaning may not be understood by the congregation, is believed to be eminently pleasing to the deity concerned, and therefore most efficacious in persuading that deity to be favourable, and to grant petitions. Next to these come the more artificial hymns, composed by religious experts for special occasions such as the greater ceremonial sacrifices. Many of the hymns in the Rig-Veda are of this kind, and were no doubt composed by priests skilled in making such compositions. Later, towards the axial age, hymns of a didactic or philosophical character come into existence. These, although subjective poems, are regarded as valuable in reviving and renewing religious experiences and states of consciousness, and although not specifically addressed to any deity, can be recited profitably as part of an act of worship if the latter seems to require that a certain state of mind or disposition is to be induced in the worshippers.

This brings us to the main function of a corpus of sacred literature when fully developed. Its purpose is to preserve, transmit, and renew a specific group of religious experiences. Thus, although the possession of such a corpus may be common to most religions, the kind of experiences which it is intended to foster, transmit, and revive will differ according to the tenets of each individual religion. For example, although many historical religions will be found to possess collections of hymns both spontaneous and artificial which are intended to be used objectively in address to the various deities of some pantheon or other, the character and content of the hymns will differ immensely according to the nature of the divinity to whom the hymns are addressed. If the latter be a benevolent one, the type of hymn will be different from that addressed to one who is thought to be dangerous or in need of propitiation. Again, many hymns are addressed to deities of a departmental character, and it is only sophisticated persons of an age much later than that which composed them who say they are addressed to one single deity in his various aspects, rather than to a number of individual deities.[1] The Gathas of Zarathustra are probably the compositions of a single prophet, and are addressed apparently to one Supreme Being. To a still greater degree is this the case with the Hebrew Psalms. The so-called Homeric hymns are thought to have been poetical compositions made as part of a competition at some festival or other, and it may well be that they were never used in worship at all.

Another type of sacred literature is the didactic. This may take the form of short pithy sentences, intended to convey the wisdom of the elders to succeeding generations. Although mainly prudential and moral, the existence of a Divine Being who forms the background to life is generally assumed. Specimens of this kind of literature are to be found in ancient Egypt, in Israel, and in the China of the age of the hundred philosophers. Fragments have also turned up in Mesopotamia which seem to suggest that it may have been prevalent there. The axial age, as might be expected, produces more or less extended forms of teaching such as is to be found in the Upanishads

---

[1] The Vedic hymns are clearly addressed to one or another of the deities in a polytheistic pantheon, and it is only the interpreters of a much later age who try to convince the public that they are really addressed to a single Supreme God under His various aspects. The original poets were undoubtedly pluralists.

of India, the Sutras of Buddhism, and the longer discourses of the Chinese sages. In all these cases the good life which assures everyone who practises it of some kind of liberation into a state of eternal beatitude, is thought of as that which is grounded in the right kind of knowledge, so that it is the aim of this kind of sacred literature to teach that knowledge. A very good example of this sort of sacred book is the Bhagavadgita. Here a Divine Being appearing incognito as a charioteer delivers a series of discourses on the correct way of life. A somewhat similar work is the Asclepius, traditionally attributed to the more or less mythical figure of Hermes Trismegistos. Perhaps the book of Job in spite of its dramatic form, might be put into the same class; and it is significant that all three poems end in a kind of theophany including a rhapsodical hymn.

The Sutras of Buddhism differ widely from the foregoing, since unless one assumes a background to them of identity-mysticism they appear to be simply moral treatises of a humanistic character and with a purely humanistic aim. Nevertheless, the chanting of these Sutras as a kind of choir-office forms a substantial part of the daily devotions of Buddhist monks as well as of laity, and the aim no doubt of such usage is to produce and to retain the state of 'rightmindfulness' leading to complete union with the Absolute, and the waning-out of all worldly and carnal desires.

When we turn to the moral and historical treatises of China (the editing of which in their present form is attributed to Kung-futze), as well as to the historico-prophetic literature of Jews and Christians we enter a different atmosphere. In the literature springing from India the background which is assumed is mainly cyclic. The Absolute remains fixed and stable, but the world of phenomena is from eternity to eternity emitted, sustained, and re-absorbed by the Divine fiat. The object of the individual must be in this case to achieve liberation from the cyclic existence and to become one with the Absolute; but in the Chinese moral treatises on history, and to a still greater degree in the Hebrew, Christian, and Moslem sacred writings the conception of life is of a linear rather than cyclic process. The most High God speaks and works in the course of events, and by His guidance, over-ruling, and judgment He gives meaning to that course of events. Thus it may be said that the Qur'ān, though largely a series of prophetic sermons of varying lengths, is built round the conception of a linear process similar to that pictured in Hebrew and Christian scriptures, beginning with creation, and proceeding through a chain of prophets which culminates in the ministry of Mohammed and ends with the Day of Judgment. In the course of this divine pageant there is no repetition or recurrence, but certain important events stand out such as the call of Abraham, the ministry of Jesus, the call of Mohammed followed by his Hijra or journey to Medina, and the Furqan or deliverance which in its restricted sense means the crowning mercy of Mohammed's victory over his enemies at the battle of Badr.   In China the book of history is not simply a secular chronicle, but, like the historical books of the Old Testament, is an interpretation of history as seen from the standpoint of God Himself.   Whatever may be said about the correctness of the records, they are interpreted as showing the way in which the Mandate of Heaven works upon earth.   This can be seen almost as clearly in the book of Chinese annals as in the Hebrew book of Judges or Kings.

It is sometimes said that India has not totally ignored the idea of a Divine Work in history, since the Ramayana is an epic poem recounting the deeds of the pious king Rama.   There is some truth in this, but it needs to be qualified.   In the first place the original Ramayana seems to be a purely biographical poem about a human king.   Beautiful as it is, it is no more a sacred book conveying revelation than a Norse saga.   It is only when we come to the rewriting of this fine and moving story in the sixteenth century A.D. by the great Indian poet Tulsi Das that we find Rama accepted as one of the main incarnations or avatar of the beneficent Indian god Vishnu.   In the second place the story has become in the course of repetition so laden with myth that it is now hardly historical, and the Indian mind does not seem to trouble how much of it is fiction, provided that it is edifying.   In the third place the cult of Rama belongs to a minority movement in Indian religion which sprang up either at the same time as Christianity or perhaps a little earlier, and does not conform to the general pattern of Indian pantheism.   It may therefore well have been the product of some influence entering India about this time from the north-west.   The vast majority of Hindus still think in terms of a cyclic movement within a general frame of pantheism, and their most sacred literature is centred upon it.   Even the Gita, which certainly seems in the main to belong to the incarnational period, is not entirely and uncompromisingly theistic, but has many pantheistic passages, and sees in the avatars a series of recurrent theophanies going on (as it would seem) to infinity, since life is cyclic and therefore these theophanies need repetition whenever the circumstances call for them: and it seems to matter but little if these theophanies are mythical.[1]

[1] The present efforts at historicising Sri Krishna do not seem successful.   That there was a human teacher who initiated Bhaganata religion we may possibly infer; but we cannot say that we know anything about him.   The Gita appears to be edifying fiction.

At the other end of the scale we have the unique sacred literature of the Christian movement. Here the whole emphasis is upon
a linear process proceeding from the mind of the Creator of the Universe and culminating in the once-for-all appearance of a great and
genuinely historical figure, who, although appearing at a single point
in Western Asia confers by his whole career a divine blessing which is
both potent and significant for the benefit of the entire population
of the planet.

The purpose of the Bible is for this reason quite distinct from
that of any other corpus of sacred literature. Like any other corpus
it is meant to be used to foster, extend, and renew a specific religious
experience, and to this extent it falls into a class, that of the 'Sacred
Book'. But in so far as the experience with which it is concerned
claims to be of unique cosmic significance, and to be neither local nor
repeatable, it stands outside the general category 'Sacred Book', and
remains in spite of all its obviously human elements in a class by itself.

Besides possessing sacred books, Moslems, Hindus, Jews, and
Christians, resemble one another to the extent that they make commentaries upon their sacred books for exegetical purposes. There
is also something of this to be found in the sacred books of the
Parsees, since their entire corpus bears the title Zendavesta, which
is said to mean 'text and commentary'. Jews, as is well known,
depend very largely upon their traditional commentaries for the
understanding of their scriptures. Less well known are the numerous
commentaries in India which aim at interpreting the Vedas in the
interests of the various schools of thought. It is only specialists in
the west who are acquainted with these commentaries, though some
work has lately been going on in India with the intention of explaining them in substance for English readers, and new ones centred upon
the Gita have appeared in recent years, written by Radhakrishnan
and Aurobindo Ghose. However much the form of these last two
may have been influenced by Christian commentaries on the New
Testament, there can be no doubt that the older Indian commentaries
of the early medieval period are entirely independent productions,
and owe nothing to Christian influence. They do, however, to some
extent resemble in form the early patristic commentaries on the Bible,
as well as the writings of Christian scholastics. Every proposition
is nailed down with a Vedic text, and the verbal inspiration of these
texts is assumed as proceeding from cosmic vibrations heard by the
rishis in antiquity. There are also, of course, many commentaries
on the Qur'ān which have been written by Moslem divines.

The general assumption which lies behind all such commentaries
is that the original text is of such sanctity that it can be interpreted as

it stands without the aid of any higher criticism. It is noteworthy that so far only Christians, and these a minority although a growing one, have shown themselves ready to study their sacred literature in exactly the same way in which they would study any other book, in the firm conviction that if this method be fearlessly pursued, it can only lead to the recovery of the exact truth. Christians have, however, not contented themselves with applying scientific methods of criticism to the Bible, but they have led the way in extending the method to the sacred books of Parseeism, Hinduism, Buddhism, and Islam, not to mention the sacred literature of the Sikhs or of the *bhakti* saints of India. There are a few signs that scholars among the non-Christian faiths are beginning to see the importance of pursuing such study; but it is still significant that it is the Christians who have not only led the way, but have declared that their religion has gained immensely from such impartial study, and they challenge the scholars of other religions to do what they have done for their own sacred texts. Whether their lead will be followed on any scale remains to be seen; it seems, however, that its application to the sacred writings in non-Christian faiths is bound to have an even greater effect upon them than it has had upon the presentation of Christianity.

One of the most striking features about the Biblical corpus of literature is its presentation of the Living God as active in calling and choosing individuals for the fulfilment of the Divine Purpose. The Upanishadic Deity, though all-pervading, does nothing in particular, except to emit, sustain, and re-absorb the Cosmos, perhaps as a letting off of surplus energy. The God of the Bible from the very beginning *speaks* to men. In the mythical early chapters, a shrewd picture is given of the intercourse between the human spirit and the Divine. God gives man commandments and prohibitions. God calls him when he is hiding, plagued by a bad conscience, and searches him out. In the folk-tales of early history, God calls Abraham and bids him migrate to a strange country, in faith and hope. David is called from among the sheepfolds and chosen to be a king and deliverer. Solomon is called, and asked what quality he desires God to give him. We are shown a whole succession of prophetic leaders, each of whom is called and chosen to declare the Divine Purpose in national history, from Moses who leads Israel out of Egypt, to Nathan who is *sent* by God to reprove David, Ahijah who has a similar task to perform in respect of Jeroboam, Isaiah, Jeremiah, and Ezekiel, each *called*, and each in turn expressing a sense of his unworthiness. Some who are called try to evade their duty, and even, like Jonah, to run away from it.

In the New Testament, God's message comes to Zachariah, to

Joseph, to Saul pre-eminently, as well as to the immediate disciples of Jesus, to Peter at Joppa, as well as to those who are sent to visit Peter and Paul, Cornelius and Ananias; and finally to John upon Patmos, who hears 'as it were the voice of a trumpet talking' with him.

Similarly, as I once heard it put in an eloquent and timely address to Indians, Deity, as presented by the Christian movement, faces individuals and communities with a fundamental *decision*. They are not to go on all their lives 'limping between two opinions'. 'If the Lord be God, then follow Him. But if Baal, Vishnu, or Siva then follow him.' However much good there may be in other religions, however much the Logos may in a partial, one-sided, or broken way, be able to manifest His operations in men's minds, however much there may be discernible a 'relatedness' between the religions of the world, in the last resort comes the demand for a final decision which no one has the right to postpone. The pages of the Bible are full of instances of people who failed to make such a decision, but faltered and are never heard of again, men like Porcius Festus, Felix, Agrippa, and perhaps Nicodemus. They also contain the record of many who made it, if need be at a cost, men like Abraham, Moses, Elijah, Matthew, Joseph of Arimathea in his final phase, and Paul, and women like Lydia and Damaris, and of course pre-eminently the one who said, 'Behold the handmaid of the Lord: be it unto me according to Thy word.' Abraham would never have been heard of, if he had contentedly stayed in Ur. Even Mary might have made the great refusal, and have said: 'Can't you get someone else, Lord? The responsibility is too great for me.'

The above may seem a commonplace repetition of facts; and yet it still needs to be pointed out (in the face of ill-conceived statements on the part of theosophists and others), that this conception of a One Holy and Righteous God who acts and speaks, who calls, guides, warns, and enheartens, is peculiar to the Biblical corpus, as well as to any literature which is dependent upon its influence. It is certainly not to be found in the Upanishads, nor does it appear in the Buddhist scriptures, and the conception behind it is wholly alien from the immanentist experience of Buddhist mystics. Where such immanentist experience occurs within the borders of Christianity, as among members of the Society of Friends, it is always linked with the recognition of the transcendent Deity who speaks. The world of the Bible is not ignored, for the Bible is often expounded at Meeting. The Theravada Buddhist on the other hand will sometimes explicitly reject the very existence of such a Deity, while the Mahayana Buddhist who acknowledges the existence of a Cosmic Purusha, does not, unless he modifies his teaching as the result of Christian contacts, invest the Purusha with attributes at all resembling those of the God of the Lord's Prayer.   Bhakti Hinduism is, of course, more personal, but it contains no suggestion of a call by a Holy God to action of an ethical nature.   The hymns, beautiful as many of them are, express an almost erotic mysticism, and appear more Christian than they really are when translated into English.   The Saivite hymns may betray a possible covert Christian influence.   It is difficult to be sure how far this medieval Indian theism, which is never more than a minority movement in Hinduism, is really an independent development.[1]

Catholic mystical theologians call the Divine approaches to individuals 'private revelations', and reckon on principle that they can and do occur to numbers of persons outside the bounds of Scripture, because of the self-imparting and active nature of Deity; but they hold equally that severe tests must be imposed, to make sure that these events as recorded are veridical revelations, and not the individual hearing his own voice, or indulging in a fit of fraudulent exhibitionism.[2]

The world-transforming constructiveness of the Christian movement is so much taken for granted by Christians themselves, that they hardly realise how unique it is.

One has only to turn the pages of the *International Review of Missions* to see how positive is the work carried on by the sending countries overseas.   Hospitals, dispensaries, schools of medicine, agricultural and technical colleges, schools of all grades, universities and centres of university status, institutions for the blind, leper settlements, movements for land-reform and for better sanitation, housing estates, model villages, printing-presses, book-depots, efforts of all kinds to combat illiteracy—these are only some among the many activities of the overseas church.   In the sending countries themselves similar undertakings are to be observed.   Perhaps in the two fields of social welfare and hygiene on the one hand, and of education on the other, the Christian movement has been the pioneer. One notices that it is Christian revolutionaries who have championed prison-reform, and the removal of the colour-bar and other forms of social injustice.   Granted there has often been inertia among stupid and conventional Christians, it is only fair to give credit where credit is

---

[1] It is only fair to admit that on occasion one encounters quasi-erotic ebullitions of mysticism among Christians.
[2] See Fr. Poulain's *Graces of Interior Prayer*, a translation of his *Graces d'Oraison*, published by Burns and Oates.

due, and to point out that if one were to take Christian philanthropic efforts out of the world today, there would be not much light left.

Now there is a theological background to all this. The world as Christianity conceived is God's world, and is meant by Him to be 'very good'. But the Christian is only too well aware of its fallings-short, and of the way in which it tends to become perverted and to misuse its God-given freedom. He therefore recognises his duty by the grace of God to transform, restore, and reform it.

Islam may have sought to mitigate a little the lot of the slave. Christians alone have seen the logical issue as the ultimate *abolition* of all slavery. The Buddha may have spoken about waiting upon the sick; but the creation and maintenance of hospitals of all kinds, of homes for incurables and for the dying, has never been central in Buddhism as in Christianity (see page 80) and it was the voluntary hospitals which long preceded the state ones. Islam makes alms-giving a duty; but it has never had any constructive plans for the re-building of society with the money so contributed. There have been educational centres outside Christianity to which the courtesy title of 'university' has sometimes been given by historians: but the *studium generale*, although perhaps Athens may deserve the honour of first having had something of the sort, has only developed fully in a Christian atmosphere, and where today universities and colleges of university status come into existence on a neutral or secular basis (perhaps for anti-clerical reasons), it is very noticeable that sooner or later they find that for their health's sake they have to take account of religion, and that religion in most cases seems to be Christianity. In India, of course, the creation of Hindu colleges and a Hindu university has not unnaturally accompanied independence. But even now some of the best and best-known educational institutions in India are those which were founded by Christians, and Indians are glad of them, and would welcome more Christian educational workers, as well as workers in her health service.

Buddhism as such has undertaken some education, and has cared for the literacy of children by maintaining schools attached to its *viharas*; but it cannot show in all the centuries anything approaching the constructive philanthropic activities of the Christian Church. The world as conceived by Buddhists is not one which is really worth transformation. One might have expected Islam to have taken over some of the Christian philanthropic activities, and there are now, it is true, Moslem boys' schools in such places as Amman, founded in imitation of and in rivalry with Christian schools; but it is not a natural impulse with Moslems to found hospitals or model villages or orphanages, to care for the lepers or the mentally afflicted, or to give education to women. Perhaps the predestinarian fatalism of Islamic belief on the one hand, and the obviously lower status given to women by Mohammed, render such activities unnecessary to the average Moslem. The emancipation of women in Moslem countries is often accompanied by a decline in Islam, and is due largely to influence from outside, such as the education of young Moslems in France. Certainly the Hindu doctrine of *karma* (see pages 196 ff.) is, as has already been observed, a fatal obstacle to any zeal among orthodox Hindus for social service on behalf of the 'untouchables'.

One has no wish to be unfair or captious in one's criticism, and one is unhappily only too well aware that there are bad pages in the Christian record, and bad areas even in Christian countries: but the Christian conscience always sooner or later speaks out against them, and if the truth is to be faced, where, outside vital Christianity are to be found the incentive and the dynamic for world-succour and transformation except in Communism (which, as Professor John Macmurray has quite reasonably pointed out, is dialectically related to it, but works by hatred and not by love)? How often is it the case that the inspiration to individuals to undertake public service in the state, local government, welfare work, and the choice of a profession such as that of a doctor or nurse as one's life's vocation, has come from a sense of 'what Christ would have me do'?

What sort of Self-Existent Being is it Who stirs people to behave in this way?—Not Brahma, not Allah, not the cosmic Absolute of the Buddhists, but the God of the Lord's Prayer, and in a measure the Yahweh of the Shemoneh 'Esreh and the Ahuramazda of the Gathas, Who both come nearest to Him as they are conceived by Jews and Parsis.

By way of summing up, it may be well to refer to some deeper points set forth by Dr. Nicol Macnicol in his thoughtful book: *Is Christianity Unique?* He makes it clear that as a matter of observed fact, (1) the pantheistic and theistic faiths stand definitely apart, and facing in opposite directions. They represent two views of Reality which are radically discordant. What if one of these should be wrong? (2) Within the theistic group, Christianity stands apart also, not merely on account of its claim (which might be an exaggerated one, were it not that it has substantiated itself by the capability of its missionaries to establish outposts of it in practically every country in the world, and amid every sort of population), but because of the *kind* of Self-Existent Deity it claims to reveal, One Who controls history—which has a linear purpose, and is not merely cyclic—One Who deals with individuals not as mere underlings, but as personal friends; One Who by His Supreme Initiative acts in Gracious Self-giving once and for all time.

If for the sake of brevity I have paraphrased the author, he must forgive me.

Finally it may be said that one of the best modern appreciations of the fundamental differences between Christianity and other religions is that from the pen of Miss Evelyn Underhill (Mrs. Stuart Moore), but I defer the consideration of it to the end of Chapter X ('Theological Revaluation').

Additional notes on

(i) KARMA AND REINCARNATION

It is well known that there is an important and fundamental difference between Western and Christian beliefs about the destiny of the soul and about the future life, and those of Asia as represented in Hinduism and Buddhism. The general principle in the latter ties up with a cyclic view of what goes on in the cosmos, and takes for granted that what is called *samsara*. an indefinite and continuous series of reincarnations, is the correct description of it. This series is held to be controlled by the inexorable law of Karma, by which what one does in this life determines one's destiny not in respect of *one* future life but in respect of the *next* in a chain of future lives. This was a theory which was worked out in India many centuries ago, and is still the background of much popular and semi-educated thought in that country. Of course some kind of belief in the transmigration of souls has been held in other parts of the world as well (we hear of it among the Druids in Britain, and in connection with Pythagoras in Southern Italy in the fifth century B.C.). But although the theory was supposed to represent the moral justice of the universe, it has always been the desire of Asians to get free from the cycle of *samsara*, and a large part of the technique proposed by the Buddha is directed to setting the individual free by inducing in him such a state of permanent consciousness (or whatever it can be called) that the illusory and defective outlook on life ceases, and the individual becomes one with the Absolute and undergoes no further rebirths.

The belief in Karma and reincarnation here pre-supposed as a background to the Buddhist way of life, and still accepted as a working theory by many Indians, has, however, suffered some blows in recent years.

In the first place, the assertions of various persons who claim to have been able to remember details from previous births have not stood up to investigation, partly in some cases owing to their having been fraudulent, but in others owing to their having been found quite easily explicable by telepathy or E.S.P.   Moreover it has been pointed out that if such feats of memory were possible, claims to be able to perform them ought to be much commoner than they are, whereas it is only in odd cases here and there that they are made, and usually in a context where the belief in their possibility already exists.   Yet continuance of personality without memory seems a contradiction in terms.

In the second place, the tragic death of Mr. Gandhi seemed to many thoughtful Indians to have impugned the justice of Karma. So good and virtuous a man could not be believed to have had a bad Karma, and ought not to have met with such an unhappy end. Nevertheless the fact remains that he did; and therefore a serious flaw in the theory would seem to be exposed.

But for a good many years criticism has been gathering round the theory, and some of the main points in this must now be set forth, since the last argument may be thought to be rather of an *ad hoc* character.

First of all, there is the difficulty that the science of biology seems to favour the idea of life on the planet as a one-way system. Characteristics of individuals may be inherited, and species of organisms, higher and lower alike, may go on repeating themselves from generation to generation.   But each individual is regarded as a fresh emergent, and not as a repetition in essence of what has gone before.   In the second place, the doctrine of Karma as cosmic justice is in itself abhorrent.   As a theory, it might have been regarded as an advance upon that which thought of suffering as capriciously inflicted.   But it cannot be regarded as truly righteous, since it is vindictive and merciless.   There is no escape, no doctrine of Divine forgiveness in response to penitence.   Further, it is imperfect, since it does not necessarily do away with the injury that a sin has done to others, nor does it necessarily regenerate a soul.   It does not even make the punishment fit the crime, since the greatest offenders sometimes suffer least, while others suffer out of all proportion to the gravity of the sin committed.   Christians themselves are sometimes puzzled and distressed at the suffering of the innocent, but they do not feel satisfied at explaining it along these lines.   They find it easier to think of God Himself as suffering in and with such people, and of the world as explicable in the terms outlined in 'Presuppositions' (page 43).   And again, the theory is abhorrent, because, as Miss Dougall has put it, 'It makes the purity of childhood a gigantic lie.   The most innocent child may really be an aged pilgrim soul, scarred and seamed by evil experience, and only innocent in the sense in which the senile are innocent when memory entirely fails.'

But finally. The theory fails horribly on pragmatic grounds. It is abhorrent by reason of its social effects. Both Hindus and Buddhists have been known to make it the prime reason why they consider it unnecessary to engage in social service, social reform, and corporal works of mercy such as constructive sexual hygiene. Sick and indigent people are held to be suffering for wrongs done by them, in fact, for their bad Karmas. It is therefore not only unnecessary but actually an unwarrantable and impertinent interference with cosmic justice to seek to relieve them. Of course the work of the Ramakrishna Mission is in flat contradiction to this; but that is because it represents Hindu belief as *modified* by Christianity. Logically Hinduism should not regard social service for the poor and afflicted as relevant.[1] It is doubtful whether the Buddha when he spoke of compassion meant the actual relief of those in need. More probably he meant their indoctrination with his teaching; though he did say something about waiting upon the sick. Yet if this had really been central in his message, it is remarkable that it should not be more central in general Buddhist teaching, where the latter has remained unaffected by Christian contacts.

A Marxist might well write off Karma as a thoroughly bourgeois doctrine, invented by the exploiting classes in order to justify their callousness, and would say that as a theory its upper-caste origin was patent.

Some of the social service now being practised in India is not due to the Ramakrishna Mission but to a liberal humanitarianism such as would be advocated by Pandit Nehru, and has no connection with either a reformed Hinduism or with Christianity, except in so far as the latter serves to stimulate it.

(ii) THE PROBLEM OF SUPERNATURAL BIRTH

It is orthodox belief in almost all Christian denominations saving the most heretical, that the life of the historical Jesus of Nazareth is a Supreme Act of God, a Divine Initiative, and not simply a human life; although it is within the bounds of a fully human life, sin only except, that that Act of God has taken place.

The exact *mode* by which this Act of God was inaugurated has been the subject of debate for the past hundred years. Those who begin with a prejudice against miracles are usually more favourably disposed towards evidence which seems to point towards a birth in

---

[1] I do think that my Indian friends (to whom I say this with all gentleness and affection) ought very seriously to consider the fact that the most severe strictures upon the Hindu way of life came to me from two *doctors*, as far apart as Banaras and Orissa. The one from the latter even went so far as to say: 'Hinduism is something we could very well do without.'

full wedlock. Those who accept the possibility of a unique life having a unique beginning, and who decline to rule out the further possibility that events may be recorded in history which are not mere mythical additions to it, but evidences of a divine control of the spatio-temporal order, capable of altering its sequence, and not so much contrary to nature as contrary to what is known of nature, will adhere to the literal credibility of scripture in this matter, and point to the probability that the birth stories could only have been told by one person, the Mother herself, since Joseph could only testify, until he had had his private revelation, that the child was not his.[1] Such a private revelation, however, could in itself only add to the Mother's evidence, while in a court of law it would hardly be regarded as on a level with it. But the clause about the birth in the old Roman creed indicates the extreme antiquity of the belief in the birth from a virgin.

There is, however, a third position which it is possible to adopt. It is possible to start with the impression produced by the Life of Jesus, so unique in dignity, holiness, isolation, and authority as well as in self-giving love, as conveying the sense that it is indeed ACT OF GOD; and then to observe that:

(1) In the earliest strata of New Testament passages the paternity of Joseph is obviously assumed.

(2) Even in the accounts known as the Infancy Gospel a minimum interpretation would be possible that at the time of the Conception and Birth both Joseph and Mary had genuine spiritual experiences which convinced them that the Holy Thing that was coming into the world was at least 'a child of promise' like Isaac, and, more than that, 'Son of God', i.e. in Hebrew idiom Divine, in a way in which Caesar was not, nor indeed any other human prophet or sage.

If these two observations be combined, it is not hard to see why some traditions which clearly indicate the acceptance of the belief that in Jesus FULL DEITY and FULL HUMANITY were indiscerptibly united, omit anything like an expressed statement of a Virgin Birth. Where did this belief come in? The position of the third group of theologians would be that the spiritual experience of Joseph and Mary, though perfectly real and authentic, became attracted in the course of verbal recording and of popular interpretation, into the form which for many centuries has been associated with the births of persons of outstanding power, wisdom, or holiness.

[1] There was a malicious Jewish report that Jesus was the illegitimate son of Mary and a Roman soldier, but this is not mentioned in the synoptic gospels, though, as has been recognised, there may be a covert reference to it in John 8:41.

It seems only proper in the interests of truth to record here as many of these traditions as possible. It is not fair to sweep them aside as silly tales. Clearly they were symbolical efforts, at the least, to give full weight to the impressiveness of the personalities concerned. How far anyone believed in them, whether as poetry or as physiological truth we cannot say. All we can do is to clarify them as far as we are able into those which are indisputably pre-Christian, those which are probably pre-Christian, and those which are possibly or certainly post-Christian, and which may therefore have been influenced by the Christian tradition and indeed may actually have been imitations of Christian dogma.

Definitely pre-Christian

(a) The well-known passage in ancient Chinese poetry regarding the birth of the reputed founder of the Chou dynasty.

> 'his mother
> reverently offered up sacrifice
> That she might not be without children.
> Then she stepped in a foot print made by T'ien, and conceived.
> . . . .
> When she had fulfilled her months
> Her first born came like a lamb;
> There was no bleeding, no tearing,
> No injury, no pain,
> In order to emphasise his divinity.'

I note that the late Professor Haloun said that he thought this conception of a supernatural birth in China might well be traceable westward to Sumeria, but he did not give me the evidence for this. If he were correct, then the idea might be said to have travelled eastward as well as westward, *diffusing* from the Middle East.

(b) Philo, in his commentary on Exodus, says of Zipporah: 'When Moses took her unto himself he discovered that she was pregnant, but not by mortal man.' The date of this commentary is slightly earlier than that of any of the canonical gospels.

(c) Plato was sometimes described as the offspring of Apollo by a woman.

(d) According to the ancient myth, Dionysus was the child of Zeus and a mortal woman Semele.

Possibly pre-Christian

In the Buddhist versions of the life of Gautama we note certain parallels to the Christian infancy Gospels. There was an angelic annunciation by supernatural messengers—to his father. His mother was a virgin for thirty-two months before his birth.   More supernatural beings sang at his birth.   Asita, who corresponds to the figure of Simeon in St. Luke's Gospel, predicted his future greatness. Gautama held a fast for forty-nine days, and was tempted by the Spirit of Evil to turn the Himalayas into gold.   He performed thirty-two healing miracles, was transfigured, had an original band of twelve disciples, fed five hundred persons with one small cake, and had a disciple who walked on water and then sank.   There are a number of logia of the Buddha which to some extent resemble logia spoken by Jesus.   Finally, although there is no crucifixion, Devadatta, the Buddhist Judas, conspires to kill his master, and hires a band of thirty assassins for the purpose.   (Is this number thirty an echo of distorted oral tradition about thirty pieces of silver?)   But when they see Gautama, they fall to the ground.   He makes a triumphal entry into his native city; and on the day of his death there is an earthquake.

Even if we omit certain other parallels which seem to be rather strained, this short list is curiously impressive.

I have sometimes thought it possible that there may have existed in an area roughly between Palestine and Bengal a mass of conventional folk-tales about holy persons, and that some of these might have affected the type of story told on the one hand about Jesus of Nazareth, and on the other about Gautama.   It is certainly the case that Asian holy men are often believed to be able to multiply food, to walk on the surface of the water, and to float through the air (this last supernatural accomplishment is called *iddhi*).   It is equally certain that the story of the Temptation shows that Jesus, while in the wilderness, faced the invitation to do two of these three things, i.e. to make stones into bread and to float down through the air into the temple court at Jerusalem; and that he refused to do either.

I am now more inclined to think that some of the parallels at any rate in the Buddhist Canon may be slightly later than the time of Christ, perhaps hardly as late as the date of the first Nestorian missions, but late enough for them to be genuine attempts to build on the basis of an imperfectly-heard Christian oral tradition, a number of stories about Gautama, so as to give him a prestige somewhat similar to that enjoyed by Jesus.   We know that Clement of Alexandria certainly had some knowledge of the existence of the Buddha, and that in the early second century A.D. a Buddhist tale got attracted into a Christian form in the romance of Barlaam and Josaphat; while Indian folk-tales from the Pançatatra travelled as far west as Italy, being traceable in the pages of Boccaccio, and also of Chaucer, who derived them from Italy.   It is therefore just as likely that Indians in the Punjab may have heard tales of Jesus diffusing in the opposite direction, and coming either from travellers or traders, even if not from early missionaries (although the latest view is that some of the latter may have arrived in the Indus valley at a very early date) and may have adopted some of these tales into the Buddhist canon, though with variations or embellishments in detail. Tales of a similar kind occur in the Jatakas or stories of re-birth, with texts attached to them; but it seems that the Jatakas in their original form had only the texts, and that the stories were added later, and that the present form of the Jatakas belongs only to the fifth century A.D., which would give ample time for Christian influence to have crept in. On the other hand it has been pointed out that some of the Jataka tales are illustrated in the Bharhat sculptures, and are there labelled with their proper title. This could make them somewhat earlier, say about 100 B.C., but it does not appear that the Bharhat sculptures represent anything which forms a parallel to actual scenes from the New Testament, but rather tales from the Jatakas of previous incarnations of Gautama, and indeed mostly adaptations of non-Buddhist Indian folk-tales. In contra-distinction to these the sculptures preserved in the museum at Lahore (and mentioned by Rudyard Kipling in *Kim*) as showing parallels to the Christian Infancy Gospel) are Gandhara art of anything between the first and seventh century A.D. and therefore most likely to be reflections of Christian tradition. This art has actually been described as 'the easternmost appearance of the art of the Roman Empire, especially in its late and provincial manifestations'.

The poetic elaborations of what we might call the Infancy Gospel of Gautama's early life by Asva Ghosha (probably first century A.D.) suggest that a story of a temptation of a prophet may belong to the folk-lore of Asia, and those by Aryasura (fourth century A.D.), although they are late enough to have received Christian influence, do not specially show it. On the other hand, the most important of the Mahayana sutras is dateable about the end of the second century A.D.: and here we get a clear conception of Gautama not simply as a human teacher but as the incarnation of the eternal and pre-existent Buddha-spirit, akin to the Logos of the Fourth Gospel. At the same time this glorified Gautama has no connection with historical sequence. He delivers sermons; but 'He does not go anywhere, and does not come from anywhere.' He simply *is*, in a timeless state of perfection.

It may be well to append to this section the original Latin text of the passage from the fourth century A.D. treatise of St. Jerome 'Adversus Jovinianum', Lib. I.42, in which the author shows that he is fully aware of the non-Christian supernatural birth stories.

'A virginibus procreatorum fabulae.   Apud Gymnosophistas Indiae
quasi per manus hujus opinionis auctoritas traditur, quod Buddam
principem dogmatis eorum, e latere suo virgo generavit.   Nec horum
mirum de Barbaris cum Minervam quoque de capite Jovis, et Liberum
patrem de femore ejus procreatos, doctissima finxerit Graecis.
Speusippus quoque sororis Platonis filius, et Clearchus in laude
Platonis, et Anaxilides in secundo libro Philodophiae, Perictionem
matrem Platonis, phantasmate Apollinis oppressam ferunt, et
sapientiae principem non aliter arbitrantur, nisi de partu virginis
editum.   Sed et Timaeus scribit Pythagorae virginem filiam chore
virginum praefuisse, et castitatis eas instituisse doctrinis.
    Diodorus Socraticus quinque filias Dialecticas insignis pudicitiae
habuisse narratur de quibus et Philo Carneadis magister plenissimam
scribit historiam.   Ac ne nobis Dominum Salvatorem de Virgine
procreatum Roma exprobraret potentia, auctores urbis et gentis suae,
Ilia virgine et Marte genitos arbitrantur.'

Of the instances given above by Jerome, some are obviously
pre-Christian, and some possibly pre-Christian, but not certainly.

It remains to consider the alleged supernatural birth of Zarathustra.

J. H. Moulton, in his Hibbert Lectures, quotes Virgil's Fourth
Eclogue as evidence that the Roman poet, like Pliny a hundred years
later, knew of stories about the supernatural infancy of the Iranian
prophet.   Moulton, for instance, draws the inference that Virgil's
risu cognoscere matrem is evidence that Virgil was making his wonder-
child behave in the same way as the infant Zarathustra, and smile
recognition at his mother on the very day of his birth, and that since
this Eclogue was composed before the birth of Christ, therefore
stories about the supernatural infancy of Zarathustra must have been
current before the infancy sections of the Gospels were composed.

Now this tale of the *risus* appears to belong to the later Magian
version of the life of Zarathustra as known to the Greeks, and it has
been said that with it goes the story of his virgin birth.   If this were
so, it would be easy to argue that since the Graeco-Iranian world
knew stories of this kind about Zarathustra it would not be difficult
to associate them with the birth of Jesus Christ; and indeed that the
story in Matthew 2, the significance of which we miss in English by
not keeping the technical term Magoi, but translating it as 'Wise
Men', is strongly influenced by this Magian literature.

But as a matter of fact the assertion about Zarathustra's supernatural birth differs in certain important respects from that recorded
of Our Lord in Matthew 2.   What the Magian literature speaks of
is a supernatural, but not a virgin birth.   Zarathustra's birth was one
in wedlock, but was accompanied by unusual happenings, such as

that his father had previously eaten some plant which contained the *fravashi* of Zarathustra. Now the *fravashi* is a proto-Nordic concept, not unlike that of the *Ka* or guardian genius in Egyptian doctrine. It belongs indeed to the group of ideas in early psychology which may be called those of a plural or multiple soul. But when the father of Zarathustra ate the plant containing Zarathustra's *fravashi*, a birth in full wedlock followed; and further, although the Zoroastrian Messiah (known variously as the Saoshyant, Saoshya, or Saoshyans) is alleged to be supernaturally conceived, we learn that this again is not quite similar to what is to be read in Matthew 1 and 2, but that the mother of the future Messiah, or Saoshyant, would become pregnant, as we should say today, by insemination from Zarathustra, his vital substance having been preserved through long years.

At the same time it seems impossible to ignore the close association of the Matthaean story with this later, though still pre-Christian, Zoroastrianism, and this has, I believe, been felt for some years. Herzfeld, in his Schweich Lectures, has drawn attention to a curious passage in the Latin *Opus Imperfectum*, a late Latin Commentary on the Matthaean Gospel. This document, in the discussion of Matthew 2, quotes from an apocryphal book of Seth. The latter would appear to be the testament alleged to have been given by Adam to Seth, according to the so-called Armenian Infancy Gospel, which as we have it is earlier than 590, though how much earlier in its original Syriac (from which it was translated into Armenian) is uncertain. It is related that this apocryphal Testament of Seth was one of the objects brought by the Magoi and presented to the infant Jesus at Bethlehem. The *Opus Imperfectum* goes on to say that it was the custom of Magoi to climb a mountain (known as the mount of revelation) every year to look for the coming of the Messiah or Saoshyant, and it calls this mountain the *mons victorialis*. This, says Herzfeld, is obviously not 'the victorious mountain' but 'the mount of the victor', i.e. of the 'Vrathrajan', which is one of the epithets by which the Saoshyant is designated. The same epithet reappears in a later book of the Avesta, the Bahram Yasth, in the form 'Verethragna', who is the human incarnation of a Deity. This Deity, like Vishnu in India, is also incarnate in a number of sub-human forms. Herzfeld considers that there has been assimilation at this (now identified) spot—the Kuh-i-Khwaja—with Islam, since the word Khwaja means Lord, and the Qur'ān makes Mohammed 'Khwaja ba'th wa nashr' (Lord of the Judgment and the Resurrection). There is good reason for identifying the Kuh-i-Khwaja in Eastern Iran with the mountain on which the Saoshyant is expected to appear, and apparently Persians still make pilgrimages to it today, without knowing exactly why.

The important question remains to be answered, 'What could be the earliest date for the dissemination of Christian oral tradition as far as India?' The latest attempt at dealing with this is that of a former Cambridge scholar, the present Bishop of Uganda, who for many years lived in South India as an educationist. According to him, the Christians of the Malabar coast take their origin from a sea-borne Christianity brought to them perhaps as late as the fourth century A.D. down the Persian Gulf by traders. The case is somewhat different when one comes to consider the early references to apostolic work in 'India'. The name 'India' is admittedly ambiguous, and was probably sometimes used to describe southern Arabia. But the fourth-century Syriac romance known as the Acts of Thomas does apparently contain one historically correct tradition, i.e. the linkage between the Christian missionary in the story (known as Thomas) and the Indian king Gundaphorus and his brother Gad. These two latter individuals are genuinely historical figures, and ruled about 19–45 A.D. over a Scytho-Indian empire which extended at that period east and west of the Indus. It is also known that there was a considerable Jewish colony in North-West India in the first century A.D. Bardaisan, the Persian Sage, writing about 196 A.D., refers to 'Parthian' Christians living amongst pagans, and the Bishop thinks this may reasonably refer to the result of the destruction of the Indian-Parthian empire by Kushan invaders in about 50 A.D. Trading intercourse between the Punjab and Alexandria was certainly in existence at the beginning of the third century A.D., at the time when Clement of Alexandria flourished.

From these various pieces of evidence brought together by the Bishop, we may therefore conclude that it is no longer unreasonable to suppose that some knowledge of the main facts of New Testament tradition were being spread in India within a century of Christ's life on earth. When one knows the remarkable readiness with which Indians to this day open themselves to hear new religious ideas, it is quite natural to believe that the remarkable stories about Jesus would have been readily transmitted orally, and that they would have excited a certain amount of rivalry, followed by attempts at imitation on the part of the followers of the Buddha. More than that it is unsafe to say, but it is resonable to infer that we can no longer be sure that the stories depicted in the sculptures at Lahore, and recounted in some of the later Jatakas, are entirely independent of New Testament tradition.

CHAPTER IX

INDIGENISATION

An Oxford-trained African professor who is a citizen of the new state of Ghana has written lately, in effect, that although the member of a social group may wish to drink with others out of a great river, need he use only one sort of cup? He puts forth this challenge as a Christian who is desirous of keeping as much as he reasonably can of his own specific Akan culture. Must Christianity, he asks, change the cup, or cannot it remain content to be the river that fills it?

In one form or another this question has been put, ever since the Church of Christ set out upon her journey. Even on the day of Pentecost we hear of unity amid diversity, the one Spirit 'dividing to every man severally' in the great burst of praise, so that, whatever happened, it was said: 'We do hear them speak in *our* tongues the wonderful works of God.'

We might almost say that the question was asked 'in reverse' by the Jewish Palestinian converts to Christ, who seemed to want to keep their essentially Jewish customs of circumcision and eating Kosher food, as well as of appealing to the Old Testament, and to impose many of their customs upon those whom, in their turn, they evangelised. St. Paul's answer to this was both clear and uncompromising. He viewed their appeal as one not for indigenisation, so much as for syncretism; and when he saw Jewish Christians seeking to fasten the yoke of Judaism upon their converts, his indignation knew no bounds. He was quite ready to appeal to the Old Testament, whenever appropriate, but only in support of prophetic Christianity. To the Galatians he sternly declares that if they submit to ceremonial circumcision Christ will profit them nothing.

For the first three hundred years of Christianity, in fact, when the infant church was struggling for the right to live, there can have been but little thought of consecrating local customs to the service of the new religion, or even of making much reinterpretation of any religious rites, save those of the Jews. This latter, of course, was done, and we know that the Eucharist must have been an adaptation of the *kiddush*: but even so, the Master himself had given his disciples a warning about the danger of trying to put new wine into old bottles, so that there was a justifiable reluctance on their part to

206

adapt much of the ordinances of the old Torah to Christian use.
Jesus Himself had said that he did not come to destroy the latter but
to fulfil it. Yet this fulfilment soon appeared, especially in the teaching of Paul, to be an enlargement extending into the realm of grace,
not of law, and as a delivery from 'beggarly ordinances' into 'the
glorious liberty of the children of God'. Moreover, in the very
nature of the case the early Christians lived as a people apart, 'a
colony of Heaven', a spiritual Israel, a *tertia gens*, and therefore
separate, as was Israel after the flesh. Their standard was of necessity a lofty one, and it kept them from mixing much with the folk
around them. Yet this exclusiveness, though perhaps inevitable,
had its dangers, for it could easily lead to a self-righteous superiority,
to a Pharisaic 'I thank God that I am not as other men are'.

Up to 313 A.D. there must clearly have been a good deal of this
exclusiveness of the kind that is described in the anonymous epistle
to Diognetus:

IV. b. 'I think thou hast learned sufficiently that Christians are right in
holding aloof from the vanity and delusion of the pagan world,
and from the punctiliousness and pride of the Jews.'

V. 5. 'They live in countries of their own, but simply as sojourners;
they share the life of citizens, but endure the lot of foreigners;
every foreign land is to them a fatherland, and every fatherland
a foreign land.'

and between 313 and 395 only a gradual relaxation. Yet it seems
quite clear that without any explicit episcopal direction a church
like that of the district round Edessa could adopt a very different
institutional set-up from that, let us say, of Rome or even Jerusalem,
and from these, in so far as they were Greek-speaking communities,
it was separated by language. If we are to believe Professor
Burkitt's interpretation of its documentary records, it was very nearly
Buddhist as an institution, exalting celibacy, and reserving baptism
for celibates, although in other respects substantially orthodox in
doctrine.

It is only perhaps from the time of Theodosius onwards that we
get a sort of studied policy of syncretism, which finally comes to
concrete expression at the end of the sixth century in the famous
letter of Gregory the Great to Mellitus and Augustine, which is at
the moment so frequently being quoted, that we cannot avoid
recording it here.

'When Almighty God shall bring you to the most reverend Bishop
Augustine, our brother, tell him what I have, upon mature deliberation
on the affairs of the English, determined upon, viz., that the temples
of the idols in that nation ought not to be destroyed; let holy water
be made and sprinkled in the said temples, let altars be erected, and

relics placed. For if those temples are well built, it is requisite that they be converted from the worship of devils to the service of the true God; that the nation, seeing that their temples are not destroyed, may remove error from their hearts, and knowing and adoring the true God, may the more familiarly resort to the places to which they have been accustomed. And because they have been used to slaughter many oxen in the sacrifices to devils, some solemnity must be exchanged for them on this account, as that on the day of the dedication, or the nativities of the holy martyrs, whose relics are there deposited, they may build themselves huts of the boughs of trees, about those churches which have been turned to that use from temples, and celebrate the solemnity with religious feasting, and no more offer beasts to the devil, but kill cattle to the praise of God in their feasting, and return thanks to the Giver of all things for their sustenance; to the end that, whilst some gratifications are outwardly permitted them, they may the more easily consent to the inward consolations of the grace of God. For there is no doubt that it is impossible to efface everything at once from their obdurate minds, because he who endeavours to ascend to the highest place, rises by degrees or steps and not by leaps. Thus the Lord made Himself known to the people of Israel in Egypt; and yet He allowed them to use the sacrifices which they were wont to offer to the devil in His own worship so as to command them in His sacrifice to kill beasts to the end that, changing their hearts, they might lay aside one part of the sacrifice, whilst they retained another; that whilst they offered the same beasts which they were wont to offer, they should offer them to God and not to idols; and thus they would no longer be the same sacrifices. Thus it behoves your affection to communicate to our aforesaid brother, that he, being there present, may consider how he is to order all things. God preserve you in safety, most beloved son.'

The fifth Canon of the Council of Ratisbon, in 742 states as follows, however;

'We have decreed also that each Bishop so order his diocese that God's people do nought that is pagan, but rather cast from them and utterly eschew all the contaminating filth of heathenism; whether it be the heathen sacrifices in connection with the dead; or resorting to divination and unlawful prying into knowledge hidden from us; or participation in sacrificial offerings, which foolish men offer in the very church's precincts but in the pagan manner, daring to name in their offerings holy martyrs and confessors; these and all other such rites of paganism are to be unremittingly forbidden.'

In the tenth century, when Olaf Haraldson became king of Norway, and

'succeeding in establishing Christianity as the national religion, he summoned an assembly at which a code of laws was drawn up known as Olaf's Kristentet which was apparently the joint work of Olaf and Bishop Grimkill. The law which related to the observance of heathen customs is of special interest from a missionary standpoint. It made no attempt to suppress the social customs connected with heathenism, but endeavoured to associate them with the observance of Christian customs. It directed that wherever three families could meet together and have a common feast and custom of drinking beer was to be observed, the beer having first been blessed "in honour of Christ and the Blessed Virgin for good years and peace". Fines were imposed in the case of a breach of this law. A step towards the abolition of slavery was made by the law which provided that, instead of offering a slave as a sacrifice at the meeting of "the assembly of people", one slave should be set free, and that one should be liberated every Christmas.'

In the twelfth century

'Otto in Germany made a clean sweep of temples and idols. He proposed to the assembled people that, inasmuch as the worship of the true God could not be combined with that of idols, they should proceed to destroy the temples of the false gods. When they hung back, moved by superstitious fears, Otto and his assistants, armed with hatchets and pickaxes, and having obtained their reluctant consent, proceeded to carry out the work of destruction. The first temple to be attacked was that of the Slavic god Trigular, i.e., the three-headed, which contained an image of the god and was decorated with sculptures and paintings. As it had been the custom to dedicate to this god a tenth portion of all the spoils taken in war, its temple contained much treasure. The Bishop having sprinkled the spoils with holy water and having made the sign of the Cross, distributed them amongst the people. The heads of Trigular he afterwards sent to Rome. A sacred oak, which was valued for its shade, the Bishop allowed to remain, but he insisted that a horse which was used for purposes of divination should be sent out of the country and sold.'

In all these instances, says Bishop Lucas of Masasi, we may trace the working of the same principles laid down in apostolic times which we have summarised as the law of charity, the law of liberty, and the recognition of the holiness due to God. Pope Gregory directs that care be taken to avoid any grave dislocation of the people's customs; they are to be modified and redirected and enriched, but idols were to be destroyed. The Council of Ratisbon suggests that things had gone too far in the direction of toleration, and offerings to the dead and divination come under special condemnation. Bishop Grimkill treads closely in the steps of Pope Gregory. Otto's actions suggest that paganism had again become a danger, and the horse also used in divination had to go; but the distribution of the blessed spoils and the preservation of the sacred oak show the same spirit careful not to bind on man burdens too grievous to be borne.

The subject of syncretism versus indigenisation has been dealt with historically at some length within the last fifty years by Professor Ernst Lucius of Strassburg. He begins by describing how in a number of cases in the early centuries of Christianity pagan temples were razed and churches erected in place of them, though, in some cases, there was a partial adaptation of an existing building. In this practice we may see an observance of a widely-accepted principle that sacred sites may well be transferred from the use of one religion to that of another. If numinous experience has been sought and found in any particular spot, it may well be regarded as wise policy to continue to let people find it there, albeit in a different form, so long as they don't go on worshipping the old *numina*. Lucius describes how building material from the temples was utilised in the construction of churches. This did not matter in the case of pillars or blocks of stone, but it was another question altogether when it came to the employment of friezes and statuary, or of building with painted walls. How far could non-Christian material rightly be used for merely decorative purposes? It seems quite clear that laxist as well as rigorist views prevailed in this matter from early times. One has only to look at some church mosaics and catacomb paintings to see how easily non-Christian motifs were retained in some cases, while in others there is not the slightest evidence of their use. I have been told that in Egypt some of the monks converted temples into monasteries, but described the frescoes of Egyptian gods painted on their walls as representing devils. But there seems evidence that other monks steadfastly refused to do this, and themselves would not go near the ruined temples, nor even allow their novices to do so. In England it has been said that there is considerable evidence for the utilisation by the Saxons of old pre-Christian sites for the building of parish churches, as shown by the number of circular or elliptical churchyards, with the church itself built on a mound inside—obviously cases where a 'high place' has been taken over from paganism and utilised for Christian worship.

Lucius continues with the consideration of what objects of veneration were taken over or adapted. He points out that fundamentally the commonest form of ancient cultus would seem to have been that of departed ancestors, heroes, and chieftains, which is practically universal and world-wide at one stage of human development. He puts side by side the cult of the departed, as it is to be seen not only among Greeks and Romans, but also among the Indo-Germanic tribes of Central Europe, among the Egyptians, and among the Arabs. He might easily have added something about its prevalence both in China and in the islands of the Pacific; but of course he is more concerned with the Mediterranean cults, as being those with which the Christian movement was first confronted. These, he says, divide naturally into the cult of the ordinary dead and the cult of heroes. Natural affection, no doubt, played a considerable part in the remembrance of the former: but the heroes stood in the view of those who venerated them only a little lower than the gods, and they performed various functions such as protectors of the country-side, deliverers from danger on sea or land, healers of disease, and revealers of the future. Their patronage was a most treasured possession. Altars were erected to them, and sacrifices offered. They obviously played much the same role as deified heroes in India, whose cultus has been described by Mr. O'Malley in his work on popular Hinduism. There was no prescribed limit to their numbers, and the famous guide-book of Pausanias shows how numerous they were.

It was not unnatural, and indeed fatally easy, for Gentile Christians to incorporate many of the practices connected with these cults into their own religious system as it developed. On the one hand the care of cemeteries or catacombs often came to be associated with the holding of funeral feasts, the details of which seem to have been taken over more or less directly from the cult of the departed ancestors as it prevailed among the pagans. There is evidence that even so convinced and pious a Christian as Monica, the mother of St. Augustine of Hippo, was in the habit of taking food and drink to the graves of the departed. It is true that she gave up the practice when she went to live at Milan, but Augustine himself said that he had the feeling that she would not have so easily relinquished it if it had not been for the influence of her son and of the great bishop Ambrose. It seems clear that the Church leaders were uneasy about these cemetery feasts, but found it difficult to control them, and Augustine in one of his letters says that he found them most prevalent in North Africa, and that they led often to evil excesses. Ambrose issued a definite episcopal prohibition, on the ground that they were only too similar to the *parentalia* rites practised by the pagans, and there are a number of other references to them of a deprecatory character in a sermon by Chrysologus, in Zeno of Verona and in Caesarius of Arles, and in a decree of the Council of Tours of the year 567.

All this kind of thing may be regarded partly as syncretism, partly as an innocent substitution of one kind of pious practice for another. But once it had begun, it was difficult to see where it was to stop. Indeed, it is not always easy to judge when a ceremony at a cemetery belongs to the category of an affectionate remembrance of a departed relative, and when it is something more. Ancestor-cult all over the world has tended to include the belief that the departed are in some way a little more powerful than the living, so that it is possible for them to grant favours, and to exercise their influence in the supernatural world on the part of their descendants. There is no doubt that very many Christians, in asking their departed relatives to pray for them, were only expressing their vivid belief that such relatives were still as much alive as when on earth, so that they could pray for their welfare, and in return ask for their prayers, in the spirit of the well-known hymn,

> 'One family we dwell in Him,
> One Church above, beneath,
> Though now divided by the stream,
> The narrow stream of death.'

But the number of requests for the prayers of the departed which occur on early Christian monuments may possibly indicate something more than this, in fact, the carrying over into popular Christianity of a genuine ancestor-cultus. The difficulty of reconciling the latter with orthodox Christian doctrine about the status of mankind has constantly been felt, and at a later date caused great heart-searching among the Catholic missionaries of the Counter-Reformation when working in China. Ricci, the Jesuit leader of the mission, advocated some kind of adoption of the cult of ancestors by the Christian Church as being simply a form of 'year's mind'; but the Pope, after giving his recommendation very careful consideration, finally decided against it. It is interesting to notice that in the discussion held in 1955 by the Christian Council of the Gold Coast on Christianity and African culture the very same problem was reviewed, though it seems without a definite decision being reached. If the reader will turn to the chapter on the Problem of Africa he will see that all the ground that was gone over by the Christian leaders of the fourth and fifth centuries is having to be gone over again at the present moment by the Christian leaders in Africa, and that much that is to be found described by Professor Lucius as being present in the Mediterranean Gentile world of the first four centuries is actually to be found in many parts of Africa today.

Lucius makes it quite clear that the pluralism so widely prevalent in the Gentile world (and so hard for the Jews themselves entirely to eradicate from their midst—as one may see from the references to devils and demons in the pages of the Talmud) led to the assimilation in many cases of the belief in the activities of angels and saints to some previous pagan cultus. Much of what he says about European pluralism reads as though it were a description of Shinto in Japan or of some forms of southern Hinduism. Whereas many educated pagans had arrived at a form of monotheism, the battle for this was only half-won, since the existence of a supreme High God did not preclude the continued belief in a multiplicity of minor supernatural daevas. Plutarch indeed recognised three grades in the supernatural, first the Supreme Being, then gods of the second rank, and thirdly the daemons who are the servants of the gods (de Fato 9). This is almost exactly the situation as it is indicated by the cultus in China connected with the Altar of Heaven. First comes Shang-ti, the Supreme. Then come various grades of *shen* (Jap. *shin*) which correspond to the lesser gods of India and to the lower grades in Plutarch's hierarchy. The daemons, according to Plutarch, convey the prayers and vows of human beings to the gods. (This belief is to be found almost completely paralleled in the description of some African religious beliefs on page 257. Very much the same scheme is also outlined by Maximus of Tyre—see Zeller, *Phil. der Griechen* III³.)

Daemons figure in the beliefs of Apuleius, Celsus, and Porphyry. Porphyry says that departmental daemons are concerned with a great variety of human affairs, such as music, gymnastic, healing, and the conveyance of votive offerings; and some are guardians of cities or states. The more remotely that Neo-Platonism sundered the Super-Essential Godhead from mankind, the more important became these intermediaries.

We thus approach the second item discussed by Lucius. He points out that Justin, Athenagoras, and Origen all affirm that Christians, besides worshipping the Triune God, believe in the existence of angels, and of these some are personal guardians, and others protectors of districts, towns, and churches. Thus the angels seem to take place within the Christian scheme previously occupied by the ministering daemons. He then proceeds to show how the saints and martyrs gradually but gently put the angels into the background, taking over from them many of their duties and services, though perhaps leaving them their function as personal guardians, since these are allotted to them in the Gospels. Lucius continues:

'The angelic beings are therefore to be regarded not only as the successors of the daemons but as the actual forerunners of the saints. They paved the way for the cultus of the saints. They broke up the original stubborn monotheism of Christianity and developed and made legitimate within it an almost polytheistic way of thinking. They shivered the conception of One Single Providence into fragments. They peopled the universe with a whole category of beings who were intermediate between God and man, a category so elastic that it not only included beings from above but also those from below, men and women elevated by God as a recognition of their special services rendered.'

It is plain to Lucius that these latter quite simply and easily slipped into the place previously occupied by the heroes of pre-Christian paganism. He shows how this occurs. There were two main ways in which Christians could manifest heroic virtue. The one was by asceticism, involving the renunciation of all kinds of worldly goods for the sake of reaching perfection, 'even as your Heavenly Father is perfect'. The other was by martyrdom, the specific sacrifice of one's life in conflict with the powers of evil as manifest in the pagan Empire and its persecuting officials. The whole conflict between the Empire and the Church was seen as a gigantic battle with invisible forces of evil, with the devil and his angels, and with those human beings who were in subjection to them (as we read in the Epistle to the Ephesians: 'Our wrestling is not against flesh and blood, but against principalities, against powers, against the rulers of the darkness of this world, against spiritual wickedness in high places'). The new heroes soon came to be venerated with only a little less esteem than the pagan heroes, and it was natural to invoke their aid, to ask them for their prayers, and to seek for their patronage and protection.

It remains a serious question as to whether this kind of syncretism was one which the Church ought ever to have countenanced. Granted that the martyrs and confessors, as well as the holy and humble men of heart, often provided admirable examples for weaker Christians to follow, their veneration as patrons raises the acute question as to whether any human being can justly be regarded as meritorious. Indeed, if we stick to the New Testament, it is hard to escape the conviction that when Jesus says that when we have done all that is required of us, we are still bound to describe ourselves as unprofitable servants who have only done our bare duty; and when St. Paul says: 'All have sinned and fallen short of the glory of God', they both mean exactly what they say.

But of course this adoption of a hero-cult into Christianity is only one item among many. The veneration of sacred spots and sacred natural objects or even statues raised many delicate questions. One old custom after another tended to creep into Christianity from outside, and the more that illiterate barbarians received mass-baptism, the more they were prone to carry over into their new life remnants of the old.

It was obviously a matter of sincere concern with Christian bishops as to what to allow and what to forbid, and we know that both Boniface and Gregory the Great ordered sacred trees to be cut down, whereas holy wells were often simply rechristened and dedicated to a saint. The famous letter sent by Gregory to the members of the Roman mission to Kent previously quoted, makes it clear that the Bishop of Rome was in this instance prepared to render the transition from the observance of pagan to Christian festivals as easy as possible, though we must admit he did it in no really unsatisfactory way, since only the day and place were to be retained. The object of worship and the mode of worship were to be entirely Christian, even though some *social* customs were allowed to pass on without change.

Bishop Lucas of Masasi has expressed his anxiety that, as far as possible, his clergy in Central Africa will observe the same principles. He says:

> 'We must do our utmost to keep far from us the attitude of mind which considers customs that seem perhaps to us uncouth, bizarre, far removed from European ways to be therefore bad.   Our first aim must be to conserve all that possibly can be conserved of essential native life. . . . The whole world will suffer a loss if the African forsakes the contribution which he alone can make through striving to confine himself in moulds that are not his. . . . Older and responsible non-Christians continue to hold aloof from Christianity, distrusting its influence and misliking what they imagine to be its message . . . because the evils of detribalisation have filled them with a right alarm. . . . It is impossible to regard the religious systems of savage and barbarous people as merely the work of the devil.   That they do invariably contain elements which are directly opposed to Christianity, and must therefore be destroyed, cannot be denied; but the more they come to be understood, the more they show that the light that lighteneth every man that cometh into the world has not been without its witness in the darkest parts of the earth; and in the providence of God a substructure has been prepared to which the firm building of Christianity will wisely be related.'

Little matters will occur to many of us at once, which are mainly concerned with good manners.   Thus I was warned in India never to salute people with the left hand, because the latter is considered unlucky, and therefore to greet in this way was discourteous. Again, the European when he beckons holds his hand with the fingers uppermost, whereas the African when he beckons holds the fingers pointing down, so that the European movement seems to him rude and unseemly.   But indigenisation, as distinct from syncretism, means very much more than this.   It means, as we know, the use of the vernacular in worship and preaching, the use of local architecture and furnishing for church buildings, the use of indigenous music, the adaptation of local customs to the expression of Christian doctrines in such a way that people can understand them better, and above all, a ministry of persons who belong to the country and are not importations from elsewhere, a Christian educational system conducted by teachers drawn from the same source, and a corpus of indigenous though orthodox theology.   But most of all it means loving the people of a country and their ways as Christ loves them, and so helping them to make the best of themselves without de-nationalisation.   The difficulties inherent in carrying out such a programme and the dangers of either too much stiffness in checking and

15

too much readiness in granting steps in the progress towards indigenisation before its time, are patent to all.   We who are English cannot
but remember that, although we eventually had English bishops and
clergy, we began by having Italian ones, and one early archbishop,
Theodore of Tarsus, was a Greek.   Later we suffered from Norman-
French ones.   No one could deny that there was certainly a period
when the Christian faith was not indigenised in England.   Some
might even say that it did not become fully indigenous until after
the Reformation in the sixteenth century, and that then it may have
over-nationalised itself so as to become insular.   The balance between Catholicity or ecumenicity on the one hand, and a reasonable
nationalism on the other, is always a delicate one.   Even the
centralised organisation of the Latin Communion allows a considerable number of local variations in customs and some concessions in
the matter of vernacular; and it has at times been so zealous about
indigenisation as to err in the direction of tacitly, if not explicitly,
tolerating syncretism.

Mr. Malcolm Macdonald in his account of official journeys in
Sarawak made during the past twelve years, furnishes some striking
and unexpected examples of the problems of indigenisation.   The
Ibans whose customs he so vividly describes, and for whom he has
obviously developed so great an affection and respect, represent a
community roughly resembling the pagan Anglo-Saxons of the sixth
century A.D.   He gives examples of Christian evangelisation undertaken among them by a Dutch Roman Catholic priest, an austere but
efficient American Methodist minister, and an Australian Puritan
working as a free-lance; and describes how these in their several ways
were trying to ease the transference of the simple Bornean peoples into
our perplexing modern world.   Mr. Macdonald shows some apprehension lest there should be a wiping out of innocent tribal cultures.
He evidently fears lest in creating a new Christian culture, much
should be destroyed which is really worth preserving, and he does not
want to see the Ibans or their neighbours turned into replicas of the
Middle West or of suburban Sydney.   He describes how a beautiful
pagan girl, in going off to a Christian Mission School, became involved in having a hair-do, using lipstick, and wearing high-heeled
shoes.   For a time at any rate she was neither a good Iban nor a
really pleasing example of a modern Christian.   It is very doubtful
whether in a climate like that of Borneo, the complete covering up of
the torso is in the best interests of hygiene.   After all the Christian
doctrine is that the body is the Temple of the Holy Spirit; and
Christian missionaries from the Scandinavian countries at any rate
should feel no difficulty about cultivating a healthy attitude towards

it. Mr. Macdonald's obvious regret at the cutting off of the splendid black manes of hair possessed by the Dayak boys has of course another side to it. How much is necessary in the interests of cleanliness? Does the possession of such masses of hair tend to make the Bornean lousy? It is good to read that the Australian evangelist used the old folk tunes of Sarawak, fitting new words to them and turning them into hymns; and it seems fairly clear that the Roman Catholic missionaries were doing all they could to salvage the local cultures. The story of the sudden burst of enthusiasm for baptism on the part of the chiefs is fascinating, and reminds one vividly of the days of Augustine of Canterbury and Ethelbert of Kent, with the mass-baptism of his subjects in the river Swale. But how history resembles itself! A situation followed uncannily resembling that prevailing after the conversion of Ethelbert, when one of his successors sought to maintain a kind of combination of pagan and Christian worship, and for a time forced the church leaders of south-eastern England into exile. Temangang Koh, that fine old Iban chief, must greatly resemble what the chieftains of Anglo-Saxon England were like, and it does not seem that the drinking customs of those days can have been greatly different from those of twentieth-century Sarawak, to wit impromptu singing at meals and the oft-repeated toasting of one another by men and women.

A somewhat striking piece of indigenisation, which must be set off against what has been said elsewhere under the heading of China since 1911, comes to me from the head of the department of music at Yenching College, Peking. He points out that in 1936 a volume called *Hymns of Universal Praise* was published in China, and he claims that it is now in use by every Christian denomination in that country, and that there is no other hymnal in all Christendom which serves such diverse groups of worshippers. The lead in the formation of this was taken by the Anglican group of Christians, the Chung Hua Sheng Kung Hui in 1931, but other groups soon followed, and the remarkable fact is that not only within the Anglican group is the new hymnal used by both Catholic and Evangelical schools of thought, but that outside it some twenty other denominations also use it, while as to its contents, the following remarkable features must be recorded.

Fourteen per cent of the words are original Chinese compositions, one from an ancient Nestorian hymn the MS. of which was discovered in 1907 in a cave in West China, and another from a hymn written by a Roman Catholic Chinese bishop in the period of the Ming Dynasty. There are sixty-seven tunes which are either Chinese or composed in the Chinese mode, and of these fifteen are indigenous tunes, eight of them genuine folk-melodies, one a chant used in Confucian ceremonies, one used by Buddhist monks, two from a Chinese repertoire of music written for a special Chinese instrument with seven strings, and three which are used in the chanting of Chinese poetry. Dr. T. C. Chao, who has also composed fifty-four original 'hymns for the people', has in addition adapted a Confucian ceremony so as to make it into a piece of Christian worship.

Bishop Lucas of Masasi (Central Africa) has enumerated a number of points in which he considers there should be a sympathetic approach to non-Christian customs. What he says must we admit primarily concern conditions in Africa, but the list is such that in general it could be applied in almost any part of the mission field.

Clothing. Christianity should not involve any change in customary native dress, since to interfere with it, especially in tropical countries, may easily involve damage to health. People usually tend to dress in a way which is suitable for the climate, and to interfere with this simply on the grounds of propriety involves a false view of the human body, which is the temple of the Holy Ghost, and may cause people to become verminous or to develop pulmonary disease. It is somewhat significant that Moslems are perhaps stricter than Christians and certainly than non-Moslem pagans about covering up the body, and although formally they lay great stress upon ablutions, it seems likely that since many Moslem countries have a hot climate, there may be a good deal of disease as well as dirt attached to this practice.

Dancing. This perhaps is a greater problem in Africa than in most countries, and it is so universal a recreation that except where it is accompanied by gestures which are erotic, obscene, or suggestive, it should be retained under reasonable control as a social institution. It is, however, noticeable that the dancing of men and women together as partners, which is an accepted practice among Europeans and Americans, seems in Africa to all but the most sophisticated coast dwellers, shocking beyond belief, and in the old days it would probably have been frowned upon in China.

Divination. This in any form is clearly incompatible with Christianity, and probably also with Buddhism in a pure form. There can be no compromise with it, and those who are admitted as catechumens should be expected to promise that they will have nothing more to do with it. The practice must be held to include the drawing of horoscopes, the looking for auspicious days, the taking of omens, any kind of fortune telling, witchcraft, and the use of charms.

Funeral rites. There are probably a number of pious and touching customs in connection with funerals which may be retained without any serious harm, though sometimes with a new significance attached to them. But all these need carefully to be reviewed, as sometimes they are not edifying or involve a pure piece of superstition.

Hospitality. All over the world customs of hospitality ought to be preserved. Indeed the decay of hospitality is one of the tragedies of modern life. Linked up with it are many ideas which are deeply concerned with the practice of the right Christian attitude towards one's neighbour and those in need, and the beautiful ceremonies of African hospitality or for the matter of that of its Arab counterpart deserve to be cherished. Bishop Lucas considers that the analogy of these customs provides a simple and effective way of teaching converts the preparation which is necessary for the right reception of Our Lord at Holy Communion.

Housing. Here again there should not be any hasty interference with native custom. Very often the architecture of houses or huts is that which is most suitable for the climate, and this applies equally to the nature of their furniture and effects. But hygiene has necessarily to be considered. Christ is the Lord of Health, and Christians must be expected to wish to be both clean and healthy. But the co-operation of converts should be sought in the promotion of sanitation, in drainage, disposal of sewage, and the provision of a pure water supply. It is always difficult to abolish practices which clearly involve contagion, such as the one in Africa in which a tobacco cheroot is passed round the whole company, each taking a few puffs. It is easy to wound people's sense of good manners by suddenly prohibiting this. The only thing to be done is patiently to explain the dangers of passing on disease by contagion, and to initiate people into the meaning and use of antiseptics. Medical missions are of course chiefly concerned with these matters, and sometimes beliefs about the causes of sickness are bound up with false ideas of religion. But wherever some simple remedy proves to be the correct and sensible one, discovered by long experience, such as the genuine efficacy of a certain herb, it would be wrong to disturb it.

Initiatory rites. This is a most difficult subject, and needs the most careful and detailed consideration in each country. It has been said that the answer of almost all European missionaries in regard to these rites would tend to be condemnatory. It is unhappily true that many of the ceremonies are morally dangerous, and are often accompanied by the singing of definitely obscene songs and a certain amount of undesirable dancing. Nevertheless in almost all primitive communities there are features in the rites of initiation which are necessary and even harmless, and leaders like Bishop Lucas have taken immense pains to sift out the good from the bad, and to make a new rite of initiation which shall be distinctively Christian and culminate in a Christian act of worship, but nevertheless retains as many as possible of the old ceremonies duly adapted. The Bishop worked out a separate ceremony for the boys and for the girls. To what extent other Christian Communions have followed his example I cannot ascertain, but it seems clear that some of them have adopted the policy of a clean cut.

Marriage. Here, of course, there are a great many ceremonies from which a selection may be made, and which, having regard for the very conservative character of folk all the world over where weddings are concerned, it is most desirable to preserve. Thus in India the sign of marriage is a wreath of flowers, and it is clear that although the ring is bound to be introduced, this should not mean the disuse of the wreath. Again, Hindu married women have always put on their foreheads the painted red dot or *tilaka*, as the sign that they are married. There seems no reason why Christian women should be expected to renounce the use of the *tilaka*, and I have noticed that a great many of them still put it on.[1]

Music. Little need be said here. There is every reason for preserving as much as possible in a Christian community the forms of music indigenous to the country. As Bishop Lucas says, it is a definite loss to religion and worship if use is not made of native melodies, provided that they are sung to suitable words, and that the original words are not likely to be such as might cause scandal by being remembered.

Names. It has often been the practice to give converts names from the Bible, and where, as for example in India, the pre-conversion names are so often those of Indian divinities, there seems good reason for encouraging the practice.[2] But there is a danger lest the banishment of names belonging to the country should seem to suggest that there is something foreign about becoming a Christian. Bishop Lucas thinks that the best way is to try to make up names on an indigenous basis which, although possessing a Christian meaning, are formed according to the custom of the country, and in harmony with its language.

Religion in general. Whatever shows that Christianity is the

---

[1] I am told that in many cases the *tilaka* on girls has now nothing to do with marriage, but is just 'a lucky dot'. Its continuance in this case seems more doubtful.

[2] Still, as long as we continue to call Christian girls by such names as 'Diana', and Scandinavian Christian boys by such names as 'Thor', it seems hard to be fussy about this.

fulfilment of what has already been adumbrated in the immemorial customs of the past will do perhaps more than anything else to help the Church to become really indigenous. Bishop Lucas says that many African peoples tend to regard it as a beautiful European religion into which certain specially kind Europeans are prepared to enrol them as associates. This will not do at all. The convert must be made to realise that Christianity is an African religion in a very real sense, and that God has been preparing his fathers for it until the time of the full revelation should come. It is surely a most fortunate circumstance that in the Bishop's own diocese of Masasi it proved possible to build the cathedral church on the slopes of a conical hill, the name of which, as far back as man could remember was Mtandi, which means the Hill of the Sacrificial Flour or in plain English the Hill of the Living Bread.

It has been pointed out that in India what is called *bhakti* or devotion to God has nine spiritual degrees:

    (i) Devotion to the Most Holy Name.
   (ii) Devotion to the Most Holy Feet.
  (iii) Hearing or reading the Holy Scriptures.
  (iv) Devotion by means of song.
   (v) Worship or oblation.
  (vi) Devotion to the saints.
 (vii) Work for God as his servant.
(viii) Friendship with God.
  (ix) The offering of self in thought, word, and deed.

It is obvious that this scheme can very easily be adapted to Christian use, and I have heard that in parts of India the preaching of retreats based in this way on *bhakti* has met with a wonderful response, because it establishes the truth that in Christianity is found the interpretation of the best in their own religious past, the fulfilment of what without it remained partial, and since this skeleton for retreat addresses is derived from the Gita, it makes them feel that Christianity is Eastern and not European.

Visual aids. Here there is little need to elaborate. Nothing does more to dispel the idea that the Christian faith is something foreign than the use of painting and sculpture indigenous to the country. Very beautiful work has in recent years been done on these lines in India and China, and some African sculpture is most impressive.

Vows. It seems to be a normal human instinct to vow an offering to some supernatural being or other if a request is granted. There seems no reason why this instinct should not be purified and made to take its place in Christian practice on the principle that God is the sole Giver of all our good, and that any benefit should be met by a thank-offering as an appropriate response.

Other problems created by the desire to make the church indigenous are those created by a composite community of converts. For example, it will not do to have too distinctively Hindu ceremonial in a church where a moiety of the congregation are ex-Moslems. Another problem is that tribal initiation tends to over-emphasise the sexual element, and anything which does so cannot be incorporated into a Christian initiation ceremony, which emphasises the responsibilities of adult life, and the disciplining of the body. Other points in this connection are that non-Christians prior to the initiation of their children make no effort to give the latter any conscious instruction or correction. The proper Christian view is, of course, that the training of a child should begin from the beginning, and that there should be discipline throughout the whole period of childhood. (It is easy to see how even in countries with a Christian tradition, slack parents slip back into this way of treating childhood. They take no personal responsibility for the training of their children, although the state compels them to send them to school. But there is no real home training.) In parts of Africa, parents do not send their children to the mission school until just before the time of initiation. When the latter approaches they realise that they have got to do something about it, and there is a hustle to get the children to their classes.

I cannot forbear to add my own personal testimony as to the need for the present policy of indigenisation in India to be still more faithfully pursued, especially in the rural areas. Many of the Christian congregations I have visited have been excellent people, but the buildings in which they worshipped and the furniture in them were European, and the hymns they sang were often in English, and sung to European melodies, and one fancies that relatively poor communities cannot afford to renew their books easily. This is not, as I am well aware, everywhere the case. Indian hymns and melodies are being increasingly used, and I have heard some of them; and some Indian churches are Indian in architecture. But a sane Christian Catholicism will, I am sure, endeavour to bring Indian villagers to the worship and service of the Eternal Christ by an extended transformation of existing institutions of worship, and avoid excessive pruning, or 'too much stiffness in refusing'.

Thus the wandering Hindu ascetic is often a real 'jongleur de dieu'; he goes round (I have seen him) singing not secular love-songs, but bhakti lyrics about the Love of Hari or Shiva. There is a real opportunity for Christian 'jongleur de dieu' to go round singing vernacular songs to Indian melodies about the Love of Jesus. It was encouraging to find Indian carol-singers going round in one place on Christmas Eve, but a little shattering to hear them burst out into Charles Wesley.

Then, again, even the daily worship of a Siva temple, so often stigmatised as gross and unspiritual, could be purified and built up into something nobler, as doubtless is already being done by faithful and enterprising Catholics in some areas. But let me tell what I had the opportuinity of seeing. The village, a large one, was awakened daily at 6 a.m. by the procession of holy water to the local Saivite temple, the vessel, borne on the shoulder of a devotee, being preceded by minstrels with two drums and wood-wind, playing an appealing melody. No excuse was offered the community of forgetting or ignoring the claims of Divine worship, and, by the passage of the urn, the whole village was symbolically lustrated from end to end. On arrival at the temple, the sanctuary was swept, and the symbol of the Divine Being ceremonially lustrated. At sunset food was brought and offered in front of the symbol, and after offering and consecration divided between the celebrant and the congregation, each of whom received a portion reverently in the right hand. Incense had already been offered, and other acts of worship followed, the offering of fire, the waving of peacock fans, the waving of a candelabra, and the ringing of a bell: and the whole time there was the chanting by the congregation of an ancient Vedic hymn, the archaic language of which they possibly did not understand, with the added recitation of a mantra in which the Divine Being was addressed, in effect, as 'Thou art He who is. Thou art the Alpha and the Omega.' Then came individual acts of submission to the Divine Will on the part of each worshipper, on whose bowed head a golden helmet was held, surmounted by a crest consisting of small models of the feet of Shiva, accompanied by a short sentence of benediction. As J. B. Pratt said, three years ago, 'the worshippers emerged from the sanctuary with a look of spiritual satisfaction on their faces'. I asked how old this ritual was, and was told, at least eighth century A.D. in form, contemporary with Anglo-Saxon England.

The above, of course, as I know very well, is only one side. The A and Ω in this instance is the personification of the Life-Force, ruthless tropical nature, itself creaturely, and subordinate to Him Who is The Lord and Giver of the Life-Force; and the symbol of the God, though on this case of silver, and enormously elaborated and robed, is ultimately that of a gross pre-Aryan fertility symbol, even though now disguised and interpreted in a different sense (some say the word *lingam* only means 'symbol', others that it means 'the rod of continence'). Moreover there was still present in the temple an element of crude polytheism, the effigy of a female consort for the deity, as well as representations of other subordinate divinities. And yet one feels that Our Lord would have said: 'I am not come to destroy but to fulfil', and that the innocent and natural ritualism of the Indian peasant might well be preserved and re-directed upon new symbols, and upon a different concept of the Self-Existent A and Ω. This I believe has already been done in some areas by Catholics. It clearly needs to be done in many more. Daily evening worship in Christian Catholic hands could retain many of its existing features, detached from their old associations, cleansed, and oriented upon the pure and holy Deity of the Bible, the Word Incarnate, victorious and glorified.

Since this was written, a small but important book has been published entitled *Appreciating India's Music*: The Christian Literature Society, Madras. It is expected to help on the indigenisation of India's Christian psalmody.

CHAPTER X

THE CHANGE TO THE MODERN WORLD

(A) THE MACHINE AGE AND THE RISE OF MARXISM

In Chapter V we have sought to trace the story of Christian expansion, and during our survey we were bound to observe the change which coincides approximately with the capture of Byzantium by the Ottoman Turks in 1453. From this point onward we seem to move with increasing rapidity into the modern world. Up to that time, except for the mission of the Franciscan friars into China (and the travels of Marco Polo), the range of the world for the purposes of evangelisation seems to lie between Ireland and Persia, Scandinavia and North Africa. But from about 1453 human travel so far as Europeans are concerned tends to increase.[1] We hear of explorers

[1] The following list of the achievement of fifteenth-century explorers and travellers, with their dates, is not only impressive but gives some idea of the maritime activities of that age:

1416	First voyage of Prince Henry the Navigator.
1418–19	Portuguese expedition to Porto Santo and Madeira.
1419–22	Embassy from the Shah Rukh of Persia to China.
1419–44	Voyage of Nicolo Conti to India and China and the islands of the Pacific.
1420	Voyage of an Arabian ship round the Cape of Good Hope.
1422	A Chinese embassy to Arabia.
1432	Pilgrimage of Chinese Moslems to Mecca.
1432	Discovery of the seven islands of the Azores.
1434	Gil Eannes circumnavigates Cap Bojader.
1436	Baldaya advances across the Bay of the Rio d'Oro.
1438	The Byzantine explorer, Laskavis Cananos, penetrates to Iceland.
1441	Abyssinian embassy to the Pope.
1441	Discovery of the White Cape.
1443–5	Discovery of the Gulf of Asquin.
1445 or 1447	Discovery of Senegal.
1446	Diego Fernandez discovers Cap de Verde.
1447	Discovery of Kap Verga.
1447	Juan Fernandez penetrates up country in N.W. Africa.
1447	Antonio Malfante reaches the Tuat Oasis.
1447	Reported discovery by the Portuguese of the American continent.
1448	Däne Wollert in Senegambia.
1455	Usodimave's journey to the river Gambia.
1456–8	Discovery of the first Cap de Verde islands.
1457–8	Discovery of the two westernmost islands in the Azores.
1461	Discovery of Sierra Leone and the Pepper Coast.
1462	Discovery of the western Cap de Verde islands.
1466–73	Journey of the Russian, Nikitin, to the borders of the Punjab.
1469	Benedetto Dei reaches Timbuktu.
1470–3	Exploration of the Gulf of Guinea as far as the Equator.
	Beginning of the project to reach the Far East by sailing across the Atlantic.
1473–6	The Danish admirals Pinnig and Pothorst reach Greenland, and the pilot, Skolp, lands in Labrador.
1480–97	English explorers cross the Atlantic as far as the West Indies, and Sebastian Cabot reaches Labrador.

who make great sea voyages, Columbus, Vasco da Gama, Sebastian
Cabot, and Prince Henry the Navigator.   Whatever one may think
about the methods of the Conquistadors and their ruffianly followers, the Church of the Counter-Reformation clearly believed it to
be her duty to use the opportunities which their expeditions afforded
of carrying the Catholic Faith into the New World across the
Atlantic.   We also find in the seventeenth century increasing communication between Europe and the Middle East.   Merchants and
traders extend their operations as far as Mesopotamia and perhaps
even beyond, and it is not long before the Jesuits embark upon a new
and in many ways extremely successful mission to the Chinese
empire.

   But side by side with all this travel and expansion begins in
Europe the earlier development of modern science.   It must not be
supposed that there had been none in the Middle Ages, for it is surprising how much skill and ingenuity, as well as enterprise, survived
from earlier generations within the monasteries.[1]   It is, however,
clear that with the revival of interest in Greek free thought which
begins in the latter half of the fifteenth century, the way is marked
out for new developments based on observation and research, and
no repression on the part of conservative churchmen can avail to
check the movement once it has been begun.   Indeed, the movement
itself would not have been possible if there had not been first the
laying of a sure foundation through affirmation of belief in the
unitary control of the universe by a Wise and Omnipotent Being, so
that it was felt credible that one could study the works of his creation

---

1482–3	The Pope sends a Franciscan mission to Abyssinia.
1482–3	Discovery of the Congo and the coast of Angola.
1483	The first Portuguese in Timbuktu.
1484	Bartolommeo Diaz' alleged circumnavigation of Africa.
1485–6	Diego Cão and Martin Behaim explore the S.W. coast of Africa.
1487	Martin Behaim's alleged discovery of America and of the Straits of Magellan.
1487–93	Covilham makes a journey to India.
1488	Bartolommes Diaz discovers the Cape of Good Hope.
1488–9	Cousin's fictitious reconnaissance from France in the direction of America.

[1] It has been concluded from the diary of Anna Comnena that in Byzantium at the
time of the First Crusade (1096) there were hospitals in which the dangers of sepsis
were understood and guarded against, and it has been said that medical and surgical
science were by no means at such a low level as has been supposed.   'Operations on
nerve and skull; the true origin of venereal diseases; the use of red rays in cases of
smallpox (with accurate statements of their results—knowledge which had to be re-
discovered in the nineteenth century by the Danish scientist, Finsen, who gained the
Nobel prize for doing so)—this and more was known and used in the thirteenth century,
and was largely forgotten two hundred and fifty years later' (see Martindale: in his
short account of St. Camillus de Lellis).   The forgetting of acquired knowledge is a
serious matter.   I sometimes find that rational information on religious matters which
was beginning to be quite well known between the two world wars is now by no means
to be counted on as part of the mental equipment of the present generation, who are
often quite ignorant of its existence.

with the confidence that one could obtain rational answers to one's inquiries. Many feel that with the foundation of the Royal Society in England a great step forward was taken which had its influence beyond the confines of Britain, and it is worth noting that the founders were all of them Christians who owned allegiance to churches of the Reformation. It would be foolish to deny that even here a certain amount of biblical conservatism (now seen to have been both unjustifiable and unwise) led later on to a severance of partnership between some leading Christians and some men of science, but it must never be overlooked that this severance was far from being as complete as has often been supposed.

The work of John Ray, a distinguished seventeenth-century pioneer in the scientific study of living nature, and one of the early Fellows of the Royal Society who was also a Christian, has received attention in the last decade. It has also been shown that John Wesley, long before Darwin, was beginning, perhaps unconsciously, to think along evolutionary lines, and was displaying remarkable freedom and liberalism in his treatment of the early narratives of Genesis, a freedom which was, of course, exercised many centuries earlier by the Alexandrian Jew, Philo, though it seems to have disappeared from Christianity after the time of Origen, whose speculations had perhaps alarmed the ecclesiastics of his day.

Mr. Hoyle thinks that Newton's rather curious tendency to dabble in alchemy and in the numerological interpretation of ancient writings such as the book of Daniel involved him in a strong belief about the possibility of gaining a greater measure of predictability as to the future, and that without this he might never have had enough imagination to conceive the immense scope of the *Principia*. But this is perhaps a matter of opinion, and all will not agree with him.

Hort, the well-known nineteenth-century Cambridge divinity professor, and Charles Darwin were friends, and Hort wrote to Darwin appreciatively about his work; while it is clear, if one takes the trouble to read the letters and memoirs of Darwin, that he was a deeply religious man, embarrassed by the crudity of his evangelical upbringing and antecedents, and that if he had been educated in his early days upon the kind of view of the Bible which is now commonly taught by authority in this country, he would never have felt the embarrassment which led him at times into the desert of agnosticism.

Nevertheless, the change to the modern world which went on faster and faster from the middle of the eighteenth century, and which continued strangely enough as a parallel movement to some of the most ardent and successful Christian missionary enterprises of the first half of the nineteenth century, has had a profound effect both in the theoretical and the practical direction.   On the theoretical side it has expanded human knowledge beyond all expectation in regard to the nature of the physical world, the origin of living organisms, and the past history of the human species.   On the practical side, by means of what we call applied science, it has provided a series of mechanical appliances by which travel has been increased, and made simpler and more speedy; and communication between the different continents has thus become easier; while in the most recent times visual and auditory aids to popular education, the unlocking of the storehouse of atomic energy, and the simplification of labour by the processes of automation, have all helped to initiate the most astounding and revolutionary changes in human habits.   The world of my own childhood knew nothing of motor transport, air travel, radio, television, atomic power stations, or the organisation of the welfare state.   Its chief novelty was the pedal bicycle with tyres. Everything else has come since, most of it in the last forty years.

The delicacy and complication of the machinery by which the operations of human brains and limbs can now be extended, accelerated, and controlled, would of course have seemed miraculous to our forefathers.   Anyone who has looked at the works inside a large modern aeroplane will understand what is meant.   Such machines, though complicated to make and needing great skill to repair, seldom need more than 'minding' when they are actually at work; and the impression which they make on the public is that of the *power of man*, especially in unlocking and applying new forms of physical energy, and in performing delicate mathematical calculations.   Popular feeling, intensified by the invention of artificial space satellites, would often still endorse Swinburne's hazardous paean:

> 'Glory to man in the highest.
> For Man is the master of things.'

although that mastery does not seem to extend to the choice between the good and the evil uses of the energy and skill so suddenly made available.

It would seem then that the whole fabric of Christian enterprise has also been faced with complete alteration within about half a century.   The difference between the period when I entered a public school, and that in which I find myself engaged in writing this book, so far as the world-outlook upon religion is concerned, has undergone a development which it is hard to exaggerate.   Not for a moment would one wish to depreciate the value of many of these changes. They have opened up possibilities, which it is true, it is just as easy to misuse as to use rightly, but if one believes that no real permanent good can come from activity which is based upon either ignorance or falsehood, then one is bound to welcome all the new knowledge which has poured in upon us in a little over half a century. When one compares the text-books of about 1890 with those available today, one can see how immense has been the change for the better. But of course this has meant that much which we thought we knew about the peoples of Asia and their beliefs and practices has had to be drastically revised, and that our interpretation of the documents and traditions upon which we depended for our knowledge of the nature and claims of the Christian faith has also had to undergo revision. But if all this revision has led us nearer to a knowledge and appreciation of the real truth, we cannot but welcome it.

Another most important and far-reaching as well as rapidly accelerating change during the past century has been the urbanisation of a large part of the world's population. Of course, there were urban areas in antiquity in the Indus valley and Mesopotamia, and at any rate in legend one of them, Nineveh, was described as 'A city of three days journey'—presumably one which in a period of slow civilian transport, it might take that time to traverse from one side to another. Antioch, in the first century A.D., had many miles of paved streets. But nothing in antiquity or in the Middle Ages can really compare with the enormous stretches of conurbations which have lately developed. It is said that the built-up suburbs of Los Angeles cover an area as large as the English county of Norfolk; while on the Atlantic seaboard of the United States there is an urban frontage of some depth extending for a length of six hundred miles. Even the seaside towns on the south coast of England, which are now rapidly joining up into an almost continuous line, cannot match this. London in the nineteenth century could already be described as 'a province covered with houses', and its suburban development since then has more than trebled. Most large towns in England as well as on the Continent now sprawl in all directions, and the growth and planning of satellite towns and dormitory villages is more and more tending to obliterate the distinction between town and country life. A glance at a map will show that many of the towns in the North and Midlands of England are already joined up, or soon will be joined to form one vast urbanised population; while along the north of the Chilterns, between Baldock and Dunstable, now stretches an industrial built-up area of many miles.

But this is not the whole story. Uncontrolled industrialisation and the utilitarian development of the countryside have destroyed and are still destroying natural beauty in all directions, and this horror may be seen all over the world, on the Copper Belt of South Africa as much as in the factory districts of Bombay. It is unnecessary here to enlarge upon the outrages which have come to be known collectively as the establishment of subtopia. The menace of ugliness is world-wide and shows few signs of being checked. Its sinister and devastating clutch is to be seen descending upon landscape after landscape in photographs taken as far apart as Rome, Delhi, Calcutta, and the Republics of South America, and it is usually accompanied by an orgy of advertising, whether on the roadside, on the walls of buildings, or even on the trunks of trees.

Mechanisation and ugliness are bound inevitably to produce harmful results upon world-religion, for they foster a sub-human species of life. Religion and beauty are so intimately connected, that even a spiritual puritanism has not always ignored comeliness, but has been productive of austere forms of art. The lives of people in subtopia may well end by being increasingly nasty and brutish, even if of longer duration than in the days of Thomas Hobbes. No world-wide Christian movement can afford to tolerate or to ignore the serious effects which may result from such changes in living conditions, and it should join in whole-hearted support of any attempt at their abolition or amendment. It may well be, however, that much of the better kind of urbanisation has come to stay, and will have to be accepted, but its long-term effects on the minds of human beings in the matter of spiritual values must be taken into account and faced constructively. By all means let the squalid and insanitary village be abolished, in whatever continent it may exist. But let the great nature reserves and national parks be cherished, and where necessary extended (as for example in the preservation of the long Ridge of Delhi), and in every built-up area let there be not only careful designing, but also plenty of good gardens and spacious parks. It is time that these matters were proclaimed as intimately associated with the delivery of the Christian message. To foster ugliness, whether visual or auditory, is as wicked as to commit manslaughter; since it involves the slaughter of the spiritual values of human minds. It should be branded as a deadly offence against God and man.

Meanwhile the most serious and searching challenge which has come to the Christian movement during the past 120 years has been in respect of its relation to the human social order. Prophets have arisen amongst us who have dared to assert that perhaps in some of its manifestations the Christian movement was after all not so admirable, but that it had actually obstructed beneficent work, had resisted enlightenment and progress,[1] had supported an established order of society based on the exploitation of one group of human beings by another, taught a wrong kind of other-worldliness, and instead of continuing to be a world-transforming dynamic force, had become a tool of an oppressive and selfish economic order. It is not that every one of these accusations was wholly just, but there was enough serious truth about them to make them arouse considerable doubts in the minds of many intelligent people of good will. Coming as they did after a century of biblical criticism, it was only too easy for a good many of the younger generation of people who had grown up since 1918 to wonder whether they were not living in a post-Christian world which had lost its old fixed standards (for whatever they were worth), and to see nothing obviously ready to take their place except the Marxist proposed reconstruction of society which had emerged in 1848, and had been gathering force ever since.

This was perhaps the position five or six years before this book was begun. The tide since then had seemed by some to have turned a little, but it is difficult to judge with exactitude whether this turn of the tide is the result of an emotional shrinking from the consequences of change, or whether it is partly due to perverse reactionary thinking, or, again, whether it is due to a gradual recovery of balance by the world in general.[2] Meanwhile the phenomenon of the social revolution is before us, and is having the deepest effects in every continent. It is therefore necessary at this point to devote serious attention to it.

---

[1] The accusation has been made against ascetic and Puritan Christianity that it tended to represent sex-life even of a normal sort as an unclean and shameful thing; that older people, largely as the result of this, were cruel to their sons and daughters who desired to marry, and that in consequence a repressed and neurotic generation grew up in some areas dominated by this kind of Christianity. It is hard to rebut this charge entirely.

[2] In almost every country where Marxism has established itself there are now signs of discussion, unrest, and deviation. Mao-tse-tung, in speeches delivered while this book is being completed, seems to have indicated that China might well be allowed a certain degree of liberalism. It is impossible to foresee whither such a relaxation might lead; but some report that already there has begun another tightening up process. Professor Shen Chin Jui of Peking, however, informed me during a personal interview that the *official* policy of the Chinese People's Republic was one of toleration of varieties of religion, both Christian and non-Christian, so long as they refrained from counter-revolutionary activities; and that even some repair of temples was being encouraged. I hope one can believe this. If it were correct, one feels that Truth would be big enough to take care of itself.

CHAPTER XI

THE PROBLEM OF MARXISM

Its cause can be summed up in one phrase: 'revolt against the exploitation of one human being or group of human beings by another.' The phrase occurs in a recent speech by the Polish Minister Gomulka, who said that it was the only essential feature in Socialism, binding the different varieties of it together in opposition to other types of human polity; and the sense of it has never been absent for long in any human community: indeed one can find glimmerings of it at points all over antiquity. Even those who kept slaves sometimes queried whether it was right to do so. For Western Europeans perhaps the most familiar passages in ancient literature in which exploitation is condemned occur in the Hebrew Old Testament.[1]

In the first century A.D. Stoicism, with its approximation to a doctrine of the brotherhood of mankind, showed some signs of a theoretical attempt to improve the condition of the depressed classes, and may perhaps have actually done something to increase the number of slaves who were freed. But the Christian movement, with the Old Testament at its back, while it does not immediately attack the institution of slavery, introduces such a high doctrine of the worth of the individual soul, that in process of time, albeit very slowly, that institution is dissolved, and when it recurs, as in seventeenth- and eighteenth-century Europe and nineteenth-century America, Christian opinion vigorously and successfully opposes it. Even so, there is still a large mass of diluted or conventionalised Christianity (not to mention unregenerate paganism) which does not feel itself outraged either by actual chattel-slavery, or by its mitigated form of wage-slavery, in which the wage-earner, being at a disadvantage in bargaining with his employer, is compelled to accept an inequitably small wage as compared with the size of the profits

---

[1] It is superfluous to quote all these passages in full; but I give the references to most of them herewith.

Amos 1:6–8; 4:1–3 the condemnation of the rich and careless women; 5:12; 8:4–6.
Micah 2:1–2; 3:1–4; 6:10–12.
Isaiah 3:14–15 which contains the reference to 'grinding the face of the poor'; 10:1–2.
Ezekiel 18:7–9; ch. 34, the indictment of the shepherds.
Deutero–Isaiah 58:3b–7.
Malachi 3:5.

accruing to his employer from that labour; so that the nineteenth century opens with a state of affairs in which, whether in agriculture or in factory-industry, such exploitation is widely prevalent.

Exploitation is not in itself a necessary consequence of differentiation of functions.[1] Even in the most primitive society such differentiation occurs, and among the various endowments which God has been pleased to bestow upon mankind is that of administration, of organising and directing human affairs, whether in agriculture, industry, local government, or statecraft. The basic sinful tendency, however, towards self-centredness and the pursuit of self-interest, which clearly occurs in all human beings, and which vitiates their lives, is specially manifested when those human beings take unfair advantage of one another, and use their endowments not for the public good but for private advantage. That this situation was recognised at a fairly early date by some leading Christians is evident from the treatise *De officiis* written in the fourth century by the famous St. Ambrose, who was Bishop of Milan. Ambrose before his consecration had been a government civil servant, and had been educated with a Stoic background before he became a Christian. In his writings he seems to be trying to baptise the best that he knows in Stoicism into Christianity, and this is especially seen in his treatment of the social problem. So remarkable is this, that one has even heard it said that, if one wants to, one can find Marxism in the pages of Ambrose. Briefly what he says is in effect that without the Fall of man there would have been community of the means of production, but that human sin has led to the existence of a society based on private profit, and with class divisions involving property-owners and

---

[1] Exploitation as a key word recurs almost like a cliché in statement after statement made to this day by party politicians. Thus the leaders of one well-known trade union have issued a memorandum in which they declare that the Press is so much under the control of those who seek to *exploit* the working classes that no newspaper can be relied on to give a truthful report of what is said at any trade-union meeting. It may be doubted whether some of those who talk most loudly are not just as ready themselves to exploit the brainworker, the creative inventor, and the artist, not to mention persons of a different colour. But exploitation as an ugly phenomenon is world-wide, and there are still only too many rich and prosperous folk who care little or nothing as to the living-conditions of those by whose toil their own prosperity and comfort are secured to them. Stories of such callousness come from many parts of Asia, from South Africa, and even from Italy, with its claim to contain the spiritual centre of Christendom. It is not clear that the Papacy has ever excommunicated those Catholics who have condoned the horrors of the Neapolitan slums.

One cannot entirely repress an uneasy suspicion that in any social structure exploitation may occur, since it is the result of an inadequate sense of the value of individual personality. The administrators of a socialist state may only too easily have this inadequate sense, and may therefore come to treat individuals as impersonal units or cogs in the social machine. However obstinate may have been the kulaks in Russia, their ruthless liquidation admits of no excuse: but there have been already cases in the nationalised industries of non-Communist states where elderly individuals have been treated in a callous and soulless manner; and centralisation in such an organisation as a National Health Service may, no doubt unintentionally, lead to the impersonal treatment not merely of patients but of subordinate officials who are engaged in operating the service.

property-less people. He does not necessarily consider that in such a world all private ownership must be wrong or sinful, but its existence involves the obligation of those who have property to use it as stewards. This, of course, is in itself fundamental New Testament doctrine, since in the Gospels Our Lord emphasises again and again the principle of human stewardship as against any idea of absolute ownership. Much has been made of this idea of primitive communism. It has been a satisfaction to some to find that in the interesting Qumran community, which preceded the development of the Jewish Christian community, and may even have had some influence upon it, there was a form of communal ownership, and most people are familiar with the statement that the early Christians in Jerusalem 'had all things in common'. Acquisitiveness, or the inordinate pursuit of riches, is clearly a sin to Christians, though some early writers like Clement of Alexandria were inclined to argue that if a man who had great possessions became a Christian he need not necessarily renounce them, provided that he recognised that he was only a steward of what he had, and administered it for the common good. It is clear, however, from the numerous instances recorded where leading Christians (like Cyprian in North Africa) sold their extensive property, and became poor for Christ's sake, believing that His challenge in the Gospels to the rich young man was a challenge to them, that the Christian conscience favoured a stewardship for the common good, coupled with a drastic reduction of private income. It has even been said that Ambrose gives an ideal picture of a Christian society as being one of 'happy, voluntarily poor people'.[1]

In spite of such teaching, in spite of the condemnation of usury, and in spite of the preaching of the friars, and attempts by the Church at defining what was the just price to pay for labour and for commodities, it must be admitted that the unfair treatment of one set of people by another still went on, and among other protests was that of the peasants' revolt in fourteenth-century England. Such protests were mostly made by minorities, and after the Reformation there seems to have been a serious decline in the witness of the Christian community and of individuals (except among some of the radical sects) against the excessive taking of unearned increment, and the exploitation of the poor. And so the stage was set for God's judgment to begin, and the weapon of that judgment was a non-religious humanism. The spectacle in eighteenth-century Europe of a corrupt and reactionary Catholicism and of a woefully world-affirming and complacent Protestantism turned a number of rationalistic thinkers in the direction of creating a new social order. The

---

[1] Quoted in Dr. Homes Dudden's life of St. Ambrose.

movement began in France, but in the early nineteenth century it expanded into an almost world-wide and sweeping protest against exploitation, and this was partly due to the extensive development of mechanised industry, partly to the gradual growth of literacy, which rendered the workers more articulate, partly to the aftermath of the French Revolution, but especially to the genius and industry of the German Jew from the Rhineland, Karl Marx.

The intellectuals in France whose doctrine gave inspiration to the leaders of the French Revolution, if not to its rank and file, were quite plainly atheistic humanists, and it was within the range of this latter humanism that Karl Marx was born, in the year 1818. It is true that his parents were of orthodox Hebrew stock, and that in his ancestry he could count a number of Rabbis and scholars. But while it seems as though he could never entirely divest himself of Jewish traditions of thought, the formative elements in his youth were those of the immediate post-revolutionary period. When at the student age he declared himself an atheist, it is plain that this declaration was due on the one hand to his disgust at the anti-Semitism of Christians in Germany, and to the hypocrisy tolerated by his father in having his children baptised as Lutherans in order to avoid persecution, and on the other hand to the influence of various post-Revolution University teachers, who, although Germans and not French, could not fail to have been influenced by the kind of rationalism prevailing at this time both east and west of the Rhine.

It is not difficult to see these various strands combining in the teaching of Marx. On the one hand is a kind of philosophic pantheism. Nature is the impersonal Self-Existent which is working dialectically and purposefully towards the perfection of human society, through the negation of the negation, until at last there are no more possible negations which can be negated, and a kind of Nirvana (as Zaehner describes it) has been reached, in which there is no more craving and no more conflict. But on the other is a belief in a terrestrial good time coming, and in the existence of a suffering messianic community, the exploited proletariat, which certainly looks like the vestigial remains of apocalyptic Judaism in the thought of Marx. It always needs to be remembered that Jewish religion in the Old Testament has practically no belief in personal immortality. 'It is the unequivocal teaching of the Torah that the righteous man will find his reward on earth, either for himself or his heirs. No promise of future life is given to the believer, as in the New Testament, and no hope of re-birth under happier conditions, as in some kinds of Indian thought.'[1]

[1] Bienenfeld, *The Religion of the Non-Religious Jews*, Museum Press, London, 1944.

If these facts are borne in mind the attitude of Marx towards the religion of his day becomes somewhat less difficult to understand, and his own belief or disbelief less unnatural and less monstrous. Let it be granted that he was not always easy to work with, that he was a good hater, and that he was not free from the prejudices of the generation of Europeans into which he was born, he was still a very great man. His passion for social righteousness was at least as fiery and sincere as that of the prophet Amos. His industry was immense. He was unworldly almost to exaggeration. Frau Marx once said dolefully of him, 'If only Karl would make some capital instead of simply writing about it!' He is, of course, credited with being the evil genius who has elevated materialism to the level of a substitute-religion, and given people an excuse for discarding spiritual values. But who has a right to judge him? He saw the half-starved and sweated work-girls in the back-rooms of the dressmaking establishments in Regent Street.[1] He saw the domestics of the great houses in the West End of London doomed to dwell in sunless basements. He saw the miserably housed agricultural labourers at Gamlingay, in the county of Cambridge. He saw, or at least was told by his friend Engels, about the evils connected with the industrialism of northern England, evils which still existed, in spite of pious ambulance work, almost unchecked right up to the beginning of the First World War: and these things stung him to profound indignation, especially as they seemed to be tolerated by people who professed to be Christians. If he did not always write justly, he at least wrote with a desire to help the poor and the under-dog. 'The Church of England', the words may be those of Marx or of Engels, but they occur in the pages of *Das Kapital*, 'will tolerate the sacrifice of one of its Thirty-Nine Articles rather than one thirty-ninth of its income'.

It is necessary to remember that although Marx was the most dynamic force in the creation of revolutionary Socialism on the continent of Europe, he was in England by no means the only person who had a profoundly troubled conscience over the social wrongs of the early nineteenth century. Charles Kingsley, Frederick Denison Maurice, and their friends, were at this time quite independently striving to arouse the public conscience, and especially the consciences of all Christians, upon this matter. One gets rather tired of having to remind people that it was Kingsley, and not Marx, who first used the phrase about religion being the opium of the people, though Marx doubtless saw its propaganda value and quickly adopted it. Moreover, as is well known, a good deal of the same kind of enthusiasm for social reform as that felt by Kingsley and Maurice,

[1] The kind of people about whom Thomas Hood wrote *The Song of the Shirt*.

and later by Westcott, had a little earlier been stirring in Methodism, and especially in the radical wing of it known as Primitive Methodists, and this may almost be said to have formed the cradle of the British Labour Movement.

But all this does not mean that the fruits of Marxism have not been evil, or that it has not turned out to have developed after a fashion which in attempting to free mankind from the tyranny of exploitation, has ended by fastening upon him another tyranny of a different sort.

It is perhaps easier to see the significance of Marxist Communism if we think of it as in one aspect a new variety of humanism. The early Greek humanists, disillusioned in regard to the existence and nature of the gods, and not altogether convinced as to the truth of dynamic monotheism, clearly thought of man as capable of being the architect of his own life, and made him, in effect, 'the measure of all things'. A great deal of Marxism, especially of the more popular sort, is inclined to take the same line. For those who hold it, God, as certainly many Christians think of Him, or are believed to think of Him, does not exist, and man's purpose must therefore be to achieve his own perfection, to work out his own earthly salvation and prosperity by obeying the natural laws which appear to govern the development of matter in motion, and to pursue the methods which the scientific approach to the physical universe has made familiar, and by the application of which apparently a great deal of success has already been achieved in breeding new and improved species of food plants and of living creatures, in providing mankind with the equipment of health services and preventive medicine and all sorts of useful appliances, with chemical apparatus for the promotion of scientific agriculture, and with improved means of communication, and various sorts of labour-saving devices both in home and factory, as well as new forms of recreation.

It is, however, quite possible to be a thorough-going humanist without being an orthodox Marxist. Many British and American non-religious and rationalistic humanists would repudiate Marxist doctrines about the development of society, as going beyond what is strictly scientific, and as being already obsolete. They would say, what it is difficult to deny, that Marx, in his passion for the deliverance of the workers from exploitation, often wrote rather as a prophet than as a scientist, and even indulged in wishful thinking. He wanted the dialectic of society to work out in a certain way, and so he said that it would, in spite of the fact that scientific analysis, although it might show that certain things had happened in the past, could not safely predict that certain other things would happen in the future, since the movement of dialectic plainly made it possible that certain other alternative developments might occur which were not forecast in Marx's scheme. On the other side, a good many Marxists who accept the full diet of Dialectical Materialism, while they expressly repudiate any suggestion that they are religious, have clearly fallen into the profession of a faith which is not at all unlike some Asian pantheistic systems. Nature is the Impersonal Self-Existent (if indeed so intelligent an entity can really consistently be described in impersonal terms) which is working dialectically and purposefully towards the perfection of human society.

The retention of a quasi-messianic hope by Marx as the basis of his struggle to secure perfect justice for the exploited, is combined first with his inversion of Hegel's dialectic (so that instead of the working-out of the Idea we have substituted for it the evolution of Matter); and secondly, with the anti-religious projectionist theory of Feuerbach, in which all conceptions of Self-Existent Deity are mere myths constructed by man to compensate for the hardships and disappointments of life. While some religion has doubtless taken this form, and while the theory of Feuerbach seemed plausible enough in his day, the more detailed study of religious phenomena on a world-wide basis which has taken place since then has shown that Feuerbach's simplification is excessive, and is not borne out by the facts as collected and co-ordinated by anthropologists.

Feuerbach, however, can hardly be blamed for rejecting theism as it was presented to him, since it can seldom have been seen in a more unattractive or unsatisfying guise. It was not so much its theoretical aspects which roused Marx to join with Feuerbach in rejecting it, as his anger at the seeming indifference of its official representatives to the obvious sufferings of the proletariat. It was the day of Disraeli's *Two Nations*. It was the day when a prayer could actually be composed by a reputable clergyman which contained the petition: 'O God, make the rich liberal and the poor patient', a prayer which one blushes to think was still being used at some clerical meetings in London as late as the year 1912. Marx's rejection of religion, in spite of his theory, was not so much metaphysical as pragmatic. Christianity did not produce the results which it ought to have done in justice, mercy, and loving-kindness, and therefore it must be false. Yet the curious feature of this condemnation is that the standard by which the failure and disloyalty of Christians is judged is the Christian one. Christians stand condemned in effect not for being too Christian but for not being Christian enough. Marxism is thus a judgment upon the Christian movement for having failed in its plain and simple duty to denounce and labour for the utter banishment of the exploitation of one human being by another. But Marx himself was by birth and tradition a Jew, and he rejected, quite consistently from his own point of view, the Christian claim to reform society by love only. It is for him and his colleagues too soft a method, and enables those who practise it to tolerate abuses which they ought to hew down and extirpate root and branch. Although Marx declared himself an atheist, he had, like many of his disciples, an objective standard by which he judged defaulters. For him there seems to be a Law of the Universe which it is a human duty to respect, and of those who violate it he seems to say: 'Do not I hate them who break the Cosmic Law? Yea, I hate them right sore, even as though they were my enemies.'[1]

It is a common practice of those who wish to make out a case against Marxism to stress the materialism of its exponents, and of course this is quite legitimate. If one looks at a pamphlet written by Josef Stalin and published in 1941, this can be seen clearly. Although it lays great stress upon the dialectical principle as governing the development of the natural world of phenomena, it re-affirms the total rejection of that world as the embodiment of an Absolute Idea, a Universal Spirit or Consciousness. The world develops in accordance with the laws of matter in motion, and stands in no need of a Universal Spirit. This means no more than simply conceiving nature just as it exists, without any foreign admixture. It is said that Lenin quoted the ancient Greek Heracleitus as saying: 'The world, the all-in-one, was not created by any god or any man, but was, is, and ever will be a living flame systematically flaring up and systematically dying down', and adds, 'A very good exposition of the rudiments of dialectical materialism.' Stalin goes on to quote extracts from the collected works of Marx, from which the following may be selected as relevant.

'Matter is not a product of mind, but mind itself is merely the highest product of matter.'
'It is impossible to separate thought from matter that thinks.'
'Matter, nature, being, the physical—is primary, and spirit, consciousness, sensation, the physical—is secondary.'

It must be obvious that in these sentences the placing of matter and mind in antithesis, while at the same time saying that mind is the highest product of matter, involves a confusion of thought, since if matter in motion is the equivalent of the Absolute, then what emerges as its highest product must have been inherent in it from the beginning. But this makes it impossible for matter and mind to be antithetical. If matter is capable of producing mind as its

---

[1] Quite good rabbinical doctrine.

highest emergent, it cannot be set over against mind. Although therefore the Marxist says that he rejects idealism, as asserting that only the mind really exists and that the material world exists only in mind, he can only maintain this opposition by using the term 'matter' first in one sense and then in another, first as absolutely opposed to anything that is mental, and, secondly, as that out of which mind can derive. If Engels says that one cannot separate thought from matter without committing a great error, it is only fair to retort that in logic it is an even graver error to separate matter from thought. Quite obviously the mind of the dialectical materialist as exhibited by Stalin is in a state of confusion. On the one side, it seems to accept a deterministic reading of the universe, as though the struggle between contradictions and opposites, which as Lenin said, is within the very essence of things, is something which is inevitable, so that no individual can be held responsible for a movement in society which is simply bound to go on; but on the other it assumes that those who seem to be resisting the movement are responsible for their actions, and therefore should, and must, receive punishment; while those who work in submission to the dialectical process are equally responsible for their choice, and should therefore receive rewards and decorations.

Julius Hecker, an American-trained Russian working some years ago in Moscow, while declaring that Communism is atheistic, uses the word ambiguously. For him the Universe is eternal, real, independent, and prior to human consciousness: but like Mr. Hoyle in a work mentioned elsewhere, he does not define the Universe. All he says is that the Dialectical Materialist accepts both quantity, quality, extension, *and mind*, as the attributes of Ultimate Reality. But there is confusion of thought here. This is hardly a philosophy replacing religion so much as one kind of philosophical theology replacing another, and to include mind as an attribute of the Ultimate is so amazing a concession that one would almost have expected the author of the *Moscow Dialogues* to be liquidated as an arch-heretic. Hecker speaks of the withering away of the supernatural which was dominating Christian culture, but he never satisfactorily defines what he means by the supernatural. It is clear that in a confused way he is interested in religion in a manner in which Stalin was not.

It has been a practice to stress the grim and unlovable personalities of revolutionary leaders, and to represent Stalin in the guise of a monster. For this there may be much to be said. The leaders of a totalitarian communist state have on principle a great deal of absolute power, and we know from experience that such power tends to corrupt. Moreover, if the logical principle upon which they work is that 'right and good' simply means that which ministers to the success of the progress of their movement towards a final goal which is beyond the horizon; and that 'evil and wrong' represents those factors which seem to be obstacles to the achievement of that distant goal, then ruthlessness in sweeping aside such obstacles will be quite legitimate. It is no question of proceeding by gradual persuasion, or on the assumption that one's opponents may have something to contribute to a final synthesis. It does not in the least matter inflicting suffering of an untold nature upon the present generation by wrecking and pulling down an existing social order in order to build a new one. But one can understand the fanaticism of a Russian revolutionary; because his great country had so often in the past been stigmatised for being backward (which it certainly was) and beaten by others in world struggles on account of its backwardness, he would naturally see the urgency for getting rid of a past of which he was ashamed, and might almost be forgiven for taking drastic steps to catch up with and to surpass the rest of the world within a short period, like five or ten years, and to show that Russia, if given a chance, could under a socialist régime do everything that the alleged capitalist world had been doing, and do it better. It does not seem that those who dislike the Russian régime of the last thirty-five years have always tried to regard the situation as it might be seen from the point of view of a patriotic Russian, and the latter is after all as much entitled to his patriotism as we are to ours.

But it will not do to be content with parading bogeys. Behind the Marxist movement as its ultimate inspiration, however misguided its principles may be, is the burning desire to put an end to exploitation, and to construct an order of society in which work will invariably be undertaken from the motive of service to the community, and not of private gain to oneself.

It may well be to quote at this point from the memorandum on Communism drawn up by a committee of Anglican bishops at the time of the Lambeth Conference of 1948, and included in the official report of that conference.

> 'Churchmen must begin by entering into the despair as well as the hope that has inspired modern Communism. They must proclaim human rights without equivocation. They must practise corporately what they preach, and so cleanse the household of faith that the Spirit of God is able to work through it with power.
>
> Secondly, they must do full justice to the truth in Communism, both its critical insights into history and its desire to help the oppressed. The Church ought not to allow itself to be identified with social reaction. Its members should be ready for social and economic change, and quick to welcome into the councils of the Church men and women with the workers' experience of living conditions.

Thirdly, they must realise that those who accept an economic theory of communism as distinct from Marxian atheism do not thereby put themselves outside the fellowship of Christ's Church. Experiments in communal living have always been a feature of the life of the Church, and in our time its life and witness are being strengthened by fresh ventures of this kind.'

The effect of this memorandum was to lead the Bishops to pass, apparently without any dissentients, a series of resolutions on human rights, of which five seem specially relevant here.

5. The Conference believes that both the recognition of the personal responsibility of the individual to God and the development of his personality are gravely imperilled by any claim made either by the State or by any group within the State to control the whole of human life. Personality is developed in community, but the community must be one of free persons. The Christian must therefore judge every social system by its effect on human personality.

6. The Conference declares that all men, irrespective of race or colour, are equally the objects of God's love, and are called to love and serve Him. All men are made in His image; for all Christ died; and to all is made the offer of eternal life. Every individual is therefore bound by duties toward God and towards other men, and has certain rights without the enjoyment of which he cannot freely perform those duties. These rights should be declared by the Church, recognised by the State, and safeguarded by international law.

7. The Conference declares that among such rights are security of life and person; the right to work, to bring up a family, and to possess personal property; the right to freedom of speech, of discussion and association, and to accurate information; and to full freedom of religious life and practice; and that these rights belong to all men irrespective of race or colour.

25. The Conference, while recognising that in many lands there are Communists who are practising Christians, nevertheless declares that Marxian Communism is contrary to Christian faith and practice, for it denies the existence of God, Revelation, and of future life; it treats the individual man as a means and not an end; it encourages class-warfare, and it regards the moral law not as absolute but as relative to the needs of the State. The Conference holds that while a State must take the precautions it regards as necessary to protect good order and peace from all subversive movements, it is the special duty of the Church to oppose the challenge of the Marxian theory of Communism by sound teaching and the example of a better way; and that the Church, at all times and in all places, should be a fearless witness against political, social, and economic injustice.

26. The Conference believes that Communism is presenting a challenge to Christian people to study and understand its theory and practice, so that they may be well instructed as to which elements in it are in conflict with the Christian view of man, and must therefore be resisted, and which elements are a true judgment on the existing social and economic order.

The Conference also called upon all Church members to find their incentive to work not only in security and gain, but *chiefly in service and good workmanship*, as an offering to the glory of God.

One wishes that more stress had been laid upon the fundamental element in Christ's teaching that we are *stewards* from God of all that we possess, and not absolute owners.

Those who desire to get rid of the exploitation of one human being or group by another may well ask: 'Why should such a campaign have the objectionable Marxist technique compulsorily tied on to it?' The only answer so far as one knows is that it is a quick and effective way of getting things done. It is a kind of 'Reformation without tarying for anie'. The misfortune, of course, is that it sacrifices too much in the process, the result being that it produces a state of human society in which the old sort of exploitation is replaced by a new one. The Marxist ideology proposes that a certain sort of happiness is to be desired and sought, and those who may find it boring are not allowed to seek any other, and if they dare to, are frowned upon, persecuted, or liquidated. As Father d'Arcy said: 'The prospect of the classless society with all its adjuncts going on for ever is a grim one, even if the first years are pleasant.' Security from exploitation has no doubt been gained, and ought to be gained, but not necessarily in this way. Whatever it may be, this ideology cannot progress after the manner in which Christian ideology has progressed and is progressing. From its very nature it is bound to be stationary, and a society formed in this way may well fail to attract many. The new morality imposed on the world by Marxism declares that those who do not like it must be forced under pains and penalties to accept it; but this is persecution, and is merely exploitation of the dissenter in the interests of the orthodox —just the very thing which some forms of Christianity in the past have been rightly blamed for practising.

Of course it may be urged, in criticism of the foregoing, that in some countries today, even without complete nationalisation of industry, a system of checks and balances, of wage tribunals and arbitration courts has come into being which, without destroying the incentive to enterprise, has rendered exploitation much less possible; and that with the rise in the West (and especially in Britain) of a higher standard of living, of National Insurance, of Health services and Pension schemes, the general condition of the industrial workers is unbelievably better than it was fifty years ago ('they have never had it so good'). This is true. But the memory of past wrongs has bred suspicion, and this means a constant watchfulness to see that one is not being taken advantage of. Even where no unfair profits are being made, there is still an uneasy feeling on the part of those employed that they are not being justly treated. There is the continual consciousness that in a privately-owned business the interests of the owners and of the employees are bound to be at least a little different, even if they are not totally opposed to one another. Hence the unhappy continuance of strikes. In any event it is always difficult to justify the *ownership* of any industrial undertaking or business by a particular set of people, who are not the whole community but only a small part of it, over against those who labour in it. Co-partnership at the very least would seem to be the implied solution.

The position of workers in industry in Britain or America may seem not to warrant any very violent strictures today, but Christians must not blink the fact that in many other parts of the world, and especially in Asia, there is still most grievous poverty and malnutrition, which may sometimes be due to bad and ineffective food production, but as often as not to the bad distribution of wealth, since the poor are found to be living side by side with people of great luxury, and are sometimes the victims of selfish landlords and money-lenders, while the festering growths of bribery and corruption still flourish.[1]

Quite clearly, unless the entire Christian Church is prepared to take the lead in eliminating everywhere all possibilities of exploitation, she cannot successfully oppose the spread of Marxist Communism. It is a race between her and the alternative propagandists, and a purely individualist and other-worldly type of Christian propaganda seems bound to fail.

If one only considers the doctrines contained in the moral treatises of the great seventeenth-century Anglican divines, Laud, Lancelot Andrews, and Jeremy Taylor, to say nothing of the more radical teachers of the Commonwealth period, one finds a continual denunciation of social injustice, and a determination to work for the welfare of all. It is also worth remembering some of the plain teaching given by Maurice, Westcott, and Gore during the last hundred years. Such utterances have certainly borne fruit in this country: but it may be questioned as to what extent their echoes have penetrated into the corners of the mission-field. Could not for instance the evangelists who went to China have attacked the social abuses of that country more strongly than they did? One cannot help wondering.

It seems to have been assumed only too readily that in a fallen world there is bound to be economic oppression, exploitation, and cut-throat competition, and that all that can be done is to ease the

---

[1] I am told that the Urdu (north Indian) word for a 'bribe' is 'what is customary'!

situation by persuading the rich to give to charity which can be dispensed by the church so as to relieve the distress of the poor. But Jesus Himself, like the prophets before Him, was quite as much concerned with how one makes one's income as with how one spends it; and His Spirit still speaks to the churches telling them to give true witness. Any impact upon society of the real Christianity of Christ as distinct from a muffled or diluted Christianity is bound to challenge a social order which permits social injustice between man and man, and to insist that conversion of the individual means something that goes down to the very roots. One regrets to observe that there is very little reference to Marxism and its challenge in Dr. Kraemer's latest work, although what there is is to the point; and there is still less in his earlier volume. The grievous problem of exploitation as a cardinal sin seems hardly to enter into his purview. Yet it *is* a deadly sin, and its wickedness has been clearly denounced from the time of the great Hebrew prophets onwards. Only too seldom have Christian missionaries quoted as on *their* side the burning words of these ancient social revolutionaries.

Doubtless the actual philosophical theories behind Marxist government do not greatly concern the vast mass of the proletariat in Asia or anywhere else, for the latter tend to do 'as their leaders tell 'em to'. What they catch hold of is that the Communist system promises them freedom from social injustice whether by landlords or employers. The tragedy is that while these two evils may be somewhat drastically disposed of by Marxism, yet in spite of the protestations about the withering away of the state, the new order of Communism seems only to fasten upon the population another and more oppressive tyranny, springing from the undervaluation of the dignity of human beings—probably the nemesis of any system founded upon an illogical materialism. Marxism produces a sub-human organisation of society taken as a whole, whereas the old exploitation tended to confine this sub-human condition to the poorest and most defenceless citizens—and that was bad enough. But this is no excuse for inertia or reactionary behaviour. There is still before us the vision of Dr. Otto Simons, Chancellor of the German Reich in the early days of the armistice period, and himself a devout Christian: 'We must have a better Communism.' Marxism, with a good deal of the Jewish sub-Christian element in it, quite apart from its materialism, is from a strictly religious point of view a step down rather than a step up. It should be replaced by a *Christian* new order. This, I believe, was what Dr. Simons meant; and Christians, if they wish to get beyond Marx, must both think and live beyond Marx.

Marxism naturally finds its most fertile soil in countries where distress and frustration are widespread. Although since 1953 many schemes such as the establishment of the Colombo plan and the economic section of the Baghdad pact, as well as the work of the Food and Agricultural Organisation of the United Nations, have been undertaken, and are now operating, there is a long journey ahead of those who are seeking to rescue mankind from starvation, and it is therefore reasonable to summarise briefly the dangerous condition in which the world's populations are still living.

In 1953 it was estimated that some 1500 million persons, roughly two-thirds of the world's population, were living in conditions of acute hunger defined in terms of identifiable nutritional disease. The twelve poorest countries in the world comprised one-third of its total population, but only 4 per cent of the total world income. Twenty-five countries with over half the total world population enjoyed only 9 per cent of the total world income; while the eight richest countries with just over one-tenth of the total world population enjoyed 56 per cent of the total income.

From these rather shocking figures it thus appears that the individual inequalities of riches and poverty which have defaced many societies are also to be found distributed on a wide scale between countries as well. The Christian evangelist cannot and ought not to be indifferent about this matter. His Lord had compassion on a multitude who had been with Him several days without adequate food, and told the disciples: 'Give ye them to eat.' To be so much concerned with saving souls *out of* the world that one ignores the conditions under which they are existing *in* the world is neither good policy nor good Christianity, and it is fortunately true that some of the best missionaries have realised this, and have sought to create new communities *from the bottom* out of the converts they have made, setting up model villages and establishing agricultural institutes. But much more remains to be done; and it is imperative that Christian churches throughout the world should pledge their support to the efforts which governments are making in many countries to improve the standard of living and the quality and health of the population.

As an example of urgency, we may take the situation as it was in India in 1952. Here, out of a population of 360 million, 14,000 persons had an income of more than the equivalent of £3000 a year, while the average income per head of population was £19 a year. A quarter of the babies born alive were reported as dying before reaching the age of 12 months and only half reached the age of 20, and 40 per cent died before their 5th birthday. The average expectation of life for a male in India in 1950 was estimated at 26 years, as against 69 for one in America. Much of this distressing state of affairs was due directly to malnutrition, though a great deal also to preventible disease. Outside India it is recorded that in Cuba a family of five has to live on the daily energy-intake actually required for one person. In New Guinea 8 out of 10 children die before reaching puberty, and Dr. Wollaston said that he rarely saw a man in the island who was over the age of 40. It is most necessary to take a balanced view of the causes of this distress. Not all of it is due to exploitation. A large measure of it results from ignorance of the best ways of producing the maximum yield in agriculture, and some of it through ignorance of the principles of tropical hygiene. No doubt lack of imagination plays a large part in the continuance of the concentration of land and money in the hands of a few; but it is not enough to redistribute the land in the form of small holdings, or to impose a steep income tax, unless people are taught how to use the land rightly when they have got it. The Gospel and the Plough may well prove to be a true partnership. Primitive man is exceedingly wasteful in his use of the soil; and even in countries where agriculture has been practised in a more scientific manner, as in times past in Italy, there has been woeful deterioration, and little effort until recently to reclaim waste lands, marshes, and marginal areas so as to provide home-grown food of good quality for a rapidly increasing population. The improvement of conditions in southern Italy is only one example of what may be done. Another is the restoration of the agriculture of North Africa, which, under the Romans, was not only the granary of the Empire, but had vast olive plantations. Here the work was begun by the Italians, but has been carried on since under the British Mandate, and is now being extended in an independent Libya by the F.A.O., by British and Americans working in co-operation with the Libyan government, and by the Libyans themselves. It seems impossible that the great desert areas south of the coastal plain which centuries ago used to produce valuable crops, should be allowed to remain fallow for lack of proper irrigation and failure to use the best methods of mechanised agriculture.

But another cause of distress is the almost entire absence over a large part of the world's surface of any systematic planning of population. It is certainly not the will of God that people should multiply indiscriminately, and without any thought as to whether they are physically capable of bearing and rearing normal healthy children. Here again all Christians should support a sound programme of eugenics and family planning. It was said that in 1953 the world population was on the increase at the rate of 25 million per annum—

two more mouths to feed every fifteen seconds, or at the rate of a population equal in size to that of greater London every four months. In the case of the area embraced by the Colombo plan and South-East Asia its population of 570 millions was expected to rise to 720 millions by 1970. It is useless to augment food-production if the expansion of population continues to increase ahead of it all the time.

All these sinister facts are, of course, handled in the plan proposed by Marxists; but the method of dealing with them along Marxist lines is bound on principle to involve a tyrannous curtailment of human liberty. No doubt there must be some control. But in a happy world this comes best from inside, and it is far better to respect individual personality by educating citizens in the practice of good agriculture, family planning, and hygiene, and in the duty of practical goodwill towards their neighbours, than to liquidate recalcitrant farmers and impose compulsory birth-control. What is perhaps worth re-emphasis is that an escapist form of religion, whether Christian or non-Christian, cannot avail in these matters and that in the face of it Marxism is bound to seem a better way. It is only a genuinely world-transforming Christianity which can successfully compete with a Marxist programme.

One feels compelled to end this section by re-affirming two maxims, which, if they are not biblical, at least spring from Christian sources, and are profoundly Christian in sentiment: first, that freedom is not the right to do what one likes, but liberty to do what one ought; and second, that a large part of the art of good living is to put into society more than one takes out.[1] Such rules of life certainly ought to be proclaimed right round the world. But who is sufficient for their practice? Our sufficiency is and can be only from the Living God.

Additional comment

Any observer of present controversies among Communists cannot help noticing that the majority, holding to Marxist orthodoxy, have insisted that conversion to the latter must involve a complete and radical break with other modes of thought and practice. Thus in China they use such phrases as 'brain-washing', which, strange to say, bears a close resemblance to the Hellenistic Christian word μετανοία, the true meaning of which has been blanketed by translating it 'penitence', whereas its original meaning is 'complete change of mind'.

There is indeed a very real sense in which to become a Christian disciple involves becoming a καινὴ κτίσις, and to some extent

---

[1] This one may at any rate be traced back to the logion of Jesus guided by Paul in Acts: 'It is more blessed to give than to receive.'

Kraemer and his friends are right in stressing this. Yet further study of Communist controversies reveals that there is a growing tendency for local groups to demand that they shall follow their own paths, while adhering to fundamentals, and, as we have seen, the Polish leader has reduced these to one single point. This is in its own way a plea for 'indigenisation' so far as Communism is concerned.

Again, the orthodox Marxist denies that change to a new order of society can come gradually. He rejects altogether 'reformism', and says that correct analysis of social changes demonstrates that the new order must come as a discontinuous jolt of a revolutionary character. Here once more the Christian can see a parallel. Quite a number of evangelists have held that conversion to Christ must be sudden and discontinuous. They reject the idea that man or society can be gradually and peacefully reformed into Christianity, and that there is a possible state of 'being saved'. 'Bow thy head, Sigambrian. Adore what thou has burned and burn what thou hast adored.' And do it quickly.

But are these inevitable antitheses? Psychologists have said: 'No'. They have declared that conversion may be either fulminant or progressive. And according to them there may be a third variety in which a progressive conversion may suddenly end in a jolt into a completely new life.

It would seem then that a study of Communist controversies tends to throw light upon Christian ones. In both socialism and Christianity there can be gradualists according to some evangelists, but not to others. But the Marxist will not allow the option. Like Dr. Billy Graham, he is committed to the necessity of making a sudden decision which effects a revolutionary change. One day a man is a pagan. The next day his old life is in ruins, and a new one is being recast. It is no accident that a groupist once wrote a book called: *Life Began Yesterday*. A convert to Marxism could do just the same.

To sum up. The Marxist goes about declaring that all hitherto existing religion is an illusion: that to be a convert from non-Christian to Christian faith is to exchange one superstition for another: that Christianity is subsidised by bourgeois capitalists and is not really interested in raising the standard of living for the poor, in Asia or anywhere else: and that the achievements of Russia and China show this to be the best way to improve the world. Unless these four propositions (which obviously contain some dangerous half-truths) are convincingly disproved, it is hard to see how the world can avoid awakening some day with a groan to the discovery that is has become Marxist, and has only exchanged the present unsatisfactory situation for a new tyranny.

CHAPTER XII

THE CHANGE TO THE MODERN WORLD

(B) AFRO-ASIAN EMANCIPATION. THE DOMINANCE OF AMERICA

Almost half a century ago, just after I was ordained deacon, there met in London a new kind of religious gathering. Up to that time there had been held about every ten years what was called The Lambeth Conference, a consultative meeting of Anglican bishops under the chairmanship of the Archbishop of Canterbury. In 1908, owing largely to the inspiration of Bishop H. H. Montgomery, Viscount Montgomery's father, a congress of Anglicans, both lay and clerical, was held, which read and discussed papers on every conceivable kind of subject which might be thought to have a bearing upon religion. As a young person I found it, despite its limitations, a most stimulating affair. The lay speakers were on the whole a brilliant assembly drawn from many different walks of life, and included Professor F. C. Burkitt, Mr. G. K. Chesterton, Mrs. Edward Compton, and George Lansbury, to mention only a few. So far as I know, the experiment has never exactly been repeated in England. It was, however, followed in 1910 by a great missionary conference convened at Edinburgh; and this perhaps, as a kind of unconscious outgrowth from the Student Christian Movement, was organised on inter-denominational lines, though without any Roman Catholic co-operation. Many of my readers will know as much about this conference as I do, but I mention it because in forty-five years it may have faded from public memory, and because it deserves to be recorded as a decisive step forward. Something similar to it was held at Birmingham in 1923, dealing with politics, economics, and citizenship; and this, like its predecessor at Edinburgh, showed that in future it was likely that such gatherings would mainly be conducted on an inter-denominational basis. Thus, although the various denominations of Christians have continued to convene their own domestic councils, so that the one held at Minnesota in 1954, while it included a considerable number of lay representatives who were non-European and non-American, was nevertheless strictly pan-Anglican; it was somewhat overshadowed by the much larger inter-denominational and international conference held in the same year at Evanston, Illinois. Between the gatherings at Edinburgh and Evanston lay two

world-wars and the establishment of Marxist Communism as a mili-
tant rival to the Christian Faith; and during the armistice period
between 1920 and 1939 what we now know as the ecumenical movement entered into full swing, and gatherings connected with 'Faith
and Order' and 'Life and Work' met at fairly frequent intervals, and
culminated in the setting up of the World-Council of Churches.

But just as important as this ecumenical trend among Christians
has been the revolutionary change throughout the whole of Asia,
which has led to the resurgence of her ancient religions, followed by
the birth of new self-governing communities in one part of Africa,
and the sinister clash between Europeans and Africans in other parts
of the continent.

No longer can what used to be called 'the sending countries'
assume that the others will without question be 'receiving countries'.
Fifty years ago Asia and Africa were on the whole passive. Their
citizens did not put up any serious resistance on behalf of their own
religions. There were open doors nearly everywhere, and if enough
money and man-power had been available many more entries could
have been made than actually took place. But it is now common
knowledge that the prestige of the Christian world has declined; and
that with the accession of many states to political freedom and independence, there has come a desire in those states to try the experiment, at least for patriotic reasons, of making the best of the religions
which they themselves have inherited.

A striking instance of this was to be seen recently on Clydeside,
where a vessel built for the Government of India was launched by the
High Commissioner of India, Mrs. Pandit. The ceremony began with
an invocation to Varuna, the Vedic deity who had once very nearly
equalled the Hebrew Yahweh in majesty and moral holiness, but who,
from being a sky-god, had gradually been demoted to the position
of a sea-god rather like the Greek Poseidon. The mantra recited in
Sanskrit was a prayer that Varuna would be propitious, and after its
recitation the usual offerings were made of rice and flowers.

It would, of course, be possible to say that Varuna for Indians
represents as nearly as possible the equivalent of 'Our Heavenly
Father', and that if indigenisation of Christianity is ever to take place
in India, it might be suitable to use Varuna as the synonym for the
God of the Lord's Prayer. But I do not imagine that the Indian
Government, which is theoretically neutral in respect of religion,
was thinking along such lines at all. Its spokesman would have said,
if asked, that since the vast majority of the citizens of the Republic
of India are still registered as Hindus, any public ceremony of this
kind ought to be a Hindu one, celebrated with Hindu rites; and the

justice of this seems clear. But fifty years ago one can hardly imagine such an event taking place. The British Raj was then ruling India, and any religious ceremony that might have been held, despite the legal impartiality of the Raj, would probably have been Christian. Even if Indians had asked to be allowed to function they might have done so apologetically, but in 1957 no apology was felt to be needed. India stands on her own feet. She cherishes her ancient heritage, and who shall deny her right to do so? If she choose in years to come to crown that heritage by an acknowledgment of the supreme claim of Jesus Christ, it will be, and should indeed be, her own free choice. Those who would wish to see her undoubted religious genius and capacity for self-sacrificing spirituality laid at the feet of Jesus, would not want that homage to come in any other way. Meanwhile in the centre of the campus of the great Hindu University of Banaras a temple which looks like being on the scale of St. Paul's Cathedral is being erected for the corporate worship of the students, while Indian students in the University of London publicly present their votive offerings to the goddess of learning, Sarasvati, and get photographed in the act of doing so.

But what is happening in India tends to go on in many other parts of Asia. One of the communities of sect-Shinto (the Konko Kyo) is making its bid, perhaps not very successfully, to become the religion of Japan. Pakistan, as well as the new Arab states, has written Islam into its constitution. Many educated Africans, even though they may believe Christianity to be the religion which most appeals to them, and which is doing most for their welfare, are looking with nationalist emotion at the cultural heritage of their own peoples, and wondering whether they cannot salvage some good things from that heritage and incorporate them into Christianity; and in this they are receiving no small encouragement from missionaries and from European Christian leaders.

I propose then in this present chapter first to make some kind of survey of the situation in those Afro-Asian countries which are experiencing emancipation; and then to go on to consider the very different but equally important factor embodied in the growing dominance in world affairs of the United States of America.

(i) THE PROBLEM OF AFRICA

What used to be called in one's earlier days the Dark Continent presents us with an almost unique situation. Nowhere else in the world has there existed a whole area of the same size which almost up to the beginning of the nineteenth century might have been described as continuing in a pre-axial condition so far as religion is concerned. Here and there in India are to be found animistic jungle tribes which are only gradually coming under the influence of either reformed Hinduism or of Christianity. In islands like Borneo or Papua, or the smaller islands of the Pacific, pre-axial religion has survived until the advent of Christianity, or as in the case of Indonesia until the arrival of Islam. But nothing on the scale of Africa has occurred anywhere else upon the planet. The cause of this has doubtless been climatic. Even until lately it has been difficult for Europeans to live and work for any length of time in certain parts of Africa. Parts of the west coast before the advent of scientific hygiene and tropical medicine were regarded we know as the White Man's Grave. Africa was in the main remote, cut off from the fertile crescent and from most of Europe by deserts, swamps, and forests. Navigation in earlier centuries, before the introduction of mechanically-propelled vessels, was difficult, and sometimes hazardous. The people of Africa were therefore left to a large extent in a state of arrested development, in which their ways of life became stereotyped, and determined by what had been done before throughout the course of innumerable past generations. It is often said that when an African is asked the reason for some curious piece of ritual which seems to have a magical or religious significance that is not immediately clear, his answer will be: 'It is our custom.'

From this condition the African has found himself almost suddenly jolted into a different world. Unlike Indians, he has not developed his own prophets or sages, who have reformed his religious beliefs and practices from within. Such prophets and sages may have yet to develop, and there are signs perhaps that some of them are beginning to emerge. But in the main, change has come to the African from outside. Islam has gradually crept in from the northeast, and Christianity has arrived by sea, and penetrated up-country all round the coast.

Perhaps, however, it is necessary to be a little more precise, and to go back to some records of earlier history. Geographically both Egypt and the Valley of the Nile are part of Africa, although the story of the Christian movement in those regions belongs mainly to that of early Church history. The establishment of the Christian kingdom of Ethiopia clearly goes back to the early centuries of the Christian movement. But beyond that we simply do not know what effect, if any, the presence of Christianity in the north-east corner of the continent may have had upon the enormous dim populations of the centre, the south, the east, and the west. There are those who see in the various scattered remains of monotheistic belief throughout the continent vestiges of colonisation from the north. It is difficult to find any certain evidence which can prove this, although it seems clear that all over Africa there are pockets of people whose physical traits are hamitic rather than negroid, and who may therefore be the descendants of migrants coming from the north, and who have sometimes established themselves as ruling aristocracies in negroid areas. But nothing is known as to the date at which such migrations may have taken place. The drift of population may have gone on during pre-Christian centuries. On the other hand there may have been a south-western drift from Ethiopia after the time when it became Christian, or some of the monotheistic features of belief may have penetrated along trade routes. Against this possibility may be set what seems to be the fact that some of the religious ideas which look like introductions from the north are found to be so deeply embedded in the life and traditions of the tribes where they occur, that anthropologists have tended to prefer the conclusion that they are separate and independent developments.

The northern coastal area of Africa is deserving of separate treatment. Bordering as it does on the Mediterranean, it has always been more under the influence of Europe than any other part of the continent except Egypt. There are obvious affinities between the prehistoric peoples of Spain and the Pyrenees and those of North Africa, and we know that at a very early time there was a land bridge in at least one place between the two. Later, as the distribution of sea and land came to assume its present proportions, and especially as the great coastal plain or *gefara* emerged in Libya, colonists came from Hellas, and later from Italy. They found there peoples, like the Carthaginians, who were of semitic stock, and they created there a number of cities with a civilisation which was European rather than African. In process of time, and especially after the defeat of Carthage by Rome, the whole of this area became organised as part of the Roman Empire, and when after 313 Christianity became a privileged religion, and after 395 was established as official, a considerable African Church developed, with a very large number of bishops, and a vigorous though stormy life of its own. Into the details of its history we cannot here enter, but some of its great figures are familiar to all, Tertullian, Cyprian, Augustine of Hippo among them. The tragic and disastrous fact, however, is the almost complete disappearance of this Church. Dr. Frend of Caius College, after an exhaustive study of its history, comes to the conclusion that it was always somewhat of an exotic, and never really an indigenous church. Although widely distributed among the Roman provincials, to the great mass of the people it must have seemed a foreign intruder. Hence when the successive invasions of the Vandals and

Arabs wrecked it, it was not difficult for the populace to accept a new and thoroughly Semitic creed, with a strong democratic basis brought to them by people who were more nearly related to them than the Italians. The same features which have at the present day made Islam attractive to the African peasantry, may well have been in-fluential at an earlier date, namely, the tolerance given to polygamy, the offer for acceptance of an attainable and not too lofty moral standard, and the claim 'know ye that every Moslem is the brother of every other Moslem'. How much monotheism may have filtered down from the north, we can never tell, but if any did, it has long ago been absorbed into the polydaemonism of native Africa.

The major object of study in the world of Africa, therefore, apart from Christian and Moslem infiltration, is the ethnic religion of pagan and predominantly rural Africa in its multiplicity of forms. Europeans engaged in exploration, evangelisation, or administration, did not for a long time apply themselves to this study. Much was misunderstood, many mistakes were made, and there was often so much more interest in the displacement of whatever religion the Africans already possessed, that very little trouble was taken to discover what the religion was, and to consider whether it was possible to build anything upon it.

But times have changed. Many missionaries, with praise-worthy zeal and charity, have made studies of the religious and social customs of the people among whom they are working. Anthro-pologists, working either as pure scientists, or as the colleagues of European administrators, have also been busy, and have sometimes sharply and not without justice reminded the missionary of what he ought to have done and has left undone. On the whole the lesson has been learned, and some of the results of it may be seen in the composite volume, *African Ideas of God*, issued from the Edinburgh House Press a few years ago, and edited by the veteran pioneer, Dr. Edwin W. Smith,[1] who has himself engaged in a detailed study of the social and religious customs of the Ila-speaking peoples of Northern Rhodesia. This work, to which twelve separate authors have con-tributed, covers a wide field, although it does not include contribu-tions from the French dominions, from Somaliland, or from certain parts of East and West Africa. Twelve different areas are con-sidered, and the object is to give twelve typical pictures of religious belief, in each case sketched by people who have been personal observers on the spot. They do not profess to produce a complete

---

[1] I desire to express my extreme indebtedness to the work of Dr. Smith and his col-leagues in the whole of this section.

conspectus either of African mythology or of all the African ideas of God.

What are the main conclusions which are arrived at?

First and foremost, the universal belief of pagan Africans of the existence of Deity in some form or other. In bygone days travellers were wont to say sometimes that they had come across an African tribe which had no religious belief. No one would think of saying this today. Closer study, and more patient attention to the conversation of Africans, has made it plain that there is really no need to persuade any of them to accept the existence of God. Though they are uncertain as to his precise power in their lives, they are quite sure that He is there.

If we take in order the areas considered by Dr. Smith and his colleagues, we shall see how true this is. Beginning first with northern Nyasaland, the contributor, Mr. T. Cullen Young, after twenty-seven years' experience, declares that although there seems to be a certain amount of vagueness as to the exact nature and attributes of Deity (which is after all felt equally, it must be admitted, by a great many people all the world over) it is quite clear that the people of this area believe in a Power who is concerned with everyday life, is personal, and over-ruling, in fact the sort of being implied when English people speak of 'Providence'. Mr. Young quotes an example of where some youngsters in an African village on the Rhodesian border were heard sniggering at a mentally afflicted woman, and were rebuked by one of their elders with the words: 'Do not deride the witless: God will know.' I cannot help feeling that I have come across this proverb somewhere in the *sebayit* literature of Egypt. It may therefore be a universal African proverb, or (which is more likely) it may have at some remote period diffused southward from Egypt. The main point, however, of course, is what word is here used, which we translate 'God'. Mr. Young admits that his area is one which has been much traversed by Arab raiders and traders, and that therefore it is impossible to be sure that some of the 'beautiful names of Allah' have not diffused there. He gives, however, four names by which the Supreme Being is called. In these the first two seem to mean a 'Great Person', yet not an ancestor, and in two of the four names there seems to be the idea of One who gives nourishment, in one case the One who gives rain. In a single case the name seems to imply an autocratic Being, but in the others Mr. Young thinks that there is an idea of a Being thoughtfully concerned with the existence of human beings for whose original creation He was responsible. He tries to put the conception into modern speech and uses the analogies of a Managing Director, and a

Principal of a University. These are not entirely unsuitable, since they leave room for the possible existence of a number of inferior beings, including ancestors, in between the human individual and the Being at the top. Still the dim belief in the Being at the top exists, and plain folk are quite sure that He has come concern for those below, and that He grants something that no lower being has the power to grant. It will be clear that the Christian preacher or teacher finds something here which he can use, a hazy view of the highest Power which He can sharpen by focusing Christian belief upon it. He can do in fact what Dr. T. R. Glover declared that Jesus did for His contemporaries, making clearer and more definite that which to them had been vague and uncertain.

One of the four names quoted by Mr. Young, Mulungu, has been adopted in various forms as the name of Deity in translating the Bible into some twenty-five East African languages; although in one of the tribes at least the word is used in two entirely different senses, first as the Creator, the Most High God, and second, as an impersonal supernatural force, something like *mana* among the Melanesians. This, I believe, is a situation which is not unknown elsewhere, for I recall a statement made by Mr. Richard St. Barbe Baker concerning another East African tribe, who, he says, have a conception of a High God whom they call N'gai, and whom they seem to worship with animal sacrifices rather like the Yahweh of the earlier Old Testament records. But the same word is also used, so he says, to refer to the impersonal supernatural. Mr. Young quotes a statement made by one of the reigning chiefs, but a man of rather exceptional intellectual development, who was not entirely unfamiliar with both Christian and Moslem beliefs, and whose language may therefore have been influenced by the latter. 'Mulungu,' he said, 'has no face, hands, legs, or body. He does not speak, but he hears and sees. He is everywhere at once. He does whatever he likes. There is nothing to which he can be likened, although he is the lightning, and the thunder is his voice. The good are rewarded by him, and the bad are punished. Mulungu is sheer mind and a very great mind.' It happened, however, that when this chief performed sacrifices to ancestors he called upon Mulungu, while the most backward people in the tribe thought of Mulungu as an impersonal force pervading everything. Mulungu to them was in curative medicine and also in the evil power of the witch doctor. It seems fairly clear that Mulungu means something primarily very much like the Latin *numen*, and that with development the term is used in progressively varying senses. In 1878, when Nyasaland was still untouched by either European Christian or Moslem influences, the tribe of the Yao was reported as saying that Mulungu was 'the Great Spirit of All Men, formed by adding all the departed spirits together'. Although this may seem to embody rather an abstract idea for an African native, there seems no doubt that the usage has been confirmed by careful observation; and it is, of course, a very instructive statement, since it shows how in the minds of primitive people the veneration of ancestors may well have been linked up with the veneration of a Supreme Being. Nevertheless, whether personal or impersonal, Mulungu seems to have no plural form.

The next writer, Mr. C. R. Hopgood, deals with a group of people living in Northern Rhodesia to the south-west of Nyasaland. These people, when untouched by European and Christian influences, are essentially animistic pluralists, and specially venerate the *mizimu*, who are spirits of departed ancestors. At the same time they are said to have a very definite belief in the existence of one Supreme Being, the commonest name for whom is Leza. They seem to refer back all kinds of natural happenings directly and ultimately to Leza. 'Leza falls', of the rain; 'Leza is intense', of the heat; 'Leza blows', of the wind; 'Leza shines', of the lightning; 'Leza is killing us with hunger', or 'with disease'. Mr. Hopgood adds that vagaries of climate and other natural phenomena are spoken of as directly caused by Leza. Yet they sometimes speak of Leza as: 'our father who saves us from disaster'. The same people express puzzlement at the problem of suffering and death. Why, if Leza exists, does he bring trouble upon us? 'What man is there who has begotten a child and would wish to kill his own offspring?' The relation of Leza to the *mizimu* is ambiguous. Sometimes he is conceived to be the greatest of the *mizimu*. At other times the *mizimu* seem to be regarded as intermediary between Leza and mankind. The remark is quoted which was made by the leader of a hunting party when they had for some time failed to find game: 'I am tired of petitioning the *mizimu*. Let us pray to Leza'; and the man's prayer is translated as follows:

'O God, our father, do not turn thy back upon us. We know that all the animals are thy children; we too are thy children, and thou gavest them to us for food. Other people come to this place and kill game. Why should we go home empty-handed? We pray thee give us success in our hunting.'

In one village a discussion is recorded about the nature of Leza. He is said to be similar to the *mizimu*, who, although they are not seen, are venerated. In another conversation a young man, after questioning is father about Leza, showed that he was sceptical as to the very existence of such a Being. Mr. Hopgood records with some surprise that he does not find that people ever think of Leza in any physical or anthropomorphic sense. Leza is spirit, and is usually thought of as sexless, though this may be a development from an earlier idea, of which traces still remain, that Leza combines male and female characteristics. In this area there are also several other names used for the Supreme Being, one of which, Munamazuba, seems to mean 'the Ancient or Eternal One'. Other names signify 'the Owner', 'the Limitless One', 'the Changer', i.e. 'the One who brings round the seasons', 'the Keeper', 'the Preserver', 'the Deliverer', and 'the Angry One'. Mr. Hopgood thinks that, in spite of all the evidence, it is unwise to conclude that these Africans have reached the same point as the prophet responsible for the later chapters of Isaiah. While the proverb, 'Leza is not mocked', though spoken by a pagan, looks exactly like the saying in Galatians 6:7, the verb is also used in the opposite sense, so that if a man is suffering from some physical infirmity, it is said: 'Leza has mocked him.' This verb therefore may mean something more like 'to suffer' or 'cause to suffer'. But it would be wrong to conclude that Leza was definitely an ethical deity. One tribe have a creation story about Leza in which they say that he came from the east and went to the west, where he climbed up by a ladder into heaven. In the course of his journey he arranged and laid out the whole country, and he is now conceived as living in a great village in the sky, seated on a metal throne, and judging the heavenly people. This myth seems to show traces of a connection with sun-worship, and again there is what may be a faint trace of Egyptian influence, since the heavenly ladder is certainly to be found in Egyptian mythology.

Dr. Smith himself deals with the religious ideas of the South African tribes, and draws his conclusions after a rather substantial survey, which includes the Bushmen, the Hottentots, the Zulu, the Xhosa-speaking peoples, the Swazi, the Bechuana, the Herero of the west, and the Bantu of the northern region. Very many of these have now become Christian, so that it is not always easy to determine with security what their pre-Christian religion was. Some of them, like the Bushmen, may possibly have not reached to the conception of a Supreme Being. These latter are said to have more mythology than the Bantu, and seem to venerate the heavenly bodies and certain animals. They have a name, *Kaang*, the meaning of which is ambiguous. Some Bushmen seem to think of him as the Creator. One old Bushman, when asked where *Kaang* was, replied, 'I know not, but the elands know; wherever elands graze in herds, there is *Kaang*.' An early missionary in Basutoland reported that *Kaang* was described there by the Bushmen as a Chief in the sky, and the Master of all things. But the word *Kaang* again is ambiguous, and sometimes seems to mean a man with magical powers, who once lived, and made the moon out of his shoe, but who is not really a deity, but a sort of mischievous Puck.

The Hottentots, or as they call themselves, the Khoikhoi(n) are now nearly all Christian, but a careful record compiled in 1881 seems to make it clear that before their conversion they already believed in a great god called Tsuigoa, Tsuigoatse, or Tsuigoab. To him they offered animal sacrifice, and addressed prayer in the form of hymns. The moon was also venerated.

The Xhosa-speaking tribes use a word for God which is a modification of the Khoikhoi(n) one, but there seems some doubt as to whether these tribes, before their conversion to Christianity, were not pluralists. One of the Pondo, however, seemed to suggest that the Supreme Being, Tixo or uTixo, is a High God, who, though regarded with reverence, is really worshipped through the medium of the spirits of ancestors. Dr. Smith' quotes a Xhosa hymn written by a Christian in which uTixo occupies exactly the place as Yahweh in the Hebrew Psalms.

In dealing with the Zulus one finds again a certain amount of ambiguity. The name by which Bishop Colenso translated the word God into Zulu was uNkulunkulu, the chief objection to which, as he admitted, was its length! Dr. Callaway, however, raised another objection, namely, that this word did not really mean Supreme Being, but the 'very ancient one', rather as we might call Adam 'our first parent'; and further, that the word sometimes means a sort of caterpillar, the grub of a fly. A learned Roman Catholic missionary thought to have solved the problem by his alleged discovery that the Zulu language, like Chinese, makes use of tones, so that words which when written down can be spelt in the same way, when pronounced may have different meanings according to the tone with which they are spoken. Unfortunately other students of the Zulu language have not agreed with this, and say that although there may be as many as nine tones in Zulu, uNkulunkulu is always pronounced with the same tone. If, however, uNkulunkulu means a man, it is fairly clear that he is sometimes described as Creator, so that perhaps it only means that the Creator was personal. It seems more probable that the real word for God in Zulu is not uNkulunkulu at all but *Inkosi epezulu*, which may be translated 'the Lord who is above'. This latter Deity, however, had no proper name, or was perhaps not allowed, from motives of reverence, to be addressed by this title, in which case the other word, meaning 'first of men', was substituted, just as the Jews for the same reason used Adonai instead of Yahweh. There are a number of other words in Zulu by which the Supreme Being is sometimes known, and which mean 'He who thunders from the beginning', 'He who roars so that all nations be struck with terror'. Dr. Smith compares the latter with the name given by the Greek poet, Hesiod, to Zeus, βαρύκτονος 'Εννοσίγαιος. Other epithets are 'He who is irresistible', 'He who bends down so as to have the mastery over others', 'He who is immense like the ocean', and finally, Uzivelele, which means, 'He who came of himself into being; He who is of himself'. This last, as will be seen, is a much more theological and abstract epithet than any of the others, and the nearest approach to it would seem to be the phrase in the Book of Exodus variously translated as: 'I am that I am', or 'I will be that I will be'. It is noticeable that among these epithets there is nothing referring either to love or mercy.

The Swazi have a word, Umkhulumcandi, which seems to mean the First Being, and is doubtless identical with a Zulu word, umVelinqangi, which sometimes means Creator. But this god is never the object of prayer or sacrifice. He does not intervene in human affairs, and the Swazi are not really interested in him, but in the ancestral spirits of their people.

The Shangana-Tonga also deify their ancestors, but above them there exists a Power which for most of the people is not clearly defined, but is called Tilo. Tilo in the first instance means the bright blue sky, but beyond that it means the Power which sends thunder, lightning, rain, and sunshine, so that finally it means much more 'the Power in the sky', and so 'the Deity who controls everything and is omniscient'.

The people we have known as the Bechwana, who should more properly be called the Tswana, have a word Morimo, or Modimo, which seems to mean the Supreme Being, but does not appear to signify an ethical God, since Robert Moffat said that it always seemed to imply Power rather than Righteousness. 'I never once heard that Morimo did good or was supposed to be capable of doing so.'

An explorer who went to Basutoland in 1833 did not find there any belief in a supreme Creator, but said that the people believed that men and animals came out of the bowels of the earth by an immense hole or out of a marshy place where reeds were growing. This, as will be seen, greatly resembles the cosmogony of some Australian aborigines as described by Professor Ratcliffe-Brown. The people in this part of Africa are also recorded sometimes to have prayed to Modimo as 'the Earth Mother'. The conclusion here seems inevitable that within this area various types or stages of belief have co-existed.

Passing on to the Bantu of the northern region of South Africa,

we note somewhat the same combination of High Gods and ancestors. The Mashona, which include a number of tribes, call their
High God Mwari, who, they say, is not interested in individuals,
but has left family and individual affairs in the charge of the *medzimu*,
the family spirits of the dead. A hymn, however, to Mwari is
quoted, which somewhat resembles the Hebrew Psalm 104. Nevertheless such worship of Mwari as has existed seems to be localised
in a cave temple. There is so much about the Mwari cult which is
unusual, that a Swedish missionary has regarded it as the degenerate
relic of an ancient religion brought into Africa from the Near East.
Thus Mwari sometimes has a human consort, who is the wife of a
priest, and Mwari is even thought of as a divine triad in which
Sororezhou is Father, Vamarumbi Mother, and Runji Son. This
looks suspiciously like Mohammed's well-known misrepresentation
of the Trinity, and it may well be that there was really somewhere a
pagan triad of this description.

In south-west Africa we have the Herero and the Ovambo.
Once again we have an ambiguity. The first missionaries, from
Germany, in 1844, adopted the name Omukuru for God, among the
Herero; but later on there was some doubt as to the wisdom of this
choice, since the Herero themselves said that it ought to be Ndjambi
Karunga, who is 'up in the sky, a god of blessing, angry with nobody
and punishing nobody'. Omukuru is clearly only an ancestor. But
the other dual term seems to be a combination of two names, that of
a sky god and a god of the underworld. This at any rate, was the
explanation of a Dutch anthropologist in 1933. But Dr. Smith
thinks it more likely that the conjunction of the two words indicates
the combination of names for deity belonging to different tribes.
Ndjambi is the heavenly god, who is benevolent, but Kalunga is
mentioned as far back as 1654 by a Roman Catholic missionary who
went to the Congo, and who says that the kings of Angola worshipped
Kalunga as the personification of the sea, the mysterious Atlantic
Ocean. But another derivation suggests that Kalunga was after all
an earth god. The Ovambo use this word Kalunga almost universally
to signify deity. They say he has never been human, that he is personal, omnipresent and omniscient. He cannot do anything, and he
receives no sacrifices, since he does not need them. He is never seen,
but he is all-seeing. He is the Author and Sustainer of life, man's last
hope and resort in trouble, yet not an object of human love. He is
'impassible'. He is, however, not described as a law-giver, since the
moral code is not rooted in him but in tribal custom. Other tribes
also use the word Kalunga, but with slight variations. Thus the
Mufifi say that Kalunga has a wife or consort. The Mbangu seem

to keep the title of Kalunga for use only during thunderstorms. Nevertheless these tribes say that Kalunga expects good behaviour on the part of men, such behaviour meaning conformity to tribal ethics. Here we seem to get an instance of the stage at which there is a transition from the idea of the moral code as man-made to the conception which is found in ancient Mesopotamia of the code as bestowed by a god, and coming wholly from above (e.g. Shamash, the sun-god, and the code of Khammurabi).

Dr. Smith adds at this point a long note on the name which we have noticed before, and which appears in various spellings, sometimes as Ndjambi, sometimes as Nyambe, Tsambi, Yambe, Zam, etc. He says that this God-name is spread over a very large part of western equatorial Africa, and that although in some cases it has certainly been introduced by missionaries, it is possible that the African people themselves may have contributed to its spread, long before missions entered the country. Thus it has a considerable resemblance to the Akan name of God, Onyame. It is always possible that we have here a survival from the ancient past before the Negro peoples had got divided up into different groups; or it may be possible that after such division had taken place there was some borrowing, in which case it is difficult to determine who was the borrower. The whole question is obscure and complicated, since a story about Nyambe told by the Barotse of the Upper Zambesi, in which some men built a high wooden tower made of logs in order to climb up into Nyambe's dwelling-place—but the weight of the logs was too great and the tower collapsed—is almost exactly the same story which Mr. St. Barbe Baker found among the Ba-kikuyu of East Africa, and Professor J. H. Hutton among some peoples in India, far away on the other side of the Indian Ocean. Who can tell, therefore, how much migration in the distant past has been responsible for the transference of religious ideas, and how much peoples themselves have moved about? We know that the people of Madagascar have racial and cultural affinities with India, and not with the negro peoples, and we cannot tell how much commerce there may have been in ancient times between India and the east coast of the African continent.

Dr. Smith ends by quoting the testimony of Dr. H. A. Junod in 1927: 'It is wonderful to notice how easily the idea of the Christian God is accepted by the Bantus. It seems as if one were telling them an old story with which they had been quite familiar, but had now half forgotten'. Others have said that the vague belief which they found to exist among so many Africans must be the decayed remnant of a clearer monotheistic faith. Elsewhere the story is quoted of the old African woman who, after she had been listening to a Christian preacher, turned to her companions and said, 'There; I always told you that there must be a God like that'. This was in the Belgian Congo. Mr. J. Davidson, of the Baptist Missionary Society, speaks of the same part of the world and says that they have a special name, Akongo, for the Supreme Being. Akongo is not impersonal, like Mana: indeed the people make a clear distinction between the latter and Akongo himself. He is over and above all spirits, human and superhuman alike, although he has a special relationship to the ancestors of the whole tribe. In this respect he seems to resemble some of the other African High Gods. On the other hand, he is not universally benevolent, for if people have misfortune, they sometimes say 'Akongo is unkind, or has done me harm'; and sometimes the Akongo of a certain place is spoken of, rather as villagers in South India refer to a Village Mother, or as Italian peasants may speak of a particular local Madonna. But they are quite clear that Akongo has never been a man. He is what he was from the beginning; he is spirit. He is worshipped with five praise-names, one of which means 'the Moulder', i.e. the Creator, another 'the Everlasting One'—the word in this case indicating 'the unendingness of the forest'. Mr. Davidson says that people on the Congo who have never seen anything but forest, and hardly know that anything else exists, think of the forest as infinite and eternal. Deity, they say, is like that. Akongo is also called 'the one who clears the forest'. Since clearing is heavy work, this epithet means 'the Mighty One'. He is also called 'the One who began the forest', and in another case 'the One who helps people to find things'. He is also known as 'the Master of the forest', 'the One who fills everything and is everywhere', and finally 'the One who is mysterious and unknown and cannot be explained'. Here again Akongo has no direct connection with a man's way of life. The moral law is the work of the ancestors. Nevertheless some old men have been found to claim that Akongo himself gave these laws to the ancestors in the first place. The tribe known to Mr. Davidson had four moral commandments prohibiting incest, witchcraft, adultery, and theft. Deceit and cunning are looked upon as accomplishments.

In the highland country on the Congo-Nile watershed are the two kingdoms of Ruanda and Urundi. The people of both these realms believe in one Creator God whom they call Imana, but they also believe in a number of other spiritual beings, to wit, the spirits of ancestors, local nature spirits who are essentially malicious, and sometimes cause fits, severe internal pains, or paralytic strokes, and two malignant deities, Ryangombe and Rwuba. Ryangombe,

18

among the Ruandi people, is known as Kiranga. Among the Ruanda, Rwuba is unknown, but his place is taken by two other evil spirits. Nevertheless Imana, though venerated, does not really enter at all into daily life. Since he can do no harm to human beings and cannot be influenced by them, there seems to be no point in praying or sacrificing to him. It should be said that very much the same situation prevails in regard to Akongo, who has just been mentioned. He needs no priests, no temple, and no sacrifice, and yet any ordinary lay individual can approach him, and there are direct evidences of chants in the form of prayers and invocations addressed to Akongo in connection with hunting and war. Imana, in the same way is often mentioned by people. They will say, 'May Imana give you good fortune', or if cursing, 'May Imana give you a stroke'. The latter invocation is said to cause more grief than any other kind of curse, since Imana is not generally thought of as hostile. Although Imana is not often addressed in prayer, Miss Guillebaud says that when in great distress an appeal can be made to him. Imana is thought of more as a convenience than as an actual influence for good. In fact he makes very little positive difference to one's conduct. One only brings him in as a last resort when in real trouble.

In Uganda there is strong evidence of the belief in a High God having come down with Hamitic immigrants from the north, perhaps from Ethiopia. In this case it may have a Judaeo-Christian origin, but the names given to this deity vary all over the area, showing how the culture of these early invaders has become absorbed into that of the Bantu aborigines. Apart from this there seems to be the usual cultus of ancestors and local spirits, and there is also among the Archoli and Lango peoples a belief in another puckish spirit known as Jok who is associated with anything of an unusual nature, and who has been identified by Christian missionaries, perhaps not altogether wisely, with Satan.

Passing further north, to the Anglo-Egyptian Sudan, Mr. R. C. Stevenson considers the beliefs of the people in the Nuba mountains, who have only in recent years come under observation. Here, he says, there seem to be three levels of religious thought. First, the notion of a High God who is the Creator and Parent of all things, and is omnipotent and above all other spirits. He was never human and has never been seen. He is treated with reverence, but his name is not often spoken, and like the Imana of Ruanda, he is only invoked in times of great trouble. On a second level is the belief in spirits residing in natural objects and local to them. This belief is pretty definite, and leads to a variety of spirit cults. In the third place there is a belief in a wonder-working force dwelling in and functioning through visible objects. It is, like the Polynesian *mana*, impersonal, and corresponds to the same idea as that of the Arabic *barakah*, so prevalent in North Africa, i.e. an independent force which is neutral, and may be either called into operation for good or for evil. We are here getting nearer to the Moslem world, so that sometimes it is possible to detect its influence. Nevertheless there are a number of words for deity which do not seem to have been introduced from outside. Thus in one tribe the Creator is called Abradi and is thought of as a superhuman person. In the southern tribes of the Nuba mountains there are several tribes which use matrilineal descent, and among these God is the great Mother. Other words are Epti, who seems to be like Abradi, Elem, a very old word in the Koalib tribe for a High God who is a Creator, Bel, meaning spirit, and a number of words for natural forces, each of which seems to be deified. One of these, Rimwa, meaning 'rain', is often used in a wider sense to mean 'Providence'.

The great West African peoples are dealt with in four sections, first the Yoruba and Ewe groups of Nigeria, second the Akan people of the newly constituted state of Ghana, thirdly the Kono people of the East Central part of Sierra Leone, and fourthly the Mende people of the same state. The religion of the first group is a system of polytheism presided over by a Supreme Creator. The Akan have a highly complex system, in which there are (1) a High God called Nyame or Nyankopon, (2) a group of subordinate deities known as Abosom; (3) spirits of the departed; and (4) various minor bogeys such as Sasabonsam, the forest ogre. There was some doubt as to whether Nyame was an Akan god at all, but it seems now definitely decided that he is really native to the country. He is apparently a sky-god, though it is doubtful how much philosophical theology can really be deduced from his various praise-names. At any rate, he is Creator, and is eternal, omniscient, and benevolent, and unlike some High Gods has temples and priests and a small altar made out of a tree cut so as to leave a triple fork at the top, on which is placed a basin or pot for sacrificial offerings. Temples of Nyame are rare, and found exclusively in the compounds of chiefs, and the priests are dedicated for life to the god's service, and can be distinguished by their shaven heads and their gold and silver ornaments. At the annual festival they wear white vestments and smear their bodies with white clay, and a number of sacrifices are offered, sheep, white fowls, and vegetables. In opposition to Nyankopon but inferior to him is a malevolent Deity called Nyankopon Kweku.

Mr. Evans, who writes about the Akan, concludes from the

evidence that their religion certainly has one strong element of monotheism, and that it has very likely deteriorated in the direction of
polytheism, and he quotes the illuminating and controversial remark
of Captain R. S. Rattray that had the Akan been left to themselves
sooner or later, perhaps, some African Messiah would have arisen
and swept their religion clean off its pluralistic animism, so that in
that case West Africa might have become the cradle of a new religion.
Mr. Evans doubts himself whether this would ever have happened.
Anyhow, whether from the direction of Islam or of Christianity,
this clearance seems now to be taking place. It is to be hoped
sincerely that in the long run the religion of the new state of Ghana
will be an enlightened and indigenous form of Christianity, which
may be of service to other parts of the continent.

Mr. R. T. Parsons writes on the Kono in Sierra Leone; and here
again we find the combination of some kind of monotheism with the
existence of lesser gods, numerous spirits, especially those of ancestors, and the usual dynamism, in which an impersonal all-pervasive
force is clearly believed in. Two words are used as names of the
Supreme Being. The first of these, Meketa, is the older, and is now
only used occasionally; it appears to mean 'the Everlasting One'.
The second name, Yataa, means 'the Great One who is omnipresent'.
Nevertheless Yataa is said to be far away in the sky, and only
addresses people indirectly through subordinate deities. The Kono
worship the Earth Mother, and say that she is the consort of
Yataa.

The last people to be considered in this series of essays are the
Mende, who are scattered over some ten thousand square miles of
the Protectorate of Sierra Leone, but are only about half a million
in number, and whose religion has been overlaid by a not very pure
form of Islam. Mr. W. T. Harris has tried to separate out the pre-
Moslem beliefs of the Mende, and says that the commonest name for
deity is Ngewo, which seems to mean the Great Chief. The latter
again is usually approached through an intermediary, in this case
a succession of ancestors; and this prayer takes time and needs some
preliminary, since the place of prayer, either hill or river, has to be
selected, and then notice has to be given in advance by some agreed
sign, that one is coming to pray. The principle is that the ancestors
will receive the prayer and convey it to the spirits of hill or water,
and these in turn will convey it to Ngewo. As to the way in which
these prayers are answered, there seem to be different opinions, since
some say that up to a point the ancestors themselves can answer
prayer. Others say that the answer in the last resort comes only
from Ngewo and is only conveyed by the intermediaries. In any

case all prayer ends with the formula *Ngewo jahu*, which means 'Under God's protection may it be so'. In emergency short prayers to Ngewo may be offered direct. But all these prayers seem to be in the form of petition or request. A little piece of mythology may serve to illustrate popular thought about this prayer. It is said that in the beginning, immediately after Ngewo had created the world, there was no kind of prayer. Nhewo sat and thought of all the people he had made and how there was no way of making them know his wishes. Then he made a big mountain near the place where the people lived and gave it power to talk to human beings. For He said, 'If the people get used to hearing the voice of the mountain and if they keep the laws of the mountain, then in future they will hear my voice and keep my laws'. He also gave people the power to dream, and out of the dream to gain information as to the will of Ngewo. If this is a genuine piece of Mende folklore, and not a corruption of something learned from missionaries, one is tempted to speculate whether it is something which has filtered down to this area from the north-east, since anyone can see that it sounds like faint echoes from the Book of Exodus.

It is now time to try to draw some general conclusions from this series of studies in the various pre-Christian and pre-Moslem religions of the African people.

(1) The universal extent of religious belief is obvious. There are no non-religious people anywhere.

(2) There is extreme difficulty in completely disentangling indigenous from diffused belief.

(3) The survey, though it only covers a selected list of twelve different groups in the whole continent, gives representative examples, from which we may clearly see that the different types of religious experience, ranging from dynamism to monotheism, are widely distributed, and to be found nearly everywhere. Since they exist side by side, it is perhaps not easy to be sure whether this situation means that there has been a kind of evolutionary development, with the earlier types surviving and co-existing side by side with the later ones, or whether the different types were present side by side from the beginning, or again whether the earliest form was a primitive monotheism, while the various pluralisms represent a decline from this. Some of the problems connected with this have been dealt with in the earlier part of Chapter II, and it seems that the only possible way of deciding what has really happened is to try to find out what was the earliest belief of the least developed types of human being in the country. One thinks naturally of the Bushmen, who of course are almost on the point of disappearing, and it will

be remembered that the latter are said possibly not to have reached the conception of a Supreme Being. Nevertheless this conclusion was not accepted by some of the early missionaries. It may well be that even the beliefs of the Bushmen have themselves passed through a certain degree of development, but in the main what seems to have survived among them is predominantly a pluralistic animism. On the other hand, some observers whose work has not been included in Dr. Smith's volume, have paid special attention to the beliefs of the pygmy peoples who still exist in some of the Central African forests. Father Schmidt of Vienna, having put together all the evidence, has maintained that the pygmies are the earliest surviving forms of human beings, and he has drawn attention to the fact that similar small human beings also exist in other parts of the world and that they all seem to share a crude and primitive belief in monotheism. He has deduced from this that some such belief was held by the most primitive men when they emerged from their simian antecedents. Many anthropologists have not accepted Schmidt's conclusions, since they hold that the pygmy form of human being is only a local contemporary diminutive of existing forms and is not earlier than them in the date of its emergence. Another difficulty in agreeing with Schmidt is that some kind of naïve monotheism is obviously found among many simple peoples who are not pygmies; and, as we have seen, this is especially true throughout Africa. Nor is it the case that the High God is invariably, as used to be thought, a Being to whom no worship is offered. While this is sometimes the case, it is not always so. Some High Gods receive no worship, but others are worshipped indirectly, or in cases of emergency. It is not universally the case that the monotheism looks like fading out, though here and there this is clearly the case.

(4) Whatever the origin of the monotheism which survives, whether it be diffused or indigenous, it is clearly some sort of foundation upon which the Christian teacher can build. Quite clearly the expression of the belief is generally of a very simple order, and combined with mythology expressed, as we might say, in the language of children's fairy tales. It is seldom adult or philosophical. Is it, however, just to dismiss it on this account, and not to allow that even the minds of Africans living in the pre-axial stage of belief may be motivated and guided by the Divine Logos? The quotation from the American poet, Longfellow, was much quoted in years gone by, and has now perhaps become rather trite and hackneyed, nevertheless it still expresses what many of us are bound to feel about the peoples in the great forests and wide spaces of the African continent:

'That in even savage bosoms
There are longings, strivings, yearnings,
That the feeble hands and helpless
Groping blindly in the darkness
Touch God's right hand in the darkness
And are lifted up and strengthened.'

If some will feel in Africa or elsewhere that the use of the word savage carries with it a very slight sensation of patronage, it is perhaps permissible to quote another and perhaps more generously worded judgment by the Jesuit, Father C. C. Martindale, who says that we must always regard it as possible that even early man 'by a pure jet of his spiritual nature has been able at times to pierce through to Reality'. The latter would seem to be the officially recognised Roman Catholic doctrine about sincerely religious non-Christians in general, since Père Jean Daniélou, in a work published in 1956, which carries the *nihil obstat*, asks whether it is not right to deduce from the naïve stories of Enoch and Noah that there is from the emergence of mankind, apart from the covenant with Israel, a 'cosmic covenant' (*alliance cosmique*). He prefers this phrase apparently to that of natural religion, and goes on to affirm that such a covenant denotes a grace-embodied relationship with God, a continuing revelation to all men through nature and conscience, and a response to that revelation by some human beings in all times and in all places. In regard to such persons he falls back on a phrase borrowed from Journet, who says, 'They belong invisibly to the visible Church'. In the same work Daniélou quotes Aquinas as saying that if one explicitly believes in Providence, one must logically be held to believe implicitly in Christ, who is the supreme instance of Providence; and he expresses the hope that in thus diverging from Karl Barth in the latter's antagonism to natural theology, the difference may be found as one of emphasis rather than of radical disagreement, though in this perhaps he is being rather an optimist. In one remarkably Pauline sentence he says, '. . . le chrétien infidèle sera condamné, tandis que le païen fidèle sera sauvé'[1].

A reference to the section on Greek and Roman religion and to the chapter on indigenisation will show the reader, without any need for its repetition at this point, how close are the parallels between the graded conceptions of the supernatural which have been described in this chapter as occurring in various parts of Africa, and those which are to be found in ancient China and in Japanese Shinto.

Africa, however, has so far not developed a philosophical stage in the evolution of her own indigenous religion, and it may seem as though she is going to miss this out altogether.

[1] Friends in India might well ponder Père Daniélou's remarks.

What, however, interests most of us is the consideration of what the religious condition of Africa is likely to be in the future. It is quite clear that the Christian faith, considered in the broadest sense, has made remarkable and substantial progress in many areas. Thus, for example, in Ghana it is said that 50 per cent of the citizens of this new state already belong to one or another of the great Christian denominations. Dr. Nkrumah has himself said that in the matter of self-government his people owe everything to the missionaries, by which he means that they have always aimed at establishing a Christian community which has its own African ministry, and supports its churches by its own voluntary contributions, as well as administering them by councils of Africans. Large numbers of Christians also exist in Nigeria and in various parts of East Africa, as well as in Southern Bantu areas such as Zululand. But this is far from being the whole story. Over South Africa hangs the gloomy and threatening cloud of *apartheid*, and all that is connected with it. It remains to be seen how far Africans will stand by the Christian Church if the latter seems to tolerate injustice and exploitation of the inhabitants of Africa by white peoples. Furthermore, many educated Africans know all about Communism, and in some cases have passed into Christianity and then out again into Marxism. A considerable number have come to study at the London School of Economics, where they have gained insight into advanced ideas both political and economic. Dr. Nkrumah himself is one such African, and although he appears to be a Christian rather than a Marxist, this does not prevent him from viewing the possible future development of his own and of other states on lines which will certainly be collectivist. Development has been unexpectedly rapid. A writer in a recent article who knows the Gold Coast and is the Africa Secretary of the Methodist Missionary Society reminds us that whereas in 1928 administrative officers were saying: 'Africans will one day govern this country, but it won't come in our lifetime', in 1957, only twenty-nine years later, the same areas has received its independence. It is well known that Dr. Nkrumah has visions of a great federation of African states, all of them self-governing, and it is clear that although the vision may not be for many days, it could be realised in just the same unexpected way. The problems of the Christian Church are, of course, closely related to this development in self-determination. It may seem that these problems are more matters of administration and of morality than of higher education and philosophical theology. Thus it is said that one of the subjects which is needing urgent and serious thought is Christian marriage and Christian family life, and further, that the enlargement of the

African ministry in such a way as to prevent the more experienced pastors from being overweighted with administrative duties which include a great deal of travelling, is an urgent matter.   The shortage of good men of training and intellectual integrity to fill posts in the higher Civil Service which is being experienced by the new West African Governments is felt quite as much by the churches, and although it may be hoped that the situation will be easier in ten years' time, today it is critical.

Nevertheless, this does not mean that the intellectual need of Africa hardly exists.   On the contrary, if the development of a sane and reverent African theology in the vernacular does not keep pace with the progressive education of African people, the situation may easily become dangerous.   The more educated African may feel that the standard within the Christian churches is rather that of the nursery than of an adult population which is not only getting a higher education in Europe and America, but is now creating important centres for it in the whole land in such places as Ibadan. There is therefore urgent need for the training of competent African theologians, who are able, on the one hand, to put the best modern theology and Bible exegesis into African language, but who are also able to make a right assessment of traditional African thought. Some sentences from the article referred to above may well be quoted:

'The true synthesis waits for those within African life who know the treasures both of their own heritage and of the Christian faith. There are many ways in which the strength of African life has still to flow freely into Christian worship.   From the present generation of Christians, set free from the real fear which their fathers faced as they turned away from worship at older shrines, yet strengthened with the same deep trust in the Lord Jesus which freed their fathers from bondage, there may come a richer African liturgy.'

What is said here may equally apply to the intellectual training and creative thought necessary for the production of educated African readers.   While it is good that some Africans should be sent to universities in Europe and America, it is also most necessary that Christian centres of education outside Africa should send freely of their best to live and work in the colleges of Africa.

It must be made quite clear that the great bulk of Christian opinion inside and outside Africa is solidly against racial segregation. It is also clear that in a multi-racial church there is bound to be a difficult transition period when non-Europeans have to face the risk of taking appointments which will give them a certain degree of responsibility in respect of the church life of Europeans.   This difficulty will pass as soon as Africans in sufficiently large numbers attain to the requisite educational and cultural standards, and some have done this already. Although there are perhaps fewer Europeans in India than formerly, there are certainly multi-racial Christian communities in some of the cities, where an Indian ministry, often with its own bishops, ministers to non-Indians without any sense of strain. In the world of the future such conditions must necessarily increase, must be expected to increase, and ought to be welcomed. The situation is bound to be different in some of the great Asian countries where there has been for many centuries a high and ancient standard of culture, but Africa has been rapidly catching up. American negroes have now for a long time received high education and have come to occupy posts of great responsibility; and the newly formed Afro-Asian alliance of peoples, with its accompaniment in the sending of African students to Asian universities like Delhi and Calcutta, is bound to hasten the process.

Nevertheless, it does not do to underestimate the difficulty which the Christian communities are experiencing in the fulfilment of their desire to show that they do not practise a colour bar, and that they are ready to take the initiative as Christians in significant action which makes the breaking down of bad social customs. The writer quoted above has given us the unwelcome reminder that in this context the Communists and the scientific humanists might even be said to be going into the Kingdom of Heaven before the Christians.

Africa, like the rest of the new Christian world, will most certainly demand a greater unity among Christians. The scandal of competing denominations is there to see. It is said that town-planners in colonial Africa have often set apart a zone for church buildings, so that in one African township on the Copper Belt there are eleven different denominational buildings standing side by side in a row. Obviously this cannot be allowed to go on. On the other hand it is said that there are signs of the beginning of attempts to copy what has been done in South India. In December 1955, Bishop Sumitra, the Moderator of the Church of South India, visited Nigeria to hold conversations there with that end in view, and similar stirrings are to be noted in Ghana and in Northern Rhodesia. It will be nothing less than tragic if the church divisions and the errors and aberrations of Christian thought which disfigure the churches of Europe and Asia should be transferred to the African continent. If the peoples of Africa in desperation turn either to Islam or to some form of humanism the Christian churches now engaged in missionary work will have only themselves to thank for it.

At the conference on 'Christianity in African Culture' previously referred to, a number of questions were provided for sub-

sequent discussion by its members.   These are sufficiently interesting
to deserve some notice, and I propose to summarise them here as
briefly as I can.

The first group asked whether there was an agreed interpretation
of nature on the part of Christians, and if so whether the African
attitude to nature could be regarded as contrary to it.   It was then
asked whether animism could fairly be regarded as inconsistent with
Christian belief, and if so why and in what sense, and further
whether anything of value to Christianity could be found from a
knowledge of African traditional religious beliefs and practices.
Since some of the pre-Christian festivals express the African people's
sense of solidarity and their common interest in the things upon
which their group life depends, is it possible for Christianity to find
a place for these festivals?   What is the problem of evil as faced in
African traditional thought and in the Christian context, and how
does the African doctrine of man in his relation to God compare
with that held by orthodox Christianity?   Is the reverence for one's
ancestors and the custom of pouring libations to them as an expression of gratitude and of a sense of dependence, to be regarded as
compatible with Christianity?   Is there a sense in which the reverence for the Stool or throne as a symbol of the institution of chief-
tancy can be regarded as consistent with the profession of the
Christian faith?   What should be the Christian attitude to what
appear to be certain facts lying behind fetishism and witchcraft?
Should witchcraft be countered by faith-healing, and should the
Christian Church still practise exorcism and the driving out of
devils?   Is it feasible and desirable today to introduce for practice
by Christians new customs which, while linking up with African culture, at the same time also provide elements of value for Christian
nurture?

It is significant that those who took part in this conference
belonged to a number of different Christian denominations, including Presbyterians and Swiss Protestants.   The discussion seems to
have been attended by great friendliness, and by a recognition that
there might be more than one answer possible to some of these
questions.   One Swiss missionary delegate seemed doubtful as to the
desirability of practising exorcism, while Catholics may well have
taken a different view.   Perhaps it may be permissible to quote some
of his words:

'The danger of exorcisms as performed by the sects is that it may not
be Christ who is working, but group hysteria and suggestion.   The
even greater danger is that it will not bring a real healing, but only a
temporary patching up of the split personality.   I am, however,

convinced that in a quiet way much can be done for the real healing of the supposed witches by intercessory prayer during our Friday services and elsewhere. And I think that even more it will be very important to admit these "witches" into the Christian fellowship of say, a Youth Guild or a Women's Class, helping them by sympathetic encouragement to assert their personalities in a healthy way. So the reassuring love and healing power of Christ may be extended to them.

We must show that in faith—but in faith only—there is a new unity of man's personality in the middle of the conflicting strains of the cultures, that there is also a new unity for the family in faith, and a new unity of society: The Kingdom of God is amongst us, though not always a visible entity. We will help people to stand patiently and bravely in the spiritual struggle, arming them with the spiritual weapons of the Christian (Ephesians 6). We also must help men to see how God can transmute the evil of disease and suffering into a blessing bringing us nearer to Him.'

One more general remark may be permitted in conclusion.

The total panorama of African religion must surely lead the observer to the conclusion that although it includes no great system of philosophical theology, yet the simple ideas spread so widely over great areas of the population must be held to indicate the operation of the Divine Logos in the minds of Africans. Not everything that occurs can be written off as perverse, misguided, foolish or obscene. To repeat a previous quotation, it is striking how naturally Africans respond to Christian belief and the Christian message. Plainly there is that within them which naturally awakens a response to what is offered. This fact alone, observable over such a vast area of the earth as the African continent, should lead those who so strongly emphasise the discontinuity between pagan religion and Christianity, to halt, and to indulge in second thoughts. I cannot find in Dr. Kraemer's two great books any reference to the data which Africa provides, and I think that a theory which omits to take account of them, when judged on the principles of scientific method, can hardly be expected to yield a valid result.

(ii) NEO-HINDUISM

The position of Hinduism since about 1800 has steadily been changing. It is certainly true that religion in India has had great teachers in the past, and that during the long period when India was relatively cut off from the Western world, religion did develop independently and with many important internal variations of its own. It is also true that India, in the main, has exhibited great religious and philosophical genius. But two points need to be stressed. First, the general religious situation has been remarkably like that which might have developed in Europe if the Christian movement had never appeared there; and owing to the time-lag, and to India's isolation, this situation has been greatly prolonged, so that the observer is constantly reminded by survivals which he comes across in nineteenth- and twentieth-century India of similar features which belong to European non-Christian religion in the days of Plutarch. Indians indeed might very profitably make a study of Plutarch, and consider why it was that he did not succeed in stemming the advance of the Christian movement in his own day. Second, the whole development of Indian society past and present has been profoundly affected by the peculiar climate of the sub-continent. No doubt, those who are born in it exhibit a certain degree of hereditary adjustment; but its seasonal fluctuations are always and inevitably bound to exercise a degree of control over the members of the human species inhabiting it, and so to affect both intellectual and social progress.[1]

Some Indians today hold the view, tinged to some extent, they would probably admit, with a certain amount of nationalist pride, that the religion of their country is at its best capable of developing so as to become the universal religion of the future. What in effect they propose is a non-Christian Catholicism as a serious alternative to a Christian Catholicism. How far such a movement could ever succeed may well be doubted, but it would be uncharitable to ignore the activity or doubt the sincerity of those engaged in it. A writer like Professor Murti, of the Hindu University, Banaras,[2] who has spent much time in this country as a student at Oxford and also as a lecturer, is a good example of this. He says:

'The need is for the spiritual regeneration of the world. Denominational religions with their dogmas and organisational sanctions deservedly stand discredited. There is something inherently secular and unspiritual in any organisation. It tends to create vested interests and to breed corruption. In stifling freedom of expression and setting up a norm of dogmas to which the votaries are required to conform, organised religion (the church) succeeds only in antagonising other religious groups and creating schisms and heresies within its own fold. What we need is the realisation of the spiritual which is the bed-rock of all our endeavour. Only mystical religion, which eminently combines the unity of Ultimate Being with the freedom of different paths for realising it, can hope to unite the world.'

It is clear that the criticism is here levelled more at the Christian Church than at the House of Islam, and those who belong to the former would do well to pay heed to it. Whereas the relative formlessness of Asian religious systems is an inherent weakness, the

[1] It is no doubt this peculiar climate which made even so warm a friend of India as C. F. Andrews speak with regret of the continuance of unpleasant customs, and of a lack of moral fibre in leaders of public opinion, and tolerance of evil, which have to be taken account of by everyone in India who sets out to be a reformer.
[2] Not to be confused with Professor Murty of Andhra University.

institutionalism of Christians also has its serious dangers. Nevertheless a movement which seeks to be world-transforming cannot
escape the necessity of some form of disciplined organisation. To
understand, however, the rise and progress of this non-Christian
Catholicism it may be well to turn to a recent account given by Mr.
Sarma of the Vivekananda College at Madras, which shows clearly
what has been happening. The first attempt at modernising Hinduism was of course the Brahmo Samaj movement begun between 1772
and 1838 by Ram Mohan Roy. It secured the abolition of *sati* (wife-
burning), discouraged caste and idolatry, and promoted education in
the sciences, but it favoured a rational theism as against Vedanta non-
duality, and gradually became more and more Christian and less and
less Hindu, splitting into three sub-sections, and steadily shrinking
in membership. It produced one outstanding personality, the poet
Rabindranath Tagore, but is now not very influential. Its neighbour, the Arya Samaj movement, has on the contrary grown steadily.
Founded between 1824 and 1823 by Swami Dayananda, it has sought
to remain steadfastly Hindu, although modernist in spirit. It takes
its stand on the Vedas alone, deprecates caste and idol worship, and
in Europe often claims to speak as the true exponent of Hinduism.
Closely akin to the Arya Samaj, but perhaps carrying its work
further is the group of teachers and social workers who claim to be
followers of the Indian saint, Sri Ramakrishna (1836 to 1886).
Ramakrishna was neither a scholar nor a logical thinker; but from
contacts with Islam and Christianity as well as with Hinduism and
with various hybrids existing in India, such as Sikhism, he came quite
honestly to believe that all existing religions are but aspects of one
universal religion of the future. In spite of this, though perhaps
because of it, he remained essentially a Hindu. His disciple, Swami
Vivekananda (1863 to 1902), continued and extended his work, and
founded the well-known Ramakrishna mission, which has hospitals
and other kinds of more strictly Christian and humanist forms of
activity connected with it. It is genuinely syncretistic, and it may
well be that its intellectual background is provided by the teaching
of Sir Sarvepalli Radhakrishnan. Nobody can doubt that it is
doing a most beneficent work, and that it is both enterprising and
progressive in a way in which some Christian Groups are not. It is
said at the moment to be planning to train 100 new missionaries for
its work, it runs good film shows for children, and it includes Christmas in its calendar of festivals.

It is interesting to speculate what kind of worship will be offered
in the great new University temple at Banaras (referred to above), and
it seems not unsafe to predict that it will be modernist in type,

perhaps more closely approaching in its worship to that of the Arya
Samaj, though it may, of course, develop as a kind of comprehensive
or union temple similar to the Birla institution[1] at Delhi.

The work of Radhakrishnan as well as that of the late Rabindranath Tagore and Aurobindo Ghose all tends towards the creation
of an Indian religion which can invite converts from other countries,
and offer itself as an alternative to Christian Catholicism, while at
the same time seeking to include elements from Christianity within
its borders.

With some of the points put forward by these 'Hindu Catholics'
it is possible to agree.   There are, as they say, many different levels
of development among human beings, and it is no doubt necessary
to provide opportunities for religious faith and self-expression suited
to these different varieties.   Yet here caution is needed.   Catholicism of any sort always tends to pay great attention to what it has
called 'the faith of the charcoal burner', and sometimes seems to be
unduly ready to let him hold on to any kind of superstitions that he
likes.   But the gradual levelling up of education is bound to sweep
away many of these types of believers, and if a religious institution
is felt to be too tolerant of foolish, bad, unworthy, and even immoral
or obscene types of religious beliefs and practices, education will very
likely sweep the simple peasant off into an opposite extreme of crude
secularism, as in many cases it has done in Russia.   Again Indians
may rightly urge that a properly developed theology should have a
sound philosophical background for those who are able to appreciate
it.   But this cannot be secured by a *return* to the Upanishads, any
more than it can be secured by a static adherence to the philosophy
of Aquinas.   The idea of the Divine Self-Limitation in creation, if
honestly held, belongs certainly to both Christians and Hindus.   It
is also obvious that Christians share with Hindus the conception of
Deity as ultimately beyond human definition, but this must not be
taken as implying that Deity is beyond good and evil in the sense of
being arbitrary or non-moral, nor must it be taken to mean that Deity
is in any way less in quality than the symbols by which He is known to
our finite natures, or that He is in the last resort totally unknowable.

The most serious difficulty for the Christian in facing Hindus
has in the past been their general attitude towards the time-process
which they regard not as part of reality, but as an actual misperception of reality by us.   They have therefore rejected the possibility
of any historical action by Deity within the spatio-temporal order.

[1] This edifice, built at the expense of a wealthy Indian, aims at providing a common
spiritual home for all types of Indian religion.   Saivites, Vaishnavites, and Buddhists
all have separate sanctuaries within its walls.

If any such seems to occur, it is held by them to be nothing more than an edifying drama of a fictional nature, performed as a kind of concession to the weakness of finite human beings, and in any case capable of being almost endlessly repeated. This is at once a rejection of the possibility of a genuinely historical Incarnation, and also of such an Incarnation as unique and once-for-all. Yet, even here, it is possible to see signs of a change. Indians have for some time begun to feel the reproach of 'not being interested in history', and once their prejudice abates, it should be possible to do what has been done elsewhere, and to secure the recognition, on the basis of the principle of diffusion and a correct doctrine of the Logos, of the unique religious significance of the historical Jesus for dwellers on this planet.

One cannot resist the conclusion that a sober and liberal Christian Catholicism at its best will provide the line along which Indian religion could easily advance. There is a vast deal of it which could be adapted to indigenous forms, but Latin Catholicism is in itself still in need of reformation, and cannot therefore wisely be used as the sole vehicle for an Indian Christianity of the future.

I wish that I could have given more space to some account of the Sarvodaya movement, now led by Vinoba Bhave. This has an importance which can hardly be overrated, and is a real answer to the violence of Marxism. But Vinoba is neither a profound and scholarly theologian nor a professional philosopher. He is pre-eminently a social reformer by ahimsa, in the true Gandhian tradition, and his mind runs in the traditional Hindu groove, but has also been, like Gandhi's, profoundly modified by certain Christian contacts. Sarvodaya is really a social philosophy developed by Gandhi after he had read Ruskin's *Unto this Last*. Some of its sentiments are profoundly Christian. It would indeed be possible to have a Christian Sarvodaya, even though Sarvodaya as it exists assumes certain axioms which the Christian could not accept, because he does not believe them to be true. But in its noble idealism it deserves our greatest respect: 'Revolution consists in embracing your enemy, in forgiving the criminal, in uplifting the down-trodden.' Vinoba insists on daily morning and evening prayers, and his hymn book contains at least one Christian hymn. His favourite prayer opens: 'O King of humility, whose abode is in the simple cottage of a poor sweeper, help us to search for Thee . . . Grant us an open and receptive heart.' The aim of Sarvodaya is the establishment of a classless, casteless society, with equality of the sexes.

(iii) NEO-BUDDHISM

The problem of Buddhism during the past fifty years has reached its acute stage since the Second World War. Before that for some considerable time the Buddhist movement in Asia had seemed relatively quiescent. This situation may have been due to a variety of causes. Burma and Ceylon were not independent states, and although the British government maintained a policy of comparative neutrality in regard to indigenous religion, nevertheless facilities were given for Christian missionary work, and it can hardly be said that British officials or European residents in general were inclined to treat Buddhism very seriously. But this was not the case in Siam or in Japan, which were sovereign states, and in the former Theravada Buddhism and in the latter the Mahayana experienced no discouragement, except that in Japan there was a revival, largely for political purposes, of State Shinto. In China the imperial dynasty was tottering to its fall, and as we shall see in another chapter was trying to prolong its existence by a feverish patronage of Confucianism. But in both China and Japan the practice of what has been called 'plural belonging'—that is to say, membership of two or more religious movements at one and the same time—rendered it possible for people to be Buddhists and something else as well.

But during the past half century there have been signs of a real effort on the part of Buddhists to come to terms with the modern world, to copy and absorb elements in and from Christianity, to introduce Western studies into the monasteries, and finally, since 1945, to issue a definite challenge to the Christian Church. It is now quite half a century since one first heard of the adaptation of Christian hymns to Buddhist use in Japan, and of the formation of a Young Men's Buddhist Association in Ceylon. Professor Pratt, who made a tour of the Buddhist world of Asia during the first and second decades of the twentieth century, found that a number of the monks in the different Buddhist countries were learning English, and reading Western authors like Bertrand Russell, Bradley, and Lowes Dickinson. I can remember myself in the year 1920 encountering a Buddhist monk in the church of St. Martin-in-the-Fields, and from the questions he asked me I could have no doubt that he was making notes of the methods being used at that church, with a view to introducing them into some Japanese temple.

Since 1945, however, matters have gone much further than this. To begin with, all Asia knows that the first atomic bomb was dropped by Christians upon Buddhists, and they draw their own conclusions from this, whatever justification may be alleged on the

19

American side. Then there has come the accession to independence of Burma and Ceylon, the French exit from Indo-China, the establishment of a new sovereign state in Indonesia, and the humiliation of State Shinto in Japan, which is bound to have influenced the status of Buddhism in that country. Finally, the nationalist enthusiasm which has sprung from newly-won freedom, and emancipation from what has come to be regarded as colonialist tyranny, have caused people of the new independent Asian states, where they have not become Marxists, to look with renewed pride upon their own national heritages, whether of art or of religion. All this has led to a resurgence of Buddhism. It has been easy for ardent Buddhists to point to the use of violence by so many professedly Christian governments, or at any rate by governments representing and supported by large masses of professing Christians. Look, say the Buddhists, at what a state the world is in. Might it not be a good thing to give us a chance to try to run it on the basis provided by the teaching of the Buddha? It is difficult to answer such a challenge without incurring the stigma of being a special pleader, but adherence to observed fact compels one to point out that Buddhism, perhaps like some forms of Christianity, has always had a dual standard of conduct, one for the monastic orders, the other for the laity. Just as Christians have held that it is not right for ministers of religion or members of monastic communities to carry weapons or to engage in lethal acts, but that the laity may be permitted to do so; so in Buddhism we have an almost exact parallel, where monks and nuns are certainly forbidden to kill their fellow creatures, but there has been no prohibition of the Buddhist laity from serving in armies. Indeed the military might of Japan must have largely depended upon numbers of Buddhist laymen being ready to fight for her, while as is well known, Zen Buddhism was popular among the officer class. Nevertheless the challenge has been thrown down, and it is stimulating for Christians that it should have been.

The efforts which have been made to restore Buddhism in Burma and Ceylon to a position of dominance as a national religion, have met so far only with qualified success. One has heard that the younger generation of government officials in Burma have not very much use for it, and do not feel confident that it will help them in building a satisfactory Burmese commonwealth. At the same time, they are said to look askance at the Christian Church, because it has been very successful in evangelising the Karen section of the population, and since the Karens have been restive over their incorporation in a Buddhist state, and have even engaged in rebellion against the central government, there has been no small suspicion that Christianity may be a means of fomenting sedition. (The same charge has been levelled against the representatives of some Christian churches among the Nagas of Assam.)

Ceylon, or Lanka, as it would like to be called, presents a rather different picture. Here the Christian movement is rather older than in Burma, and has gained a good many adherents from among the Sinhalese themselves. But the monks of Ceylon are highly intelligent and well educated, and have sought in recent years to increase their political influence. Most important of all, they have succeeded in putting forth what is in effect a substantial manifesto, and it will be necessary to devote our attention to it.

This manifesto takes the form of a large book[1] published at Colombo and sponsored by the abbot of one of the leading monasteries, Pahamune Sri Sumangala of the Malwatta Vihara, at Kandy. The book itself is the work of a Buddhist layman and former Cabinet Minister, Mr. D. C. Vijayavardhana, and as we shall see, his Buddhism is of a somewhat liberal order, so that it is difficult to be certain that in spite of his protestations it would have been acceptable to the Founder himself. His work is a long one of nearly 700 pages, and it covers a great deal of ground, including a brief history of the island of Lanka before and during the British occupation. It may in fact be compared not unfairly to Pandit Nehru's *Discovery of India*, which he wrote in prison some years ago. Our author, who has obviously had a Western education, displays enormously wide reading, and positively encyclopaedic knowledge, but I do not think that he has by any means completely digested it. Here and there, for instance, he advocates theories which have been given up, as for example Jeans' theory of the development of the solar system. Nevertheless, it seems clear that we ought to welcome his very honest statement of a point of view which is in many ways different from ours, and yet with which on occasion we cannot help being in sympathy. It is like looking at Britain from the other end of a telescope, and we are so much accustomed, whether in London or New York, to think that the Western point of view is the only one that matters, that it is a salutary tonic to read something written from the Asian standpoint, even though at times the author may seem to us to be unfair in his judgments. What perhaps is surprising is that Mr. Vijayavardhana comes down somewhat heavily in criticism upon the monks of the Sinhalese viharas. Admittedly he does so out of what he believes to be loyalty to the essential teaching of the Buddha, who, he considers, proclaimed a much more positive world affirming ethic than

[1] *Revolt in the Temple.*

his commentators have usually allowed; but his strictures are severe.

Mr. Vijayavardhana's acceptance of the total atheism of the Buddha fundamentally affects the whole of his work. He would like to see in the Buddha an early outstanding exponent of scientific humanism, and at this one is not in the least surprised. I myself indeed have been expecting that sooner or later this kind of apologetic would be put forward. A decade ago a Buddhist monk was kind enough to send me a copy of a sermon which he had delivered in London, and it was evident, when one read it, that here was nothing at all except an exposition of humanistic ethics. There was not a word about religion from beginning to end, but only an analysis of certain evil modes of conduct (which, it was held, had produced the painful situation of 1945) and a commendation of their opposite virtues. The analysis was beautifully phrased, and one could find no fault with it; but no reason was given beyond 'virtue as the best policy' as to why anyone should accept it if he did not think it was in his own interests to do so.

But it is far from certain that primitive Buddhism was nothing more than this. Most scholars who know the early Buddhist texts now seem to hold that the Buddha himself was an off-shoot of the Upanishadic age, and that in his earliest utterances he speaks of the Great Self in a typically Upanishadic manner. They would certainly concede that he did not consent at any time to venture upon a definition of this Absolute Being, and that he was content, as much as any Upanishadic teacher, to say, 'neti neti'. Indeed, many of the arguments which he is described as conducting with his disciples display a 'neti neti' technique. He refuses again and again to say that something exists, and to say that it does not exist. For him on these occasions the question is not properly posed, and he will not allow himself to be misunderstood by giving an answer favourable to one side or the other. But it would never do to infer from this (as some clearly have done), an admission on his part that there was no Self-Existent Being at all. He himself was, however, chiefly concerned with man, and with man's deliverance from the ills of life. Scholars would with equal certainty agree that as the Buddhist and Jain movements developed they did become more and more atheistic, and ended in being merely societies for the practice of a certain kind of mental technique which would deliver their members from the pressure of life in a tropical disease-ridden country. Of course, some of their monastic sages had much more than this under consideration, but the net effect of these movements in India was to stress the ethical at the price of starving the religious element. Had they succeeded, India would have remained Buddhist, with probably also a strong Jain element as well.   But this did not happen, and one cannot help noticing that a recent Hindu essayist claims that the development of Indian theism and of *bhakti* (emotional devotion to a quasi-personal Deity) during the medieval period was a reaction against this atheism, and that in his view such *bhaktas* as the Alvars drove Buddhism out of India by their religious songs and reduced Jainism to a minor movement.   Further, it is a matter of observed fact that Mahayana Buddhism restored theism by positing the existence of the Dharmakaya or Cosmic-Buddha Spirit, Who is in effect the self-expression of the Absolute and Self-Existent, and that the Absolute, through this self-expression—which so much resembles the Logos of the Stoics—voluntarily limits Itself, in order to create and to communicate with the Cosmos of Its creation.   In this process of communication the Bodhisattvas are the successive incarnations of the Dharmakaya.

Having all this in view, one cannot but recognise that the Buddhism championed by Mr. Vijayavardhana is really an interim Buddhism lying between the Buddha himself and the Mahayana. This Buddhism has grown into what we know as the Theravada type; but it has only managed to maintain itself as a religion for the masses by tolerating the existence within its borders of polytheism and polydaemonism.   The Buddha himself always recognised the existence of *daevas* or super-human beings, but they were to him only super-human, and were never regarded by him as self-existent, being as much subject to the laws of flux and decay as mankind itself.   Hence we find Sinhalese Buddhists recognising the existence of gods on the mountains near Kandy, and Nepalese Buddhists of gods on the peak and slopes of Everest.   But these gods are only *daevas*.   They are finite beings, subordinate to the Absolute, and in no sense self-existent, though it may well be prudent to keep on good terms with them, just as a small state might like to keep on good terms with a Great Power.

The result of this is that Mr. Vijayavardhana, being quite logical, uses only the *ethics* of the Buddha to commend Buddhism to the world as a panacea for its ills.   Like most Theravada Buddhists he is really a humanist, and on one page, as I have said, he virtually admits this.   He wants people to be happy (in itself a laudable thing) and he sees the whole-hearted adoption of the Buddhist ethics, read in his own manner, as a true way to this.   He does not start from God but from man, and seems to assume that man has only to say, 'I *will* be good', and to try very hard, and the results will follow.   It may well be thought that in doing this he is heading for disillusionment.   The general experience of the human-race has been that to start from humanism and to exclude or ignore the idea of a morally holy Self-Existent is to end in a situation in which people say: 'Why on earth should I observe your precious principles of conduct if it suits my purpose to break them? I have no authority but your bare assertion. If you say that the Buddha as a human teacher exalts me to Right Speech, i.e. to telling the truth, why should I accept him more than my Marxist leader who says that if it will serve the Cause of the Dialectic Process, I am justified in telling a great big lie.'

In the third part of his book Mr. Vijayavardhana comes right into the open. He begins by describing the rise and development of the Buddhist movement, and its transformation into its two main types. The details of this are already fairly well known, and some of them have been referred to in a previous chapter. It will not therefore be necessary to delay long over them here, though a brief résumé is desirable. The actual ministry of the Buddha lasted forty-five years, but was confined to a comparatively small part of North India, the territories now known as Oudh and Bihar. This is the 'Eastern Land' and was so distinguished as opposed to the 'Western Land', which was the ancient home of Vedic culture, where the Brahmin caste was strongly established. It does not seem that this western area ever became as strongly Buddhist as the eastern. But the latter, like most territories in India, was on a large scale, and the distance between the capitals of the two chief kingdoms contained in it was about 400 miles. After the death of the Buddha the problem naturally arose as to how his work was to be carried on. He did not designate any individual successor, but appointed the whole body of the Sangha to this responsibility. Even this did not prevent dissensions and jealousy. To begin with, a large council of disciples was held immediately after the death of Gautama, at which certain collections of the Master's sermons and sayings were recited. But during the next 100 years the Sangha became divided on a number of points of doctrine and discipline, and it is by no means clear that any of the original teaching had even yet been committed to writing. Indeed by the end of the first century after the Master's death, when a second council was held at Vaisali to settle ten questions of monastic discipline, the Sangha had already split into eighteen different sects, comprising four different schools of thought. This unhappy condition prevailed until the accession of the famous king Asoka, who was the third sovereign of a united North Indian kingdom which had been formed to resist the possible aggressions of Alexander the Great's generals. Asoka favoured the Buddhist movement because he found it less disposed to interfere with politics

than the Brahmins.   What kind of Buddhism it was which he favoured it is not easy to say; but it seems clear that it appealed to him
as a layman, and it also seems clear that he was anxious to see its
influence extended outside his own empire, for he sent Buddhist
teachers not only to all parts of India, but even to Syria, Egypt, North
Africa, Macedonia, and Epirus.   There is no suggestion that at this
time it was a specifically atheistic creed.   Indeed, many of the
converts, while accepting the Buddhist ethics of the noble eightfold
path,'felt no difficulty about retaining some of their old Brahmanical
doctrines.   Under Asoka's patronage a third council was held at
Pataliputra 100 years after the second one.   The empire of Asoka
disintegrated after his death, and then came Greek invasions which
certainly had some influence on the shape of Buddhism and especially
upon its art.   Next came a Scythian invasion, which also founded an
empire, and the greatest of whose kings, Kanishka, embraced
Buddhism and summoned a fourth council at Jalandhara in Kashmir.
It was at this point that Buddhism divided into the Theravada and
Mahayana schools.

Mr. Vijayavardhana makes it quite clear, as I have said, that he
regards the original teaching of Gautama as an early form of
humanism, much closer to the former of these two main schools: and
indeed he deliberately links it up in so many words with a scientific
humanism of the present day such as that of Dr. Julian Huxley.   He
describes the Mahayana as developing the original doctrine in a
mystical, theological, and devotional work, and the Theravada as
trying to preserve its rationalistic, monastic, and puritanical elements.   Yet while he rejects the former, he also rejects what he calls
the 'monastic pessimism' of the latter.   This is rather startling, since
the Theravada is the Buddhism of his own country, and it is worth-
while devoting a moment or two to seeing the way in which he
develops his attack.   He says: 'The Buddhism taught by some
members of our Sangha is downright pessimism.   They lay stress on
the presence of suffering in the world to the exclusion of all else.
Life, in their eyes, is a bleak and dismal procession to the grave.
This emphasis on sorrow is a disastrous way of teaching the Buddha's
Way of Life.   The Sangha, by parodying sorrow and suffering, is
tying what are virtually mill-stones round the necks of the people,
and it becomes a strain on the State, whose duty it is to make the
people stand erect as men, and behave as men.'   He goes on to say:
'the Sangha also teaches the faithful that if they make gifts to the
order it will effect the condition under which they are reborn in
another existence', the inference being that those who have contributed to the Sangha in their past births are those who are rich in

their present ones. This may be logical doctrine, but if it is logical it is disastrous in its effects, for it encourages rich people to think that they have deserved their wealth for some meritorious act in the past, while there is no need to do anything about other people's poverty, since that is obviously deserved for some misdeed or other, equally in the past. (I have found the same kind of doctrine used among Hindus to justify the amassing of riches and the neglect of the untouchables.) He says that the Sangha also teaches the doctrine of the transference of merit, so that one can help one's departed relatives and friends by making gifts to the Order. He concludes:

'The members of the Ceylon Sangha, as a whole, have degenerated, and no longer are they leading the selfless lives the Master exhorted them to do. The main reasons for the deterioration are the selfish motives and considerations of the bhikkhus themselves, their self-interest, greed and ignorance, and their failure to adhere to the principles of the teaching of the Master. The Siam *Nikaya*, the principal sect of the Sangha of Ceylon, is not only caste-ridden but also class-conscious. It grants the *Upasampada* or higher Ordination to one particular caste only, and the Malwatta Chapter, which controls the largest number of bhikkhus, has always been dominated by Kandyan monks, although the largest number and the most learned bhikkhus of this sect are of the Low-country.'

It appears, then, that Mr. Vijayavardhana actually rejects the Theravada Buddhism of Ceylon, since it is difficult to deny that its implications are such as to lead to exactly the kind of abuses which he condemns. A careful analysis of Buddhist ethics, as they appear placed side by side with Christian ethics, which has been recently made, confirms this. The Pali documents make it abundantly clear not only that to be 100 per cent Buddhist it is certainly necessary to withdraw from the world and to join a monastic community, but that the virtues which one is then enjoined to practise, though they sometimes seem to resemble those of the beatitudes, and of the thirteenth chapter of I Corinthians, are really much paler. For instance the virtue of mettā, which has often been compared to the Christian Greek word agapē, is really a rather more negative term, closer perhaps to the Indian term *ahimsa*, which means 'harmlessness'. Mr. Vijayavardhana says that he desires a reborn Buddhism, which would not profess the passionlessness of the Theravada ideal, but instead would be a social religion, based upon the acceptance of the brotherhood of all mankind, which would practise a life of active love, and would regard dogma, ritual, and creed as non-essential.

'A life, not a creed, would be the test. As its first concern it would encourage a Buddhist way of life lived seven days a week, fifty-two weeks a year, not only on Poya days and on special occasions; the

Dhamma is a way of life, meant to be followed every day, to influence every activity of ours. It would be a religion of all the people, the rich and the poor, the high and the low—a true kingdom of righteousness.'

But all this is something which is so distinct from ordinary Buddhism, and approaches so nearly to the principles of the Christian life, by which it is obviously stimulated, that one is bound to ask what here is left of the old, distinctive Indian Buddhism beyond the conception which we find in the Mahayana of the Buddhist saint, or Bodhisattra, who aims at the highest good for others as well as for himself. If this is really Buddhist doctrine, as put forth by its founder, then it is not unreasonable to see in Gautama 'a Christian before Christ'. Where his teaching might be said to have fallen short was in that, though telling men to be loving and virtuous, he did not show by what means they might attain to the habitual practice of virtue and love. But, here again, we cannot be sure that the Buddha himself, as a good disciple of the Upanishadic age, did not teach that people were to live by the Inner Light afforded by the Great Self. Mrs. Rhys-Davids declares, of course, that this is the actual meaning of the Pali text, and if she is right, then all we can say is that the Buddha was a Quaker long before Quakerism!

One interesting feature about the new democratically based governments in those Buddhist countries which have lately become independent states is that by the mere fact of their now having direct responsibility for the welfare of their citizens they cannot be world-denying or world-negating institutions, and it is obviously embarrassing if large numbers of their citizens contract out of their obligations by entering monasteries to practise a contemplative life. They are therefore faced with a dilemma. Are they to tell their Buddhist citizens that world-negation and the doctrine of *anatta* are both mistaken deductions from the teaching of the Buddha, which a good many monks will certainly regard as an heretical statement, or are they to assent to these doctrines as of the very *esse* of the Buddhist position? If they take the former line, they will certainly have to face opposition from conservative Buddhists. If they take the latter, then they will clearly have to submit to a fundamental ethical dualism among their citizens. Such dualism would seem to have been quietly acquiesced in by the Japanese government, even if with rather doubtful logicality, but it is clear that the Marxist government of China will have nothing to do with it, and has made the monks and nuns come out of their seclusion and do useful and productive work; while in Russia monasteries of all kinds, both Christian and Buddhist, have been rather ruthlessly liquidated. It seems that in a community which accepts some measure of this-worldly interest and responsibility, the only possible status for the 100 per cent Buddhist can be as a member of a monastic order, yet how is this to be reconciled with the universal proclamation of *dhamma*?

Some recent items have lately come to my notice from Burma, and although they partly confirm what has been said already, they make a few additions to our knowledge, and also include some comments both by Christian and Buddhist Burmans which seem applicable to a wider field.[1] I give this account of the situation in greater detail partly because nationalist enthusiasm has been leading the Burmese seriously to consider the despatch of Buddhist missionaries to the west.

It would appear that out of a population of 12 million Burmese only 12 thousand are as yet Christians. Although among the minority communities Christianity has spread most largely among the Karens, even among these latter 60–75 per cent are still Buddhists. It must, however, be made clear that a great deal of this alleged Buddhism is mixed up with a survival of animism, which to the vast majority of the less-educated folk is of much more importance than the rather difficult doctrines of the Theravada. This condition may, however, be partly due to the neglected education which is said to have followed the sixty years after the otherthrow of King Thebaw. Such, at any rate, is the view of the Honourable U Win, the present minister in Burma for Home and Religious Affairs. He declares that after the fall of King Thebaw the community of the Buddhist monks became split up into different sects, that the monks lost touch with the laity, that there was a dearth of learned men, and that devotional habits were neglected. Whereas in the past it had been the almost universal custom for children to get their rudiments of education in the monasteries, during the British occupation this practice declined, and has only now been resumed. The standards of the monks themselves deteriorated, and sometimes criminals joined the Sangha in order to escape detection and arrest. It may well be that from the point of view of a sincere educated Buddhist the above is true. Much as British administrators may have tried to act impartially, it is hardly likely that many of them would have been actually interested in the success of Buddhism, and they do not appear to have given it as much protection as the British Government has almost always given to Islam in occupied countries. This was probably due partly to the fact that even at the time when the British came to power they did not think Buddhism in Burma to be in a very healthy condition, but partly also to the fact that they did

[1] For access to these, as also for a number of other items in this section, I am deeply indebted to the Reverend George Appleton, formerly Archdeacon of Rangoon.

not understand it. Some of them may have lumped it together in ignorance with Hinduism; and because it was less like Protestant Christianity than Islam, they were less attracted to it. The present Burmese government from 1950 onwards has made it a matter of policy to help in the restoration of Buddhism in Burma. It has passed several acts of parliament to aid in promoting the study of the Buddhist scriptures and the education of Buddhist monks, and in a way, has 'established' Buddhism. It has even voted considerable sums towards the establishment of a general Buddhist Council, and for the repair of pagodas.

Some words spoken by the present Attorney-General, U Chan Htoon, may well be quoted:

'Now we are threatened with another global war and total annihilation of mankind. The people of the world are greatly alarmed and very anxious to find some way out of this impending catastrophe. Buddhism alone can provide the way, and thus the World Buddhist Conference was held in Ceylon during May 1950. It was attended by Buddhist delegates from twenty-nine countries, including delegates from almost every important country of the West; and one thing was noticeable at the Conference, and that was the unanimous belief of all those people present there that Buddhism is the only ideology which can give peace to the world and save it from war and destruction.

What was aimed at the Buddhist conference was not to attempt to convert the followers of other religions of the world into Buddhists. But what we hoped for was this: people may profess any religion they like, but if their moral conduct is such as is in conformity with the principles of Buddha's teachings or in other words, they lead the Buddhist way of life, then there will be everlasting peace in the world. . . . The present is the opportune moment and long-hoped-for time to win the West over to the principles of Buddhism. We also see unmistakable signs and indications that the time has come for the revival of Buddhism in India, the country of its origin.

We are of the firm conviction that the time has come for us to make every one in the country live according to the Teachings of the Buddha. All aspects of national life, including civilisation, culture, literature, law, and customs, etc., of all the indigenous people of Burma, have risen from and still have their roots in Buddhism. According to history, Buddhism has taken root in Burma for more than 2000 years and Burma may be said to be the leading Buddhist country.'

U Chan Htoon, speaking about the Constitution, points out that while Article 20 guarantees to all persons equal freedom of conscience as well as the right freely to profess and practise religion, Article 21 recognises the special position of Buddhism as the faith professed by the great majority of the citizens of the Union. He adds that if all the Buddhists in Burma become true Buddhists and lead a genuinely Buddhist life, there will be no interference with the adherents of other religions in the enjoyment of their rights. The Attorney-General does not define these rights explicitly except in so far as he speaks of freedom to profess and practise religion. It is not clear whether this involves freedom to evangelise, or whether even if it does, such evangelisation is confined to Burmese citizens, or whether the right to practise it extends to persons of other nationalities.

The Prime Minister, U Nu, spoke in Parliament in support of one of these Acts for the promotion of Buddhism, and he said that one of its provisions was to send Buddhist missions abroad in the same way in which other countries had been in the habit of sending their missionaries to Burma. He continued:

'Another object is to counter the machinations of those who are out to destroy the very foundations of our religion. Their methods are very subtle and their intention is undoubtedly sinister. From certain quarters Lord Buddha's omniscience[1] has been questioned and ridiculed. Worse than that some even go to the extent of declaring that Lord Buddha was a lesser man than Karl Marx. It will be one of the functions of this Buddhist organisation to combat such challenges in the intellectual field. Any doubt regarding the existence of omniscience must be promptly dispelled. We must be able to explain what omniscience really is. If any Marxist comes out with the statement that Karl Marx was a very wise man, it is not our concern to question it. But if he encroaches on our sphere and ridicules Lord Buddha whom we all adore and revere and if he has the effrontery to say that Marx was wiser than Lord Buddha, it is up to us to retaliate. It will be our duty to retort in no uncertain terms that the wisdom or knowledge that might be attributed to Karl Marx is less than one-tenth of a particle of dust that lies at the feet of our great Lord Buddha. . . . In introducing the Bill it is far from our intention to disparage in any way other religions like Mohammedanism, Hinduism, Christianity, or Spirit worship. We have been prompted by the sole consideration to combat effectively anti-religious forces which are raising their ugly heads everywhere.'

It is perhaps only fair to recall that although the examinations in the study of the Buddhist scriptures held annually by the Burmese kings from the seventeenth century onwards were suspended by the British in 1855, they were resumed by the latter in 1895, after a lapse of forty years, and then continued till the outbreak of the Second World War, after that the disturbed condition of the country led to their suspension until the present Burmese Government revived them in 1947. It is also right to record that although in 1851 General Cunningham, having discovered certain sacred Buddhist relics at Sanchi in India, took them to London and deposited them at the British Museum, recently these relics have been returned to the government of India by the British Government, and have been taken

[1] This is a dangerous claim, and would hardly be made by orthodox Christians for their Master, who is reported to have said: '. . . of that day and that hour knoweth . . . *not even the Son of Man*'.

for exposition both to Burma and to Ceylon, and some of them have actually been allowed to remain in Burma as a focus for popular devotion.

A Burmese Christian, U Pe Maung Tin, has spoken frankly about some of the causes for the failure of the Christian movement to spread more widely in Burma. He himself is evidently clear that in the long run essential Christianity is preferable to Buddhism, yet he says:

'The Buddhists of Burma blame the Christian missionaries for causing, as they say in Burmese, the division of blood among Burmans. A Burman is synonymous with a Buddhist, and so when a Burman turns Christian he is looked upon with suspicion; he is pro-British, pro-American, a traitor to Burma. Some twenty-six years ago when Stanley Jones first came to Burma he had a meeting with educated Burman Buddhists at a Burman's house not far from Bishopscourt. I was invited as a Christian conversant with Buddhism. At the end of Stanley Jones' talk, the late U Tin Tut got up and thanked him for the sincerity of his address. He said that he had a complaint to make, namely, that when Burmans turned Christians they ceased to mix with their Buddhist friends and formed a separate community whose allegiance to Burma, on that account, was questionable. That complaint has always stuck in my memory, because it is to a great extent true. The Burman Buddhists are thankful to the few Burman Christians who attend their weddings and funerals. But they note with regret the entire absence of Burman Christians at their religious functions such as the initiation ceremony for their sons and the ear-boring ceremony for their daughters, their charities and feeding of monks. Some Buddhists send out Christmas cards as Christians do, but how many of us Christians take part in the water-throwing festival? To meet a monk is irksome to us Christians because of the Buddhist way of saluting and addressing him. When a Burman Buddhist has to adopt the English Christian manner of addressing and greeting an Anglican Bishop, why should not a Christian adopt the Burman Buddhist manner of addressing and greeting a Burman Buddhist monk? If you do not wish to talk to a Buddhist monk because you refuse to pay the respect due to him, how can you find out what he is thinking about? How can you make progress in your Buddhistic studies? A conversation with a learned Buddhist monk is something you should not miss, so full of love and compassion and yet without a hint of aggression born of an ardent desire to convert you.'

Another Christian, U On Kin, comments as follows (and it is well that the Western world of Christians should take his utterances to heart):

'You and I stand as ambassadors for Christ as King of kings and Lord of hosts. In days gone by, during pre-war years, I heard some preachers representing America and the British Empire as God's own country and the chosen people of God. They even went so far afield as to justify their military conquest over Asia and extolled imperialism. At the same time they condemned Buddhism. They therefore incurred the displeasure of Buddhists. We must bear in mind that we are commissioned to preach nothing but Christ, and to bear witness to the saving power of Christ.

As followers of Jesus, missionaries have come to us and shared with us the dynamic philosophy of Christ's life which has given them their ways of living and thinking, and which has also given them breadth of view, a new lease of life, and spiritual birth to national life, still imperfect though in the process of time and history. We deeply appreciate the missionary enterprise and we do claim that we are heirs of the spiritual heritage of the west.

But you missionaries come from a life of gadgets, movies, schools, mass production, more or less good food, cars, juke boxes, radio, and corner drug-stores. In the west you have the most, the best, the biggest, the tallest, the greatest, the finest, the deepest, the superlative in everything. You vaguely expected the Orient to be a lusty, glamorous, exciting, and somehow mysterious place. What you find is poverty. There is nothing in your scale of values by which you could measure and accept the filth and the stench and the bitter subjection in which you find millions of people, crowding about you in their great cities or toiling like dumb animals on the land. Your initial reaction of shock, pity, perhaps even indignation, is usually soon dissolved. You get used to it, as you get used to the smell of a stock yard. You have to live with it and adapt yourself to it.

There are many who catch something of the agony and striving of Asiatics, who hear a little of what it means to a country to be under foreign colonial rule for two centuries and to be caught under the twin burdens of subjection and backwardness. They do not blame the Asiatics for their own poverty and try to understand the immensity of the Asiatics' struggle for survival. They are convinced that if only these teeming people of Asia had the dynamic philosophy of Jesus Christ, they would come up on to the stature of men and women that should be in the sight of God, the Father of mankind. This type naturally will appeal to the Burmans. For this is the type who is willing to treat the Burmans as though they too are men, without pity, without patronage, but simply with equality.'

A third Christian, U Kyaw Than, comments on the defects which he sees in the approach which has hitherto been made by Christians to Buddhists. He admits that some will say that 'approach' is the wrong word and that we ought to speak rather of 'confrontation'. Two writers, he says, D. T. Niles and U Tha Din, have sought to convey comparisons and contrasts between the two faiths and their scriptures by using words and concepts familiar to the Buddhist. But even so he thinks that Christians in the past have never taken enough time to understand the fundamental structure of Buddhist thought, and so have never known where the Christian witness is most relevant and the message most revealing. The result has been that the Christian has had neither the knowledge nor the terminology which would enable him to proclaim the gospel in such a convincing manner that it would ring the bell for the Buddhist listener. And, he says, the Christian gospel comes in just where Buddhist thought stops. It presents the living God as available to direct experience.

It resolves the frustration which naturally results from the inability of human beings to do the right in spite of their knowledge and willingness to do the right. The basis of Buddhist thinking is life. The premise of Christian thinking is God. The Buddhist thinks life is self-interpreted. The Christian sees that this is wrong, and that the interpretation of life lies in God. Of course in reply to this it may be said that this is more likely to be the case if the Buddhist one is dealing with is really a kind of humanist. If on the other hand he believes in a Cosmic Spirit manifest to him in a series of Buddhas, and views his goal as that of 'buddhification', then it is possible to say, as St. Paul said to the Athenians, that the Christian declaration concerns One who is already imperfectly the object of belief. U Kyaw Than ends with a plea for indigenisation, and challenges the church in Burma to rid itself of everything in its life, expression, and administration which mis-represents it to the Burman Buddhist. The church must be not a pot-plant but a growth out of the soil, a natural shoot of a seed sown in the soil.

The most recent estimate of the situation in Burma comes not from a missionary but from one who has been until recently a professor of history at the University of Rangoon, and who may therefore be regarded as devoid of prejudice. He is quite clear that as an outsider he is not in a position to assess the inwardness of what he sees, but he confidently asserts that public opinion in Burma now regards religious observance as an essential duty. The Communist attack on religion has horrified the good patriotic Burman, and even if the Government contains some persons who call themselves Marxists, they are always careful to treat Buddhism with respect.

> 'As in early Victorian England open disregard of religion stamps the Burman with a position in society as a man apart. Neither the Deputy Commissioner nor his clerk would pass a pagoda in their town without stopping to make obeisance at the shrine. . . . The Prime Minister, U Nu, in accusing Than Tun of being a man capable of despoiling the Shwe Dagon, was employing the vilest epithet in his vocabulary.'

Professor Tinker considers that the Burmese leaders and especially U Nu show a remarkable self-control, serenity, and selflessness, which he attributes to their sincere acceptance of the best in Buddhist ethics. Again, one cannot be sure how far this driving force is orthodox Theravada Buddhism, or how far it is a Buddhism modified by contact with devoted Christian missionaries, and which therefore lays stress upon those very features in the personality and teaching of the historical Gautama which can be assimilated to those of the historical Jesus.

One has to think carefully what can be meant by the development in the character of U Nu. Professor Tinker says that he has utterly confounded the dictum that power corrupts.

> 'As a hasty hot-tempered young man, full of prejudices and dogmatic assertions, he was plunged into supreme responsibility, and supreme power; and amidst unceasing trials and upheavals he has emerged a selfless being, completely relaxed, without tension, inspired by vision and compassion; and his driving force is a Buddhism which permeates his every thought and action.'

But is his Buddhism a pure article, or is it one which has been modified by the precepts and example of some Christian with whom he has been in contact?—One cannot but wonder. So many of the new nationalist leaders owe a good deal of their education to mission schools or colleges, where they have been taught by people who, full of Christian idealism, have devoted their lives to work in non-Christian countries. It cannot be uncharitable to point this out.

The state of modern Thailand, which earlier generations have always known as that of Siam, deserves a section to itself. Nearly thirty years ago, when J. B. Pratt wrote about it, he quoted a recent American Consul-General at Bangkok as calling it:

> 'The one officially Buddhist state, the one remaining absolute monarchy, the one nation with an inconvertible paper currency, with more than its nominal gold value, the one nation whose national debt is less than five dollars per capita, one of the few nations without strikes, lockouts, unemployment, or Bolshevism and with a large excess of exports over imports, a paying state-owned and state-operated railway system, and a gilt-edged credit in the world's money market.'

Such a description would not apply today in all details, but the fact still remains that in spite of a number of constitutional changes Thailand is still a state which looks towards London and New York rather than Moscow, and which is still officially Buddhist.[1] Unprejudiced observers give it as their considered opinion that the Theravada Buddhism of the country is respectable, well-organised, universally esteemed, dignified, and satisfying. We may reasonably look to find some reason for this. I venture to suggest that it is largely due to the fact that for over sixty years the leaders of Thailand have been educated in the West, and have, during the period of their education, conformed to Western customs. Prince Chula of Thailand, who has spoken much in public of late, frankly confesses that although he counts himself a Buddhist, he attended an Anglican school chapel while he was at a public school in England. The general description given by Pratt of the institutional worship which

---

[1] Like many Asian countries which have non-Communist governments, it is inclined to consider the policy of *neutralism*, partly perhaps because it wishes to trade freely with Communist states This renders the general position unstable (see end of Chapter XI).

he attended in some of the temples or wats of Bangkok gives the impression not only of reverence and order but of the performance of a dignified choir office accompanied by a sermon not at all unlike what might be witnessed in parts of Europe or in America. There is no doubt that the Thailand government, which until recently was a personal monarchy, has for some decades taken a great interest in the promotion of an enlightened Buddhism. It has even made regulations to improve the education of the monks. Indeed, a rather curious situation arose some years ago with the introduction of state military service. According to principle a monk as a 100-per-cent Buddhist would expect to be exempt from such service, and there was in consequence rather a large, and to the government alarming, increase in the number of young men who desired to take monastic vows, and so to evade national service. The government countered this by imposing the regulation that all these young men were to take an examination in Buddhist theology, and were only to be granted exemption if they succeeded in passing up to rather a high standard. This accounts for the spectacle of crowds of young men gathering for examination, or waiting for the results of it, which visitors to Thailand have noted and upon which they have commented. But the salutary effect of all this upon the standard of education among the *bhikkus* of Thailand is obvious, and Pratt noted the enthusiasm of the students and the generally good quality of education displayed by the average Buddhist monk, and also the interest among the more earnest of the laity in the intellectual side of their religion.

But what is this religion? Quite clearly it varies in expression, and in some cases the learned abbot will respond to a question about it not very different in terms from that of any other scholarly Theravadin. But what is one to make of this? Here is a very short sermon which was given to Pratt by an educated lay preacher:

'The use of Buddha to the world is to make people cease to be selfish and jealous. Also Buddha teaches us that death is not the end but that man is immortal, and that only the body dies but the soul lives on. We shall have everlasting life in Nibban. We shall have eternal happiness there. It is a happiness that cannot be lost. But Buddha said, "If you are to be happy in Nibban you must obey the Teaching and do good". The man who really puts his heart into his prayer will get a blessing from it. The Buddha hears and knows our prayers, and is doing his best to help us.'

One does not wish to exaggerate, but surely this kind of thing is a serious modification of orthodox Theravada. How much of it exists in Thailand one would not like to say, but it is clear that contact with

20

England has not been without its effect upon the educated classes whose influence is strong in this 'officially Buddhist' state Once again we are conscious that an Eastern religion is itself changing, and modifying its teaching as the result of contact with Christians.[1] Nationalist pride compels it still to call itself Buddhist, but the Buddhism which it allows sometimes to be expounded is clearly not primitive, but is undergoing change and showing signs of syncretism.

There can be no doubt that when the Christian movement comes face to face with Buddhism, it really encounters a unique situation. Islam may still be treated as arising partly out of a misunderstanding, partly out of Arab nationalism, partly out of an imperfectly conceived desire to restate the Hebraeo-Christian message in simpler terms. Hinduism, until touched by Christianity, is an ethnic religion, and makes no universalist claims. Buddhism, however, a universalist movement deriving from Hinduism in a way slightly analogous to the way in which Christianity derives from Judaism, makes a claim very similar to that of the Christian movement. So similar in fact, especially sometimes in its institutional expression, that it is impossible not to ask whether by the time it had become fully universalist it had not already been overtaken by Christian missions, and profoundly influenced by them. I think it is possible to overstate the likelihood of this. Yet the evidence now seems to push back the operation of Christian influence in India to a much earlier date than was formerly supposed. It may well have reached the Indus valley by some time during the second century, and the most Christian items in the stories about the Buddha's life are now thought to have taken form at a time when the missions from the Middle East had had time to penetrate into the centre of North India.[2] Yet, though we may have to write off some of the items in the Buddha's life as assimilation from Christianity, we are still faced to a great extent with a parallel development; and it is rather surprising that until the twentieth century no Christian ever seems to have tried to talk to Buddhists in the way that Christians had tried to talk to Moslems or Hindus. One would almost have thought that Christians found Buddhism at its best and purest to be so exalted that they felt themselves somewhat daunted by the prospect of the task of trying to replace it, while it is certain that Buddhists in countries like Siam have often expressed themselves as so much satisfied with their institutional faith that they do not feel the need to exchange it for any other.

[1] One can only hope that the monk with whom Mr. J. A. Michener associated in Bangkok (see *The Voice of Asia*, pp. 186 ff.) was not a typical member of the Sangha. But that he and his fellows could exist there argues a rather sad lack of discipline in the community, due perhaps to the practice of making too many boys into novices.
[2] See additional note to Chapter VIII.

Yet the issue raised by the juxtaposition of the two faiths cannot be evaded. Are Buddhists to be asked to replace the figure of Gautama by that of Jesus in the centre of their devotion, or may they reverence both?—The Emperor Alexander Severus apparently would not have thought the latter course improper, since he is reported to have placed statuettes of Jesus, Abraham, Orpheus, and Apollonius of Tyana side by side in his private oratory. Yet the universalist claim of orthodox Christianity does not allow of a twin devotion, or of two Incarnations, one for the West and the other for the East. It seems inevitable that Gautama should have to step down, like John the Baptist, and assume a secondary even if honoured place. Those who see in the Buddha merely an atheistic humanist will not of course allow him even this place of honour, but if, like Streeter, we say that where the Buddha is most himself (i.e. where he is least influenced by contemporary Indian ideas) there he is nearest to being Christian, we shall not hesitate to give him due esteem; and while the positive additions put him as much out of court as the Baptist, and perhaps even more so, he may still keep his place as one of the most eminent forerunners of Christ. There might perhaps be a place for the Christian Buddhist as there has been for the Christian Platonist.

But there is more to be said than this; and it is a misfortune and a reproach that there has been no central and well-thought out scheme of address by the Christian to the Buddhist. Information of the kind that would be needed for such is scattered up and down in a number of different places, and if one tries to gather together here some of the *disjecta membra* of this corpus of attempts at communication with Buddhists, it is with no sense of thereby furnishing anything like a complete record of all that might be said.

The work of Professor J. B. Pratt has already been referred to. From his conversations he makes it quite clear that there is a wider gap between different types of Buddhist than between different types of Christian teaching. Some of the monks he spoke to seemed quite clear that the Buddha no longer existed, that there was no future life for the individual beyond the grave, and indeed that to suppose that there was any individual who could survive in this way was a misperception of the facts. Others, however, did not seem by any means so sure of all this. They argued about it with one another in undertones, and eventually led Pratt to a senior monk who gave the correct Theravada answer with scholastic precision. On the other hand Pratt had a small discourse addressed to him, the speaker of which (a Thai monk) clearly thought of the Buddha as in some sense a divine being who had come into the world in the person of Gautama to save mankind from ignorance and suffering, and to follow whom would eventually lead the believer to a kind of celestial paradise. It is true that here and there latitudinarian Christians exist whose views differ so widely not merely from those of the conservative Catholic or Evangelical but even from those of the liberal orthodox modernist as to seem hardly specifically Christian at all. But such persons are rare, and at most constitute a small minority among the total number of Christians. But in Buddhism there are large bodies of both sorts. Very many, without acknowledging any Christian influence, hold that the historical Buddha is a manifestation in the flesh of the Cosmic Buddha-spirit, that his compassion led him to a self-sacrificing pastoral career, that he is now in glory (Nirvana, though an ineffable state of bliss, is not held to imply extinction), and that what we do now with our lives determines whether we will go to Heaven or Hell.[1] Here it seems that only the Passion is missing in order to provide an exact parallel. But very many Buddhist monks, as well as laity, not only profess complete agnosticism about any Cosmic Deity, but say that the historical Gautama is no longer in existence, and that there remains in store for all of us nothing more than an absorption into the Absolute, which, although it is said to produce bliss unspeakable, does not seem to be accompanied by any 'social joys'.

The clue to this curious dichotomy of belief seems to lie in the doctrine to which Streeter refers, and which in Japan is called *hormon* (accommodation). This teaches that besides the full metaphysical and severely scholastic Buddhism, with its paradoxes, its teaching about the Void, and its refusal to define what, in harmony with its founder, it holds to be the Indefinable, there can also be an exoteric teaching for the non-philosophically minded multitude, with an *accommodation* to the needs of the simple and uneducated, in which myth and symbolism may justly have a place. *Hormon* has its equivalent most certainly in philosophically conceived modern Hinduism, and also in the Buddhism of the countries which we have lately been invited to call Lanka and Thai, as well as in Japan, and it would be dishonest to deny that it has sometimes found a place in the teaching of Christianity, as for example in visual representation of the Ascension and in similar representations of the worship and the joys of Heaven. But it does not hold the place in the Christian movement which it occupies in the religions of Asia. If symbolism is employed, Christians say that it should be used sparingly, and that people are entitled to be told that it *is* symbolism, and that the truth is not some-

[1] Cf. a sermon recorded by an observer in a Japanese village and quoted in my *Sacred Books of the World*, p. 159.

thing inferior to or radically different from the implication of the symbol. The whole idea of at any rate Reformed Christianity is that a high standard of education should be aimed at for all, so that as far as possible all may be taught on the same level. There is here no easy acquiescence in illiteracy and naïve ignorance. Symbolism no doubt may still have its place in the representation of beliefs about matters which it is really beyond the capacity of human language to depict 'photographically', but ideas which are avowedly and totally contradictory of one another may not be held with propriety by different classes of Christians. It is unthinkable that even the most philosophically defined doctrinal statements taught either in a Catholic or Anglican seminary for clergy, or in a Presbyterian or Methodist college, should in essentials contradict what is said from a pulpit to a mixed congregation by its minister.

Hormon or its equivalents, is in Buddhism a clear derivative from Hinduism, and the acquiescence in it is one of the points at which Roman Catholicism has seemed to approximate at times most nearly to the religions of Asia.

The situation which Streeter describes as prevailing in many Japanese Buddhist temples, where lucky charms are manufactured and distributed, would be unthinkable in Reformed Christianity, and one doubts whether even the use by Catholic Christians of blessed medals and palms, or of little images of St. Christopher ('protecteur des voyageurs') upon motor cars, as charms or mascots, would be officially allowed or deliberately tolerated by any Catholic authority, though the latter may perhaps sometimes turn a blind eye to it.

But the problem of communication remains an outstanding one. It seems quite certain that educated Buddhists and instructed Christians repeatedly misunderstand one another, because they do not know the basic meaning of the terms which each side is using. Thus a Burmese monk once said to me that of course he and his colleagues did not believe in a Personal God, but when I quoted to him certain definitions in Christian theology: 'God is Spirit' and 'There is but One Living and True God, everlasting, without body, parts, or passions, etc.', he seemed surprised, and asked where they were to be found. I told him, in the Fourth Gospel and in the first of the Anglican Thirty-Nine Articles; and his rejoinder was: 'If that is the official doctrine, we should feel no difficulty over it.'

I must admit that when this same monk sent me a copy of one of his sermons it turned out to be an entirely ethical discourse on the evils of greed, anger, and delusion, and the virtues of unselfishness, good will, and wisdom, while there was not a single reference of a theological character, not a word about the Absolute, the Self-Existent, much less of God, as One 'from whom all Holy desires, all good counsels and all just works do proceed'. It was in fact indistinguishable from anything that might be said by a pure humanist, and this leads one to suspect that it is only too easy for the modern Theravada Buddhist to slide over into humanism.

But again this is not the whole story. It would hardly be fair perhaps to judge the whole of this monk's teaching from a single sermon, since, with his background of identity-mysticism, he might say in reply that if he was speaking as one who was conscious of his own unity and even identity with the Absolute, and was practising the precept of 'right speech', then his sermon *proceeded from* the Absolute, and was of the nature of a meditation by the Absolute on its own virtue! But this would leave unanswered the problem as to how such things as greed and anger could exist. Could the Absolute actually misperceive itself, or must there not be a differentiation of finite points within the Absolute which are capable of error? And further, as Professor Slater with his long experience of Burma has pointed out, Buddhist theologians, if so we may call them, frequently use the language of paradox and of negation (neti neti) in speaking of spiritual entities such as *Nirvana* or *atta*, and this is misunderstood by many Christians, who think the speakers are *denying* the existence of something which, with the central Asian penchant for metaphysics, they are merely trying to avoid expressing in concrete terms such as they feel might involve contradiction or misunderstanding. It is noticeable that here Professor Murti, writing in his *Central Philosophy of Buddhism*, would seem to agree with Slater.

Pratt, Streeter, and Slater would all concur, I think, in admitting that the linguistic problem is critical. The meanings of sentences on both the Christian and Buddhist side must be carefully weighed, and as much trouble should be taken over the explanation of words as happened in the fourth century, when the Greek and Latin theologians were considering such terms as ὑπόστασις, οὐσία, persona, and *substantia*.

Yet even so, certain fundamental differences seem to emerge. To begin with, the multiple manifestations of the Cosmic Buddha-spirit seem, in many cases, like the *avatars* of Vaishnavite India, to be lacking in a true historical basis. Thus the famous incarnation of the Buddha-spirit in the person of Amida or Amitabha seems to be entirely mythical, and Sir Charles Eliot thinks that perhaps it was the name of some central Asian divinity which crept into Buddhism over the North-West frontier of India, and has got transmitted to Japan. A Japanese scholastic might say that, for the multitude, it was a convenient symbol (*hormon*) of the unselfishness of the original Buddha, but that is not the way that the public takes it; and yet there is no evidence at all for the existence of any primitive Buddhist saint of the name of Amitabha. The multiplication of concrete symbolical figures is a feature of Asian theology and also of its art. Hence the enormous repetitiveness in the decorations of the great temples in South India, and the great multiplication of statuettes of Buddhas in many Japanese temples and shrines. This repetitive symbolism may not mean to the Asian mind the same thing that it would mean to us westerners. We may not feel disposed to express intensity by repetition. But when all is said and done, repetition of a non-historical symbol does not convert it into an historical one, any more than saying a thing three times makes it true.

Again, the historical story of the Passion makes it quite clear that the Christian belief about the evil in the world is based upon a deeper apprehension of its seriousness than is possible for any system which develops straight out of an ethnic pantheism. It is not enough to be compassionate towards the ignorance of the multitude. Positive wickedness, and the misdeeds of carnal liberty, are perversions of the will which cost more than that to put right. And again it is not by any means certain that the supreme virtue in Buddhism is quite the same as it is in Christianity. Much discussion has taken place over the meaning which ought to be given to such words as *mettā*, *karuna*, and *anukampā* on the one hand and agapē and caritas on the other. But it now seems clear that the Buddha himself thought in terms of pity and compassion rather than of constructive goodwill. It is true that in the Mettā Sutta or Discourse on Compassion, Gautama is represented as saying: 'As a mother, even at the risk of her own life, protects her son, her only son, so let him cultivate goodwill without measure among all beings. Let him cultivate goodwill without measure toward the whole world, above, below, around, unstinted, unmixed with any feeling of differing, or opposing interests. Let a man remain steadfastly in this state of mind all the while he is awake, whether he be standing, sitting, or lying down. This state of heart is the best in the world.' The word translated here as 'goodwill' is *mettā*. With such a programme before him one might have expected that the Buddhist movement would have produced many constructive philanthropists and social reformers. Yet the curious fact seems well established that this is not the case. When the Metta Sutta is translated into English it probably looks more Christian than it really is. It seems likely that the Buddha himself thought of *mettā* as expressing pity and compassion towards individuals who were living in a state of ignorance and misperception rather than as involving any constructive goodwill. *Mettā* was in fact more like the benevolence of the Stoic. It was a habit of mind which, coupled with the Stoic belief that nothing could happen to you which was not ordained by the constitution and course of nature, never issued in active attempts to change the conditions of life for anybody. It is doubtful whether Gautama would have thought that attempts at changing the structure of society or the circumstances of individuals were relevant to the situation as he saw it, or even, in so evanescent a thing as the world of space-time, really worth while. Pity and compassion are noble enough in themselves, but they have not dynamic force enough to transform a whole society, though they may lead one to kindness to individuals. The Buddha is represented as saying on one occasion: 'He, O monks who would wait upon me, let him wait upon the sick', which sounds of course like an echo from the gospels, and has been thought to indicate a borrowing from the New Testament. If it could be proved that the *logion* first appeared at a later date than the ministry of Christ, this might not be beyond the bounds of possibility, but it seems fair to suppose that something like it was said by Gautama, for we are told that the Emperor Asoka, whose date is certainly B.C., gave temporary expression to the logion by fostering the institution of hospitals within his dominions. Yet, whereas the constructive care of the suffering has for generations formed a major practical expression of Christianity it does not appear to do so in the Buddhist movement, and Buddhist hospitals as regular and permanent expressions of belief do not exist except where the stimulus of Christianity has led to their foundation.[1] And further, the positive, activist character of *agapē* would seem to show that this Christian virtue is one which carries its possessor even beyond mere ambulance work (though it greatly intensifies this) towards a Christian reconstruction of society and Christian planning. Buddhism even at its best does not seem naturally to produce reformers. Historical figures like St. Camillus de Lellis, Lord Shaftesbury, General Booth, or Josephine Butler and Elizabeth Fry, do not seem to grow naturally out of it, in the way that they do out of the Christian movement. This is not said in disparagement of Buddhism at its best. It is only meant to indicate that just as much that was noble in Stoicism was carried over into and baptised into Christianity (as for

---

[1] One wishes it were possible to say something different from this, but in spite of all that neo-Buddhist propaganda may put forward, it still remains true that in Burma practically the whole of the care of the sick and afflicted still remains in the hands of the small Christian community created there by devoted missionary work. This statement has been confirmed for me by an observer who has visited the country during the last year. The main interest seems to be in the acquisition of merit by the decoration of pagodas. A rich Burmese would rather add gold leaf to the covering of the Shwe Dagon than give its equivalent in value to a hospital.

example by such persons as the great St. Ambrose) so all that is good and noble in Buddhism might well be carried over into and baptised into Christianity. And yet it would still be true that the ethics of Stoicism and Buddhism and the character of those endeavouring to practise them, would continue to fall short of the supernatural graces of the Christian Saint, who says that he or she has no merits, but is simply trying to surrender day by day to the indwelling of the Spirit of Christ.

(iv) CHINA SINCE 1911[1]

Some of the tendencies to be seen at work in China at the present time (1958) were already in operation nearly half a century earlier.

If we consider the present almost total decline in Confucianism, it is worth observing that the cult of Kung-fu-tze reached its peak exactly fifty years ago, when the Manchu rulers, seeing their power on the point of collapse, sought to bolster it up artificially by an edict which placed sacrifices to him on a level with those offered to Heaven. This subterfuge failed, and four years later came the first revolution. But those who promoted the latter did not wish at the time to disestablish the new cultus. On the contrary, a great many leading men, with the sympathy of some British and Americans, favoured the idea of making Confucianism explicitly into a real state religion, which they said it virtually was already. The Republicans in 1913 at first declined to take this step, but subsequently, in article 19 of the new constitution which they proceeded to frame, they went so far as to declare 'In the education of citizens, the doctrines of Kung-fu-tze shall be regarded as the basis of moral cultivation'. A year later the ambitious President Yuan Shih-K'ai, who aspired to revive for himself the office of Emperor, decreed the resumption of the sacrifices to Heaven and to Kung-fu-tze, both of which had been suspended in 1912. Two years later he died, and after that the pro-Confucian movement declined. In 1923 a fresh constitution said that any citizen of the Republic of China was to be free to honour Kung-fu-tze and to prefer any religion he pleased, 'honour' in this case meaning only 'respect as a national hero', not 'worship'. This, of course, meant general toleration and neutrality, as opposed to the

---

[1] It is to the credit of the United States Universities that more has been done in them than in European centres towards the study of recent Chinese thought. Mr. Wing-tsit-chan was appointed in 1942 as Professor of Chinese Culture and Philosophy at Dartmouth College, and has since then visited China and collected materials for a most useful survey: Religious Trends in Modern China, which is an expansion of lectures delivered in 1950 at Columbia University. In this section I am greatly indebted to his work. One cannot help noticing from his footnotes what a lively interest there must be in the subject in North America.

sponsoring of a state religion. Meanwhile, there were critics who said that the attempt to bolster up Kung-fu-tze involved the pretence that he knew all about modern thought, which was absurd, and ribald parodies appeared in America. It was also seen that Yuan's attempt to revive the sacrifices had been a disingenous political move. The sacrifice to Kung-fu-tze, however, continued to be offered in the temple of Kung-fu-tze itself, until 1928, when it was abolished by order of the Nationalist Government. About 1930 it was again offered, for political reasons, in some of the provinces; but, in general, the Chinese public paid little attention to these actions. Confucianism as a state religion was defunct, and Chinese scholars began to dispute whether it could in fact be called a religion at all. In this perhaps they went a little too far, for we have seen from the classical records that although Kung-fu-tze himself was chiefly concerned with behaviour, and sometimes expressed himself in agnostic terms, yet he certainly believed in the Mandate of Heaven, and said that Heaven had entrusted him with a mission, and confessed that he prayed. None of these considerations, however, proves that Confucianism in the beginning was a religion, but only that it had a religious background of a rather vague sort, partly theistic, partly pluralistic.

Yet even as a system of ethical culture the Chinese repudiated Confucianism during the pre-Marxist period. Between 1917 and 1942, during a time of intellectual renaissance, two of its leaders, Ch'en Tu-hasiu and Hu Shih, especially between the years 1911 and 1930, attacked the Confucian ethic as 'not suitable to modern life'; as 'a big factory for manufacturing obedient citizens', and as 'absolutely incompatible with Republicanism'.

Thus by the time of the establishment of the Chinese People's Republic, Confucianism on any estimate was already completely undermined, and the introduction of the teachings of Marx and Lenin only gave it its coup de grâce. Hu Shih had already pointed out the ineffectiveness of Confucianism in stimulating good social reforms. It had tolerated licensed homosexuality, judicial torture, the subordination of women, foot-binding, and other abuses. Small wonder that Mao Tse-Tung and his colleagues had no use for it. As far back as 1935 a straw effigy of Kung-fu-tze was being burnt: but now it is the case that the Confucian classics are no longer studied in schools, and the government has even abolished the observance of the birthday of the sage as a public holiday. In 1948–9, Dr. Wing-tsit Chan found one temple of Kung-fu-tze used as a barracks, another as a dormitory, another as a hospital, one as a refuse dump, and another left in complete ruin. The downfall is most impressive.

Nevertheless, Dr. Chan maintains that it may only be institutional Confucianism that has perished. The fundamental doctrines of the sage may remain, such as the belief in the Mandate of Heaven, in the duty to respect one's parents, and also especially in the pre-eminence of 'jên'. One wonders whether Dr. Chan is really right at this point. Marxism would seem clearly to deny a transcendent Deity and to substitute for it an Immanent Process. Marxists have certainly been encouraging the young to denounce their parents, whenever they think them to be anti-revolutionary, and have substituted for 'jên' (universal benevolence), loyalty to the party programme, which certainly involves hatred of one's enemies.

But this is only one side of the picture. The other side is the possible revaluation of Confucianism. Mao Tse-Tung in his earlier writings attacked Confucianism as semi-feudal, but in a later work, entitled 'On entering the new stage', he says that one should be ready to learn not only from Marx and Lenin but also from the ancient sages of China, and perhaps some of his more recent speeches confirm this softened attitude.

In the course of the three large volumes of the works of Mao Tse-Tung there are scarcely any references to religion, and I think none to Christianity. This is no doubt partly due to the fact that the works selected for translation are almost entirely political, and evidently intended to demonstrate for English readers the Marxian orthodoxy of the author, and his freedom from any deviationist tendencies. But it is also due in part to the indisputable fact that out of a total Chinese population estimated in 1950 at 483,870,000, the total estimated Christian community was still only 1 per cent. Mao would therefore consider himself mainly concerned with the 99 per cent of non-Christians, vast masses of them both illiterate and superstitious. It is not surprising that the few references to religion concern only the domination of the Chinese by 'a system of gods and spirits, including the system of the nether world ranging from the King of Hell to the City Gods and local deities, and that of supernatural beings ranging from the Emperor of Heaven to all kinds of inferior gods and spirits'.[1] Mao describes with approval the smashing of idols, the forbidding of superstition, and the appropriation of the temple revenues (as being 'public revenue derived from superstition') to maintain schools for Chinese peasants. So far, he might be a fourth-century Christian in Alexandria, approving the sack of the Serapeum. His speech to the peasants of Hunan (quoted on pages 48–9 of his collected works) might even come from the pages of Tertullian or St. Augustine of Hippo. No doubt in his numerous

[1] Investigation into the Peasant Movement in Hunan.

hostile references to foreign imperialistic influences he has in mind the missionary propagandist institution set up by foreign agency, and Dr. Rosencranz has described some of the causes of such hostility very effectively in an article in the *International Review of Missions*. No doubt also correct and orthodox Marxism is strongly opposed to Christian missions, especially to Roman Catholic ones, the Vatican being ever an especial object of its dislike. There is, of course, always the difficulty that is bound to be felt by any government about an international organisation which has its centre of loyalty outside the country, and in this particular case so rigid a spiritual totalitarianism as that of Rome can hardly fail to evoke hostility on the part of a totalitarianism based on an entirely different principle. It is a question whether the communities established by the churches of the Reformation awaken as much enmity. Recent information brought over to Europe by Bishop Ting or circulated by the Bishop of Hong Kong would seem to suggest that these latter communities have in many places won the respect of the new Republican Government, and are not now generally being persecuted. It is said that they are even increasing in numbers, that their right to exist has been conceded, and that two of their leading members have actually come to occupy high government appointments. Since then a number of Anglican Bishops from Australia have been allowed to visit their opposite number in China as a denomination (the Chenghuashengkunghui), and it has been announced that Chinese bishops may be allowed to attend the Lambeth Conference of 1958.

All this tempts one to speculate whether the victory of the Christian faith over Marxism may not begin in the Far East, where the latter is confronted not with old, enervated, and possibly corrupt and unreformed churches, but with entirely new, earnest, and untarnished Christian communities. The situation might then come to be comparable to that in South India, where Christian reunion has already far outstripped its comparatively feeble manifestations in the West, again largely because the Christian churches in India are new ones, relatively free from vested interests and embarrassing traditions, and so able to forge ahead untrammelled.

The kind of criticisms levelled by Marx against religion might be held inapplicable to a church set up by missionaries from a Republican country, ardently interested in social welfare and in cooperative movements. But one word of warning has to be given. Some of the most enthusiastic mission work, especially in western China, has been prosecuted by fundamentalists, and it is therefore not impossible that it may come under fire from the Marxist criticism for being naïve and anti-intellectual.

Also the grim and undeniable fact remains that the Chinese People's Republic has made a systematic effort to exterminate the Christian missionary movement. Mr. Chester Bowles, late U.S.A. Ambassador to the Republic of India, has described how in April 1953 he saw some 6,000 expelled missionaries cross over the steel railway bridge from the mainland to Hong Kong. Was this God's judgment upon Christian propaganda which had been based on a wrong foundation, and had in any case failed to attack the manifest abuses of the social order? Might we perhaps parody Isaiah and say, 'Ho! China, the rod of Mine anger; the staff in whose hand is Mine indignation'? This is not to belittle the devoted labours of Christian workers. But they were the victims of a previously outlined policy, based upon inequitable treaties, or the agents of a country which in some of the utterances of its public men showed a lack of wisdom.

It does not seem that Taoism in its later and corrupt form can play any effective part in the life of modern China. Its fortune-telling, alchemy, and general superstition render it just the kind of religious phenomenon that Marxism is out to destroy. But the older mystical doctrines about the great Tao as we find them in the writings traditionally referred to Lao-tzu and Chwang-tzu could possibly come to be regarded even by Chinese Marxists as a part of their cultural inheritance which was capable of being harmonised with Marxist thought. The principle of surrendering to the motion of the Great Tao, and of not interfering with Its onward sweep has hitherto been interpreted quietistically, and *wu wei* has been taken to mean: 'Don't interfere with the constitution and course of nature. Don't overgovern your citizens. Just let life go on of itself. Let things happen as it were automatically; and all will be well.' But this doctrine of *wu wei* could just as easily be twisted round so as to give an activistic meaning to daily life, and in this case the Great Tao could be equated with the Dialectic Process, so that it could be said: 'Do not resist the Process, since if you do, It will inevitably destroy you, because It is fundamentally irresistible. Surrender to It, let your self be used by It, and the Socialist Millenium you desire will come—if not in your own generation, at least in the fulness of time.' As a matter of fact, in Chapter 30 of the Tao-te-King we read: 'Whatever is against Tao will perish.'

Equally also, of course, the Tao could be equated with the Divine Logos (as has already been done in the Chinese Protestant version of the Fourth Gospel). In this case again surrender will be activistic. 'Let the Word of God dwell in you richly in all wisdom and spiritual understanding.' 'His Kingdom cannot fail. He rules o'er earth and Heaven.' 'We see not yet all things subdued unto Him.' Martyrs and confessors for the Christian Faith and Way of Life may not see the Kingdom established in their own lifetime, but they know that 'God's Word for all their force and craft one instant cannot linger'. The Commonwealth ordained by the Living God is bound to come in the future in power and in the Holy Ghost, and is only hindered by man's carnal misuse of his divinely bestowed freedom. But the patience of God can afford to wait, since βιὰ οὐ πρόσεστὶ τῷ θεῷ, and in the end all things shall be subdued to His Sovereign Purpose, and God shall be all in all.

(v) JAPAN

A consideration of the latter has been partly covered by what has been said in the section dealing with modern developments in Buddhism. But it is desirable to make some reference here to the various attempts in Sect-Shinto, especially Konko Kyo, to produce an indigenous type of Japanese religion. These attempts have not achieved perhaps any spectacular success, although they have certainly gained some adherents, and have put forth an appreciable amount of propaganda literature, some of it in English. But they provide a warning, not wholly unneeded, against any attempt to encourage the spread of the Christian movement in Japan by an excess of non-Japanese influence. A serious reaction might set in if it were thought that America, or any other country, was seeking unduly to control the religious future of Japan, even with the best intentions. By all means let Christians seek to be brotherly, and helpful, as they should also be doing in India, Burma, and Ceylon, not to mention self-governing parts of Africa. But let them beware of even appearing to wish to dominate proud and independent peoples. Japan is clearly seeking to think out her religious problems for herself. By all means let her be helped and encouraged in the task. But she must find the answer for herself, especially if it is really to be of lasting value to her. Let Christ be put before her with all the skill and devotion that are possible. But Our Lord is able to take care of His own honour, and in the last resort, the citizens of Japan must make their own independent decision and their own surrender—if they wish to.

(vi) THE JEWS

The position of the Jews in the modern world is both difficult and complicated. Up to 1918 they had been for centuries a people without a territory of their own; but by the Balfour Declaration they were allotted an area at the Eastern end of the Mediterrean which their forefathers had certainly occupied and ruled centuries before, but which they had acquired by conquest, and which had since been successively under the sway of Greeks, Romans, Byzantines, and Turks. At first this 'national home' was controlled by a Mandate under the League of Nations, but the Jews did not like the restrictions on immigration imposed on them, and were impatient to obtain total self-government, so that after an unrestful period of agitation they eventually, with the aid of external help from Jews and their sympathisers in other countries, especially in America, established the new Republic of Israel. This step was resisted by the non-Jews resident in Palestine, many of whom disliked the prospect of living under a Jewish government, and after a short period of hostilities, in which the Jews from a military standpoint were successful, and a great many of the non-Jews were either killed or went into exile, an armistice was reluctantly agreed to by both sides, which left the country partitioned clumsily between the Jews and the non-Jews, and Jerusalem itself divided into two sections, with the old city in Arab hands.

After this, immigration continued, but neither Egypt nor the other adjacent non-Jewish states ever really approved the presence of the Israeli republic, and regarded it as an intruder. The industry of the Jews, and their determination to build up a strong army to defend their territory, immensely strengthened their position, though their somewhat congested population and their inability to trade with their immediate neighbours have tended to endanger the viability of their economy. At the time of writing this account there is still no sign of really peaceful agreement between Israel and her non-Jewish neighbours.

The foregoing paragraphs may seem to be mainly concerned with political affairs; but that these have an important bearing upon religious problems cannot be denied.

After the downfall of the Jews before the Romans, which resulted from their two unsuccessful rebellions of 70 and 133 A.D., and after the severance of relations between Jews and Christians resulting from what Baron has called 'the great schism', Judaism became the religion of a scattered minority, with no Holy City and no Temple as a rallying point, but with a remarkable capacity for cohesion around the Torah and its commentaries, and the worship of the various synagogues, and with a pathetic trust in the future advent of a Messianic deliverer and the restoration of the nation to its ancestral home—'Next year in Jerusalem' as the saying used to go at each Passover. Before 70 A.D. there were, of course, many Jews dispersed throughout the Mediterranean world, but they still had their rallying centre in their old capital, and theoretically were expected not to live more than ninety days' journey from it, so that they could once a year if possible travel to attend an annual festival in it, and also to pay the Temple tax each year. After the destruction of the Temple, and later after the prohibition by Hadrian of any Jews approaching or remaining domiciled in Jerusalem, the Jewish community became, as it were, truncated. Deprived of political rights, tolerated to varying degrees in the different countries of their dispersion, the Jews nevertheless preserved a sense of their uniqueness, which their misfortunes probably sharpened; and they consoled themselves for their unhappy condition by the obstinately held belief that they were still a people singled out by Almighty God to be for Him a priestly nation. 'I have chosen thee above all nations' was their charter. But this spiritual election tended more and more to be given a materialistic emphasis—the very thing which Yahweh in the Old Testament is represented as not approving. In the latter we read 'I did not choose you because you were more in number than any people', but are told that Abraham was elected for a mission to the world because of his obedience and faith—'In thy seed shall all the *goyim* of the world bless themselves (or be blessed)'. John the Baptist very clearly expressed the danger when he said: 'Repent . . . and say not to yourselves, we have Abraham to our father, for I say unto you that God is able of these stones to build up children unto Abraham.' The Christian claim has ever been that from the coming of Jesus of Nazareth the *material* Israel has been superseded by and fulfilled and enlarged into the *spiritual* Israel. The material Israel clearly had its place in the working out of the Divine Purpose, but the Jewish Church was not intended to be God's permanent instrument, but to be enlarged into a Universal Church of all peoples, nations, and languages (as in the vision of Daniel), inheriting the riches of the Jewish past, but fulfilling, enlarging, and transforming rather than destroying, and doing so under the guidance of the Spirit of Jesus, who was not only born physically of the seed of David, but in whom dwelt all the fullness of the Godhead bodily. He was in an amazingly true sense God's Messiah or Anointed One; and in his new and enlarged Messianic kingdom there was to be neither Jew nor *goy*, neither slave nor free, neither male nor female, but only one standard of citizenship, that of being 'in Christ'. According to this, to be a Jew meant exactly the same as being a Frenchman or a Japanese, no less and no more; it was in fact a national and political, but no longer a religious label.

Now the Jewish people have never as a whole accepted this belief. Yet their attitude has been by no means uniform. Some certainly became Christians at once, others gradually; and in driblets throughout the centuries there have always been conversions, though never a mass-movement. Some infiltrations have been made out of expediency, and to avoid persecution, as when the father of Karl Marx had all his children baptised as Lutherans. The sympathy of Christians for Jews persecuted by the Nazis has perhaps slightly increased the numbers in recent years who have crossed over; but against it must be set the miserable hostility of the intervening centuries, when again and again the Jews were the objects of brutal cruelty as being the alleged descendants of the accursed race who killed Jesus Christ. This in itself had the effect of hardening the Jews against the Christians, of whom Spinoza said bitterly: 'They differ from us mostly in their opinions', meaning that they did not display any real superiority over Jews in the beauty and charity of their lives.

The great bulk of dispersed Jews have therefore remained, in so far as they have not become secularised, fixedly Jewish in religion, and have steadfastly adhered to their ancestral forms of synagogue-worship and private devotion, still believing in the material election of the Jewish race, still endeavouring to keep their stock pure, and still looking for a future Messiah who will reign over them politically. Perhaps only a great wave of loving-kindness, and a growing sense of the need of reparation for past injustices on the part of Christians can bring about any fundamental change.

Modern Jews have, however, tended to divide into a number of groups, perhaps four or five. First, there are those who maintain a legalistic orthodoxy; second, those (and especially Polish Jews) who have become more and more attracted by a mysticism which has modified their attitude towards the Torah, and have sought to diminish the dominance of the rabbis and to increase the dignity of the laity; third, those who through a study of science and philosophy and the tenets of other religions have become liberalised, so that while retaining a kind of political pride in their nation they have ceased to observe literally the precepts of the Torah and have become so to speak Jewish Unitarians; fourth, those who through the same studies have become secularised, and have turned into agnostic humanists, though still conscious of their Jewish ancestry. An important variety of these latter are those Jews who have frankly adopted Marxism.

The last two groups have obviously abandoned anything like a specific Jewish religious belief, but the first three or at any rate the first two and a good many of the third have a definite religious attitude towards Gentiles or *goyim*. They do not consider that there

21

is any necessity for Jews to become Christians in order to attain closer union with God. Ever since the day of the ancient covenant with Abraham, all his descendants, they hold, have been elected by Almighty God, and therefore they need neither baptism into Christ nor the redemptive sacrifice of Christ to reconcile them to God. They consider themselves, like the Brahmin caste of India, to be a biologically superior people, formed in creation to be a spiritual Herrenvolk. The Christian no doubt will regard this conception as completely out of date; but it has in the past exercised a very considerable influence, and in India and in Jewry alike has seemed a perfectly legitimate hypothesis. Those Jews who hold it do not necessarily repudiate the idea that they have any responsibility towards non-Jews. They have first of all to maintain their own priesthood, i.e. to offer on behalf of all nations the example of a pure and spiritual sacrifice of devoted lives. But in the second place they claim that in the Hebrew scriptures Yahweh declared that he had mercy upon the sons of Noah, i.e. the *goyim* as distinct from the seed of Abraham. Accordingly it is the bounden duty of all Jews not to Israelitise the *goyim*, or to make them into Jewish proselytes (though that was certainly tried in the past and has perhaps even now not been entirely abandoned), but to make every *goy* a true son of Noah, who acknowledges God in holy awe and keeps his commandments as they were given to Noah in the beginning.

Rabbinical Judaism declares that the sons of Noah were given by God seven positive commandments, to abstain from idolatry, unchastity, the shedding of blood, the profanation of God's name, robbery, and the mutilation of animals, and to observe justice in all their dealings; and the great medieval Jew, Maimonides, who had many Christian friends, is recorded as saying:

'Whosoever receives the seven commandments, and is careful to observe them, he is one of the pious (*chasid*) of the nations of the world (*goy*), and has a share in the world to come.'

'Thus Moses our master has commanded us by Divine tradition, to compel all that come into the world to take upon themselves the commandments imposed upon the sons of Noah, and whosoever will not receive them is to be put to death.' (Maimonides H. Mel. 8.10.)

The above are quoted by Dr. Hans Kosmala in the *International Review of Missions*, July 1941.

So optimistic are some observers about this revival of Noachism, as it is called, that one of them, Dr. Schoeps, has written: 'Christianity is left behind by the universality of Judaism. Israel will be the world-religion of the future, while the Church will decline. It is on the noachistic ground that we can all meet.'

Noachism was certainly the belief of many of the medieval Jews regarding their Gentile neighbours. They obviously did not see any great access of *goy* converts to the belief, but they compensated for this by saying that man's heart is naturally evil and always adverse to God, and that the prophets foretold that the number of God-fearers on the basis of Noachism will always be small, until the advent of the Messiah, when the sons of Noah will flock to Zion.

The emancipation of the Jews since 1918, and later, the establishment of the Israeli republic, have undoubtedly given a stimulus to the revival of this doctrine of Noachism.   Jews are now not only brought into free contact with the Gentile world in a way which was not possible so long as they were despised and segregated groups; but as citizens of a sovereign state they feel that they can speak to Gentiles with a sense of freedom and equality which they did not previously possess.

It seems quite certain that, like the Buddhists of Burma and Ceylon, Jews will use this newly-won status not only to revive and re-establish their own religion, but to engage in propaganda.   There are many of them who are as much convinced of their capacity to do this, as the Buddhists are in *their* way of theirs; and the groups of Jews and Christians which have been formed in various countries in recent years are often welcomed by Jews not merely as signs of Christian friendliness and of the cessation of persecution, but as opportunities to put the Noachist point of view, and to interpret all non-Jewish religion on Noachist lines.   That theological developments on this basis are bound to take place, and indeed are actually taking place, cannot be doubted.   It seems quite probable that Jews will say to Christians, Hindus, Buddhists, and Moslems: 'By all means keep your own ways of serving God if you like them, but be sure that you at least adopt the Noachic injunctions—which approach closely to the ordinary moral law of any secular state, and may even be regarded as resembling some of the provisions in the United Nations' Charter of Human Rights.'

Certain liberal Jews who, apart from their nationality, hold virtually Unitarian beliefs, will no doubt deem this kind of propaganda unnecessary; but the Jew who retains a certain measure of orthodoxy will feel that it is not mere rationalisation, but that it has scriptural authority, and does justice alike to the ancient Jewish inheritance, to the responsibilities of Jews towards non-Jews, and to the undoubted religious yearnings of many *goyim*.

Christianity is not necessarily approved.   In its Catholic and Greek Orthodox forms it is felt by many Jews to be idolatrous.   But it is accepted provisionally as a stage in the conversion of the *goyim* to Noachism, and the belief is held that when this has taken place, the more specifically Christian doctrines will gradually fade.   Jesus, a Rabbi in Israel, becomes the advocate of Noachism. This is clearly the position of such modern Jews as Buber, Klausner, and Stephen Wise, as well as of the Frenchman, Pallière, who in his book *The Unknown Sanctuary* claims to have been converted to Noachism from Christianity. I have given some space to this account of the Jewish attitude, not because it seems that Noachism is a particularly convincing doctrine, but because it seems right to do it justice.

It would be manifestly unfair to make no mention of the influence in modern Judaism of the Chassidic communities. Until the return of many Jews to take up their residence in the newly formed state of Israel the Chassidim were somewhat isolated from the rest of Jewry owing to the fact that they were mostly to be found in Eastern Europe. But with the gathering together of Jews from all over the world into one national centre, they have found themselves side by side with co-religionists of other traditions, and there can be no doubt that their zeal and piety must be exerting a strong influence upon the spiritual life of their neighbours. Martin Buber, the man who has written most about them, is himself in Jerusalem, or was in 1952, and it is from him that one is able to obtain most of one's information.

The origin of this strange mystical movement belongs to the beginning of the eighteenth century, when there was born in a town on the old frontier between Poland and Turkey a humble villager who possessed a most magnetic personality. He had no great intellectual gifts or education, and was indeed regarded by the Rabbis of his day as an ignorant person who knew little of Talmudic scholarship; but it is remarkable that he first became famous because of his alleged power to work miracles. Although himself no Rabbi, he rapidly became recognised as a stimulating teacher, and the laity were drawn to him by his anti-clerical outlook, his rejection of asceticism, and his generally cheerful and world-affirming attitude. There must, one imagines, have been some striking originality about him which attracted disciples, and he and they dedicated themselves to a career of unworldly spirituality. Buber himself is disposed to see in him some resemblance to Jesus of Nazareth. It is difficult to know how far this resemblance may be due to a deliberate policy of behaviour on the part of the teacher himself, and how far to the natural tendency of Jewish prophetic leaders to develop along similar lines. The actual name of this man is only known as that by which his disciples called him: Israel the Master of the Good Name, or in Yiddish, Israel Baal Shem Tov, or the Besht. He wrote no book, and for many years his sayings were transmitted orally, and this undoubtedly led to additions, embellishments, and interpretation passing into the body of authentic logia, so that it is not easy to separate out what is original. There can be no doubt, however, that the Besht stimulated many to follow him as teachers, and there now exists a vast Chassidic literature, made up of sayings and anecdotes, which, although as compared with the Old Testament it has no actual canonical authority, is greatly valued by the Chassidic community. It is now some 250 years since the birth of the Besht, and until recently his influence and that of his followers may be said to have been largely confined to Poland. Nevertheless the westward drift of Russian and Polish Jews has not infrequently brought isolated members of the Chassidim to England and to America, and this movement obviously increased as the result of the Nazi persecution. How many of the Chassidim perished in the massacres it is hard to say, but the number must have been considerable. At any rate a substantial number of survivors have now established themselves in Jerusalem, and their zeal and earnestness cannot fail to be noticed by any who visit their numerous synagogues. Within the state of Israel they certainly exert a certain amount of political influence, since the weight of their vote naturally tends to be thrown on the side of the conservation of Jewish religion, as against that of secularised Jews who care little or nothing about it. But how far the Chassidic vote would be large enough to turn the scale decisively at an election or to influence public policy cannot be determined. Meanwhile the movement is there, and granted its continuance for some lengthy period, it may end by having a considerable influence in moulding the spiritual life of the citizens of the new republic.

The Christian attitude to Jewry must, it seems, depend entirely upon what type of Jew is being encountered. If it is a question of agnostics, humanists, or Marxists, obviously no specific attention need be paid to Jewish beliefs which have already been discarded. Evangelism in this case can and should be attempted on the same basis as in dealing with any other déraciné secularist. But if the Jew in question retains any belief in the physical election of the Jew as such to be a Herrenvolk, with the *goyim* relegated to an inferior Noachic status, this must clearly be combated as intellectually and anthropologically indefensible. A common world-faith can never be built on such a foundation, and to try to do so is to indulge in wishful thinking.

It may be asked: What relation does the doctrine of the Logos bear to all this? Let it be said in reply that no one ought to wish to refuse to the many earnest Jewish religious sages of the past and present a share in the inspiration which the Divine Word affords to all those in mankind who seek to serve God in Truth. But the historical Jesus, though born of the seed of David according to the flesh, occupies a unique position in the world. He belongs not to Jews, Europeans, or Asians exclusively, but to the whole world and yet, as born in Israel, he is the fulfilment of the true hopes of Israel.

The future would surely seem to lie in the recovery of establishment of a Jewish National Christian Church, with a Hebrew ministry, liturgy, and indigenous customs, to which all religious Jews might belong, but which could be regarded as part of a wider Catholic Church with which it would be in full communion and from which it might derive its orders. Such a church might have its headquarters in an Israeli sovereign state, wherever constituted, just as English Christians tend increasingly to look towards Canterbury, and the Latin races almost invariably to the patriarchate of Rome.

But it is difficult to regard revived Noachism as anything more than a parallel movement to neo-Hinduism or neo-Buddhism, an expression of natural exuberance born of sudden emancipation.

Of course what I have described above is not the view held by all liberal Jews. They probably feel that it is a rationalising view, framed to meet the desires of those who don't want to have to give up their Judaism; and they probably sense that if it were really true, more people would accept it in preference to Islam or Unitarianism. Of these two they probably regard the latter as preferable, since it agrees with most of their criticisms of Christianity without dragging in on the one hand the dogma of the physical election of Israel, or on the other the dogma of the unique revelation to Mohammed. It naturally depends a good deal what sort of Christianity is the target of any particular Jewish criticism. Jews, as has been said, condemn those Catholic practices which seem to them to savour of idolatry. But they equally criticise Protestant acceptance of Trinitarian doctrine, Protestant evangelical insistence upon the Fall, sinful corruption, Hell, and Eternal Punishment. They insist upon the freedom of the will to obey God's law, yet they equally admit that man never really *does* completely obey, and that therefore the Yom Kippur or Day of Atonement has its proper place in the scheme of events, though they regard God's forgiveness as His response to man's expression of penitence to sin, and do not see the need for the intervention of anyone's propitiatory sacrifice (nevertheless many of them still surreptitiously practise some small blood-sacrifice). Again, Jews criticise much Christianity for its asceticism and its depreciation of the joys and labours, the family ties and interests, of ordinary earthly life. Celibacy, they say, is improperly exalted above marriage, suffering is glorified, world-renunciation is commended. 'Christian piety is passive, and the monastery is held to be superior to the family.' Of course this is certainly true of some sections of the Christian Church, though it is certainly not a fair representation of them, and there is a perfectly good answer to the critic, provided that one recognises that different circumstances call for different attitudes towards the married state. But Catholic apologists are not always in a very happy position in dealing with such charges. Judaism on the other hand has often been excessively this-worldly, though there is certainly a kind of Judaism which is as balanced in this connection as much Christianity.

Criticisms of Christian ethical teaching such as the sayings 'Resist not evil', 'love your enemies', and 'whosoever would save his life shall lose it, but whosoever shall lose his life for My sake shall save it', as Montefiore agrees, and as might well be expected, have not proved very effective or just. Indeed, it may fairly be said that some Jews in such matters do not show themselves quite at their best. Much as we may admire Jewish piety and family life and the treasures of Jewish liturgy and mysticism, there is the uneasy feeling that in a world which has such a long expectation of life ahead of it, Judaism cannot as it exists play a vital part. It cannot really be the effective nucleus for a common world Noachism, nor is it at all clear that this was really the Divine intention. If there is to be a nucleus, it must surely consist of a Church in which any human being can share, not of a Church with a racially restricted membership. The attack on the glorification of suffering comes rather pathetically from those whose forefathers are reported as saying of the Crucified One: 'His blood be on us and on our children.' I hardly think it can be a common attitude among Jews, especially those who are admirers of the Besht and his disciples, and I do not believe that the pride (so justifiable) that Jews take today in the memory of the martyrs during the Hitlerite massacres is consistent with such an attack.

It is impossible to end this section without a renewed expression of the sorrow and shame which a Christian must feel at the past iniquities of professing Christians where Jews have been concerned, and with continuing pleasure at the work of the Society of Jews and Christians, in which such friendly conversations between both groups have become possible and are still being carried on.

(vii) REFORM IN ISLAM

The main features in the reforming movements have been adequately set forth by Professor Gibb and Professor Lawrence Browne. They fall naturally into two groups, first those which seek to get back if possible to Islam in its purest and most primitive form, and second those which seek to modernise it and to bring it into a condition in which they think it can satisfy the needs of the modern world. The first group naturally makes but little of tradition, and would go back to the plain teaching of the Qur'ān. We think of it chiefly in connection with the Wahabi movement in and around Saudi Arabia, in which a strict Puritanism prevails, and any modernism is forbidden; but there is another kind of reformed Islam which had its rise in Cyrenaica and takes its name of Senussi from the family of its founder. Of my own experience of it I have spoken elsewhere. It is earnest, devout, and of exemplary piety, and favours the simplification of life, with perhaps a good deal of stress upon meditation. Although it has become associated through its king with the political form of the State of Libya, it is a genuinely religious movement; but at present it shows no signs of wishing for any strong or deep rapprochement with the modern world. In this it differs widely from the reforming movements in Egypt and Pakistan. In both these countries the educated classes have for a long time been in contact with Western culture, and it is therefore not surprising that they should have tried to come to terms with it. In Pakistan many educated Moslems have received their early training in schools and colleges founded by Christians, and although in these there has often been no attempt at putting pressure upon them to be proselytes, the students cannot but have been conscious of what was going on around them both in the worship, teaching, and practice of their Christian leaders. It is therefore not unnatural that Indian Moslems should have produced, prior to the partition, a number of reforming sects whose purpose has been both to modernise Islam and to assimilate it to Christianity. In Egypt the name of Mohammed Abduh is well known as that of one who sought to liberalise Moslem teaching, and to make room for development by reviving the principle of *ijtihad* or interpretation. There are probably a good many individual Moslems who, although they do not openly belong either to the Ahmadiyyahs of Pakistan or to any other corresponding body in Egypt or elsewhere, nevertheless are in sympathy with any project for developing Moslem teaching in such a way as to meet the criticisms of Christians and of scientists, without abandoning what are felt to be the fundamental tenets of Mohammed's original observation; but these are rather nervous about declaring themselves openly, and are no more a majority than modernists of any kind are in the total membership of Christianity. It is often forgotten that the largest single Christian Church is officially very conservative, even though it is now slowly on the move.

Mirza Ghulam Ahmad (*c.* 1889) was a Panjabi visionary whose claims and experiences bear a considerable resemblance to those of Mohammed himself. He certainly had visions and locutions, and although interested in both Hinduism and Christianity, never really understood either of them properly, nor made any serious investigation into their tenets. He claimed at one time to be the Messiah, and that his appearance constituted the second Advent. He also seems to have claimed equality with Mohammed on some occasions, but on others that he was the latter's supersessor. In 1904 he declared that for the Hindus he was an avatar of Krishna. He urged reform in all three religions and after his death a schism arose in 1914 among his followers. A minority, the Qadianis, still hold him to be a prophet, and apparently support his extravagant pretensions. The majority section, however, centred upon Lahore, merely think of him as a stimulating reformer and nothing more, and go beyond him in their ideas of what reform should be.[1] It is curious that with this reduced estimate of their founder, they nevertheless call themselves Ahmadiyyahs. They say that Christianity is too idealistic to be practicable, whereas Islam is eminently suited to human beings as they are. This of course makes a certain appeal, but limits any aspirations to spiritual progress. Orthodox Sunnis naturally regard these Ahmadiyyahs as heretics, since they insist upon having a liberal and rational Islam animated by a free use of reason and a free interpretation of the Qur'ān in view of present world conditions. Nevertheless the movement certainly had life. There is always the possibility that it may throw up some religious and intellectual genius who will give the entire group a firm and reasonable policy, but with its present trend it is difficult to see it heading for anything but an Asian type of an eclectic Unitarian Christianity. It was an Ahmadiyyan Mosque which was established some years ago at Woking in Surrey.

In Egypt Mohammed Abduh (1849–1905) really owed much of his inspiration to a less well-known reformer, Jamal-ad-din-ad Afghani, who was himself a Sufi, but by no means confined himself to mysticism, since he clearly believed in political action as the means of reviving Islam in a religious sense. He wanted a new and live Caliphate to unite all Moslem people under one spiritual head, but he seems to have found no really friendly reception in any of the various Moslem countries which he visited. Mohammed Abduh, however, held him in high esteem, and used to attend meetings at his house in Cairo. In 1895 Abduh, who had become a lecturer in the

[1] This body actually declares that the historical Jesus was really crucified (thus disagreeing with the Qur'ān), but that He subsequently revived in the tomb, escaped, and made His way to Kashmir, where He died at the age of 120. Needless to say, there is no historical evidence whatsoever for such an assertion.

al-Azhar Mosque (the Moslem University), succeeded in getting a committee appointed by the government for its reform. Four years later he himself was appointed Mufti of Egypt, and thus had the duty laid upon him of interpreting the *shari'a*. This gave him his real opportunity, for he had for a long time insisted upon the necessity for the revival of the practice of *ijtihad* in order to give a freer interpretation of Islamic law on its practical side, and he now claimed the right to use *ijtihad* himself. The natural question which arises is: How much of the influence of Abduh has survived his death in 1905? The answer seems to be: A good deal. In recent years the religious and political situation in Egypt has been fluid, so that it is not easy to discover what is the most dominant group. But it is certainly the case that the followers of Abduh are a distinct and not uninfluential party, with a journal, *al Manas*, as the medium for the propagation of their ideas. Some of Abduh's own works have been translated into Urdu and Turkish, and may therefore be regarded as circulating both in Pakistan and North India, as well as in Turkey; while Dr. Lawrence Browne reports that a reform movement among Moslems in Indonesia is specially influenced by Abduh's ideas. In Egypt one curious piece of rather drastic reform from above in recent years has been the tendency on the part of the police to suppress the popular observance of the festivals of various Moslem saints, known as the Moulids.

The Baha'i movement, which at one time was thought by Professor E. G. Browne to show promise of a great spiritual force, has moved outside Islam, and claims to be an entirely new founded universalist religion. It has an impressive new temple at Haifa and its largest one is in America, but it does not seem to be maintaining itself in the Middle East so far as numbers go, but has dwindled there; and it shows no sign of being able to supersede Christianity. There are certain not very edifying features about its early history, and while one would not wish to deny that some of its teachings, although not original, are salutary, the idea of an hereditary spiritual leader is repugnant to Christians. In 1931 an article by Mr. J. R. Richards in *The Moslem World* maintained that the conversion of a Moslem to Baha'ism, so far from being an advance, was actually a step on the road to materialism, and that Baha'ism itself as a religion did not stand very high. Probably its chief appeal has been to those who, having no very deep religious roots, thirst for a novelty. My own experience has been that young students who belong to the sect, while certainly showing both earnestness and spirituality, display a considerable confusion of thought, and that if they were once to grasp the significance of the Logos doctrine, would be much better and happier as Christians.

No reform in Islam can really remove from it certain essential features in which it differs profoundly from Christianity. Its claim is that it is a practicable religion, whereas Christianity is so exalted as to be impracticable. This is a taunt to be taken with gladness. The glory and greatness of the Christian programme for human life is that it does not limit man's ideal to what is within his unaided powers, but invites him to strain after supernatural virtues, to be perfect, even as his Father in Heaven is perfect, and in spite of weakness to live a strong life in a strength greater than his own. As Professor Lawrence Browne says: 'It would be distressing to learn that man had already reached his goal and could advance no further.' The good observant Moslem is rather in the position of the boy scout who, having done his good deed for the day, is permitted to untie the knot in his handkerchief. The Christian has a knot which he is never allowed to untie, since he is under an obligation to love God and his neighbour without limit, and even when he has done all that seems for the moment to be required of him, is taught to say that he is still only a servant who has done what it was his duty to do (some texts even read 'An unprofitable servant'). We do well to remember the gentle rebuke of Sir Sarvepalli Radakrishnan: 'You Christians seem to me to be very ordinary people making extraordinary claims.' Such a remark ought certainly to keep us humble, but the point, of course, is that the extraordinary claims are made. The Moslem seems rather to pride himself on the fact that he does not make them.

The ascetic element in Christianity is challenged by those Moslems who say that the teaching of the Qur'ān does greater justice to man's duty to his body. One has heard the same claim put forward by certain Hindus, and one has read it in the pages of a Jewish controversialist. Although it is quite possible that this challenge can be made in full sincerity, I fear that here and there there are those who make it (perhaps unconsciously) because they desire a religion which will give them greater liberty for their carnal appetites. But in any case the claim that Islam puts the duty towards the body on a level with that towards the soul must of necessity imply either an undervaluation of the soul, or an overvaluation of the body. Asceticism may well have been exaggerated by, for example, some of the hermits of the Nitrian Desert, just as it has been exaggerated by some Indians, perhaps notably by some Jains, but it clearly has a right to a place of honour in religion, as von Hügel has vigorously demonstrated; and it involves the important principle that the soul is one's real self, and is meant to be the master and controller of the body as its instrument. But even Moslem asceticism exists. Witness the observance of Ramadan. Some dervishes actually seem to practise self-torture (eye-gouging) as a votive offering to Allah.

And further, there are two features in Islam which even for educated Moslems it does not seem possible to explain away: first, belief in *Jinns*, and the use of magic against them: second, the unsatisfactory treatment of women, which, although deprecated by a few, who would like to see some reform, is still approved of by the great majority of educated Moslems. Both these features are historically part of Mohammed's original *kerugma*, and not excrescences which could be easily removed without undermining the authority of the prophet and his sacred book in the eyes of the orthodox. It is true that there is a quibble by which monogamy is now justified, namely that since the Qur'ān declares that a man may only have a plurality of wives provided that he treats them all equally and alike, and since such treatment is humanly speaking impossible, the inevitability of having only one wife is implied. But we have only to compare this with the original principles about matrimony enunciated by Christ in order to see on what a different level the latter stands.

Finally, it seems impossible that an orthodox Moslem could ever accept free criticism of the Qur'ānic texts. Christianity has no official doctrine of inspiration of its scriptures which prohibits such criticism. But within the Qur'ān itself again and again its verbally supernatural origin is asserted in such a way that no room is left for any fallible human element. Even the Papacy, albeit with some caution, bred no doubt from anxiety not to disturb the simple faith of the peasant, has lifted the embargo on biblical criticism, and has given scholars rather more elbow room; and in practically all the churches of the Reformation there is now full liberty to interpret the scriptures freely on the lines of general literary criticism. It is hard to see how Islam could be developed on similar lines without ceasing to be Islam.

The greatest need is the resumption on a wide scale of friendly discussion and conversation between Moslems and Christians. Not only have they a good deal to learn from one another, but the removal of misunderstandings is only possible where such free discussion prevails. Is it too much to hope that the time may come when Mohammed may be revered in the same way as some of the great sages of Hellas, India, and the Far East, not as equal with Christ, but as manifesting even though in an imperfect and partial way the inspiration from the divine Logos? It might surely be possible for an indigenous Arab church to arise, worshipping in the vernacular, having its own distinctive liturgy and perhaps ceremonial, reverencing its prophet as at least as great as Isaiah or Jeremiah, and even being allowed to read some of its sacred scriptures alongside of the Old Testament. But this vision is perhaps not for many days.

Moslems sometimes point out that their religion is nearly 600 years younger than Christianity, and that it would not be fair to judge the latter by what it was in the age of the great Papal Schism and the Lollards. How much less then should one judge Islam by what it is now? But the answer to this is two-fold. First, Islam and Christianity must be compared in their initial stages, and their religious founders set side by side. If this is done, it is not difficult to see which way the conclusion lies, however much credit one may give to Mohammed himself; and in any case one cannot build truth upon misunderstanding. And so, in the second place, one is bound to recognise that starting out from this beginning Islam could not, if kept isolated and pure from accretions, ever develop into anything possessing the virtues of the Christian faith; and that if it took anything substantial from Christianity into itself, it would cease to be genuine Islam. Hence it seems impossible that it should ever successfully be reformed without losing its identity, whereas experience has already shown that the bulk of reform in Christianity has not disturbed its fundamentals.

It is, of course, difficult to persuade educated Moslems to make any study of classical Christian literature, whether of biography or devotion. I cannot think of any Moslem who has written about Christian mystics in the way in which Professor Nicholson and Dr. Margaret Smith have written about their Moslem counterparts. If such there be, I should be glad to know of them.[1] Nor do Moslems seem ready to engage in Qur'ānic higher criticism. The lengthy Ahmadiyyah annotated English version of the Qur'ān, issued from Lahore, is the nearest approach in recent years to such a rapprochement; but it represents, of course, the work of an heretical minority movement, and is much concerned with explaining away inconvenient passages in the Suras by means of a good deal of special pleading and strained argument. One looks in vain for any move on the part of orthodox Sunni scholars; yet it is difficult to see how much longer they can keep blinkers on themselves.

(viii) THE DOMINANCE OF AMERICA

In 1945 the population of the United States of America was reckoned approximately at 134 million. Of this total rather more than 67 million were recorded as belonging to some religious denomination. The figures included children in the families of adult

---

[1] I have heard that a Pakistani Moslem scholar has lately been engaged on such a book, but I have not been able to see it.

members, and as church rolls of membership are seldom devoid of a certain amount of deadwood, due to removals, deaths, and lapses, it seems probable that the real total was less than the figure given above. Nevertheless, it has been alleged that during the period immediately before this census, church membership was increasing faster than the birth-rate to the extent of about 3 per cent, while since 1945 it is alleged that there has been a considerable increase all over the United States in the number of new church membership registrations. According to the information supplied at Christmas 1954, more than 30 million of new church members had been added to the denominational rolls in fourteen years, giving a total increase from 67 million to 94 million, and a percentage increase throughout the whole population from less than 50 per cent to 60·3 per cent.

Going back to the 1945 years, where details are available, it is said that out of the 67 million recorded, 23 million were Roman Catholics, $4\frac{1}{2}$ million Jewish, and nearly a million and a half Eastern Orthodox. This leaves a block of non-Roman Christians of about $38\frac{1}{2}$ million, divided among some 243 denominations, 200 of which, in the Middle West and the Deep South, account for 3 per cent of the total church membership. Admittedly, some of these latter groups are exceedingly small. Thus we find 'The Fire Baptised Holiness Church of God', united with 'the Mount Moriah Fire Baptised Holiness Church of Knoxville, Tenn.', which in the whole of America has between sixty and seventy congregations, while the 'Church of Daniel's Band' has only five congregations. Countless small sects are found among the negroes. Dr. Sperry[1] only mentions eleven of the chief ones, the most remarkable perhaps being the 'Apostolic Overcoming Church of God', which has a sort of cathedral at Mobile, Alabama, where the hymns are accompanied by an amazing jazz orchestra, and the congregation prophesy in unknown tongues, and engage in sacred dances. The main groups are seven in number, and comprise the Protestant Episcopal Church which belongs to the Anglican Communion, the Presbyterian, the Lutheran, the Methodist, the Baptist, and the Congregationalist, but with the exception of the last, and of the Episcopalians, the remaining groups are subdivided into between ten and twenty denominations. The seventh group, the Disciples of Christ, contained in 1945 rather more members than the Congregational Church, but as it originated from the Baptists, it might almost be counted as the twentieth sub-division of the latter.

It will thus be seen that in its profession the United States is

[1] *Religion in America*, Cambridge University Press.

predominantly Christian, and that the strongest element in it proportionately is Roman Catholic. We have to remember, however, that we are speaking of a country which is on the scale of Europe, India, or China, and not of Great Britain. Were we to consider Europe as a whole, we should have to confess that in some corners of it there still existed some rather curious forms of Christianity, and that in others there were very strong irreligious elements; but it would not be fair to judge European religion by these alone, or by stressing them unduly in relation to the large blocks of soberly religious people. Similarly, if we were to look at the sub-continent of India we should be bound to recognise the vast size of its population, its partition between two republics, one neutral and the other Moslem, and the enormous number of sectarian bodies to be found in the former. These considerations should at the outset moderate any judgment we may make upon religion in the United States. We have also to remember the influence which the very fact of the U.S.A. has had upon all the various religious bodies which have migrated to it. The constitution precludes the existence of any kind of Established Church, while the constitution itself was, strange to say, originally drafted by men who perhaps favoured Liberal Deism rather than orthodox Christianity, and were under the influence of eighteenth-century rationalism as expressed in France and England; so that theoretically the state is neutral as far as religion is concerned. There is an intense individualism, and an immense and, until recently, indomitable optimism. Some of the migrating denominations, where they exist in relatively out-of-the-way places, have preserved old-fashioned Protestant customs and even costumes. The time-lag clearly operates, and it is hard to feel certain that some of the changes which have been acutely felt in Europe will not eventually come to be felt in America.

With all these considerations it must be borne in mind nevertheless that a very large part of the settlement of North America was undertaken by people who were desperately in earnest about their religion, and who, whatever creed they may have acknowledged, did put it at the centre of their lives, and were often migrants to the New World for liberty of conscience sake, even though they may have sometimes in their turn become persecutors. These traditions play a considerable part in determining the present attitude of American people to religion.

One observer has lately queried how the high percentage of Christian worshippers in the United States can have been correctly calculated, since American periodicals and films reaching Europe seem to reflect the activities of a wholly secular and materialistic society. Of course, the answer to this might be that the reflection is a false and partial one, and that only a single aspect of American life is represented in print and on the screen. Yet the curious fact remains that young men who come over to Europe to bring for performance intolerably vulgar and discordant music, erotic songs, and barbaric dances, nearly always describe themselves on interview as 'really very religious, you know', this being apparently a certificate that what they are bringing over is respectable.[1] One would be almost tempted to wonder whether a great deal of American life was not the manifestation of a kind of corporate split personality, or whether the position of religion in the U.S.A. might not be similar to that in a large part of Germany as described by Rudolf Eucken in the early years of the twentieth century as 'the embroidery on a life mainly devoted to other interests'. In a recent article a well-known British scholar and mission preacher spoke of 'the appalling religiousness of America', and said he feared that many were using religious institutions and observances as a kind of shock-absorber between themselves and the possibility of a shattering encounter with the Living God.

Yet one must be careful to avoid any kind of impatience or show of superiority. Plenty of criticisms could be passed on the defects in the British way of life so far as religion is concerned, and America, with all its materialism, its anxiety to sell things to people, its luxury, its wasteful extravagance, and its obsession with what is known as 'consumptionism', is still very far from being an irreligious country. On the initiative of Thomas Jefferson, the Virginia Legislature passed a statute of religious freedom in 1786, which was further developed in the constitution of the Federal Government to such an extent that even so moderate a provision for the religious instruction of the young as that made in England by the post-war Education Act is something which, without a fundamental change in her constitution, the United States has not the slightest prospect of being able to enact. Yet, on the other side, the United States has splendid and highly-organised Sunday Schools, and the property of religious denominations is exempt from taxation. This latter is a privilege which, as Dean Sperry says, implies a tacit vote of confidence in the contribution made by the various religious denominations to the life of the American people; and one of its results is that in Cambridge, Massachusetts, 47 per cent of real property in the State is for this precise reason tax-exempt. Opportunities for Sunday rest and worship are, on the whole, it is said, better protected than they are in

---

[1] Of course this does not mean that they represent the main stream of Christian life in America, for they do not. But the undisturbed prominence which is given to them is alarming to the onlooker.

England. Indeed, at the time of writing the American republic gives the impression of being swept by a religious revival, although this impression is a false one.[1]

The size and wealth of the United States give it a dominance in the world of the twentieth century which it is hard to overestimate. Americans have greater financial resources for the propagation of ideas than any other communal group, the U.S.S.R. not excepted. Hence, if they feel called upon by conviction to spread any sort of ideology or religious teaching, they can easily find the funds needed to equip its missionaries.[2] Their immense resources have in this way enabled them, in the past half-century, to flood Asia with more missionary agents than other Anglo-Saxon countries. They have given generously to such fine institutions as the Theological College at Jubbulpore in Central India, and the large Andhra Christian College at Guntoor,[3] and they have subscribed to the re-establishment of St. Augustine's College, Canterbury, as an ecumenical centre, to the repair of cathedrals, and to many other good works. It would be both unfair and ungenerous not to record all this with thanksgiving. The hospitality afforded to great congresses in recent years, such as those held at Evanston and Minneapolis, is beyond praise. But such generosity, when coupled with American individualistic philosophy, has serious dangers. It is quite clear that the ease with which religious projects can be subsidised from America tends to upset the balance in the religious world, and often gives to minor religious movements a degree of support which from the point of view of scientific theology, and even of a liberal orthodoxy, they do not deserve. Sometimes religious movements which in the ordinary course of events would decline or even collapse, have had a stay of execution granted them by the naïve and unthinking financial support which they have received. It was a rich American who provided the new Buddhist temple at Sarnath near Banaras in India. It was almost certainly large sums collected in America which enabled the Bahai movement to erect its costly new mosque at Haifa. And the largest Bahai mosque in the world is actually at Evanston! It is American money which keeps alive the denomination known as Jehovah's Witnesses. It is largely American resources which have

[1] There are many signs of a widespread increase of interest in religion, but perhaps not more than that.

[2] The high cost of living makes it precarious to compare clerical incomes in the United States with those in Great Britain, but it is a fact that a deacon on ordination can expect a stipend equivalent to £1000 in England, and some incumbents receive as much as £5000 per annum. Giving is generous, and the weekly contribution to church funds, though voluntary, is honoured as strictly and conscientiously as if it were a compulsory church rate. A critic adds here that most American ministers' salaries range from the equivalent of £1300 to £2000 p.a.

[3] This institution is the largest affiliated college to Andhra University, and has an unusually high percentage of Christian students.

22

equipped the headquarters of the Christian Science Movement in London. It was American money which built the large Seventh Day Adventist Church in Calcutta.

While a great many American missionaries are intelligent, well educated, and liberal, as well as earnest, a considerable number are sent out by Christian communities which have not really come to grips with the problems of the modern world, and still hold on to very uncritical and old-fashioned views about the Bible. It is best and safest in this connection to depend on what Americans say about themselves. A work entitled, *Religion in Crisis and Custom* published in New York in 1955, and described in an introduction as probably the most important contribution of its kind since the famous work by William James on *The Varieties of Religious Experience*, states that the great majority of American Protestants, something like three-quarters of them, adhere to the old-fashioned pre-critical view of the Bible, and look askance at any critical study of it. 'It is true', says the writer, 'that an increasing number of persons in all our major churches do not look upon the book of Genesis as an authority regarding the age of the earth and the process of creation, and these people, the *Liberals*, regard the Bible as the record of the religious experience of the Hebrew people, and seek religious authority in the tested experience of today; while they are ready to make use of the methods of science in the domain of religion itself. *But this group is still a minority.*'[1] As far back as 1932 the Laymen's Missionary Commission in America reported on enquiry that the great majority of American missionaries in India, China, and Japan knew next to nothing about Socialism; and were uncritically opposed to Communism, and just as uncritically supporters of Capitalism. This simplicity is altogether too childlike for those who are seeking to build a Christian community in modern Asia upon solid foundations. It may be that some European missionaries have been no better. Possibly in the last twenty-five years the situation has somewhat changed; but it is doubtful whether it is actually much different in many areas today. During the last twelve months before this was written, the author of a serious appraisal of the religious situation in the United States came to the conclusion that whereas there was more earnestness than ever about the cause of religion, there was a serious gap between those who were most in earnest and those who represented the most vigorous intellectual life of the sub-continent.[1] This is perhaps reflected in the enthusiasm with which Americans have received the ministrations of Dr. Billy Graham, and have sent him

[1] A critic observes that nevertheless the main stream of American theological thought in all denominations, even though not that of the majority of theologians, is not liberalistic.

forth as an advocate of evangelical Christianity to all parts of the world. Of the sincerity and humility of Dr. Graham there can be no possible doubt, but a perusal of his sermons and writings, and a study of his personal confession as to the circumstances which led him to adopt his own particular kind of preaching, equally leave no doubt that his theology is defective, and his use of the Bible naïve and anti-intellectual, to such a degree that if it were not balanced by certain other good elements in his outlook, it could only too easily sink into superstition.[1]

That such folk as Dr. Graham are in earnest, and that their loyalty to Our Lord is undoubted, no-one wishes to deny less than I do myself. But they gravely under-estimate the degree to which their opinions have been controverted in recent years, and their intellectual background is at times astonishingly naïve, and is by no means equal to their undoubted skill in eloquent writing and preaching. They have launched a monthly periodical, again with considerable help from American funds, and the number of free copies circulated must in itself have cost a great deal. It is, of course, a perfectly legitimate enterprise, and no one would wish to prevent people from circulating opinions in which they sincerely believe. The size of their organisation may be gauged from the list of contributing editors and correspondents in all parts of the world which is printed at the beginning of each number. It is gratifying to see that the movement uses its great influence on the side of racial integration as opposed to segregation and apartheid, and that it disowns some of the more peculiarly radical and unconventional sects such as Jehovah's Witnesses and Christian Science, although one supposes that it is hardly fair to group together two such very different kinds of aberration from the main highway of Christianity. It may well be that such a theological group as this may in time come to move theologically in those directions in which it is obviously at present weak,[2] though this does not mean that one in any way wishes it to take the strength out of some of its strongest affirmations. One of the leading contributors to the journal has been the senior United Nations truce delegate at Panmunjon, Lieut.-Gen. William K. Harrison. In all probability his interpretations of the Bible will not commend themselves to everyone, nor his treatment of the Second

---

[1] Dr. Graham declares that at a certain moment of crisis, when walking in the woods, he was moved to kneel down and make an act of surrender, to accept the words of the Bible *at their face value* as delivered by Almighty God, and to preach them in that way, without any modification. No Moslem of the orthodox persuasion could have expressed himself more clearly and uncompromisingly when speaking of the Holy Qur'ān.

[2] There are signs already that it is doing so, and that its fundamentation is intellectualist rather than wholly obscurantist.

Advent—he regards the period between the First and Second Coming of Christ as one in which society must inevitably face the death and destruction of wars, and says we are not to expect that even with Divine help mankind will be enabled to establish peace upon earth. But he is certainly right in saying that a non-Christian cannot be won simply by an exposure to the Christian ethic, but must be born again. A watered-down message, a social ethic without the Gospel, robs Christianity of its main power in dealing with the Marxists. Merely to see that the Christian ethic looks rather nice and attractive is not in itself enough, because one can do that and still remain humanistic, man-centred, and fundamentally selfish. One can adopt the Christian ethic because one thinks it pays, or is comfortable, or makes things a bit easier in the office or the works. But this is not at all the same thing as the recognition of the basic fact that people cannot be converted with any success to the habit of treating one another properly, to giving up exploitation, cut-throat competition, racial superiority, or class-preferences and the colour-bar unless their whole being is transformed, and they adopt the deliberate policy of placing the Living God at the centre of their lives. Yet this is a desperately serious undertaking, and is one which cannot be achieved with any hope of its permanence unless those who approach the unconverted are known by the latter to be respecters of truth. If the folk who are the objects of an evangelistic campaign become aware that the evangelists themselves are clinging to obsolete and petty views of the universe, or are proclaiming an obscurantist theology, they may well turn a deaf ear to their appeals, and feel that they have a good excuse for doing so.

The sober truth, I fear, is that a great deal (only too much) of Christianity, and especially American Christianity, is as unfitted to guide the future of religion in the world as the Marxists of Russia and their friends are to dispose of it.

On what, then, is the cause of vital religion to depend? Some would say 'upon Rome'. It would be foolish and unfair to deny the immense spiritual resources of the Latin Communion, and the revival of spiritual power which has come to it in recent years. The mere fact that there are now said to be 33 million Roman Catholics in the United States of America, out of a total Christian population which is now said to reach 100 million, makes it evident that the weight of Christian opinion in that country is not by any means entirely Protestant, and a single religious body of that size, well-knit and well-disciplined, is likely to have a greater influence by its vote alone, than the 58 millions of Protestants, with their strong individualism and their enormous number of sub-divisions. Yet the prominent features in Roman dogmatic theology over the last hundred years have been the tendentious justification of new dogmas, the intellectual foundation for which is but frail. The 'infinite variety' which is sometimes claimed for Latin Christianity may conceivably find room for such tendencies side by side with undoubtedly earnest efforts to improve biblical study and to face the issues of literary criticism of documents and historical evidence, and the discoveries made in the physical sciences; but it is still true, one fears, as von Hügel wrote some years back:

> 'Catholicism was in the time of Aquinas and even still in that of More a great intellectual culture and rich mental training school, as well as the home of saints; but since say 1720, and still more since the French Revolution, it has shrunk more and more to being, usually and easily, just that home[1]; and, I do not say to gain, but even fully to retain such culture and such training within the Roman communion is now distinctly difficult. But pray let us have no exaggeration; though they are all *un peu á côté*, and though they do not dominate the popular presentation of the Catholic faith, ripe scholars and ripe minds exist sure enough now still within that great church.'

But of course this is a problem which does not concern America only. At the same time American dominance adds weight to it from that direction. It is, to me at any rate, an unwelcome task to have to stress the embarrassment which proceeds from these various disquieting features in transatlantic life, for I have many friends in America and I have had many pupils from across the Atlantic. I am sure that the United States contains a substantial number of enlightened and cultured Christians: but they appear to be seriously in a minority. An old pupil of mine, holding a responsible position in a well-attested college in the States, told me with dissatisfaction some time ago that any efforts to present a modern view of the Bible encountered active opposition and plainly-manifested disapproval on the part, not only of the parents of his pupils, but of the pupils themselves, who had clearly been brought up from early years to hold an impossibly conservative position with regard to the Scriptures. One cannot help noticing that on the basis of the 1945 figures, out of 144 millions only 67 millions have recorded themselves as belonging to a religious denomination, and of these $4\frac{1}{2}$ millions were Jews. No doubt on the Pacific coast there would have also been some Buddhists. But what of the other half of the population of the United States who did not get recorded as having any religious connection at all, and who, on the evidence of the most recent census figures, must have also increased proportionally during the past twelve years? Are they all

[1] A similar appraisal of Roman Catholicism in U.S.A. appeared recently in a well-known and reputable Roman Catholic periodical in Great Britain, and here again a charge was made of deficiency in intellectual power and leadership.

wicked persons? Is it not possible that they include many who find that their intelligence will not accept the kind of religious teaching frequently provided for them in the United States?

Here perhaps is something in which the accusing finger may be pointed at Britain as well. It has been declared with some frequency of late that in the author's own country only 10 per cent have a strong connection with any Christian denomination. Although beyond that 10 per cent there are probably a good many others who would not wish to be considered irreligious, but who worship in public a few times a year, and say some prayers privately; and although a good many more would say that they were sympathetic to religion but were not aware of the necessity of belonging to any specific denomination, beyond these groups there is a great mass of people who are puzzled as to what it is reasonable to believe, and who are beset by considerable doubts. Some of them, it is said, remembering what they were taught in the infant school, are inclined to regard the Bible as 'a book of tall stories'. It seems, in fact, that it is idle to throw stones of criticism at one another, for on both sides of the Atlantic we are living in glass-houses. Yet, upon the enterprise and honest facing-up to the realities of the religious situation by all English-speaking Christians during the next fifty years, by those on both sides of the Atlantic (in Canada as well as the U.S.A.), and also by those in Australia and New Zealand, may depend the whole religious future of the planet.

Of course it may be said quite justly that the intellectual frequently suffers from pride and vanity and from a false sense of superiority; that he is sometimes a crank, quite as much as his obscurantist sectarian brother; and that the wisdom of this world needs to be baptised and humbled before it can serve the Christian cause. But this is not the whole case, and if the Christian faith cannot command the respect of honest seekers after the truth, it can have little chance of becoming the common world religion of the future.

The special conditions of American life have modified the traditional set-up of some of the European denominations. The Rev. H. C. Snape, speaking at the Conference of Modern Churchmen held at Cambridge in 1956, pointed out that the Episcopal Church in America (in communion with Anglicans) has no archbishop and no provincial organisation, and that in fact if not formally the laity have so much power that it possesses virtually a system of government after the presbyterian model, in which laymen share with ministers the government of each congregation. He thinks that American Roman Catholics, in spite of intellectual deficiencies, are on the whole progressive in politics (Al Smith stood for Roosevelt's New Deal),[1] and that if ever the American hierarchy should come to dominate the College of Cardinals, or an American be elected to the papacy, the Vatican might well come to adopt a less cautious social policy, and its attitude towards Protestantism might become less intolerant.

It is on the whole correct to say that only three faiths, Catholicism, Protestantism in its various well-recognised denominations, and Judaism are really accorded a place in the national system. 'To be a declared atheist, agnostic, or humanist is to be not quite American, if not un-American, and to be a Buddhist or Moslem is to be foreign. The fancy religions do not quite belong in America, even though they may be tolerated there, while the really popular form of faith is that which claims to give to the hustling American citizen restfulness and repose, and perhaps this is not altogether a bad thing, although at times a tranquilliser may come dangerously near to opium.

A few more words from Mr. Snape's paper may be worth quoting. After describing how this popular religion is purveyed by such means as a well-known song: 'You have a friend upstairs', or by a telephone service, in which when worried you dial a certain number and immediately hear a prayer for peace and comfort, he continues:

'Peace of mind depends on faith, so that the core of American religion seems to be the power of faith in faith. . . . Up to now Americans have never failed to achieve the object of their desires and have known nothing but space and abundance. In these last years they have discovered that they cannot exclude themselves from the tyrannies, wars, and rumours of wars both to the East and the West of them. They possess neither the phlegm of the Englishman bred of a long experience of self-development within a troublesome environment, nor the hard scepticism of the long-suffering European peasant. Hence their apprehensions for the future of mankind strike deeper than we are aware. That is why there comes to them a desire for faith in faith. It may and often does verge on idolatry, but it is also a faith that somehow the plan of God is being accomplished and that His ways are those of mercy and love. Science, economics, and politics have failed to allay the fears for the future, which the American feels much more acutely than we do, just because his sensitiveness and his imagination have not been blunted and dimmed by hard experience. He believes in the future, but is aware that his belief needs confirmation. . . . The frugal mind of a visitor from the Old World cannot help but be appalled by the prodigal use which is being made of the natural resources of the country, symbolised by the mountains of disused motor-cars to be seen wherever one goes.[2] When it is

[1] Throughout the whole era of the New Deal, support for Roosevelt's policies came from a democratic party largely dependent on Roman Catholic support, while the major opposition to it, except for a minority of liberal social gospel leaders, was undoubtedly lodged in upper class American Protestantism.

[2] Yet again, I am afraid, *waste* is almost world-wide—a universal sin.

found that conservation must replace profligacy, a revolution of standards and modes of living with all manner of social re-adjustments is to be expected. Faith will be shaken, and perhaps tried in the fire.'

Lest anyone should feel that only a partial, unfair, or ungenerous account of the situation has here been given, let it be said that, in spite of all possible criticisms, one is bound to give thanks without reserve for the wonderful witness of many Americans to Christ as the Sole Hope of the world. How can one forget the contributions to the riches and vitality of the Christian movement coming from Bishop Phillips Brooks, John R. Mott, and Reinhold Niebuhr, to mention only a few; to the vast sums generously bestowed upon all manner of works of mercy and the relief of the distressed; to the support of many idealistic movements such as the World Student Christian Federation, which apparently originated in America, and to the devoted labours of United States missionaries in all parts of the non-Christian world? True, their zeal, like that of some of our own minor sectaries, is not always entirely according to knowledge, and because of their greater numbers and immense financial backing they are apt to create suspicion among those whom they are genuinely wishful to help, and are thought to be agents of American imperialism and trade-expansion in the countries to which they go. But perhaps it were more gracious to say that, however mixed may be the motives, Christ is preached, and that, to that extent, we ought to rejoice, and indeed do rejoice.

CHAPTER XIII

THE CHANGE TO THE MODERN WORLD

(c) THEOLOGICAL REVALUATION

The contemplation by Christians of other forms of religion than their own goes back, as we have seen, as far as apostolic times. There were moments in history when contacts reached an acute stage, as when such men as Boniface were confronted with Teutonic paganism, or Cyril and Methodius engaged in work among the Slavs, or again when the Franciscans went to China, Raymond Lull to the Moslems, and the Spanish friars to the Americas—the latter often protesting bravely against the cruelties inflicted by the soldiery of the Conquistadors. But these were mostly examples of what has been called radical displacement, and although some of the missionaries to Central America noted and wrote down certain superficial resemblances between the sacramental practices of Mexicans and Peruvians to those of Catholics, they attributed these to the machinations of the devil. It is now known that Luther was not by any means unaware of the problem presented by non-Christian faiths, especially Islam; that in 1542 he brought out a German translation of the Qur'ān, and that he sought by every means in his power to understand the religion of the Turks, who had in 1529 besieged Vienna, and were threatening Central Europe.

Apart from this, it is evident that in the pre-Christian period, Herodotus on the one hand and Plutarch on the other engaged in observations about the different religious beliefs which they saw around them.

But it was not until more extensive travelling took place, roughly from the time of Prince Henry the Navigator and Columbus onwards, that wide views of the world, and increasing freedom from the restrictions of ecclesiastical authority, combined to produce among Europeans attempts at framing *general theories* of religion. Perhaps the first of these was that of the Dutchman, Baldaeus, in the seventeenth century, but in Britain the first it would seem to try his hand at a general theory was Lord Herbert of Cherbury, who died in 1648 (the year of the Peace of Westphalia). Herbert based his work upon scrappy and inadequate information, and it is therefore perhaps today only of a historical interest, but his initial assumptions are as good as when they were first put forth, namely that human beings as a species are distinguishable for their propensity to try to establish relationship with the Self-Existent, and that there are in consequence no real atheists, since the maximum unbelief that is possible is for a man to reject all other concepts of the Self-Existent than his own, as being either unworthy or impossible of credence. (Here Zähner would be in agreement with him regarding the Process-Philosophy of the Marxists.) Herbert's five definitions of true religion are those of a Deist, and omit any reference to Christianity, although they are obviously influenced by it. They represent what he considers to be the basic principles of natural religion, and similar analyses are to be found in the slightly later writings of Locke and Collins; while the general principle of the Deists is, of course, that natural religion receives a kind of republication in the teaching of Christ, a view which no one today would regard as an adequate description of the latter.

As the eighteenth century advanced, versions of Asian sacred books became available in Latin, French, or English, while travellers went further and further afield, and commerce extended so as to bring more and more Europeans into contact with the peoples of Asia and Africa. This inevitably led to a suspicion that previous theories had been based upon insufficient evidence, and although theorising was not abandoned, it was controlled and put into a secondary position as compared with the empirical study of past and present religion phenomena, and their classification. The process of empirical study thus begun has continued right up to the present day, and the methods of conducting it have been gradually sharpened and made more systematic. Field workers in anthropology have increasingly undertaken *to live with* the peoples they are studying, and not merely to visit them; and have tried to take down in writing the substance of what their hosts have said about themselves. In this way many earlier misunderstandings have been removed, and a sympathetic approach has been made, which has, of course, had to run the risk of being exaggerated, but which has certainly led to a juster appreciation of the basic feelings of those who are sincere non-Christians. We may compare in this respect the work of Abbé Dubois in India from 1765–1848, of C. F. Andrews, also in India, during the twentieth century, and of the Austrian journalist and diplomat, known usually by his adopted name of Muhammad Asad, all of whom have helped us to an appreciation of the spirit behind Hinduism on the one hand, and Islam on the other. It is difficult to include among these the brilliant renegade Christian, Verrier Elwin, since in spite of his vivid analyses of Indian tribal life, he somehow seems to lack the moral earnestness of Andrews and Asad. In the last half-century a small number of Europeans have embraced Buddhism, and have tried to interpret it to the West, but they have hardly succeeded in this as well as the American Episcopalian, the late J. B. Pratt, who about the year 1915 spent a considerable time in Buddhist monasteries talking to monks, and attended many services in Buddhist temples.

The first really scientific classifiers of religious phenomena appear on the Continent, the Frenchman, Benjamin Constant, and the German, Christoph Meiners of Göttingen. They are followed by an increasing band of other investigators, Dieterich and Hackmann, Chantepie de la Saussaye, Ratzel and Frobenius, Kuhn, and Max Müller, and in Britain Sir Edward Tylor, Andrew Lang, Sidney Hartland, and Sir James Frazer, with a long line of distinguished anthropologists and 'religiongeschichtliche' scholars on both sides of the North Sea, stretching right up to the present day. It is beyond the scope of this book to deal in detail with the work of this goodly company, or with the various conclusions at which some of them arrived, though brief references will have been found to them throughout its pages.

What matters for our main purpose is that their work stimulated a number of Christian theologians to devote themselves to a new revaluation of Christianity in the light of all this access of fresh information. It will therefore be my endeavour in the remainder of this chapter to select and describe the work of some of these theologians, and to see whether we can draw any serviceable conclusions from such a survey. In doing so I shall probably find myself leaving out those who have composed what are mainly text books on the subject, and I shall confine myself in a general way to those who have tried to construct what the French would call a *théorie générale*. I have only included a brief reference to Tillich because his work has already been so fully dealt with by Dr. Kraemer in his most recent book. Confining one's self to chronological order has, of course, a certain disadvantage, in that it does not necessarily bring out the most satisfying synthesis as the final term in the series, but, like an alphabetical series, it has on the other hand the merit of impartiality, while at the same time exhibiting a graph of European thought in its true sequence. But this section, to preserve its balance, must be prefaced by a few words on another weighty subject.

Besides what we may term the *external* theological revaluation, there has also proceeded, during the same period, though in spite of strenuous opposition, a corresponding *internal* revaluation. This was necessitated in the first instance partly by the application of scientific methods to the study of the text and contents of the canonical Christian scriptures, partly by a substantial extension of our knowledge of the history of those countries which formed the cradle of Hebraeo-Christian religion, and partly by a revolutionary re-casting of our views of the physical universe, including the human species, as the inevitable result of prolonged empirical research. This internal revaluation is still not yet complete, and indeed cannot be, so long as there remain problems in each of the three realms of study to be attacked, and regions in each still unexplored. It is impossible to do much more than to refer to it here, since to deal justly with it would need at least another volume of the size of the present one; but I have tried to give due weight to it throughout the whole of my work, and especially in Chapters II to VI.

Many zealous Christian evangelists have ignored this process of internal revaluation, and have continued to evangelise upon a comparatively naïve traditional basis; and it may well be that their work will in consequence be lacking in permanence and stability. They have won, and are undeniably still winning successes from among the great masses of mankind whose minds continue to function in a maze of pre-axial superstition; and the intense personal appeal of the historical Jesus makes itself felt, even through the medium of preachers and teachers who are themselves blinded to the fact that He does not Himself endorse everything that they teach in His Name. But Truth must prevail in the long run; and it certainly cannot be in the interests of honest religion to shut one's eyes and ears to what is going on in that world where the sincere intellectual study of life's phenomena is proceeding dispassionately.

Such reflections may stir to impatience those who seek a rapid conversion of the world to some sort of Christian belief, perhaps to an evangelisation in this generation. But is there real wisdom in such impatience? The Eternal, Self-Existent, and Living God has always eternity in which to build: He is in no hurry, and it cannot be His will that we should be either. Hence this internal theological revaluation should be gladly embraced and studied, and such study ought not to be fettered by the misuse of authority. It is quite clear that mistakes have been made and probably are still being made during the course of it,[1] partly through the tendency of some scholars to ignore the evidence which may be gained from the study

---

[1] Some will remember that the original survey of New Testament study produced by Dr. Schweitzer was entitled, *Von Reimarus zu Wrede*. We are now badly in need of someone to produce a second volume which might be entitled: 'Von Schweitzer zu Bultmann', and which would do justice not only to the work of scholars on the mainland of Europe but to that of British scholars like Burkitt, R. H. Lightfoot, T. F. Glasson, J. M. Creed, Vincent Taylor, and C. H. Dodd on the one hand, and of Hoskyns and the Barthians on the other; and even have something to say about Guignebert, and Bishop E. W. Barnes.

of Christian corporate experience and tradition as well as from individual experience. But freedom of thought must mean freedom to proceed by trial and error; and far too much may be made of the value of limiting the operations of the mind by the authority of an external governing body.

No doubt it saves a good deal of trouble and anguish to stop thinking in certain directions, and to be content to operate mentally within a certain well-defined sphere, and in some countries of the world there has been for centuries a tradition of this sort, so that even when a new theology is set up in them, it assumes the same kind of authority as the old, and imposes upon a not unwilling public the same type of intellectual restrictions. But this is not the way in which mankind can become mentally adult or mature, as one is sure God means it to do; and if Christian belief really contains a core of eternal truth, as I sincerely believe that it does, it cannot be ill-advised to slow down evangelisation in order that those who teach may have a deeper and more thorough intellectual training, the better to appreciate what that core is.

Nevertheless I am sure that to detach the study of documents from the wider study of the life of persons and communities is to cripple the former by isolating it from its context. It was for this very reason that some of the earlier revaluation went astray and will certainly have to be done over again.

And now let us come to our survey of the external revaluation, and let us begin with one who flourished during the first half of the nineteenth century, but whose work was somewhat overlooked until recent years, when it has again attracted attention.

(i) FREDERICK DENISON MAURICE

In the year 1691, Robert Boyle, in a codicil to his will, directed that eight sermons (or rather lectures) should be provided at his expense, to be delivered at stated intervals in a London church, 'proving the Christian Religion against notorious Infidels, to wit Atheists, Theists, Pagans, Jews, and Mohametans'. (It does not seem quite clear why he should have included 'Theists'. One may suppose perhaps that he was thinking of people such as Socinians and Unitarians who denied the divinity of Christ.)

The inspiration behind this bequest may conceivably have been that of Lord Herbert of Cherbury: but it is not without significance that it was drawn up only a few years earlier than the foundation in 1698 of the Society for the Promotion of Christian Knowledge, and in 1699 of the Society for the Propagation of the Gospel. It was in fact the period in the reign of Queen Anne when Christians, after the disastrous Civil War and the revolution in 1688, were reviving their religious life, showing anxiety about their responsibilities towards their non-Christian neighbours both at home and abroad, and becoming increasingly conscious of mission. Boyle himself, who lived from 1627 to 1691, was active in supporting work among the North American Indians. A society for the promotion of the gospel in New England had been first initiated in 1649 with the appeal of the Long Parliament. Boyle, in 1662, obtained from Charles II a charter incorporating this society, and later he obtained its extension to the East Indies. The work of Xavier in Asia had stimulated Christians belonging to other religious groups to emulate him, and Boyle insisted that when England acquired from the Portuguese the district of Bombay, something should be done, as he said: 'to bring to those countries some spiritual good things whence we so frequently bring back temporal ones' and in 1678 the foundation stone was laid of the Church of St. Mary at Madras.

During the next 150 years the Boyle lectures do not seem to have attracted much attention, and one does not find them referred to in the well-known English Church History of Hunt and Stephen; but in 1847 the post of lecturer was held by Frederick Denison Maurice, and it is he who may be said to have initiated a new kind of approach, and perhaps to have laid the foundations for a new study of the religions of the world, for he made use of the latest and most scholarly information available in his day, and brought to bear upon his subject the freshness and originality of his own mind.

We should probably today not adopt the same outline method as Maurice. He did not approach his task either historically or chronologically, but began with the one non-Christian religion which in his opinion was at the time exercising the most influence in the world, namely Islam. With some courage he declared that he saw in it a sign of the judgment of God upon base, unworthy, and degenerate forms of Christianity. Almighty God, he says, often raises up strange and unexpected instruments for working his will. (The words might have been spoken with regard to Marxists in our own day.) Maurice sees in Mohammed's proclamation certain positive contributions, namely:

(1) that if God exists, His will must indeed be the law of the universe,

(2) that the life of man is and must be a continual spiritual warfare against evil,

(3) that there are errors and evils in the world which it is not our duty to tolerate with complacency.

He turns no blind eye to the defects of Islam, which he sees as clearly as does Kraemer in our own day.   But he also sees in the Divine Permission for its uprising 'a Divine hand regulating outward circumstances and the wills of men'.   Such generosity of approach has not always been common.   But it seems clear that unless Christians can practise it, it will be difficult for them to gain the attention of Moslems, and persuade them to look steadily and objectively at their origins—a matter which as we have seen is vitally necessary.

Maurice passes on to discuss Hinduism and Buddhism.   It is obvious that he had not the information available regarding these which was at the disposal, let us say, of Sir Charles Eliot in 1921, when he composed his four great volumes (the final one posthumously published).   Maurice, nevertheless, made full use of what he had.   Some of his judgments, which, be it remembered, were delivered about ten years before the Indian Mutiny, may reflect the situation as it stood in his own day.   Thus when he says that although the 'priest' of Buddha is really an intelligent man, the mighty portion of the globe over which Buddhism presides is nearly the most ignorant, he is no doubt partly hampered by lack of intimate knowledge of the best that has been achieved in Buddhism, and partly by the fact that the nineteenth century was a time of decadence in Buddhist education in certain areas such as Burma; but partly also to the fact that he tended to look rather too fixedly, as indeed so many have done, at the curious alliance of Bön-Religion and Buddhism which characterises Tibet, and did not know apparently the great literature of the Buddhist philosophers and theologians. (Max Müller's series of translations had yet to be published, and the Pali Text Society had not yet been founded.)

It may, however, be said with some justice that Maurice was a pioneer in insisting upon the comparative study of religion by his own fellow Christians, and he meant it to comprise the *whole* of world religion, past as well as present, defunct as well as living. Thus he includes some discussion of Graeco-Roman religion.   His references to China and to Egypt are scrappy, and except for Iran he hardly discusses the Middle East, where archaeology had then scarcely begun its task; and since, like most of his contemporaries, he had had a classical education, he gives a good deal of space to the religious ideas of Greeks and Romans, although he refers briefly to the religion of the Teutons and of the Manichaeans.   In his sixth lecture he discusses sympathetically the doctrine of the Logos in relation to Hinduism, and in fact, although his treatment of all these topics is only too brief, it is quite clear that he, at this point, sketched the outline which those who succeeded him were bound to follow.

Some of his concluding remarks are still worth listening to. If, as he says, Englishmen were to abstain rigidly from all contacts with Asians, not even trading with them, then there might be some excuse for ignoring the operations of their minds, but if we are to communicate with them, and in doing so to recognise them as being spiritual creatures like ourselves, then it is clearly our duty to understand their point of view. It may seem surprising that this should still need to be said at the present day, and yet even within the last ten years one has heard the remark from an educated man that, being a Christian, he thought that the production of a book on Hinduism was really a waste of time.

Part of what Maurice says is worth quoting in full:

'A faith which boasts to be for humanity cannot test its strength unless it is content to deal with men in all possible conditions. If it limit itself to England, it will adapt itself to the habits and fashions and prejudices of England, and of England too in a particular age. But doing this, it never will reach the hearts of Englishmen. You say, "Try your Christianity upon the cotton-spinners of Manchester, upon the hardware men of Birmingham; if it fails with them, do you expect it will succeed in Persia and Thibet?" But we know it will fail, it must fail in Birmingham and Manchester, if it addresses the people in those places mainly as spinners and workers in hardware. This has just been the mistake we have made. We have looked upon these "hands" as created to work for us; we have asked for a religion which should keep the "hands" in the state in which they will do most work and give the least trouble. But it is found that they are *men* who use these hands; and that which is a religion for hands, is not one for men. Therefore it becomes more evident every day that there is a demand in Manchester and Birmingham for that which, till we understand human beings better, we cannot supply. To acquire that understanding we need not grudge a journey to Persia or Thibet; we need not think it an idle task to inquire what the people want, who are not called to spin cotton or work in hardware, but who are creatures of the same kind with those who do. When thoughtful men say that a working age of the world is about to begin, they mean I suppose an age in which those essential qualities of humanity which belong to working men as much as to all others, shall be more prized than the accidents by which one class is separated from another. Most important is it then to ascertain whether we are holding a faith which addresses us as members of a class, a class of fine gentlemen, philosophers, divines, or any other; or one which addresses us as men, which explains the problems of our human life.'

(ii) 'ESSAYS AND REVIEWS', 'LUX MUNDI', AND J. R. ILLINGWORTH

Essays and Reviews was the first of a number of collections of theological essays which have continued to be issued every few years since about 1860, by groups of scholars working together in harmony, on the problem of relating the Christian faith to contemporary thought. Compared with later composite volumes, it is a slight production, and comprises only seven essays, one of which was in the end withdrawn; whereas later collections contain more like twelve to twenty essays.[1] Moreover, it is in the main concerned with the first beginnings of internal rather than external theological revaluation.

There is, however, one essay, that by Frederick Temple, at that time Headmaster of Rugby and subsequently Bishop of Exeter and Archbishop of Canterbury, in which some attempt is made to deal in outline with the larger problem. Under the title 'The Education of the World' Temple describes what he sees as the periods of training through which the human race has passed, and indicates the contributions made successively by Israel, Greece, and Rome. Towards the end of this survey he comes to the consideration of Asia, but he does not seem to extend his gaze beyond the Middle East, referring in explicit terms only to Assyria, Babylonia, and Persia. He takes the conventional view that Asia sought and still seeks her inspiration in rest and contemplation, and he speaks of Athanasius as a thorough Asiatic, both in sentiment and in his mode of argument. He then continues:

'Western nations are always inclined to confine all doctrines within the limits of spiritual utility. Asia supplies the corrective to this by perpetually leaning to the mysterious. When left to herself she settles down to baseless dreams, and sometimes to monstrous and revolting fictions. But her influence has never ceased to be felt and could not be lost without serious damage. Thus the Hebrews may be said to have disciplined the will, Greece the reason and taste, Asia the spiritual imagination. Other races that have since been admitted into Christendom also did their parts, and others may yet have something to contribute; for though the time for discipline is childhood, yet there is no precise line beyond which all discipline ceases.'

That is as far as Temple goes, and in itself his conclusion is a good one; but he is quoted here at some length partly in order to show what an immense gap there now is between an extremely able liberal orthodox Anglican theologian of 1860 and one of any

[1] Readers may perhaps wonder why I have apparently left out of consideration the last two of these composite volumes, *Foundations* (1912) and *Essays Catholic and Critical* (1926). In the case of the former, the volume is entirely concerned with *internal* theological revaluation. In the case of the latter, it is only the first essay which matters, and this I have tried to deal with in so far as it is relevant, during the course of Chapter II. The argument developed in it which depends upon the genuineness of the Piltdown skull (now established as a forgery) cannot, of course, any more be held valid.

Foundations was followed by a number of similar volumes, mostly edited by the late Canon Streeter, and sometimes referred to as 'the Cumnor series' because they were the fruit of collective study by a group of friends held at a house in Cumnor; but these again were mostly concerned with internal theological revaluation, except for two essays by Miss Lily Dougall upon Theosophy, and the ideas of Karma and Reincarnation. With these I have tried to deal in a separate excursus.

23

denomination today, when dealing with the subject of comparative religion. This gap is due not to a widening of sympathy so much as to an extension of knowledge. The pages of Temple's essay contain remarkably little factual detail and not a single footnote quoting from the sacred books of the East. Between him and us now stands nearly a century of exploration, translation, and study of Oriental classics, and familiarity at first hand with those who profess non-Christian religious faiths.

Essays and Reviews ran through ten editions, aroused heated controversy mainly on account of its attitude towards biblical exegesis, and is today almost forgotten: but after an interval of nearly thirty years it was succeeded by another volume, issuing from an Anglo-Catholic group of scholars.

This volume, entitled *Lux Mundi*, first appeared in 1889, and went through fifteen editions. To some of the older Anglo-Catholics it came as rather a shock, and provoked in its way almost as much opposition as the earlier volume: but in the main it was welcomed, since those who wrote it did so as responsible scholars and clergy of the Church of England, three of whom, including the Editor, subsequently became Bishops of repute; and in a number of quarters it was hailed as a liberating publication.

To the Rev. J. R. Illingworth was allotted the fifth chapter, which dealt with the Incarnation and development. The second chapter on the Christian doctrine of God was by the Rev. Aubrey Moore. In both these essays there is an avowed acceptance of the doctrine of the Logos, but it is in Mr. Illingworth's essay that it is specially brought to bear upon the problem of the non-Christian religions. Of these there is no detailed account, but Illingworth recognises that their comparative study, though still young, has already reached some general results, and of these he enumerates three. First that the universality of religion has been established as an empirical fact. 'The notion that religion was an invention of interested priestcraft has vanished, like many other eighteenth-century fictions, before nineteenth-century science. Even in those races where priestcraft is most conspicuous, the priest has never created the religion, but always the religion the priest.' Secondly, although there is a progressive tendency observable in the religions of the world, none of it happens by the improvements of a committee, but only by more or less insensible modifications. These are generally the work of reformers, and are counteracted by degeneracy; for individuals elevate, but the masses degrade religion. Hence from the golden age of religious creativity, the torch is handed on from one great teacher to another, while in the interval it is often degraded or vulgarised. Thirdly, the nature of this progress involves the consequence that all the pre-Christian religions have been partial, and have emphasised unduly if not exclusively one requirement or another of the religious consciousness, but never its complex whole. However great the individual teacher, he cannot proclaim with prophetic intensity more than one aspect of a truth; and his followers invariably tend to isolate and exaggerate this aspect, while any who attempt to supply its complement are regarded with suspicion. Hence the sects and heresies of which religious history is full. Nevertheless from the day of man's first appearance in the dim twilight of the world, God has not left Himself without a witness. In short, the history of pre-Christian religion is like that of pre-Christian philosophy, a long preparation for the Gospel. The principles of religious development laid down in the Epistle to the Hebrews admit of no limitation to any single race of men. In a writing addressed to Hebrews it is most natural that they should be illustrated from Hebrew history; but their scope is universal. They compel their own application to every religious history which the growth of our knowledge brings to light, and from this point of view the many pagan adumbrations of Christian doctrine, similarities of practice, coincidences of ritual, and analogies of phrase and symbol, fall naturally into place. Illingworth sums it all up with the words: 'The pre-Christian religions were the age-long prayer. The Incarnation was the answer.'

That was the situation as Illingworth saw it in 1889. Of course it is easy to put forward the criticism that he, like Westcott some years later, in speaking of 'pre-Christian religions', ignored the obvious fact that Islam is *post-Christian* and not pre-Christian, and that therefore some modification of the theory, such as that which makes Islam into a Christian heresy, is needed, if it is to be fitted in. What, however, is of importance for our purpose is that these distinguished and scholarly Anglicans declared their allegiance to the view of religion in general which is to be found in the Greek Fathers. Elsewhere in Illingworth's essay we find the assertion that all great teachers of whatever kind are vehicles of revelation, each in his proper sphere, and that therefore we may consistently accept their verified conclusions as divinely true, though the moment they transgress their limits, they are deprived of the Divine Assistance which was the secret of their previous success, so that in this case their conclusions are to be rejected. He adds that the Divine Reason assists but does not supersede the human. Many earnest and successful thinkers have been and are if not atheistic, at least agnostic; but the difficulty raised by this fact is only superficial. The method,

education, and experience involved in different studies are so distinct
that few in a single lifetime can reach the eminence and intelligence
which is able thoroughly to appreciate more than one department of
the complex world of thought. It is encouraging to find that
Illingworth pursues the Logos doctrine beyond the time of the Greek
Fathers through Athanasius to the Schoolmen of the Middle Ages,
quoting the following passages from St. Thomas Aquinas:

'As the thought of the Divine mind is called the Word, Who is the
Son, so the unfolding of that thought *per opera exteriora* is named
the word of the Word.'
'The created intellect is the imparted likeness of God, and every intellectual process has its origin in the Word of God who is the Divine
Reason.'
'Christ is our internal teacher, and no truth of any kind is known but
through Him; though He speaks not in language as we do, but by
interior illumination.'
'The philosophers have taught us the sciences, for God revealed them
to them.'

Illingworth adds:

'With pantheism, materialism, rationalism surging all around them,
the Schoolmen, perfectly conscious of the fact, met these errors, not
by denying the reality of matter or the capacity of reason, as later
apologists have often done, but by claiming for both a place in the
theology of the Word. And this theology was . . . an inheritance from
the patristic tradition which the Fathers in their turn had not invented
but received as apostolic doctrine, and had only made more explicit
by gradual definition during centuries when, as it has been fairly said
by Mark Pattison: "The highest reason, as independently exercised
by the wise of the world, was entirely coincident with the highest
reason as inspiring the Church."'

This last brief quotation from one of the contributors to *Essays
and Reviews* may have added to the alarm which was felt by such men
as Liddon at the appearance of *Lux Mundi*, but it does not appear
that the work for that reason received any public condemnation.
No doubt it avoided some of the features which rendered the former
volume obnoxious, and its obvious determination to show that the
views set forth in it were those either expressed or implied in the
writings of the early Fathers, as being fair and reverent deductions
from Scripture, safeguarded it from attacks. Whereas in *Essays
and Reviews* the treatment accorded to the early chapters of Genesis
sometimes jarred upon the minds of devout Christians, the writers of
Lux Mundi much eased the situation by pointing out that both St.
Athanasius, Clement of Alexandria, and St. Anselm had treated the
stories of the Creation and of Adam and Eve in Paradise as allegorical
and figurative. It seems clear from a quotation in a medieval Greek
writer, referred to by Bishop Gore in the eighth essay of the volume,

that the same freedom was claimed by Irenaeus, in a work no longer extant.

We see the effect of the spirit of these essays in the general attitude of Anglo-Catholics of subsequent generations upon the matter of the Logos doctrine, and it is clearly to be observed in the volume *Essays Catholic and Missionary* to which reference is made elsewhere.

(iii) BROOKE FOSS WESTCOTT

It is sometimes thought that there was no serious attempt on the part of any British theologians, other than Maurice, the contributors to *Essays and Reviews*, and *Lux Mundi* to deal with the problem of non-Christian religions, but this is not the case, for in the last decade of the nineteenth century a quite serious and even more systematic attempt was made by the famous Bishop Westcott of Durham to write a fresh introduction to the study of Christian Doctrine, based upon a proper recognition of the non-Christian religious systems of Asia. The work came out in 1892, had a second edition three years later, and was thought important enough for its publishers to re-issue it in a cheap 6d. edition in 1906. As, however, Westcott's work, which he entitled *The Gospel of Life*, does not seem to be very well known today, it is only right and just to give some account of it here, especially since it is not a mere journalistic effort, but was composed with the precision and systematic method which are so characteristic of Westcott's scholarship. Moreover, it does not belong to any particular school of thought, either Catholic or Evangelical, but proceeds from Westcott's own individual study of the problem, based upon his immense learning. Westcott of course had carried the study of the New Testament a good deal further than any of his contemporaries, though many of the more recent conclusions of scholarship were not known to him, but there is a certain breadth and open-mindedness about his work which recalls to us that he and his colleague, F. J. A. Hort, were contemporaries of Charles Darwin, and that Hort was on very friendly terms with the latter, and wrote appreciatively of his work. This can hardly have been unknown to Westcott, for in his treatment in Chapter Six of his work of the early stories of Genesis, though he writes with caution, it is quite clear that he treats them as a revelation of spiritual mysteries and not as a realistic narrative.

Let us then see how Westcott deals with the subject of religion in general. He begins by reminding us that the Christian religion, of which Christian doctrine is the intellectual expression, is, like every other religion, an attempt to answer questions which are suggested by human life itself. It does not introduce fresh mysteries into the world: it meets mysteries which already exist. They are the material on which it has to work, and they are an essential part of everyone's consciousness. Everyone, he says, is conscious of what he chooses to call 'self', of the external world, and of that which is Self-Existent and Eternal. The consciousness of these three given elements underlies in some degree all human thought: it may be and in many cases is imperfectly defined, but it belongs to the nature of man. Each of these elements, or if we like categories, admits of a good deal of analysis, and again such analysis is inescapable. We cannot refuse to consider it except at the cost of abdicating our loftiest privileges. The Christian religion does not create this analysis, for it can be and has been engaged in by many who are not Christians. In dealing with the category of the external world Wescott's essay is somewhat dated, for he cannot go beyond the work of his contemporaries, of whom Professor J. Clerk Maxwell, at one time a colleague of his at Trinity College, Cambridge, is the physicist on whose work he chiefly depends: but the fact remains that he does attempt to keep pace with the scientific findings of his day, and if he had lived at the present time he would no doubt have made use of the work of modern physicists and astronomers, such as Eddington, Thomson, and Rutherford, and Hoyle and Lyttelton. He then goes on to stress the duty and necessity of seeking a solution to the problems which arise from a contemplation of the data of consciousness. What is the self? What are its status and prospects? Can we learn anything of the meaning and purpose of the external world from a detailed study of its structure? What can we justly say about the nature of the Self-Existent Being and of our relation to it? These questions are unavoidable. As Plato has said, the unexamined life is not really livable. Under what condition are we to seek for a solution of these problems? Clearly it will not do to investigate only the nature of the self, to turn inward and study only what appears to be the nature of mind, the process by which it works and the principles of a theory of knowledge: we are compelled also to look continuously without, to study by scientific method the world of inorganic matter, far and near, and the manifold pageant of living organisms. And then when we come to man we have to consider history. The conditions therefore under which we seek for the solution of our problems are those in which we investigate and accumulate truth, psychological, mathematical, physical, and historical.

This is not at all the kind of approach that we usually encounter when we read the doctrinal treatises of continental theologians. It is not for example at all the kind of thing with which Karl Barth opens the pages of his monumental *Dogmatik*, and it does not appear in Kraemer, though he may have a few covert references to it.[1]

Having established himself on this basis, Westcott then goes on to maintain that in the contemplation of the Self-Existent there is room for another type of truth, another method of enquiry, and another kind of certainty. This type, he says, is not unscientific, but is simply a new science, a positive science of theology, which like the other sciences must have its own appropriate facts. How can we obtain these facts? How can we be sure that they are facts? And how can we use them as the basis of further deductions and generalisations? Westcott's answer is threefold. First, he says, we must recognise that although all scientific method proceeds from observation to classification and generalisation, each branch of scientific study is distinct, so that although there may be a marvellous harmony between the different parts of the universe, it is not necessarily possible to pass directly from one science to another. Secondly, the investigation in any one particular department proceeds by abstraction, and we cannot expect this abstraction to yield principles which apply outside the sphere of the abstraction. Thirdly, the methods employed in introspection are bound to be different from those employed in the study of the external world. I am not quite sure that we could pass the latter statement of Westcott's without challenge. The modern worker in the psychological laboratory would say that he was using delicate machinery to measure items in human mental behaviour just as the physicist and the chemist might be using machines to take readings of physical and chemical phenomena. But it is quite clear what Westcott means. He means to imply that in the scientific study of knowledge of the Self-Existent Being we cannot proceed by the same methods as if we were analysing the behaviour of an electrical technician, or splitting up a chemical compound into its component parts, and studying their properties and reactions in the presence of other elements.

Westcott continues with the postulate that if there is a Self-Existent Being, there must be some kind of communication between that Being and us who observe Him. Such communication is what is commonly called Revelation, and the study of it will involve enquiry into the veracity of those who claim to receive it; but the

[1] Nurtured upon this kind of approach from my youth up, I can remember finding myself in an unfamiliar atmosphere when lecturing in 1935 at a theological Seminar held in the University of Geneva, where I had to follow in the wake of Barth, and was told by the chairman: 'You Anglicans are so empirical in your approach.' Anyhow, it *is* our tradition, and one can see that it is our association in university life with those who are engaged in scientific investigation which makes us differ from those who appear to be much more shut up inside their own theological faculties.

proof of Revelation is primarily personal, and springs from a realised fellowship with the unseen. Thus the truths of theology must be investigated mainly along the lines of historical science, in which we first ascertain by a study of records what has really been said, and then go on to consider the credibility of what has been recorded. It is plain that this kind of treatment of theology was suggested to Westcott most naturally by the scientific study of history which was developing in Cambridge at the time when he was Regius Professor of Divinity, and a Fellow of Trinity College. I am not prepared to say that Westcott's description of the relation of theology to the sciences was completely satisfactory, but it is clear that his aim was to keep theology on a sober and well defined path, and to show that as long as it kept to this path it could claim to be a respectable colleague of the other sciences, though he himself asserted boldly that it was the crown of all of them, and that religion was their synthesis. 'True theologians', he concludes, 'will strive to guard themselves alike against the temptation to refuse to other sciences the fullest scope as far as they reach. . . . They will not withdraw one document which helps to define their faith from the operation of any established law of criticism.'

Having then laid this foundation, Westcott goes on to consider what he calls the work of the 'prae-Christian' nations towards the solution of the problems of life and being, and it is here that he boldly engages in an exposition of what he sees to be the main features of religion in India, China, Iran, and the Buddhist world. I do not think that any theologian in England had attempted this kind of treatment before on the same scale, not even Maurice. This is not to say that our knowledge of the facts and details of these religious systems has not been immensely increased since Westcott wrote. But the point is that he, as a Christian Bishop, with his immense interest in the missionary work of the church, with his profound respect for the great literature and philosophic thought of Hinduism, openly declared that it was right and proper as a preliminary discipline to study the 'prae-Christian' religions and to see what lessons could be learned from them.[1] No one would wish to pretend that what he said here was final, though as one reads one is conscious of the way in which his penetrating intelligence grasped the essential features of each, and he gives us a good object-lesson

[1] He had been foremost in securing the establishment of a Christian college for higher education of men in the city of Delhi, for the purpose of bridging the gulf between the best theological thought in Britain and the best thought in India; and he was heard to say on one occasion that we should never have a proper understanding of the Fourth Gospel until we had had a commentary written upon it by a Brahmin convert to Christianity.

in setting over against one another, for example, the confession attributed to Lao-tzu about the nature of the great immanent power of the Tao, and the Vedic hymn to Varuna, remarking that we feel the partial truth in both, though perhaps we feel the partial truths more keenly when they are presented to us separately.

The basis and justification for this treatment is to be seen in the middle of Chapter Four of his essay, where he takes his stand firmly on the same side as Justin Martyr and Clement of Alexandria.

Having then sought to do justice to what he conceives to be the work of the Divine Logos in the minds of great pre-Christian teachers, Westcott moves on to a consideration of the specifically Christian claim to have solved finally and absolutely the problems set out at the beginning of the essay. First, there are the assumptions and presuppositions which Christianity makes. It assumes that the world was made by God, that man was made in the image of God, and that man by self-assertion has broken his rightfulconnection with God. From these three assumptions it follows that the world is for the Christian in all its parts an expression of the will of God (he means, of course, sin only except). This is the charter of a true Christian humanism. Secondly, it follows that man is capable of fellowship with God; and thirdly it follows that man needs the grace of God for the fulfilment of his destiny in the sense that he needs not only further growth but restoration. It will be clear from this statement of the Christian position that Westcott, for all his tenderness towards the non-Christian faiths, is fundamentally orthodox in his doctrine of man. Indeed, when he speaks about the completeness of the potential communion between man and God as marred by sin, there is little difference between him and Kraemer. Westcott goes through the mythical story of the fall of man in Genesis III, and declares that no criticism can rob it of its sublime majesty and pathos.

In his seventh chapter Westcott faces the problem created by the miracles in the New Testament and pre-eminently in the gospels. Here again, while he is essentially conservative, he is clear that to many of his day stories of miracles are an embarrassment. He appears to assume that a supreme revelation will be accompanied by physical signs which are important not so much in themselves as in what they are calculated to indicate. Such signs suggest the idea of the action of a personal spiritual Power, but while they suggest it they cannot in any intelligible sense be employed to prove the existence of that Power. Yet as acts of that Power they will be essentially creative, though they will always be in accordance with the moral government of the universe by that power. Westcott appears to refer only very briefly to Christ's reluctance to give 'signs' when he is asked, or, when he is tempted, to yield to the suggestion that he should compel belief by a supernatural descent through the air into the temple courts. He does indeed say that it is wrong to speak of miracles as being in a primary sense proofs of a revelation, or of Christianity in particular, since no such claim is actually made for them in the New Testament. On the contrary he declares that the external testimony of facts is distinctly subordinated to the testimony of words. But he is obviously anxious to avoid wounding the feelings of those who adhere to the old way of regarding miracles, and he seems to waver between two ways of approaching them, for while avoiding the actual use of the word 'proof', he says, in the last paragraph but one, that they are in the gospels in fact a revelation of the Person of Christ, and set vividly before the believers through whom they were wrought a personal relation of God to themselves. It is fairly clear, however, that Westcott had comparatively little realisation of the difficulties which many devout scientists have felt over these strange stories, and he does not seem to notice the statement of St. Augustine the Great which has been noticed elsewhere, and in which the latter says that a miracle is not something contrary to nature, but only to what is known by us of nature.

In his next chapter Westcott states the two signal characteristics of Christianity as being absolute and historical. It cannot be said that he deals in any fullness with the former, since he only states it as a claim which is presented from the first. On the other hand he proceeds in his ninth chapter to lay great stress upon the historicity of the gospel story, and indeed on the foundation of the Christian faith in its antecedents as essentially historical. It grows out of a belief that the Living God is Lord of History, while Christian belief is neither in a code of laws, nor in a structure of institutions, nor in a system of opinions, but in the life of a Living Person with whom we ourselves can live in fellowship. Whatever legendary and mythical elements may have come to be attached to it, it is in essence completely free from myth and legend, so much so that it would be possible to recount the events in it with such boldness as to make it a neutral account of something entirely humanistic. Thus belief in their orthodox interpretation is not compelled: but follows only from an experimental act of faith. It is true that Westcott does not put it in this way. He himself would probably have regarded some of the events as in themselves, apart from the interpretation put upon them by the experiment of faith, overwhelming evidence as to the nature of the Person with whom they are concerned. But in this he was probably taking the same line as most of his contemporaries, and he would not have approved of the statements which are so often to be found in works dealing with the theology of the New Testament.

Westcott finally declares that the proferred Christian solution of the problems of life finds its verification in the twin testimonies of history and experience. Both, he says, are needed for complete assurance, and when the voice of society expressed in history and the voice of the soul agree, we have the highest conceivable assurance of the truth of their message. We may wish that the Bishop had gone further in justifying some of his statements, and in giving full weight to the difficulties which some must undoubtedly have been feeling in his own lifetime; but however much we may regret the limitations of his work, he undoubtedly stands out as a pioneer in the broader treatment of the religion of mankind as something which must be studied as a whole, and not by having nine-tenths of it excluded from consideration. At the end of his book he makes one statement which later generations have hesitated to endorse exactly in the form in which he expressed it. 'If', he says, 'it could be shown that there is one least truth in things for which the Gospel finds no place; if it could be shown that there is one fragment of human experience with which it does not deal: then, with whatever pathetic regret it might be, we should confess that we can conceive something beyond it: that we still look for another. But I can see no such limitation, no such failure in the Gospel itself, whatever limitations and failures there may have been and may be still in man's interpretation of it.' Professor J. M. Creed in his Hulsean lectures ventures to suggest that within the limits prescribed for it by Divine Providence, the Christian revelation may well be absolute, but that there may be other spheres of experience of a different nature within which there may be room for other absolute truths. (The foregoing is actually a paraphrase of what Creed says, but it gives the substance of his meaning.) Somewhat the same conclusion is arrived at by Dr. E. C. Dewick in his Hulsean lectures, where from long experience in Asia, he too draws the conclusion that there may be enunciated in the deliverances of non-Christian teachers truths which are as valid in their way as the truths of the Christian Gospel, although they may not find actual expression in the pages of the New Testament or in the acknowledged experiences of famous Christian teachers. It would seem then that further study of the non-Christian religions has led in some quarters to a modification of the rather uncompromising assertion of Westcott.

I have devoted some considerable space to the consideration of the Bishop's work, because the study of it seems to me to show the great development which has taken place in the expansion of

Christian thought on this august subject. Westcott himself stands on the borderline. In one sense he belongs to and speaks the language of the older Victorians, such as H. P. Liddon, and J. B. Mozley. On the other he stretches out to meet the modernists of the twentieth century.

(iv) ERNST TROELTSCH

Troeltsch was the son of a Bavarian doctor and was born in 1865. He studied theology, mainly under the influence of Ritschl, and served after ordination for a time at a Church in Munich. After that he returned to academic work, and was at Göttingen, Bonn, Heidelberg (for 21 years), and finally Berlin, where he remained as Professor of Philosophy till his death in 1926. He was an immensely learned man, and his book, *The Social Doctrines of the Christian Churches and Groups* (1912) not only displays his intense interest in the social implications of Christianity, but will remain for many years a standard work on the subject. It is, however, with his smaller work on the *Absolute Validity of Christianity*, published in 1909, which in the year 1921 I had the privilege of translating, that we are here concerned. That he did not succeed in establishing his thesis in no way detracts from the importance of his essay, since it may be said that if absolute validity cannot be established by his argument, the attempt to do so along these lines cannot be carried any further. Kraemer indeed considers that Troeltsch in fact lands himself in a cul-de-sac. He was somewhat doubtful about the validity of stressing the historical element in Christianity, since history, he says, is concerned not with the abstract and universal but with the concrete and relative, with that which happens only once; and Christianity is a product of history. It may therefore be difficult to construe the absoluteness of Christianity within the realm of historical thinking. This in itself provoked rejoinders, especially from two Anglicans, William Temple and F. C. Burkitt. The former published his thesis in the form of a small book called *The Universality of Christ*, while the latter published an essay with the clause in the Apostles' Creed 'Under Pontius Pilate' for its text. Burkitt, of course, was not a philosopher but a New Testament critic, but Temple remained a philosopher to the end. Both, however, insisted upon the reality of time, and upon the credibility that Deity might discontinuously act within the spatio-temporal order if it were His Will to do so; and that the essential difference between Christianity and Asian pantheism lay in its acceptance of the significance of historical sequence. Troeltsch does not seem to have gone as far as this. Paying very little attention to the more primitive religions, he divided the higher ones into two groups, the prophetic-personalist and the pantheistic-monist. We must, he concluded, decide in favour of the first group, because it would never do to abandon personalism. But within this group, as he held, Christianity was the highest, because it was the strongest and most concentrated revelation of personalistic religion. He therefore claimed that it was not only the goal of convergence in an evolutionary process of religious development, but the point of culmination. But here, as a Christian, he landed himself in a difficulty. His work as a scientific historian led him to add that one could only say: 'Christianity is the point of culmination up till now' (bis jetzt), and he went on to say that the conviction that it would *always* be the culmination point could not be demonstrated, but must be a confession of faith. Further, his preference for personalist religion, as Kraemer has since pointed out, could quite easily be answered by a Hindu or a Buddhist with the assertion: '*We* prefer the impersonalistic systems of Asia, and *we* are just as much entitled to regard *them* as leading to a point of culmination in the religious development of humanity.' It is curious that Kraemer omits mention of the fact that towards the end of his life Troeltsch accepted an invitation to come over and lecture in England, and prepared a paper to be delivered in 1923 in the University of Oxford. He died before he could deliver it, and it is possible that Dr. Kraemer has never seen it and may not know of its existence; but in this paper, which was translated in England, and carefully revised by Professor C. C. J. Webb and Troeltsch's great personal friend Baron Friedrich von Hügel, the author develops a theory which he had hinted at some years earlier, namely that of polymorphous truth, to wit that a religion in the several forms assumed by it, always depends upon the intellectual, social, and national conditions among which it exists, while his further study of non-Christian religions convinced him more and more that their naïve claims to absolute validity were also genuinely such. He says that he found Buddhism and Hinduism to be at their best really humane and spiritual religions, capable of appealing in precisely the same way as Christianity to the inner certitude and devotion of their followers; and he did not see that it was possible to rule out the idea that other racial groups than those of the West, living under entirely different cultural conditions, might experience their contact with the Divine Life in quite a different way, and might themselves also possess a religion which has grown up with them, and from which they cannot sever themselves so long as they remain what they are. The extreme honesty of this statement cannot but command respect, but of course Troeltsch himself recognised that if accepted it was bound to have a profound and revolutionary influence upon the question of Christian missions. He saw that Christianity 'is at a critical moment of its further development, and that very bold and far-reaching changes are necessary, transcending anything that has yet been achieved by any denomination'. Troeltsch concludes:

'so far as human eye can penetrate into the future, it would seem probable that the great revelatiors to the various civilisations will remain distinct, in spite of a little shifting of their several territories at the fringes, and that the question of their several relative values will never be capable of objective determination, since every proof thereof will presuppose the special characteristics of the civilisation in which it arises. The conception of personality itself is, for instance, different in the east and in the west; hence arguments starting from it will lead to different conclusions in the two cases. Yet there is no other concept which could furnish a basis for argument concerning practical values and truths save this concept of personality, which is always itself already one of the fundamental positions of the several religions, and is determined by them according to these respective general attitudes of theirs.
This is what I wish to say in modification of my former theories. I hope you feel that I am not speaking in any spirit of scepticism or uncertainty. A truth which, in the first instance, is *a truth for us*, does not cease, because of this, to be very Truth and Life.'

Troeltsch died soon after composing this lecture, and I doubt whether he ever delivered it in person anywhere. During his lifetime, as Kraemer reminds us, his thesis became the centre of a dramatic battle between theologians. A Dutchman once described it as a piece of disguised theology, because the author began by taking the superiority of Christianity to be self-evident, while at the same time trying to prove it. It will be seen, however, that this attempt broke down even within his own lifetime. Ten years after his first book he wrote an article for the *Review* known as 'Logos', in which he showed that he was moving further away from his earlier position. 'It is conceivable', he wrote, 'that the whole European Christian civilisation might submerge, and that new and mighty religious creations might arise (elsewhere) in some future hundred thousand years. In that case Jesus would remain the religious centre of the European Christian world. . . .' His close friendship with von Hügel led him to a greater appreciation of the Roman point of view than is often the case among Lutherans, and he is especially tender to the conception of a supernatural ethic, one which is not bred of nature but leads out beyond nature.

(v) RUDOLF OTTO

In the year before the end of the first World War there appeared in Germany a work *Das Heilige*, composed by one of the Professors of Theology in the University of Marburg, which had a most unusual career. In six years it passed through ten German editions, as well as a number of translations, and in the year 1931 the author, though seriously ill, was still the centre of attraction for numbers of foreign students visiting his University. Otto was not only a Christian theologian but an expert student of the religious literature of ancient India, which he was able to read in the original. One of his later works was a critical edition of the Gita, and he is also noted for his comparative study of the teachings of Sankara and Meister Eckhart. His main work (*Das Heilige*) is in consequence an essay which makes use of material drawn from Asia as well as Europe, though not I think from Africa, and its scheme was the elucidation of what Otto called *das numinöse*, or as one might say in English 'the awesome holy'. This concept according to Otto is, like Professor Moore's concept of 'the good', an *a priori* object of consciousness which is basic and final, and incapable of being analysed into anything else without remainder. He gives examples of this concept from a wide field, and shows that whereas in its crudest form it is simply the uncanny, or the spookish, as religion develops into its highest and more refined forms it comes to represent the incomprehensibility of Deity, the majestic holiness of Deity, and the righteous indignation of Deity. Otto gives examples of this kind of consciousness from the sermons of St. John Chrysostom and the writings of Luther, and he calls the recognition of the numinous, 'divination', tracing it from its simpler forms until he reaches the Biblical prophets, who, he says, correspond in the sphere of religion to creative artists in the sphere of art. The prophet is full of the Spirit which enables him not only to hear the voice within, but to recognise whence it comes, and to give utterance to its message. But beyond the prophet there is an even higher stage, that of one:

'in Whom is found the Spirit in all its plenitude, and Who at the same time in His person and in His performance is become most completely the object of divination, in Whom Holiness is recognised as apparent. Such a one is more than a prophet. He is the Son.'

Otto, as Kraemer recognises, is a thinker of a very different order from Troeltsch. Although he approaches his subject from the standpoint of the scientific study of religion, and although he has a profound knowledge of Hindu religious thought and piety, nevertheless he does not come to adopt the polymorphous theory about religious truth. He is fully aware that in the history of religion many parallels and convergences appear, but at the same time he never loses the conviction that there is something about the Christian faith fundamentally different in it from that which one finds for example in the Hindu *bhakti* or the most ardent devotion of any Moslem. He has his own way of classifying religious phenomena, and he ventures to call the whole of what so very largely occupied the attention of Sir James Frazer in all his works 'pre-religion', which develops from a groundwork of strangely confused spiritual states and ideas recurring with strange similarity and regularity amongst all the peoples who are living in what we have called elsewhere the pre-axial state of existence. Otto does not here give quite as much weight as he ought to the probability that much of this similarity and regularity is due to diffusion, so that he makes what he calls 'this disconcerting similarity' point to a uniform and constant function of human psychology as the underlying determining factor. But this will hardly do. The magical use of cave-paintings by the Australian aborigines of the centre and the north can hardly be satisfactorily explained as a purely independent invention, but is better understood as a practice brought into Australia by prehistoric tribes who came in thither when Australia was joined on to Asia by a land bridge, and wherever the practice originally diffused, the similarity of usage, as well as some of the objects depicted, make it impossible not to draw the conclusion that the rock paintings of India and of various parts of Africa as well as those of France and the Pyrenean region[1] have all of them diffused from some centre.

Otto was I think the first to recognise the more or less concurrent emergence of the higher religions in the axial age, and he is perhaps the first explicitly to recognise the resemblance between the Tao of Lao Tzu and the *Logos* of Heracleitus. He also notes the parallels in what he calls Saviour-Mysticism, though here again it is difficult not to suspect that the coincidence between the emotional Saviour-Pietism of India and the catholic emotional Pietism of the West must be due to some common cause. Nevertheless Otto is quite clear that there is a substantial difference between Indian *bhakti* and Christian devotion. He quotes the experience of *bhaktas* (devotees) who have become Christians, and who say that they seem to have entered quite a different world; and he explains this as being due to the fact that India has not the same sense of the seriousness of sin as that occurring in Christianity. It is possible that this conclusion also may need some modification. If the contrast is between a Saivite devotee and an evangelical Christian (especially one with a Lutheran background), then no doubt it will be true, but it is doubtful whether the contrast is so much marked between a Hindu *bhakta*

[1] If the cave-paintings in an island off the coast of Sicily, found in 1955, be genuine ones, we must now add: 'the Mediterranean region'.

and a Roman Catholic convert, not because the latter is deficient in a doctrine of sin, but because the doctrine is different as between Catholicism and Lutheranism, being in the former case a fall from supernature into nature, in the latter a fall from a state of grace into a state of sin. But in any case the difference exists, and is due to the Christian belief on the one hand in a morally holy God, who is contrasted with creaturely imperfection; whereas, on the other hand, with the Indian, Absolute Deity is beyond good and evil. Even where Otto sees immense similarities between Sankara and Eckhart, he also sees considerable divergences, due probably to the fact that Eckhart is thinking of the Christian God and Sankara of the Absolute of Hinduism. But even here one could go further than Otto, since in spite of the fact that some of Eckhart's utterances verge dangerously near to pantheism, in other places Eckhart leaves the identity-rapture of the mystic for the Hebraic consciousness of the Divine Transcendence, and says that even at the peak of ecstasy God stays God and soul stays soul.

Nevertheless, although Kraemer shows greater sympathy with Otto than with any other members of this school of thought, he sees what it is difficult to deny, that Otto still stands within the sphere of the science of religion, so that however much he may detect and describe the differences between the Christian and non-Christian faiths, he cannot establish the uniqueness of Christianity from within the range of operation of that school. This is seen most clearly in the final sentence with which *Das Heilige* concludes. Although the Son appears as the highest category in the unfolding of the numinous, it is not shown why there should be only *one* Son.

(vi) JAMES MAURICE WILSON AND FREDERICK TENNANT

In 1905 a series of essays on some theological questions of the day was issued by members of the University of Cambridge under the editorship of the Regius professor of Divinity, Dr. Henry Barclay Swete. One does not hear much today about this volume, possibly because some of the essays, especially those dealing with the Bible, are rather marked with a date. The essay by Dr. Duckworth on 'Man's Origin and his Place in Nature' has been mentioned in an earlier chapter. But there is one other essay, contributed by Canon J. M. Wilson of Worcester, which deserves not to be forgotten, since although it may not possess complete finality, it presents a theory about revelation which in this volume we cannot afford to disregard. The spirit of modern science and philosophy, says Dr. Wilson, has compelled us to regard the universe as a continuous, purposeful, reasoned whole, evolving under conditions of unbroken law. In

24

this continuous whole, from hidden sources of life within, which we call Divine, mysterious and ordered movements spring out, progressing towards some remote end. Revelation, from this point of view, is regarded as the growth or evolution of the Divine Life, and of the knowledge of its own nature, in the human race. The earth has been slowly turning to the sun. On the other hand we can think, and perhaps indeed we must think of the universe and Divine personality, as of two things apart, objective to each other. From this standpoint revelation is to be regarded as the history of God's successive gifts in self-disclosure to man whom He created, this revelation reaching its climax, if not its completion, in the manifestation of God in Christ. In other words, the sun has been slowly rising on the earth. Wilson sees that these two ideas of revelation, though they have much in common, are clearly distinguishable, and at the time he wrote, the former idea seemed to be taking the place of the latter. One can certainly think of a number of statements issuing at various times during the past one hundred years from Cambridge scholars, which seem to imply that during that period the second view was gradually coming into favour. Charles Darwin wrote in one of his letters that he did not think there had ever been any revelation in the old-fashioned sense, although he would not exclude the possibility that by discovery, within the bounds of the Divine Providence, much might be known about the ways of the Supreme Being (I paraphrase his words). Professor Gwatkin began his Gifford lectures (for the year 1904–5) with the words 'All knowledge is in some sense revelation'. Dr. Tennant in the second volume of his massive work on philosophical theology defines revelation as: 'God causing Himself to be understood', and compares the growth in Divine knowledge to the unveiling of a previously veiled statue, or the unfolding of a landscape which was already there, by the act of climbing a mountain. Neither Wilson nor any of these other writers, introduces or recognises the concept of the Divine Initiative, wherein the self-disclosure of God is achieved not merely by His *exposing* Himself to the contemplation of human reason, but by revelatory and redemptive *action* within the course of historical events. Wilson in another essay invites us to get over the difficulty of the conflict which appears to exist between the old idea of revelation and our growing conviction of continuity and progress, by assuming that revelation and discovery are two aspects of something that is going on to a varying extent all the time. Looked at in this way, the element of discovery and the element of revelation are present throughout in man's 'getting to know'. Wilson would have been the last person to doubt or deny the supreme act of divine self-disclosure in the historical Jesus, but he would still say that without an equal element of receptiveness that self-disclosure would have been barren of results. God in causing Himself to be understood plainly cannot, without doing violence to His own purpose, over-ride human free-will. As in the Fourth Gospel we read of 'as many as received him', which implies that there were also many who did not, so in the total self-disclosure of Deity, in the works of creative evolution as much as in the events of history, 'only he sees who takes off his shoes'. Discovery and revelation are thus the *obverse* and the *reverse* of the same entity. Wilson in fact, in his second essay, actually used the metaphor of the coin to illustrate this.

Of course, objections were raised to this theory, partly on the ground that it seemed to make revelation entirely subjective, and partly that it seemed to pave the way for a levelling down or levelling up which would put all religious experience, Christian and non-Christian, on the same level. But Wilson was ready to reply that a subjective view of revelation did not destroy certitude, but only substituted for what must seem like the over-riding of human free-will, the acceptance of the claim for humanity expressed in the epistle to the Ephesians as being 'Filled with all the fullness of God . . . according to the power that worketh in us' He implies, and no doubt would have been ready to admit if challenged, that there are degrees of revelation, as well as of discovery, and that it is possible that the proportion between the two varies in different cases, so that sometimes the human element is present in a larger degree than the Divine, God being ever ready to allow Himself to be understood by those who in sincerity seek him, but equally not always displaying his responsiveness to man's quest in the same way, or acting for the same reason.

It is perhaps permissible to introduce at this point a mythical illustration which I believe in its original form owes its origin to Archbishop William Temple, the younger, and which I have adapted and frequently used myself in lecturing. Temple, I believe, employed it to illustrate the relation of 'general' revelation to 'special' revelation. John Smith is a respectable bank clerk. He observes in his life an extremely regular routine and time table, rising regularly at the same hour, catching the same train daily to and from work, observing the same office hours, and during his day's work performing the same kind of tasks with the utmost order and precision. His home life is equally regular in its habits, and to some might seem monotonous, though to his wife and children as well as to his neighbours it gives a sense of confidence, in that they know that he can always be relied upon and trusted in all his dealings. One day, however, the normal routine of his life is suddenly and severely interrupted. On his way to work he encounters a run-away horse and van, and sees a small child in danger of being run over. He rushes forward, rescues the child, and flings it into safety, but as he is doing so, he is struck down by the run-away horse and van, and fatally injured. This event happens obviously but once in his life, and from the nature of the case is irrepeatable: but in it a deeper knowledge of John Smith's character is disclosed not only to the bystanders but to all his friends and relatives, and colleagues at the office, who may afterwards get to hear about it. Some of them may say: 'We never knew he had it in him'. Others will say: 'We always thought he had it in him, and now we know'. If one may compare small things with great (and there have certainly been people like John Smith in the course of history) and if we apply the principle of *analogy*, we may justly say that in the process of creation, preservation, and the many blessings of life, the Divine Nature is constantly and continuously being revealed to those who will use their faculties of discernment to discover and receive it, and that this is true in a partial and broken way throughout the religious quest of mankind, but that nowhere is there such a self-disclosure of the Divine Nature as in the career of Jesus of Nazareth. I do not think that Wilson would have had any hesitation about assenting to the foregoing, but some might say that in his emphasis upon unbroken continuity, which was a concept strongly felt by the scientists of his day, and perhaps rather less felt by the scientists of a later generation, he unnecessarily weakened the emphasis upon the uniqueness of the self-disclosure of the Divine Nature in Christ, which is of the nature of a discontinuity or unique intensification in the Activity of the Living God.

(vii) 'MANKIND AND THE CHURCH' ESSAYS BY SEVEN BISHOPS

This work, published a year before the Pan-Anglican Congress of 1908, marks a great step forward, not only in Anglicanism but in missionary thinking as a whole. Each of its seven authors represented a different area in the world, and its general thesis was that the peoples of each area must necessarily have their part to play in bringing to its fullness the knowledge and the glory of Jesus Christ and the fullness of the whole Church of God. The Editor, Bishop H. H. Montgomery, described the writers as 'Seven Dreamers', but claimed that dreams and visions must be an indispensable part of the life of the Church. National, racial, and religious characteristics in the different areas were carefully described; and the contributors aim at showing how these can play their part in the full development of a truly universal Christian faith, the common world-religion of the future.

The generosity of such an outlook certainly betokens a profound change from the naïve antagonism of a century earlier. While it aims at being constructive, it does not ignore any of the weaknesses, aberrations, and deficiencies to be seen in the various paganisms. The Archbishop of the West Indies writes of the negro, the Bishop of South Tokyo of the Japanese, the Bishop of Hong Kong of the Chinese, the Bishop of Lahore of the Moslem world, and the Bishop of Bombay of 'the possible service of Hinduism to the collective thought of the Church'. The Bishop of New Guinea speaks of the contribution to be made by the more primitive peoples.

It must be admitted that fifty years have gone by since this book was written, and that circumstances have greatly changed. Yet the work is of more than merely historical interest, since it stands for a great principle which is still valid, but which 150 years ago was hardly conceived.

Among the special features mentioned are the marked steadfastness of the Chinese under persecution, their extreme practicality, and their diligence in communicating their Christianity to their neighbours: the contribution that Moslems themselves make to the reality and sovereignty of the One God, and their remarkable persistency in claiming that a dogma about the Divine Nature lies at the root of all true social and political order: the cheerful patience, proper estimate of wealth and subordination of individual interests, showed by the Japanese: the four-fold contribution of the negro races, which is said to be (1) stress on the emotional element generally in the presentation of truth and on the experimental realisation of it, (2) a strong sense of brotherhood, shown by community in service, and sympathy in affliction, (3) cheerful acceptance of all providential arrangement as the acts of a wise and loving God, (4) a strong appreciation of authority and discipline in the Church.

The longest and most detailed essay is that on Hinduism by Bishop Mylne, who claims that in its philosophic form it has actually a profound contribution to make to the enrichment of Christianity by its stress on the Divine Immanence as against a crass and godless materialism. We do not hear much about this quality today, though it was extremely evident to the Bishop. More indeed seems to have been made since then of the deficiencies of Hinduism, especially in its under-valuation of the historical and factual and its lack of moral indignation. These may be real; and yet one cannot help wondering whether perhaps there ought not still to be a more generous recognition of the priority of the spiritual in the life of the average Indian citizen, leading him to an unworldliness, a readiness to self-sacrifice, and an inclination towards pacifism and non-violence which are admirable and precious contributions to an enrichment in the expression of the Christian faith.

Yet, although it must remain a matter of opinion as to whether one can agree with the various analyses successively presented, the great principle of *positive contribution* assuredly remains as one which was worthy of emphasis.

A curious gap, must, however be mentioned. There is not a single reference to the possible contribution which might come from Buddhist converts, and there are no chapters dealing either with Burma or Ceylon. Japanese Buddhism, in so far as the Bishop of South Tokyo is acquainted with it, is not rated very highly by him. He thinks it has left its best elements behind, and has allowed many degrading superstitions to take their place, while its temple schools, as he sees them, are hotbeds of immorality. One imagines that here there has been a clear improvement. Canon Streeter, during his year in Japan (1929) met many Buddhists, and neither he nor Professor Pratt seem to endorse the Bishop's account. It may well be that Christian contacts in Japan during the early years of the twentieth century galvanised Japanese Buddhism into new life. Streeter indeed actually speaks of what he saw going on as a kind of Buddhist Counter-Reformation, caused by the example and stimulus of Protestant Christianity. I do not think that those who praise Buddhism realise that what has been happening in Japan has been happening elsewhere as well, and that the Buddhism we see today owes more than it dares to acknowledge to assimilation to Christianity. The Buddha himself, as presented and revered by many today, is really a composite figure, possessing the attributes of Christ rather than those of an Indian mystic of the fifth century B.C. Since the work described in this section appeared before this Buddhist Counter-Reformation had got well under way, it is hardly surprising that there is practically no reference to it, except a slight one in Bishop Montgomery's introduction; but the reader will have noticed that considerable details regarding it have appeared in the chapter preceding this one.

(viii) WILLIAM ERNEST HOCKING

During the armistice period the work of re-valuation was continued by Anglo-Saxon liberal theologians. Among these there stands out the figure of Professor Hocking, though he is only one of a number which includes A. G. Widgery, E. S. Brightman, C. S. Braden, J. N. Farquhar, Nicol Macnicol, and E. D. Soper. As Dr. Kraemer remarks, most of these are inspired by the necessity to come to terms with the question: 'Why should Christians so ardently engage in missionary work?' That this was the feeling, especially in America, is clear from the events of 1931 and 1932. At that time American Protestantism was seriously concerned with the problem of the right approach to non-Christian faiths, and a Commission was sent to Asia, consisting of laymen, of whom Professor Hocking was one. The report of this Commission was published in the autumn of 1932 under the title: 'Re-thinking Missions'. Hocking was perhaps intellectually the most important member of this Commission, and on his return he delivered a number of lectures in the United States, and the Hibbert Lectures in England, partly at the University of Cambridge. It is only fair to remark that his presuppositions are those of a Congregationalist Christian of Unitarian tendencies, so that he does not experience any serious difficulty in treating the various religions of the world on a level, nor of accepting on the Christian side, a 'reduced Christology', and it goes without saying that his point of view, like that of most of his contemporaries mentioned above, is not acceptable to Dr. Kraemer, the chief reason being that it is not sufficiently a *theological* approach to the subject. Admittedly Hocking's definition of religion: 'a passion for righteousness conceived as a cosmic demand', is probably far less satisfactory than that of Otto, and it is certainly one which few religious philosophers would be found to endorse. It is also noticeable that Hocking adopts a completely opposite view to that of Whitehead, in that the latter regards it as 'what a man does with his solitariness', whereas Hocking defines it as 'clearly a step out of privacy, a rejection of the illusion of privacy'. Hocking's main outline is that the whole trend of global life is in the direction of a single world-religion. The minds of men are being wafted towards a community of outlook, and the forces of applied science are bringing the inhabitants of the planet into a relationship which may almost be compared to that of the various dwellers in a huge block of flats. What then is to be done about all this? Are we to leave the growth of a world-faith simply to the kindly offices of time, or are we to take what might seem to be the dangerous step of encouraging it ourselves, which might seem rather like 'blossoming the flower'? Like most Christians, Hocking feels that the policy of laissez faire is precluded by the injunctions of Christ himself. But his travels and conversations with non-Christians led him to a strong sense of the worthiness of much that he found in the ordinary exponents of the older Asian religions. Thus he describes vividly a conversation which he had with a young Japanese Christian who described to him the faith and piety of his old Shintoist mother, and he says that he never enters the realm of

Buddhist literature without feeling that 'certain traditional fetters and browbeatings had dropped away'. He goes on to consider three possible ways by which the Christian may seek to establish a world-faith. The first of these he describes as that of 'radical displacement', the second as that of 'synthesis', and the third way as that of 'reconception'. The first method has obviously very much of the traditional about it, though the rise of Barthianism involves a return to it, and American fundamentalism has, of course, never abandoned it. As he remarks, the decisiveness of this policy makes short shrift of any kind of relativity doctrine. 'No one can learn whether wine suits him by mixing it with milk. The experiment must be clean. A half-way experiment is no experiment.' Something approaching this point of view is represented by Dr. Kraemer, yet in justice to him it does not appear that it has always been his policy. For instance, when establishing a mission in the island of Bali, his wish was to conserve what was characteristic in the harmonious and in many ways beautiful native culture. The objections to doing this came from the Balinese themselves. For them, religion was so much a way of doing things in everyday life, that to become a Christian and to retain Balinese customs seemed to them a contradiction in terms. One seems to have heard something of the same kind of story from the Orokolo Bay area of New Guinea. It was not the agents of the London Missionary Society who ordered the abolition of some of the cultural practices of the people in this area, but the people themselves. Once they became Christians, without any initiative on the part of the missionaries, they ceased to be interested in preserving any of their artistic pageantry, by adapting it to the service of the new faith. This is, of course, very interesting, because it seems to suggest that some particular presentations of the Christian faith have in themselves a deadly effect on the cultural life of the people who receive them. Yet we know that this has not always been so, and indeed that when engaging in the conversion to Christianity of the Anglo-Saxon inhabitants of Great Britain, Gregory the Great sent instructions to Augustine at Canterbury to allow the people, after their conversion, to retain as many of their old customs as possible, and to adapt them to the service of the new faith, with the result that many of these old customs became grouped around the festival of Christmas. A commentary on this is the opposite behaviour of the Mayor of Canterbury in the days of Oliver Cromwell. The Mayor was a Puritan, and he proceeded to abolish what he called 'the heathen festival of Christmas'. It is evident that radical displacement is not so much a policy of Christians, qua Christians, but of Christians of a certain sort, and a case can certainly be made out for it.

Hocking's second possible way is that of synthesis. Now synthesis may be of more than one kind. It may for instance be the adoption into a new religion of certain words or ceremonial acts which belong to the old one, but which in their adoption for the purposes of the new religion have their meaning modified or even changed. This, one can see, was certainly the case with early Islam. Mohammed and his disciples took over a number of terms from the Christianity of the Middle East, as has been shown by Dr. Bell and Dr. Sweetman, and also from the pre-Islamic religion of the Arabs. The word 'Allah' itself is pre-Islamic but as used by Mohammed it is filled out with a fresh content. This is not syncretism in the bad sense. It is merely giving fulfilment to religion by endowing the vocabulary of the worshippers with a new richness of content. The second kind of synthesis may be what has been mentioned above in connection with Gregory the Great. It involves the taking into the new religion of certain practices of ritual behaviour, but of changing their meaning. Most people know that Mohammed, in making Mecca a centre of pilgrimage, retained a certain number of the ceremonies, such as perambulating the Ka'aba, running between two specified spots and throwing stones, and sacrificing sheep. But those who perform these ceremonies either have no notion what they mean, or attribute to them a meaning different from that which they had before the time of Mohammed. Similarly, quite apart from the usages connected with Christmas, many of which have now no religious significance at all, but are simply 'nice old customs such as the hanging up of the mistletoe', Catholicism, following the tradition of Gregory the Great, has uniformly endeavoured to preserve, and, so to speak, to baptise as many pre-Christian customs as possible, so as to make the transition from one faith to another not more difficult than it need be. This has sometimes led, so people think, to a rather too favourable treaty with the ethnic religions, and Mexico is sometimes quoted as an example of this, many Mexican peasants keeping up their old pre-Christian customs side by side with Christian ones, apparently as a kind of insurance policy, since it seems that they still believe in the existence of their former objects of worship, though now perhaps subordinated to the Christian god. In the same way, it has been noticed and recorded that in Malaya Moslem fishermen will pay due regard to their *mullahs*, and obey their Moslem precepts, but at the same time will have their boats and tackle blessed by a non-Moslem medicine-man before setting out on a fishing expedition. How much this is done in secret and how much of it is known to the *mullahs*, but winked at, it is not easy to say. Clearly, however, a distinction ought to be drawn between syncretism, or rather in this case synthesis, which is officially permitted, and syncretism, or perhaps parallelism, which is indulged in by the people themselves, without the permission of their religious leaders. Hocking himself does not seem clear that the way of synthesis is invariably a good one, though he would probably favour what is now called a policy of indigenisation. He passes on to a third way, that of reconception. For this he regards the intimations of synthesis as a natural preparation.

Reconception, as he says, has its own dangers. It involves getting down first to the essence of an individual faith, and then trying to see how both it and the essence of another individual faith can be included in an enlargement of faith A by the inclusion in it of what is valid in faith B, thus producing an enlargement of A which he symbolises as A_1 and by a further enlargement of the same kind as A_2 and so on indefinitely up to A_n. This search for essence, he says, is progressive. It comes to no final stopping-place; since for every reconception there is conceivably a better one still to be had. It is also the natural process of religious growth, because it is growth within sameness. This way of thinking, says Hocking, escapes the fallacy of a kind of modernism which insists on the relativity of all stages of religious teaching, whereas religion from its very nature ought to be able at each stage to unite mankind with that which is everlasting and changeless. The change is only in our apprehension, which we can hardly pretend is in no need of improvement. Every judgment which we make about the essence of Christianity contains an element of certainty together with an ingredient of hypothesis, and on account of this latter factor there is a call from time to time for further induction based on wider groups of facts and on better insight into their nature. On the basis of Christ's discourses in the Fourth Gospel, Hocking evidently considers that this reading of the future falls within the limits of orthodoxy, since he adds that it is a special feature of Christianity that in its view God's revelation of Himself is progressive and unfinished: this being one of the meanings of the doctrine of the Holy Spirit, namely 'the perpetual contemporaneousness, personalness, and novelty of the unfolding of the meaning of its truth. No one who declines to admit that form of change which means the arrival of new light—He shall guide you into all truth—has understood this doctrine'. It is, however, a little doubtful as to whether Hocking combines with this doctrine the acceptance in any sense of the absoluteness of the Person of Jesus. It is true that he says: 'Christianity is the only religion which inclines to substitute its founder for its entire doctrine, and knows that it has gained rather than lost by so doing'; but in the same section he speaks of the greatest strength of Christianity being its 'symbol', having previously said 'We know so little of the factual life of Jesus that it is possible to imagine (and for some scholars to believe) the narrative as a myth.' This seems dangerously near adopting the Hindu position.

Hocking then goes on to consider the merits and demerits of Christianity as we see it. He begins by saying that Christianity has a superior power of self-expression. By this he does not mean merely that it is better organised and is free from what he calls the formlessness of much Asian religion. In addition to that it has, as he points out, wider resources of self-definition and of apology. It may be best to quote his own words:

'It has lived for two millennia in company with a diverse activity in western philosophising and in letters, and for three hundred years with a group of independent sciences. Alone among the great religions, Christianity has fought out its issues with the natural sciences, has passed through the purge of the scientific study of itself as an object, its "higher criticism", its comparative science of religion, its psychology of religion. It has met outspoken criticism on the part of these free agencies; and it has gained from this ordeal a capacity not alone to defend itself but to perceive what is defensible and what not defensible. It no longer feels the necessity of denouncing scientific results in the interest of a literal biblical loyalty. It has ceased for the most part, to identify itself with scientific absurdities; it has been disciplined, hardened, and made agile. By reducing its appanage of cumulative fancy, science has given Christianity the fighting benefit of its inherent simplicity, and a language soberly responsible to experience.

It is hardly accurate to call this advantage accidental, since (contrary to the common reading of history) Christianity is largely responsible for this very independence which makes the arts and sciences such telling critics. It is Christianity which has set the arts free, and defined the grounds of their secular operation. For example, John of Damascus stated the separation of philosophy from theology; Augustine used and expanded the distinction; Thomas Aquinas gave it a systematic place; on this basis Descartes could give philosophy a wholly secular head, and propose for it a method derived from mathematics and physics. Since Galileo, Christian theology has had the criticism not alone of science and philosophy but also of a social order increasingly disposed to conduct its affairs on an experimental basis. All religions have had an attendant corps of scholars; but it is one thing to discuss with a group of minds submissive to an ultimate authority; another to debate with minds who have thought out and apply their own criteria or truth and reality.'

Within most British Divinity faculties these words of Hocking would for the most part be endorsed, but against them must be set the relative conservatism of the great Roman communion on the one hand and of the still greater conservatism of some American and British evangelical protestantism (typified by Dr. Billy Graham and his supporters) on the other.

Other points in the superiority of the Christian faith enumerated by Hocking are: Firstly, *Its capability of a free social application.* Other religions find themselves embedded in a set of social customs, either the caste system of India or the adherence of Moslems to the precepts of the Sharia. Even Buddhism, though less confined than these, seems to assume a social background very different from that of the modern world. A Japanese Buddhist said to Hocking in 1932 that although Buddhism was his religion, its social thought was neither vigorous or swift enough for the great period of transition through which Japan was passing, and that they must rely upon Christianity for help. Since Hocking wrote, the spread of Marxism has perhaps made it a little difficult to be quite so positive about this. But on reflection one can see that it is still true, since the Marxist doctrine of society is completely bound up with a very rigid though by no means intellectually secure theory, and with a denial of human rights to those who do not agree with it. Secondly, *its interest in ordinary people.* These have always been the first objects of its care. Its preaching has been to them rather than to specialists. The Buddha spoke first to his fellow ascetics, and is represented as addressing them, according to the S.B.E. translation as 'young men of good family', presumably implying that they were reasonably high caste Indians.

As to disadvantages, he sees Christianity as having become pre-eminently a Western religion. Yet it is not incurably Western, and it can almost as easily be said that Western civilisation is in many respects secular rather than Christian. The Christian movement cannot compel any state to accept its advice. It remains free to advise, if it has advice to offer, and through its members it is free to criticise the State or to influence its policy by the votes of individual Christians. But unlike Marxism it does not deny the right to be in opposition. Men and governments must be free to go wrong. Hocking concludes that while in its ideal character Christianity is the anticipation of the essence of all religion, in its empirical or actual self, it is still not yet ready to serve as a world religion, since on many matters it has still not solved some of its own problems, more particularly that of how to achieve unity without destroying diversity, and secondly because there are, he thinks, still values in other religions, which we think ought not to perish. He considers that whatever may be true of exceptional Christians, Islam among its members exhibits as a whole an awareness of a dignity, a sweep, a sense of the instant majesty of God, which we lack, or rather which lacks saliency in our religious expression and in our lives. Islam has also, he thinks, an effective fraternity which crosses racial bounds with an ease which Christianity professes, but Christians seldom attain. I am not sure that it is not possible to exaggerate this. The solidarity of Moslems depends very largely upon the solidarity of Arabs. And although Hocking declares that Islam has no proletariat, it is difficult not to be aware in Moslem countries of sharp social differences such as those in Egypt between fellahs and effendis, and between wealthy Moslems in India and Pakistan and the very poor ones in the same areas.

(ix) T. R. GLOVER AND NICOL MACNICOL

I have grouped together these two scholars of Protestant Christianity (the one a Baptist and the other a Presbyterian) because the one slightly precedes the other, yet the second of the two clearly endorses the main thesis of the first, and is inspired by it in the later chapters of his work. Glover, who was a distinguished Classical scholar at Cambridge about forty-five years ago, became well known for his three attractive books: *The Conflict of Religions in the Roman Empire* (which described the religious situation in the Mediterranean world of the first and second centuries); *The Jesus of History*; *Jesus in the Experience of Men* (a striking passage from which has been quoted at the end of Chapter IV). In his first work Glover wrote: 'If Christianity had depended upon the Logos, it would have followed the Logos into the limbo whither went Aeon and Aporrhoia and Spermatikos Logos. But that Logos has not perished is due to the one fact that, with the Cross, it has been borne through the ages on the shoulders of Jesus.' It is this attitude towards the Logos which inspires Macnicol in his final chapter, and makes him cautious in the acceptance of it. We shall return to this in a moment. In the meantime it must be said that the treatment of Dr. Macnicol's work by Dr. Kraemer is sufficiently unfair to make one wonder whether the latter has really read his principal work. Macnicol was an eminent and scholarly missionary in India; and in the latter part of the Armistice period he returned to Europe and held at Oxford the Wilde Lectureship in Natural and Comparative Religion. In the first two courses of his lectures he expounded objectively the living religions of the Indian people. But in the third course he directed himself towards a more general survey of the faiths of the world, and made an attempt at an appraisal of their religious value. It is this work which we must here discuss, more especially as a good deal of the material was delivered not only in Oxford but in America, Canada, and at Geneva. The learning and long experience of Macnicol in the mission field ought to have led Kraemer to treat his work much more seriously than he has, since it cannot be airily dismissed as simply a modern version of Justin Martyr. After a brief introduction, Macnicol comes down straight away face to face with the fundamental differences between the great religions of the world, and he appeals to fact. There are fundamental differences and it is idle to ignore them. There are certainly among them at least two distinctive views of God's relation to the universe, the one which views the natural as the obscuring of the supernatural, the other which views it as its revealing. This, of course, does not sever Christianity from the other religions by declaring it to be the one and only true revelation, but it certainly divides off the pantheistic religions from those concerned with transcendence. Like Dr. Harold Smith, Dr. Macnicol perceives that between these two broad divisions there are a number of sub-types, and he considers them in relation to the reality of the world and the freedom of human personality. This kind of analysis, as being a scientific one, would not unnaturally seem to make the author incur the criticism of Dr. Kraemer. But the succeeding chapters make it abundantly clear that for Dr. Macnicol, Christianity is not simply a type of theism bracketed together with other types, but a type which stands apart on its own.

In his third chapter Macnicol considers the fruits which the various religions bear, and here his experience of Asia comes out clearly. He quotes the saying not of a Christian but of a Hindu Indian Professor of Physics: 'The western world plays with pantheism, and perhaps then pantheism may not do much harm, but the eastern world takes it seriously, and it sucks the blood.' He adds his own comment:

> 'Whatever Hinduism has been (and it has been many things) it has never in all its long history escaped wholly from the petrifying influence which follows pantheism in all its forms like its sombre shadow. That this is so is written all over the history of the Hindu people, and is revealed in their ideals, which represent a life of moral indifference as the highest sainthood, and the supreme attainment as a peace of stagnation and death.'[1]

Something of the same, he feels, may be the effect of the sense of apathetic submission to fate which is so largely a characteristic of Moslem peoples. Dr. Macnicol deals with Buddhism further on in a separate chapter and does not mention its fruits here; but pure Buddhism not infected by contact with Christianity is an extension outside India of the Indian point of view, with the result that while it makes a great deal of the spirit of compassion and of ethical seriousness, it develops a world-outlook which empties it of reality.

---

[1] Another friend of India has written regretfully of the absence in Hinduism of anyone like the writer of Isaiah I or the prophet Amos.

The result is that only in a modified Buddhism can there be any development of social service, social planning, or even scientific study of the external world, and a theory, as Macnicol says, which makes God superfluous (or at any rate, as we may say, substitutes the Absolute for the living God) cannot create true religion even in the hands of so deeply religious a personality as the Buddha.

In his fourth chapter Macnicol goes on to survey the effect of oriental influences in the west. This is useful, since it has often been overlooked that Asia and Europe are not two islands remote from one another, but portions of one great land-block. When from the middle of the eighteenth century Asian books came to be known in Europe and in America they had quite a considerable influence on the continent of Europe. The French read the Chinese sages and the Germans the Upanishads. Many will be familiar with the effect of these latter upon Schopenhauer and Heine in Germany and Amiel in Switzerland. But there has been a more recent development of the same kind in the twentieth century among the members of the Irish literary renaissance. We find W. B. Yeats translating the Upanishads and escaping from the trammels of life not merely to the lake island of Inisfree, but into a Celtic twilight, which, as Macnicol says, bears an unmistakeable resemblance to the night of Brahman. George Russell has allowed himself to be bound more completely by the spells of India; while Joseph Plunkett in one of his poems has dissolved the figure of Christ into the world of nature, so that, as in the apocryphal Acts of John, the Incarnation and the Crucifixion are just phantom ideas. Macnicol shows that the American mystics Thoreau, Emerson, and even Walt Whitman were attracted by certain elements in the teaching of the oriental sages, and he concludes by referring to M. Romain Rolland and Mr. Fausset. Since this lecture was originally delivered about twenty years ago there has, of course, been a notable increase in the respect shown in Europe and America to the mystical literature of Asia, and perhaps nothing has shown this more than the extraordinary number of new editions and translations of the Bhagavadgita.

(X) ERICH PRZYWARA

Most of the theological revaluations which appeared during the Armistice period proceeded from the Churches of the Reformation; but there was one published in Munich,[1] which came from the pen of a

[1] In a composite volume on Philosophy. The essay in question was entitled 'A Catholic Philosophy of Religion', and was published in an English translation in 1935 under the title 'Polarity'.

Czech Jesuit, and which eventually appeared side by side with another essay from the pen of the Swiss Protestant, Emil Brunner, in a composite volume on European philosophy. Przywara himself, apart from this essay, is best known as the author of an anthology drawn from the works of St. Augustine the Great, as the editor of a journal *Stimmen der Zeit*, which was the Catholic rejoinder to the Barthian publication *Zwischen den Zeiten*, and also as the leading Catholic philosopher attending the International Congress of Philosophy held in 1934 at Prague. Although the author displays a good deal of ingenuity, as Father Wilfrid Knox said, in the way in which he accommodates his thesis to the definitions of the Vatican Council and the anti-Modernist oath, and is in effect formally orthodox, it is clear that his whole attitude, if followed to its logical conclusion, would be fatal to the stricter ultra-montane orthodoxy of many Romanists. Knox concluded that apart from a few details it would stand very well as an exposition of the dominant philosophical system prevailing in the Anglicanism of his day.

Przywara attempts to construct a system which will find a place for every type of religious experience, outside and inside Catholicism. While he concludes that the latter provides a stable synthesis for the various fluctuating types which come and go in the world outside it, he finds a place for various types of Chinese thought, as well as Indian, and for a number of non-Christian systems which have appeared in Europe since the sixteenth century. It is strange that Kraemer never mentions him once (and it is certainly a defect in Kraemer's otherwise fine and comprehensive work that he devotes so little space to the Catholic point of view, and indeed, after dealing very briefly with Aquinas, only mentions one other Catholic theologian, Sertillanges).

Przywara bases his system on the data provided by ordinary human consciousness. The latter is divided into three main activities, immanence, in which the ego is conscious of itself as self-contained, transcendence, the consciousness of an external unity of completeness to which the ego is objectively related, and transcendentality or 'becoming-actualness', which is the activity of striving outwards in an infinity of endeavour. This gives three kinds of religious consciousness, in which the Self-Existent is seen (1) in the depths of the ego, (2) in the distance of the height above, and (3) in life as process.

The system is further based upon the general principle in the scholastic philosophy which is known as *analogia entis*. According to this principle, Self-Existent Deity is entirely separate from the universe, yet there is nothing in the universe that is external to Him, for although the universe is in no way necessary to Deity, everything in the universe is derived from Deity, made in His image, and pointing to Him, so that knowledge of Deity may be had as it were by extrapolation.[1] Creation is the free act of Deity and is not indispensable to His being. Knox queries whether the statement *liberrimo consilio* should be interpreted to imply that Deity is free to create in any way that He chooses, for this raises grave difficulties. Deity may be free not to create at all, but can hardly be what is meant by Deity if He is not bound to create in the best way possible.

On the principle of the *analogia entis*, Przywara proceeds to apply his analysis of human consciousness to Deity, who is at one and the same time self-sufficient, yet goes out from Himself in the very act of creating, and is the whole time immanent in the continuous process of evolution and maintenance of His created universe. Human beings thus experience Self-Existent Deity in one or another of these modes, and the religious phenomena of their world, their theology, and their worship, tend to correspond to one or other of these three types of activity. It is observable, however, that outside the Catholic Faith there is a certain instability to be seen in these phenomena. There is oscillation between the three different types as between three poles, and this results in hybrid types of experience, in which the religious person swings from the contemplation of immanence to that of transcendence, or vice versa; from transcendence to the contemplation of process, or vice versa; from the contemplation of process to the contemplation of immanence, or vice versa. There exists therefore the possibility of at least nine types of experience, but not one of these succeeds for long in satisfying the demands of the religious consciousness. The overwhelming transcendence of orthodox Islam produces Sufism, and yet the latter is not really at home in Islam, but seems to belong much more to Indian thought, or to neo-Platonism. Throughout the whole essay a strong Hegelian background is noticeable. Terms are taken over from the Logic in their usual sense, and the assumption is accepted that the progress of religious experience is dialectical. The various poles of experience play the part of thesis and antithesis, held together or related in a 'Spannung' or tension. The British are not so

[1] The method of analogy, or *via eminentiae*, is certainly to be found in the teaching of Jesus. It animates most of His parables, especially that of the generous householder, commonly called that of the prodigal son, where the inference is that if a human father can yearn after the reclamation of his son, and can divide his whole estate without any favouritism, and run to meet the sinner when he returns, how much more will God deal generously with the human race, and respond when it shows signs of penitence. Analogy also finds expression in the logion: 'If ye then being men of the world know how to give good gifts unto your children, *how much rather* shall your Heavenly Father give the Holy Spirit to them that ask Him.'

25

familiar perhaps as their continental cousins with this dialectical outlook, and it is noticeable that Karl Barth, Przywara, and the Communist philosophers, are all at one in taking pains to see that it is not forgotten. Dialectic considered as pure logic is neither realist nor idealist, but is merely an account of the process of thought considered as a process of growth or development; and as pure logic it is (as`MacMurray says rightly) 'one of the supreme achievements of the human mind, the final discovery of how all movements of an organic character can be thought about and understood—the mind's instrument for exploring the world'. This is clearly Przywara's position, though, as we shall see later, he strictly subordinates this dialectic process to the operations of another law.

Rarely, if ever, do we find any one of the three modes of experience and activity in a state of mutual exclusiveness except by a process of abstraction. In reality we find each single one usually combined, though in a fluid state, with one or both or the other two, so that what we observe tends to look more like nine and not three types of experience. Into this group of (as it were) nine pigeonholes Przywara seems to be able to fit all the different examples which he goes on to give, but he is not content even with this, for he manages to divide Deism into four different varieties. There is, however, no stability about all these efforts at a synthesis of the various contradictions. The tension in which they are held together is according to him an *explosive* one. The two sides in each type fly apart again sooner or later, and man is ultimately disappointed of his quest.

Przywara then goes on to a second analysis, which he calls that of the consciousness of the concrete ego; and here he sees four tensions; the relationship of body to spirit or vice versa; and the relationship of individual to community, or vice versa. Each of these four, as he points out, connects with one of the three fundamental modes of active experience, producing, in relation to every one of these three modes, a corresponding variety of types of thought and practice.

Finally he engages in a third analysis, undertaken in answer to the question: Is religion Act of God, moving from above downwards, or is it Act of Man, moving from below upwards? To accept the former would give us absolute supernaturalism, or theopanism. To accept the second would give us absolute rationalism, or pantheism. Religion, says Przywara, comprehends on one side the innermost life of man: in the tidal movement of life it seeks to find the Absolute Point outside itself. Yet on the other hand, this

Absolute seems, as such, unable to stand separate from all that is relative in the creaturely. Solution is sought along the lines of the three main roads of experience, and the attempt is made to hold them in synthesis. But again the result is an explosive tension, and not, as desired, a tension in unity.

Is then religion impossible, and is man's quest for a synthesis of his modes of experience a mere hunt after a will-o'-the-wisp? Clearly neither the pantheism of India, nor the Barthianism of Europe, nor the dialectic atheism of the Marxist will suffice. All three, and many other sub-types leave man baffled and dissatisfied.

Przywara claims that it is only in Catholic philosophical theology that a final solution is to be found. To begin with, in this theology Deity and the creaturely are related in a tension, but it is one which is not 'explosive', but merely 'open'. In some respects the Deity of Przywara is not unlike that of Barth. He is Other, and not simply an absolutised relative, as in the three modes of what we may call natural religion, which really destroy Deity, while at the same time demanding His existence as Necessary Being. But in the principle of *analogia entis* the essentially super-creaturely absolute fixed point is really to be found *in* Deity, and Przywara thus not unnaturally claims that the God of orthodox Christian theism is the only truly transcendent Deity. The difference between the two thinkers is seen in the rejection by Barth of the *analogia entis*. He will not allow the existence of similitude between the creaturely and Deity. It is true that the inconoclastic biblicism of Deutero-Isaiah, let alone that of the Decalogue, would seem to exclude analogy. Yet what is really excluded is the limitation of worship to the symbol, not the worship of the Other through that wherein He is veiled, yet figured on the principle of analogy.

Przywara then goes on to show that this principle of analogy preserves in Catholicism the three fundamental modes of active experience and their sub-types, while at the same time depriving them of their explosiveness in relation to one another, and so furnishing them with a real and enduring synthesis.

Anyone who takes the trouble to read this essay as a whole cannot fail to be conscious of its great richness. It not only contains as much in 140 pages as might be found in many works of two large volumes, but it shows an extraordinary range of knowledge. Buddhism, Taoism, Rabbinic speculation, the doctrines of Luther and Zwingli, Augustine, Aquinas, Suarez, and Newman, as well as most systems of European philosophy from the sixteenth century to today jostle one another within its pages. Nevertheless, it is perhaps understandable why this work would not appeal to a thinker like

Dr. Kraemer, assuming the latter to be acquainted with it. Przywara's system seems to be aimed at bringing Catholic and non-Catholic, Christian and non-Christian religious thought all within the bounds of one complete scientific theory, and this the European neo-Protestant cannot approve of. Przywara very rarely quotes or refers to the Bible. Not that he would depreciate its importance. Whenever such a reference is made, as in the quotation from a Pauline speech in Acts, or a reference to Moses on Mount Nebo, the record is reverently accepted without question. But it is clear that to the Catholic theologian the Bible is the instrument in the hands of the Church, and not, as it seems so often in Kraemer, an independent authority, sometimes treated critically, and sometimes not. Actually, Przywara, by setting Catholicism over against the oscillations and explosive tensions of natural religion, clearly means us to infer that there is a serious qualitative difference between the former and the latter, so that I do not think there is really as much difference at this point between Przywara and Kraemer as there might seem to be. Both accept that Something has entered into the spatio-temporal order at a point in history which has permanently changed the relationship between Deity and the creaturely. But it would seem that Kraemer almost regards the Bible as an independent witness of this, although at one point he seems inclined to accept the authority of the Church in establishing the Canon of Scripture.

The point at which there is greatest divergence between Catholic and non-Catholic theologians so far as non-Christian religions are concerned is in the use made by the former of the principle of analogy. This is a very large subject, and is, I believe, to be dealt with in another volume in this series, so that what is said about it here may seem to some inadequate, but it is necessary to emphasise that its acceptance by Catholic thinkers leads them to see in the ideas of many non-Christians a remote but real approach to true belief. The gap between Divine and human personality is not such that it is impossible for men to form partial and incomplete yet not wholly erroneous notions of God. The neo-Protestant on the other hand is inclined to say that *analogia entis* is an invention of the Devil, and that there is such a discontinuity between God and mankind that the former is Wholly Other, and cannot be known at all by analogical deduction but only by an exceptional and unique revelation. And it is sometimes added: 'Not every time is revelation-time.'

Readers must judge for themselves which is the more rational way of approaching the problem. But it will be seen in the section dealing with the work of Archbishop Söderblom and Archbishop

William Temple[1] which follows that the latter, while not explicitly avowing their acceptance of the principle of analogy, are yet, much more than might be supposed, on the same side as Przywara in their attitude towards non-Christian faiths.   There is, of course, a strong tradition in favour of an approach by analogy to the problem of Divine Personality, running its course from Butler to Illingworth, but a tradition need not be accepted without query.

(xi) NATHAN SÖDERBLOM AND WILLIAM TEMPLE

This great man stands in a class by himself.   Born in 1866, a Swede of much intellectual distinction, and of strong and noble character, he was educated at the University of Upsala, where he began his studies in Iranian religion, which remained always his special interest.   After ordination, he spent seven years in Paris, and in 1901 returned to Upsala as a Professor of Theology.   From 1912 to 1914 he held the Chair of the History of Religions at Leipzig, and contributed during that time to Hastings' *Encyclopaedia of Religion and Ethics* an article in which he actually anticipated Rudolf Otto's famous theory regarding *Das Numinöse*.   Finally he returned to Sweden to become Archbishop of Upsala, and during his tenure of this office made himself one of the most prominent and useful Christian leaders in Europe.   Not only did he do much to relieve suffering during the First World War, and to handle the difficult questions connected with prisoners of war; but he subsequently took the lead in a number of ecumenical movements, Life and Work, Faith and Order, and Church Unity.   All these various experiences rendered him uniquely qualified to say something constructive and decisive on the problem of the relation of the Christian Faith to other religions; and in 1931, the year of his untimely death, he delivered the first series of Gifford lectures on this very subject at Edinburgh.   He was unable to see their publication and it is a misfortune that he was also unable to complete the draft of his second series, in which no doubt he would have developed further some of the themes which appear in his first series.   The title he chose was

---

[1] How clearly this emerges when one tries to talk to some neo-Protestants was shown to me some years ago when at the John Calvin House in Geneva I was engaged in a friendly disputation with some German Lutherans, and ventured to use the arguments of Temple as outlined in his Gifford Lectures. 'Why', came their reply, 'you are really giving us the Roman Catholic doctrine'—as though that immediately put it out of court.   This is not a denominational or ecumenical issue.   It involves a fundamental question of religious philosophy which cuts clean across denominational divisions.   *Analogia entis* could be rejected by an Anglican; while not all Protestants, continental or otherwise, would necessarily refuse to accept it as a principle.   The very last thing I desire to do is to caricature the opposition to the principle of *analogia entis*. But I do wish to draw attention to the very serious situation which is bound to arise if people try to be more orthodox than Our Lord Himself; and since, as we have seen, He clearly makes use of analogy in His teaching about the Nature of God, who are we that we should reject it?

The Living God, and he treats his matter under ten headings. In the first of these sections he is mainly concerned with magic, worship, and witchcraft in primitive religion. He then comes to grips with the greater non-Christian achievements, and groups what he has to say under the following headings:

(1) Religion as Method, in which he considers the Yoga of India.

(2) Religion as Psychology, in which he deals with the phenomenon of Jainism and the Theravada or Hinayana form of Buddhism.

(3) Religion as Devotion, in which he has much to say about the phenomenon of *bhakti* both in Hinduism and Buddhism.

(4) Religion with a 'Salvation Fact', which he describes mainly in connection with Mahayana Buddhism.

(5) Religion as a fight against evil. His subject in this is the teaching of Zarathustra, and he was here in his own special field, so that this chapter is rather longer than the others.

(6) The Religion of Good Conscience, in which he deals mainly with Socrates.

This brings him to the idea of revelation in history, where of course he is pre-eminently concerned with Hebraeo-Christian religion. He then goes on to his two final chapters, the Religion of Incarnation, and Continued Revelation. He is thus mainly concerned with the comparison of different types of personal religion.

One cannot help feeling that if Söderblom had lived he would certainly have revised this scheme of classification. So far as it goes in defining topics it is a good one. But if one is going to put the different kinds of religion into pigeon-holes, one is bound to do it completely. For instance, under the heading of Devotion one is bound to consider *bhakti* in Christianity as well as outside it, and it is not quite easy to sever the idea of Salvation Fact from Incarnation; and again, if one is having a section on Incarnation, one is bound to put in this section multiple as well as once-for-all Incarnation, and docetic types of it as well as genuinely historical ones.

The real importance of Söderblom's work lies in the fact that he was at the same time both a scientific student of religion and also a distinguished theologian and a great Churchman. Kraemer is quite right in saying that he thought of his work primarily as concerned with theology, and as done on behalf of the Church of which he was an ordained minister. This attitude of his lends great weight to the argument of his final chapter, in which he attempts to answer the question: 'Does God *continue* to reveal himself to mankind?' No one doubts that Söderblom was fully convinced from experience that the unveiling of the character of God in Jesus Christ was in a very real sense supreme and final. But it is equally clear that he did not regard Divine Revelation as finished with Christ or the Bible. He says, in fact, in so many words, that that idea is absurd. The whole idea of Revelation, he implies, needs to be seen in a much wider context. We are bound to think of what is involved in the idea of God as self-revealing. If that is truly a supreme attribute of His, then the operation of that attribute must be one which is ever present. If man is always seeking, God is always responding; and therefore long before the supreme Revelation in Jesus Christ, revelation had already been going on, while since the period of that Supreme Revelation, an ever-present revelation clearly continues. Because God is the Living God, he is active in the whole of history, past, present, and future. How much Söderblom would have developed this theme if he had been able to deliver a second series of lectures we cannot tell. Obviously what he says in his tenth chapter lacks completeness. He goes on to maintain that the continued revelation of God is to be seen in creative genius. Life he says is essentially a continued creation, not merely the regulation of things created, for in genius new things appear, things which have never before existed. This is the fundamental distinction between genius and mere talent. Genius appears as part of the Almighty's continuous creation. This may seem a daring conception to be uttered by a Christian Archbishop, but there it is, and it is quite clear that Söderblom felt no uneasiness in stating it. He at any rate, whatever may have been the attitude of some of his contemporaries, belonged to the category of forward-looking Christians, of whom it is certain that there must be many more in the future if the Christian movement is not merely to survive, but to do its full work in the future. Söderblom goes on at this point to consider one specific kind of genius, namely that of the prophet, and true to his heritage he sees the signal instance of this in the personality of Luther, though he also refers briefly to other prophets such as George Fox, and Grundtvig the prophetic genius of Denmark. Here perhaps he might well have said more about Kierkegaard. The argument at this point rambles a little and breaks off. Söderblom never completed his work. But he has left us with a challenge which cannot be ignored.

It is hardly to be expected that this method of treatment would commend itself to Dr. Kraemer as satisfactory. He sees Söderblom as 'caught in the trap of not clearly distinguishing between religious experience, and revelation as God's Act, independent of any experience'. He thinks that Söderblom over-estimated the competence of scientific research, and supposed that it could enable one indirectly to determine where revelation was at work in any religion and where not, and even to determine whether its quality was that of general or special revelation.   But it was unlikely that the two men could agree, since the Archbishop, in an earlier study published in 1913 entitled *Natural Theology and the General History of Religion*, had already declared his acceptance of the Logos-doctrine which, as we have seen, is clearly the heritage of the undivided Christian Church.   Indeed he welcomed it strongly, and said that as expressed by Justin Martyr it had gained new relevance and fresh actuality from the results of modern research in the sphere of non-Christian cultures and religions. The whole of mankind shares in the inspiration of the Logos whom the Christians call Christ the Son of God.   He calls this doctrine a grand one,[1] and says that for many centuries it could not come to the point at which it could be really fruitful, but that now in our day theology is ready for it.   Thus for him all religions are rooted in Divine Self-disclosure.   All genuine religious experience proceeds from Divine Self-disclosure, and we are bound to say either that there is real revelation outside the Biblical sphere, or there is no revelation at all, not even in the Bible.   Something very closely akin to this has been said by the Anglican Archbishop, William Temple, both in his Gifford lectures[2] and in a paragraph in his commentary on the Fourth Gospel, and one is tempted to speculate whether in this matter Temple was influenced by Söderblom, whom he certainly knew and respected, and with whom he must have worked in the ecumenical movement.

Kraemer, of course, recoils from Söderblom's conclusion.   He has a very real respect and even affection for the venerable figure of the Archbishop, but for him the gap between the best non-Christians and Christ is so important and even overwhelming that it reduces the element of general revelation in them almost to nothing.   For instance, he says of Socrates that he displays 'an enigmatic unimpairedness, untouched by the humility and self-abandonment which is revealed, in Christ'.   The Logos, he says, presses in upon a man like Socrates, but his self-respect leads him to evade that pressure.   For Kraemer to become a disciple of Christ always means a radical break with the past, never a gradual transition, since Christ is the *crisis* of all religion.   Kraemer considers that Söderblom was too much impressed with the upsurge of the Comparative Study of Religion.   He feels that he was dazzled by it, and had not really arrived at any satisfactory reconciliation between scientific truth and his own

---

[1] grosszügig.
[2] 'Revelation and its Mode' (Lect. xii).   See additional note at end of this section.

deep-rooted religious conviction, to both of which he tried to be loyal. Kraemer calls Söderblom the Clement of the twentieth century, and by doing so he implies his profound disagreement with the great Alexandrian Father of the Church. He goes on indeed to criticise Clement, who, he says, 'neglected the radically theocentric orientation implied in Biblical revelation, and made wisdom and knowledge the common denominator both for revelation and for philosophy'.

I have dealt at some length with Kraemer's criticism of Söderblom, not because I think that the latter at the time of his death had really arrived at a final decision, but because between these two men there is a fundamental difference of approach which is bound to be decisive for the whole of Christian theology in the future. Söderblom, on the one hand, although standing loyally in the Lutheran tradition is of a very liberal temperament. He has not deserted the belief that in the general progress of thought within the Church there is such a thing as Divine Guidance; while on the other hand he sees the fundamental necessity of accepting the work of scientific method in all its bearings where honestly and sincerely pursued, as the vehicle of God's further self-revelation. It does not appear that Kraemer is disposed to accept these two preliminary considerations for Christian theology and Christian work. Hence he is prepared to criticise the progressive thought of the Church as sometimes misdirected and erroneous, and he does not seem to be interested in study conducted along scientific methods as such, when it seems to conflict with his own reading of Biblical doctrine.

This involves fundamentally a most serious situation. One has heard it said that a very large number of continental Protestants who are sincerely interested in the missionary work of the Church have been led to adopt the position indicated by Kraemer; and if this is really the case it indicates a difference of belief which could easily and fatally split the Christian missionary movement, as well as endangering ecumenical efforts towards Christian unity. It has certainly resulted already, in many quarters, in a tendency for conversations between Christians and non-Christians to be broken off, and if it persists it may seriously hinder that growth of world-unity which is so sorely needed, and may damage the reputation of Christian theology, by giving the impression that it declines to come to grips with all the available facts. I hope that in this I am not overstating the case, nor do I desire to do anything to wound the feelings of my Protestant friends. But the situation has got to be faced, and it involves for weal or woe, 'speaking the truth in love'.

Additional note on Archbishop William Temple

The latter has written:

'We affirm . . . that unless all existence is a medium of revelation no particular revelation is possible. . . . Only if God is revealed in the rising of the sun can He be revealed in the rising of a man from the dead. Only if He is revealed in the history of Syrians and Philistines can He be revealed in the history of Israel. . . . If all existence is a revelation of God, as it must be if He is the Ground of its existence, and if the God thus revealed is personal, then there is more ground in reason for expecting particular revelations than for denying them.'— 'Revelation and its Mode' (Ch. xii in Gifford Lectures).

I have not devoted a separate section to Temple's work, since he is himself chiefly concerned with philosophical theology, and only incidentally at this juncture touches upon the topic of non-Christian religion. But what he says is obviously of great importance, though it comes curiously from one who, as I have said, previously commended Kraemer's earlier work as a preparatory study for the Tambaram conference. One is almost tempted to wonder whether that commendation can have been composed in haste, without a careful scrutiny of what he was commending; and whether Temple in this connection, can have been guilty of what his father had said of Moses in composing the Pentateuch that 'he must have written unadvisedly with his pen'.

(xii) ALTHAUS, FRICK, GUSTAV MENSCHING, J. H. BAVINCK, FRIEDRICH HEILER, J. WITTE, AND VAN BAAREN

I venture to group these continental scholars all together although they are referred to at separate points by Dr. Kraemer, because they all belong to much the same generation, and have made their contributions in the last quarter of the century. The salient points about them may be briefly summarised as follows. Althaus and Frick emphatically distinguish between the revelation in Christ and Christianity as an empirical historical religion. This distinction is certainly accepted by a good many, though probably not all of the neo-Protestant theologians, and naturally separates them somewhat from their Catholic neighbours. But Witte goes further still, and regards all religion except the revelation in Christ as totally abandoned by God (Gottverlassen). It deserves nothing but condemnation, and there is no way to God through it at all. Heiler on the contrary, with Catholic generosity, sees in non-Christian religions a true *praeparatio evangelica*, and regards the sacred scriptures of Indian religion as possibly the equivalent in part of the Old Testament for the Christian Church in India. This has made considerable appeal to loyal and patriotic Indians, who sometimes mention it to one in conversation; but it does not seem at present to have been carried much further, and perhaps requires fresh consideration. The difficulty will be, of course, over deciding what passages to select, since most of the Puranas would never do, while some of the ideas embodied in the Upanishades are really incompatible with Christian doctrine.

Mensching occupied himself partly with an objective comparative study of the various expressions of higher religion—for example, the practice of silent prayer. His essay on *Heilige Schweigen* is a valuable contribution from this point of view. Mensching also entered into the controversy over 'Absolutheit', which arose out of the essay by Troeltsch, mentioned previously. He drew a distinction between 'intensive' and 'extensive' absolutism. By the former, according to Kraemer, he meant that every kind of serious religious conviction, whether held by those who do or those who do not belong to a world-religion, depends upon a sense of subjective absolutism, presumably a sense that through that conviction one has immediate access to Deity. 'Extensive' absolutism, on the other hand, is that which characterises the claim put forward by any religion, whether Christian or non-Christian, which explicitly asserts its universalism. This claim is based upon logic rather than upon experience. Mensching warns against an over-dependence upon rationalism, and lays almost exaggerated stress upon the non-rational element in religion.

Bavinck, a Dutch Professor of missions, has written an essay on 'Religious Consciousness and Christian Faith', in which he attempts a classification of his own, resembling in some respects that of Przywara, for it starts out from the fact of religious experience rather than from the fact of Deity or the Self-Existent. Once again, therefore, we get a phenomenology rather than a theology, and Bavinck leaves us with the impression of having merely classified and described various types of human belief, without attempting to show whether they are related to one another by reference to any objective standard. Yet his conclusions seem capable of arrangement under four headings: first, the existence of one group of religions in which man experiences himself as part of a Cosmic Whole; second, the existence of another group in which there is a consciousness of being related to a Norm or World-Order which is above and beyond us. Bavinck sees these two types as intermingling, and in the third place he sees in both groups alike the experience at times of a more or less vague relationship with a quasi-personal Self-Existent. Fourthly and lastly, Bavinck sees a number of religions as characterised by the sense that life is a contest between humanity and superhuman fate, between an indifferent or hostile Infinite, and finite souls. This classification seems to leave out the third element, which is recognised by Przywara, that of process, transcendality, or 'becoming-actualness', and to that extent alone it is defective. But in any case it omits any recognition of the possibility of a completely normative or absolute religion. The analysis is mutual and relativist.

I would finally append to this group some mention of the work of another Dutch scholar, van Baaren, who has endeavoured to evaluate in a phenomenological manner the conception of Divine self-communication (revelation, self-impartation, Divine initiative, Offenbarung, Openbaring).

He concludes that it is possible to enumerate thirteen different types of self-communication, of which the first three may be described as 'unintentional', and the second ten as 'intentional'. The 'unintentional' he further classifies as dynamistic; the 'intentional' he divides into pluralist and monotheist. But only intentional self-communication should, he says, deserve the name of revelation: the unintentional ought only to be called manifestation.

We may perhaps be allowed at this point to cast our thoughts back to the chapter entitled 'Pre-suppositions'. If we do so, we cannot fail to notice that unless all hope is abandoned of any self-communication on the part of the Self-Existent there referred to for the first time, we are compelled to choose between an unintentional manifestation on the part of a Total Universe, or an intentional self-impartation by a Super-Personal Self-Existent 'by divers portions and in divers manners', wherever the Divine Logos is active, with the possibility of a supreme culmination at a single central point.

Mention has been made in another section of Dr. F. R. Tennant. It is perhaps fitting to say here that in the second volume of his *Philosophical Theology* he has drawn attention to the tendency of those who accept the fact that the latter kind of revelation has really taken place, to make such self-impartation appear coercive and 'above reason', and he clearly considers that this tendency has been harmful to the credit of honest religion, in that it has appeared to make Deity deal with finite persons as less than personal, which, he says, must be wrong and unworthy of any Being who besides being Supreme and Super-Personal is also said to be ethically good. But this attempt to fasten a coercive authoritarianism upon the expression of Christianity—for that is what it amounts to—is to desert the Christianity of the Gospel records. Christ, it is true, spoke with ἐξουσία, with first-hand prophetic freshness, and with clear consciousness of his isolated and immediate union with Deity; but he never displays any desire to override human freewill, or to appeal to anything but the truth. Indeed the famous words of Dr. Oman correctly represent his method. 'There is only one way of persuading, and that is to present what is true in such a way that nothing will prevent it from being seen except the desire to remain in darkness.'

(xiii) G. VAN DER LEEUW

Like Dr. Kraemer, Dr. van der Leeuw was a Dutchman, and his work, *Religion in Essence and Manifestation*, only appeared in an English translation just before the outbreak of the Second World War. At that time many us us were looking to the free Universities of the Netherlands to supply what seemed lacking in most of those in Germany which were suffering from Hitlerite servitude. In the same year, 1938, appeared Dr. Kraemer's earlier and most provocative volume. Kraemer refers with respect to Dr. van der Leeuw's work, although at certain points he disagrees with it. It would seem that van der Leeuw in an earlier book, *Der Mensch und Die Religion*, had adopted a line more like that of Kraemer over the doctrine of the Logos: but in the work here considered he rather shocks Kraemer by saying that taking account of the present state of our knowledge the only way to formulate the relation of Christianity to the non-Christian religions open to us is a return to the theory of the Logos as it is to be found in the Greek Fathers. Van der Leeuw presents quite an original treatment of his subject. In the first part he deals with what he calls the object of religion, and in the second part with its subject, considered as the individual, the community, and the soul-within-man respectively. In the third part he considers object and subject in their diverse reciprocal relations both outward and inward: in the fourth part the treatment of the external world in religion: and in the fifth part what he calls 'forms', by which perhaps he means institutions. Under this head he considers thirteen different types of religion and six different types of founder. It will thus be seen that he is concerned mainly with the description of the various types of religious phenomena rather than with the formulation of a general theory, but it is nevertheless clear from his concluding chapters that unlike Kraemer he does not draw a sharp line between biblical realism and the rest of religion. My own personal impression of van der Leeuw, whom I had the privilege of meeting and listening to only a few weeks before his death, was that he was too good a scholar to allow himself any such arbitrary division in dealing scientifically with what he calls the phenomenology of religion. Indeed I think he felt right to the end that he was dealing with what was still a young field of research, and that phenomenology itself was still in its childhood. At the same time he was no positivist, and was never content to take religion as 'the voice of humanity, in which mankind has unfortunately spoken falsely'. On the contrary, in his preface he says quite the opposite: 'It is not man himself who is the active agent in the situation, but, in one mode or another, God. A Divine activity sustains all phenomena alike, from their more primitive types to their culmination in Christianity as well as those religious movements which are now concealed by our largely secularised civilisation.' It is clear from this that although van der Leeuw in his great work writes with restraint about the vast mass of material with which he shows such an amazing familiarity, in the end he arrives at the same position as Dr. Harold Smith whose work is dealt with in the next section. It would take an undue amount of space to discuss the whole of the detail in the chapters in this encyclopaedic work. The author's background is of course that of Dutch Reformed Christianity, but he does not allow himself to be biased, and shows sympathy and fairness as well as knowledge in dealing with Catholic religious experience. The one hundred and ten chapters vary a good deal in length and probably also in quality, and there are some topics which one would have liked to have seen dealt with rather more fully, as, for example, conversion, which ought to have found a definite place in Chapter 94, though it is barely mentioned, under the heading of Revivals. In general one feels that this remarkable book deserves more attention than it has received. It never had a chance, since it was originally published at Tübingen in 1933, and the English version of 1938 was swamped from the outset by public attention being immediately diverted to the conflict with Nazi Germany.

(xiv) HAROLD SMITH

Almost at the end of the armistice period the Lecturer in the Comparative Study of Religions at King's College, London, Dr. Harold Smith, issued a judiciously written approach to what he called *Comparative Theology*. This was a typically British approach. Dr. Smith did not begin by laying down any preliminary theory, but in a series of five chapters surveyed the concepts of Revelation, Sacred books, Deity, Cosmogony, the doctrine of Man, and Salvation, as they appear in the different religious systems of the world. His survey was based upon a direct examination of the sacred literature and doctrines of each religion, and might therefore be regarded as empirical, but in the course of it one can see that a general theory is tacitly assumed, i.e. that the last word in each case lies with Christianity. The different types of religion are in each chapter grouped in such a way that Christianity appears as the final term, if not as the apex. I do not think that this is anywhere explicitly stated by the author, but it may reasonably be inferred from his arrangement that he would regard it as a fair deduction, if not as his own.

Let us now look at his scheme in detail.

Theories of revelation he groups under six categories. Into the first of these he puts the relatively late sacred books of Shinto, which are accompanied by no theory of revelation: the sacred books of Confucianism, in which the authors imply their belief in some kind of indirect revelation which is due to the Heavenly Mandate; and the sacred books of the Buddhists and Taoists, in which the idea of an objective revelation is replaced by a belief in the mystic sympathy of their authors with the universe. The second category contains two items, to wit the Vedas and the Upanishads of Hinduism, which it is said became treated as records of revelation by an age later than that in which they were composed. Whether Hindus would agree with this description may be doubted, since the Vedas are now claimed as the verbal recordings of cosmic vibrations perceived by the *rishis* or seers of primaeval antiquity in India, while their interpretation in the Upanishads is held to be divinely inspired, so that Indian commentaries expound the words of them in much the same way as that in which St. Thomas Aquinas expounds the words of the Christian Scriptures. But of course it is difficult for the textual and literary critic to accept this claim. Under the third category are grouped sacred records associated with an original claim to direct revelation: i.e. the sacred literature of Zoroastrianism, pointing back to a single personal prophetic founder to whom was mediated the 'Good Thought' of Deity; the sacred literature of Judaism, pointing back to a number of personally inspired prophets; and the single sacred book of Islam, delivered, it is asserted, to a single prophetic individual, and amplified by a corpus of authenticated traditions. The fourth category contains only one item, that of incarnational Hinduism, in which a number of divine persons descend directly, though not necessarily in a historical so much as in a visionary and illusory manner into the order of space-time, leaving behind an account of their activities in the form of epic poems. The fifth category again contains only one item, the records of the successive appearances of a plurality of Buddhas; and the sixth or final category differs from all the others in conceiving Revelation to have taken place in history once and for all in a factual and not mythical manner, the record of this being contained in a corpus of sacred scriptures guaranteed by the movement or society proceeding from the original once-for-all act of Incarnation, and in this case the revelation is regarded as in the first instance coming directly through the life of a historical person.

In dealing with the ideas of God and Reality, Dr. Smith works with six categories, though he has a good many sub-divisions, and it is quite clear that he accepts the dichotomy of the history of religion in the manner in which it was set forth in our second chapter, except that he prefers to call it the division into 'elementary' and 'advanced' religion. Under the former heading he includes pre-animism, animism, and primitive pluralism, as well as the (possible) primitive monotheism. The advanced section he divides under five heads, religions which conceive of Deity as personal; those which seem to conceive Deity as impersonal; those which exhibit impersonal tendencies within personal religion; and those which exhibit personal tendencies within impersonal religion. Under the first of these groups he would place Vedic polytheism with a growing tendency towards a unitary conception of God; Shintoistic polytheism with a growing tendency to accept the existence of one Supreme Divine Ruler; the pre-Confucian system with a personal Heaven ruling supreme over a number of minor deities; early Zoroastrianism as a pluralism in process of transformation into a prophetic monotheism; later Zoroastrianism, as an antithetical dualism with the expectation of the ultimate victory of the Good Personal Power; Judaism as ethical monotheism giving room for free will in the creaturely; and Islam, with its omnipotent monotheism allowing little for human freedom except bare submission to the will of Allah. In the second group he would put all the various types of monism, Taoist, Hindu, Buddhist, Confucian, in which Reality is divested of any personal features, however exalted. The third group includes the pantheistic mysticism of Moslems and Jews, that of the Sufis and that of the Kabbala, in both of which a strongly personalistic conception of Deity swings towards impersonalism. The fourth group has two items, Mahayana Buddhism, in which the idea of a Supreme Personal Cosmic Spirit emerges within a system which to begin with did not seem to require it, and sectarian Hinduism, whether Saivite or Vaishnavite, in which the idea of a personal Deity manifested in human or sub-human form emerges within a system of impersonal monism with which it does not seem directly consistent. The final or sixth category is the Christian one, in which many of the various elements seem to be combined. The Triune Deity, though certainly not sub-personal or impersonal, is not anthropomorphic, but implies in its symbolism a grade of personality which might perhaps be described as the extrapolation of personality to infinity.

Cosmogony is graded by Dr. Smith under three heads. The

first of these, emanation; the second, teleological creation, non-Christian; and the third, creation as conceived by Christian believers. This classification is perhaps a little difficult to accept. Some pre-Christian accounts of how the universe was made are frankly mythical, while others seem to imply a view of emanation not very different from that which might be that of some philosophically-minded Christians. Thus the Shinto account of creation seems to be frankly mythical, whereas the conception to be found in the doctrines of the Hindu medieval scholastic Ramanuja (in which the Supreme Deity, who is distinct from the universe of his creation, is said to emit, sustain, and reabsorb it), is not at all unlike the belief held by the Alexandrian Christian speculative philosopher, Origen, and might be said almost to be forced upon us by some modern astronomical theorists with their doctrine of continuous creation ex nihilo, and continuous annihilation of stellar matter. There seems, however, one supreme difference between the ideas of emanation put forth to the east of Persia and to the west of it. Eastward there seems little idea that there is any purpose in creation. The Iranian prophet Zarathustra, and all Jews, Christians, and Moslems, seem to hold on the contrary that creation is the definite working out of a Divine purpose, though this may sometimes be thought of as arbitrary, and at other times as seeking to be undertaken with the co-operation of the creaturely.

Regarding the doctrine of man and the conception of the good life, Dr. Smith sees four different types. The first of these, which is exceedingly widespread and begins early, concerns itself in the main with the benefit of man. To this end, as Dr. Leuba has reminded us, Deity, though a necessity, is not an end in Himself, but is merely *made use of* for the advantage of man. This, in the period of advanced religion, swings over into two very different types. The first of these, which is in the main world-negating, is closely connected with impersonal conceptions of the Absolute, and varies from the passive non-action of Taoism, in which one allows the Absolute to rule everything without interference, to Hinduism of the Advaita variety, in which the individual is urged to see himself as one with the Absolute, and the Absolute is not conceived as having any purpose in its cyclic activities within the spatio-temporal order, these being in fact nothing more than the expenditure of its surplus energy for its own amusement. The latter merges in Buddhism into the idea that the cyclic order is the realm of suffering and evil, and that therefore the good life for man is to purge oneself of the craving for life in any of its forms. There is some controversy, as we have seen, as to whether this represents the primitive form of Buddhism, but

26

Dr. Smith seems quite correct in placing it here as the standard Theravada doctrine. Against this, which he calls 'de-humanistic religion', is set the doctrine of man inspired by the various of theism, in which man's life, it is said, should be centred upon the service of the Super-Personal God. Here, Zoroastrianism has no place for asceticism, and stresses the freedom of human choice. Judaism, while equally having little or no place in its standard form for the ascetic life, modifies the belief in human freedom by stressing the presence of what it calls the evil inclination. Islam, by virtually denying human freedom, makes the good life, centred upon Allah, little more than one of total submission. Finally, in theocentric Christianity are to be seen a number of varying types, though the fundamental conception is that the good life is the grace of God working upon human consent, which is thought of not as the submission of a slave, as in Islam, but as the free consent of one who desires to be a friend and fellow-worker of the God who has loved us and given Himself for us. Dr. Smith gives full weight here to the divisions in Christianity. While in its orthodox forms it insists that all have sinned and fallen short of the glory of God, it interprets this 'fallenness' in various ways, some of which can hardly be regarded as representative of Christianity as a whole.

In his final chapter on salvation Dr. Smith's classification is easier to follow. That human beings, as William James has said, are almost uniformly conscious of an uneasiness, or lack of balance in their lives is broadly true. But whereas many of the earlier types see this uneasiness as needing deliverance from ceremonial defilement, from material distress, or from the dominance of evil spirits or malevolent deities, more advanced religion seeks profounder explanations for it, and correspondingly seeks to provide appropriate remedies. Thus Taoism sees the uneasiness to come from excessive finite concentration upon activity, and proposes deliverance by the adoption of quietism, while Hinduism sees it to proceed largely from ignorance which leads people to immerse themselves in the cyclic activities of the world, and offers them salvation from this ignorant state of mind through *vidya* or esoteric knowledge. Buddhism sees the uneasiness to arise from sorrow, suffering and physical craving, and offers salvation by a total change of outlook accompanied by meditation upon the Absolute, leading to total bliss through total absorption in the Absolute.

The theistic religions, Judaism, Islam, and Christianity see the uneasiness to lie in the mis-direction by man of his own will, which thus causes a barrier or separation to arise between him and true fellowship with the Living God. Salvation in this case comes by surrender of the will, followed by the bestowal of Divine Grace, which fills the life with divine power, and heals the breach.

(xv) EMIL BRUNNER

The range of Dr. Brunner's writing has been wide, and he has done good service in the field of ethics with his large work *Das Gebot und die Ordnungen*, and his smaller work on the conception of Justice. Here we are only concerned with his *Offenbarung und Vernunft* (Revelation and Reason) which was published at Zurich in 1941, but fortunately did not appear in a British edition until 1947, when there was more opportunity for it to be studied. Whether we agree with it or not, it is certainly of importance to understand why the usual order of the words has been reversed in the title. Catholic theology tends to start with the foundations of religion in nature and reason, and then proceeds to consider what it is that Man is unable to find out for himself, so that he has to depend for the knowledge of it on the supernatural self-revelation of Deity. Brunner's object is to show that from the Protestant standpoint the proper way of approach is to begin with revelation, and then to work outwards to reason. We have, he says, to learn afresh to read the Bible 'biblically'. By this he does not mean a return to the doctrine of verbal inspiration. Far from it, he considers that the latter has broken down as the result of modern scientific knowledge both in respect of natural and of historical science. What he means is that although the collection of documents which we call the Bible must be unhesitatingly studied by scientific methods, it will still be possible to find behind the words of the Bible certain facts and events which, taken altogether, constitute a *unique* body of knowledge about the living personal revelation of the Living God. 'The God of the Bible, as the Holy and Loving One, is the God who seeks Man.' Deity in many non-Christian systems may or may not be considered in relation to Man, but the God of the Bible is essentially one who is responsive, who goes out to meet Man, who takes the initiative, and whose desire is to impart himself. Although, therefore, the idea that Deity, in whatever form, may send some kind of message to man, sometimes about very trivial things, the essential feature about Deity as revealed in the course of events recorded in the documents of the Bible is one whose very nature it is to reveal himself wholly and fully. The God of the Bible is one who is continually being *encountered*. The foregoing represents the essential doctrine of the early part of Brunner's work, and it is difficult not to agree with it. It may well be that one of the great reasons for the remarkable spread of the Christian faith is this sense (which is derived from the whole corpus of biblical literature), that the Spirit of the Living God does not merely repose in His own dignity, but goes out to seek and to save. Once the truth of this has been felt, it is so powerful that it tends to sweep other religions out of the field. Perhaps it has been the duty and function of Protestantism to re-assert this fundamental truth, which in Catholicism is sometimes in danger of being blurred, as also in some kinds of Liberalism.

But this being the case, what may be justly said about the various non-Christian beliefs?—May it not be possible for a non-biblical religion partially or in some measure to point the way towards this self-revealing God?—Or is the exclusive claim: 'No one cometh unto the Father but by Me' still tenable, even in view of the facts of the history of religions?—Of course, every religion, however primitive, has some traces of the idea of human intercourse with a Divine Power or powers which can manifest themselves and can be encountered, and in so far as this is the case it is not unfair to say that there is encounter, even if it be in a dim or broken way, with the Living God. Brunner, in other words, does not, like Barth, totally reject the possibility of some general revelation, though one surmises that he would say if pressed, as some of the rest of us do, that no one can come to exactly the full knowledge and realisation of what is involved in 'the Fatherhood of God' except through Jesus Himself. Brunner rightly sees that the illumination which occurs in Buddhism, though it seems like an event of a supernatural character, is really more an intuition than a revelation. It involves instructions on the right path which man has to tread in order to achieve indestructible spiritual happiness. It is therefore primarily man-centred. There seems to be no communicating, self-disclosing Deity, who is either believed in or experienced. Brunner thus comes to the conclusion at which many have arrived after the consideration of the original experience of Gautama. But I have suggested elsewhere that although many later Buddhists have interpreted what happened to Gautama in this way, it may be that that was not the real meaning of the experience, and that we ought rather to regard his enlightenment as welling up within him in a context in which the identity of Deity and the finite self was widely assumed. Then the enlightenment would mean the self-revelation of the Infinite as *within* the finite. I have suggested this elsewhere, and only refer to it again because it does not seem to me that Brunner gives quite enough weight to the possibility that something like this may have happened in the case of Gautama. Quite clearly the latter does not say as does the prophet Amos: 'Thus saith the Lord.' Brunner sees that this kind of experience outside Judiasm and Christianity can only be detected in the message of Zarathustra, and in that of Mohammed. He differentiates strongly between these and the experiences of the Hebrew prophets. That Zarathustra and Mohammed both experienced some kind of encounter with the Living and Transcendent God it is difficult to deny, but Brunner sees in the case of the former a considerable difference in the nature and content of that which is revealed. The God of Zarathustra is a good, holy, and righteous Being, but He is not yet known as the generous giver of grace and pardon. Deity is here only the moral law, heightened and personified into the Absolute. Mohammed's alleged revelation seems to be lacking in creative originality. It is, says Brunner, a blend of Old Testament Judaism plus some secondary Christian elements, a fair amount of ancient Arabian paganism plus the elements of personal religious and poetic imagination. He agrees with Kraemer that the result is 'a superficial religion that has almost no questions and no answers'. It is possible to think that Brunner, and perhaps Kraemer too, here under-estimate the contribution of Mohammed and do not do justice to his greatness. However much the latter may have misunderstood the significance of what he was dealing with, it can hardly be denied that the material passed through his own very earnest prophetic mind, and received the original and individual impress of that mind. That it had its imperfections we may not doubt. But it is easier to think justly of Mohammed if we compare him with Luther. Both came some centuries *after* Christ, and it is not correct to say that Mohammed 'said no to Him'. His attitude to the great figure of Galilee was doubtless heretical and full of misconceptions, but he did recognise the Figure. Where Brunner is undoubtedly right is in seeing that the God of Mohammed is not conceived as engaging in personal self-communication, in the bestowal of divine grace upon the sinner whom he loves. It is a legalistic religion (perhaps owing to its over-indebtedness to Talmudic Judaism) in which one can be saved through one's works.

Brunner concludes that the common assumption that the Christian claim to revelation is opposed by a variety of similar claims of equal value is wholly untenable. The amazing thing, he says, is the exact opposite, i.e. that the claim of a revelation possessing universal validity in the history of religion is rare, and that the claim of revelation made by the Christian faith is in its radicalism as solitary as its content, the message of Atonement. Only at one place, and only in one event has God revealed Himself truly and completely. No other religion can assert revelation in this radical unconditional sense, because no other religion has the full and exact knowledge of God which is contained in the Christian faith. Of course the decisive words here are 'truly and completely'. To what extent would Brunner allow that the non-Christian religions were linked to the Christian through the principle of the Divine Logos? Brunner takes the line that in the doctrine of the Apologists and of Origen, as well as in later writings, a synthesis was accomplished which dangerously dimmed the purity of the biblical idea of God. In this way he seems like Kraemer to turn his back upon the Logos-doctrine of the Fourth Gospel, with the interpretation of which he does not actually deal at this point, though in his 20th chapter it seems clear that he takes the same line as Kraemer.

(xvi) E. C. DEWICK

In 1953 Dr. Dewick published his Hulsean Lectures. He had spent many years in India, and his familiarity with both Hinduism and Islam made him peculiarly well qualified to undertake a valuation of them, in relation to the Christian faith of which he had been for very many years a faithful missionary. His sensitiveness to the weaknesses and mistakes of missionaries involved him in the task of attempting to restate the message of Christ and in recovering first principles in the task of its dissemination. His obviously first-hand knowledge of the facts of missionary life and indeed its dependence throughout upon observed fact and original authorities make it impossible for those who disapprove of his conclusions to sweep it upon one side because they dislike it. With a great deal of what Dr. Dewick says one is bound to be in agreement. He covers much of the same ground as myself in the course of this book, and there are so many items in it which I have not myself noticed, and which I would have fain incorporated in these pages if they had come my way, that I gladly refer my readers to Dr. Dewick's work and hope that they will read it. But I am not quite sure whether in his third lecture he has not laid a little too much emphasis on the *message* of Christ, and rather less than he should have done upon the *action* of Christ. This probably affects his entire theology, and exposes him to the criticism of Dr. Kraemer, who thinks that his theology is neither sufficiently articulate or substantial, and that, therefore, his plea for inter-religious co-operation and mutual appreciation while maintaining the supremacy of Jesus Christ leads him into fatally blurring the true issues. It is significant that Kraemer groups Dewick with three other British scholars,[1] who in effect all produce what he calls in disparagement 'a modern version of Justin Martyr'.

Some of Dr. Dewick's quotations are especially worthy of mention. He reminds us for instance, that in 1928 a volume called

---

[1] Farquhar, MacNicol, and Soper.

Essays Catholic and Missionary[1] appeared in England in which the majority of the contributors, which included Miss Evelyn Underhill and Bishop Lucas of the U.M.C.A. mission in the African diocese of Masasi, endorsed the suggestion that Christianity is the fulfilment and completion of the best elements in other religions, and one contributor maintained that in the policy 'not to destroy, but to fulfil' Catholicism is nearer to Christ than Protestantism.   He continues that in 1930 the Lambeth Conference affirmed: 'We gladly acknowledge the truths contained and emphasised in the great religions; but . . . each of them is less than the Gospel of the unsearchable riches of Christ.   The majesty of God in Islam, the high moral standards and profound truth in other Eastern religions, are approaches to the truth of God revealed in Christ.'   He points out that so far as Judaism is concerned, the theory of fulfilment has substantiated its claim beyond reasonable doubt, and receives the approval of Christ Himself, but, as he says quite rightly, there is a case for disagreeing with the idea of 'fulfilment' in relation to Buddhism or Islam, since so much in each seems to differ fundamentally both from its neighbour and from Christianity.   That there should be a sympathetic rather than aggressive approach by Christians to non-Christians need not involve a sacrifice of any principle, and Dewick points out that it was no less a person than the Cardinal Archbishop of Algiers (Lavigerie), in the middle of the nineteenth century who, when passing a mosque, used to alight from his carriage and walk past it bare-foot.   Yet the Cardinal was a zealous and successful missionary who won many converts from Islam.   Dewick concludes that while he finds nothing to disprove and much to confirm the belief that through Christ God has given a revelation of truth that is for all mankind central, distinctive, supreme, and satisfying, he does not consider that this excludes the possibility that God may also have truly spoken to men through other channels, and that we should be ready to examine any evidence adduced in favour of or against this without fear or prejudice.   At the same time he considers that if we try to test all religions by Christian principles, it becomes clear that it is quite impossible to maintain that they are all fundamentally alike, or of equal value.   This in itself would seem to indicate that he does not himself approve of the 'fulfilment' principle, if it is held in any sweeping fashion.

(xvii) HENDRIK KRAEMER

We here approach a consideration of the ablest and most learned opponent of the more liberal attitude towards non-Christian

[1] See a later section in this chapter.

religions, and one to whom frequent reference has already been made. One might indeed almost say that the shadow of Kraemer looms over the whole of this book, and certainly over the present chapter, and the one on the doctrine of the Logos.

Dr. Kraemer published his first work, *The Christian Message in a Non-Christian World* in the year 1938. This book was written in preparation for an international missionary conference at Tambaram in South India, and rather unexpectedly received the commendation of Archbishop William Temple, all the more surprisingly since Kraemer himself disagreed subsequently with certain statements made by Temple in his Gifford Lectures about the relation between general and special revelation (the former term, he says, is quite alien to the Bible). The appearance of Kraemer's essay largely determined the form of the discussion at Tambaram, and some delegates agreed with it, while others vigorously opposed it. It is certainly the case that the more liberal and friendly approach which was manifested at the earlier Jerusalem conference of 1928, where some delegates urged the co-operation of Christians and non-Christians in opposing secularism, was largely absent from Tambaram, and this may well have been due to the weighty influence of Kraemer. He has since, in 1956, published another large work, *Religion and the Christian Faith*, in which, incidentally, he answers some of his critics, but in which he renews his attack, and aims at showing that if the Christian faith is properly conceived there really can be no inter-religious co-operation.

Kraemer sets out by drawing a sharp distinction between biblical realism and the naturalist religions of transempirical realisation. This is really not a new division, but a new way of describing an old one, quite familiar among Protestants on the Continent, where it appears sometimes as 'Das Evangelium und die Religionen'. 'Biblical realism' denotes the message from God which comes through and indeed unites into one corpus the diversified literature of the Bible. For Kraemer, and indeed for a good many other Protestants such as Karl Barth, it is not the same as the religion of the church (by which they chiefly mean the Roman). This, they think, is so much infected with naturalism that they prefer to put it on the same side of the line as for example, Hinduism; and such being the case, it would seem that for Kraemer the witness of churches other than those of the Reformation must be seriously defective. Indeed, in his second volume, he has very little indeed to say about the witness of the great Roman Communion, and dismisses it in nine pages, whereas he devotes seventeen to Radhakrishnan. Kraemer's versatility as a Biblical scholar, a philosopher, and a missionary in

Indonesia, makes him a formidable antagonist, and indeed, it would be extremely dangerous to say that his wide learning and shrewd power of observation do not lead him on many occasions to a correct conclusion. There are, however, certain points in which he seems to go wrong. First of all, his attitude towards the Bible, like that of Brunner, seems to detach it too much from its context, and so to give it just that exaggerated degree of authority which it certainly had among the earlier Protestants.[1] Kraemer declares that he is perfectly prepared to avail himself of the results of Biblical criticism. He is quite clear that if one uses it aright, the Bible 'demythologises itself'; and he shows that not only sober history but myth, poetry, and drama can be used by God as the medium of revelation, yet he adds that although the Bible is composed of many writings produced over a range of more than a thousand years, from the time it was made into one book it functioned as one book, because in spite of its multiform composition it was held together by its one great theme. In spite of this, when it comes to the exegesis of the Bible, Kraemer shows a certain individualism which is perhaps characteristic of the Protestant group of commentators. I have tried to show elsewhere why I do not think that he is right in his treatment of the prologue to the Fourth Gospel. Like most continental Protestants, he lays immense stress upon the teaching of St. Paul, and especially on the Epistle to the Romans, and one doubts whether such emphasis is really justified, and whether it has not the effect of making one's theology lopsided, and of even distorting just a little the meaning of St. Paul himself. In any case it is hazardous to put forward what seems something perilously like the infallibility of the apostle, and it is surely improper to make so little relative use of the Gospels. And this brings me to what seems to be a very serious inconsistency in all Protestant exegesis of this school, mainly that whereas it claims to accept the full benefits of literary criticism, and to have abandoned any doctrine of verbal inspiration, it seems to be continually slipping back into something very like the latter. Kraemer's treatment of certain passages in the book of Genesis seems to come very close to this, and when he says that he is only concerned to get at the real sense of the Bible text, whether it suits him or not, and to try as best one can to take it as it wants to be understood, to try to find out what is its peculiar mode of thinking, and to try to present this thinking according to its peculiar genius, he seems to overlook the possibility that this way of thinking might prove to be an impossible one for

---

[1] One recalls the statement of Chillingworth, 'the Bible, another Bible only, is the religion of Protestants'. But Chillingworth, like Hooker before him, would allow a place of honour to *reason* in his interpretation of the scriptures.

the world of the present day, and that it might also be necessary to do as Dr. Jowett advised many years ago,[1] and interpret the Bible with the same detachment and impartiality as any other book; although there is, of course, a sense in which he is perfectly right, mainly that the literature of the Bible does imply a theocentric outlook of a unique character.

There is too much in both these volumes of Kraemer for one to be able to do justice to them in a short survey such as this. In his earlier volume he has many pregnant remarks to make about the nature of the religions of Asia, and in his more recent volume he covers an immense amount of ground, and includes one whole very apposite section upon Indian religious thought with special reference to Radhakrishnan, and a long treatise at the end upon the work of Paul Tillich. Kraemer recognises that some of the criticisms of his earlier book were valid. Thus he considers that Dr. Farmer was quite right in saying that Kraemer and many others holding similar opinions have too much neglected the awareness of God which is to be found in the non-Christian religions. He defends himself in the controversy over the 'point of contact' by saying that in this matter there are two levels of concern which must not be confused, i.e. the level of practical evangelism and ordinary human contact, in which he is pretty well in agreement with his critics, and the level of exclusive concern about the question of truth, where he holds strongly to his main thesis, that there is really no way through from the non-Christian religions to the Christian faith, since the former start from different assumptions, and the latter is wholly given, and does not work *through* them but *independently* of them. But this, of course, is just what so many great Christian propagandists in past and present have not accepted.

There are certain further criticisms of Dr. Kraemer's treatment of his subject which one feels bound to make, and in which I find myself in general agreement with something which has recently been written about it by Dr. Dewick. In the first place it seems very questionable whether he is right in not allowing either our human reason or our moral sense any right at all to form a judgment upon the nature of Divine Revelation. By all means let us recognise that human reason has its limits, but that is not at all the same as refusing it any validity, and it seems as though Kraemer himself is blind to this, since throughout his book he certainly makes an appeal to reason, and himself reasons carefully. Again, if the use of analogy in philosophical theology be completely cut away, as it is by Kraemer and other neo-Protestants, this means that the truth con-

[1] In *Essays and Reviews*.

cerning God has no relation to any human conception, and consequently to human conceptions of good and evil. Hence on this count God appears to be beyond or above moral distinctions. But this is surely not a Christian view at all. It completely disposes of our natural tendency to judge various religions by an absolute moral standard, the moral consciousness of mankind of which Dr. Rashdall wrote so much. Yet in both the Old and New Testaments it is certainly assumed that both the righteousness of men and human love are akin to the righteousness and love of God, though the latter far surpasses them both in perfection. This total rejection of analogy can only mean that the decision about what to accept as Divine Revelation depends solely upon faith, which must in consequence be blind faith, and is in fact itself a divine gift, so that to be logical one must say that Almighty God decides for us what we are to believe, and we have nothing to do but to submit. But this is not New Testament Christianity at all. This is Islam ('It shall be as Allah pleases'). How can we tell that what is offered us really is Revelation, if the choice is made for us, in which case the operation of our own minds ceases to exist? This seems absurd. Is it possible that Dr. Kraemer is exercising here subconsciously some kind of personal preference?

It may be, as Dr. Dewick says, that Dr. Kraemer would retort that he bases his faith on what is *given in* the Bible. But if so, he ought to base it upon the *whole* Bible and not upon part of it, as Dr. Dewick says: 'Not upon a text here and a passage there, often without taking account of other Biblical passages which point towards different conclusions.' Although he declares his general acceptance of modern Biblical research, and repudiates any idea that he is a fundamentalist, he really makes very little use of critical studies, and again and again treats the text of the Bible, and especially that of the Old Testament, exactly in the way that a fundamentalist does. And while he sometimes affirms the definition of the Canon by the Church as due to Divine guidance, at other times he clearly rejects it, and relies on his own individual judgment, just as Luther did.

The same kind of individualism besets him in his treatment of Church Theology. He begins by admitting that the Church has a divine commission, but he has clearly his own definition as to what this divinely commissioned Church is. It is clearly not the Church of the first four centuries, since the chief Doctors of the latter are all found fault with. It is not Augustine; it is not Aquinas; it is not even all the reformers, since Zwingli is excluded, and by implication the Anglicans. Apparently it is only in Luther and Calvin that for the first time in the history of the Christian Church we find a true theology of religion. It is all very puzzling, and since even Barth and Brunner are not entirely excluded from criticism, while there is a drastic treatment of Paul Tillich, one is left with the sensation that Dr. Kraemer is really almost in the position of the old Scotchwoman who said she thought that the only two elect persons in her village were herself and the Minister, and 'she whiles had doots aboot him'. I don't suppose that this is really the case, but the matter is a serious one, and again cannot be settled along denominational lines. May it not be that the Great Church is still in the womb of the future and that therefore all our theologies are to that extent provisional and imperfect? A genuinely ecumenical theology need not be that of Dr. Kraemer, but neither need it prove to be exactly that of Fr. Przywara.

(xviii) RUDOLF BULTMANN AND PAUL TILLICH

The importance of Bultmann's theological revaluation centres round his notion of 'de-mythologising' Christianity. It is sometimes thought that this merely involves a renewal of the earlier attempts at modernism, such as the allegorisation of the early narratives of Genesis, or the recognition that the account of the birth of Our Lord has been attracted into forms widely current in the Gentile world. But Bultmann actually means much more than this. He holds that the entire world-outlook of the first century A.D. was dramatic rather than scientific, mythological rather than empirical; so that as we receive the gospel in the New Testament, it is presented to us there wholly by persons who accepted such an outlook, which is not naturally today that of persons who have been brought up with a scientific education.

Bultmann, whether successfully or no, therefore endeavours to detach the Gospel from this first-century setting, and to show that the historical Jesus has a value and message which are as essential for the twentieth century as for the first. It has lately been suggested that Bultmann is mistaken in identifying the expression of the religion of Jesus Himself with the mythological beliefs of the first century, and that in de-mythologising he may only be discarding that which Jesus Himself rejected. In other words, the mythology of the first century may have been a perversion of the non-mythological. Jesus may have used myth to express His message, but He did not allow myth to use Him, and we see Him best as superior to the mythology of His day, though He does not always seem to have troubled to detach the essence of what He had to say from the current mythological terms used by His contemporaries.

The critic would thus suggest that the task of de-mythologising is not that of taking us on to a more mature form of Christianity but of restoring the latter to its original form, as it took shape in the mind of its Founder.

Nevertheless it is fair to say that behind and beyond the views of modern empirical scientists, the dramatic element persists and is inescapable. Good and evil are realities, and the best of men are still conscious that there is a mystery of ungodliness against which they are battling, and which often seems to confront them with frustration. As stated in its negative form by the astronomers, with their picture of a race of earth-dwellers doomed to extinction, of stellar matter in a myriad forms waxing and waning, and of their ignorance as to the meaning of it all, we have at least drama in its most tragic form. With such before their eyes, Christians have no need to to be apologetic when they affirm the possibility of a victorious dénouement when God shall be all in all.

Tillich, to the consternation of Kraemer, affirms positively in his various works that the Logos-doctrine is the foundation and starting point of Christian theology, and also its meeting point with philosophy. The Logos who has become concrete in Jesus, is at the same time the Universal Logos, and wherever the latter is at work it agrees in fundamentals with the Christian message. No philosophy which is obedient to the Universal Logos can contradict the concrete Logos who 'became flesh'.

There would seem to be some over-statement here. The agreement of the Universal Logos, when at work outside Christianity, with the Christian message, is certainly not everywhere apparent. A measure of agreement in places there may be, but it is only fair to suppose that some distortion or brokenness may occur at times as the result of the human element, with its imperfection and finitude. Moreover, it is possible for there to be a good deal of philosophy which is not obedient to the Universal Logos, and may therefore contradict the concrete Logos.

Tillich gets over this by adherence to the doctrine of the Fall, which, although it does not destroy reason, blinds or blurs it in action (verblendet).

Kraemer's criticism of this may be summed up in two of his paragraphs. First, he queries the centrality of *reason,* as it was affirmed by the Greeks. Modern psychology in its analysis of man's nature seems somewhat less confident about it, and tends to lay greater stress upon the libido. Secondly, he maintains that in biblical epistemology also the heart rather than the reason is central.

In effect, the affirmation of the Bible is that mankind is repeatedly and constantly offered the friendship of God and that the Fall, therefore, is the rejection of that friendship, a rejection which in varying degrees is perennial and universal, but which vitiates human thought as well as human action.

To allow for development, Tillich defines Christianity as final revelation only in the sense of being decisive, fulfilling, and un-surpassable,[1] but he leaves room for a continuous (post-axial?) revelation in the history of the Christian Church (this without safe-guards might lead to an acceptance of the Ultramontane Roman position) as well as in the various contacts between Christianity and the other religions of the world.

The Continentals use the term 'ontology' more than we do. It would seem that by it they mean a mode of thinking about the being of the world in naturalistic terms rather like that of Julian Huxley or R. B. Braithwaite, in both of whom the element of doubt is strong. But, says Tillich, faith and doubt belong together, since faith in-cludes doubt or presupposes it as rejected (there is courage to risk what still remains not wholly secure). The task of biblical religion is to correlate itself with ontology, by seeking, on the basis of the Logos doctrine, the intellectual conversion of the latter.

Kraemer rejects the friendliness of Tillich towards mysticism, which he always considers as Eros rather than Pistis. He finds it difficult to understand how Tillich, with his biblical background, can join hands so easily with Orientals like Aurobindo Ghose. Although he feels that Tillich is quite sincere in his 'Sisyphus-job' of keeping the two dimensions under one common denominator; he doesn't quite see how he does it. It may well be that Tillich, in spite of his immense learning, is here guilty of a confusion of thought from which a scholar like Heiler or Przywara is delivered by his essentially Catholic background and tradition. There is, as we have seen elsewhere, a fundamental distinction between pre-Dionysian Chris-tian mysticism and that which is either completely non-Christian or post-Dionysian Christian.

(xix) KARL JASPERS

Mention has been made as far back as Chapter II of this re-markable Swiss philosopher of the mid-twentieth century. That he has a profound sense of the importance of religion cannot be doubted, and in one respect he is of special importance for the present work,

---

[1] A critic writes: 'The real point (which you do not make) in Tillich's position over the finality of the revelation in Christ is that it "negates itself without losing itself", by bringing a judgment against all culture and all religion, Christianity included.'

because of his development of the idea of an 'Achsenperiode der Weltgeschichte', which had previously been discerned by Otto, and also by Henri Masson. Jaspers attributes immense importance to this 'Achsenzeit' in the history of the human race, but, as we saw in Chapter II, he makes it begin later than the prevalence of the earlier *sebayit* literature in Egypt, and terminate before the emergence of Christianity, yet nevertheless suggests that it is also the acme, the culmination and normative point in human history.

He confesses that although he himself does not believe in revelation, he nevertheless derives the whole of his faith from the thought of the Bible, which he declares is something that does not belong exclusively to any single religion, but to the world. He rejects revelation partly because for him it spells exclusiveness, which is abhorrent, but partly because he prefers as a philosopher to reach God through 'Erdenken' (excogitation). He stops short before he reaches the New Testament, and would fain content himself with some version of the prophetic religion of the Old Testament; and he feels that the Christian thesis, being that of one religion among several, cannot possess universal validity. It is evident that this position can have no finality about it, since it starts from a prejudice against listening to Christianity as it gives its own account of itself. The New Testament is treated by Jaspers in an old-fashioned 'liberal' way, and is not allowed to tell its own tale.

Though exciting our sympathy, and certainly making some contribution towards the discovery of a *Ziel der Geschichte* ('goal towards which history is tending'—he would rather say 'axis on which it revolves') Jaspers cannot be said to succeed in relating his biblical inheritance with any comfort to his own special brand of existential philosophy. He actually ends by saying that the Christian universalist claim is a purely human one, and does not come from God at all. Thus in the last resort he opens the way to neo-Hinduism, and gives up the task of making sense of the biblical postulates. Yet the curious fact is that Jaspers' insistence upon an Achsenperiode is no more invulnerable as a theory than the insistence upon Christianity as the culmination of religion upon earth. If anything, the latter claim strengthens the whole position, and Jaspers' exclusion of Christianity weakens his theory by taking a vital part out of the picture.

(xx) ARNOLD TOYNBEE

Professor Toynbee is best known for his monumental study of History, in which, following Spengler, with massive learning and considerable originality he has sought to interpret the various phases in the story of the human race. In his Gifford Lectures delivered at

Edinburgh in 1952 and 1953 he has turned his attention to an interpretation of the history of the various religions of mankind. He had begun the consideration of this in his Reith Lectures on the world and the West which were also delivered in 1952, and in which he had pursued the subject previously dealt with some years before by Professor Joad on the impact of the East upon the West. One recognises in these Edinburgh lectures his now familiar technique in classification and generalisation, and in the invention of strange adjectives, such as Buddhaic and Hinayanian. He has his own division of the subject, splitting it up for consideration into (1) the worship of nature, (2) man-worship in which local communities are made into idols, (3) man-worship in which large communities, such as the Roman Empire, are made into idols, (4) man-worship in which a philosopher is made into an idol, the obvious examples being Kung-fu-tze and perhaps Gautama the Buddha.

From these he passes to what he calls the higher religions, and sees the latter in collision respectively with idolised empires and with philosophers as well as with attempts to capture and divert them from spiritual to mundane tasks. He then passes on to what he calls the idolisation of religious institutions. It is rather curious that he seems to list ten higher religions as once existing in the Hellenic world, of which he sees six as still in the field today, in addition to two philosophies. It is difficult to feel quite happy about all this classification. To begin with, it seems to draw the line between the higher religions (so-called) and the earlier ones at the wrong point, and so to blur the distinction between the developments of the axial age and those which preceded it. Moreover, Buddhists, one feels sure, would resent the placing of the Mahayana in one pigeon-hole as religion, and the Hinayana or Theravada in another pigeon-hole as philosophy. And further, Confucianism is now so much on the decline that it is difficult to know what one can wisely predict about its survival. Finally, is it justifiable to classify the worship of Cybele and Isis under the heading of higher religions?

In his second series of lectures Toynbee deals at some greater length with what he calls religion in a westernising world. Here he seems to consider rather too exclusively the various western expressions of Christianity. He brings under observation in turn the reaction of the West against the distinctive medieval Christian way of life, and especially its reaction against coercive persecution, and the general secularisation of the western world in which the technician became idolised instead of the inspired saint. He sees this worship of technology and its exponents as going on right up to the present day, and as being mainly responsible for the great spiritual decline of

society during the first half of the twentieth century. The release
of atomic energy in 1945 has in his judgment brought this idolisation
to a sudden end. The technician 'after having been undeservedly
idolised for a quarter of a millennium as the good genius of mankind,
has now suddenly found himself undeservedly execrated as an evil
genius who has released from his bottle a jinn that may perhaps
destroy human life on the earth'. But not only has the technician
ceased to be worshipped. He has also lost the intellectual freedom
which he enjoyed for the past 250 years. Science, instead of being
a purely beneficent rationalistic occupation, has in many quarters
come to be regarded as 'a shocking vent for Original Sin, and a
serious threat to man's welfare and perhaps even to his existence'.

With most of this analysis there might be some measure of
agreement. But what is going to be substituted for this idolatry?
Toynbee recognises that the disillusionment of the West with what
has been until lately its idol, has brought it back once more face to
face with religion, which means in many cases with traditional
Christianity. It cannot avoid this re-encounter, and it finds itself
compelled to reconsider how it stands towards its earlier religious
heritage which it had discarded. But in doing so, it finds the situation in which it stands complicated by a much closer contact with the
non-Christian religions. Unless, therefore, it is going to be rigidly
conservative, shut its eyes to these, and refuse also to consider
any of the effects upon the expression of Christianity which have
come from the modern scientific and critical approach to the Bible,
to Church History, and to religious experience, it is bound to take
some serious notice of Buddhism, modern Hinduism, Judaism, and
Islam, as well perhaps as of the religion of the Parsis which has been
striving within the limits of a small community to modernise itself.

By this time Toynbee has approached the last two chapters of
his book, and it is significant that in making his own analysis he
almost completely ignores Judaism and Islam, and has very little to
say about Hinduism. He urgently commends the spirit of toleration.
Religious conflict is not just a nuisance but a sin; and religious persecution also, of whatever kind, whether Catholic or Communist, is
equally sinful. But he goes further, and in this respect seems to
unite with the neo-Hindus. 'Absolute Reality is a mystery of which
no more than a fraction has ever yet been penetrated by—or been
revealed to—any human mind' and he follows up the latter by a
quotation from Symmachus which occurs in the course of a controversy with Saint Ambrose:

'The heart of so great a mystery cannot ever be reached by following
one road only.'

27

He continues:

'However strong and confident may be my conviction that my own approach to the mystery is a right one, I ought to be aware that my field of spiritual vision is so narrow that I cannot know that there is no virtue in other approaches. In theistic terms this is to say that I cannot know that other people's visions may not also be revelations from God—and these perhaps fuller and more illuminating revelations than the one that I believe that I myself have received from Him.

Moreover, the fact that I and my neighbour are following different roads is something that divides us much less than we are drawn together by the other fact that, in following our different roads, we are both trying to approach the same mystery. All human beings who are seeking to approach the mystery in order to direct their lives in accordance with the nature and spirit of Absolute Reality or, in theistic terms, with the will of God—all these fellow-seekers are engaged in an identical quest. They should recognise that they are spiritually brethren and should feel towards one another, and treat one another, as such. Toleration does not become perfect until it has been transfigured into love.'

In his final chapter he contents himself with placing in contrast Buddhism and Christianity. He appears to accept the fact of Original Sin without either defining it or criticising, but he seems to agree with basic Buddhism that the suffering in life mainly proceeds from emphasis upon self-centredness. But many will say that suffering is not necessarily the greatest evil in life, and that a self-centredness which aims at the escape from suffering, even by a spiritual technique, may be a greater evil. Toynbee would choose the way of the Mahayana rather than that of the Theravada. Whereas both are agreed that it is right to seek to extinguish self-centred desires, the Mahayana goes on to diagnose a desire which is not self-centred and which therefore can be pursued because it is a good desire, that of self-sacrifice; and this may not be self-extinction, but the devotion of the self in loving service to others at the cost of whatever suffering this service may bring with it.

This, as Toynbee sees, brings Christianity and the Mahayana on to the same side as against the Hinayana, and, of course, at this point he is brought up face to face with the problem as to which is the original form of Buddhism. Is the Mahayana the Buddhism of the Buddha's own school, or is it a reinterpretation due to some kind of external influence? Toynbee seems to be of the opinion that if the former is the case, then the Buddha, refusing access to Nirvana, is to be equated with Christ resisting the temptation not to drink the cup of suffering. We may well agree that in this matter the Buddha of the Mahayana and Christ draw very near together; but of course the important question remains: is the Mahayana picture historical?

According to many of the early stories about the Buddha, he saw detachment as meaning 'to wander alone in the forest like a rhinoceros', and when he was confronted with the appealing figures of his wife and her little son, met the spectacle with complete indifference. Toynbee does not seem to consider this, except in so far as he admits that for the *arhat* or Buddhist saint who is pursuing detachment, every other self in the universe is not a 'thou' to be loved, but an 'it' to be repudiated; and a desire that treats persons as if they were things is self-centred even when its only use for them is to be quit of them.   One answer to this, however, as Toynbee sees, may be to say that the Buddha was not preaching what he was practising, and that when he engaged in a long ministry to help other people to release themselves from suffering he was tacitly countermanding his own previous teaching.   It seems that this very difficult question demands a more detailed enquiry than Toynbee has given it.   Were it the case that the historical Gautama both taught and practised self-denial in the loving service of others, Toynbee's logical inference that the Buddhist and the Christian ways to heaven are equally valid would be justified.   But this really remains to be established.   In any case he seems totally to ignore the Logos doctrine.

Toynbee in conclusion comes back again to Symmachus, whose argument for tolerance, he says, has never been answered by his Christian opponents.   We may well agree that the forcible suppression of the old Roman religion by the secular arm of a Christian Roman government was no answer at all.   But the way to answer Symmachus, in whatever form he reappears, is not by penalising him, but by proving that what he says, however attractive it may look, is something which is not properly phrased.   The heart of so great a mystery may certainly be pursued by more than one road: but it does not follow in reason that all roads are necessarily equally good or direct.   They may not even be roads going in the right direction. They may be blind alleys.   Or they may not be roads at all.   Such considerations do not seem to enter into Toynbee's argument in the final pages of his volume.   One feels that his conclusions are based rather upon sentiment than upon genuinely scientific enquiry.   It is not necessarily true that the visions of the higher religions are not competitive but complementary.   They may be related, and in many respects doubtless are.   But that does not necessarily place them all upon a dead level.   One cannot avoid the conclusion that the whole problem, though illuminated by Toynbee in many ways in his highly original work, demands for its solution a more detailed enquiry than he has seen fit to give it, and that in framing any general theory it will not do to leave Judaism and Islam so much out of account.

(xxi) R. H. L. SLATER AND H. H. FARMER

I am glad to be able to include here a reference to an article published in the *Canadian Journal of Theology* by Professor R. H. L. Slater of McGill University (who was a pupil of mine over thirty years ago), in which he sums up the present position from the point of view of one who has for some time been working in transatlantic countries, and was before that for a good many years at Rangoon. Dr. Slater points out that for the newly populated countries of the Commonwealth and for the younger churches of emancipated Asia, faced by a resurgence of the great rivals of the Christian faith, a revaluation of the Christian attitude to other religions is not academic, but a sheer matter of life and death. He begins by quoting an attempt by Archbishop Temple the younger to reconcile the two divergent opinions of Kraemer and of his more liberal opponents, which occurs at the beginning of his commentary on the Fourth Gospel.

> 'All that is noble in the non-Christian system of thought, or conduct, or worship', says Temple, 'is the work of Christ upon them and within them. By the word of God—that is to say, by Jesus Christ— Isaiah and Plato, and Zoroaster, and Buddha, and Confucius conceived and uttered such truths as they declared. There is only one divine Light; and every man in his measure is enlightened in spite of veils of prejudice and obsession ... and when it blazes out more fully, men refuse it. For these reasons it is true both that Christ is indeed the Desire of All Nations,[1] and yet that He is always more and other than men desire until they learn of Him. To come to Him is always an act of self-surrender as well as of self-fulfilment, and must be first experienced as self-surrender.'

This, of course, is a typical example of Temple's capacity, which almost amounted to genius, for combining two separate points of view in a single sentence or paragraph. But this attempt to hold together conflicting points of view, as we know from personal experience of Temple, did not always maintain itself successfully outside the committee-room, or the House of Convocation, and the curious thing is that as we have already observed Temple subsequently commended Kraemer's famous first book as 'likely to remain for many years the classical treatment of its theme'. Of course it may have seemed obvious that the rather facile liberalism of the 1920s had somewhat overstepped the mark in its readiness to adopt large chunks of material from Asian sacred books as a sort of Old Testament for converts from Hinduism and Buddhism, but it may be thought equally that the influence of Dr. Kraemer on the meeting of the International Missionary Council at Tambaram in 1938 was

[1] It is regrettable to see Temple assenting here to a mistranslation of the Hebrew text of Haggai.

excessive. Slater rightly draws attention to the Gifford Lectures of
Professor H. H. Farmer, to whose work, published in 1954, it is
appropriate here to draw attention. Farmer is perhaps justifiably
suspicious of a purely detached, objective study of the religions of the
world by any Christian. He thinks it an *ignis fatuus*. In a way it
is possible to agree with him, since to be what Dr. Inge called 'an
honorary member of all religions' gets one nowhere. Nevertheless
I do not think the discipline of making an objective study of the
religions of the world, and of listening to what each has to say about
itself before fitting it into any general theory of one's own, is one
which ought to be discarded. I consider it a good discipline for the
mind of the would-be theologian, provided that he also masters
thoroughly the meaning and claims of Christianity, and knows it
in worship and practice from the inside. After that he can go back
again to the non-Christian faiths and appraise them in the light of
his Christian experience. But if he begins this appraisal before he
has heard what they have to say for themselves he will run the
danger of being unjust, and will in any case be acting in violation of
the best principles of scientific method. I consider also that it is only
fair to allow the general public to share in this objective study, since
if it is discouraged, the suspicion may be aroused in the minds
of many that the Christian faith cannot stand comparison with
other faiths, and that its exponents know this, and are apprehensive
of what will happen if they allow too many facts to be known.

Having said this, one can then whole-heartedly support Dr.
Farmer's plea for the proper recognition of one's own personal
experience of the God claiming to be revealed in Christ, because this,
studied in worship and daily life, is a proper subject for empirical
investigation, and both in its very nature and its effects is *sui generis*
and unique—something quite distinct from any experience (however
much it may be that of what Slater calls 'depth-religion') which
may be found anywhere else. 'Christus-mystik' (the phrase comes
from Schweitzer) is a thing apart; otherwise how are we to account
for the many converts to it from other faiths? Conversions in the
opposite direction are not only rare but always seem to have something just a little odd about them. This is no disparagement of
whatever good may be found in other kinds of 'depth-religion'—and
it is certainly to be found there. It is simply a case of the better
replacing the good, of that which has the greatest capacity of solving
the problems of life and so of being of universal value, diffusing
itself, and by diffusion superseding what went before; and as it goes
along, possibly absorbing and baptising something of the old faith to
the service of the new.

One thing at any rate is certain, that diffusion, if it is to be good, must proceed in a friendly, peaceful, and comradely spirit. I heartily endorse Slater's remark that a great many people today, being sensitive of a growing concern for world peace, feel equally that religion ought to be on the side of peace, and that it is intolerable that a conflict of religious ideologies should menace this peace.

(xxii) ESSAYS CATHOLIC AND MISSIONARY (Miss Underhill and Professor Laurence Browne)

I have left to the last the consideration of this somewhat important work (even sacrificing chronology in order to do so), partly because the first two essays which it contains seem to me the clearest and most sympathetic which have appeared during the process of revaluation. That they have not attracted more attention is I think partly due to the fact that when they appeared in 1928 they were published in conjunction with fourteen other essays, most of which, though quite excellent in their way, were concerned in the main with the domestic problems and principles of the mission field, but partly perhaps because the title of the book suggested to observers a pure piece of propaganda, in which the conclusions were already prescribed. This, however, would not be at all a fair estimate of its contents. The essay by Bishop Lucas upon non-Christian customs has been published elsewhere as a separate pamphlet, and has been referred to already in the chapter on Indigenisation. But the first two essays dealing with the claims of other religions than Christianity, and with the presentation of the Gospel to the greater religions deserve detailed consideration here, and I venture to think that were they better known they would be found to answer a good many of the questions which the educated but not theologically-trained public has been asking frequently during the past five or ten years.

Miss Underhill begins by describing the obvious situation, namely that Christians can only make good their claim that theirs is *the* world religion by proving it to be distinct in kind and superior in effect as compared with other systems. Of course this would not in itself establish that a Christianity is the *final* world religion, but only its distinction and superiority as far as the history of religion has as yet proceeded. That there was nothing ahead would thus be an act of faith based upon considerations of probability. But to return to Miss Underhill.

She considers three possible attitudes: to dismiss the other religions as wholly false; to regard them as imperfect revelations of the one true God (some might here retort that the Christian faith was another of the partial revelations); or thirdly, to maintain that the

Christian Gospel is not merely the fulfilment of the others but also cuts across them in a manner of criticism.

In her essay she recommends the third of these attitudes. She begins by granting that there are similarities as well as differences. Like Islam, the Christian faith subordinates all things to the will of the Eternal and Infinite God. Like the Hinduism of the Vedanta, it offers a sublime vision of infinite Deity. Like the Bhaktas of Hinduism and the Sufis of Islam it declares God's accessibility and responsiveness to man's love, as well as His demand for entire surrender. Like Buddhism and Confucianism at their best it sets a lofty ethical standard. It proclaims a doctrine of grace, not unknown elsewhere. Such similarities when observed have appealed to some missionaries of the modern type. But on the other side she sees that for many Asians the Ultimate is strictly impersonal, and against this Christianity comes into the world 'as a revelation of the Absolute God, made through man to men, which discloses in the essential nature of the very Godhead *the perfection of all that we mean by personality*'. It is the consciousness of this which makes the great Christian mystics so different from the non-Christian ones. Non-Christian theism may give us the sense of the 'numinous'; but it fails to bring the latter into close relation with the actualities of human life; and she points out that the efforts of the great medieval reformers in Hinduism were mainly directed to this end, even though they may not have succeeded. In the distinctive Catholic doctrine of the Incarnation in history once and for all, grounded upon the witness of the New Testament, she sees the real fulfilment of the religious need of the world. But in this, the Christian revelation cuts right across the Hindu conception of a God who is simply equally immanent in the whole world, and the Moslem conception of prophecy as the only means by which the exclusively transcendent Deity is disclosed to man.

The anchorage of Christianity upon history is a very strong one, and Miss Underhill rightly points out that one has only to compare the story of Krishna with the story of the Cross in order to show how strong it is.

Moreover, there is a greater richness and depth of reality revealed by the Cross than can be found elsewhere. Taoist or Buddhist ethics may be noble as far as they go, but Christianity goes on where they stop. The act of God and the interpretation of human life offered in the story of the Passion is so profound and yet so simple that as St. Augustine has said 'an elephant can swim in it and a lamb can wade'.

The Christian doctrine of God, says Miss Underhill, possesses three points of manifest superiority over its rivals. They may all have ideas about what is holy, about what needs to be set right, and about Divine activity; but the Christian conceptions of ethical holiness, of the redemption of life not by rejecting it but by transforming it, and of the supreme priority of God which makes everything in life, and especially the rescue of man from self-centredness, a free gift, not an achievement, a generous dower of life given from above, not a task laboriously worked out from below, these are all of them unsurpassed elsewhere.

Miss Underhill readily admits that there is much in the language of the mystics which makes it difficult when a sentence is taken out of its context, to say whether it comes from Christian or non-Christian sources; but she points out quite rightly that when put back into their context the non-Christian sentences are seen to be expressions of piety directed towards a Deity who is often unattractive and seriously deficient in the beauty and excellence of the Christian God: while on the other hand some of the greatest non-Christian mystics, such as Hallaj the Sufi, are also found to be heretics within their own religion, and even if not declared as such, are seen to draw from Christianity some of their most characteristic ideas. I would add here, what she does not mention, that the Saivite mystical hymns of South India in their content strongly suggest that they have been influenced by ideas coming from the ancient Christian Church in that part of the sub-continent. But again, the non-Christian saint is usually the lonely soul who does not get much support from the religious system into which he is born, and does not contribute much to it. He is either a Sufi who stands aloof, a Hindu Yogi who lives a hermit life, or a Buddhist monk who is a recluse. It is true that there have been hermits and recluses within the Christian Church, but in general they are linked up with the worshipping community of which they are members. Even the Christian contemplative spends much time in intercession for the community and for individuals within it, and at stated intervals worships corporately, and receives sacremental communion.

Miss Underhill appropriately quotes the words of Father Maréchal of the Society of Jesus in defining the opposition between Christian and non-Christian mystics.

'Christian asceticism is not directly ordered to the attainment of mystical states. It has as its end the perfection of supernatural charity. The Church knows of methods and schools for the attainment of spiritual perfection, but not, properly speaking, of schools or methods for procuring the mystical states, far less of procuring ecstasy.'

She sees rightly that where Christianity is strongest, there Bhakti and Sufi experience are weakest. They are not only lonely but they are not creative; they never achieve that divine fecundity which is the goal of the supernatural life for the Christian saints. She quotes Radnakrishnan in giving an account of the *bhaktas*, but points out that some of his propositions could hardly have assumed their precise form without the help of the New Testament and of Christian theology; and yet that when he gives the most favourable account of it, it still remains a lonely and aristocratic type of spirituality, very different from the humble and self-giving life of the Christian mystic as delineated by Father Poulain in his *Graces of Interior Prayer*.

She ends this section by a useful quotation from Cardinal Mercier:

'The interests of a Christian are not a private matter. They are the interests of the whole community. All that you do, for good or for evil, either benefits or damages the whole society of souls. By your work, your purity of life, your participation in the common suffering, you can intensify and extend the Kingdom of Love.'

Her final point is the well-known but perhaps not sufficiently emphasised one, that the Christian ethic is not a code which is satisfied by obedience to it, but the free application of a principle which is centred upon God and not upon even a sublimated self-interest. Sublimation there may be, but it is sublimation which is centred upon a vision of God and an obligation towards God. Miss Underhill sees that this ideal is not always completely fulfilled in the Christian movement as we have it; but she sees also that where there is fulfilment Christianity can face without fear or apprehension the claims of any other systems which may exist outside it.

Professor Laurence Browne has himself been a missionary, and writes with inside knowledge of Islam.

He begins by warning us of the danger which we may encounter if we try to assert the superiority of Christianity as containing a greater measure of truth. Truth is not a commodity which can be measured in units, and truth and error cannot in this case very well be computed after the manner of book-keeping. Such a comparison could only make Christianity out to be superior in degree to other religions, but could not demonstrate its finality. But we must learn to think of Christianity as different in kind, so that although it may contain many points of resemblance, and may even share much that is good with the best which is to be found in the other great faiths, it possesses in itself one really original thing, namely the historical Jesus, from whom all the rest of its originality proceeds, and in whom the various

28

truths which may be found existing separately in many religious are brought into one great synthesis.

He faces the fact, which we noticed right at the beginning of this book, that each of the great non-Christian religions is today undergoing a severe crisis, not only as the result of the impact upon it of Christianity but also that of Western culture. Many Japanese students are agnostic: so are many Hindu students. The growing materialism and indifference to religious practices which he himself has seen among the educated Moslems of Cairo and Constantinople are instances of this. Had he been writing today he would no doubt have had much to say about the influence of Marxism. He does not welcome the break-up of other religions, because he sees that in most cases it does not lead to Christianity but rather to materialism and agnosticism.

As he sees the situation, each of the great non-Christian systems only provides an imperfect synthesis, so that when it receives blows from either of these external forces it is disturbed, though it does not completely collapse, but being pushed out of its posiition, may rest in another position of unstable equilibrium. This has certainly happened in regard to Hinduism. It has been greatly disturbed, so that now almost all educated Hindus who have come under Western influence, but have not ceased to be religious, have accepted certain elements from Christianity. But this attempt at a synthesis between Christianity and Hinduism cannot succeed, without altering Hinduism to a point at which it ceases to be itself; so that the present position, though different from what it was before, is still unstable, and there must be of necessity a preparation for the next move, which may be an attempt at a further reform of Hinduism (which may create another temporary stage of imperfect equilibrium), or a complete collapse of Hinduism either in the direction of agnosticism or of a landslide in the direction of Christianity. But even if the latter happens, it is too much to expect that there will be an uninterrupted advance.

Dr. Browne reminds us of the possibility of a check wherever the presentation of Christianity falls short of the full truth or is inconsistent with the best modern thought. He points out that in the past there were wonderful successes of the Christian faith in the Middle East, and apparently over Zoroastrianism itself, which was in its origin a spiritual religion of high morality. Yet we know that there followed a gradual decline ending in failure and practical extinction. Dr. Browne does not think that this was particularly due to the Nestorian heresy, which as he says, was hardly held at all even by those who called themselves Nestorians; but rather by the excessive adherence of the Eastern Church to the ascetic ideal on the one hand and to the excessive cult of images on the other.   These two facts made it an easy victim in the face of Islam, which was strong in the very two points where the Christian Church had become weak, but it also meant that since asceticism and idolatry have been both agreeable and prominent where the Far East is concerned, there has not seemed to be a very strong case for conversion, so far at any rate as India was concerned.

Dr. Browne concludes by giving an outline of some of the leading elements in the Christian Gospels as they appear in its relationship to the greater non-Christian faiths of the present day.

1. None of the non-Christian religions have any full conception of salvation, because they are not aware of the depths from which we need to be saved.   Some of them have no real sense of sin, and the relentless theory of Karma rules out the possibility of forgiveness. Judaism has an adequate sense of sin, yet even the Day of Atonement does not really bring any completely atoning sacrifice.   Only basic Christianity can save from the sense of fear.   Even Moslems live their lives in fear and superstition, just as those do who have an imperfect and inadequate form of Christianity.

2. In spite of all that may be said about the non-Christian sages, none of these other religions have anything to offer comparable with Christ as the Way, the Truth, and the Life.   It is the experience of countless missionaries that men are drawn irresistibly to the person of Christ long before He comes to occupy a unique place in their minds and hearts.   Moreover, the ethical character of the Christian God is presented by far-and-away the best method, not as an abstract proposition, but as arising out of a study of the Person and teaching of Christ.

3. The person of Christ adequately sets forth the ideal in which 'Martha and Mary combine'.   The East loves the mystic way, but needs to learn social service.   The West may have the latter, but it cannot learn from the East the true mystic way.

4. The familiar point is made of the importance of Christianity as based on fact not on edifying fiction.

5. The conception of the Holy Catholic Church is not only a cardinal item in Christian belief, but it is a greater idea (however imperfectly presented by a Church which is not yet reunited) than one which stresses racial particularism, the divisions of caste, or the restriction of brotherhood to those who are believers.   The Christian recognises nothing less than human brotherhood.

6. In the great religions of the world, as Browne points out, there is a very sharp cleavage in the matter of the relationship between the material and the spiritual, which is specially seen in

the antithesis between idolatry and iconoclasm. The Christian faith with its doctrine of sacraments and its sacramental life guards against excess in either direction, and preserves a right balance of relationship between the spiritual and the material.

7. Finally, says Browne, the Christian faith in its fulness has a conception of the future life which is not only more satisfying than others, but avoids the materialism of the Qur'ānic heaven (which admittedly the modern Moslem is disposed to allegorise) but following Christ it goes beyond the agnosticism of earlier prophetic Judaism, while refusing to define the indefinable ('eye hath not seen nor ear heard'). The value of the Gospel of the life eternal with God cannot be over-estimated when it is confronted with either a dreary scheme of endless rebirths, or the absorption of the individual as a drop of rainwater in the sea. Whatever proper limits there may be to the Christian definition of eternal life, it is certain that it includes social joys, the knitting up of severed friendships, and a life in God which is richer and fuller than anything in this present one.

In this chapter I have been compelled, for the sake of brevity, to paraphrase a good deal of the language of the theologians with whose work I have been dealing. I hope this will not have prevented me from preserving the substance of their teaching, and that it may not have led to any inaccuracy or unfairness.

I regret that I have not made any reference to the work sponsored in 1936 by the Dean of St. Paul's, the General Editor of the present series. This contained one essay by the late Principal Sydney Cave, which dealt in outline with the relation of the Christian Faith to the non-Christian religions. On reading it, however, I have come to the conclusion that while summarising the situation as it existed in that year, it did not specially set out to break any fresh ground, but re-emphasised the view which is to be deduced from the writings of Söderblom and William Temple, as against that of Kraemer. Its importance, however, lay in the fact that it was from the pen of one who had spent many years of his life as an educational missionary in South India, and therefore knew Hinduism at first-hand.

Summary

The issue raised by Dr. Rudolf Otto, and mentioned in the Introduction may seem to have been left for rather a long time out of sight; but it must now be dealt with.

What values exist in the non-Christian faiths which ought to be preserved, even if those faiths should be displaced by a full Christianity.

As to general principles:

First, if the various faiths are *related*, through the universal operation of the Divine Logos, then there can be nothing wrong in holding friendly conversations with those who have hitherto been believers in the non-Christian faiths, even if this is intended to lead up to some kind of supersession.

Second, any really sub-Christian elements in belief and practice cannot be accepted for preservation. Already some institutional Christianity finds itself encumbered by sub-Christian elements which have become embedded in it, and which its more earnest adherents would fain get rid of. It would never do to increase the number of such unwelcome survivals.

Third, some of the pre-Christian literature may still be of cultural value to Christians and may have an educational value as showing how earnest seekers in the past have expressed what they thought to be the right approach to Self-Existent Being. But here again there must be a strict testing of that inheritance by the words of Jesus Christ: 'It was said by them of old time, but I say unto you.'

With these provisos, it may not be improper to consider in outline some of the main features which it would not be a good thing to destroy.

1. There is the sense of worshipfulness, which may be encouraged by being redirected.

2. There are many words and practices which can be retained while being invested with a new meaning, so as to preserve a sense of spiritual continuity. Something has been said about this in the chapter on indigenisation.

3. Especially in the case of India, there is the wonderful capacity of her people for self-sacrificing spirituality, which again needs to be redirected and supplemented. The spiritual riches of India can hardly be overrated; but it is abundantly clear that much of that spirituality has not been of a world-transforming character, but rather of a world-negating one, or at least of a retirement from the world. This, which may easily minister to a spiritual selfishness, is to be deprecated, and must be replaced by an active world-transforming spirit. Bishop Mylne's claim that India may help us by her greater stress upon the Divine Immanence in nature is worthy of attention, and the reverence for animal and bird life which is involved is certainly something in which India can teach the West.

4. Buddhism tends to call forth somewhat similar remarks. There are clearly treasures in it in which it goes beyond Hinduism, such as in its denial of caste. Other treasures are its insistence upon universal benevolence, its inculcation of a serenity of temper, and its system of ethics, which might well be a preparation for an advance into Christianity. Like Christianity it inculcates gentleness and non-violence, but like Christianity in its outward expression it has tended to divide life into two levels, an upper and a lower, so that Buddhist laity are to be found serving in the armies of Asia. Buddhism as practised is often a man-centred system of acquiring merit in order to attain to some sort of future blessedness. But so alas is some Christianity, though fortunately by no means the majority of it. Observers say that the Buddhist laity of Ceylon are much more honest

than the non-Buddhist laity of a city like Calcutta, and it is certain that if Buddhist ethics are properly taught in the schools of the various Buddhist states, they can be very beneficial in the production of good citizens. But of course there are serious gaps, and it is no use simply telling people to be good if they are given nothing but themselves to depend on, and if there is no provision for those who find themselves defeated in the struggle for virtue, to enable them to rise and go on again. Buddhism when all is said and done is very largely for the public an Asian humanism, and if the theology of the Lord's Prayer be true, then Buddhism must be declared to be deficient. Yet it ought not to be impossible for the best in Buddhism to be incorporated within a Christian Catholicism just as St. Ambrose declared that the best in Stoicism could be.

5. China is in a more difficult position, since she seems to be rejecting her ancient systems on a large scale. But if anything in them can be salvaged, it should surely include the highest expression of goodwill as it appears in the virtue of *jen-ai*; the conception of moral responsibility to the Living God as it appears in the idea of the Mandate of Heaven; the assertion of the divine immanence in the doctrine of the Great Tao; and the expressions of filial piety, which have sometimes taken a very beautiful form. It is no doubt the fashion in some quarters to denigrate the work of Kung-fu-tze and to say that his doctrines stressed patriarchal authority, aristocracy, and graded love. But those who do so have perhaps not read the Lun-Yü as carefully as they should, since there are many jewels in the latter which are worthy of the appreciation of Christians.

6. Judaism, as we have seen, is trying to revive itself, and has much in the pieties of family life and in its steadfastness under persecution in which it can command the admiration of Christians. In the section dealing with it one has perhaps sufficiently emphasised what seem to be its deficiencies; but it is still a duty incumbent upon all Christians to make reparation for past unkindnesses to Jews, and to seek, by friendly and brotherly conversation, to draw into the fulness of Christ those who are in many ways not far from the Kingdom of God.

7. Islam always contributes to the fulness of religion a sense of the majesty of God, a demand for an ordered simplicity as against an overloading with ritual, a realisation of brotherhood, and a regularity in exercises of devotion which may prevent one from ever being for any length of time unmindful of the over-ruling presence of Deity.

8. One may hesitate perhaps to claim any positive contribution for Marxism. Yet surely as a sharp reminder of the deadliness of

the sin of human exploitation it has a very real and austere part to play in the sifting of good religion from bad.

9. Perhaps as a general summing up one may call to mind the oft-repeated but alas oft-forgotten maxim that religious heresies are protests against the neglect or abandonment by Christians of some essential part of Divine Truth, and that like heresies non-Christian religion (and even substitute-religions) may be used by Divine permission to recall an unfaithful church to a fuller faith, and a more obedient performance of her duty.

Additional note on Sir Sarvepalli Radhakrishnan

We are only just beginning to get attempts at theological revaluation from the Asian side. The exclusiveness of Islamic dogma has made it unlikely that even a modernist Moslem would do more than try to frame a theory which would include Jews and Christians. We have had an expression of the Shi'ah point of view from Syed Ameer Ali, and how much further Mohammed Ikbal would have carried his attempts at syncretism if he had lived we cannot tell. Perhaps the most substantial contribution has come from Sir Sarvepalli Radhakrishnan, who is at present the Vice-President of the Republic of India, but who has been Indian Ambassador to Moscow, and who was for many years Lecturer on Eastern Religions in the University of Oxford.

One of the best features in Dr. Kraemer's most recent work is his section dealing with Radhakrishnan, and it is the one with which in the abstract I feel least inclination to disagree. One would certainly not wish to say over again what has been said there so effectively.

Nevertheless one is bound to try to express one's own sensations regarding this distinguished Indian, and they involve a somewhat different approach. I desire above all not to say anything that will hurt, or leave behind the sense of unfairness, more especially as I have received both courtesy and hospitality from him, and I think the best way will be to consider how matters must seem when looked at from his end of the telescope.

First and foremost, Radhakrishnan is a patriotic Indian, with a profound and indeed just sense of the greatness of the traditions of his country. He rightly wishes to see justice done to the religious and philosophical inheritance of his people, and the apparent alliance between the former British Raj and the exponents of Christianity has left in his mind at least an unconscious bias against the latter. He has indeed spent the best years of his life in trying to interpret Indian thought to the West, and during his residence at Oxford he made a profound impression upon some whom he met there, and those who came under his spell sometimes felt as though there would be no more need of any missionaries to India, but that in actual fact India had much to teach the West.

But in the second place, the formative years of Radhakrishnan's life were spent in a Christian environment, and that no narrow or obscurantist one, but as a student at Madras Christian College, with its strong and enlightened scholarly traditions. One does not gather that he ever became a member of any Christian denomination; but it is quite clear that he owes much of his earlier training to Christian teachers, especially Presbyterian ones, and that he knows a good deal about Protestant Christianity. It does not seem that he has quite the same acquaintance with Catholic philosophical theology.

Now the effect of the two foregoing factors is that Radhakrishnan, whether consciously or unconsciously, has for a long time been trying to live in two worlds. He is a scholar and thinker of immense ability and versatility, and has a great capacity for lucid self-expression in English and, one may well believe, in his mother tongue as well. He has many friends among us Christians, and we all like him, and respect his earnestness. Thus when he told me of his long conversations with Marxist leaders in Moscow and of how he had tried to convince them of their erroneous attitude towards religion, I felt that one ought to say: 'he who is not against us is for us.' Radhakrishnan knows very well the best that can be said about Christianity, as well as the imperfection shown by us who expound it, and he may be forgiven if at times he gives way to a little impatience with us, for I daresay we deserve it. But his patriotism at times also tends to make him unfair, and to say things which are not quite worthy of his eminence. In order to be loyal to his Hindu traditions. he has sometimes to play the advocate, and to make out a case in which one feels he cannot really believe; yet in his role of apologis. he does not represent Hinduism as it really is, so much as what he would like it to be, and what he thinks he might be able to make it. He re-interprets it in the hope of making it adaptable to the modern world, and especially as an alternative to Christianity. But can this really be done? The pathetic eagerness of Radhakrishnan to do it, especially as he advances in years, invokes almost an affectionate sympathy. He would like to check Christian proselytism and to replace it by the promotion of a new kind of synthetic Hinduism. And yet, and yet,—one doubts whether he is spending his time well, and whether he and those of his generation who agree with him will have any successors. Mr. Panikkar, in spite of his brilliancy, seems too much of a controversial politician to be able to step into his shoes, let alone those of such great religious enthusiasts as Gandhi and Aurobindo Ghose. Indian Christian theologians are now arising who are dealing with Radhakrishnan on his own ground, and who show their dissatisfaction with his synthetic theology in no uncertain terms. Although for some time he has been regarded, and one believes justly, as the most distinguished of all living exponents of Indian thought to the world, is it not possible that he may have been rated just a little too highly as a critic of others? It may well be that both he and his many admirers ought to go back and consider soberly whether his estimate of the kind of religion the world needs, which is not orthodox Christianity and certainly not orthodox Hinduism, is really the final word: and whether a full-blooded but indigenous Catholic Christian faith may not be the real answer to India's quest. Christians revere the memory of the great Greeks, though without any intention of reverting to their beliefs. Cannot the great Indian thinkers be revered by those who, in spite of them, have gone on to accept Him who is the Answer to the very questions which are inevitably raised by such as Gautama, Sankara, and Ramanuja, and yet left by them, as Kraemer rightly says, to the end unanswered?

Sir Sarvepalli is actually in error in blaming St. Paul for a policy of exclusiveness in the matter of religion, and for initiating a long-continued habit of Christian propaganda and proselytism. As I have tried to show elsewhere (in Chapter V) universalism as a Christian claim goes back to Our Lord Himself, and in some sense behind Him, judged on a critical study of documents. It is possible that the attitude of Dr. Kraemer may in certain respects excite Radhakrishnan's resentment: but one hopes he will realise that some of the comments made by Kraemer are by no means endorsed by all other Christians. Although on the principle of diffusion they cannot see any objection to people becoming Christians if they feel conscientiously that even Hinduism at its best falls short of the truth; on the basis of the Logos doctrine they are equally prepared to adopt a generous and sympathetic attitude towards the great heritage of India, and always to show kindness and respect towards its most distinguished and venerable champion, who has performed an unparalleled service in making it understood and appreciated by the Western world.

EPILOGUE

Any actual summing up of what has gone before need not be lengthy, since most chapters are fairly complete in themselves. But a few points are worth reiteration.

1. It will have been observed that much of the renewed vitality of non-Christian religions, where it has taken place, has been due to competition with a missionary-minded Christianity, and that these religions have not been content to be themselves—as though they had nothing for which to apologise—but have taken over as much as they possibly can from Christianity, and then have reproduced it as part of their own systems. The inference to be drawn from this is only too obvious.

2. Yet no one ought to wish former adherents of the non-Christian faiths to renounce what is good in their own. Hence it must be said again that just as Benjamin Whichcote, John Smith, and others like them called themselves Christian Platonists at Cambridge in the seventeenth century, without one whit abating their Christian allegiance, so one conceives that at some time in the future it might not be improper for believers to exist who called themselves Christian Buddhists, or Christian Confucians, and even perhaps Christian Vedantists or Christian Moslems, without in the least abating their adherence to the Catholic Faith, and while paying a respectful tribute to the religious insights of their forefathers, and to their enlightenment by the One Logos.[1] There are already some who dare to call themselves Christian Communists.

3. Indigenisation is seen nevertheless to have its dangers, and a hasty syncretism, especially if indulged in in the interests of nationalist sentiment, is to be deprecated. The past twenty years have seen an unhappy and most heretical attempt at creating a 'German Christianity'. Those who in South Africa advocate 'Apartheid' are sometimes (perhaps not always) guilty of trying to create a white South African Christianity of just as heretical a nature. The danger in India of the rise of an 'Indian Christian community' is that it may develop a communal consciousness, exercise a communal vote, and not think enough in terms of God's will for the blessing of the whole Indian people, not to mention that of the world as a whole. But it is quite certain that indigenisation of a wholesome sort must be

---

[1] The extent to which a pre-Christian late Stoic treatise such as the 'Hortensius' of Cicero (now, alas, known to us only through quotations) was read and valued by medieval Christians should be a sufficient answer to any who feel scruples about this.

increased. It will never do for Christians in any country to be regarded by their fellow-citizens as foreigners; still less for them to be
accused (as the early Christians were, unfairly) of nurturing an
'odium generis humani'. The joint-family in India has come in for
some criticism on the part of missionaries; but Indian Christians who
have grown up under it actually maintain that in its common bearing
of burdens it is more Christian than (or at least as Christian as) the
Western system of the small independent family. In Africa Professor Phillips says that it is now generally agreed that customs connected with 'bride-price' are not necessarily incompatible with
Christianity.

4. The major issue of Revelation is seen to be the source of
strong disagreement. Readers will clearly have to take their choice
between the various views represented; but the author of this book
feels himself justified in declaring a decided preference for the larger
view supported by Söderblom and William Temple, as against the
opinions of Witte and Kraemer. At the same time it must be clear
that the Christian Gospel *does* cut across the lines of other faiths, and
that only a very shallow acquaintance with the latter can lead to the
conclusion that they are after all very much alike.

5. Moreover, the historical question is fundamental. However
much portions of the sacred books of other faiths are to be valued[1]
and even perhaps read at public worship, the prophetic message of the
Old Testament documents cannot be relegated to the background,
without serious loss to the proper understanding of Christianity.
Whether less of these documents should be read *in extenso* in public
worship is a domestic question that may well be discussed in the
councils of the Churches, and one which is already receiving different
answers from quite convinced Christians; but a knowledge of their
substance is certainly essential for the full delivery of the Christian
message. The New Testament generally is not intelligible without
the Old, and indeed it may be said that no strong or lasting Christian
Church can be built up in isolation from it. What has to be undertaken is the *translation* of the story of God's revelation in history into
terms which each separate people and also each succeeding century
can understand.

6. A much gentler and more generous view needs to be taken of
pre-axial religion. One tends to find some scientists quite as ready
as some ardent Christian reformers to dismiss it all as 'superstition'.
Yet even the most naïve and unsophisticated of non-literate and
simple peasants sometimes display a wholeness and soundness of

spiritual insight which make their prayers and their behaviour very nearly Christian, and put to shame those of some orthodox church-people.

What of the future? It seems clear that the events of the age running from 800 B.C. to 300 A.D. are as unlikely to be repeated as those of the great age of scientific discovery in which we live. Both will recede into the past, and both, though admittedly separated by some 1900 years, will eventually become very ancient history. Nevertheless the pattern of change from one type of religion to another seems likely to go on recurring, until perhaps there is no more of the pre-axial type left on the planet. What will happen then? It is inconceivable that the development of religion should cease. Doubtless within and without its existing types new kinds of philosophy will arise. At the moment it looks as though for some time the various axial forms will continue to co-exist, not perhaps peacefully, since they will seek to rival one another. One can well imagine that a fierce hostility will persist between the devotees of the Dialectic Process and Catholics who stand by their belief in a truly transcendent Deity. But there will be other rivalries as well, some perhaps of a more friendly nature. One can imagine a federated Moslem world zealous to go on modernising itself as an alternative to Christianity. One can see India once more taking Buddhism under her wing, and a federation of neo-Buddhist states anxious to maintain a kind of Asian Catholic Buddhist church as an alternative to Catholicism. It is not difficult to visualise neo-Hinduism itself as making a similar bid for world supremacy. But these latter movements will have to reckon in the long run with the difficulty of maintaining their position intellectually, and also with the advance of Marxism in Asia, where already it has laid its hand on Vietnam, Chinese Buddhism seems largely to have collapsed before it, and penetration into Japan is growing. Religion which is not world-transforming will find itself in a difficulty.

We are obviously at a stage in which startling developments are possible in unexpected places. No one can tell whether the next important step may not be taken in the region of Japan. That country has asked for the next Congress on the History of Religions to be held in 1958 at Tokyo. The Congress is the only religious fixture which U.N.E.S.C.O. allows itself to sponsor, and its occurrence in Japan might even be the occasion for some decisive movement to be initiated there, which might set alight a new wave of religious enthusiasm in the Far East. And this in its turn might react upon America. No one can tell.

One finds it difficult to believe in any case that a recrudescence of something resembling McCarthyism can for ever keep Communism out of the United States. It already has a strong hold in Mexico, on the other side of the southern frontier, and is by no means inactive in the South American Republics. Marxism indeed cannot be checked by any world-negating religion, nor by repressive encirclement. It can only be overcome, as Douglas Hyde, the ex-Marxist, has himself pointed out, by a still more radically world-transforming movement, and we may add by one which has eschewed all superstition. It is possible that Marxist dogmas themselves may gradually come to appeal less and less to the intelligentsia, and since the man in the street usually ends by taking his tone from the latter, we may expect that in time the popular use of these dogmas by the shop-steward class will decline. But this will not necessarily mean a return to Christianity; there may still be a strong appeal on the part of socialistic humanism for the allegiance of mankind, and this will always be stronger than any escapist or world-negating form of religion.

The burning need among all who see in some kind of high religion a necessary condition for giving meaningfulness and worthwhileness to this strange planetary life of ours must be to consider without prejudice which faith seems most likely to be true, and which most fruitful in truth, beauty, and goodness. However could medical (or for that matter any) science progress if it were divided up into conflicting groups, so that India had an Ayurvedic one, Russia a Marxist, and Great Britain an insular British one? Such a situation would be monstrous and absurd. Even though there must needs be one and only one single corpus of scientific truth, preferences in matters of detail might still exist, and one may legitimately assume that different temperatures, climates, and breeds of human beings might require the use of different types of medicaments and hygiene. But throughout there could only be one set of general principles, even if these had to begin by diffusing from one pioneer country to the others.

So must it be in religion. If one faith (1) is better able than the other to make good its claim to be intellectually true as a personal unveiling of the Self-Existent in action (or should one say, to be the greatest of all personal unveilings): (2) is seen to be supremely beautiful, and uniquely productive of constructive good in the formation and redemption of individual character and of social order, then that will be the religion to follow, the one which will in the last resort most successfully diffuse, and the one which will absorb all the good that is to be found in the others, and the one which will be most likely to reform and renew itself, where and when necessary.   Such a religion, however, will not be able to win through simply by making repeated universalist claims, or by mere reiteration of authority.   Assertions of that sort could by themselves amount to nothing more than skilfully publicised bluff, and would be rejected as such by many thoughtful persons.   They could only gain the assent of the easily suggestible multitude.   Moreover, such a religion, even though it might establish its uniqueness, could not do so with regard to its finality.   It could reasonably argue the probability of the latter, and indeed the very strong probability, and the majority of thoughtful persons might even be in agreement with it about its claim.   But this, while providing a competent guide for life, would not in the nature of the case amount to a complete demonstration. All that could be said would be that any religious phenomenon which might come after would not negate but would include and confirm the best of what had gone before, and that the circumstances attending the development of religion such as have been surveyed in Chapter II of the present work rendered the appearance of any such future phenomenon in the highest degree improbable.

Were the realism which is always latent in the Roman Communion (after all is said and done still the largest Christian body in the world) to assert itself more strongly, so that its leaders became ardent devotees of historical fact, no matter how shattering to their previous convictions, one has enough faith in Christ to believe that such devotion to truth, so far from disintegrating that great Communion, would only render it more truly capable of becoming the vanguard of the Christian movement of the future.   There might then follow a reunion with separated bodies such as Anglicans and Greeks.   But unless and until that new Reformation took place within the borders of Rome, such reunion would be premature, and not even worth while; since it would only weaken those other Christian bodies born of the sixteenth-century Reformation (themselves more sensitive to fact) to be federated with a church which, however large and full of piety and zeal, displayed either a policy of timid caution or of stubborn rejection in the face of the honest work of the empirical scientists.

But the pace must be quickened, for the time is short; and past history shows that the judgments of the Living God of Truth and Righteousness fall rapidly upon those who, having received His charge and message, are cowardly or unfaithful in the handling of it.

Perhaps it may be said in criticism of this work that it has laid too great stress upon the past, and has exaggerated the achievements of the axial age.   The exaggeration is more apparent than real.   If this earth continues its course, as it well might, for another three thousand years, some historian, writing of the golden age of the natural sciences, might be charged with over-estimating its significance. The truth is that all such formative periods have a permanent and unique significance of their own. But I should never wish to depreciate the importance of post-axial epochs in their effect upon axial religion. However permanent and decisive the contribution of Christ as divine revelation, it has to be appropriated and expressed in post-axial terms, and it would be foolish to ignore the extent to which our own age has decisively moulded the form which that appropriation and expression are bound to take for many future generations. It is more than doubtful whether the Christian faith can ever again be effectively proclaimed in the terms in which even such comparatively recent exponents as Liddon and Spurgeon proclaimed it, in spite of all their earnestness and undoubted eloquence. And yet we see that it is living on and still winning disciples.

It has become almost a trite thing to say that the great task which lies in front of all intelligent Christians today is to solve effectively the problem of communicating the basic Christian truths to a world which is intimidated by modern astronomy, which is aiming as never before at universal literacy (with all the risks and complications that it necessarily involves), which is solemnly dedicated to the employment of scientific method in the appraisement of all the data of the world, internal and external alike, which is more closely knit than it has ever been before by the agencies of wireless and aviation, and which above all has become rather breathless from the pace at which it has been travelling for the past fifty years. Yet there can be no post-Christian period which will dare with an easy conscience to leave behind it the whole of its Christian past, any more than there can be a post-Marx, post-Darwin, post-Einstein, -Rutherford, or -Thomson period which in the same light-hearted way can leave the whole of its scientific past behind it.

If the present work, in which the author hardly expects at the most to do more than serve his own generation, should succeed in stimulating its readers to view in proportion the entire panorama of religion, and to keep inviolate a Treasure which must never be lost, but which cannot be fitly valued in isolation from other treasures, then its preparation will not have been entirely a vain task.

But it is not merely a case of 'preserving a Treasure'—what a most exalted personage in this country not long ago charmingly and truly called 'our precious Christian heritage'. Since Christians are made by grace and not simply born biologically, the Eternal Jesus must needs go on breaking through into individual lives and into history repeatedly to the end of time, bringing His Kingdom with Him.

It is only beyond history, 'when time shall be no more', that this process can come to its conclusion, and God be all in all.

BIBLIOGRAPHY

In presenting this list of books, the author wishes to make it clear that although the works listed have been consulted by him, the opinions expressed in the pages which precede are his own, and where they differ from those of the authorities quoted, he accepts responsibility for the difference. Long as the list is, it might of course have been much longer; but the author has tried, in making his selection, to include as far as possible all works mentioned in the text, as well as those which he feels have influenced him, either to the extent of agreement or dissent.

BIBLIOGRAPHY

ABBREVIATIONS

E.R.E. = Hastings' Encyclopaedia of Religion and Ethics.
I.R.M. = International Review of Missions
       (quarterly pub. Edinburgh House Press).
I.C.C. = International Critical Commentary.
S.C.M. = Student Christian Movement.
O.U.P. = Oxford University Press.
C.U.P. = Cambridge University Press.

INTRODUCTION

Bishop STEPHEN NEILL. *The Unfinished Task.* London. 1957.
The late Dr E. C. DEWICK. *Hulsean Lectures. The Christian Attitude to other Religions.* C.U.P. 1953.
Canon MAX WARREN. *Merrick Lectures.* Ohio & London. 1956.
Dr K. S. LATOURETTE. *Missions To-morrow.* Harper, N.Y. 1936.
Dr ALBERT SCHWEITZER. *Christianity and the Religions of the World. Selly Oak Lectures.* George Allen & Unwin. 1923.

CHAPTER I. PRE-SUPPOSITIONS

Sir GEORGE THOMSON. *The Foreseeable Future.* Cambridge. 1955.
Professor F. HOYLE. *Reith Lectures. The Nature of the Universe.* 2nd ed. 1952.
— *Man and Materialism: in "World Perspectives".* George Allen and Unwin. 1957.
Dr R. A. LYTTLETON. *The Modern Universe.* London. 1956.
Professor A. C. B. LOVELL. *Reith Lectures.* 1959.
Sir JULIAN HUXLEY. *Religion without Revelation.* 2nd ed. London. 1957.
Mr ALDOUS HUXLEY. *The Perennial Philosophy.* Chatto and Windus. 1946.
Professor C. W. MORRIS of Chicago. *Signs, Language, and Behaviour.* New York. 1947.
Professor R. B. BRAITHWAITE.
  (1) *Scientific Explanation. Tarner Lectures.* Cambridge. 1953.
  (2) *An Empiricist's View of the Nature of Religious Belief. Eddington Memorial Lecture.* Cambridge. 1955.
Professor IAN RAMSEY. *Religious Language: an Empirical Placing of Theological Phrases.* London. 1957.
THE OXFORD ATLAS.
Professor GREGOR SMITH. Articles by, in the *Listener.*
Cambridge Theological Essays. 1905. Articles by:
  The late Dr W. L. H. DUCKWORTH. No. IV. Man's Origin, and his Place in Nature.
  Dr F. R. TENNANT. Essay II. The Being of God, in the Light of Physical Science.
  Also by TENNANT:
    The Origin and Propagation of Sin. Hulsean Lectures. 2nd ed. 1906.
    The Concept of Sin. Cambridge. 1912.

Mr LESLIE PAUL. *Nature into History.* Faber & Faber. 1957.
(A most interesting and original study of the problem of the transition of man from being simply an animal into a dimension of being which the animal does not share.)

CHAPTER II. A BRIEF HISTORICAL SURVEY OF RELIGION

General

Professor FRIEDRICH HEILER. *Das Gebet.* Munich. 1923.
(Eng. abridged translation. *Prayer.*)
Dr J. ESTLIN CARPENTER. *Comparative Religion.* Home University Library. 1933.
(An outline work by a learned Unitarian.)
E. O. JAMES. *Comparative Religion. An Introductory and Historical Survey.* Methuen. 1938.
(By an eminent Anglo-Catholic scholar.)
T. H. ROBINSON. *A Short Comparative History of Religions.* Duckworth. 2nd ed. 1951.
(By a learned Baptist.)
J. N. D. ANDERSON (editor). *The World's Religions*: by various authors. The Inter-Varsity fellowship. 1950.
(Conservative Evangelical, yet surprising in its recognition of standard books. Shows a considerable advance in outlook.)
AELFRIDA TILLYARD. *Spiritual Exercises.* S.P.C.K. 1927.
(A clear and simple description of the way in which people in different religions pray and meditate.)
Relevant articles in HASTINGS' *Encyclopaedia of Religion and Ethics.*

1. The broad divisions

Professor KARL JASPERS. *The Origin and Goal of History.* London. 1953. (Trans. from German.)
Professor CHRISTOPHER DAWSON. *Religion and Culture.* Sheed & Ward. 1947.
Professor R. C. ZAEHNER. *At Sundry Times.* London. 1958.
The late Dr W. R. INGE. *Confessio Fidei. In Outspoken Essays.* Vol. 2.
Dr MARGARET MEAD. Article in *The Listener.*

2. The pre-axial period

The Primitives

E. O. JAMES. *The Emergence of Religion.* 3rd ed. S.P.C.K. 1929 (in Essays Catholic & Critical).
— *The Origins of Religion.* Unicorn Press. 1937. Op. cit. above.
— *Prehistoric Religion.* Thames and Hudson. 1957.
— *The Origins of Sacrifice.* Murray. 1933.
The works of Sir JAMES FRAZER.
(Again an enormous output. It seems best to summarise.)
The *Golden Bough*, eventually expanded into a series of volumes, by the 3rd Edition. London. 1914.
In addition, the following may be noted:

The Belief in Immortality and the Worship of the Dead. 3 vols. *Gifford Lectures.* 1913.

Folk-lore in the Old Testament. 2 vols. London. 1918.

The Worship of Nature. London. 1926.

Totemism and Exogamy. 4 vols. 1910.

Man, God, and Immortality. Selections from works by J. G. F. London. 1927.

Dr W. H. R. RIVERS. *The Todas.* Macmillan. 1906.

PAUL SCHEBESTA. *With Congo Pygmies.* Hutchinson. 1933.

Professor J. H. HUTTON and Dr J. P. MILLS. Series of volumes on the various Naga Tribes, pub. over a number of years.

PAUL RADIN. *Primitive Religion.* Hamish Hamilton. 1938.

Messrs E. W. SMITH and DALE. *The Ba-ila of Northern Rhodesia.* Macmillans. 1920.

Dr GEOFFREY PARRINDER. *West African Religion.* Epworth Press. 1949.

The late Professor A. RADCLIFFE BROWN. *The Andaman Islanders.* Cambridge. 1933.

— *Australian Aborigines.* (In a volume of collected essays and addresses.) London. 1956.

Miss CHRISTINA HOLE. *English Folklore.* Methuen. 1940. (See also the *Journal of the Folk-Lore Society.*)

Dr MARGARET MEAD. *Growing up in New Guinea.* Pelican Books. 1942.

The late Dr R. R. MARETT. *Faith, Hope and Charity in Primitive Religion, and The Sacraments of Simple Folk (Boston Lectures).* O.U.P. 1932.

— *Head, Heart, and Hands in Human Evolution.* Hutchinson. 1935.

Captain R. S. RATTRAY. *Religion and Art in Ashanti.* Oxford. Head. 1927.

The late Dr EDWYN BEVAN. *Holy Images.* London. 1940.

Egypt and the Middle East

Articles in *The Cambridge Ancient History.*

The late Dr HENRI FRANKFORT. *Ancient Egyptian Religion.* New York. 1949.

Dr MARGARET MURRAY (inter alia):

The Splendour that was Egypt. London. 1949.

Egyptian Temples. London. 1931.

The writings of Professor ADOLF ERMAN and Sir E. WALLIS BUDGE.

Professor J. H. BREASTED. *Development of Religion and Thought in Ancient Egypt.* Hodder & Stoughton. 1912.

Mr A. W. SHORTER. *The Egyptian Gods.* Kegan Paul. 1937.

Sir LEONARD WOOLLEY. *The Sumerians.* O.U.P. 1928.

The writings of M. ETIENNE DRIOTON and the late Professor S. R. K. GLANVILLE.

T. E. PEEL. *Schweich Lectures.* 1931.

Documents collected by Dr J. B. PRITCHARD and translated by various scholars, relating to the Middle East. Princeton U.S.A. 1957.

The great change

Professor KARL JASPERS. Op. cit.
Professor F. HOYLE. *Man and Materialism.* Op. cit.
E. O. JAMES. *Prehistoric Religion.* Thames & Hudson. 1957.
Ch. ix.
The Intellectual Adventure of Ancient Man. Chicago Univ. Press.
1947. Various authors.
(Re-issued in Pelican Books, 1949, as *Before Philosophy*: deals with
the change in the Middle East.)

Iran

The late Dr J. H. MOULTON. *Hibbert Lectures on Zoroastrianism.*
1913.
— *The Treasure of the Magi.* O.U.P. 1917.
(Some of his conclusions no longer hold.)
Professor J. DUCHESNE-GUILLEMIN.
Zarathustra. Paris. Maisonneuve. 1948.
The Gathas of Zarathustra. Trans. from his French version.
George Allen & Unwin. 1932.
(An expert Belgian scholar.)
FRAMROZE, BODE, and NANAVUTTY. *Songs of Zarathustra.* George
Allen & Unwin. 1952.
(Translations by a Parsee modernist.)
Dr DHALLA. *History of Zoroastrianism.* New York. 1938.
(An attempt at modernizing the Parsee religion.)
MASANI. *The Religion of the Good Life.* *Zoroastrianism.* George
Allen & Unwin. 1938.

India

Professor J. B. PRATT. *India and its Faiths.* Macmillan. 1915.
Dr C. L. O'MALLEY. *Popular Hinduism.* C.U.P. 1935.
Dr A. C. BOUQUET. *Hinduism.* Hutchinson. 1946.
Dr E. O. MARTIN. *The Gods of India.* Dent. 1914.
J. N. FARQUHAR. *A Primer of Hinduism.* O.U.P. 1912.
Sir CHARLES ELIOT. *Hinduism and Buddhism.* 3 vols. Arnold.
1921.
The Writings of Abbé Jean Antoine Dubois (1765–1848). ed. Beau-
champ. Oxford. 1906.
The Religion of the Hindus. New York. Ronald Press Coy. 1953.
Seven chapters by Hindus, edited and with extracts from their Scrip-
tures and a glossary, by the Chaplain of Colgate University, U.S.A.
The late Mr C. F. ANDREWS. *The True India.* George Allen &
Unwin. 1939.
H. D. GRISWOLD. *The Religion of the Rig Veda.* O.U.P. 1923.
Dr BHARATAN KUMARAPPA. *The Indian Conception of Deity.*
London Univ. Press. 1934.
Professor BERRIEDALE KEITH. *The Religion and Philosophy of the
Veda.* 2 vols. Harvard Univ. Press. Cambridge, Mass.
1925.
Professor J. ESTLIN CARPENTER. *Theism in Medieval India.* Hibbert
Lectures. 1921.

Sir SARVEPALLI RADHAKRISHNAN. *The Hindu View of Life.*
The late Principal SYDNEY CAVE. *Redemption, Hindu and Christian.*
    O.U.P. 1919.
The following texts:
    Professor R. E. HUME. *The Thirteen Principal Upanishads.*
    O.U.P. 1931.
    SWAMI NIKHILANANDA. *The Upanishads.* 4 vols. Harper.
    New York. 1959.
        (Translation and commentary by an Indian.)
    Dr NICOL MACNICOL. *Hindu Scriptures.* Dent. 1938. Every-
    man Series.
        (Contains selected Vedic hymns and Upanishads, and the full text of
        the Bhagavadgita, in English trans.)
The Gita has been translated into English, with commentary, by
    (1) Sir SARVEPALLI RADHAKRISHNAN. London. 1948.
    (2) The late Dr AUROBINDO GHOSE. Calcutta. 1949.
    (3) Dr. E. J. THOMAS. John Murray (in the Wisdom of the
        East series). 1921.
    (4) Professor FRANKLIN EDGERTON. 2 vols. in the Harvard
        Oriental Series. Mass. 1944.
    (5) Professor RUDOLF OTTO. *The Original Gita.* Dent.
        1939.
        (Attempts to split up the poem into its various strata.)
But the above is only a selection of the many editions.

Buddhism

BY EUROPEANS

Sir CHARLES ELIOT. Op. cit. and also his fourth volume on Japanese
    Buddhism, published posthumously. London. 1935.
Professor J. B. PRATT. *The Pilgrimage of Buddhism.* Macmillan.
    1923.
Mrs RHYS DAVIDS. *Buddhism.* Home Univ. Library. 1934.
— *A Manual of Buddhism.* Sheldon Press. 1932.
        (These two latter works give the rather radical views of the authoress
        on the early texts, and on the original teaching of Gautama.)
Miss I. B. HORNER. *The Early Buddhist Theory of Man Perfected.*
    C.U.P. 1936.
Mr CHRISTMAS HUMPHREYS. *Buddhism.* Pelican Book A 228.
The late Dr F. HAROLD SMITH. *The Buddhist Way of Life.* Hutchin-
    son. 1951.
Dr EDWARD CONZE. *Buddhism.* Oxford. 1951.
Professor A. J. BAHM (of New Mexico). *Buddhist Philosophy.* 1959.

BY ASIANS

ANANDA COOMARASWAMY. *Buddha and the Gospel of Buddhism.*
    Harrap. 1916. Illustrated.
Professor SUZUKI.
    (1) *Outlines of Mahayana Buddhism.* 1937.
    (2) *Essays in Zen Buddhism.*
Professor MURTI (of Banaras). *Buddhist Philosophy.* 1957.
    George Allen & Unwin.

TEXTS

Dr E. J. Thomas. *Early Buddhist Scriptures.* Kegan Paul. 1935.
Lord Chalmers. *Buddhist Sermons.* 2 vols.
  (In the publications of the Pali Text Society, all of which are of value.)
Arthur Waley and others. *Buddhist Texts throughout the Ages.* Oxford. 1954.

Jainism

BY EUROPEANS

D. A. Guérinot. *La religion Djaïna.* Paris, 1926.
Mrs Sinclair Stevenson. *The Heart of Jainism.* O.U.P. 1915.

BY ASIANS

Jagnanderlal Jaini. *Outlines of Jainism.* C.U.P. 1940.
Vijaya Dharmi Suri. *Sermons Preached before the Maharajah of Banaras.*
Mohan Lal Mehta. *Outlines of Jaina Philosophy.* Bangalore. 1954.
  (Compares this system with others in India and also in Europe.)

Chinese Wisdom

BY EUROPEANS

Confucius

Professor R. Wilhelm. *Confucius and Confucianism.* Kegan Paul. 1931.
Mr E. D. Edwards. *Confucius.* 1940.
Dr Carl Crow. *Master Kung, A Life of Confucius.* Hamish Hamilton. 1937.
Article by Professor H. H. Dubs on 'The Ethics of Confucianism' in Sir S. Radhakrishnan's *Festschrift.* George Allen & Unwin. 1951.

China in General

P. J. Maclagan. *Chinese Religious Ideas.* S.C.M. Press. 1926.
E. D. Harvey. *The Mind of China.* Yale Univ. Press. 1933.
L. Wieger. *Histoire des croyances religieuses et des opinions philosophiques en Chine, depuis L'origine jusqu'à nos jours.* Paris. 1922.
E. P. Fitzgerald. *China.* The Cresset Press. 1942.
K. L. Reichelt. *Religion in Chinese Garment.* Lutterworth Press. 1951. (Trans. from the Norwegian.)
Mr E. R. Hughes and his daughter. *Religion in China.* Hutchinson. 1950.
Marcel Granet. *La religion des Chinois.* Paris. 1934.
Henri Maspero. *Les religions Chinoises.* 1950.

TEXTS

In general, the relevant volumes in Sacred Books of the East. (But these translations have been challenged.)

Dr ARTHUR WALEY. *The Lun-yü of Confucius.* George Allen &
    Unwin. 1945.
— *The Tao-te-King.* London. 1934.
Mr E. R. HUGHES. *Two Chinese Classics.* Dent.
— *Chinese Philosophy in Classical Times.* Dent.
Selected passages from *Mencius.* Trans. by LIONEL EILER in the
    Wisdom of the East series. John Murray. 1942.

On Sufism

    Relevant chapters in works already referred to.
Article in E.R.E.
The works of the late Professor R. A. NICHOLSON, especially his
    translations of Sufi poems. Cambridge. 1921.
    Also, *The Idea of Personality in Sufism. London Univ. Lectures.*
    1923. Pub. in Cambridge.
See also recent works of Professor A. R. ARBERRY.

Sikhism

    The standard work is still:
       Dr M. A. MCAULIFFE. *The Sikh Religion.* O.U.P. 1909.
    But chapters upon it are to be found in other works:
       e.g. Sir CHARLES ELIOT, op. cit.
See also article by H. A. ROSE in E.R.E., written by an I.C.S.
official long resident in the Panjab.

BY ASIANS

Y. C. YANG. *China's Religious Heritage.* New York and Nash-
    ville. 1943.
LIN YU TANG. *My Country and My People.* 2nd edition. Lon-
    don. 1939.
       (All the above written before the Marxist revolution.)
    See bibliography to Ch. XII.
G. K. C. YEN. *The Confucian Conception of Jên.* The China
    Society. London. 1943.
       (A most useful little pamphlet.)

Japan

Professor MAHARSARU ANESAKI. *History of Japanese Religion.*
    Kegan Paul. 1930.
Dr D. C. HOLTOM. *The National Faith of Japan.* Kegan Paul. 1938.

Hebrew religions

GENERAL

Dr T. SKINNER. *Prophecy and Religion.* C.U.P. 1936.
Dr ROBERTSON SMITH. *The Religion of the Semites.* (New edition
    by Professor S. A. COOK. 1927.)
OESTERLEY and ROBINSON. *Hebrew Religion and its Developments.*
    London. 1937. (2nd edition.)
Dr W. O. E. OESTERLEY. *Sacrifices in Ancient Israel.* Hodder &
    Stoughton. 1937.

Dr ALFRED GUILLAUME. *Prophecy and Divination.* Hodder & Stoughton. 1938.

Dr R. H. CHARLES. *The Decalogue.* (*Warburton Lectures.*) Edinburgh. 1923.

And besides the Old Testament, the following texts:

Select Documents illustrating Old Testament Thought. Ed. by Professor D. WINTON THOMAS. C.U.P. 1959.

Professor C. F. A. SCHAEFFER. *The Cuneiform Texts of Ras-Shamra-Ugarit.* (*Schweich Lectures.* 1936–39.)

J. W. JACK. *The Ras Shamra Tablets.* T. and T. Clark. Edinburgh. 1935.

POST-EXILIC DEVELOPMENTS

Dr R. H. CHARLES. *Between the Old and New Testaments.* Home University Library 1914.

THE QUMRAN DISCOVERIES

The Dead Sea Scrolls. J. M. ALLEGRO: in Pelican Books. (And its extensive bibliography.)

The principal texts, edited in English by T. H. GASTER. Secker & Warburg. 1957.

Professor H. H. ROWLEY. *The Dead Sea Scrolls and the New Testament.* S.P.C.K. 1957.

CHAPTER III. THE PRINCIPLE OF DIFFUSION

Diffusion as opposed to concurrent development was advocated in England some years ago by such writers as W. J. PERRY. A more measured view now prevails as to its relation to concurrency, though it is still held to be an important element in the development of material culture. The best book on the subject which I have read is by an American writer, and I regret that I have not kept a record of the author's name.

See also:

D. THOMSON, on *Dionysiac Religion and its Expansion.* C.U.P.

CHAPTER IV. THE RISE OF CHRISTIANITY

N.B. As this book is one in a series, it is obviously not the business of the author to devote a large space to a subject which is dealt with in extenso in other works in this series, and is pre-supposed throughout it. But he is bound in the bibliography to indicate to readers how that subject may be further studied. Such studies can however only provide a somewhat detached and external approach, and can never satisfy. It is only *encounter* and *surrender* which can provide *real* knowledge. There is the obvious difference between reading about a Person and His influence, and actually meeting Him!

HOWARD CLARK KEE and FRANKLIN W. YOUNG. *The Living World of the New Testament.* Longmans. 1959. Illustrated.
(The latest general standard introductory work on a great subject.)

Recent works in this field are by (inter alia):

Dr C. H. Dodd. *History and the Gospel. Hewett Lectures.* Nisbet. London. 1938.
— *The Parables of the Kingdom.* Nisbet. London. 1935.
— *New Testament Studies.* Manchester. 1953.

But works which may also be consulted (among a host of others) are:

The late Professor F. C. Burkitt. *Jesus Christ.* James Clarke.
— *The Gospel History and its Transmission.* Fourth impression. Edinburgh. 1926.
The late Dr Edwyn Bevan. *Christianity.* Home University Library.
H. A. A. Kennedy. *St Paul and the Mystery Religions.* London. 1913.

Larger and more detached and dispassionate works are by:

Drs. Kirsopp Lake and Foakes-Jackson. *The Beginnings of Christianity.* Seven vols. Macmillan. London. 1920.
Dr H. D. A. Major and others. *The Mission and Message of Jesus.* London. 1937.
The Rev. Sir Edwyn Hoskyns and The Rev. Noel Davey. *The Riddle of the New Testament.* 3rd ed. 1947.
Dr Lietzmann. *Geschichte der Alten Kirche.* Berlin. 1932. The first volume translated into English by B. L. Woolf. 1936.
Dr Martin Dibelius. *A Fresh Approach to the New Testament, and Early Christian Literature.* 1936.
The late Canon W. L. Knox. *St Paul and the Church of Jerusalem.* 1925. And its sequel.
Professor A. D. Nock. *St Paul.* Home University Library. 1938.
The Rev. Dr H. D. A. Major. *Jesus by an Eye-witness.* John Murray. 1925.
Dr Albert Schweitzer. *The Quest of the Historical Jesus.* London. 1910.
(This most famous and provocative work may be balanced by reading T. F. Glasson's *His Appearing and His Kingdom.* London. 1953.)

CHAPTER V. THE EXPANSION OF CHRISTIANITY

The largest and most comprehensive work is that of:

Dr K. S. Latourette, in 7 volumes. *The History of the Expansion of Christianity.* London. 1938.
See also:
Dr Latourette's *The Christian World-mission Today.* London. 1954, and *Christianity in a Revolutionary Age.* New York. 1958.

But for the earlier period, reference may be made to the scientific early twentieth century work of:

Dr Adolf Harnack. *Die Mission und Ausbreitung des Christentums.* Leipzig. 1934. 2nd ed. translated by J. Moffatt. Published by Williams and Norgate, in the Theological Translation Library.

The evidence for Christian universalism is best studied in the texts of the Old and New Testaments themselves, as the author has tried to do, and has there given also various exegetical references.

CHAPTER VI. THE DOCTRINE OF THE LOGOS

General

Article by Dr INGE in the *Encyclopaedia of Religion and Ethics.*
Professor LEBRETON. *L'Histoire du dogme de la Trinité.* Vol. I. English translation. 1938.

Justin Martyr

Various works exist in German, by Krüger and others, but the results of them are summarised in Dr A. W. F. BLUNT'S edition of the Apologies: *Cambridge Patristic Texts.* 1910.

The Fourth Gospel

The author, in the treatment of the text of the Fourth Gospel, has taken his own independent line; and the exegesis of the Prologue and 12^{35} is as far as he knows, original.   But he is of course greatly indebted to the various distinguished commentators, whose works are listed below.

Commentaries are, of course, numerous.   The principal ones, in chronological order, are:

Bishop B. F. WESTCOTT.   John Murray.   Last edition in 1902.
Archbishop BERNARD. *I.C.C.* Edinburgh. 1928.
Dr W. SANDAY. *The Criticism of the Fourth Gospel.* 1905.
Professor A. E. BROOKE (in Peake's Dictionary of the Bible.   Introduction and brief commentary).
The Rev. Dr R. H. STRACHAN.   S.C.M. Press.   3rd edition.   1943.
The Rev. Sir EDWYN HOSKYNS and the Rev. NOEL DAVEY.   2 vols. London.   1947.
Professor RUDOLF BULTMANN.   Göttingen.   1952.
Dr C. H. DODD. *The Interpretation of the Fourth Gospel.*   Cambridge.   1953.
Dr C. K. BARRETT.   London.   1955.

CHAPTER VII. THE PHENOMENON OF ISLAM

General

The late Dr RICHARD BELL. *The Origin of Islam in its Christian Environment.*   London.   1926.   Macmillan.
Professor A. S. TRITTON. *Islam.*   Hutchinson.   1951.
Professor H. A. R. GIBB. *Mohammedanism.*   Home University Library.   1949.
    (See his bibliography.)
Professor ALFRED GUILLAUME. *Islam.*   Pelican books.   1954.
    (See his bibliography.)
G. H. BOUSQUET. *Les Grandes Pratiques rituelles de L'Islam.*   Presses Universitaires de France.   1949.

442 BIBLIOGRAPHY

Muhammad

MAURICE GAUDEFROY-DEMOMBYNES. *Muslim Institutions.* Trans.
by J. P. MacGregor. George Allen & Unwin. 1950.
W. MONTGOMERY WATT. *Muhammad at Mecca.* O.U.P. 1926.
FRANTS BUHL. *Das Leben Mohammeds.* Trans. H. H. Schaever.
Berlin. 1930.
TOR ANDRAE. *Mohammed, the Man and His Faith.* London.
1936.
ESSAD BEY (pseud.). *Life of Mohammed.* Cobden Sanderson.
1938.
  (Interesting, but prejudiced.)

The Qur' ān (Translations)

J. M. RODWELL, in the Everyman Library.
  (Rather an old work now, but useful, if only for its footnotes.)
RICHARD BELL. Edinburgh. 1937–9. 2 vols.
  (The first attempt at a critical analysis of the text of the Juras.)
A. YUSUF ALI. *The Holy Qur' ān.* 2 vols. Lahore. 1934.
  (An Ahmadiyya or modernist commentary on the text.)
 See also:
Dr TRIMINGHAM. *The Call of the Mosque.*

Doctrine

J. W. SWEETMAN. *Islam and Christian Theology.* 2 vols. 1945
& ff.
  (This work is of great interest as showing the inter-locking of Christianity
  and Islam at an early date, and their gradual drifting apart.)

CHAPTER VIII. RESEMBLANCES AND FUNDAMENTAL
DIFFERENCES

Dr NICOL MACNICOL. *Is Christianity Unique?* Lectures delivered
at Hartford, Conn., U.S.A., in 1936. Pub. S.C.M. Press.

CHAPTER IX. INDIGENISATION

Bishop LUCAS. Articles in *I.R.M.*
Professor ERNST LUCIUS of Strassburg. *Die Anfänge des Heiligen-
kults in der Christlichen Kirche.* Tübingen. 1904.
The Rt. Hon. MALCOLM MACDONALD. *Borneo People.* London.
1956.

CHAPTER X. THE MACHINE AGE AND THE RISE OF
MARXISM

Fr GEORGE EVERY. *Religion in the Machine Age.*

CHAPTER XI. THE PROBLEM OF MARXISM

KARL MARX. *Das Kapital.* (With additions by Friedrich Engels.)
English translation by Eden and Cedar Paul. Dent's Everyman
Library.

Professor H. J. LASKI. *Communism.* Home University Library. 1927.
> (A Polish economist, who, though a socialist, does not wholeheartedly accept Marxist theory, but expounds and discusses it.)

Christianity and the Social Revolution. Gollancz. 1935.
> (A composite volume, which aims at objectivity.)

Dr. JULIUS HECKER. *Moscow Dialogues.* Chapman & Hall. 1933.
> (An American-trained Russian, Professor of Philosophy in the University of Moscow, tries to expound Marxism by a series of dialogues after the model of Plato.)

Professor H. G. WOOD. *The Truth and Error of Communism.* S.C.M. Press. 1933.
> (The Birmingham Professor, writing from the Woodbrooke Settlement at Selly Oak, tries to evaluate Marxism from the standpoint of moderate Labour.)

WILLIAM GALLACHER. *The Case for Communism.* A Penguin Special. 1949.
> (The first British M.P. to be elected as a Communist. His essay is clear, confident, and uncompromising.)

Monsignor DARCY. *Communism.* Pelican Books.
> (Gives the enlightened Roman Catholic point of view.)

Lambeth Conference Report. 1948. Pp. 201 ff. and the Resolutions.
> (Deals with various aspects of the Christine Doctrine of Man.)

Rt. Hon. JAMES HAROLD WILSON. *The War on World Poverty: An Appeal to the Conscience of Mankind.* London. 1953.

MAO-TSE-TUNG. *Opera.* English trans. London. 1954.

R. C. ZAEHNER. Essay on *The Religious Instinct.* In another composite volume pub. by Gollancz. 1956.

CHAPTER XII. AFRO-ASIAN EMANCIPATION

Pan-Anglican Papers. 1908.

Report of the Edinburgh Conference. 1910.

Report of the Jerusalem Conference. 1923.

C.O.P.E.C. Report. 1923.

Report of the Inter-denominational Conference at Evanston, Ill. 1954.

Christianity and the Asian Revolution. Ed. by Rajah B. Manikar. 1954. Repr. 1955.

PANDIT JAWAHARLAL NEHRU. *The Discovery of India.* Meridian Press. 1946.
> (A brilliant, though, it is alleged, not very scholarly survey by a great leader: written in prison.)

Mr D. C. VIJAYAVARDHANA. *Revolt in the Temple.* Colombo. 1958.
> (An apology for Theravada, by a leading Buddhist layman.)

African Ideas of God. Various, ed. E. W. SMITH. Edinburgh House Press. 1949.

AUROBINDO GHOSH. *The Life Divine.* Pondicherry. 1955.

Mr WING-TSIT-CHAN. *Religious Trends in Modern China.* Columbia University Press. 1953.

MAO-TSE-TUNG. *Works.* 3 vols. Selections in English. London. 1953.

(Also, articles by LIN-YU-TANG.)

The Dominance of America

Dean W. L. SPERRY. *Religion in America.* C.U.P. 1945.
The Rev. H. C. SNAPE. Article in the *Conference Number of the
Modern Churchmen's Union* for 1956.

Jews

Articles in *I.R.M.* by HANS KOSMALA.
Professor SCHOEPS: in his *Gottheit und Menschheit.* Stuttgart.
1950. And in the journal which he edits.
Liberal Judaism. Literature, especially the writings of the late
Dr ISRAEL MATTUCK.

Islam

Professor H. A. R. GIBB. *Whither Islam?*
Dr LAURENCE BROWNE. *The Prospects of Islam.* S.C.M. Press.
1944.
     (See his bibliography.)
M. T. TITUS. *Indian Islam.* O.U.P. 1930.
Articles in *The Moslem World.*
The late Sir MUHAMMAD IQBAL. *The Reconstruction of Religious
Thought in Islam.* O.U.P. 1934.
AMCER ALI SYAD. *The Spirit of Islam.* Christopher. Revised
edition. 1935. (A Shi'ah work.)

CHAPTER XIII. THE CHANGE TO THE MODERN WORLD
—THEOLOGICAL REVALUATION

Lord HERBERT OF CHERBURY
BALDAEUS. *Bibliotheca Baldaeana.* Holland. 1711.
Abbé DUBOIS. Op. cit.
BENJAMIN CONSTANT. *De la religion considérée dans sa source, ses
formes, et ses développements.* Paris. 1830. 5 vols.
CHRISTOPH MEINERS. Berlin. 1805.
ERNEST RENAN. *Etudes d'histoire religieuse.* Paris. 1864.
DIETERICH (ALBRECHT). *Religiongeschichtliche Versuche und Voran-
beitungen.* Giessen. 1903.
H. F. HACKMANN.
   (1) *Religions of the World, in Collaboration with Other Scholars.*
   London. 1931.
   (2) *Buddhism as a Religion.* Robotham. London. 1910.
CHANTEPIE DE LA SAUSSAYE. *Lehrbuch der Religiongeschichte.*
Ed. Bertholet and Lehmann. Tübingen. 1925.
RATZEL (FRIEDRICH). *The History of Mankind.* Translation.
3 vols. 1896–8.
FROBENIUS (LEO). *The Childhood of Man.* London. 1909.
(Trans. from the German by A. H. Keane.)
KUHN (ADALBERT) (inter alia):
   (1) *Mythologische studien.* Gütersloh. 1886.
   (2) *Nord-deutsche Sagen.* Leipzig. 1848.

MAX MÜLLER
(An enormous output here for one man. In addition to his editions of Asian sacred books, the following are relevant, as showing his general attitude.)
— *Gifford Lectures.*
(1) *Natural Religion.* 1892.
(2) *Theosophy.* 1895.
— *On the Origin and Growth of Religion, as illustrated by the Religions of India. Hibbert Lectures.* London. 1882.
— *On Missions.* With an introduction by Dean Stanley. 1870.
F. DENISON MAURICE. *Boyle Lectures.* 6th edition. Macmillan. 1886.
Bishop B. F. WESTCOTT. *The Gospel of Life.* London. 1892.
Sir EDWARD TYLOR. *Primitive Culture.* 4th ed. 2 vols. London. 1903.
ANDREW LANG. *Myth, Ritual, and Religion.* 2 vols. 1899.
EDWIN SIDNEY HARLAND. A large output. The chief being:
Mythology and Folktales. 1900.
Ritual and Belief. 1914.
The *Essays and Reviews* group. Bishop FREDERICK TEMPLE.
The *Lux Mundi* group. J. R. ILLINGWORTH.
Sir JAMES FRAZER. See list in bibliography to Chapter II.
(Frazer's work sometimes seems influenced by French Positivism, but starting from a Scotch Presbyterian background, and with a thorough Classical education behind him, he seems to show a respect for the prophetic element in Christianity, even where he also seems most agnostic.)
ERNST TROELTSCH. *Die Absolutheit des Christentums.* Mostly trans. by A. C. B. 1922.
(New translation in preparation.)
See also: •
A volume of his lectures, posthumously published. *Christian Thought.* London University Press. 1923.
GUSTAV MENSCHING. *Das heilige Schweigen. Eine religion-geschichtliche Untersuchung.* Giessen. 1926.
RUDOLF OTTO. *The Idea of the Holy.* O.U.P. 1923.
(A translation of his famous work *Das Heilige,* by J. W. Harvey.)
TH.P. VAN BAAREN. *Voorstellingen van Openbaring.* Utrecht. 1951.
J. WITTE. *Die Christensbotschaft und die Weltreligionen.* 1936.
ALTHAUS. *Die Christlich Wahrheit.*
HEINRICH FRICK. *Das Evangelium und die Religionen.* Nares. Oxford. 1938.
(HERMANN) BARVINK. *The Philosophy of Revelation.* London. 1909. Lectures.
JAMES MAURICE WILSON. In *Cambridge Theological Essays.* 1905. No. VI.
FREDERICK ROBERT TENNANT. 'Revelation, in the Light of Modern Knowledge and Research'. In his *Philosophical Theology.* Vol. 2. C.U.P. 1930.
Seven Bishops (Anglican). *Mankind and the Church.* Longmans. 1908.

FRIEDRICH HEILER. Address delivered at the International Congress at Tokyo in 1958.

Archbishop NATHAN SÖDERBLOM. *The Living God.* (*1st series of Gifford Lectures.*) O.U.P. 1933.

EMIL BRUNNER. *Revelation and Religion.* English trans. by Miss Wyon. 1947.

Professor WILLIAM ERNEST HOCKING. *Living Religions and a World-faith.* George Allen & Unwin. 1940.

ERICH PRZYWARA. *A Catholic Philosophy of Religion.* 1931.

Archbishop WILLIAM TEMPLE. Chapter on 'Revelation and its Mode', in his *Gifford Lectures.* Macmillans. 1935.

E. C. DEWICK. Op. cit.

Dr HAROLD SMITH. *Elements of Comparative Theology.* Duckworth. 1937.

Dr T. R. GLOVER: NICOL MACNICOL. Op. cit.

Dr VAN DER LEUUW. *Religion in Essence and Manifestation.* English trans. George Allen & Unwin. 1938.
    (A learned Dutch Protestant writes in German from Tübingen. 1933)

PAUL TILLICH. *Systematic Theology.* Vol. 1. Nisbet. London. 1953.

KARL JASPERS. Op. cit.

HENDRIK KRAEMER.
   (1) *The Christian Message in a Non-Christian World.* Edinburgh House Press. 1938.
   (2) *Religion and the Christian Faith.* Lutterworth Press. 1958.

Professor R. H. L. SLATER. Article in the *Harvard Theological Review.*

Professor H. H. FARMER. *Gifford Lectures.* 1951. *Revelation and Religion.* Nisbet. London.

ARNOLD TOYNBEE. Final volume in: *A Study of History.*

Miss UNDERHILL   ⎫ In *Essays Catholic and Missionary.*   Ed.
Dr LAURENCE BROWNE ⎭   Bishop E. R. Morgan.

Works by Sir SARVEPALLI RADHAKRISHNAN (a selection):
   A History of Indian Philosophy. London. 1929.
   The Hindu View of Life. Upton Lectures. 1926.
   An Idealist View of Life. Hibbert Lectures. 1929. Pub. 1932.
   East and West in Religion. London. 1933.
   East and West. Some Reflections. London. 1958.

INDEX